MW01155242

COURSE 1

Math in Focus®

Singapore Math
by Marshall Cavendish

Consultant and Author
Dr. Fong Ho Kheong

Authors
Gan Kee Soon and Dr. Ng Wee Leng

U.S. Consultants
Dr. Richard Bisk
Andy Clark

Published by Marshall Cavendish Education
An imprint of Marshall Cavendish International (Singapore) Private Limited
Times Centre, 1 New Industrial Road, Singapore 536196
Customer Service Hotline: (65) 6411 0820
E-mail: tmesales@sg.marshallcavendish.com
Website: www.marshallcavendish.com/education

Distributed by
Houghton Mifflin Harcourt
222 Berkeley Street
Boston, MA 02116
Tel: 617-351-5000
Website: www.hmheducation.com/mathinfocus

First published 2012
Reprinted 2012 (thrice)

Math in Focus® Course 1 Student Book B
ISBN 978-0-547-56012-0

Printed in United States of America

4 5 6 7 8 1401 17 16 15 14 13 12
4500360395 B C D E

Course 1B Contents

Equations and Inequalities

In Student Book A and Student Book B, look for

Practice and Problem Solving	Assessment Opportunities
• **Practice** in every lesson • Real-world and mathematical problems in every chapter • **Brain @ Work** in every chapter • *Math Journal* exercises	• **Quick Check** at the beginning of every chapter to assess chapter readiness • **Guided Practice** after every Learn to assess readiness to continue lesson • **Chapter Review/Test** in every chapter to review or test chapter material • **Cumulative Reviews** four times during the year

The Coordinate Plane

Area of Polygons

Circumference and Area of a Circle

Surface Area and Volume of Solids

CHAPTER 13 Introduction to Statistics

Measures of Central Tendency

Welcome to

Math in Focus®

Singapore Math by Marshall Cavendish

COMMON CORE

What makes *Math in Focus*® different?

This world-class math program comes to you from the country of Singapore. We are sure that you will enjoy learning math with the interesting lessons you will find in these books.

- **Two books** The textbook is divided into 2 semesters. Chapters 1–7 are in Book A. Chapters 8–14 are in Book B.
- **Longer lessons** More concepts are presented in a lesson. Some lessons may last more than a day to give you time to understand the math.
- **Bar models and visual models** will help you make sense of new concepts and solve real-world and mathematical problems with ease.

About the book Here are the main features in this book.

Chapter Opener

Introduces chapter concepts and big ideas through a story or example. There is also a chapter table of contents.

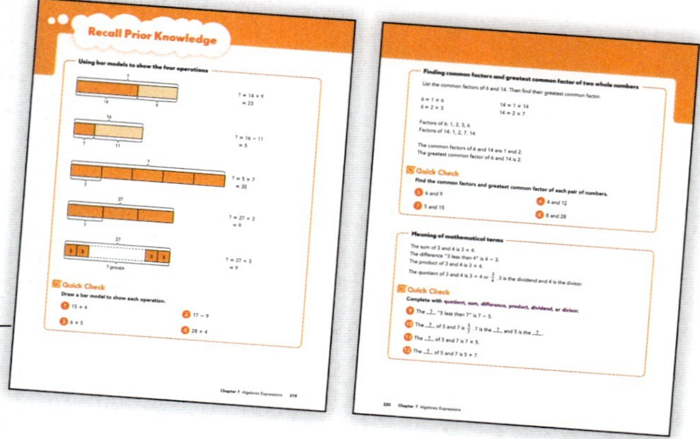

Recall Prior Knowledge

Assesses previously learned concepts, definitions, vocabulary, and models relevant to the chapter.

Quick Check assesses readiness for the chapter.

Look for these features in each lesson.

Learn shows steps that are easy to follow and understand. It often contains bar models or other visual models.

Model mathematics

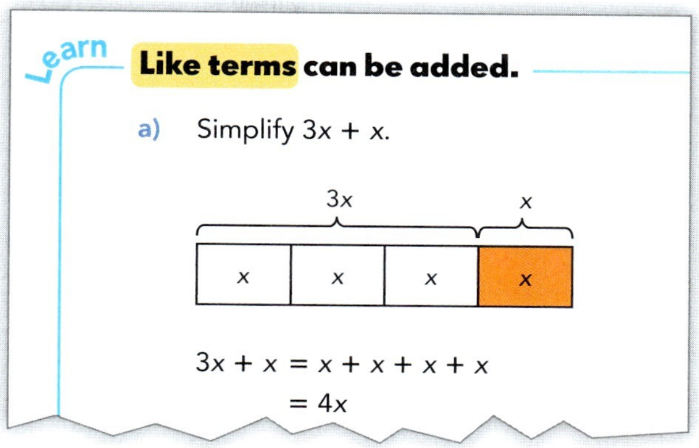

Guided Practice exercises provide step-by-step guidance through solutions.

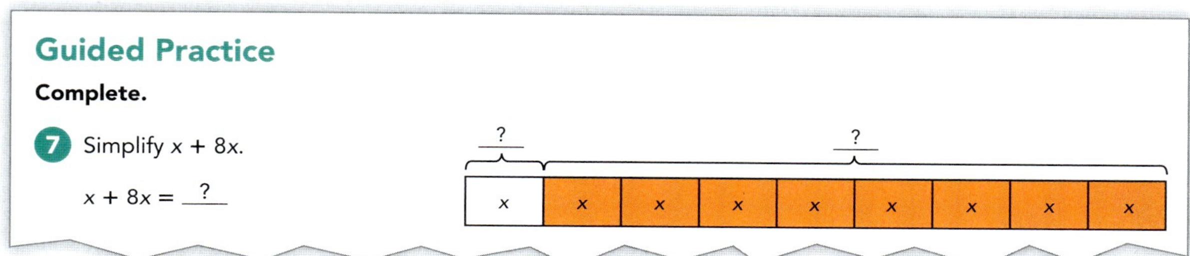

Cautions alert you to common mistakes and misconceptions related to the topics.

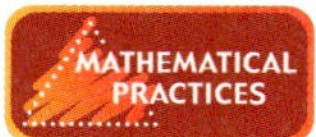

Structure, reasoning, and precision

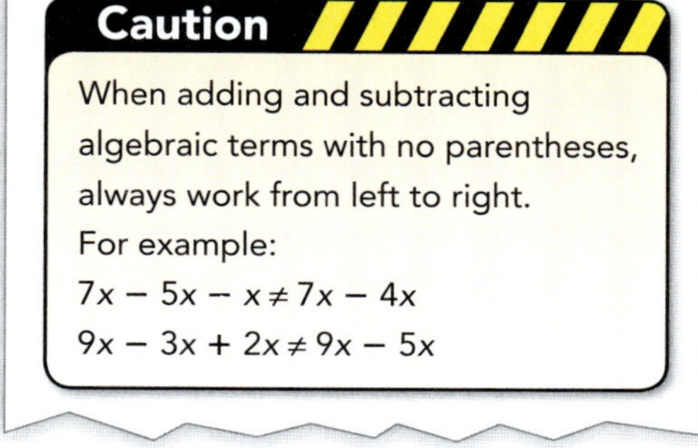

Math Note

Commutative Property of Addition: Two numbers can be added in any order.

So, $4 + a = a + 4$.

Math Notes are helpful hints and reminders.

Practice 7.3

Simplify each expression. Then state the coefficient of the variable in each expression.

1 $u + u + u + u$

2 $v + v + 5 - 2$

Practice and **Math Journal** are included in practice sets.

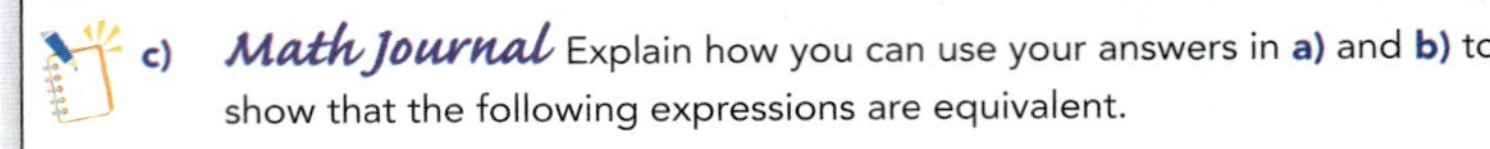
c) *Math Journal* Explain how you can use your answers in **a)** and **b)** to show that the following expressions are equivalent.

$3x + 6$ and $3(x + 2)$

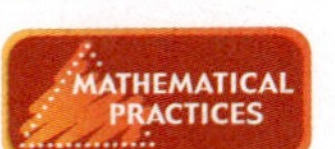

Construct viable arguments

Hands-On Activities and **Brain@Work** combine logical thinking with math skills and concepts to help you meet new problem-solving challenges.

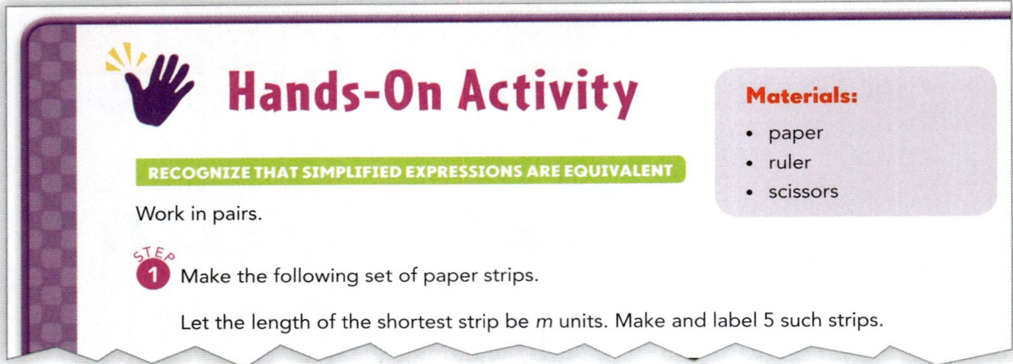
Hands-On Activity

RECOGNIZE THAT SIMPLIFIED EXPRESSIONS ARE EQUIVALENT

Work in pairs.

Materials:
- paper
- ruler
- scissors

STEP 1 Make the following set of paper strips.

Let the length of the shortest strip be m units. Make and label 5 such strips.

Hands-On or **Technology Activities** provide opportunities for investigation, reinforcement, and extension.

Reason, solve problems, use tools and models

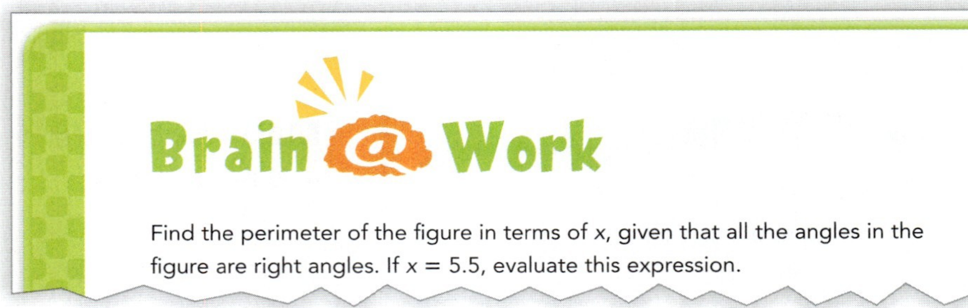
Brain@Work

Find the perimeter of the figure in terms of x, given that all the angles in the figure are right angles. If $x = 5.5$, evaluate this expression.

Brain@Work problems, found at the end of each chapter, are challenging and promote critical thinking.

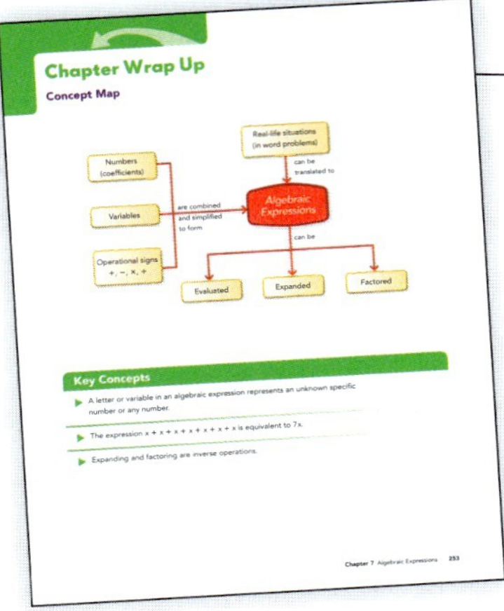
Chapter Wrap Up

Concept Map

Key Concepts

Chapter Wrap Up

Key concepts, definitions, and formulas are summarized for easy review.

The Chapter Wrap Up summaries contain concept maps like the one shown below.

There may be more than one way to draw a concept map. With practice, you should be able to draw your own.

The center box contains the big idea for the chapter.

Other boxes represent key concepts of the chapter.

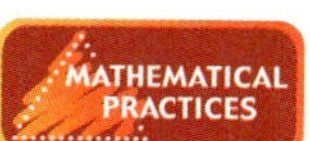

Structure, reasoning, and precision

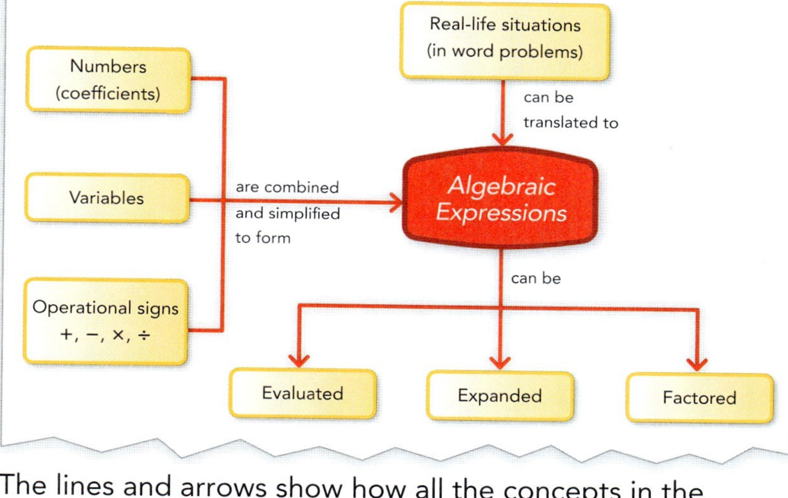

The lines and arrows show how all the concepts in the chapter are related to one another and to the big idea.

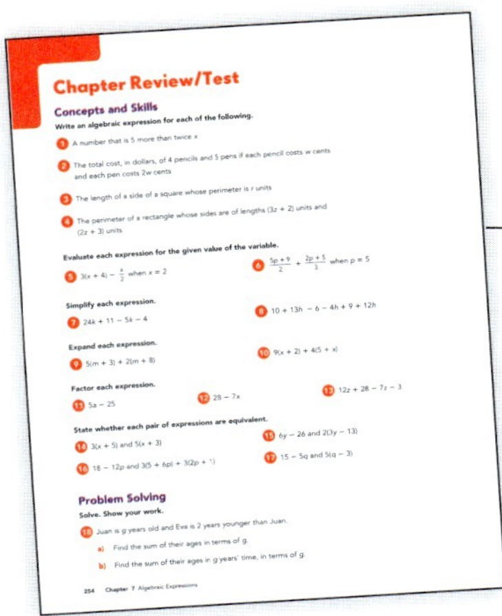
Chapter Review/Test

Concepts and Skills

Problem Solving

Chapter Review/Test

A practice test is found at the end of each chapter.

Cumulative Review

Cumulative review exercises can be found after Chapters 3, 7, 11, and 14.

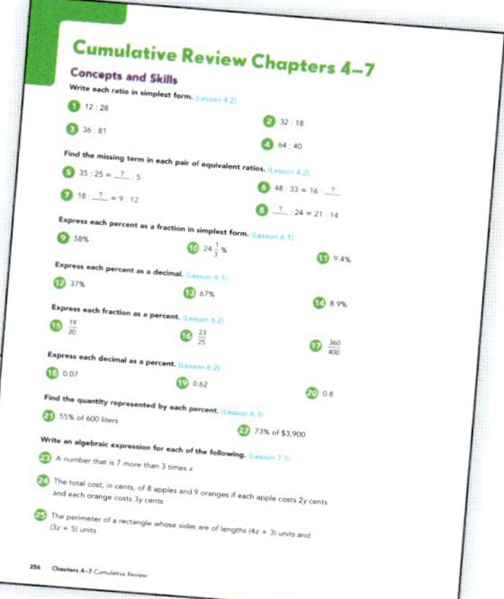
Cumulative Review Chapters 4–7

Concepts and Skills

CHAPTER

8 Equations and Inequalities

Going on a vacation?

If you travel to another country, you can use linear equations and inequalities to help you plan your finances. Before you leave, you might want to change your U.S. dollars into a different currency. The amount of money you get in the new currency depends on how many U.S. dollars you start with and also on the currency exchange rate. To find out how much money you get in the new currency, you use a linear equation.

While on your trip, you may want to set aside money to spend on souvenirs. You can use a linear inequality to find how many souvenirs you can buy. Planning finances, travel times, and distances can all be made easier by using linear equations and inequalities.

▶ Equations and inequalities can be used to describe situations and solve real-world problems.

Recall Prior Knowledge

Comparing numbers with symbols

Symbol	Meaning	Example
$=$	is equal to	$12 \times 4 = 48 \longrightarrow 12 \times 4$ is equal to 48.
$\neq$	is not equal to	$6 - 2 \neq 2 - 6 \longrightarrow 6 - 2$ is not equal to $2 - 6$.
$>$	is greater than	$0 > -9 \longrightarrow 0$ is greater than -9.
$<$	is less than	$-5 < -1 \longrightarrow -5$ is less than -1.

Quick Check

Complete with $=$, $>$, or $<$.

1. 25 ? -26
2. $12 + 12 + 12$? $3 \cdot 12$
3. $40 \div 8$? $8 \div 40$
4. -16 ? -7

Using variables to write algebraic expressions

Statement	Expression
The sum of x and 7	$x + 7$
The difference "14 less than y"	$y - 14$
The product of 8 and w	$8w$
Divide z by 6	$\frac{z}{6}$

Quick Check

Write an algebraic expression for each of the following.

5. The sum of 15 and p
6. The difference "q less than 10"
7. The product of r and 23
8. Divide s by 11.

Evaluating algebraic expressions

Evaluate $4y + 1$ when

a) $y = 7$,

b) $y = 10$.

a) When $y = 7$,

$4y + 1 = (4 \cdot 7) + 1$ Substitute.

$= 28 + 1$ Multiply inside parentheses.

$= 29$ Add.

b) When $y = 10$,

$4y + 1 = (4 \cdot 10) + 1$ Substitute.

$= 40 + 1$ Multiply inside parentheses.

$= 41$ Add.

Quick Check

Evaluate each expression for the given values of the variable.

9 $3x + 5$ when $x = 9$ and $x = 12$

10 $28 - 4x$ when $x = 4$ and $x = 7$

Plotting points on a coordinate plane

Plot points A (2, 4) and B (3, 2) on a coordinate plane.

To locate point A (2, 4), move 2 units to the right of the y-axis and 4 units above the x-axis. Then mark the point with a dot.

To locate point B (3, 2), move 3 units to the right of the y-axis and 2 units above the x-axis. Then mark the point with a dot.

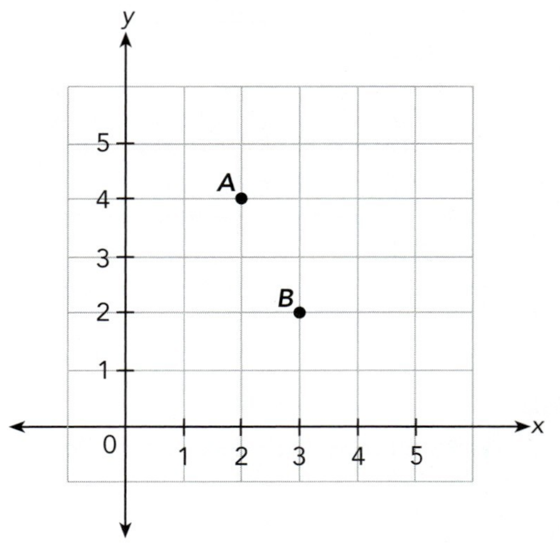

Quick Check

Plot the points on a coordinate plane.

11 K (2, 1), L (3, 3), M (0, 6), and N (7, 5)

8.1 Solving Algebraic Equations

Lesson Objective

- Solve equations in one variable.

Vocabulary
equation
solution

Learn Use substitution to solve simple algebraic **equations**.

a) The figure shows a balance scale. Find the value of x such that the left side balances the right side.

■ represents 1 counter.
[x] represents x counters.

There are $(x + 5)$ counters on the left side.

There are 8 counters on the right side.

Since the two sides balance each other,

$x + 5 = 8$.

$x + 5 = 8$ is called an equation.

You can think of an equation as a balance scale, where the left side is always balanced by the right side.

To solve the equation, you need to find the value of x that makes $x + 5 = 8$ true.

If $x = 1$, $\quad x + 5 = 1 + 5$
$\qquad\qquad\quad = 6 \quad (\neq 8)$

If $x = 2$, $\quad x + 5 = 2 + 5$
$\qquad\qquad\quad = 7 \quad (\neq 8)$

If $x = 3$, $\quad x + 5 = 3 + 5$
$\qquad\qquad\quad = 8$

Another way to solve an equation like $x + 5 = 8$ is to ask yourself, 'What number can be added to 5 to equal 8?' Only 3 can be added to 5 to equal 8, so the only solution of the equation is 3.

The equation $x + 5 = 8$ holds true when $x = 3$.

$x = 3$ gives the **solution** of the equation $x + 5 = 8$.

Continue on next page

b) Solve the equation $3x = 12$.

The equation $3x = 12$ can be represented on a balance scale:

■ represents 1 counter.

▬ x ▬ represents x counters.

To solve the equation, you need to find the value of x that makes $3x = 12$ true.

If $x = 1$, $\quad 3x = 3 \cdot 1$
$\qquad\qquad\qquad = 3 \quad (\neq 12)$

If $x = 2$, $\quad 3x = 3 \cdot 2$
$\qquad\qquad\qquad = 6 \quad (\neq 12)$

If $x = 4$, $\quad 3x = 3 \cdot 4$
$\qquad\qquad\qquad = 12$

The equation $3x = 12$ has only one solution, $x = 4$. The equation does not hold true for other values of x.

The equation $3x = 12$ holds true when $x = 4$.

$x = 4$ gives the solution of the equation $3x = 12$.

Guided Practice

Complete each ? with = or ≠, and each _?_ with the correct value.

1 For what value of x will $x + 3 = 7$ be true?

If $x = 1$, $\quad x + 3 =$ _?_ $+ 3$
$\qquad\qquad\qquad =$ _?_ $\quad$ (? 7)

If $x = 2$, $\quad x + 3 =$ _?_ $+ 3$
$\qquad\qquad\qquad =$ _?_ $\quad$ (? 7)

If $x = 4$, $\quad x + 3 =$ _?_ $+ 3$
$\qquad\qquad\qquad =$ _?_

$x + 3 = 7$ is true when $x =$ _?_.

Solve each equation using the substitution method.

2. $p + 6 = 13$
3. $r + 4 = 12$
4. $k - 10 = 7$
5. $2m = 6$
6. $4n = 20$
7. $\frac{1}{5}z = 3$

Learn

Solve algebraic equations involving addition or subtraction.

a) Solve the equation $x + 6 = 9$.

The equation $x + 6 = 9$ can be represented on a balance scale:

■ represents 1 counter.

[x] represents x counters.

When you remove 6 counters from the left side, the scale becomes unbalanced.

$x + 6 - 6 < 9$

To balance the scale, you will need to remove 6 counters from the right side.

$x + 6 - 6 = 9 - 6$

The steps above can be summarized as follows:

$$x + 6 = 9$$
$$x + 6 - 6 = 9 - 6 \quad \text{Subtract 6 from both sides.}$$
$$x = 3$$

$x = 3$ gives the solution of the equation $x + 6 = 9$.

Check: Substitute 3 for the value of x into the equation.

$$x + 6 = 3 + 6$$
$$= 9$$

When $x = 3$, the equation $x + 6 = 9$ is true.
$x = 3$ gives the correct solution.

Math Note

Compare this with $3 + 6 = 9$.

$$3 + 6 - 6 = 9 - 6$$
$$3 = 9 - 6$$

You can subtract the same number from both sides of the equation and the two sides will remain equal.

Continue on next page

b) Solve the equation $6 = x - 3$.

$$6 = x - 3$$
$$6 + 3 = x - 3 + 3 \quad \text{Add 3 to both sides.}$$
$$9 = x$$

Check: Substitute 9 for the value of x into the equation.

$$\begin{aligned} 6 &= x - 3 \\ &= 9 - 3 \\ &= 6 \end{aligned}$$

When $x = 9$, the equation $6 = x - 3$ holds true.

$x = 9$ gives the correct solution.

Math Note

Compare this with $6 = 9 - 3$.

$6 + 3 = 9 - 3 + 3$
$6 + 3 = 9$

You can add the same number to both sides of the equation and the two sides will remain equal.

Guided Practice

Complete each ? with + or –, and each ___?___ with the correct value.

8 Solve $x + 8 = 19$.

$$x + 8 = 19$$
$$x + 8 \;?\; \underline{?} = 19 \;?\; \underline{?}$$
$$x = \underline{?}$$

Solve each equation.

9 $f + 5 = 14$

10 $26 = g + 11$

11 $w - 6 = 10$

12 $z - 9 = 21$

Learn Solve algebraic equations involving multiplication or division.

a) Solve the equation $2x = 12$.

The equation $2x = 12$ can be represented on a balance scale:

■ represents 1 counter.

▬ x represents x counters.

When you divide the number of counters on the left side by 2, the scale becomes unbalanced.

$2x \div 2 < 12$

To balance the scale, you will need to divide the number of counters on the right side by 2.

$2x \div 2 = 12 \div 2$

The steps above can be summarized as follows:

$$2x = 12$$
$$2x \div 2 = 12 \div 2 \quad \text{Divide both sides by 2.}$$
$$x = 6$$

$x = 6$ gives the solution of the equation $2x = 12$.

Check: Substitute 6 for the value of x into the equation.

$$2x = 2 \cdot 6$$
$$= 12$$

When $x = 6$, the equation $2x = 12$ holds true.

$x = 6$ gives the correct solution.

Math Note

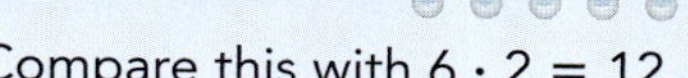

Compare this with $6 \cdot 2 = 12$.

$$6 \cdot 2 \div 2 = 12 \div 2$$
$$6 = 12 \div 2$$

You can divide both sides of the equation by the same number (except 0) and the two sides will remain equal.

Continue on next page

b) Solve the equation $\frac{y}{3} = 4$.

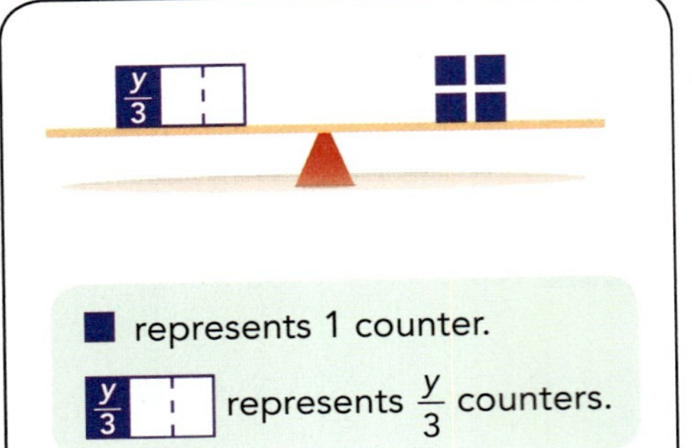

$$\frac{y}{3} = 4$$

$$\frac{y}{3} \cdot 3 = 4 \cdot 3$$ Multiply both sides by 3.

$$y = 12$$

Check: Substitute 12 for the value of y into the equation.

$$\frac{y}{3} = \frac{12}{3}$$
$$= 4$$

When $y = 12$, the equation $\frac{y}{3} = 4$ holds true.

$y = 12$ gives the correct solution.

Math Note

Compare this with $\frac{12}{3} = 4$.

$$\frac{12}{3} \cdot 3 = 4 \cdot 3$$
$$12 = 4 \cdot 3$$

You can multiply both sides of the equation by the same number and the two sides will remain equal.

Guided Practice

Complete each ? with × or ÷, and ? with the correct value.

13 Solve $3x = 27$.

$$3x = 27$$
$$3x \; ? \; \underline{?} = 27 \; ? \; \underline{?}$$
$$x = \underline{?}$$

Solve each equation.

14 $6a = 42$

15 $65 = 13b$

16 $\frac{m}{8} = 9$

17 $12 = \frac{n}{7}$

Learn Solve algebraic equations involving fractions.

a) Solve the equation $x + \frac{1}{10} = \frac{3}{10}$. Write your answer in simplest form.

Decide which operation to use. Since $\frac{1}{10}$ was added to the variable, you need to subtract $\frac{1}{10}$ from each side of the equation.

$$x + \frac{1}{10} = \frac{3}{10}$$

$$x + \frac{1}{10} - \frac{1}{10} = \frac{3}{10} - \frac{1}{10}$$ Subtract $\frac{1}{10}$ from both sides.

$$x = \frac{2}{10}$$ Simplify.

$$= \frac{1}{5}$$

b) Solve the equation $3y = \frac{2}{3}$.

Decide which operation to use. Since y was multiplied by 3, divide each side of the equation by 3.

$$3y = \frac{2}{3}$$

$$3y \div 3 = \frac{2}{3} \div 3$$ Divide both sides by 3.

$$y = \frac{2}{3} \cdot \frac{1}{3}$$ Multiply by the reciprocal of the divisor.

$$= \frac{2}{9}$$

Guided Practice

Complete each ? with +, −, ×, or ÷, and ___?___ with the correct value.

18 Solve $x + \frac{3}{7} = \frac{5}{7}$.

$$x + \frac{3}{7} = \frac{5}{7}$$

$$x + \frac{3}{7} \; ? \; \underline{?} = \frac{5}{7} \; ? \; \underline{?}$$

$$x = \underline{?}$$

Solve each equation. First tell which operation you will perform on each side of the equation. Write your answer in simplest form.

19 $k + \frac{1}{8} = \frac{7}{8}$

20 $4p = \frac{3}{4}$

Practice 8.1

Solve each equation using the substitution method.

1. $b + 7 = 10$
2. $17 = e + 9$
3. $k - 4 = 11$
4. $42 = 3p$
5. $8t = 56$
6. $\frac{1}{4}v = 5$

Solve each equation using the concept of balancing.

7. $k + 12 = 23$
8. $x - 8 = 17$
9. $24 = f - 16$
10. $5j = 75$
11. $81 = 9m$
12. $\frac{r}{6} = 11$

Solve each equation using the concept of balancing. Write all fraction answers in simplest form.

13. $\frac{5}{6} = c + \frac{1}{6}$
14. $h + \frac{5}{14} = \frac{11}{14}$
15. $q - \frac{3}{10} = \frac{7}{10}$
16. $7k = \frac{4}{7}$
17. $\frac{5}{12} = 5d$
18. $\frac{1}{2}x = \frac{1}{4}$
19. $\frac{8}{9} = \frac{1}{3}f$
20. $r + 2.1 = 4.7$
21. $9.9 = x + 5.4$
22. $11.2 = f - 1.8$
23. $j - 3.7 = 20.4$
24. $4w = 6.8$
25. $13.9 = 2.5z$
26. $3.2d = 40.8$
27. $x + \frac{1}{2} = 1\frac{3}{4}$
28. $g + \frac{5}{3} = 3\frac{2}{3}$
29. $2\frac{5}{7} = p - \frac{2}{7}$
30. $e - \frac{18}{11} = 1\frac{6}{11}$
31. $\frac{4}{3}y = 36$
32. $\frac{9}{10} = \frac{5}{6}v$
33. $\frac{2}{3}k = 28 \cdot \frac{4}{9}$

Solve.

34. Find five pairs of whole numbers, such that when they are inserted into the equation below, the solution of the equation is 3.

$$x + \underline{\ ?\ } = \underline{\ ?\ }$$

35. Find five pairs of numbers, such that when they are inserted into the equation below, the solution of the equation is $\frac{2}{5}$.

$$\underline{\ ?\ }\,x = \underline{\ ?\ }$$

8.2 Writing Linear Equations

Lesson Objectives

- Express the relationship between two quantities as a linear equation.
- Use a table or graph to represent a linear equation.

Vocabulary

linear equation
independent variable
dependent variable

Learn **Write a linear equation to represent a given situation.**

a) Caleb is x years old. His sister is 10 years older than he is. If his sister is y years old, write an equation that relates their two ages.

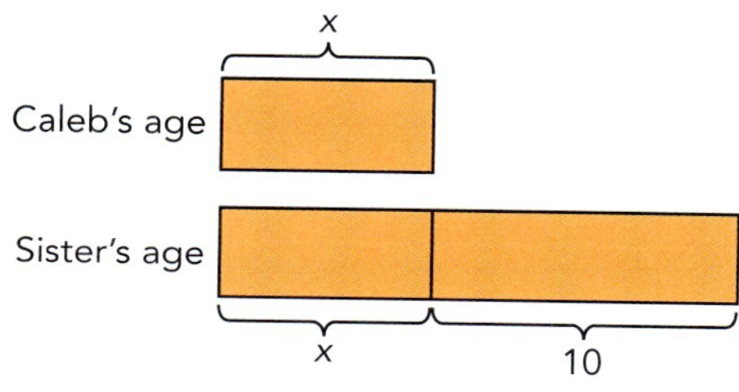

From the model, an expression for the sister's age is $x + 10$.

To make an equation using this expression, notice that the problem says that the sister's age is another variable y.

So you can write:

$y = x + 10$

The equation $y = x + 10$ is called a linear equation.

In the equation, x is called the **independent variable** and y is called the **dependent variable** because the value of y depends on the value of x.

Writing y as an expression using x is called expressing y in terms of x.

Continue on next page

b) A rhombus has sides of length r centimeters. If the perimeter of the rhombus is P centimeters, express P in terms of r.

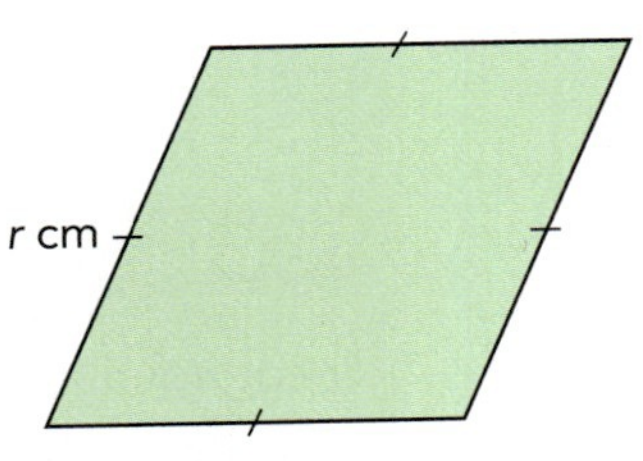

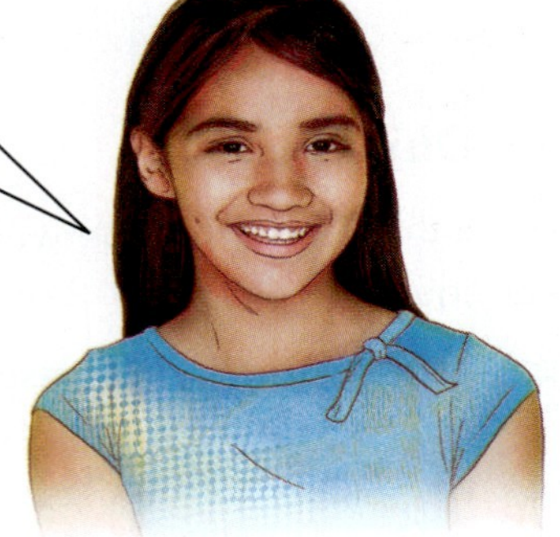

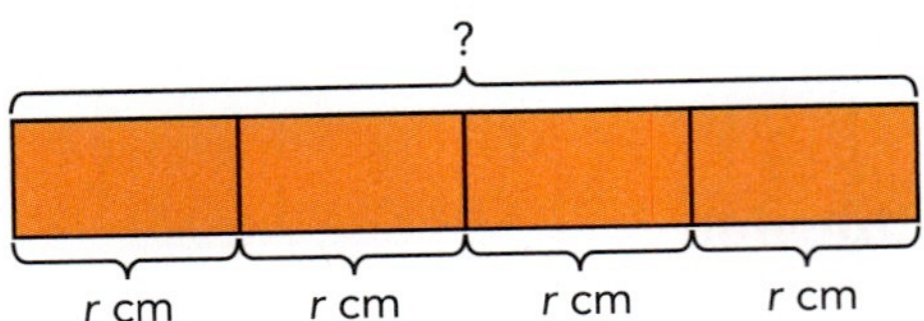

From the model, the perimeter of the rhombus $= r + r + r + r$

$= 4r$ cm

Because the perimeter of the rhombus is P centimeters, you can write

$P = 4r$.

Guided Practice

Complete.

1 Isaiah has h baseball cards. Miguel has 7 more baseball cards than Isaiah.

a) Write an expression for the number of baseball cards that Miguel has in terms of h.

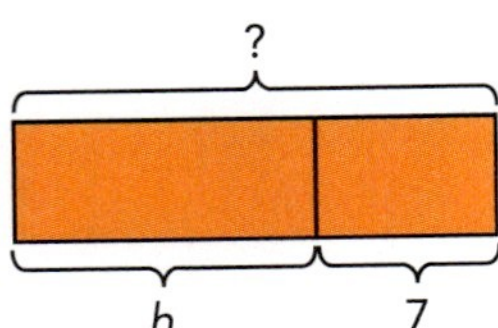

Miguel has __?__ baseball cards.

b) If Miguel has k baseball cards, express k in terms of h.

$k =$ __?__ + __?__

c) State the independent and dependent variables.

Independent variable: __?__, dependent variable: __?__

Write an equation for each of the following. Then state the independent and dependent variables for each equation.

2. Hannah took p minutes to jog around a park. Sofia took 12 minutes longer to jog around the park. If Sofia took t minutes to jog around the park, express t in terms of p.

3. A bouquet of roses costs $30. A bouquet of tulips costs m dollars less. If the cost of one bouquet of tulips is n dollars, express n in terms of m.

4. Nathan has 7 boxes of marbles. Each box contains b marbles. If he has c marbles altogether, express c in terms of b.

5. A motel charges Mr. Kim x dollars for his stay. Mr. Kim stayed at the motel for 12 nights. If the rate per night for a room is y dollars, express y in terms of x.

Learn Use tables and graphs to represent linear equations.

a) The length of a rectangular picture frame is 5 inches longer than its width. Write an equation to show how its width and length are related.

Let w represent the width of the picture frame, in inches.
Let ℓ represent the length of the picture frame, in inches.

Since the length is 5 inches longer than the width,

$\ell = w + 5.$

Many pairs of ℓ and w values will make this equation true.

Width (w in.)		Length (ℓ in.)
1	$\xrightarrow{+5}$	6
2	$\xrightarrow{+5}$	7
3	$\xrightarrow{+5}$	8
4	$\xrightarrow{+5}$	9
5	$\xrightarrow{+5}$	10

The length is dependent on the width.

The width (w) is the independent variable, and the length (ℓ) is the dependent variable.

Continue on next page

The data on the previous page can be represented in a table, as shown below. The first row of the table shows values of the independent variable. The second row shows values of the dependent variable.

Width (w inches)	1	2	3	4	5
Length (ℓ inches)	6	7	8	9	10

Use the data in the table to plot the ordered pairs (1, 6), (2, 7), (3, 8), (4, 9), and (5, 10) on a coordinate plane. Connect the points to draw a line.

The horizontal axis shows the width of the picture frame.
The vertical axis shows the length of the picture frame.

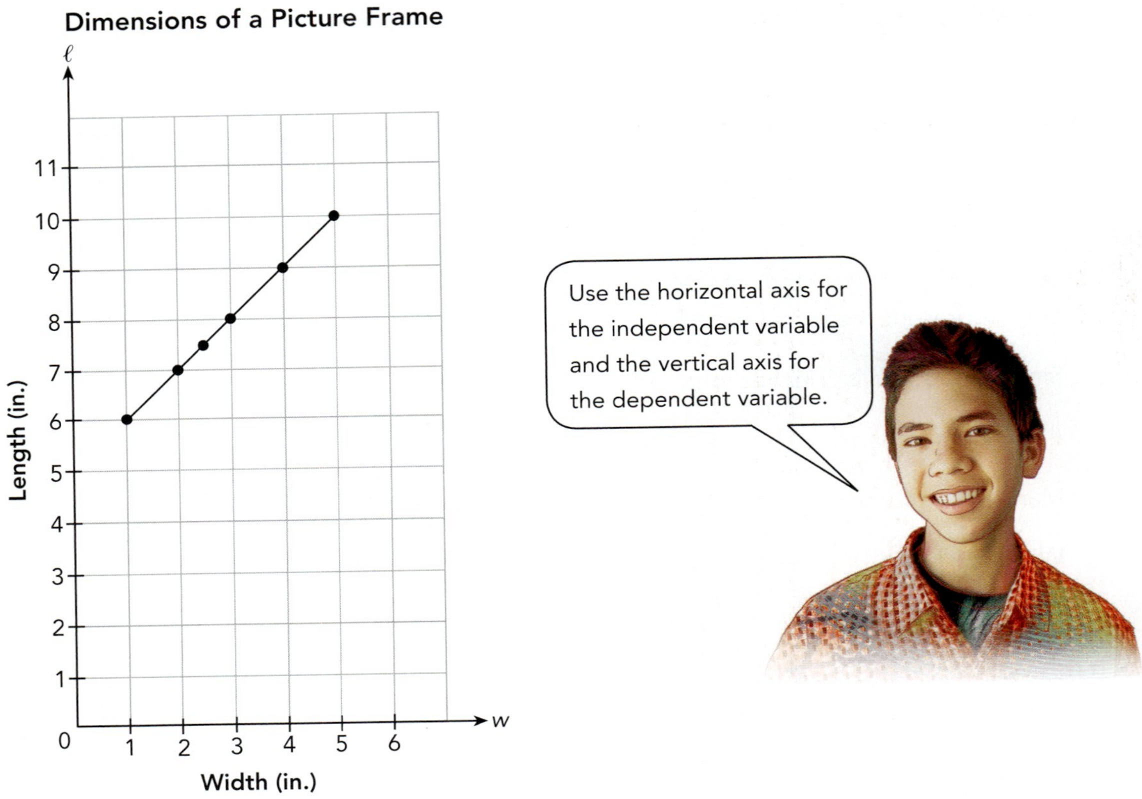

All linear equations have graphs that are lines. The graph of a linear equation contains all the ordered pairs that make the equation true.

For example, the point (2.5, 7.5) is on the graph of the equation $\ell = w + 5$. You can see that these values make the equation true:

$$\ell = w + 5$$
$$7.5 = 2.5 + 5$$

The ordered pair (2.5, 7.5) also makes sense in this situation because you could have a picture frame that is 2.5 inches wide and 7.5 inches long.

b) Each can of paint contains 5 gallons of paint. Write an equation to show the relationship between the number of cans and the volume of paint.

Let v represent the volume of paint in gallons, and c represent the number of cans of paint.

Since each can contains 5 gallons of paint,

$v = 5c$.

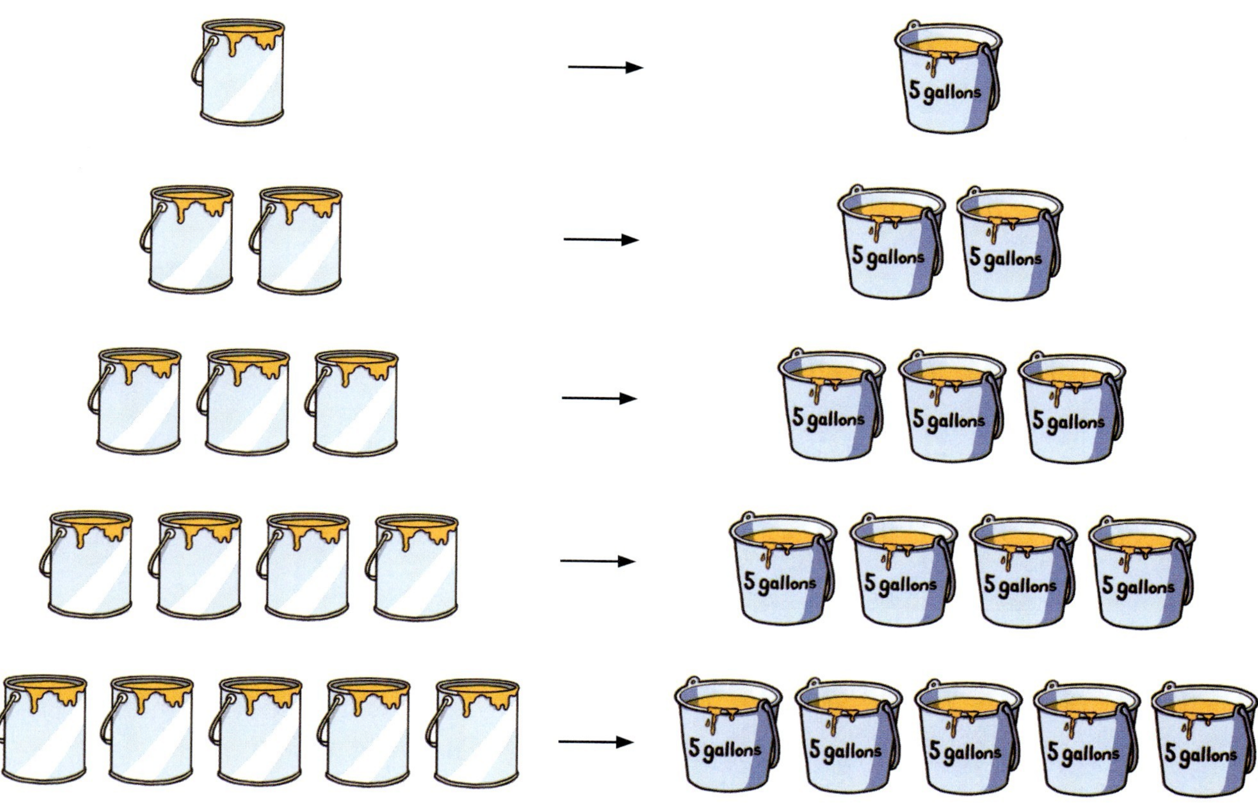

The volume of paint depends on the number of cans of paint. The number of cans c is the independent variable, and the volume of paint v is the dependent variable.

Continue on next page

The data on the previous page can be represented in a table, as shown below. The first row of the table shows values of the independent variable, and the second row shows values of the dependent variable.

Number of Cans (c)	1	2	3	4	5
Volume of Paint (v gallons)	5	10	15	20	25

You can write the data in the table as the ordered pairs (1, 5), (2, 10), (3, 15), (4, 20), and (5, 25). These ordered pairs can be plotted on a coordinate plane, and you can look for a pattern. You can connect the points to draw a line.

The horizontal axis shows the number of cans of paint.
The vertical axis shows the volume of paint in gallons.

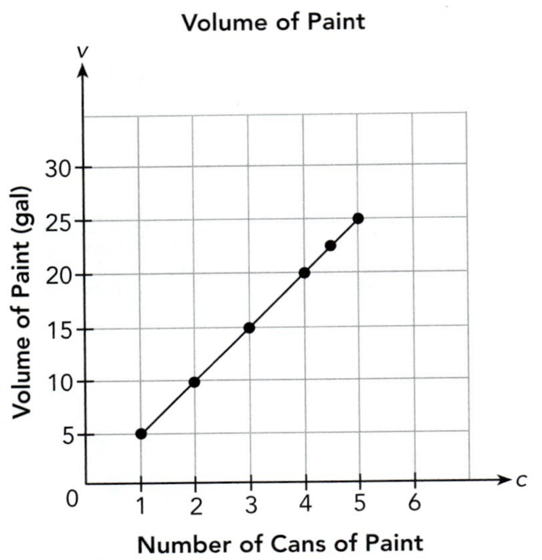

The graph of the equation $v = 5c$ contains all the ordered pairs that make the equation true.

For example, the point (4.5, 22.5) is on the graph of the equation $v = 5c$. You can see that these values make the equation true:

$$v = 5c$$
$$22.5 = 5 \times 4.5$$

The ordered pair (4.5, 22.5) and other values of ordered pairs make sense in this situation.

It is possible to have 4.5 cans of paint that contain 22.5 gallons of paint.

It is also possible to have $2\frac{1}{3}$ cans of paint that contain $11\frac{2}{3}$ gallons of paint.

Guided Practice

Copy and complete the table. Then use the table to answer the questions.

6 The width of a rectangular tank is 2 meters less than its length.

a) If the length is p meters and the width is q meters, write an equation relating p and q.

Length (p meters)	3	4	5	6	7	8
Width (q meters)	1	?	?	4	?	?

b) Use the data from **a)** to plot the points on a coordinate plane. Connect the points with a line.

c) The point (5.5, 3.5) is on the line you drew in **b)**. Does this point make sense in the situation?

Copy and complete each table. Then express the relationship between the two variables as an equation.

7 Paul and Lee went to the library to borrow some books. Paul borrowed 6 more books than Lee.

Number of Books Lee Borrowed (x)	1	2	3	4	5
Number of Books Paul Borrowed (y)	7	?	9	?	?

8 At a crafts store, Zoey bought some boxes of red beads and some boxes of blue beads. The number of boxes of red beads was 4 times the number of boxes of blue beads.

Number of Boxes of Blue Beads (b)	2	3	4	5	6
Number of Boxes of Red Beads (r)	8	?	?	?	24

Use the data in the table to plot points on a coordinate plane. Connect the points to form a line. Then write an equation to show the relationship between the variables.

Time Taken (t hours)	1	2	3	4	5	6
Distance Traveled (d miles)	50	100	150	200	250	300

Practice 8.2

Solve.

1 Joshua is *w* years old. His brother is 3 years older than he is.

a) If his brother is *x* years old, express *x* in terms of *w*.

b) State the independent and dependent variables in the equation.

2 Rita has *b* markers. Sandy has 11 fewer markers than she has.

a) If Sandy has *h* markers, express *h* in terms of *b*.

b) State the independent and dependent variables in the equation.

3 A small box of cereal weighs *k* grams. A jumbo box of cereal weighs 5 times as much.

a) If the weight of the jumbo box of cereal is *m* grams, express *m* in terms of *k*.

b) State the independent and dependent variables in the equation.

4 The area of Hank's farm is *n* acres. The area of Hank's farm is 8 times as large as the area of Stan's farm.

a) If *s* represents the area of Stan's farm, express *s* in terms of *n*.

b) State the independent and dependent variables in the equation.

5 Ethan scored *x* points in a game. His younger sister scored 8 points when she played the same game. Their combined score was *y* points.

a) Write an equation relating *x* and *y*.

b) Copy and complete the table to show the relationship between *x* and *y*.

Ethan's Scores (*x* points)	10	11	12	13	14	15
Combined Scores (*y* points)	?	?	?	?	?	?

6 There are x sparrows in a tree. There are 50 sparrows on the ground beneath the tree. Let y represent the total number of sparrows in the tree and on the ground.

a) Express y in terms of x.

b) Make a table to show the relationship between y and x. Use values of $x = 10, 20, 30, 40$, and 50 in your table.

c) Graph the relationship between y and x in a coordinate plane.

7 A rectangle has a perimeter of P centimeters. Its width is b centimeters. Its length is double its width.

a) Express P in terms of b.

b) Copy and complete the table to show the relationship between P and b.

Width (b centimeters)	1	2	3	4	5	6
Perimeter (P centimeters)	?	?	?	?	?	?

8 Every month, Amaan spends 60% of what he earns and saves the rest. Amaan earns n dollars and saves r dollars each month.

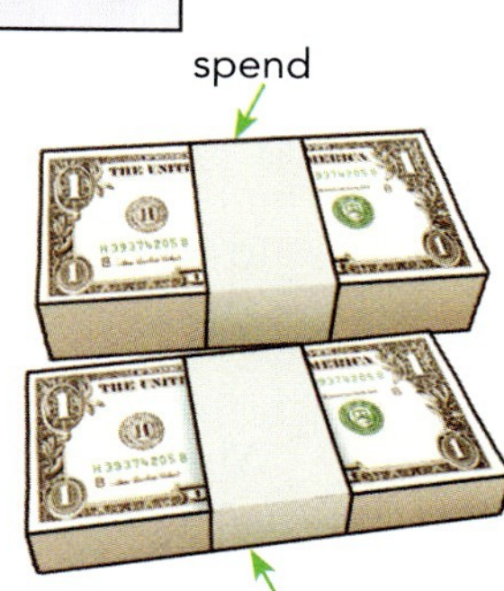

a) Express r in terms of n.

b) Make a table to show the relationship between r and n. Use values of $n = 100, 200, 400$, and 500 in your table.

c) Graph the relationship between n and r in a coordinate plane.

d) The point (287.5, 115) is on the line you drew in **c)**. Does this point make sense in the situation? Explain.

9 The side length of a square is t inches. The perimeter of the square is z inches.

a) Express z in terms of t.

b) Make a table to show the relationship between z and t. Use whole number values of t from 1 to 10.

c) Graph the relationship between z and t in a coordinate plane.

d) Use your graph to find the perimeter of the square when the length is 3.5 inches and 7.5 inches.

8.3 Solving Simple Inequalities

Lesson Objectives

- Use substitution to determine whether a given number is a solution of an inequality.
- Represent the solutions of an inequality on a number line.

Vocabulary
inequality

Learn **Determine solutions of inequalities of the form $x > c$ and $x < c$.**

a) A bag of tomatoes weighs more than 5 pounds. Find the possible weights of the bag of tomatoes. Then represent the possible weights on a number line.

Let x represent the possible weights, in pounds, of the tomatoes.

Since you know the bag of tomatoes weighs more than 5 pounds, you can write the inequality

$x > 5$.

To find the possible weights of the bag, you need to find the values of x that make $x > 5$ true.

When $x = 5.1$, $x > 5$ is true.
When $x = 5.2$, $x > 5$ is true.
When $x = 5.3$, $x > 5$ is true.
When $x = 6$, $x > 5$ is true.
⋮
When $x = 100$, $x > 5$ is true.

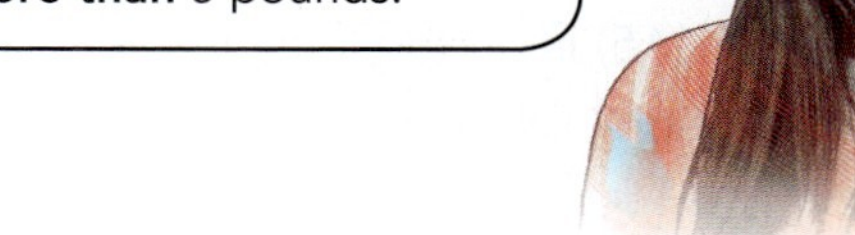

The inequality $x > 5$ is true for any value of x that is greater than 5.

Since the inequality has infinitely many solutions, you can represent the solutions on a number line as follows:

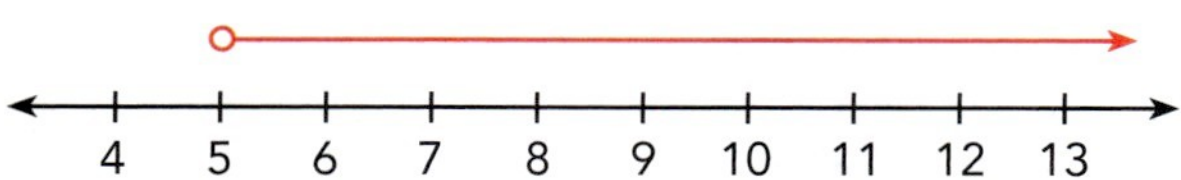

The number line above indicates that the inequality $x > 5$ is true for any value of x that is greater than 5. This value can be a fraction or mixed number, decimal, or whole number.

For example, $5\frac{3}{8} > 5$, $5.6 > 5$, and $9 > 5$.

Math Note

The empty circle indicates that the value below the circle is not a solution of the inequality.

b) The figure shows a medicine bottle.

Find the possible temperatures at which the medicine should be stored. Then represent the possible temperatures on a number line.

Let w represent the possible temperatures, in °C, at which the medicine should be stored.

You can write an inequality to show that the medicine is to be stored below 20°C:

$w < 20$

To find the possible temperatures, you need to find the values of w that make $w < 20$ true.

When $w = 19.9$, $w < 20$ is true.
When $w = 19.8$, $w < 20$ is true.
When $w = 19.7$, $w < 20$ is true.
When $w = 19.5$, $w < 20$ is true.
When $w = 19.4$, $w < 20$ is true.
When $w = 10$, $w < 20$ is true.
⋮
When $w = -4$, $w < 20$ is true.
When $w = -5$, $w < 20$ is true.

The inequality $w < 20$ is true for any value of w that is less than 20.

The solutions can be represented on a number line as shown:

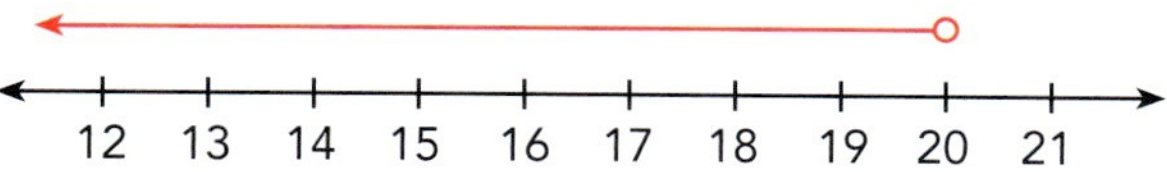

Guided Practice

Use substitution to determine the solutions of each inequality. Then represent the solution set of each inequality on a number line.

1. $h > 8$
2. $y < 10$
3. $p > 23$
4. $e < 14$
5. $m > 30$
6. $n < 5$

Hands-On Activity

WRITING INEQUALITIES

STEP 1 The figure shows a balance scale.

Write the equation that this figure represents.

STEP 2 2 counters are added to the right side. Draw what the balance scale looks like now. Then write an inequality to represent the relationship between x and the counters on the right side of the balance scale.

STEP 3 3 counters are then removed from the right side. Draw what the balance scale looks like after removing the 3 counters. Then write an inequality to represent the relationship between x and the counters on the right side of the balance scale.

STEP 4 Now, if $y > x$, write an inequality to represent the solutions of $y > x$. Explain how x and y are related using a balance scale.

Learn Determine solutions of inequalities of the form $x \geq c$ and $x \leq c$.

a) Yleana needs at least 7 feet of ribbon for her crafts project. Find the possible lengths of ribbon that would be enough to complete the project. Then represent the possible lengths on a number line.

Let p represent the length, in feet, of the ribbon Yleana needs.

You can write an inequality to show the possible lengths she needs:

$p \geq 7$

≥ means "is greater than or equal to."

To find the possible lengths of the ribbon, you need to find the values of p that make $p \geq 7$ true.

When $p = 7$, $p \geq 7$ is true.
When $p = 7.4$, $p \geq 7$ is true.
When $p = 7\frac{4}{9}$, $p \geq 7$ is true.
When $p = 8$, $p \geq 7$ is true.
When $p = 8.5$, $p \geq 7$ is true.
⋮
When $p = 20$, $p \geq 7$ is true.

The inequality $p \geq 7$ is true for any value of p that is greater than or equal to 7.

Since the inequality has infinitely many solutions, you can represent the solutions of the inequality on a number line as follows:

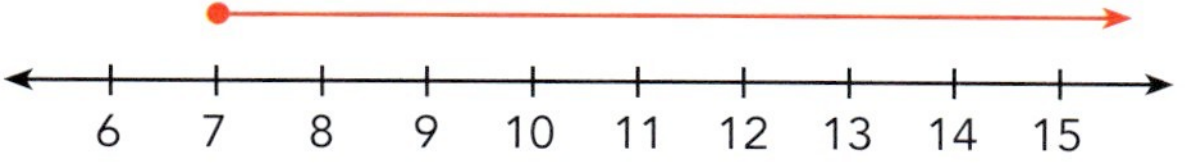

Math Note

The shaded circle indicates that the value below the circle is a solution of the inequality.

Continue on next page

b) On one winter day, Helena, Montana, had a maximum temperature of -4°C. Find the possible temperatures in Helena that day. Then represent the possible temperatures on a number line.

Let y represent the possible temperatures, in °C, of Helena that day.

Since you know the maximum temperature is -4°C, you can write an inequality.

$y \leq -4$

≤ means "is less than or equal to."

To find the possible temperatures, you need to find the values of y that make $y \leq -4$ true.

When $y = -4$,	$y \leq -4$ is true.
When $y = -4.2$,	$y \leq -4$ is true.
When $y = -4.7$,	$y \leq -4$ is true.
When $y = -5$,	$y \leq -4$ is true.
When $y = -6.7$,	$y \leq -4$ is true.
When $y = -8$,	$y \leq -4$ is true.

The inequality $y \leq -4$ is true for any value of y that is less than or equal to -4.

The solutions can be represented on a number line as shown:

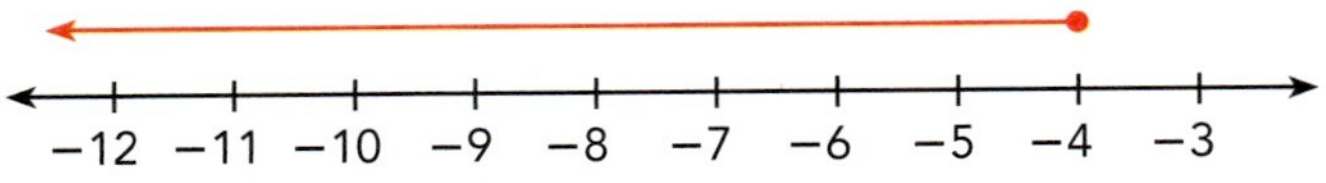

Guided Practice

Use substitution to find three solutions of each inequality. Then represent the solutions of each inequality on a number line.

7 $q \geq 3$

8 $d \leq 12$

9 $k \leq 25$

10 $m \geq -28$

Match each inequality to its graph.

a) $x < 10$ **b)** $x \leq 10$ **c)** $x > 10$ **d)** $x \geq 10$

11

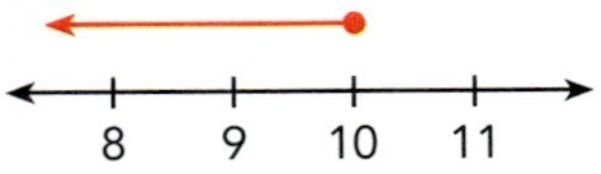

12

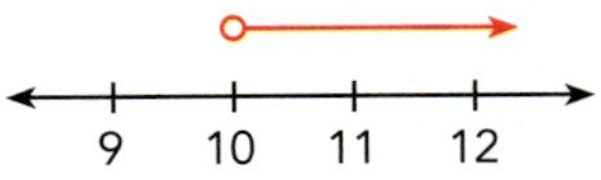

13

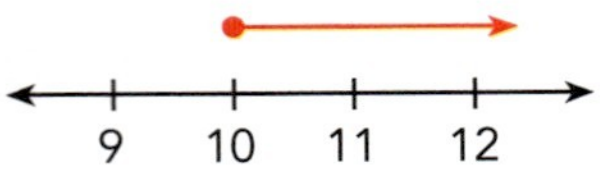

14

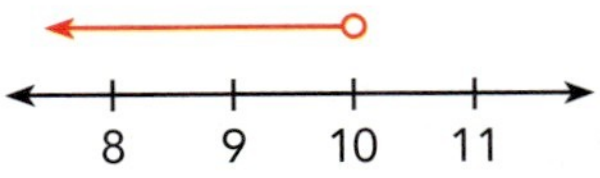

Practice 8.3

Rewrite each statement using $>$, $<$, $\geq$, or $\leq$.

1. k is less than 12.

2. d is greater than 10.

3. w is greater than or equal to 17.

4. p is less than or equal to 36.

5. A sack of potatoes weighs at least 20 pounds. Write an inequality to represent the weight of the sack of potatoes.

6. The maximum number of shirts Amanda can buy is 9. Write an inequality to represent the number of shirts that she can buy.

Represent the solutions of each inequality on a number line.

7. $x > 5$

8. $r \geq 8$

9. $m < 22$

10. $q \leq 13$

Write an inequality for each graph on a number line.

11. 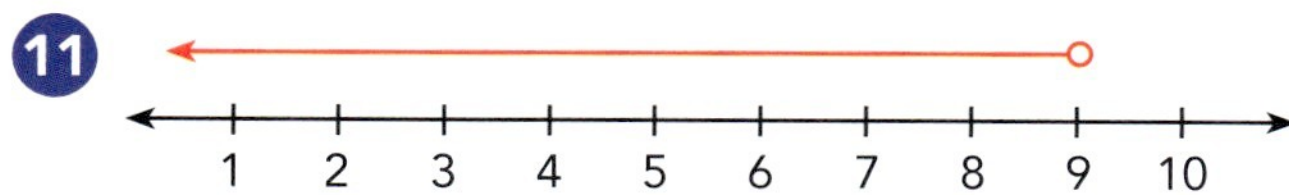

12. 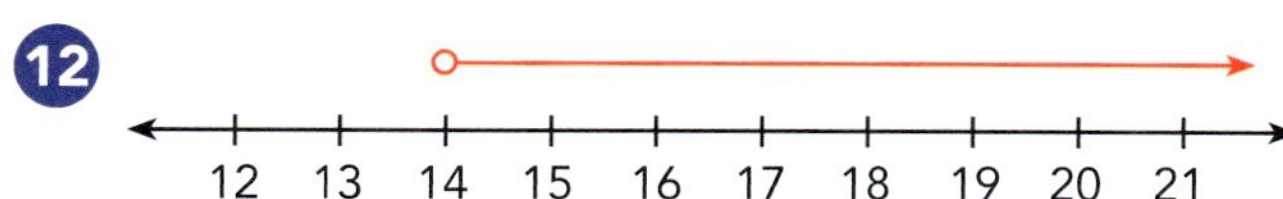

13. 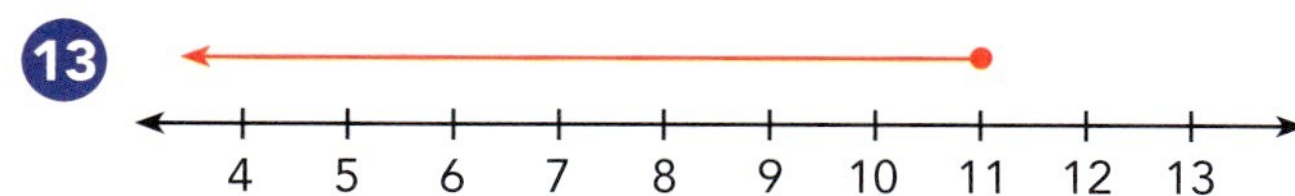

14. 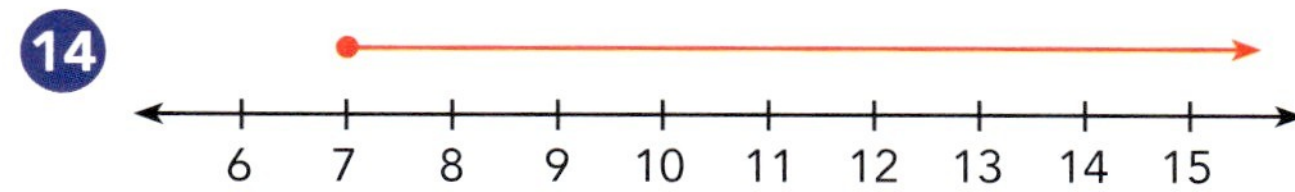

Represent the solutions of each inequality on a number line. Then give three possible integer solutions of each inequality.

15. $p < 9\frac{1}{2}$

16. $y > \frac{37}{5}$

17. $b \leq \frac{23}{4}$

18. $s \geq 6\frac{3}{7}$

19. $g > 1.5$

20. $m \geq 4.8$

21. $z \leq 9.2$

22. $r < 16.6$

Solve.

23. In the inequality $x > 9$, x represents the number of restaurants along a street.

    a) Is 9 a possible value of x? Explain.

    b) Is $9\frac{2}{5}$ a possible value of x? Explain.

    c) Use a number line to represent the solution set of the inequality. Then state the least possible number of restaurants on the street.

24. In the inequality $q \leq 24.3$, q represents the possible weights, in pounds, of a package.

    a) Is 24.4 a possible value of q? Explain.

    b) Is $20\frac{7}{10}$ a possible value of q? Explain.

    c) Use a number line to represent the solution set of the inequality. Then state the greatest possible weight of the package.

Each inequality has the variable on the right side of the inequality symbol. Graph each solution set on a number line.

25. $11 \leq d$

26. $7\frac{3}{4} > q$

27. $2.5 < h$

28. $-6 \geq w$

29. $5.7 < m$

30. $8.1 \geq n$

8.4 Real-World Problems: Equations and Inequalities

Lesson Objectives

- Solve real-world problems by writing equations.
- Solve real-world problems by writing inequalities.

Learn Write algebraic equations to solve real-world problems.

a) Yesterday Kyle had some stamps. Today his father gave him 12 more stamps. Now he has 27 stamps altogether. How many stamps did Kyle have yesterday?

Let x represent the number of stamps Kyle had yesterday.

Kyle had **some** stamps. Today he has **12 more** stamps. Now he has **27** stamps.

x $\quad + 12 \quad = 27$

The equation is $x + 12 = 27$.

To find how many stamps Kyle had yesterday, solve the equation.

$$x + 12 = 27$$
$$x + 12 - 12 = 27 - 12$$
$$x = 15$$

Subtract 12 from both sides.

Kyle had 15 stamps yesterday.

b) In a pond, there are 3 times as many koi as goldfish. If there are 48 koi, find the number of goldfish in the pond.

Let g represent the number of goldfish in the pond.

There are **some** goldfish. There are **3 times as many** koi. There are **48** koi.

g $\quad \times 3 \quad = 48$

The equation is $3g = 48$.

Continue on next page

To find the number of goldfish in the pond, solve the equation.

$3g = 48$

$3g \div 3 = 48 \div 3$ Divide both sides by 3.

$g = 16$

There are 16 goldfish in the pond.

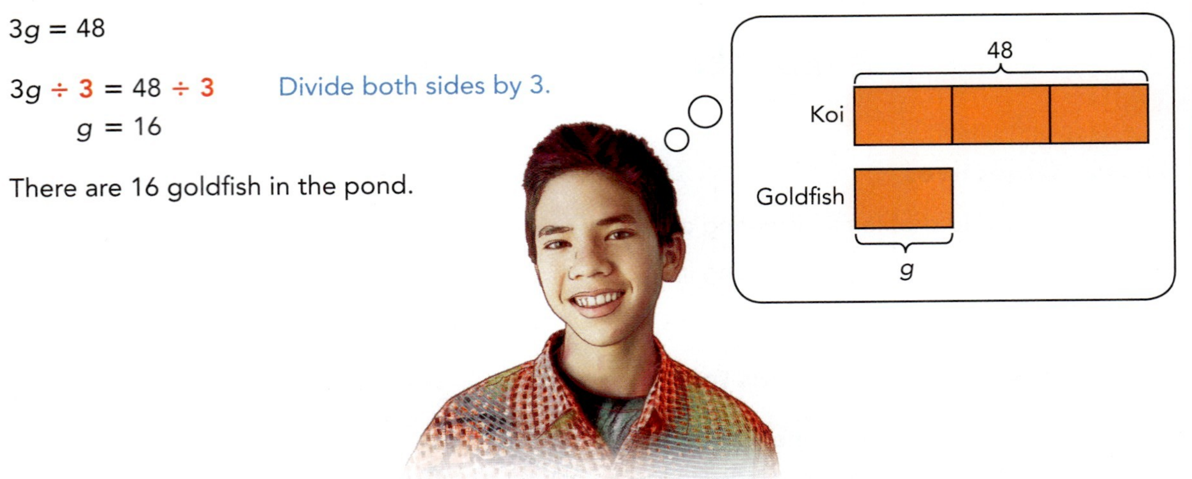

Guided Practice

Complete.

1. On Monday, Wendy had some leaves in a collection she was making for biology class. After she collected 23 more leaves on Tuesday, she had 41 leaves. Find the number of leaves Wendy had on Monday.

   Let r represent the number of leaves Wendy had on Monday.

   $r + 23 = \underline{\ ?\ }$

   $r + 23 - \underline{\ ?\ } = \underline{\ ?\ } - \underline{\ ?\ }$

   $r = \underline{\ ?\ }$

   Wendy had __?__ leaves on Monday.

Write an algebraic equation for each problem. Then solve.

2. Carlos thinks of a number. When he adds 17 to it, the result is 45. What is the number that Carlos thought of?

3. Sylvia bought some blouses and T-shirts. She paid a total of \$63. The T-shirts cost \$29. How much did the blouses cost?

4. Felicia used 153 yellow beads and some green beads for her art project. She used 9 times as many yellow beads as green beads. How many green beads did she use for the project?

5. Ivan had saved some quarters. He spent 50 quarters, which was $\frac{2}{5}$ of the quarters he started out with. How many quarters did he start out with?

Learn Write algebraic inequalities to solve real-world problems.

a) Jamal sees the sign shown in a store window.

Write an inequality to represent the situation. Use a number line to represent the inequality. Then give the greatest possible cost of a T-shirt.

Let c represent the cost of a T-shirt.

All T-shirts cost less than $16.

The inequality $c < 16$ represents the situation.

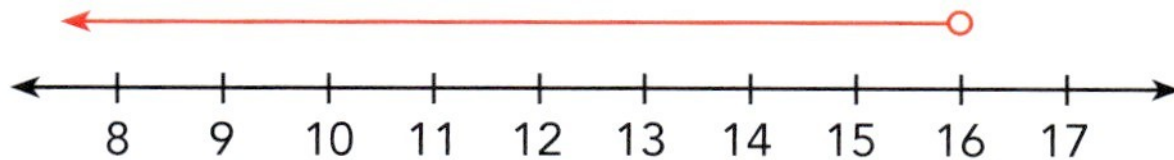

The greatest possible cost of a T-shirt is $15.99.

b) A ski club is organizing a trip. At least 20 club members have to sign up for the trip to cover the cost of the bus. Write an inequality to represent this situation. Use a number line to represent the inequality.

Let w represent the number of members who sign up for the trip.

The number of members who sign up must be at least 20.

The inequality $w \geq 20$ represents the situation.

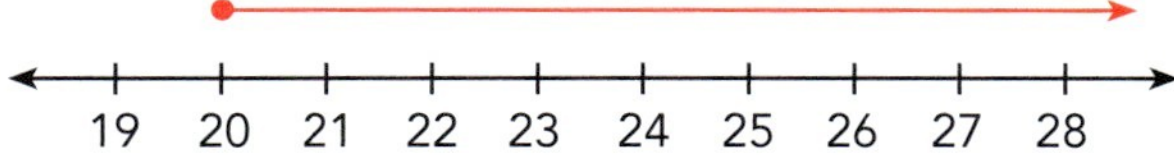

The graph shows that the least number of members who have to sign up is 20.

Guided Practice

Complete.

6 The figure shows a speed limit sign on a highway.

a) Let x represent the speed in miles per hour.

Write an inequality to represent the situation.

The inequality is ___?___.

b) Give the maximum legal driving speed on the highway.

The maximum legal driving speed is ___?___ miles per hour.

Solve.

7 More than 35 guests came to Katrina's birthday party last Sunday.

a) Write an inequality to represent the number of guests who turned up for the birthday party.

b) What is the least possible number of guests who could have come to the party?

8 In Mr. Boyle's class, the students are required to summarize a passage in less than 50 words.

a) Write an inequality to represent the number of words that the students can use to summarize the passage.

b) What is the maximum number of words that a student can use?

9 A cargo elevator has a load limit of 240 tons.

a) Write an inequality to represent the load limit of the cargo elevator.

b) What is the greatest possible load the cargo elevator can carry?

10 To get a discount coupon at a bookstore, you need to spend at least $50 at the store.

a) Write an inequality to represent the amount of money that you must spend in order to get a discount coupon.

b) Andrea has spent $45 at the store, and her friend Alex has spent $55. Which person can get a discount coupon?

Practice 8.4

Write and solve an algebraic equation for each problem. Show your work.

1. Damien thinks of a number. When he adds 32 to it, the sum is 97. What is the number that Damien thought of?

2. A baker made some bagels in the morning. After selling 85 bagels, there were 64 left. How many bagels did the baker make in the morning?

3. Claudia can text 3 times as fast as Fiona. Claudia can text 78 words per minute. How many words per minute can Fiona text?

4. Eric spent $\frac{2}{5}$ of his allowance on a jacket. The jacket cost him $12. How much was his allowance?

Write and solve an algebraic inequality for each problem.

5. In a science competition, students have to score more than 40 points in order to move on to the next round.

   a) Write an inequality to represent this situation. Use a number line to represent the inequality.

   b) What is the least number of points a student needs to score in order to move on to the next round? Only whole numbers of points are awarded to students.

6. A stadium has a seating capacity of 65,000 spectators.

   a) What is the maximum number of spectators the stadium can hold?

   b) Write an inequality to represent this situation. Then use a number line to represent the inequality.

Write and solve an algebraic equation or inequality for each problem. Show your work.

7. A bicycle store sells $\frac{4}{7}$ of the mountain bikes in the store. Then only 24 mountain bikes are left. How many mountain bikes were there originally?

8. Mabel has a total of 54 decorative beads. Some are black and some are white. The ratio of the number of black beads to the number of white beads is 7 : 2. How many more black beads than white beads are there?

9. Gary has a collection of comic books. After selling 70% of his comic books, he has 42 comic books left. How many comic books did he start with?

10. There are 30 students in the gym. If there are at least 16 girls, write an inequality to represent the number of boys in the gym.

11. The marbles in a box are repackaged in equal numbers into 6 smaller bags. If each bag has more than 8 marbles, what is the least possible number of marbles that could have been in the box?

12. Mr. Edwards is now 3 times as old as his daughter. In 15 years' time, the sum of their ages will be 86.

    a) Find their ages now.

    b) How old was Mr. Edwards when his daughter was born?

13. In a competition, each school is allowed to send a team with at least 5 members, but not more than 8 members. 12 schools participated in the competition.

    a) Find the least possible number of participants in the competition.

    b) Find the greatest possible number of participants in the competition.

A rectangular photograph is mounted on a rectangular card. There is a border of equal width around the photograph. The perimeter of the card is 40 centimeters longer than that of the photograph. Find the width of the border in centimeters.

Chapter Wrap Up

Concept Map

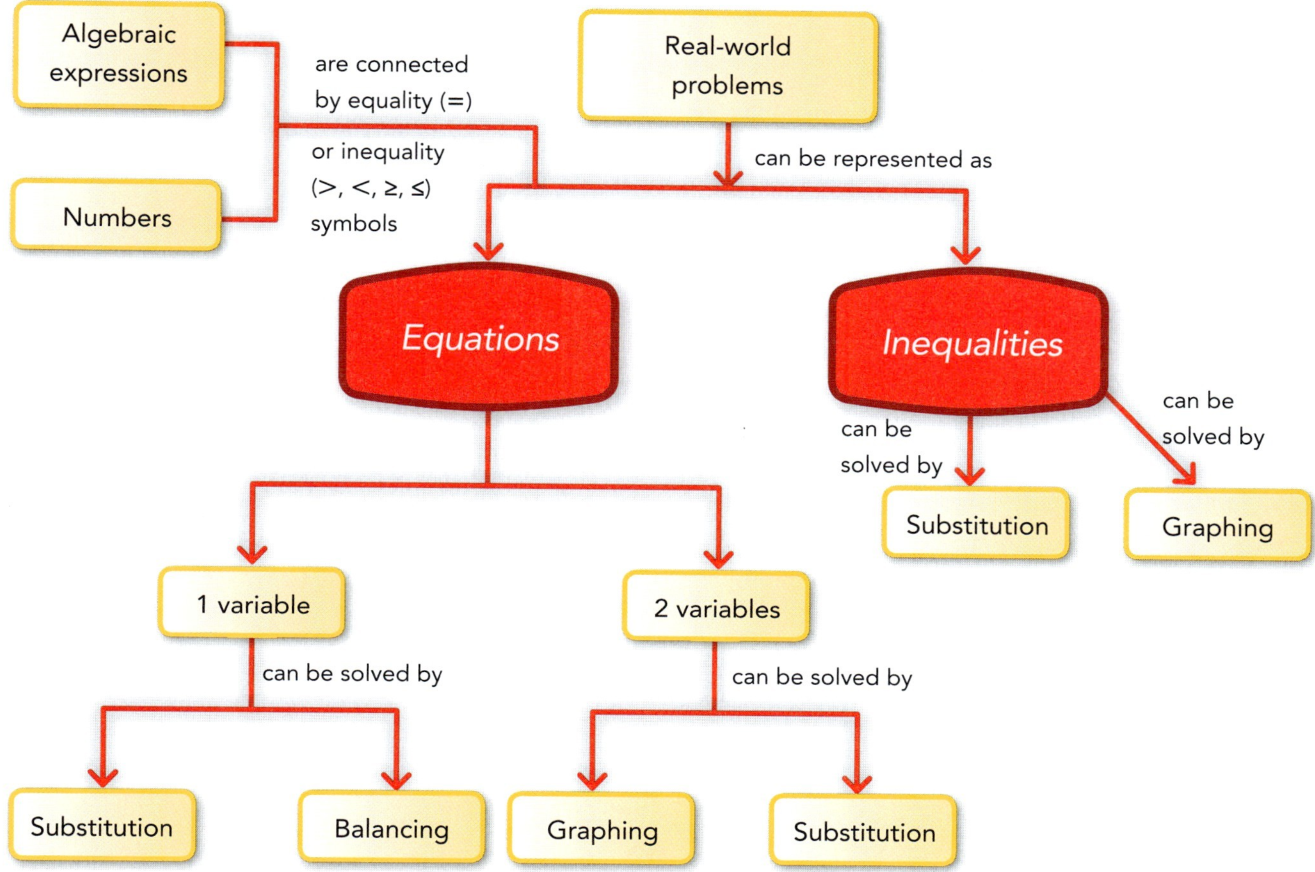

Key Concepts

- Equations can be solved by substitution, or by adding, subtracting, multiplying, and dividing each side of the equation by the same nonzero number.
- The solution of an equation is a value, or values, that makes the equation true.
- A linear equation has a dependent and an independent variable.
- The solutions of an inequality are all the values that makes the inequality true.
- An inequality can be solved by substitution or by graphing on a number line.

Chapter Review/Test

Concepts and Skills

Solve each equation using the concept of balancing.
Write all fraction answers in simplest form.

1. $x + 8 = 27$
2. $\frac{10}{11} = a + \frac{4}{11}$
3. $f + 3.8 = 9.2$
4. $42 = y - 14$
5. $k - \frac{7}{8} = 2\frac{11}{24}$
6. $n - 2.7 = 13.4$
7. $6h = 84$
8. $75.6 = 7.2r$
9. $\frac{4}{5}p = 10$
10. $9 \cdot \frac{3}{5} = \frac{8}{11}w$

Represent the solution set of each inequality on a number line.

11. $b < 7$
12. $b > 13$
13. $m \geq 24$
14. $m \leq 38$
15. $g > \frac{2}{3}$
16. $g \leq 5\frac{3}{5}$
17. $z < 7.1$
18. $z \geq 10.4$

Write an inequality for each number line.

19.

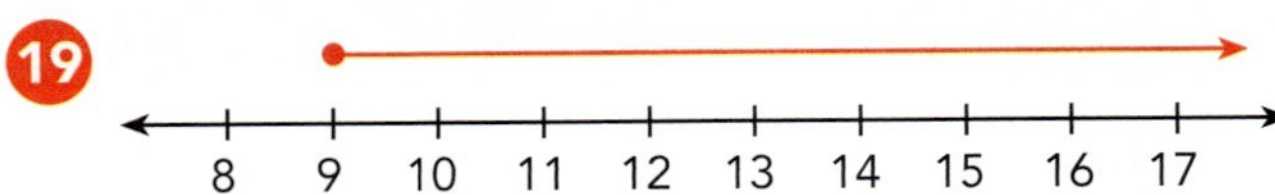

20.

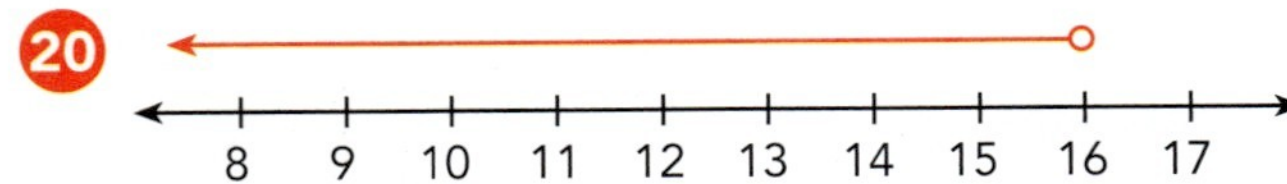

21.

$\frac{1}{10}$ $\frac{2}{10}$ $\frac{3}{10}$ $\frac{4}{10}$ $\frac{5}{10}$ $\frac{6}{10}$ $\frac{7}{10}$ $\frac{8}{10}$ $\frac{9}{10}$ $\frac{10}{10}$

22.

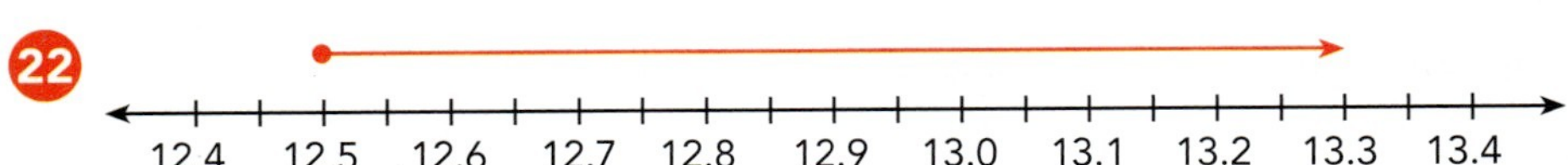

Write an equation for each of the following.

23. Patrick is x years old. His brother is 9 years older than he is. If his brother is y years old, express y in terms of x.

24. The length of a house is three times its width. The width of the house is f yards. If the perimeter of the house is h yards, express h in terms of f.

Problem Solving

Use an algebraic equation or algebraic inequality to solve. Show your work.

25. Mrs. Lewis makes some orange juice. After making another 850 milliliters of juice, she now has 4,880 milliliters of orange juice. How much orange juice did Mrs. Lewis make at first?

26. Adrian has 5 times as many stickers as Derrick. If Adrian has 325 stickers, how many stickers does Derrick have?

27. A printer prints fewer than 18 pages per minute. What is the maximum number of pages the printer can print in 7 minutes?

28. If a number is multiplied by 4, it gives the same result as $\frac{2}{7}$ of 504. What is the number?

29. Keane has a total of 96 counters. Some are green and some are red. The ratio of the number of red counters to the number of green counters is 3 : 5. How many more green counters than red counters are there?

30. A grocer bought 8 boxes of apples. Each box contains 35 apples and fewer than 40% of the apples in each box are green apples. Find the greatest possible number of green apples in all the 8 boxes.

31. A rectangular lunch tray has a length of x centimeters and a width of 15 cm. The tray's length is at least 20% greater than its width.

   a) Write an inequality to represent this situation.

   b) Suppose x is a whole number. Find the least possible perimeter, and the least possible area of the lunch tray.

CHAPTER

9

The Coordinate Plane

9.1 Points on the Coordinate Plane

9.2 Length of Line Segments

9.3 Real-World Problems: Graphing

▶ Every point on the coordinate plane can be represented by a pair of coordinates.

Have you ever used a street directory?

A street directory is useful for locating a street in an unfamiliar area. The maps in the directory use a system of coordinates to help you locate the streets easily.

When using a directory, you can look for a street name in the index. The index gives you the correct map to look at and also gives a pair of coordinates so that you can locate the street.

For example, in the map below, Fort Hill Road can be found on map 87, section B2. B2 is a pair of coordinates that tells you the location of the street on the map.

In this chapter, you will use numerical coordinates to locate points on a coordinate plane.

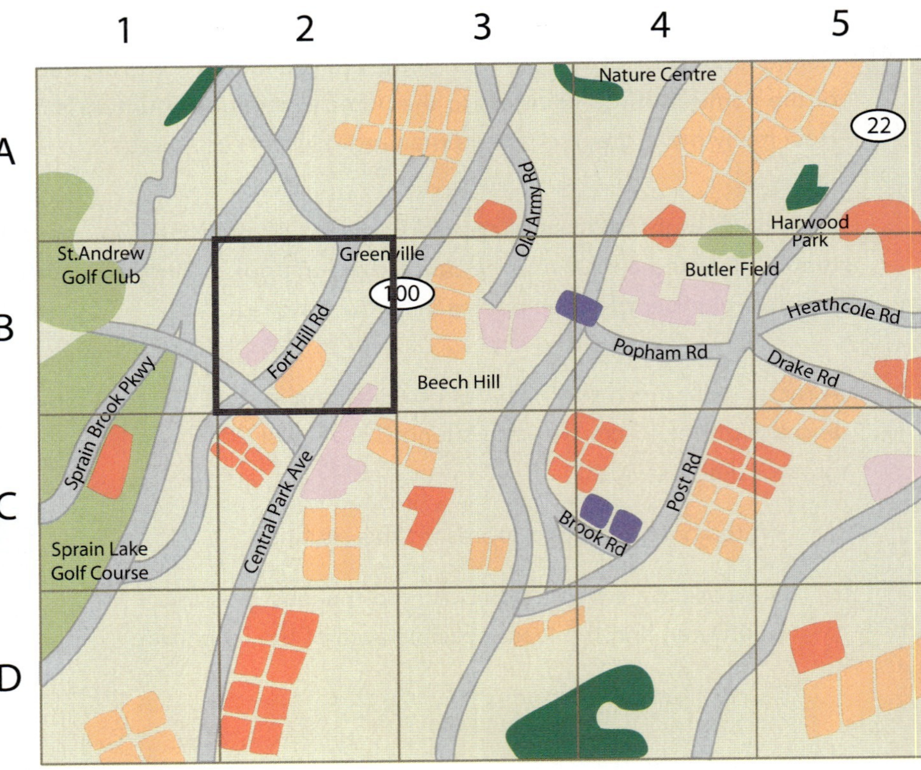

Map 87

Recall Prior Knowledge

Identifying and plotting coordinates

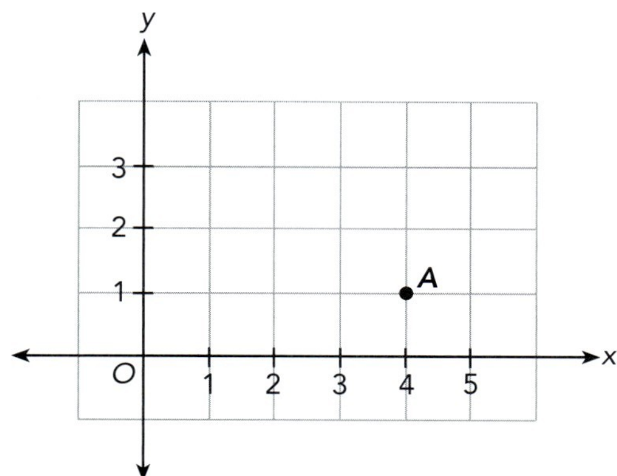

The coordinates of *O*, the origin, are (0, 0).

To find the location of point *A*, move **4** units to the right on the *x*-axis and **1** unit up on the *y*-axis.

The coordinates of *A* are (**4**, **1**).

Quick Check

Use the coordinate plane below.

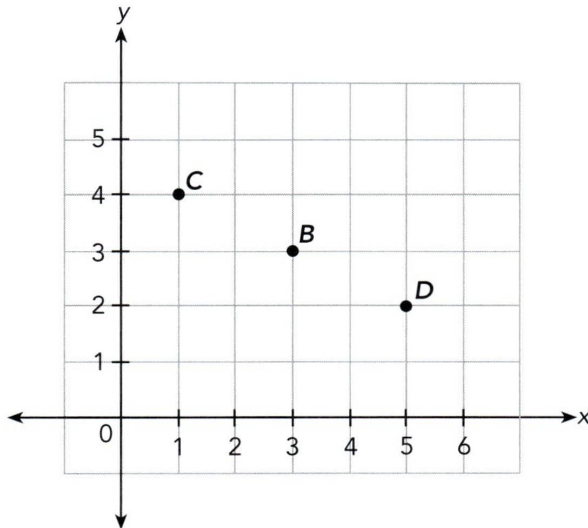

1. Give the coordinates of points *B*, *C*, and *D*.

Use graph paper. Plot the points on a coordinate plane.

2. *P* (3, 2), *Q* (2, 3), and *R* (0, 4)

Representing negative numbers on the number line

Negative numbers are numbers less than zero.

−2, −10, −23, and −134 are examples of negative numbers.

Negative numbers are found to the left of 0 on the number line.

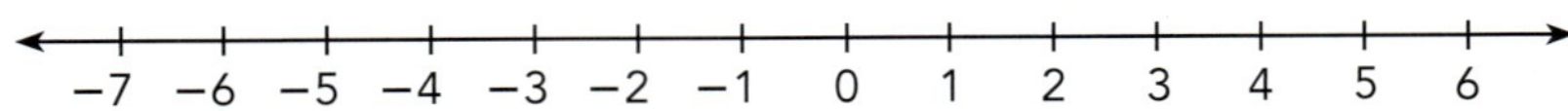

Quick Check

Identify the number that each indicated point represents.

3

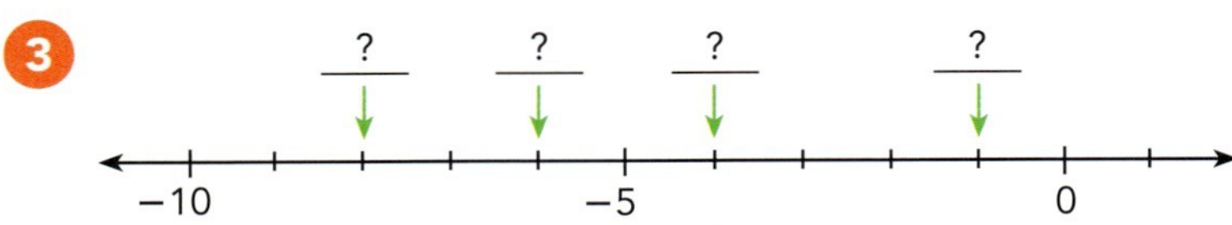

Draw a horizontal number line to represent each set of numbers.

4 −3, 0, 1, 5, 8

5 −15, −11, −9, −7, −2

Recognizing and writing the absolute value of a number

The absolute value of a number is the distance from itself to 0 on the number line. It is always positive or zero.

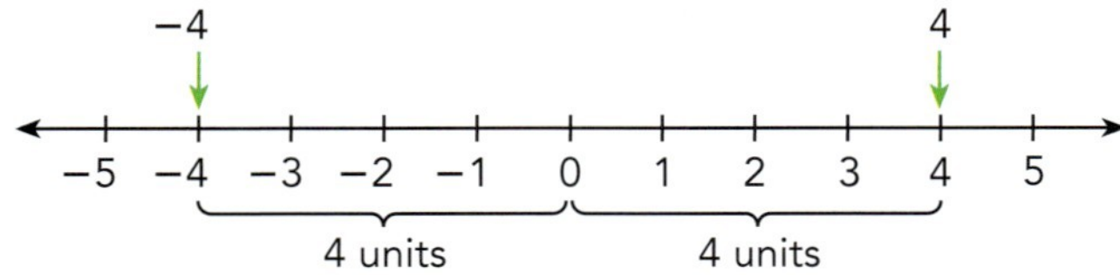

−4 is 4 units away from 0. Its absolute value is 4.
Similarly, the absolute value of 4 is also 4.
You can write $|-4| = 4$, and $|4| = 4$.

Quick Check

Use the symbol | | to write the absolute values of the following numbers.

6 11

7 −16

8 −21

Finding the perimeter of a polygon

The perimeter of a polygon is the distance around it.

Figure *ABCDE* has 5 sides — $\overline{AB}$, $\overline{BC}$, $\overline{CD}$, $\overline{DE}$, and $\overline{EA}$.

The perimeter of figure *ABCDE* is equal to the sum of the lengths of its 5 sides:

$AB + BC + CD + DE + EA$
$= 9 + 7 + 7 + 7 + 9$
$= 39$ cm

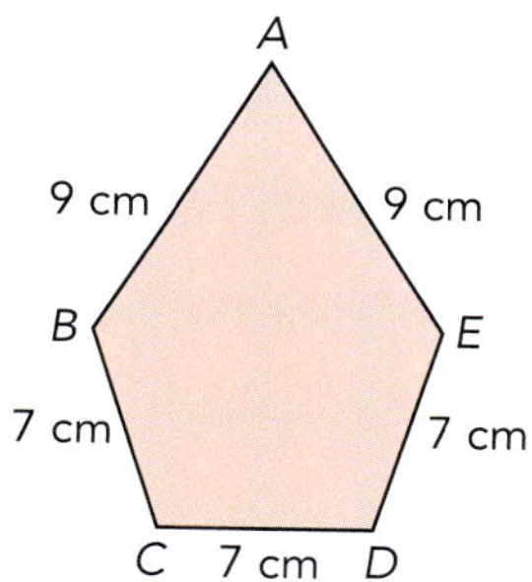

Quick Check

Find the perimeter of each polygon.

9. Figure *ABC* is an isosceles triangle.

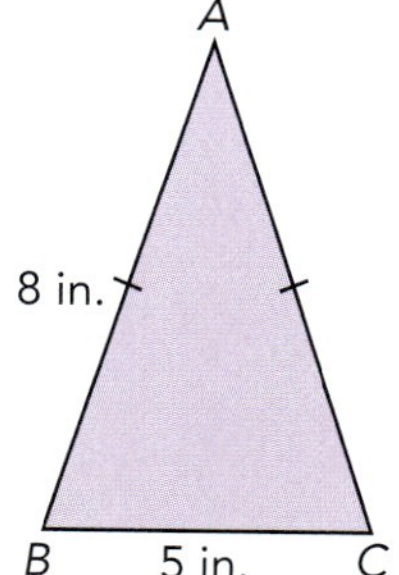

10. Figure *DEF* is an equilateral triangle.

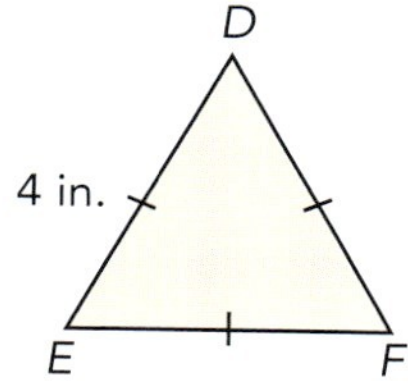

11. Figure *PQRS* is a trapezoid.

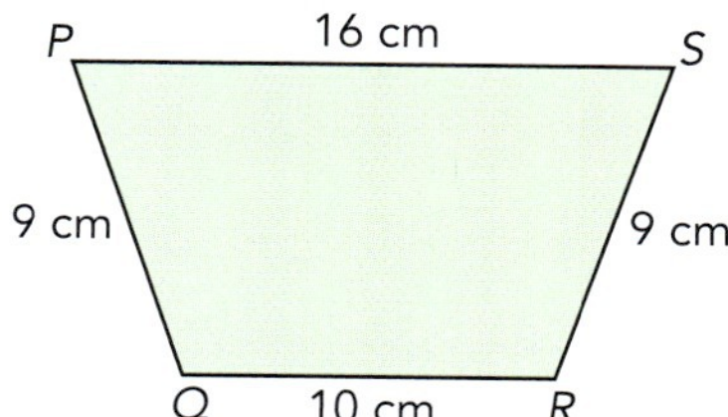

12. Figure *WXYZ* is a parallelogram.

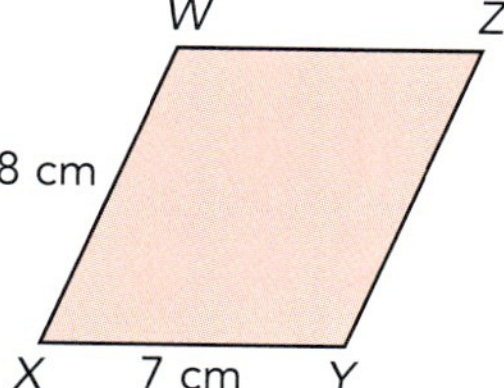

13. Figure *JKLM* is a rhombus.

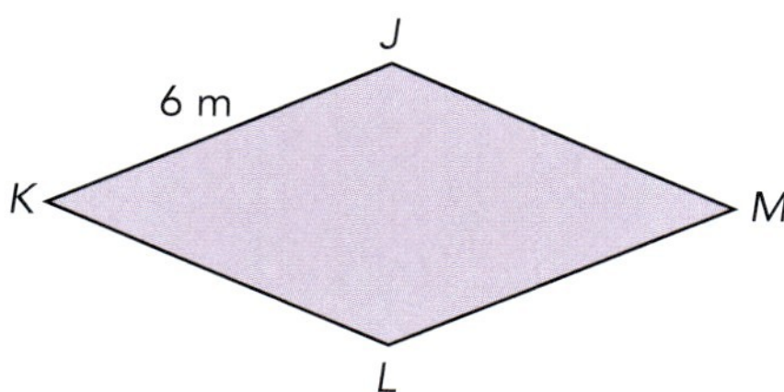

9.1 Points on the Coordinate Plane

Lesson Objectives

- Name and locate points on the coordinate plane.
- Draw and identify polygons on the coordinate plane.

Vocabulary

coordinates
coordinate plane
x-axis
y-axis
quadrants

Find the coordinates of points on a coordinate plane.

The coordinate plane is made up of two number lines that intersect at right angles. The horizontal line is called the **x-axis** and the vertical line is called the **y-axis**. The point of intersection, usually labeled *O*, is the origin.

The *x*-axis and *y*-axis divide the coordinate plane into four parts called **quadrants**. Moving counterclockwise around the origin, the quadrants are named Quadrant I, Quadrant II, Quadrant III, and Quadrant IV.

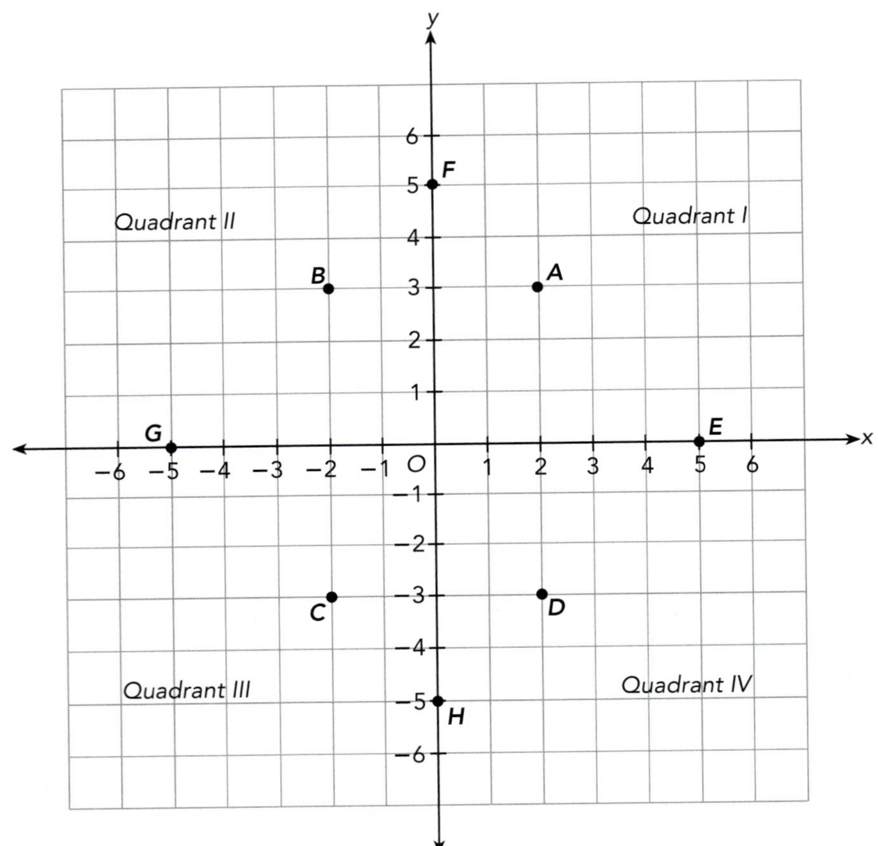

Point A is in the first quadrant.
Point A is 2 units to the right of the origin, so its x-coordinate is 2. It is 3 units up from the origin, so its y-coordinate is 3.
The coordinates of A are (2, 3).
(2, 3) is called an ordered pair.
You can write A (2, 3) to represent the location of A.

Caution

The x-coordinate comes first in an ordered pair. The ordered pair (2, 3) does not name the same point as (3, 2).

Point B is in the second quadrant.
Point B is 2 units to the left of the origin, so its x-coordinate is -2. It is 3 units up from the origin, so its y-coordinate is 3.
The coordinates of B are $(-2, 3)$.

Points A and B are symmetrical about the y-axis. Point A is said to be the reflection of point B across the y-axis.

You can also say point B is the reflection of point A across the y-axis.

Point C is in the third quadrant.
Point C is 2 units to the left of the origin, so its x-coordinate is -2. It is 3 units down from the origin, so its y-coordinate is -3.
The coordinates of C are $(-2, -3)$.

Points B and C are reflections of each other across the x-axis.

Point D is in the fourth quadrant.
Point D is 2 units to the right of the origin, so its x-coordinate is 2.
It is 3 units down from the origin, so its y-coordinate is -3.
The coordinates of D are $(2, -3)$.

Points C and D are reflections of each other across the y-axis.

Points E lies on the x-axis. It lies between Quadrant I and Quadrant IV.
Similarly, point F lies on the y-axis. It lies between Quadrant I and Quadrant II.

Point G lies on the x-axis. It is between Quadrant II and Quadrant III.

Point H lies on the y-axis. It is between Quadrant III and Quadrant IV.

Guided Practice

Use the coordinate plane below.

1 Give the coordinates of points P, Q, R, S, T, U, and V. In which quadrant is each point located?

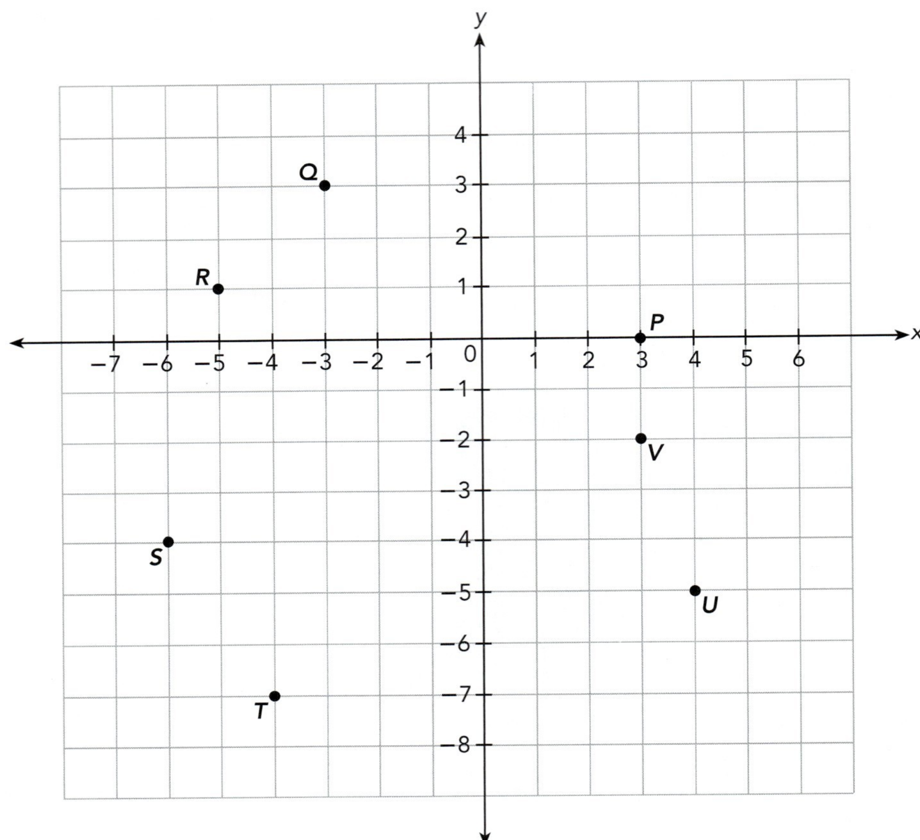

Use graph paper.

2 Plot points $A\,(-4, 3)$, $B\,(3, -4)$, $C\,(5, 0)$, $D\,(0, -5)$, $E\,(-2, -1)$, and $F\,(2, -1)$ on a coordinate plane.

3 Points P and Q are reflections of each other about the x-axis. Give the coordinates of point Q if the coordinates of point P are the following:

a) $(-6, 2)$

b) $(-2, -4)$

c) $(4, 5)$

d) $(7, -3)$

4 Points R and S are reflections of each other about the y-axis. Give the coordinates of point S if the coordinates of point R are the following:

a) $(-6, 2)$

b) $(-2, -4)$

c) $(4, 5)$

d) $(7, -3)$

Learn Draw and identify polygons on a coordinate plane.

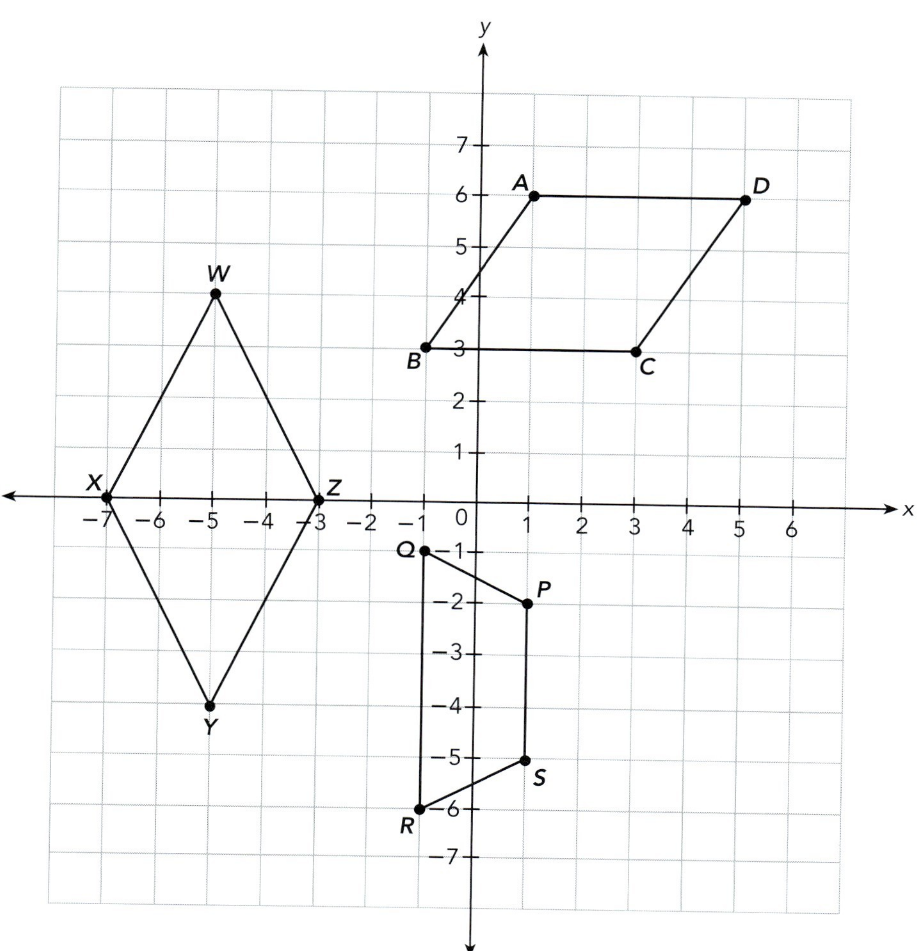

You can join points on a coordinate plane to form geometric figures.

Points A (1, 6), B (−1, 3), C (3, 3), and D (5, 6) are joined to form a parallelogram.

Points P (1, −2), Q (−1, −1), R (−1, −6), and S (1, −5) are joined to form a trapezoid.

Points W (−5, 4), X (−7, 0), Y (−5, −4), and Z (−3, 0) are joined to form a rhombus.

Guided Practice

Use graph paper. For each exercise, plot the given points on a coordinate plane. Then join the points in order with line segments to form a closed figure. Name each figure formed.

5 A (3, 4), B (−6, −3), and C (2, −4)

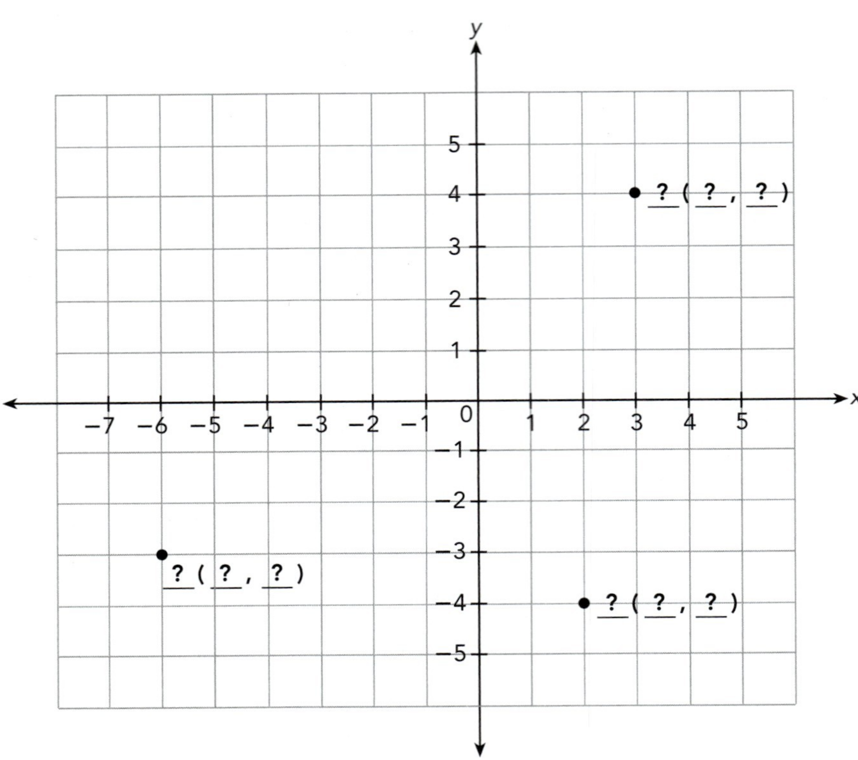

6 D (1, 1), E (0, 0), and F (−4, 4)

7 J (−3, 0), K (0, 5), and L (3, 0)

8 P (3, 2), Q (−1, 2), R (−1, −2), and S (3, −2)

9 W (−3, 2), X (1, −2), Y (3, 0), and Z (−1, 4)

10 A (−5, 2), B (−5, −1), C (−1, −1), and D (1, 2)

11 E (−2, −2), F (−5, −5), G (−2, −5), and H (1, −2)

12 J (−4, 1), K (−3, −1), L (0, −1), and M (2, 1)

13 P (4, 0), Q (0, 4), R (−4, 0), and S (0, −4)

14 W (−2, 0), X (−3, −3), Y (1, 1), and Z (2, 4)

Hands-On Activity

Materials:
- graph paper

IDENTIFYING QUADRILATERALS DRAWN ON A COORDINATE PLANE

Work in pairs.

STEP 1 Plot four points on a coordinate plane and connect them to form a special quadrilateral such as a parallelogram, a rectangle, or a rhombus. Do not let your partner see your quadrilateral.

STEP 2 Tell your partner the coordinates of three out of the four coordinates of the points you plotted in **STEP 1**. Also tell your partner the type of quadrilateral you plotted, and in which quadrant the fourth point is located. Have your partner guess the coordinates of the fourth point.

Example

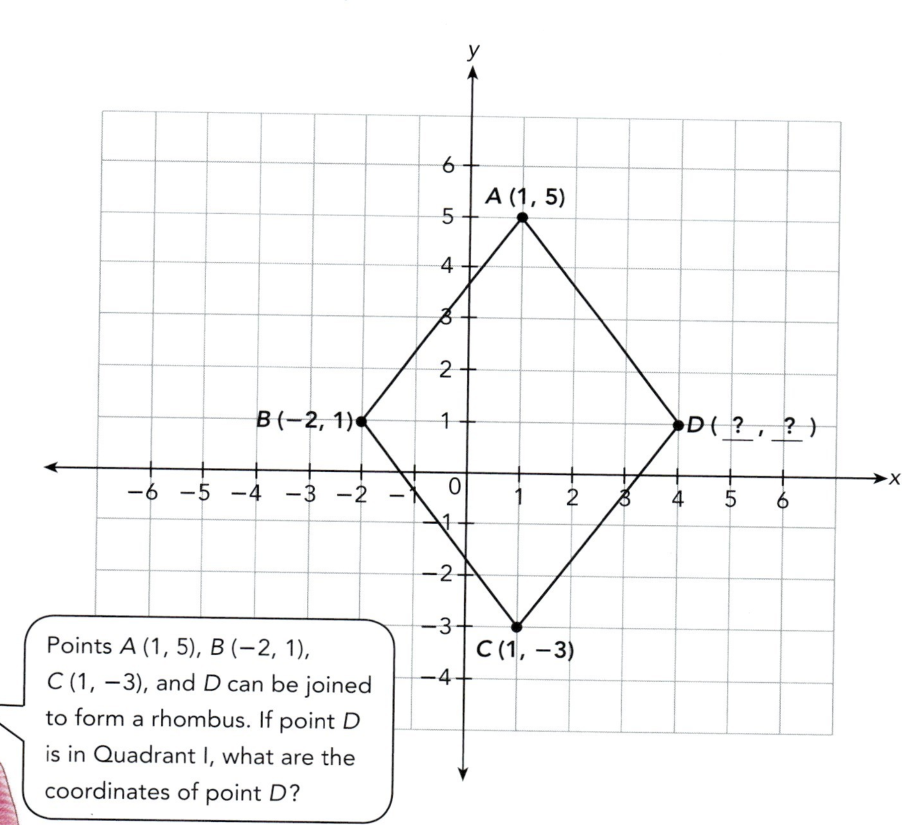

STEP 3 Switch roles with your partner and repeat the activity with other quadrilaterals.

Practice 9.1

Use the coordinate plane below.

1 Give the coordinates of each point. In which quadrant is each point located?

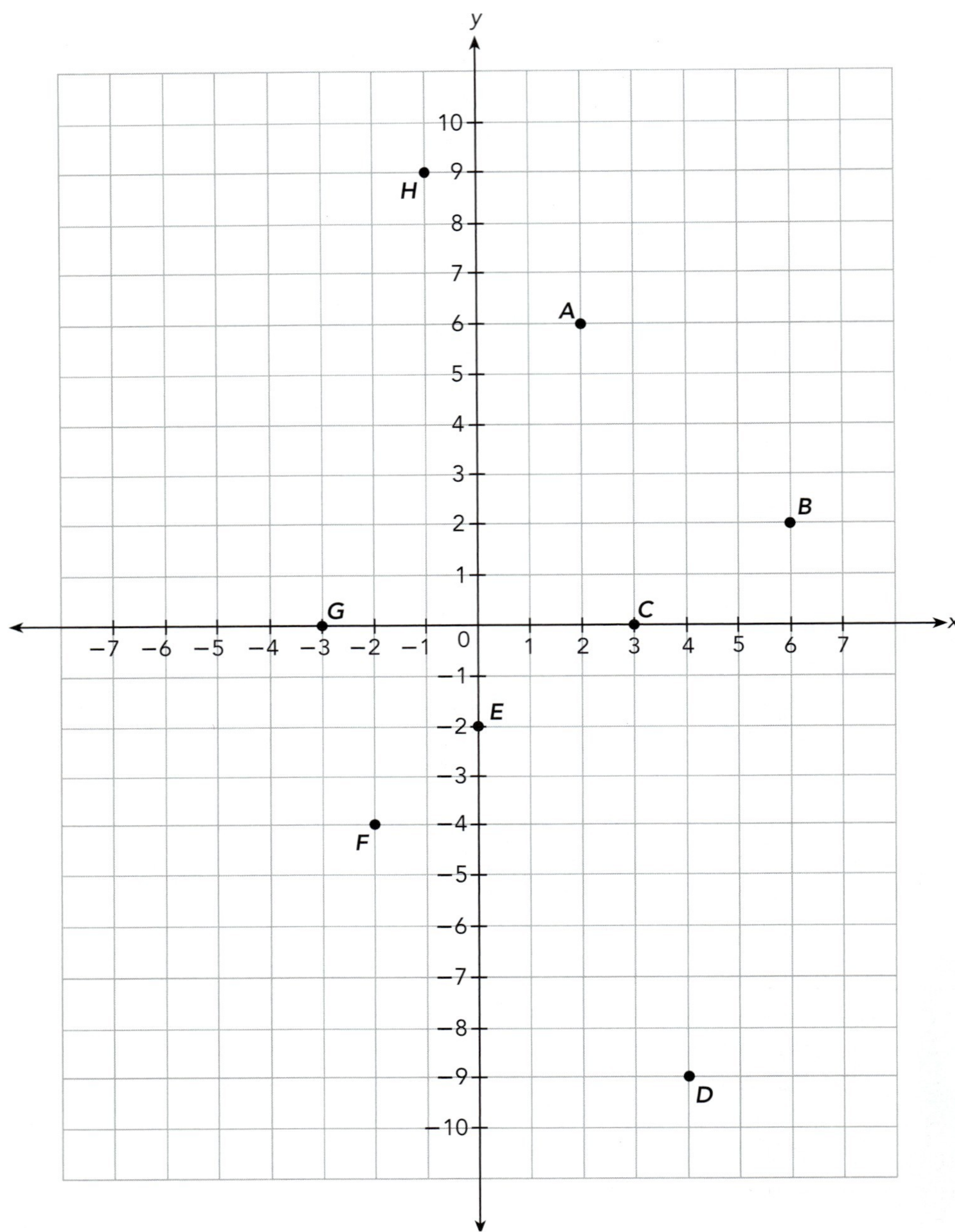

Use graph paper. Plot the points on a coordinate plane. In which quadrant is each point located?

2 *A* (3, 7), *B* (2, 0), *C* (8, −1), *D* (0, −6), *E* (−3, −5), and *F* (−6, 7)

Use graph paper. Points A and B are reflections of each other about the x-axis. Give the coordinates of point B if the coordinates of point A are the following:

3 (4, 1)

4 (−2, 3)

5 (2, −2)

6 (−1, −3)

Use graph paper. Points C and D are reflections of each other about the y-axis. Give the coordinates of point D if the coordinates of point C are the following:

7 (4, 1)

8 (−2, 3)

9 (2, −2)

10 (−1, −3)

Use graph paper. For each exercise, plot the given points on a coordinate plane. Then join the points in order with line segments to form a closed figure. Name each figure formed.

11 H (−5, 1), J (−3, −1), K (−1, 1), and L (−3, 3)

12 R (2, 1), S (−1, −3), T (4, −3), and U (7, 1)

13 W (−5, −2), X (−6, −5), Y (−1, −5), and Z (−3, −2)

Use graph paper. Plot the points on a coordinate plane and answer each question.

14 **a)** Plot points A (−6, 5), C (5, 1), and D (5, 5) on a coordinate plane.

b) Figure $ABCD$ is a rectangle. Plot point B and give its coordinates.

c) Figure $ACDE$ is a parallelogram. Plot point E above $\overline{AD}$ and give its coordinates.

15 **a)** Plot points A (−3, 2) and B (−3, −2) on a coordinate plane.

b) Join points A and B with a line segment.

c) $\overline{AB}$ is a side of square $ABCD$. Name two possible sets of coordinates that could be the coordinates of points C and D.

16 Plot points A (2, 5) and B (2, −3) on a coordinate plane. Figure ABC is a right isosceles triangle. If point C is in Quadrant III, give the coordinates of point C.

17 Plot points A (0, 4), B (−4, 0), and C (0, −4) on a coordinate plane.

a) What kind of triangle is triangle ABC?

b) Figure $ABCD$ is a square. Plot point D on the coordinate plane and give its coordinates.

9.2 Length of Line Segments

Lesson Objectives

- Find lengths of horizontal and vertical line segments on the coordinate plane.
- Solve real-world problems involving coordinates and a coordinate plane.

Learn **Find the lengths of line segments on the *x*-axis and *y*-axis.**

Find the lengths of the line segments $\overline{AB}$, $\overline{CD}$, $\overline{EF}$, and $\overline{GH}$.

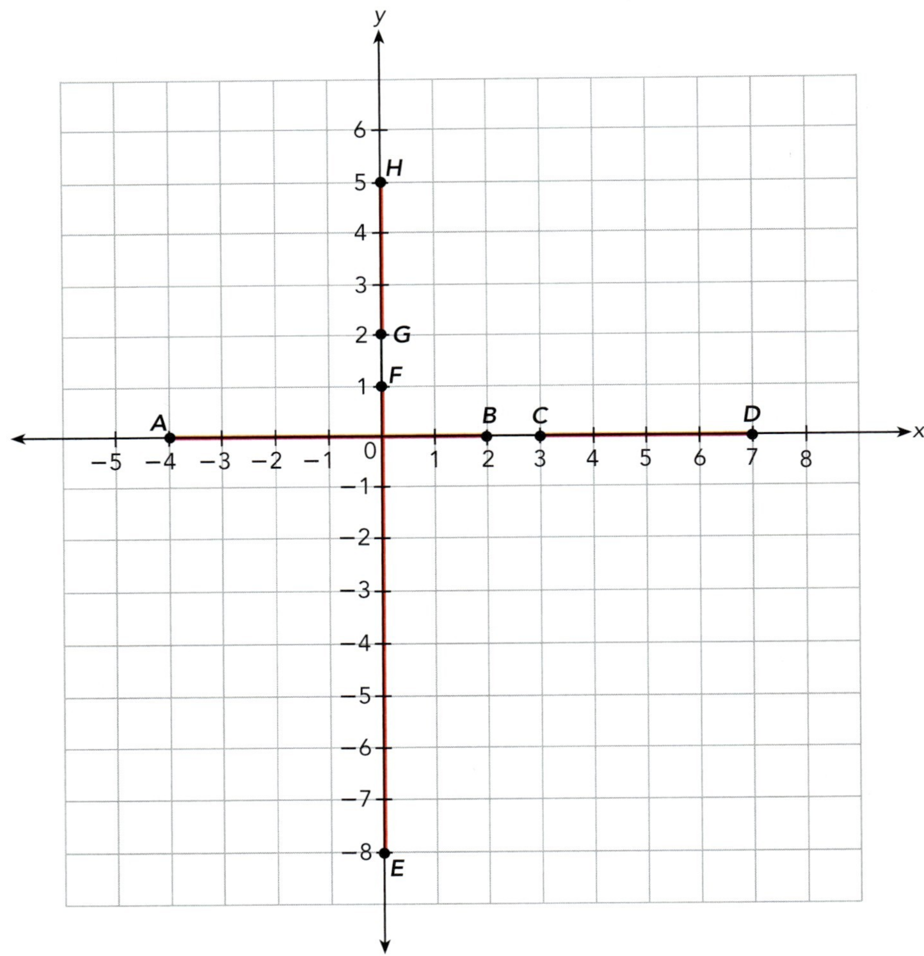

The coordinates of C and D are $C\,(3, 0)$ and $D\,(7, 0)$.
By counting the number of units from 3 to 7, you can see that the length of $\overline{CD}$ is 4 units.

The coordinates of A and B are $A\,(-4, 0)$ and $B\,(2, 0)$. By counting the number of units from -4 to 2, you can see that the length of $\overline{AB}$ is 6 units.

Math Note

Length is a non-negative quantity. It can be zero or positive.

You can also find the length of $\overline{AB}$ this way.

$$\begin{aligned} AB &= AO + OB \\ &= |-4| + |2| \\ &= 4 + 2 \\ &= 6 \text{ units} \end{aligned}$$

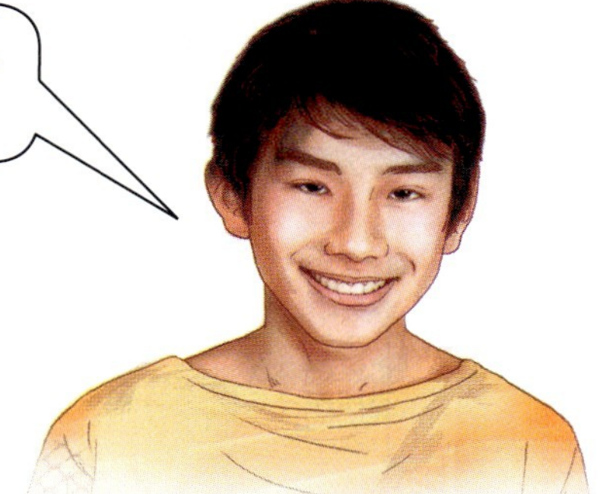

The coordinates of G and H are $G\,(0, 2)$ and $H\,(0, 5)$. By counting the number of units from 2 to 5, you can see that the length of $\overline{GH}$ is 3 units.

The coordinates of E and F are $E\,(0, -8)$ and $F\,(0, 1)$. By counting the number of units from -8 to 1, you can see that the length of $\overline{EF}$ is 9 units.

Similarly,

$$\begin{aligned} EF &= EO + OF \\ &= |-8| + |1| \\ &= 8 + 1 \\ &= 9 \text{ units} \end{aligned}$$

So, the length of $\overline{EF}$ is 9 units.

Guided Practice

Use graph paper. Plot each pair of points on a coordinate plane. Connect the points to form a line segment and find its length.

1. $C\,(3, 0)$ and $D\,(8, 0)$

2. $E\,(-6, 0)$ and $F\,(-2, 0)$

3. $G\,(-7, 0)$ and $H\,(1, 0)$

4. $J\,(0, 5)$ and $K\,(0, 2)$

5. $M\,(0, -6)$ and $N\,(0, -3)$

6. $P\,(0, -3)$ and $Q\,(0, 5)$

Learn Find lengths of line segments parallel to the *x*-axis and *y*-axis.

Find the lengths of the line segments $\overline{RS}$, $\overline{MN}$, and $\overline{PQ}$.

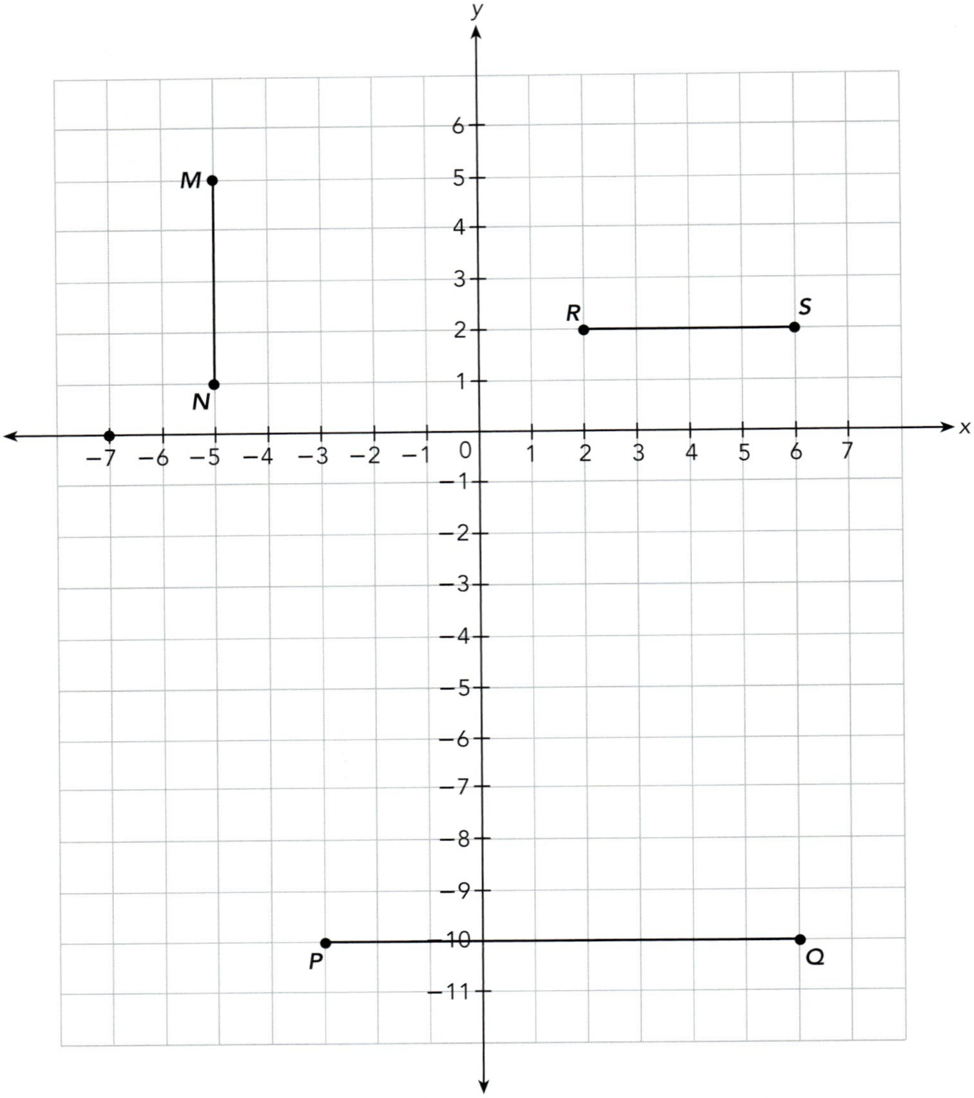

The line segment $\overline{RS}$ joins points R (2, 2) and S (6, 2). The *y*-coordinates of points R and S are the same, so $\overline{RS}$ is a horizontal line segment.

Using the *x*-coordinates of R (2, 2) and S (6, 2),

$$\begin{aligned} RS &= |x\text{-coordinate of } S| - |x\text{-coordinate of } R| \\ &= |6| - |2| \\ &= 4 \text{ units} \end{aligned}$$

So, the length of $\overline{RS}$ is 4 units.

The line segment $\overline{MN}$ joins points $M(-5, 5)$ and $N(-5, 1)$. The x-coordinates of points M and N are the same, so $\overline{MN}$ is a vertical line segment.

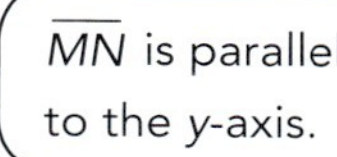

Using the y-coordinates of $M(-5, 5)$ and $N(-5, 1)$,

$$\begin{aligned} MN &= |y\text{-coordinate of } M| - |y\text{-coordinate of } N| \\ &= |5| - |1| \\ &= 4 \text{ units} \end{aligned}$$

So, the length of $\overline{MN}$ is 4 units.

The line segment $\overline{PQ}$ joins points $P(-3, -10)$ and $Q(6, -10)$. The y-coordinates of points P and Q are the same, so $\overline{PQ}$ is a horizontal line segment.

Using the x-coordinates of $P(-3, -10)$ and $Q(6, -10)$,

$$\begin{aligned} PQ &= |x\text{-coordinate of } P| + |x\text{-coordinate of } Q| \\ &= |-3| + |6| \\ &= 9 \text{ units} \end{aligned}$$

So, the length of $\overline{PQ}$ is 9 units.

Guided Practice

Use graph paper. Plot each pair of points on a coordinate plane. Connect the points to form a line segment and find its length.

7. $A(1, -2)$ and $B(6, -2)$

8. $C(-1, 3)$ and $D(5, 3)$

9. $E(-3, 4)$ and $F(1, 4)$

10. $G(-3, 2)$ and $H(-3, 6)$

11. $J(-1, -6)$ and $K(-1, 4)$

12. $L(5, 6)$ and $M(5, 1)$

Learn Plot points on a coordinate plane for a real-world problem and solve it.

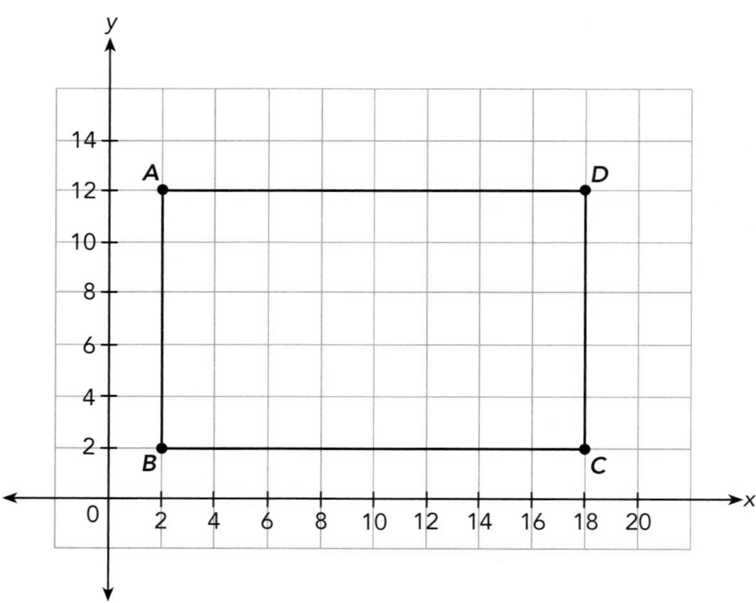

A plan of a rectangular garden is shown. The side length of each grid square is 2 meters.

a) Give the coordinates of points *A*, *B*, *C*, and *D*.

The coordinates are *A* (2, 12), *B* (2, 2), *C* (18, 2), and *D* (18, 12).

b) Find the length and width of the garden in meters.

Length = *AD*
= 18 − 2
= 16 m

The length of the garden is 16 meters.

Width = *AB*
= 12 − 2
= 10 m

The width of the garden is 10 meters.

Caution

Remember to look at the scale of a graph before finding the coordinates of a point or before finding the length of a line segment.

c) Find the area of the garden in square meters.

Area = ℓw — Write formula.
= $16 \cdot 10$ — Substitute.
= 160 m^2 — Multiply.

The area of the garden is 160 square meters.

d) Find the perimeter of the garden *ABCD* in meters.

$$\begin{aligned} \text{Perimeter} &= 2 \cdot (\ell + w) \\ &= 2 \cdot (16 + 10) \\ &= 2 \cdot 26 \\ &= 52 \text{ m} \end{aligned}$$

The perimeter of the garden is 52 meters.

e) There is a palm tree planted at point *E* in the garden at a distance of 12 meters from $\overline{AB}$ and 4 meters from $\overline{AD}$. Give the coordinates of point *E* and plot it on the coordinate plane.

First find how many grid squares from $\overline{AB}$ point *E* is.

1 grid square represents 2 meters.

$$\begin{aligned} 12 \text{ m} &= 12 \div 2 \\ &= 6 \text{ grid squares} \end{aligned}$$

For point *E* to be in the garden, the *x*-coordinate has to be 6 units to the right of $\overline{AB}$. So, point *E* is $1 + 6 = 7$ grid squares to the right of the *y*-axis. The *x*-coordinate of point *E* is $7 \times 2 = 14$.

Then find how many grid squares from $\overline{AD}$ point *E* is.

$$\begin{aligned} 4 \text{ m} &= 4 \div 2 \\ &= 2 \text{ grid squares} \end{aligned}$$

For point *E* to be in the garden, the *y*-coordinate has to be 2 units below $\overline{AD}$. So, point *E* is $6 - 2 = 4$ grid squares above the *x*-axis. The *y*-coordinate of point *E* is $4 \times 2 = 8$.

The coordinates of *E* are (14, 8).

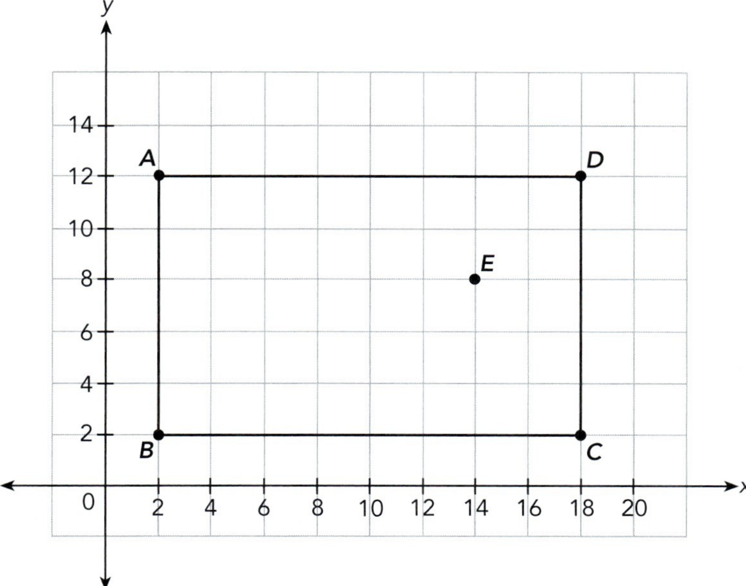

Guided Practice

In the diagram, triangle *ABC* represents a plot of land. The side length of each grid square is 5 meters. Use the diagram to answer questions 13 to 15.

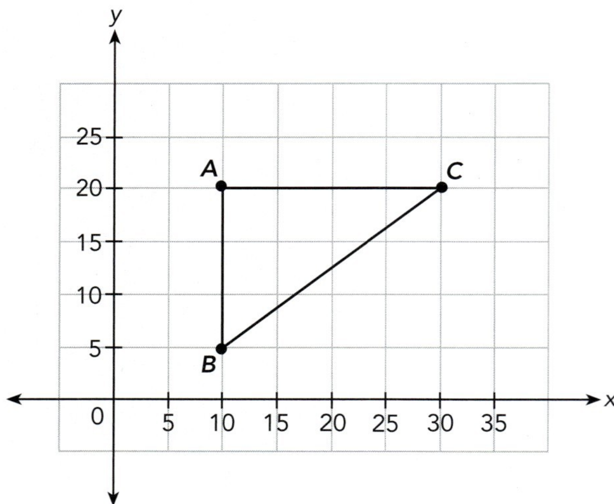

13 Give the coordinates of points *A*, *B*, and *C*.

14 Mr. Manning wants to build a fence around the plot of land. If *BC* is 25 meters, how many meters of fencing does he need?

AB = __?__ − __?__

= __?__ m

AC = __?__ − __?__

= __?__ m

Perimeter of triangle *ABC* = *AB* + *BC* + *AC*

= __?__ + __?__ + __?__

= __?__ m

Mr. Manning needs __?__ meters of fencing.

15 A pole is located at point *D* on the plot of land at a distance of 10 meters from $\overline{AB}$ and 5 meters from $\overline{AC}$. Give the coordinates of point *D*.

1 grid square represents 5 meters.

10 m = __?__ ÷ 5

= __?__ grid squares

For point D to be on the plot of land, the x-coordinate has to be ___?___ grid squares to the right of $\overline{AB}$. So, point D is ___?___ + ___?___ = ___?___ grid squares to the right of the y-axis. The x-coordinate of point D is ___?___ × ___?___ = ___?___.

For point D to be on the plot of land, the y-coordinate has to be ___?___ grid square below $\overline{AC}$. So, point D is ___?___ − ___?___ = ___?___ grid squares above the x-axis. The y-coordinate of point D is ___?___ × ___?___ = ___?___.

The coordinates of D are (___?___, ___?___).

In the diagram, rectangle *PQRS* represents a parking lot of a supermarket. The side length of each grid square is 4 meters. Use the diagram to answer questions 16 to 18.

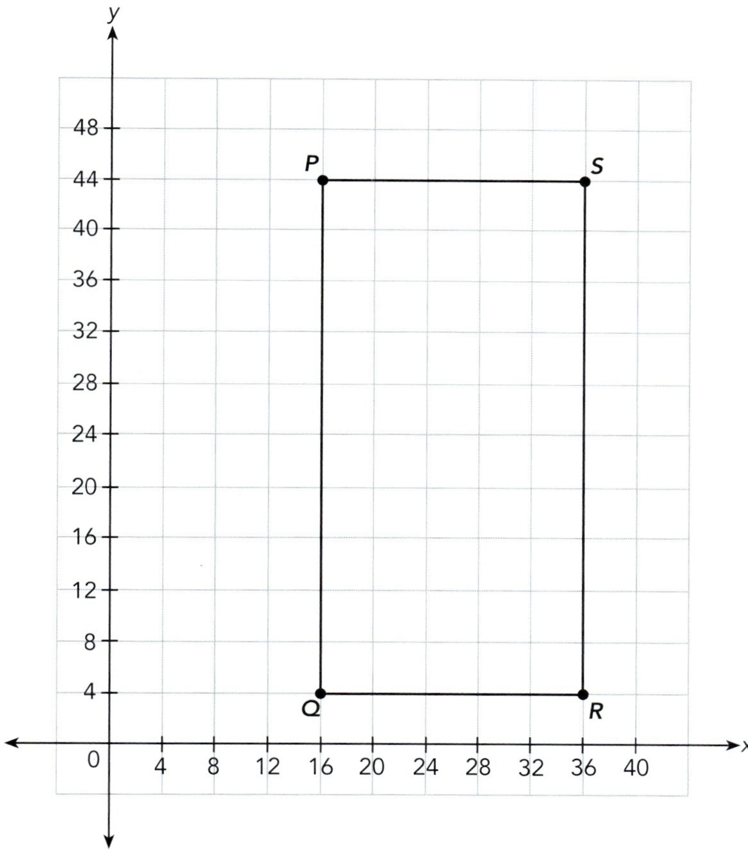

16 Give the coordinates of points P, Q, R, and S.

17 The manager of the supermarket wants to build a concrete wall around the parking lot. What is the perimeter of the wall?

18 The entrance of the supermarket is at point T. It lies on $\overline{PQ}$, and point T is 8 meters from point P. Give the coordinates of point T.

Practice 9.2

Use graph paper. Plot each pair of points on a coordinate plane. Connect the points to form a line segment and find its length.

1. *A* (5, 0) and *B* (8, 0)

2. *C* (−3, 4) and *D* (3, 4)

3. *E* (−5, −2) and *F* (8, −2)

4. *G* (0, −5) and *H* (0, 2)

5. *J* (−5, −3) and *K* (−5, −8)

6. *M* (1, 7) and *N* (1, −8)

Use graph paper. Find the coordinates.

7. Rectangle *PQRS* is plotted on a coordinate plane. The coordinates of *P* are (−1, −3) and the coordinates of *Q* are (−1, 2). Each unit on the coordinate plane represents 1 centimeter, and the perimeter of rectangle *PQRS* is 20 centimeters. Find the coordinates of points *R* and *S* given these conditions:

   a) Points *R* and *S* are to the left of points *P* and *Q*.

   b) Points *R* and *S* are to the right of points *P* and *Q*.

8. Rectangle *ABCD* is plotted on a coordinate plane. The coordinates of *A* are (2, 3) and the coordinates of *B* are (−2, 3). Each unit on the coordinate plane represents 3 centimeters, and the perimeter of rectangle *ABCD* is 48 centimeters. Find the coordinates of points *C* and *D* given these conditions:

   a) Points *C* and *D* are below points *A* and *B*.

   b) Points *C* and *D* are above points *A* and *B*.

9. Rectangle *PQRS* is plotted on a coordinate plane. The coordinates of *P* are (−1, 4) and the coordinates of *Q* are (−1, −4). Each unit on the coordinate plane represents 1 centimeter, and the area of rectangle *PQRS* is 64 square centimeters. Find the coordinates of points *R* and *S* given these conditions:

   a) Points *R* and *S* are to the left of points *P* and *Q*.

   b) Points *R* and *S* are to the right of points *P* and *Q*.

In the diagram, rectangle *ABCD* represents a shopping plaza. The side length of each grid square is 10 meters. Use the diagram to answer questions 10 to 14.

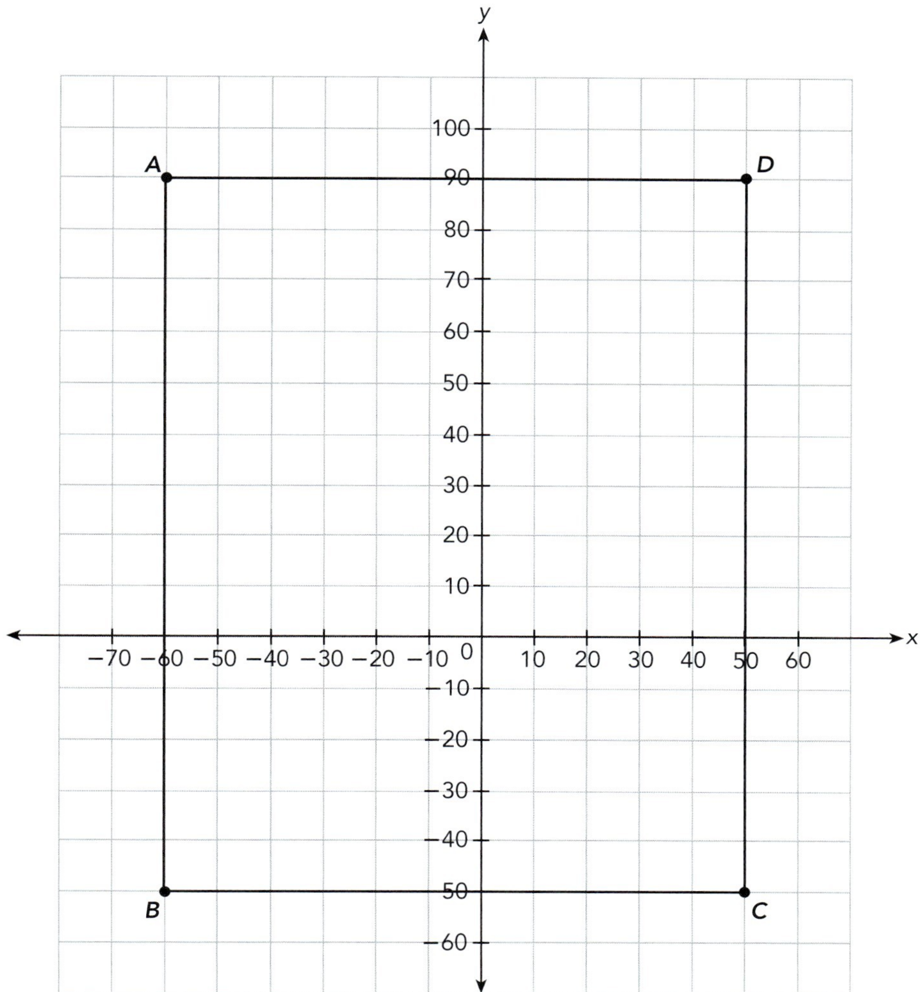

10 Give the coordinates of points *A*, *B*, *C*, and *D*.

11 Write down the shortest distance of points *A*, *B*, *C*, and *D* from the *y*-axis.

12 Write down the shortest distance of points *A*, *B*, *C*, and *D* from the *x*-axis.

13 Find the area and perimeter of the shopping plaza.

14 A man at the shopping plaza is standing 50 meters from $\overline{AD}$, and 40 meters from $\overline{DC}$.

a) Find the coordinates of the point representing the man's location.

b) Find the shortest distance in meters from the man's location to the side $\overline{BC}$.

In the diagram, triangle *PQR* represents a triangular garden. The side length of each grid square is 5 meters. Use the diagram to answer questions 15 to 19.

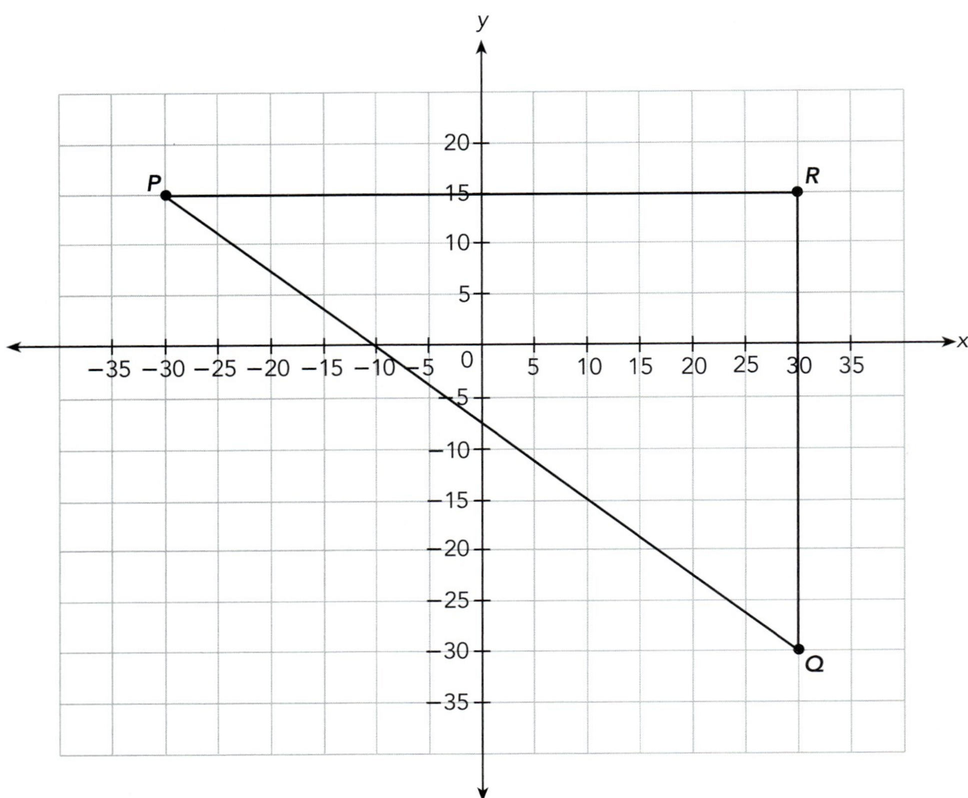

15 Use graph paper. A rectangular region *ABCR* in the garden is to be fenced in. Point *A* lies on $\overline{PR}$, and is 35 meters away from point *P*. Point *C* lies below $\overline{PR}$, and is 20 meters away from point *R*. Plot and label points *A*, *B*, and *C* on the coordinate plane. Write the coordinates of points *A*, *B*, and *C*.

16 If *PQ* is 75 meters, what is the perimeter of the triangular garden in meters?

17 Find the area of the enclosed region *ABCR* in square meters.

18 Find the perimeter of the enclosed region *ABCR* in meters.

19 If *PQ* is 75 meters, what is the perimeter of the garden that is not enclosed?

The diagram shows the outline of a park. The side length of each grid square is 10 meters. Use the diagram to answer questions 20 to 22.

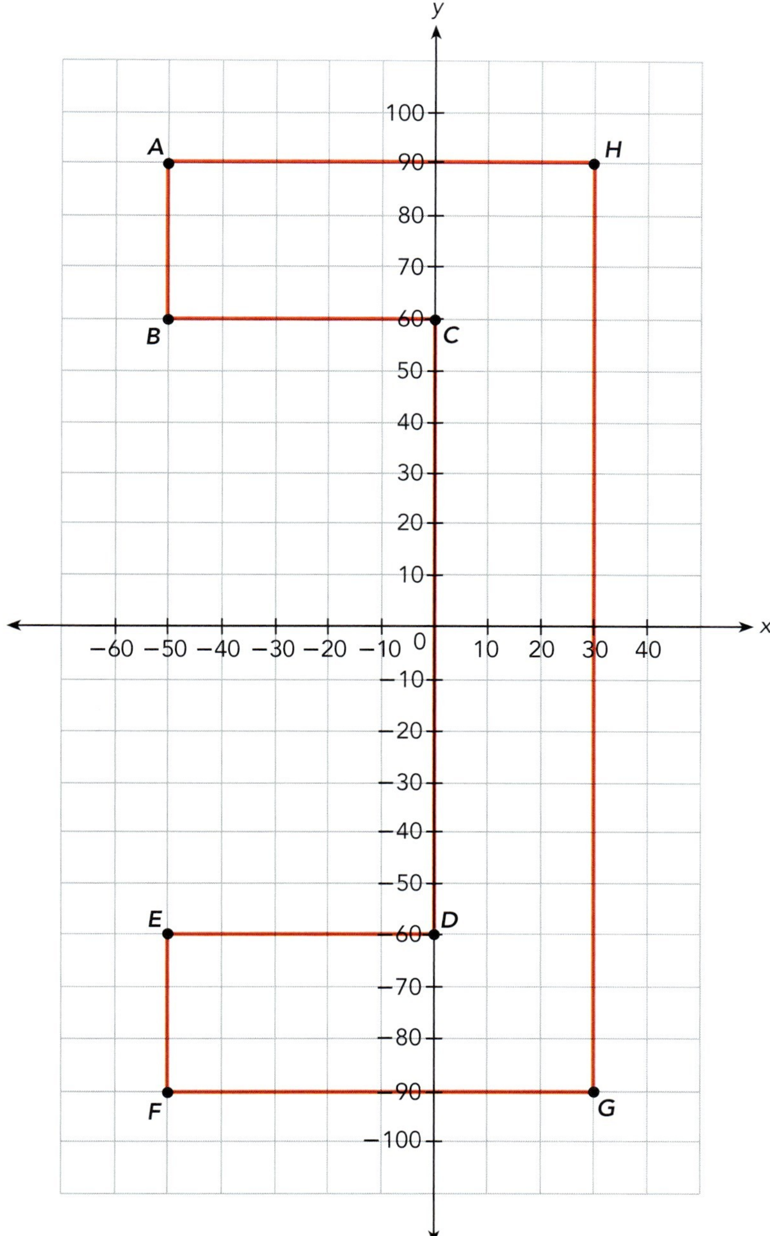

20 Find the area of the park in square meters.

21 Brandon starts at point A and walks all the way around the perimeter of the park. If he walks at 1.5 meters per second, about how many seconds pass before he returns to point A? Round your answer to the nearest second.

22 A picnic table in the park is 20 meters from $\overline{BC}$, and is closer to point B than it is to point C. Write down two possible pairs of coordinates for the location of the picnic table.

9.3 Real-World Problems: Graphing

Lesson Objective

- Solve real-world problems involving equations and a coordinate plane.

Vocabulary
linear graph

Learn Graph an equation on a coordinate plane.

Angela is driving to the Raccoon River. The distance traveled, d miles, after t hours, is given by $d = 40t$. Graph the relationship between d and t. Use 2 units on the horizontal axis to represent 1 hour and 2 units on the vertical axis to represent 20 miles.

Time (t hours)	0	1	2	3	4
Distance Traveled (d miles)	0	40	80	120	160

a) What type of graph is it?

It is a straight line graph. This is also called a **linear graph**.

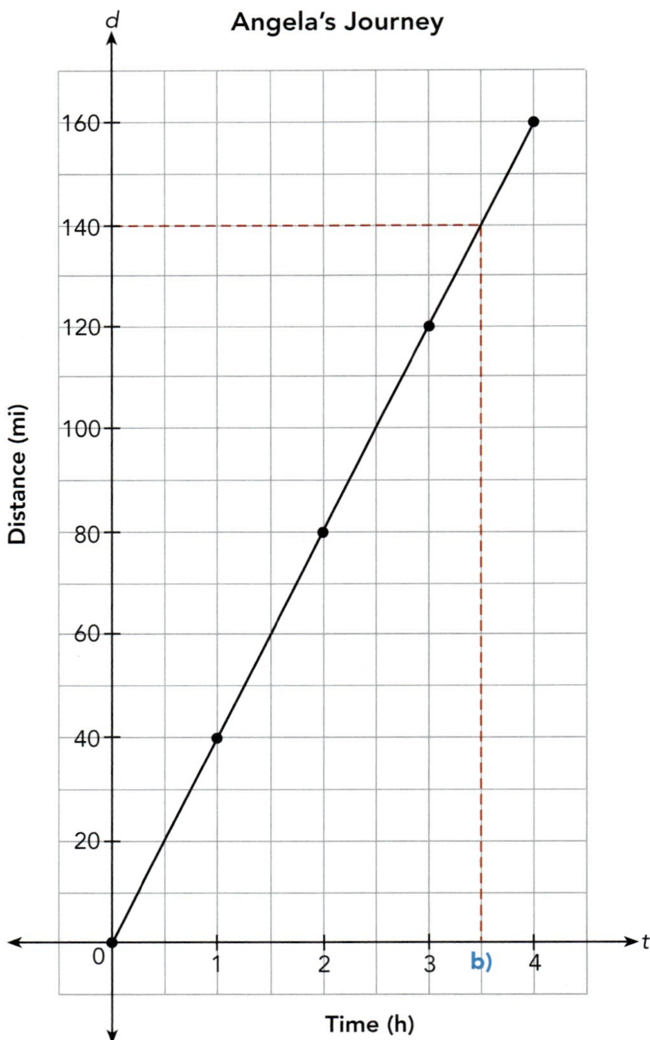

b) How far did Angela drive in 3.5 hours?

From the graph, Angela drove 140 miles.

c) What is the speed at which Angela is driving?

$$\text{Speed} = \frac{\text{total distance}}{\text{total time}}$$
$$= \frac{160}{4}$$
$$= 40 \text{ mi/h}$$

Angela is driving at 40 miles per hour.

d) Angela has driven for 4 hours. If she drives for another hour at this constant speed, how far will she drive in all?

$$\text{Distance} = \text{speed} \times \text{time}$$
$$= 40 \times 5$$
$$= 200 \text{ mi}$$

She will drive 200 miles.

e) If Angela wants to drive at least 120 miles, how many hours will she need to drive? Express your answer in the form of an inequality in terms of t, where t stands for the number of hours.

$t \geq 3$

f) Name the dependent and independent variables.

d is the dependent variable, and t is the independent variable.

Guided Practice

Use graph paper. Solve.

1 A car uses 1 gallon of gas for every 20 miles traveled. The amount of gas left in the gas tank, x gallons, after traveling y miles is given by $y = 240 - 20x$. Copy and complete the table. Graph the relationship between x and y. Use 1 unit on the horizontal axis to represent 1 gallon and 1 unit on the vertical axis to represent 20 miles.

a)

Amount of Gas (x gallons)	12	10	?	6	?
Distance Traveled (y miles)	0	40	80	120	160

b) What type of graph is it?

It is a __?__ graph.

c) How many gallons of gas will be left in the tank after the car has traveled 60 miles?
From the graph, there will be $\underline{?}$ gallons of gas left.

d) How many gallons of gas will be left in the tank after the car has traveled 100 miles?
From the graph, there will be $\underline{?}$ gallons of gas left.

e) After the car has traveled 160 miles, how much farther can the car travel before it runs out of gas?

After 160 miles, $\underline{?}$ gallons of gas were left.

The car uses 1 gallon for every $\underline{?}$ miles traveled.

Distance = number of gallons × mileage

$= \underline{?} \times \underline{?}$

$= \underline{?}$ mi

The car can travel another $\underline{?}$ miles.

f) If the car travels more than 40 miles, how much gas is left in the tank? Express your answer in the form of an inequality in terms of x, where x stands for the amount of gas left in the gas tank.
If the distance traveled is more than 40 miles, then $\underline{?}$.

g) Name the dependent and independent variables.

2 Sarah plants a seed. After t weeks, the height of the plant, h centimeters, is given by $h = 2t$. Copy and complete the table. Graph the relationship between t and h. Use 1 unit on the horizontal axis to represent 1 week and 1 unit on the vertical axis to represent 2 centimeters.

a)

Time (*t* weeks)	0	1	2	3	4	5
Height (*h* centimeters)	?	2	4	6	?	?

b) What type of graph is it?

c) What is the height of the plant after 3 weeks?

d) What is the height of the plant after 5 weeks?

e) What is the height of the plant if less than 4 weeks have passed? Express your answer in the form of an inequality in terms of h, where h stands for the height of the plant in centimeters.

f) Name the dependent and independent variables.

Practice 9.3

Use graph paper. Solve.

1 A cyclist took part in a competition. The distance traveled, d meters, after t minutes, is given by $d = 700t$. Graph the relationship between t and d. Use 2 units on the horizontal axis to represent 1 minute and 1 unit on the vertical axis to represent 350 meters.

Time (t minutes)	0	1	2	3	4
Distance Traveled (d meters)	0	700	1,400	2,100	2,800

a) What type of graph is it?

b) What is the distance traveled in 2.5 minutes?

c) What is the distance traveled in 3.5 minutes?

d) What is the average speed of the cyclist?

e) Assuming that the cyclist travels at a constant speed throughout the competition, what distance will he travel in 7 minutes?

f) If the cyclist needs to cycle for at least 2.1 kilometers, how many minutes will he need to cycle? Express your answer in the form of an inequality in terms of t, where t stands for the number of minutes.

g) Name the dependent and independent variables.

2 A bus uses 1 gallon of diesel for every 7 miles traveled. The amount of diesel left in the gas tank, p gallons, after traveling q miles, is given by $q = 112 - 7p$. Copy and complete the table. Graph the relationship between p and q. Use 1 unit on the horizontal axis to represent 1 gallon and 1 unit on the vertical axis to represent 7 miles.

a)

Amount of Diesel (p gallons)	16	14	12	10	8
Distance Traveled (q miles)	0	?	28	42	?

b) How many gallons of diesel were left after the bus has traveled 49 miles?

c) After the bus has traveled for 56 miles, how much farther can the bus travel before it runs out of diesel?

d) If the bus travels more than 28 miles, how much diesel is left? Express your answer in the form of an inequality in terms of p, where p stands for the amount of diesel left.

3 A kettle of water is heated and the temperature of the water, j°C, after k minutes, is given by $j = 5k + 30$. Copy and complete the table. Graph the relationship between k and j. Use 1 unit on the horizontal axis to represent 1 minute and 1 unit on the vertical axis to represent 5°C.

a)

Time (k minutes)	0	2	4	6	?
Temperature (j°C)	?	40	?	60	70

b) What is the temperature of the water after 5 minutes?

c) What is the average rate of the heating?

d) Assuming the temperature of the water rises at a constant rate, what is the temperature of the water after 10 minutes?

e) The kettle of water needs to be heated till the water boils. For how many minutes does the kettle need to be heated? Express your answer in terms of k, where k stands for the number of minutes. (Hint: Water boils at 100°C.)

Use graph paper. For each exercise, plot the points on a coordinate plane.

1 A (−5, 1), B (−3, −3), C (3, 1), and D (−1, 5)

2 J (4, 2), K (−2, 4), L (−4, 0), and M (0, −2)

3 S (−1, 3), T (−3, −1), U (1, −1), and V (5, 3)

4 In questions 1 to 3, what is the figure formed?

5 a) For each figure in questions 1 to 3, mark the middle of each side and connect the points in order.

b) What are the figures formed? Explain your answers.

Chapter Wrap Up

Concept Map

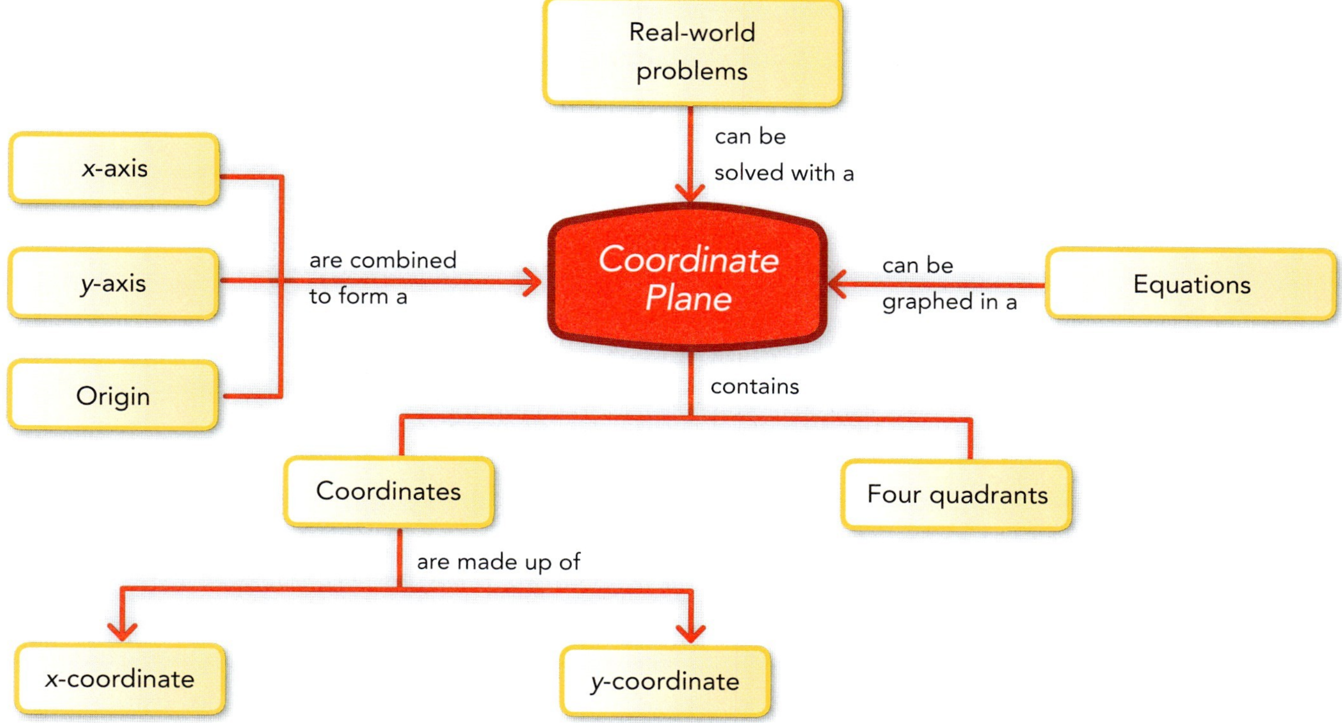

Key Concepts

- The *x*-axis and *y*-axis divide the coordinate plane into four quadrants. The quadrants are called Quadrant I, Quadrant II, Quadrant III, and Quadrant IV.

- Each point on a coordinate plane can be located by using an ordered pair (x, y).

- For any point,
  - the *x*-coordinate tells how far to the left or right of the origin the point is relative to the *x*-axis.
  - the *y*-coordinate tells how far up or down from the origin the point is relative to the *y*-axis.

- Points to the left of the *y*-axis have negative *x*-coordinates. Points below the *x*-axis have negative *y*-coordinates.

- A straight line graph is also called a linear graph. A linear equation has a straight line graph.

Chapter Review/Test

Concepts and Skills

Use the coordinate plane below.

1 Give the coordinates of points *A*, *B*, *C*, *D*, and *E*.

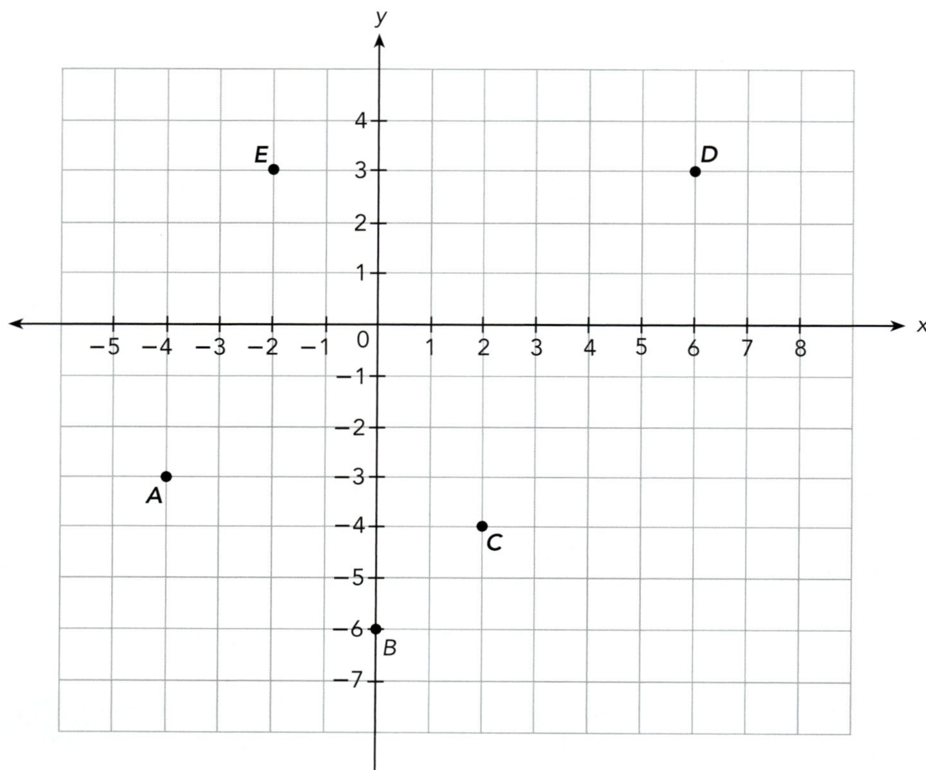

Use graph paper. Plot the points on a coordinate plane. In which quadrant is each point located?

2 *A* (3, 5), *B* (−2, 0), *C* (7, −2), *D* (0, −5), and *E* (−3, −8)

Use graph paper. Points *A* and *B* are reflections of each other about the *x*-axis. Give the coordinates of point *B* if the coordinates of point *A* are the following:

3 (3, 6)

4 (−6, 2)

5 (5, −4)

6 (−3, −5)

Use graph paper. Points *C* and *D* are reflections of each other about the *y*-axis. Give the coordinates of point *D* if the coordinates of point *C* are the following:

7 (3, 6)

8 (−6, 2)

9 (5, −4)

10 (−3, −5)

Use graph paper. For each exercise, plot the given points on a coordinate plane. Then connect the points in order with line segments to form a closed figure. Name each figure formed.

11 A (2, −4), B (2, 4), C (−6, 4), and D (−6, −4)

12 E (0, −2), F (−3, 1), G (−5, −1), and H (−2, −4)

13 J (0, 1), K (1, 4), and L (−4, 3)

14 M (6, 5), N (3, 5), P (3, −3), and Q (6, −3)

15 A (6, −3), B (4, 2), C (−1, 2), and D (0, −3)

16 E (−1, 6), F (−3, 3), G (3, 3), and H (5, 6)

17 J (6, 1), K (8, −2), L (2, −2), and M (0, 1)

18 P (2, 7), Q (−1, 7), R (−5, 4), and S (4, 4)

19 T (−2, 1), U (−6, 1), V (−6, −3), and W (−2, −3)

Use graph paper. Plot the points on a coordinate plane and answer the question.

20 **a)** Plot points A (1, −1) and B (7, −1) on a coordinate plane. Connect the two points to form a line segment.

b) Point C lies above $\overline{AB}$, and is 2 units away from the x-axis. If triangle ABC is an isosceles triangle with base $\overline{AB}$, find the coordinates of point C.

c) Points D and E lie below $\overline{AB}$ such that $ABDE$ is a rectangle. If BD is 5 units, find the coordinates of points D and E.

Use graph paper. Plot each pair of points on a coordinate plane. Connect the points to form a line segment and find its length.

21 A (−1, 0) and B (8, 0)

22 C (−2, 4) and D (6, 4)

23 E (−6, −2) and F (−6, −6)

24 G (−5, −4) and H (2, −4)

25 J (0, −3) and K (0, −8)

26 M (5, 2) and N (5, −5)

Problem Solving

The diagram shows the plan of a room. The side length of each grid square is 10 feet. Use the diagram to answer questions 27 to 30.

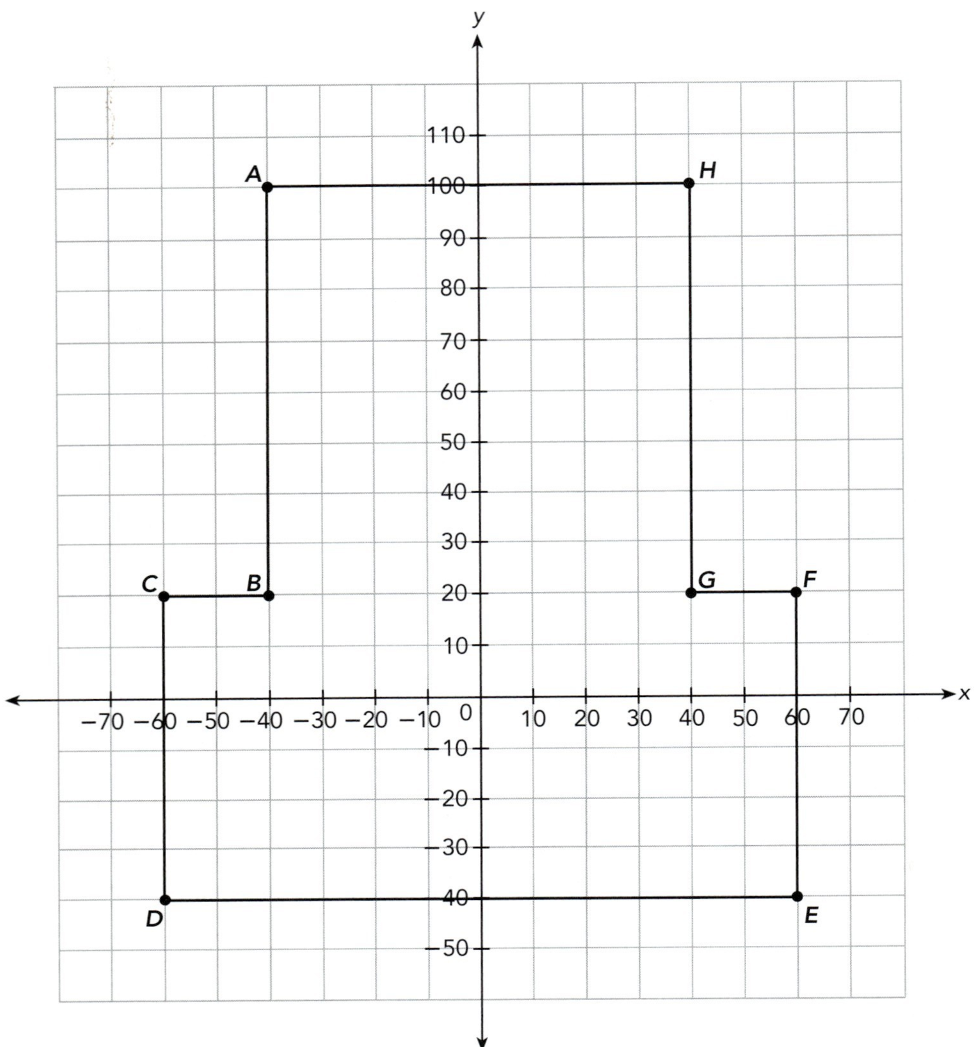

27 The eight corners of the room are labeled points *A* to *H*. Give the coordinates of each of these corners.

28 The entrance of the room is situated along $\overline{AH}$. What is the shortest possible distance in feet between the entrance and $\overline{DE}$ of the room?

29 Diana walks across the room from point *B* to point *G*, and then walks from point *G* to point *H*. Find the total distance, in feet, that Diana walks.

30 Calculate the floor area of the room in square feet.

Use graph paper. Solve.

31 An athlete took part in a race. The distance the athlete ran, v meters, after t minutes, is given by $v = 300t$. Graph the relationship between t and v. Use 2 units on the horizontal axis to represent 1 minute and 1 unit on the vertical axis to represent 150 meters.

Time (t minutes)	0	1	2	3	4
Distance Traveled (v meters)	0	300	600	900	1,200

a) What type of graph is it?

b) What is the distance the athlete ran in 3.5 minutes?

c) What is the average speed of the athlete?

d) Assuming the athlete runs at a constant speed, what is the distance she will run in 8 minutes?

e) Name the dependent and independent variables.

32 A truck uses 1 gallon of diesel for every 12 miles traveled. The amount of diesel left in the gas tank, r gallons, after traveling s miles is given by $s = 300 - 12r$. Copy and complete the table. Graph the relationship between r and s. Use 1 unit on the horizontal axis to represent 1 gallon and 1 unit on the vertical axis to represent 12 miles. Start your horizontal axis at 17 gallons.

a)

Amount of Diesel (r gallons)	25	?	21	19	17
Distance Traveled (s miles)	0	24	48	72	?

b) How many gallons of diesel are left after the truck has traveled 60 miles?

c) After the truck has traveled for 72 miles, how much farther can the truck travel before it runs out of diesel?

d) If the truck travels more than 48 miles, how much diesel is left in the gas tank? Express your answer in the form of an inequality in terms of r, where r stands for the amount of diesel left.

Area of Polygons

▶ The area of a polygon can be found by dividing it into smaller shapes, and then adding the areas of those shapes.

Have you ever made a quilt?

Quilted fabrics have been used throughout the world for thousands of years. A needle and thread are used to combine the layers of fabric that make up a quilt.

The top of a quilt may be made of bits of fabric pieced together into "blocks." To decide how much fabric is needed, a quilter needs to know the size and shape of each block and the size and shape of all the pieces.

In this chapter, you'll learn how to find areas of various geometric shapes like those shown in the quilt block below.

Recall Prior Knowledge

Finding the area of a rectangle using a formula

The longer side of a rectangle is called the length.
The shorter side is called the width.

7 cm

4 cm

The opposite sides of a rectangle have the same length. If ℓ is the length and w is the width, the formula for area is Area $= \ell w$.

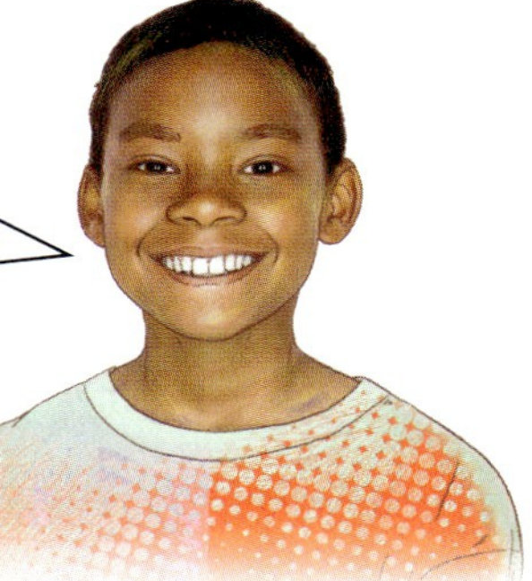

Area of rectangle $= \ell w$

$= 7 \cdot 4$

$= 28 \text{ cm}^2$

The area of the rectangle is 28 square centimeters.

Quick Check

Solve.

1. The length of a rectangle is 15 meters and its width is 8 meters. Find the area of the rectangle.

Finding the area of a square using a formula

A side length of a square is 12 meters. Find the area of the square.

12 m

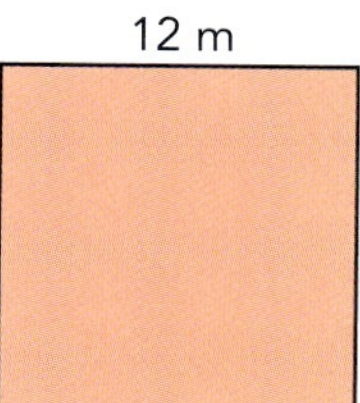

Area of square $= \ell^2$

$= 12^2$

$= 144 \text{ m}^2$

The area of the square is 144 square meters.

The side lengths of a square are all equal. If ℓ represents the side length, the formula for area is Area $= \ell^2$.

Quick Check

Solve.

2. A side length of a square is 10 centimeters. Find the area of the square.

Identifying parallelograms, trapezoids, and rhombuses

Figure *ABCD* is a parallelogram. There are two pairs of parallel sides. $\overline{AB}$ is parallel to $\overline{DC}$. $\overline{AD}$ is parallel to $\overline{BC}$.

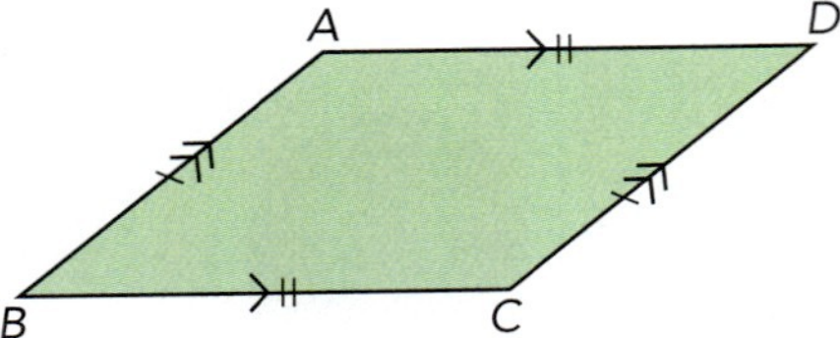

Figure *PQRS* is a trapezoid. There is one pair of parallel sides. $\overline{PS}$ is parallel to $\overline{QR}$.

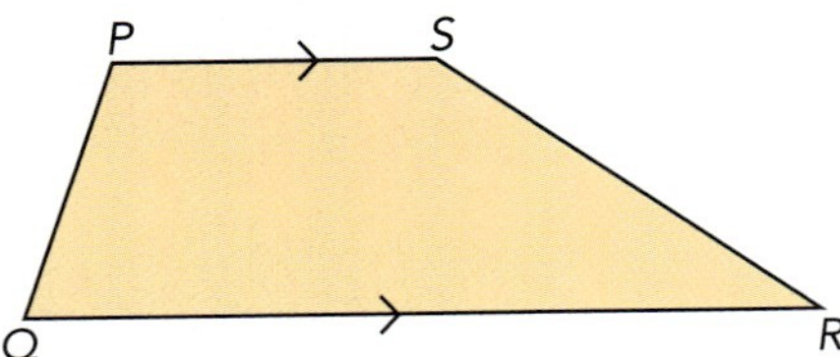

Figure *WXYZ* is a rhombus. The side lengths of a rhombus are equal, and the opposite sides are parallel. $\overline{WX}$ is parallel to $\overline{ZY}$. $\overline{XY}$ is parallel to $\overline{WZ}$.

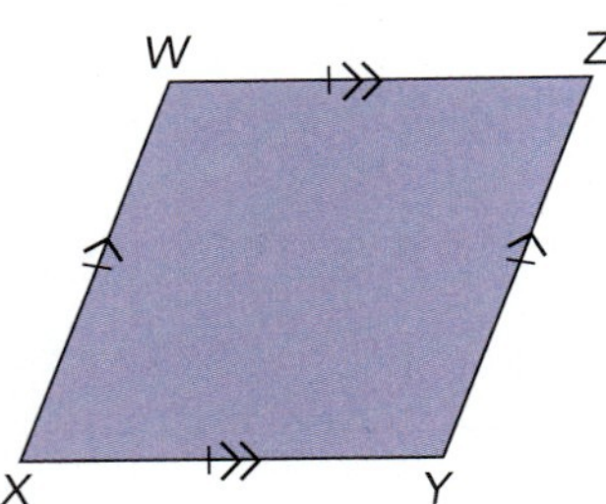

Quick Check

Name each figure and identify the pairs of parallel lines.

3

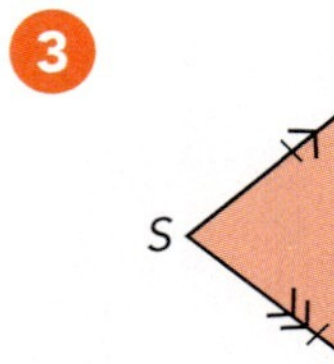

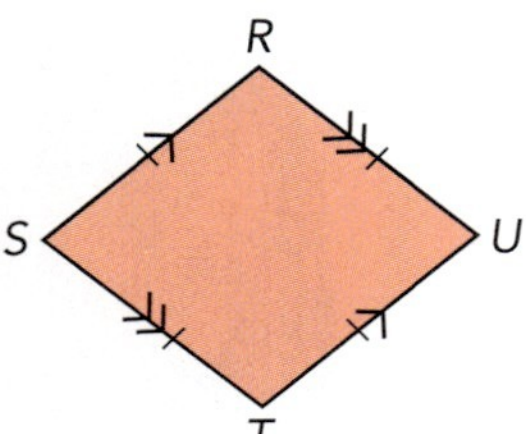

4

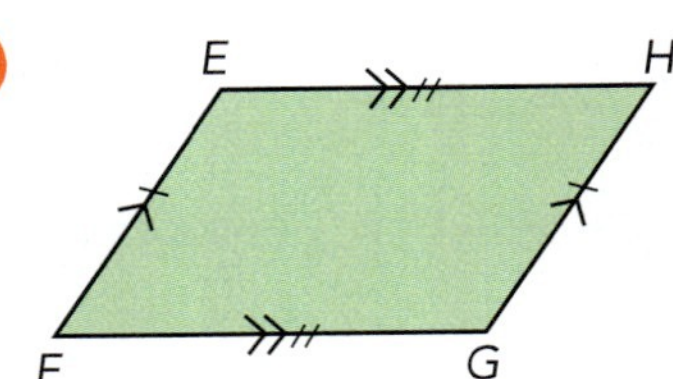

5

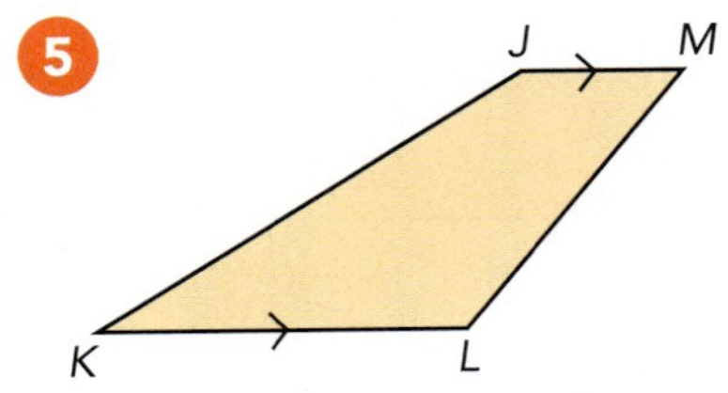

10.1 Area of Triangles

Lesson Objective

- Use a formula to find the area of a triangle.

Vocabulary

formula
base
height

Learn **Derive the formula for the area of a triangle.**

Area of rectangle $= \ell w$

The diagonal of a rectangle divides it into two congruent triangles.

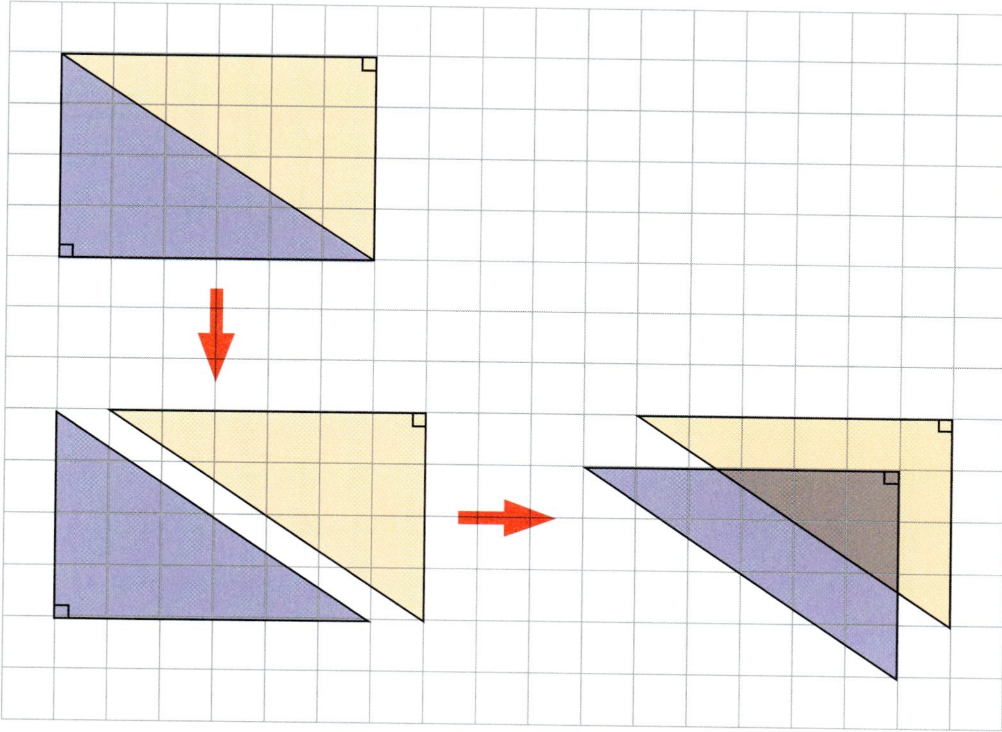

The area of the yellow triangle is half the area of the rectangle.

Area of the triangle

$= \frac{1}{2} \cdot$ area of the rectangle

$= \frac{1}{2} \cdot \ell w$

Continue on next page

Any side of a triangle can be called its **base**. The perpendicular distance from the base to the opposite vertex of the triangle is called the **height** of the triangle.

Area of triangle $= \frac{1}{2} \cdot \ell w$

$= \frac{1}{2} \cdot \text{base} \cdot \text{height}$

Using b for base and h for height, you can write the formula as

Area of triangle $= \frac{1}{2}bh$

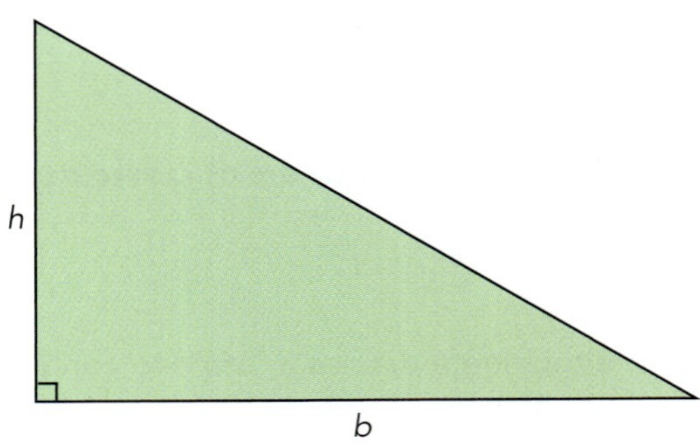

Hands-On Activity

Materials:

- scissors
- graph paper

PROVE THE FORMULA FOR FINDING THE AREA OF A TRIANGLE

Work in pairs.

Triangle PQR is an acute triangle. $\overline{QR}$ is the base and PX is the height.

STEP 1 Draw triangle PQR on a piece of graph paper as shown. Then draw and label rectangle $AQRD$.

Example

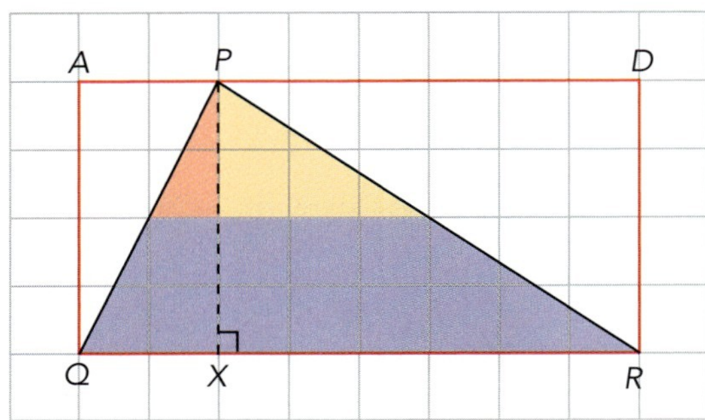

Cut up triangle *PQR* into smaller triangles. Rearrange the triangles to form rectangle *EQRF*, as shown below.

Example

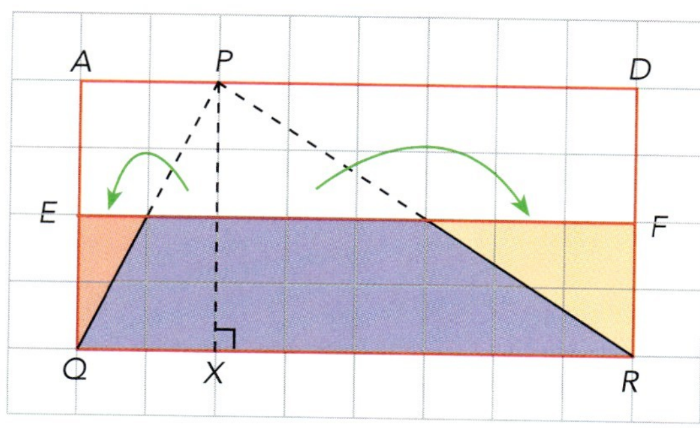

Find the area of rectangle *EQRF*. How does its area compare to the area of rectangle *AQRD*?

How does the area of triangle *PQR* compare to the area of rectangle *EQRF*?

How does the area of triangle *PQR* compare to the area of rectangle *AQRD*?

Triangle *MNP* is an obtuse triangle. $\overline{NP}$ is the base and *MF* is the height.

Draw triangle *MNP* on a piece of graph paper as shown. Then draw and label rectangle *ANPD*.

Example

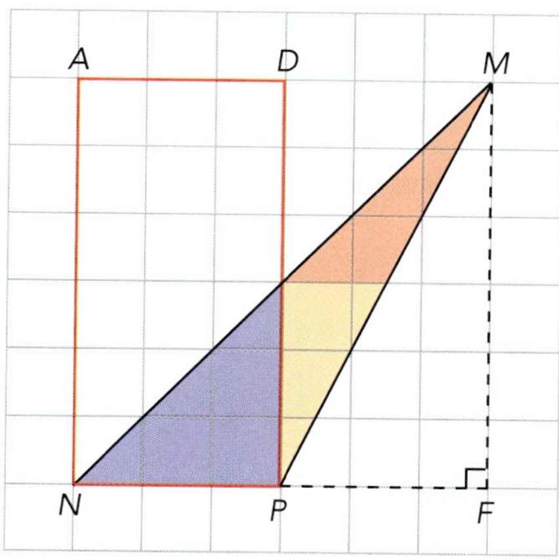

Continue on next page

STEP 2 Cut up triangle MNP into smaller triangles. Rearrange the triangles to form rectangle $ENPF$, as shown below.

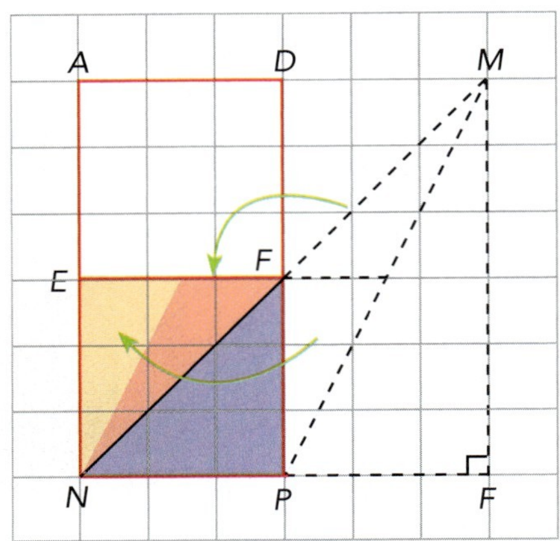

STEP 3 Find the area of rectangle $ENPF$. How does its area compare to the area of rectangle $ANPD$?

How does the area of triangle MNP compare to the area of rectangle $ENPF$?

How does the area of triangle MNP compare to the area of rectangle $ANPD$?

Learn Find the area of a triangle.

a) In triangle ABC, $\overline{AX}$ is perpendicular to $\overline{BC}$.

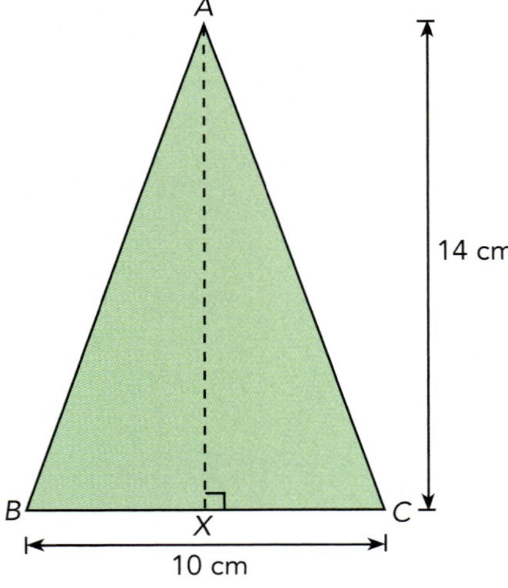

Math Note

Any side of a triangle can be called the base. The height of the triangle is the perpendicular distance from the opposite vertex to the base.

Base = BC = 10 cm
Height = AX = 14 cm

Area of triangle ABC $= \frac{1}{2}bh$ — Write formula.

$= \frac{1}{2} \cdot 10 \cdot 14$ — Substitute.

$= 70 \text{ cm}^2$ — Multiply.

The area of triangle ABC is 70 square centimeters.

b) In triangle PQR, $\overline{PX}$ is perpendicular to $\overline{QR}$.

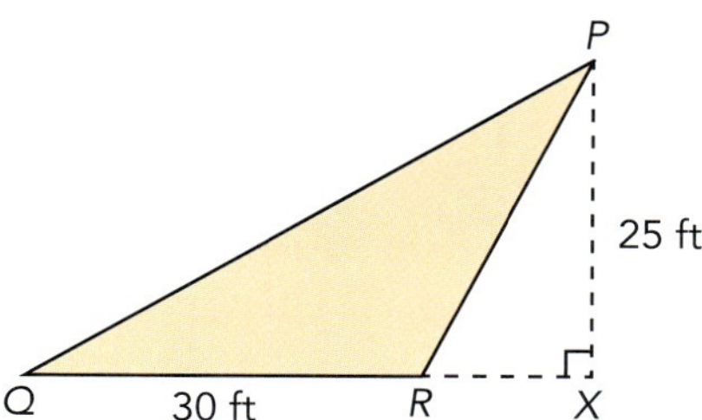

Caution

PR is **not** the height of the triangle. PX is the height because it is the perpendicular distance from P to the base.

Base = QR = 30 ft
Height = PX = 25 ft

Area of triangle $PQR = \frac{1}{2}bh$ Write formula.

$= \frac{1}{2} \cdot 30 \cdot 25$ Substitute.

$= 375 \text{ ft}^2$ Multiply.

The area of triangle PQR is 375 square feet.

Guided Practice

Complete to find the base, height, and area of each triangle. Each square measures 1 unit by 1 unit.

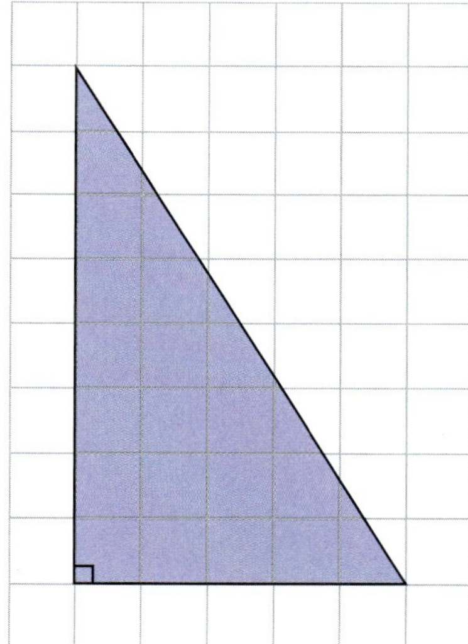

Base = __?__ units

Height = __?__ units

Area = $\frac{1}{2}bh$

= __?__ · __?__ · __?__

= __?__ units^2

2

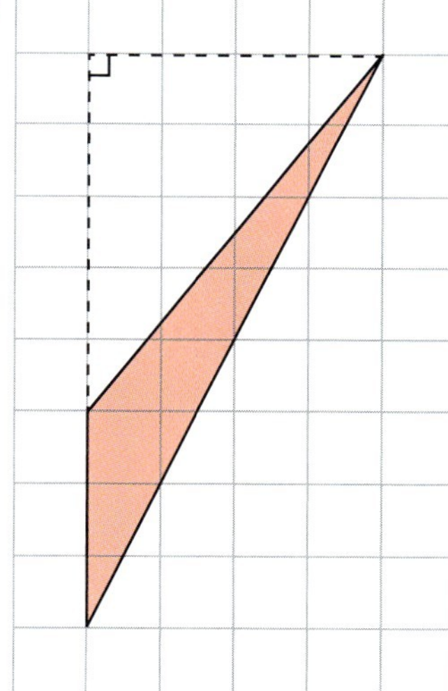

Base = __?__ units

Height = __?__ units

Area = $\frac{1}{2}bh$

= __?__ · __?__ · __?__

= __?__ units^2

3

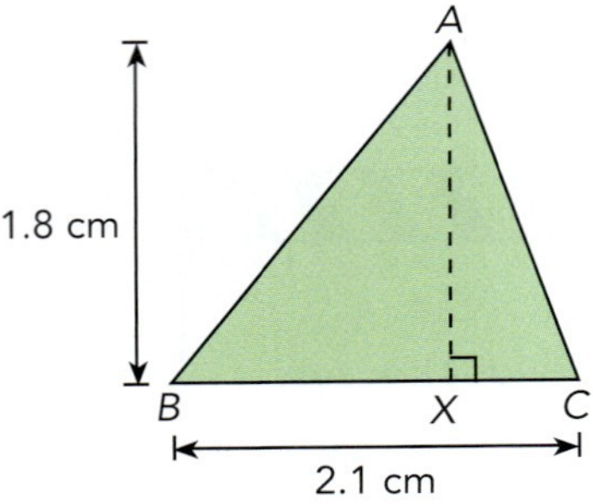

Base = $\underline{\quad ? \quad}$ cm

Height = $\underline{\quad ? \quad}$ cm

Area of triangle *ABC*

$= \frac{1}{2}bh$

$= \underline{\quad ? \quad} \cdot \underline{\quad ? \quad} \cdot \underline{\quad ? \quad}$

$= \underline{\quad ? \quad}$ cm^2

4

P
2.7 ft
X
Q
R
3.4 ft

Base = $\underline{\quad ? \quad}$ ft

Height = $\underline{\quad ? \quad}$ ft

Area of triangle *PQR*

$= \frac{1}{2}bh$

$= \underline{\quad ? \quad} \cdot \underline{\quad ? \quad} \cdot \underline{\quad ? \quad}$

$= \underline{\quad ? \quad}$ ft^2

Learn

Find the height of a triangle given its area and base.

The area of triangle *FGH* is 46 square inches. Find the height of the triangle.

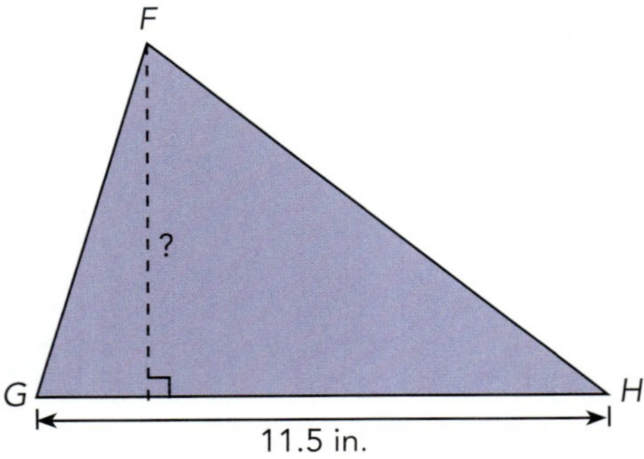

Area of triangle *FGH* $= \frac{1}{2}bh$	Write formula.
$46 = \frac{1}{2} \cdot 11.5 \cdot h$	Substitute.
$46 = 5.75 \cdot h$	Simplify.
$46 \div 5.75 = 5.75h \div 5.75$	Divide each side by 5.75.
$8 = h$	Simplify.

The height of triangle *FGH* is 8 inches.

Guided Practice

Complete to find the height of triangle *JKL*.

5 The area of triangle *JKL* is 35 square meters. Find the height of triangle *JKL*.

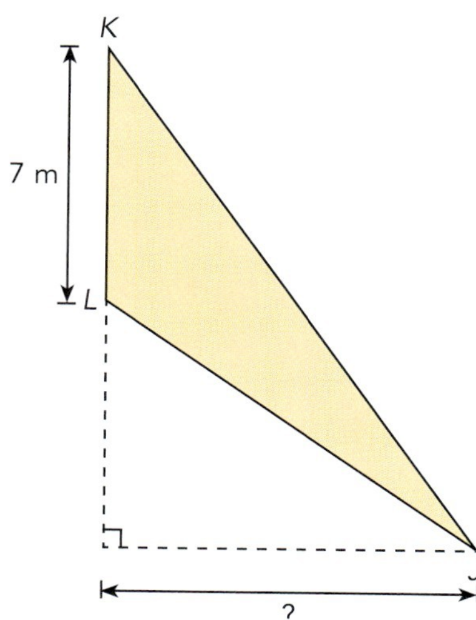

Area of triangle $JKL = \frac{1}{2}bh$

$\underline{\ ?\ } = \underline{\ ?\ } \cdot \underline{\ ?\ } \cdot h$

$\underline{\ ?\ } = \underline{\ ?\ } \cdot h$

$\underline{\ ?\ } \div \underline{\ ?\ } = \underline{\ ?\ }\, h \div \underline{\ ?\ }$

$\underline{\ ?\ } = h$

The height of triangle *JKL* is $\underline{\ ?\ }$ meters.

Learn Find the base of a triangle given its area and height.

The area of triangle *XYZ* is 36.5 square centimeters. Find the base of the triangle.

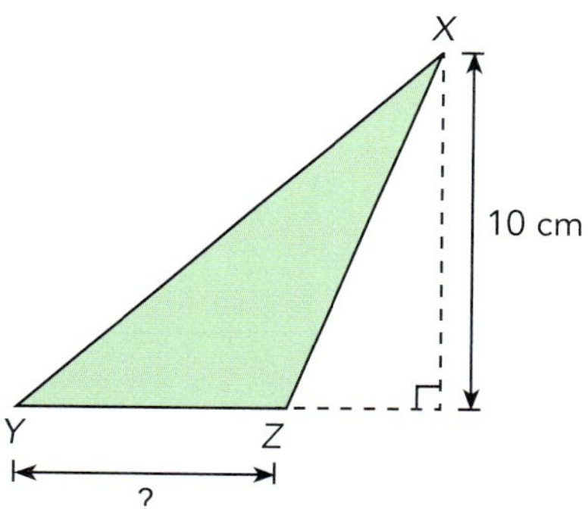

Area of triangle $XYZ = \frac{1}{2}bh$	Write formula.
$36.5 = \frac{1}{2} \cdot b \cdot 10$	Substitute.
$36.5 = \frac{1}{2} \cdot 10 \cdot b$	Commutative property.
$36.5 = 5 \cdot b$	Simplify.
$36.5 \div 5 = 5b \div 5$	Divide each side by 5.
$7.3 = b$	Simplify.

The base of triangle *XYZ* is 7.3 centimeters.

Guided Practice

Complete to find the base of each triangle.

6 The area of triangle *LMN* is 36 square inches. Find the base of triangle *LMN*.

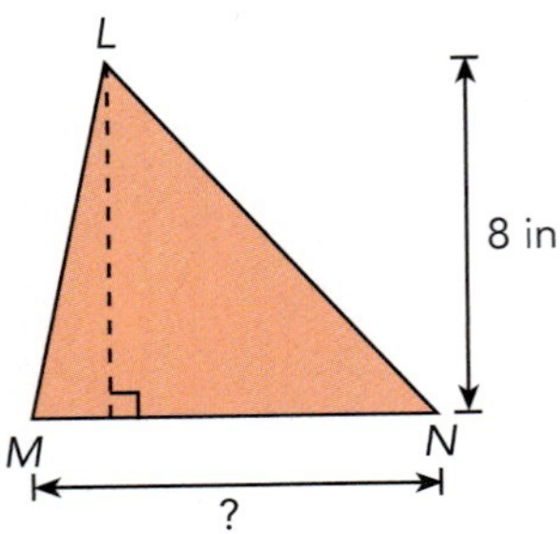

Area of triangle *LMN* $= \frac{1}{2}bh$

$\underline{\ ?\ } = \underline{\ ?\ } \cdot b \cdot \underline{\ ?\ }$

$= \underline{\ ?\ } \cdot \underline{\ ?\ } \cdot b$

$\underline{\ ?\ } = \underline{\ ?\ } \cdot b$

$\underline{\ ?\ } \div \underline{\ ?\ } = \underline{\ ?\ }\, b \div \underline{\ ?\ }$

$\underline{\ ?\ } = b$

The base of triangle *LMN* is $\underline{\ ?\ }$ inches.

7 The area of triangle *PQR* is 19.2 square centimeters. Find the base of triangle *PQR*.

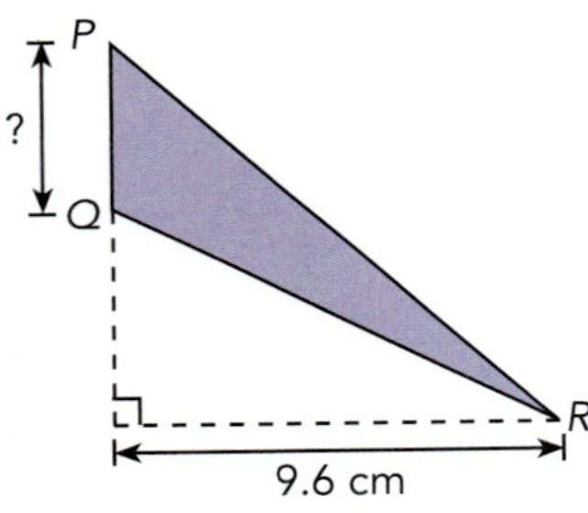

Area of triangle *PQR* $= \frac{1}{2}bh$

$\underline{\ ?\ } = \underline{\ ?\ } \cdot b \cdot \underline{\ ?\ }$

$= \underline{\ ?\ } \cdot \underline{\ ?\ } \cdot b$

$\underline{\ ?\ } = \underline{\ ?\ } \cdot b$

$\underline{\ ?\ } \div \underline{\ ?\ } = \underline{\ ?\ }\, b \div \underline{\ ?\ }$

$\underline{\ ?\ } = b$

The base of triangle *PQR* is $\underline{\ ?\ }$ centimeters.

Practice 10.1

Identify a base and a height of each triangle.

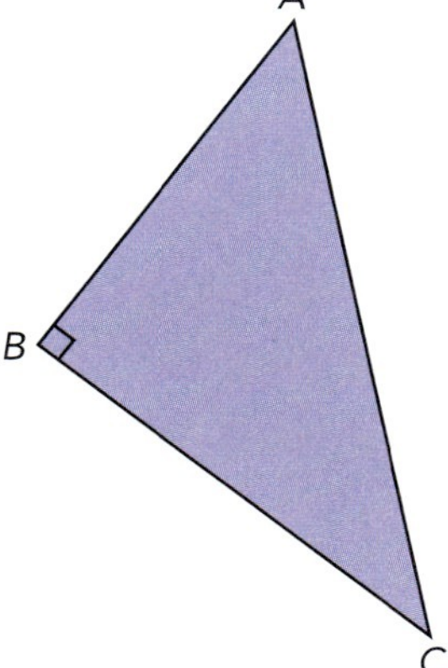

2

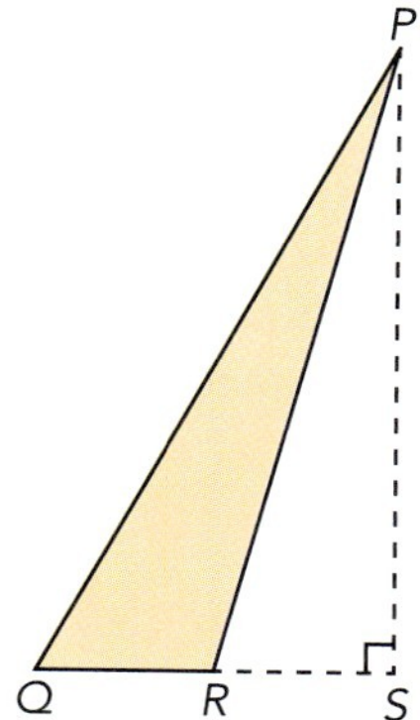

Copy each triangle. Label a base with the letter *b* and a height with the letter *h*.

3

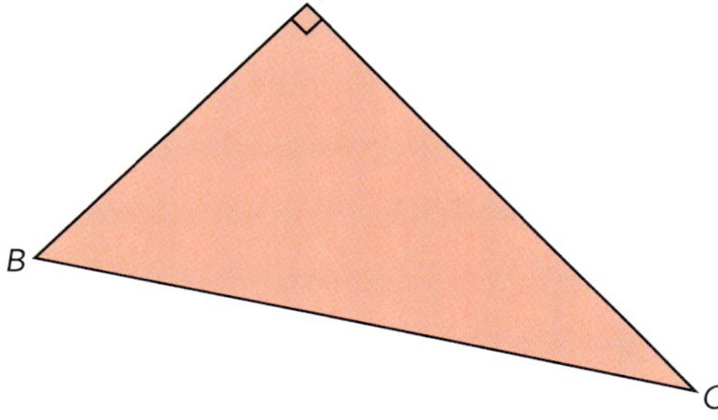

4

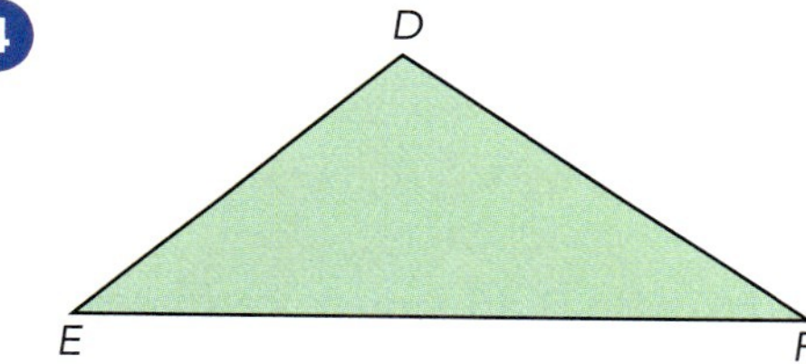

5

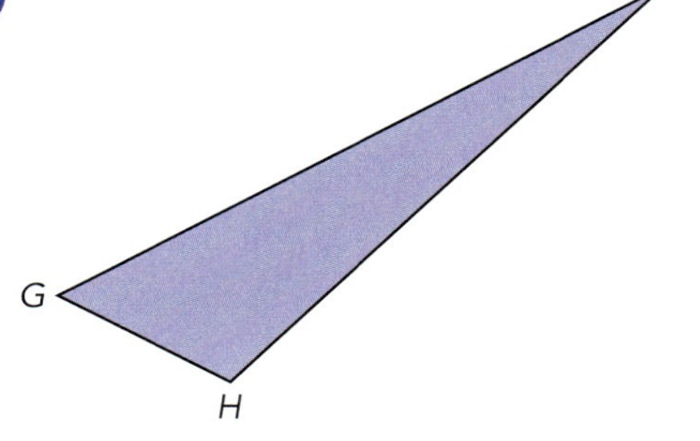

6

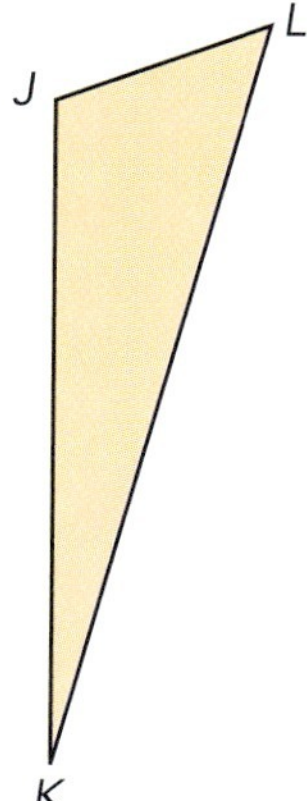

Find the area of each triangle.

7

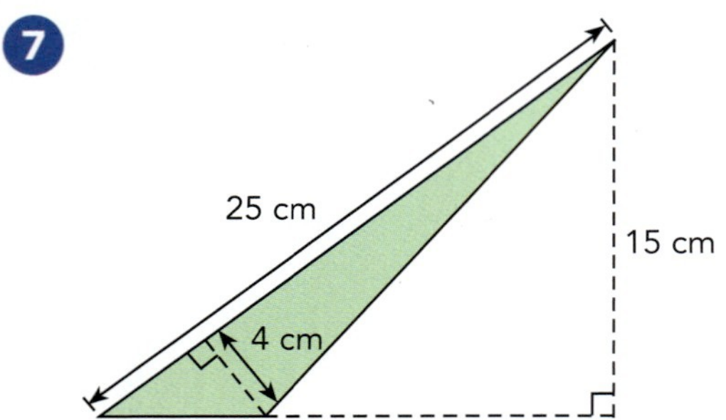

8

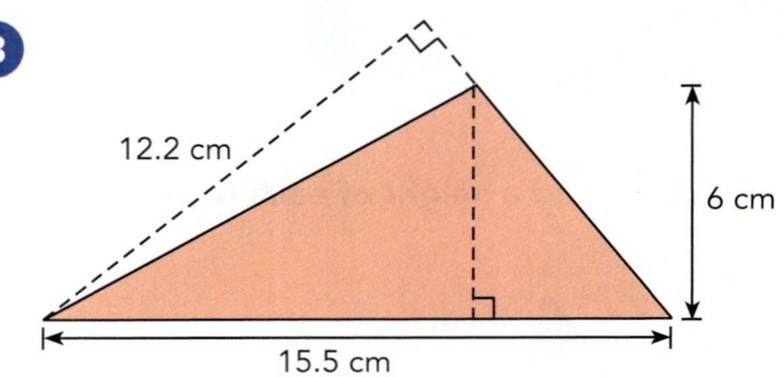

The area of each triangle is 76 square inches. Find the height and round your answer to the nearest tenth of an inch.

9

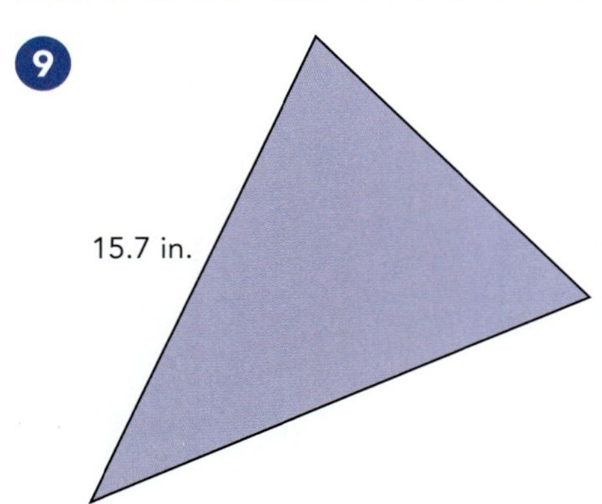

10

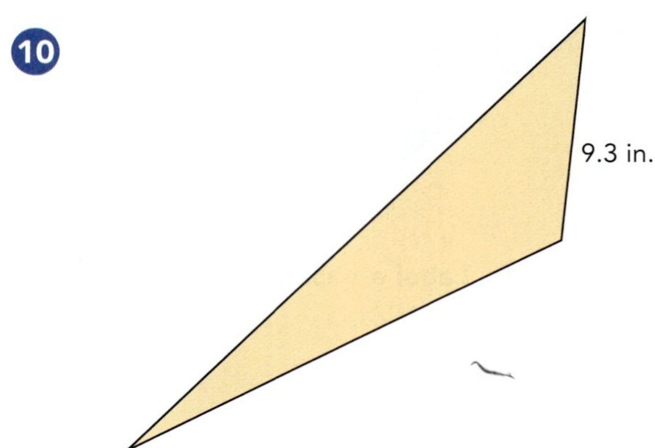

The area of each triangle is 45 square centimeters. Find the base and round your answer to the nearest tenth of a centimeter if necessary.

11

7.2 cm

12

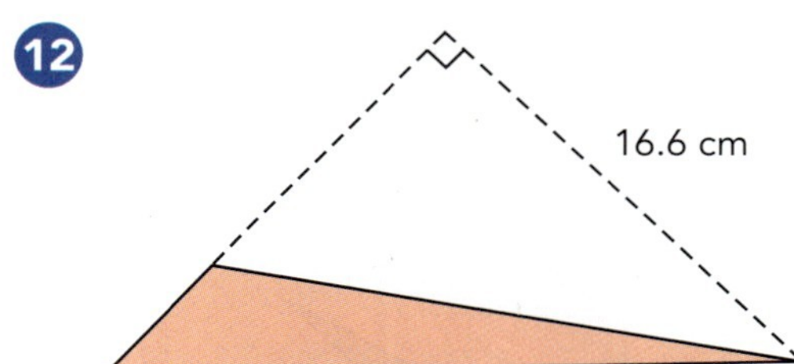

13

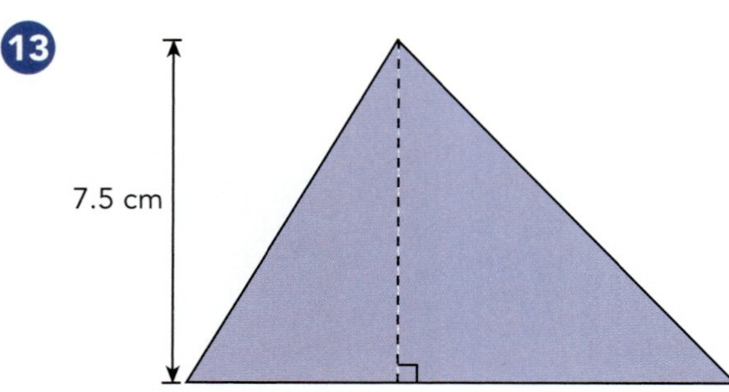

14

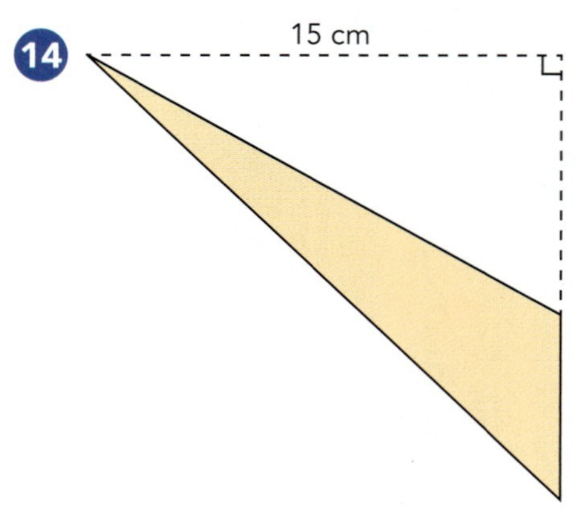

Find the area of the shaded region.

15

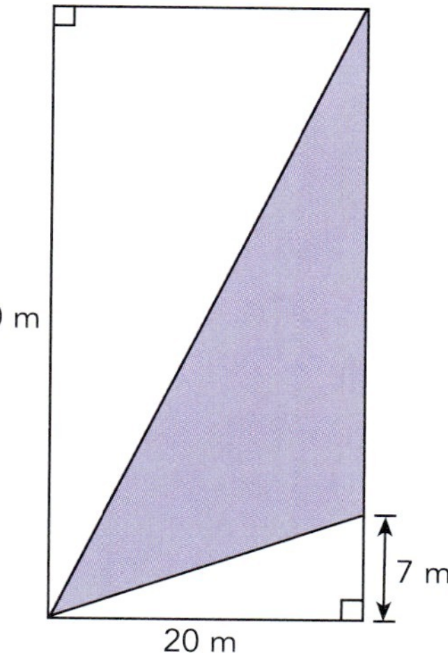

16

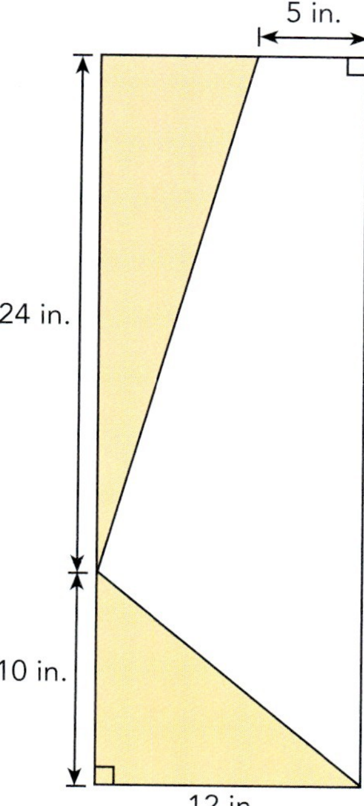

17

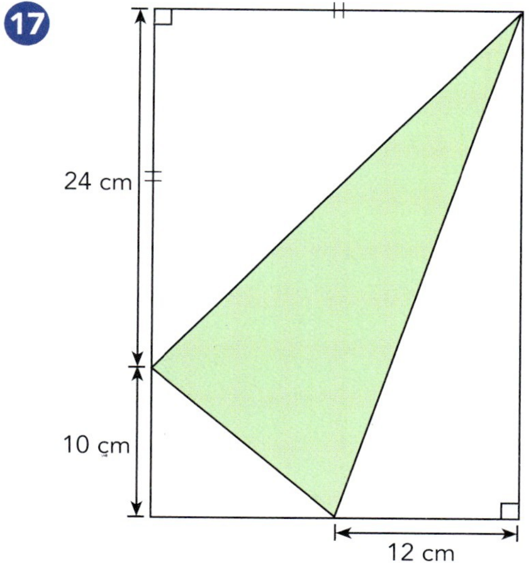

18

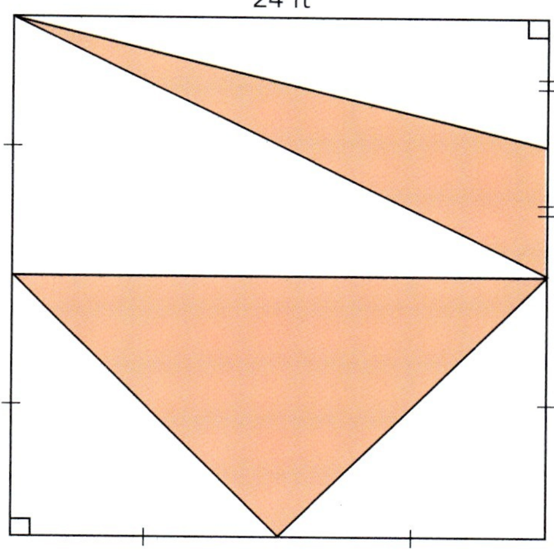

19

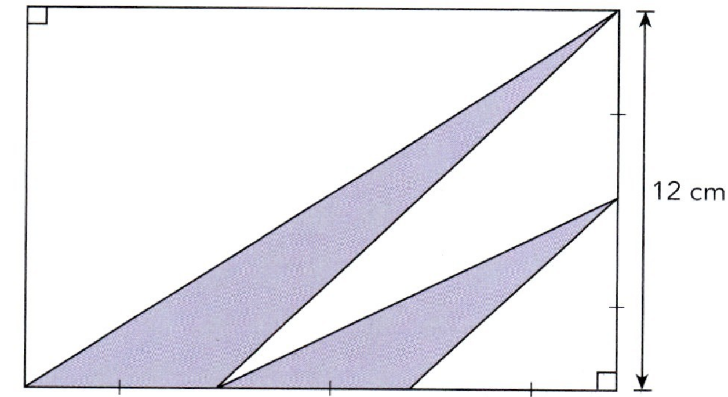

Use graph paper. Solve.

20 The coordinates of the vertices of a triangle are A (4, 7), B (4, 1), and C (8, 1). Find the area of triangle ABC.

21 The coordinates of the vertices of a triangle are D (1, 7), E (−3, 2), and F (6, 2). Find the area of triangle DEF.

22 The coordinates of the vertices of a triangle are J (−5, 2), K (1, −2), and L (5, −2). Find the area of triangle JKL.

23 The area of triangle MNP is 17.5 square units. The coordinates of M are (−9, 5), and the coordinates of N are (−2, 0). The height of triangle MNP is 5 units and is perpendicular to the x-axis. Point P lies to the right of point N. Given that $\overline{NP}$ is the base of the triangle, find the coordinates of point P.

24 The coordinates of the vertices of a triangle are X (1, 2), Y (−6, −2), and Z (1, −4). Find the area of triangle XYZ. (Hint: Use the vertical side as the base.)

25 The coordinates of the vertices of a triangle are P (−2, 6), Q (−4, 2), and R (5, 1). Find the area of triangle PQR. (Hint: Draw a rectangle around triangle PQR.)

Find the area of the shaded region for questions 26 to 29.

26 Figure $DGHJ$ is a trapezoid.

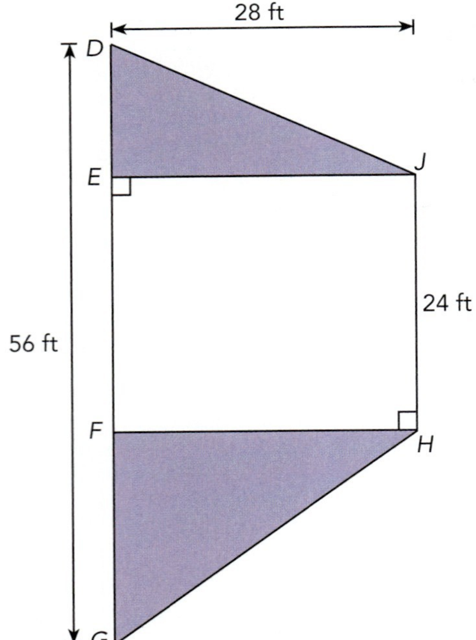

27 Figure *ABCD* is a rectangle. The length of $\overline{ZB}$ is $\frac{3}{7}$ the length of $\overline{AB}$.

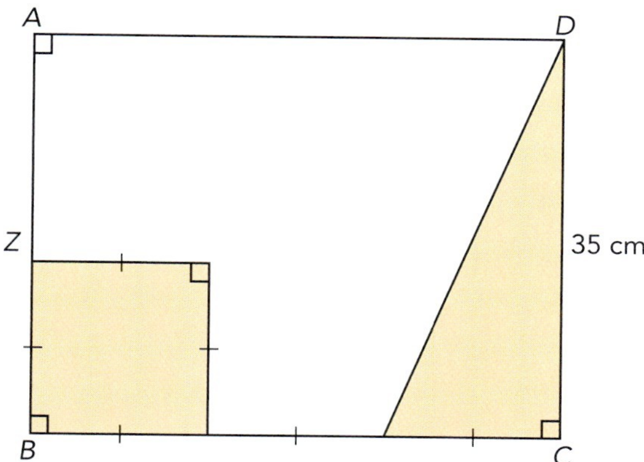

28 The area of triangle *PQS* is $\frac{7}{12}$ of the area of trapezoid *PRST*.

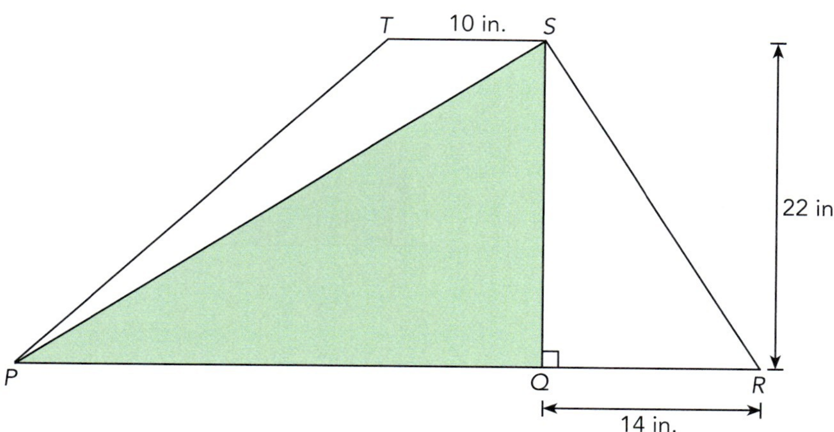

29 Figure *EFHL* is a parallelogram. The length of $\overline{FG}$ is $\frac{5}{8}$ the length of $\overline{FH}$.

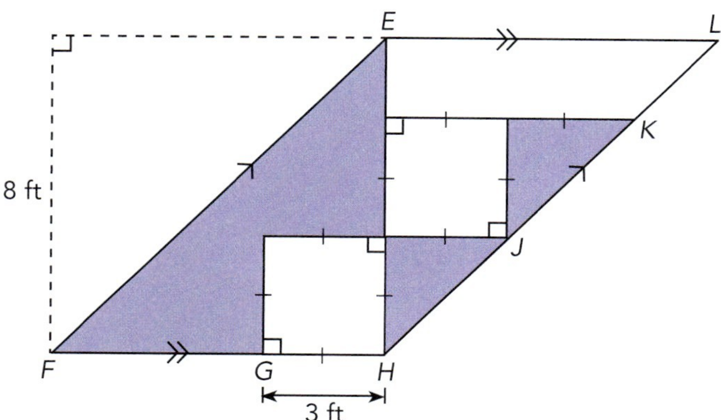

10.2 Area of Parallelograms and Trapezoids

Lesson Objectives

- Use a formula to find the area of a parallelogram, given its base and height.
- Use a formula to find the area of a trapezoid, given its bases and height.

Learn **Derive the formula for the area of a parallelogram.**

Figure *ABCD* is a parallelogram with base $\overline{BC}$ and height *AX*.

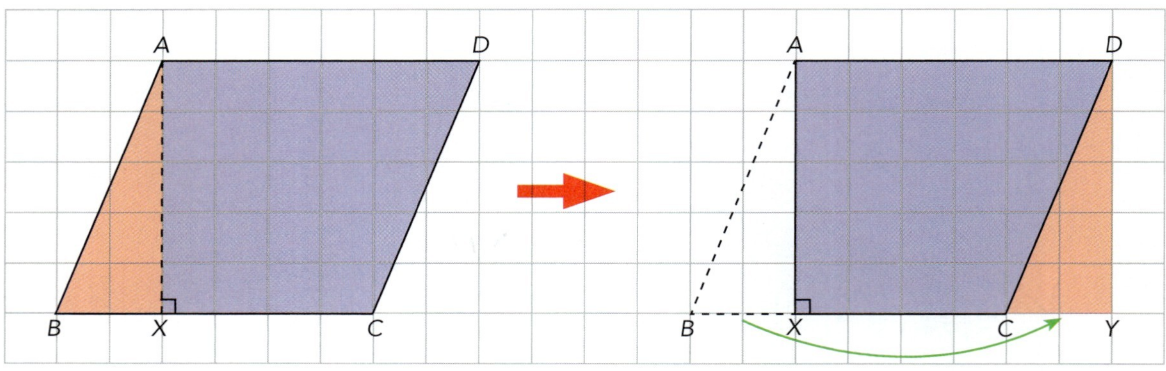

Triangle *ABX* is cut and moved to the side, where $\overline{AB}$ is placed against $\overline{DC}$. Rectangle *AXYD* is formed.

Since the area of the parallelogram is the same as the rectangle,

Area of parallelogram = area of rectangle *AXYD*

$= XY \cdot AX$

Notice that $\overline{XY}$ has the same length as the base $\overline{BC}$ of the parallelogram. *AX* is the width of the rectangle and is also the height of the parallelogram. Using *b* for base, and *h* for height, you can write this formula for the area of a parallelogram:

Area of parallelogram = *bh*

Any side of a parallelogram can be considered the base. The height is the perpendicular distance from the opposite side to the base.

Learn Find the area of a parallelogram.

In the figure, *ABCD* is a parallelogram and $\overline{BE}$ is straight.

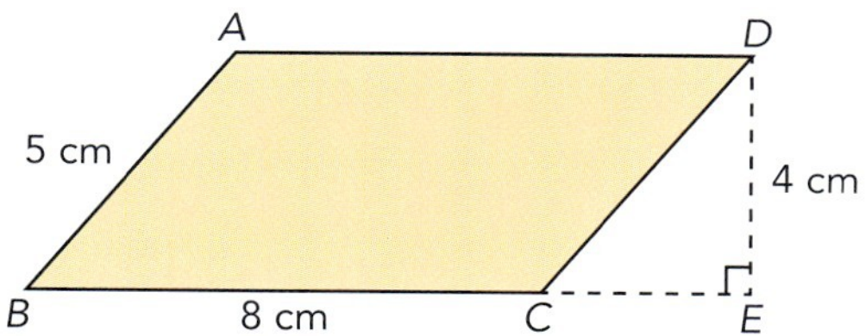

Caution

The height of the parallelogram is *DE*. *DC* is **not** the height of the parallelogram, because $\overline{DC}$ is **not** perpendicular to the base.

Base = *BC* = 8 cm
Height = *DE* = 4 cm

Area of *ABCD* = *bh* — Write formula.
= *BC* · *DE* — Substitute.
= 8 · 4 — Multiply.
= 32 cm^2

The area of parallelogram *ABCD* is 32 square centimeters.

Guided Practice

Complete to find the base, height, and area of each parallelogram. Each square measures 1 unit by 1 unit.

1

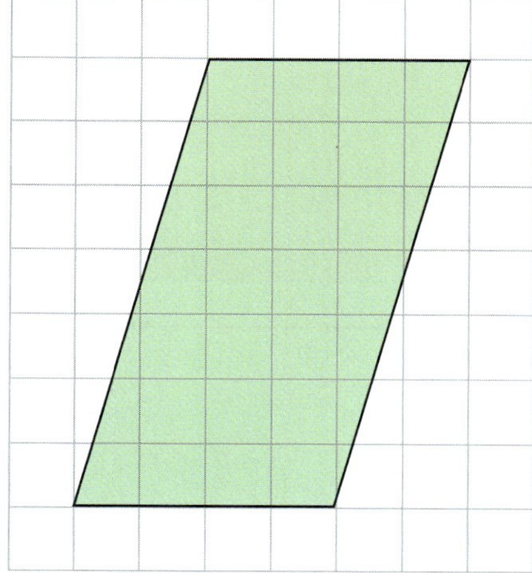

Base = __?__ units

Height = __?__ units

Area = *bh*

= __?__ · __?__

= __?__ units^2

2

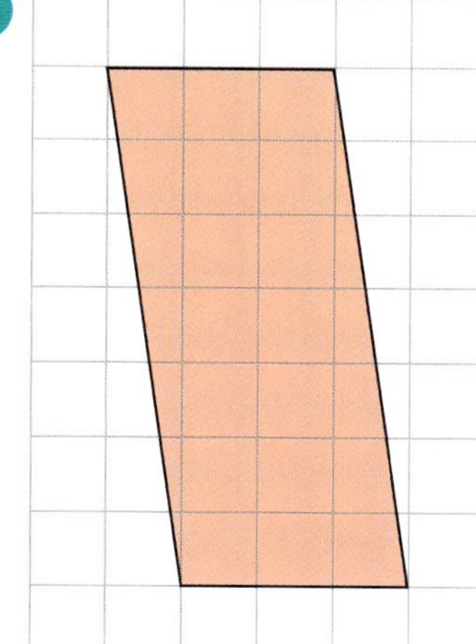

Base = __?__ units

Height = __?__ units

Area = *bh*

= __?__ · __?__

= __?__ units^2

3

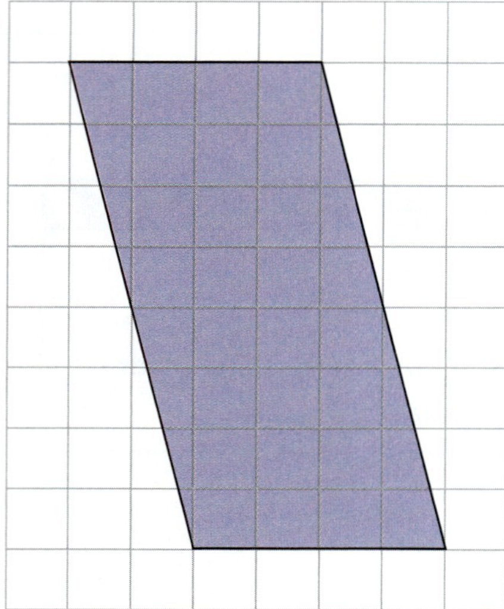

Base = __?__ units

Height = __?__ units

Area = bh

= __?__ · __?__

= __?__ units^2

4

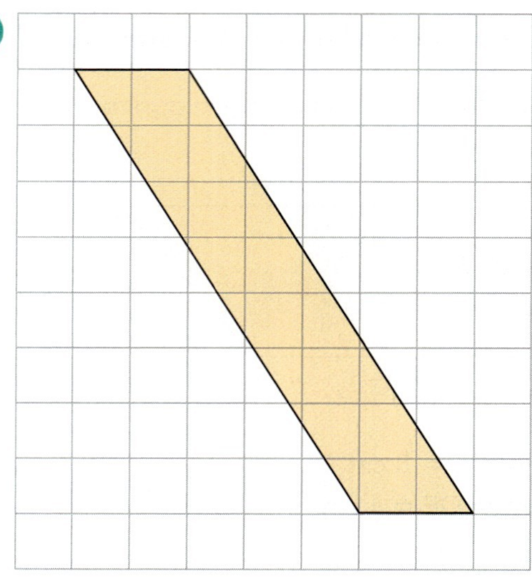

Base = __?__ units

Height = __?__ units

Area = bh

= __?__ · __?__

= __?__ units^2

Complete to find the area of each parallelogram.

5

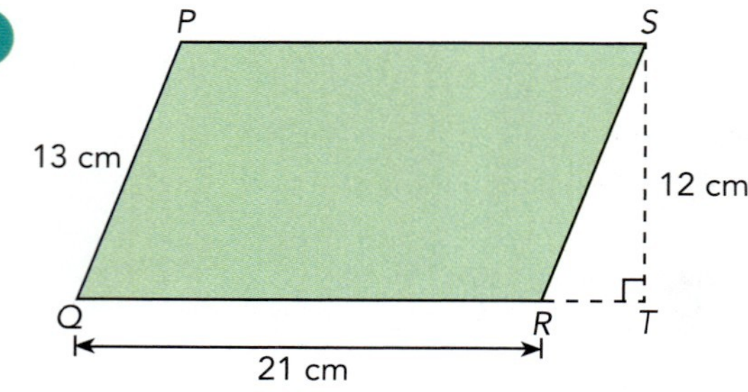

Base = __?__ cm

Height = __?__ cm

Area = bh

= __?__ · __?__

= __?__ cm^2

6

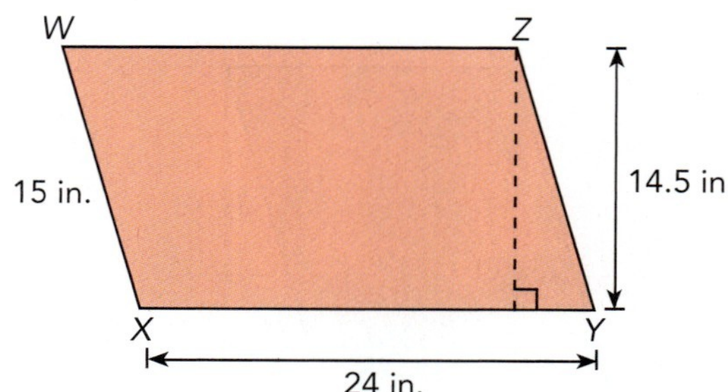

Base = __?__ in.

Height = __?__ in.

Area = bh

= __?__ · __?__

= __?__ in.^{2}

Learn

Derive the formula for the area of a trapezoid.

Figure *ABDE* is a trapezoid with bases $\overline{AE}$ and $\overline{BD}$ and height *EC*. $\overline{AE}$ is parallel to $\overline{BD}$.

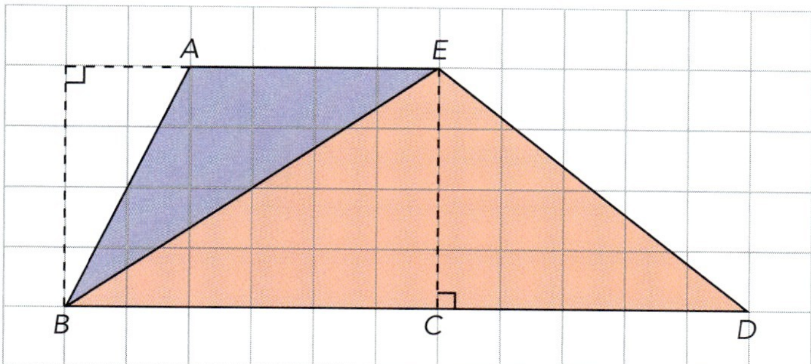

The diagonal $\overline{BE}$ of the trapezoid divides it into two triangles. Both triangles have the same height.

Area of trapezoid = area of blue triangle + area of orange triangle

$$= \frac{1}{2} \cdot AE \cdot \text{height} + \frac{1}{2} \cdot BD \cdot \text{height}$$

$$= \frac{1}{2} \cdot \text{height} \cdot \underbrace{(AE + BD)}_{\text{sum of the lengths of the parallel sides of the trapezoid}}$$

Area of trapezoid = $\frac{1}{2}$ · height · sum of the lengths of the parallel sides

The parallel sides in a trapezoid are called its bases. One base is usually labeled b_1, and the other is labeled b_2. The perpendicular distance between the bases is the height of the trapezoid. Using *h* for height, you can write a formula for the area of a trapezoid.

Math Note

b_1 and b_2 are read as "*b* sub 1" and "*b* sub 2."

Area of trapezoid

$= \frac{1}{2}h$(sum of the lengths of the parallel sides)

$= \frac{1}{2}h$(sum of the bases)

Area of trapezoid = $\frac{1}{2}h(b_1 + b_2)$

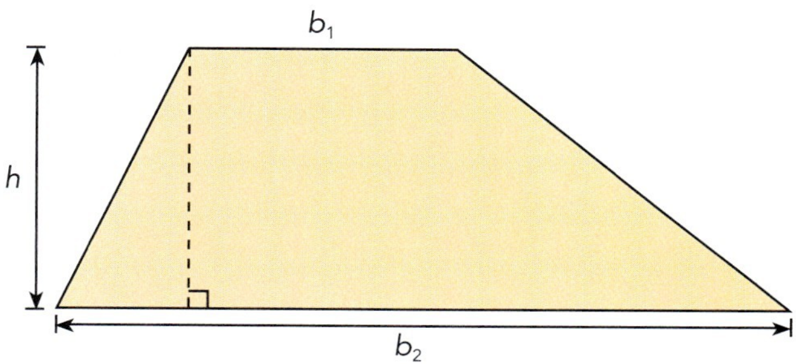

Learn Find the area of a trapezoid.

In the figure, *TUVW* is a trapezoid. $\overline{TW}$ is parallel to $\overline{UV}$. Find the area of trapezoid *TUVW*.

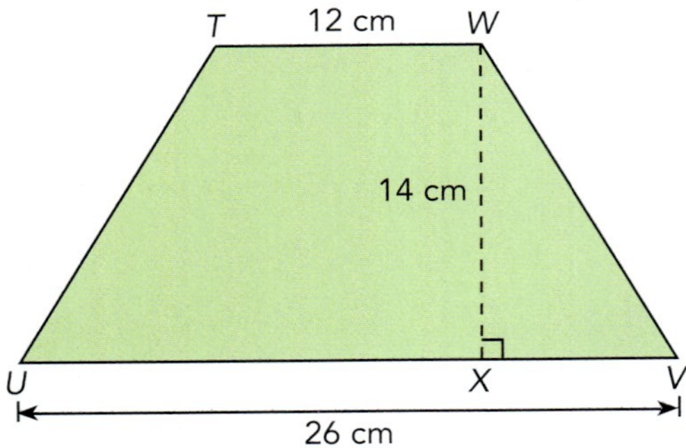

Height = WX = 14 cm

Sum of the bases = $TW + UV$

= 12 + 26

= 38 cm

Area of trapezoid $= \frac{1}{2}h$(sum of the bases) — Write formula.

$= \frac{1}{2} \cdot 14 \cdot 38$ — Substitute.

$= 266 \text{ cm}^2$ — Multiply.

The area of *TUVW* is 266 square centimeters.

Guided Practice

Complete to find the sum of the bases, height, and area of each trapezoid. Each square measures 1 unit by 1 unit.

7

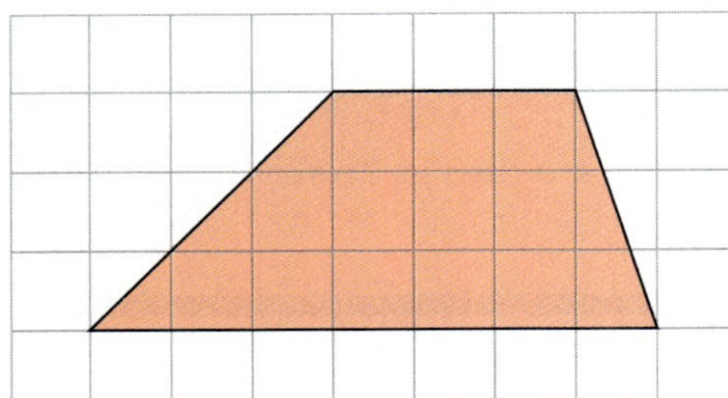

Height = __?__ units

Sum of bases = __?__ + __?__

= __?__ units

Area $= \frac{1}{2}h$(sum of bases)

= __?__ · __?__ · __?__

= __?__ units^2

8

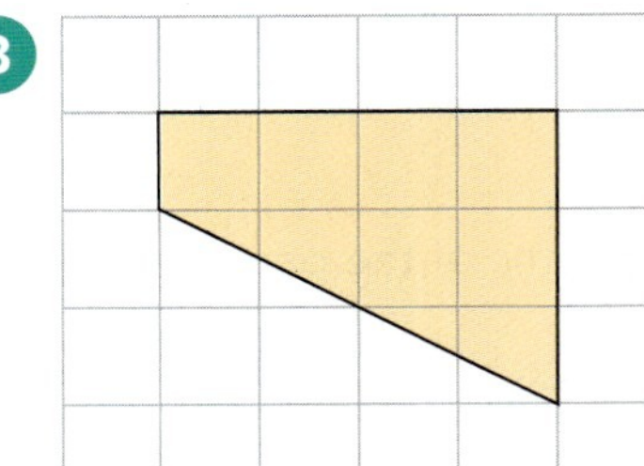

Height = __?__ units

Sum of bases = __?__ + __?__

= __?__ units

Area $= \frac{1}{2}h$(sum of bases)

= __?__ · __?__ · __?__

= __?__ units^2

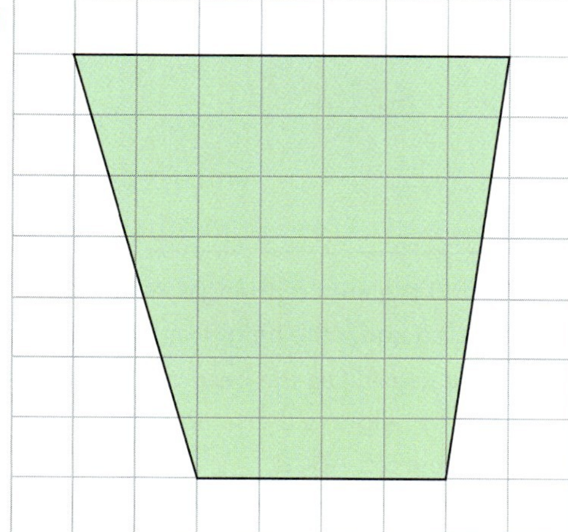

Height = ___?___ units

Sum of bases = ___?___ + ___?___

= ___?___ units

Area = $\frac{1}{2}h$(sum of bases)

= ___?___ · ___?___ · ___?___

= ___?___ units^2

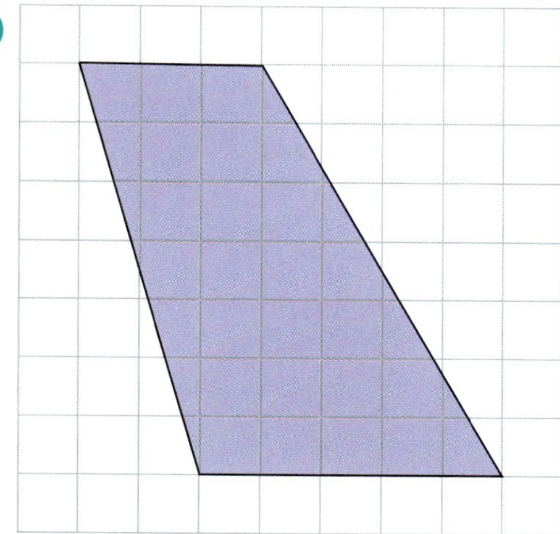

Height = ___?___ units

Sum of bases = ___?___ + ___?___

= ___?___ units

Area = $\frac{1}{2}h$(sum of bases)

= ___?___ · ___?___ · ___?___

= ___?___ units^2

Complete to find the area of each trapezoid.

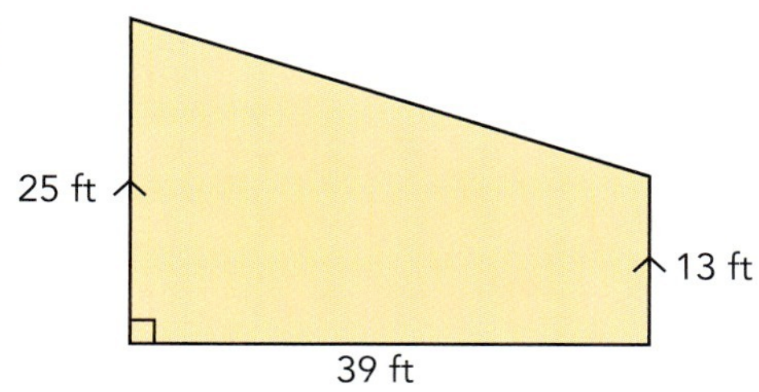

Height = ___?___ ft

Sum of bases = ___?___ + ___?___

= ___?___ ft

Area = $\frac{1}{2}h$(sum of bases)

= ___?___ · ___?___ · ___?___

= ___?___ ft^2

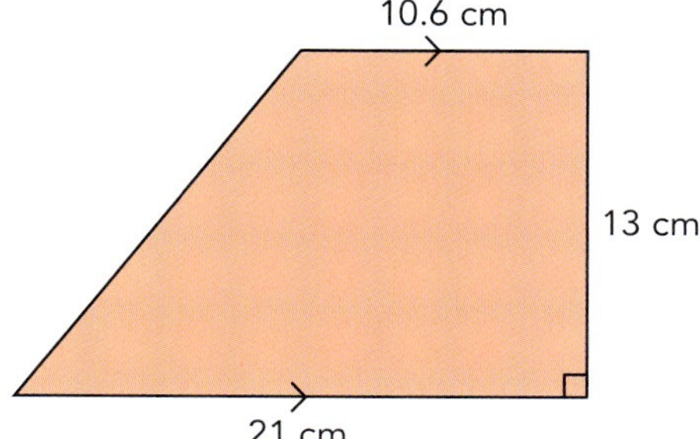

Height = ___?___ cm

Sum of bases = ___?___ + ___?___

= ___?___ cm

Area = $\frac{1}{2}h$(sum of bases)

= ___?___ · ___?___ · ___?___

= ___?___ cm^2

Learn Apply the formula for the area of a trapezoid.

The area of trapezoid *ABCD* is 4,196.5 square meters. $\overline{AD}$ is parallel to $\overline{BC}$. Find the area of triangle *ADC*.

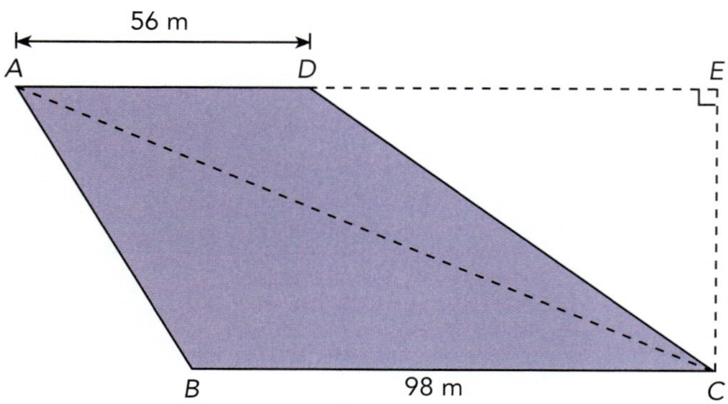

To find the area of triangle *ADC*, you need to know the height of the triangle. If you use $\overline{AD}$ as the base of the triangle, then its height is the same as the height of trapezoid *ABCD*.

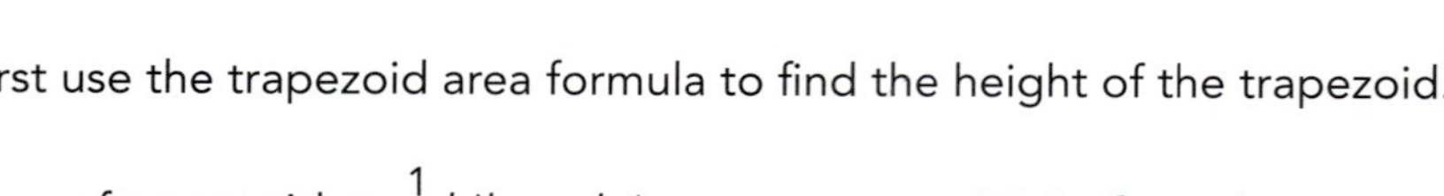

First use the trapezoid area formula to find the height of the trapezoid.

Area of trapezoid $= \frac{1}{2}h(b_1 + b_2)$	Write formula.
$= \frac{1}{2} \cdot EC \cdot (AD + BC)$	Substitute.
$= \frac{1}{2} \cdot EC \cdot (56 + 98)$	
$= \frac{1}{2} \cdot EC \cdot (154)$	Add inside parentheses.
$= \frac{1}{2} \cdot 154 \cdot EC$	Apply commutative property.
$= 77 \cdot EC$	Simplify.

Since area of trapezoid = 4,196.5 m^2,

$77 \cdot EC$ = area of trapezoid

$77 \cdot EC = 4{,}196.5$

$EC = 4{,}196.5 \div 77$

$= 54.5$ m

Height of trapezoid $= EC$

$= 54.5$ m

Then use the fact that *EC* is also the height of the triangle to find the area of the triangle.

Area of triangle *ADC* $= \frac{1}{2}bh$	Write formula.
$= \frac{1}{2} \cdot 56 \cdot 54.5$	Substitute.
$= 1{,}526$ m^2	Multiply.

The area of triangle *ADC* is 1,526 square meters.

Guided Practice

Complete to find the area of triangle *ABD*.

 The area of trapezoid *ABCD* is 1,248 square centimeters.

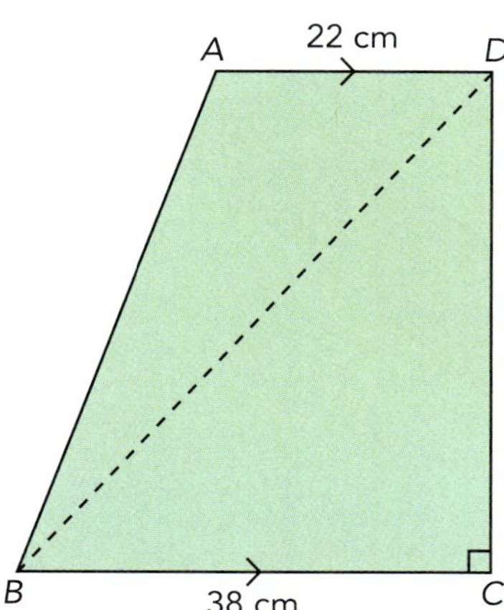

Area of trapezoid *ABCD* $= \frac{1}{2}h(b_1 + b_2)$

$= \frac{1}{2} \cdot h \cdot (\underline{?} + \underline{?})$

$= \frac{1}{2} \cdot h \cdot \underline{?}$

$= \frac{1}{2} \cdot \underline{?} \cdot h$

$= \underline{?} \cdot h$

Since area of trapezoid = $\underline{?}$ cm^2,

$\underline{?} \cdot h$ = area of trapezoid

$\underline{?} \cdot h = \underline{?}$

$h = \underline{?}$? $\underline{?}$

$= \underline{?}$ cm

Height of trapezoid = $\underline{?}$

$= \underline{?}$ cm

Area of triangle *ABD* $= \frac{1}{2}bh$

$= \frac{1}{2} \cdot \underline{?} \cdot \underline{?}$

$= \underline{?}$ cm^2

The area of triangle *ABD* is $\underline{?}$ square centimeters.

Practice 10.2

Copy each parallelogram. Label a base and a height for each. Use *b* and *h*.

1. 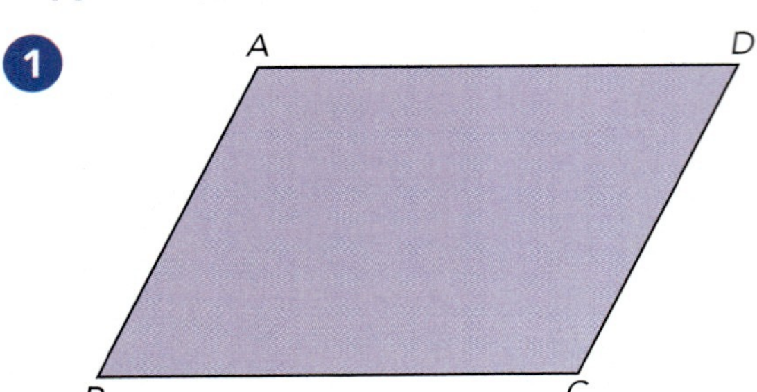

2. 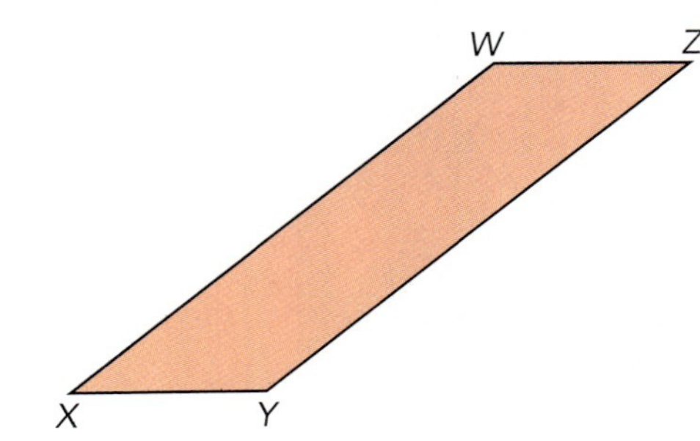

3. 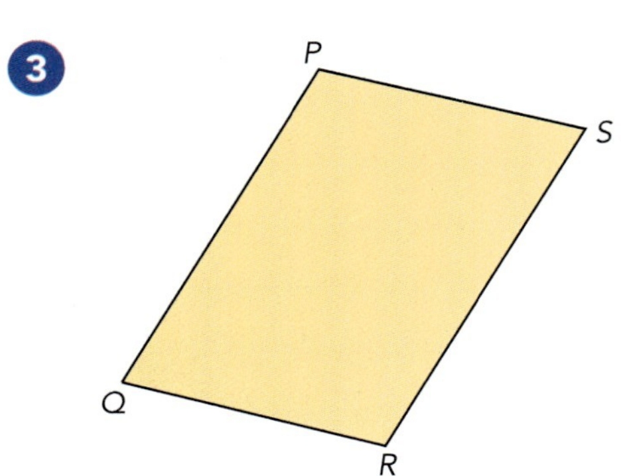

4. 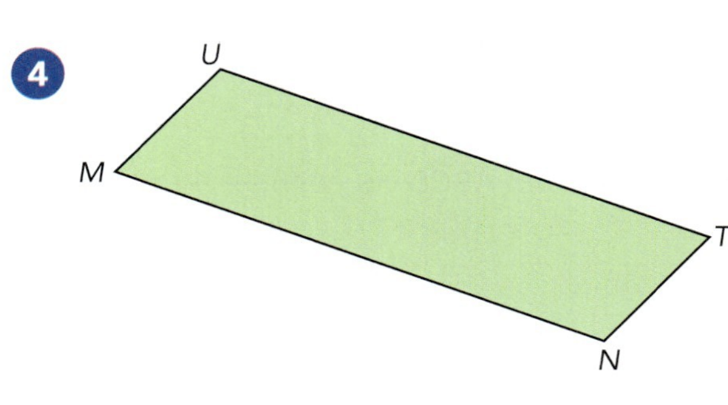

Find the area of each parallelogram.

5. 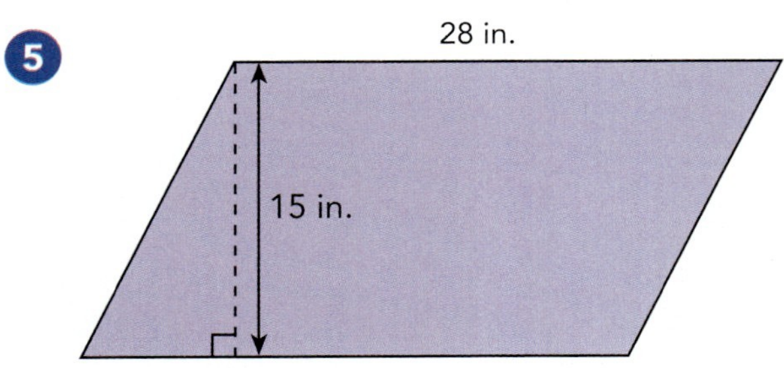

6. 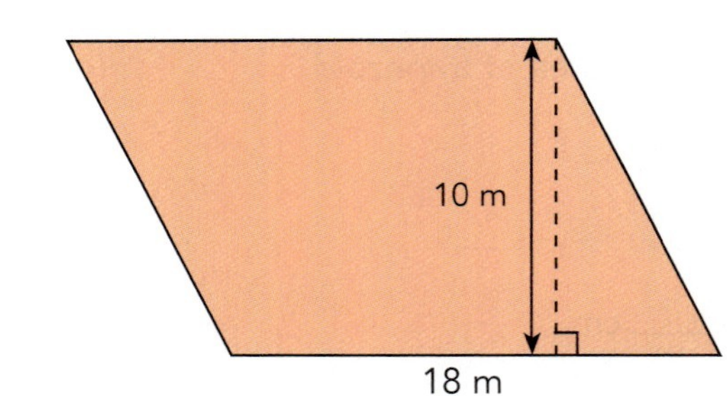

Copy each trapezoid. Label the height and bases. Use *h*, b_1, and b_2.

7. 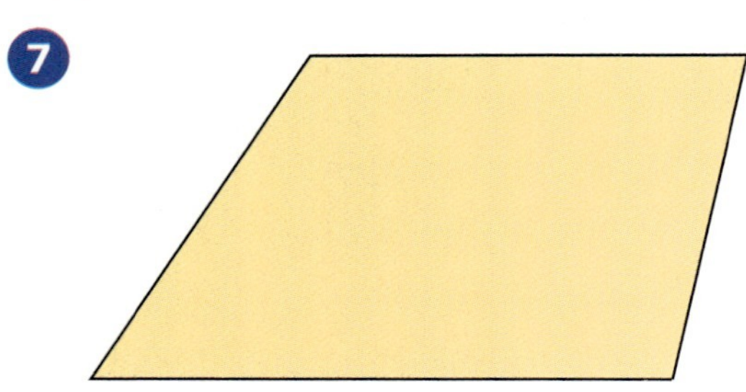

8. 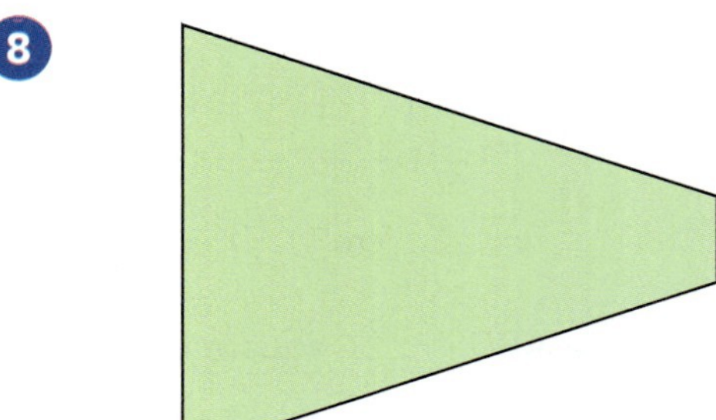

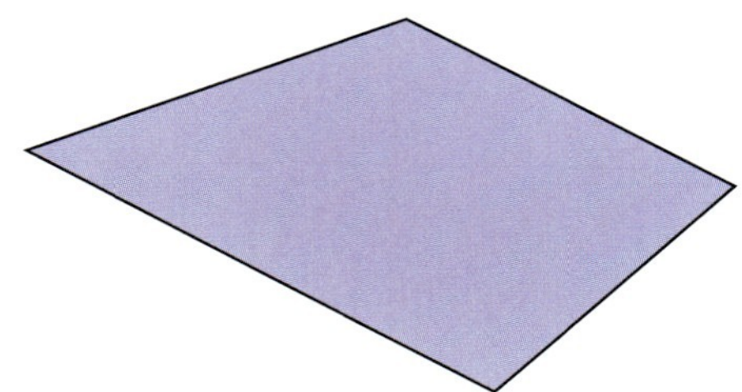

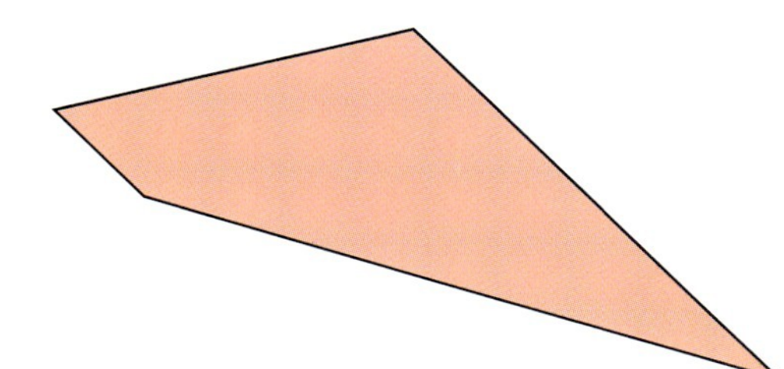

Find the area of each trapezoid.

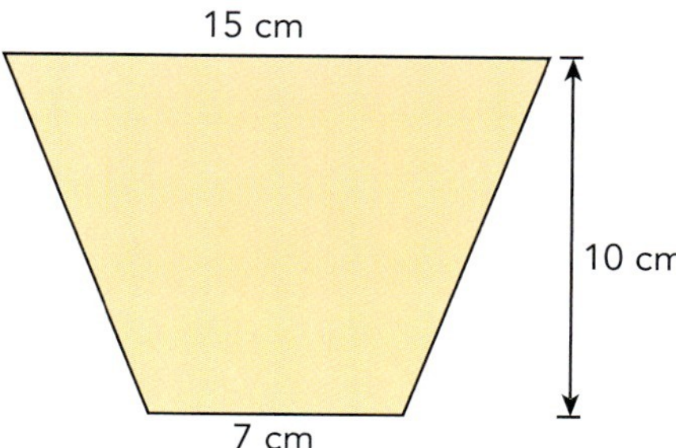

12

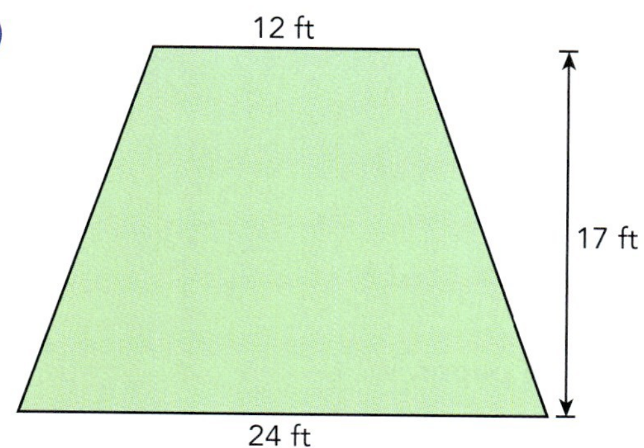

The area of each parallelogram is 64 square inches. Find the height. Round your answer to the nearest tenth of an inch.

13

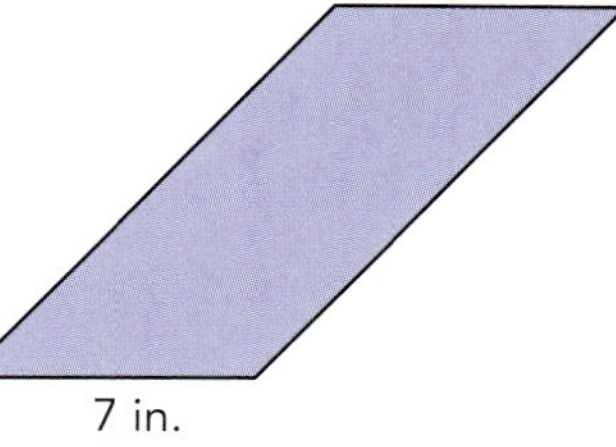

14

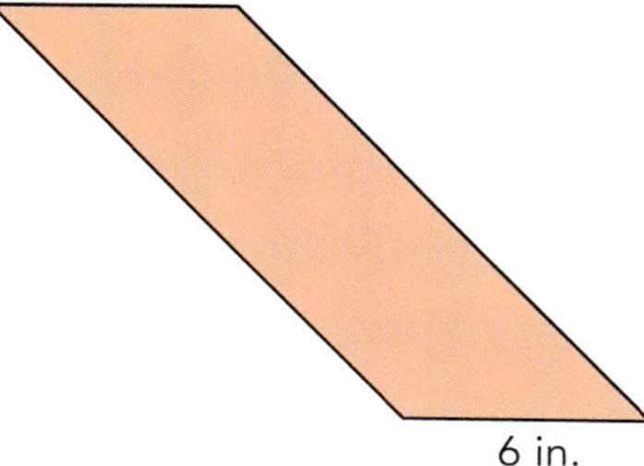

The area of each trapezoid is 42 square centimeters. Find the height. Round your answer to the nearest tenth of a centimeter.

15

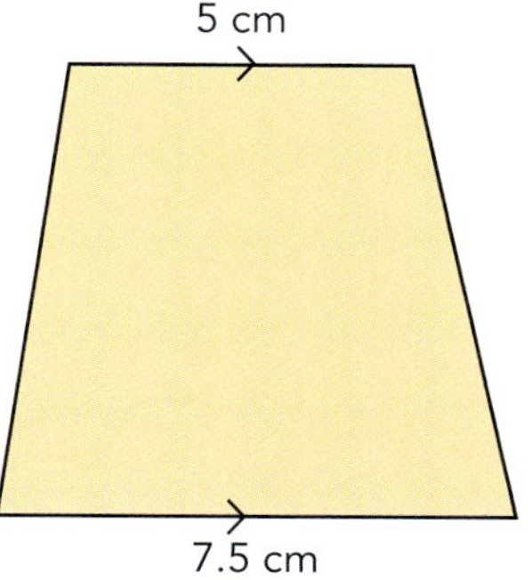

16

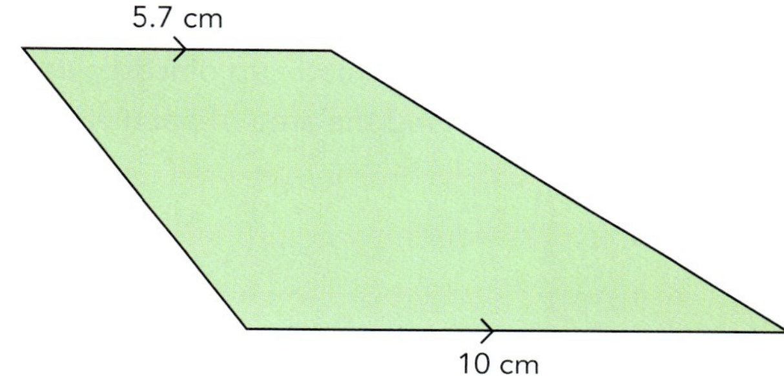

Solve.

17 The area of trapezoid $ABCD$ is 503.25 square centimeters. Find the length of $\overline{BC}$.

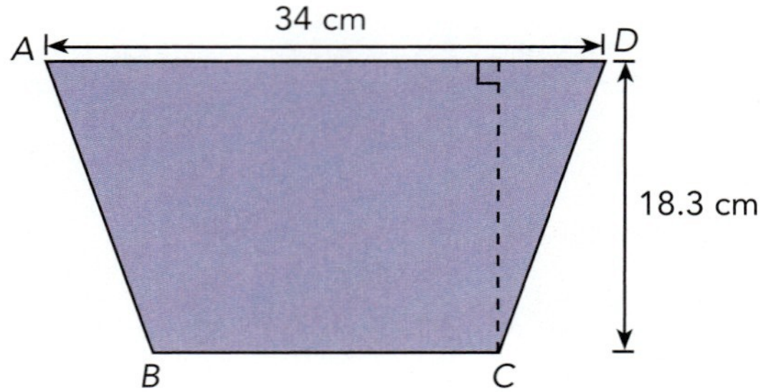

18 The area of trapezoid $EFGH$ is 273 square centimeters. Find the area of triangle EGH.

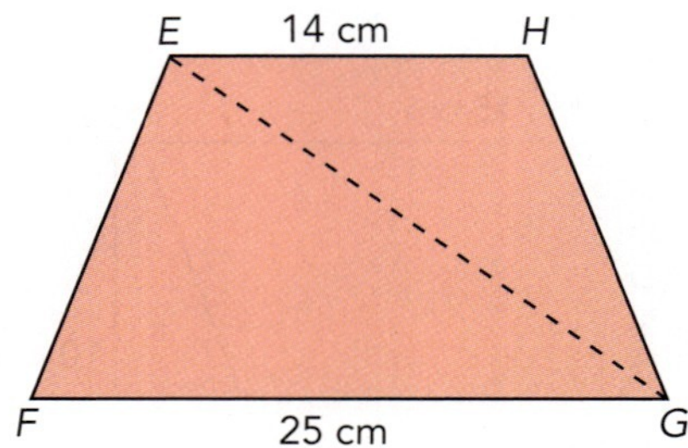

Solve. Use graph paper.

19 The coordinates of the vertices of a parallelogram are P (0, 5), Q (−3, 0), R (2, 0), and S (5, 5). Find the area of parallelogram $PQRS$.

20 Three out of the four coordinates of the vertices of parallelogram $WXYZ$ are W (0, 1), X (−4, −4), and Y (−1, −4). Find the coordinates of Z. Then find the area of the parallelogram.

21 The coordinates of the vertices of trapezoid $EFGH$ are E (−3, 3), F (−3, 0), G (1, −4), and H (1, 4). Find the area of the trapezoid.

22 Three out of the four coordinates of the vertices of trapezoid $ABCD$ are A (0, 1), B (−4, −4), and C (−1, −4). $\overline{AD}$ is parallel to $\overline{BC}$. AD is 6 units. The point D lies to the right of point A. Find the coordinates of point D. Then find the area of the trapezoid.

Solve.

23 Parallelogram $PQRT$ is made up of isosceles triangle PST and trapezoid $PQRS$. Find the area of parallelogram $PQRT$.

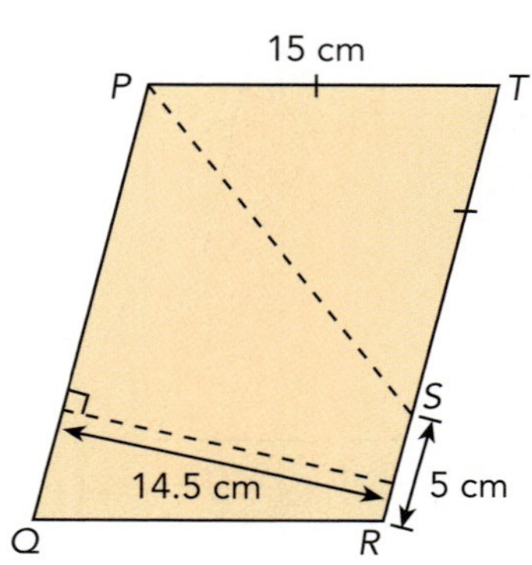

10.3 Area of Other Polygons

Lesson Objectives

- Divide polygons into triangles.
- Find the area of a regular polygon by dividing it into smaller shapes.

Vocabulary
regular polygon

Learn **Find the areas of regular polygons.**

a) Patrick drew a regular pentagon with side lengths of 16 centimeters. He divided the pentagon into 5 identical triangles, and measured the height of one of the triangles to be 11 centimeters. Find the area of the pentagon.

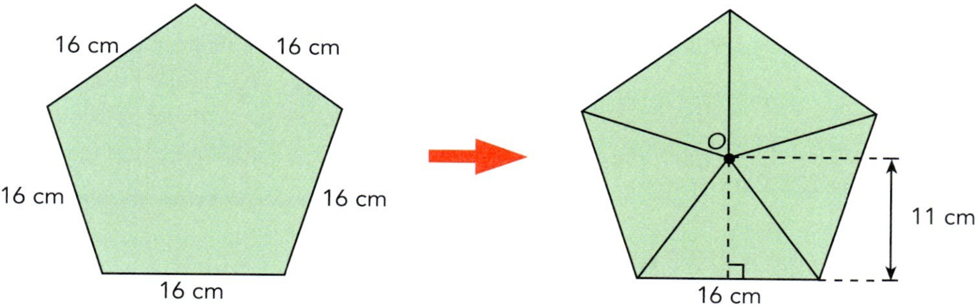

The line segments from O to each vertex of the pentagon divide it into 5 identical triangles. These triangles are isosceles triangles.

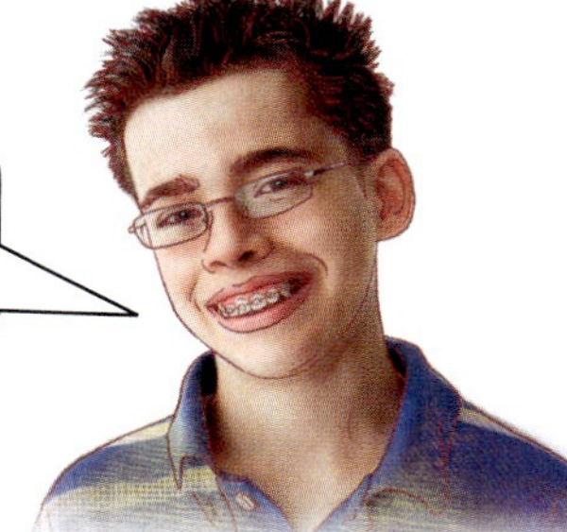

$$\text{Area of each triangle} = \frac{1}{2}bh$$
$$= \frac{1}{2} \cdot 16 \cdot 11$$
$$= 88 \text{ cm}^2$$

$$\text{Area of pentagon} = 5 \cdot 88$$
$$= 440 \text{ cm}^2$$

The area of the pentagon is 440 square centimeters.

Continue on next page

b) Johanna has a hexagonal placemat. She measured the sides and found that they were all 9.3 inches long. She then divided the hexagon into 6 identical triangles. She measured the height of one triangle and found that it was 8 inches. Find the area of the placemat.

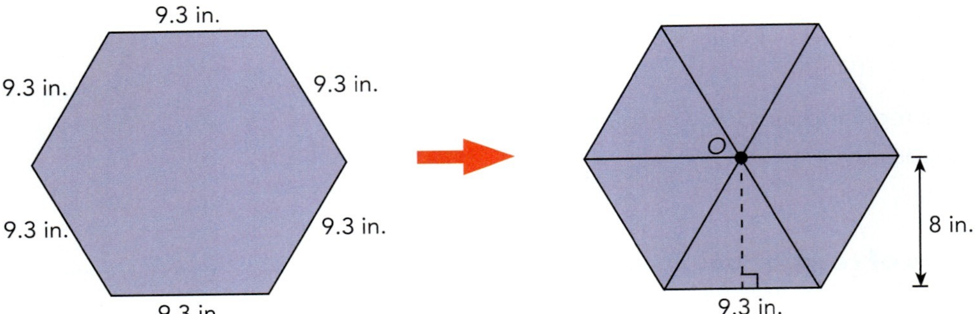

$$\text{Area of each triangle} = \frac{1}{2}bh$$
$$= \frac{1}{2} \cdot 9.3 \cdot 8$$
$$= 37.2 \text{ in.}^2$$
$$\text{Area of placemat} = 6 \cdot 37.2$$
$$= 223.2 \text{ in.}^2$$

The area of the placemat is 223.2 square inches.

Math Note

The line segments from the center to each vertex of a regular hexagon divide it into 6 identical triangles. These triangles are equilateral triangles.

Guided Practice

Give the minimum number of identical triangles you could divide each regular polygon into so that you could find the area of the polygon.

1

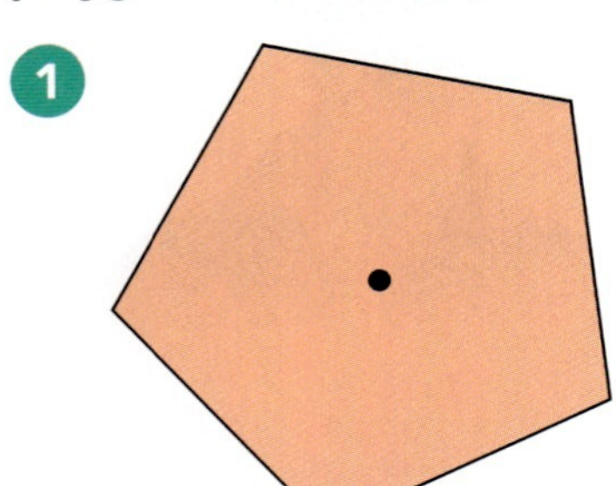

2

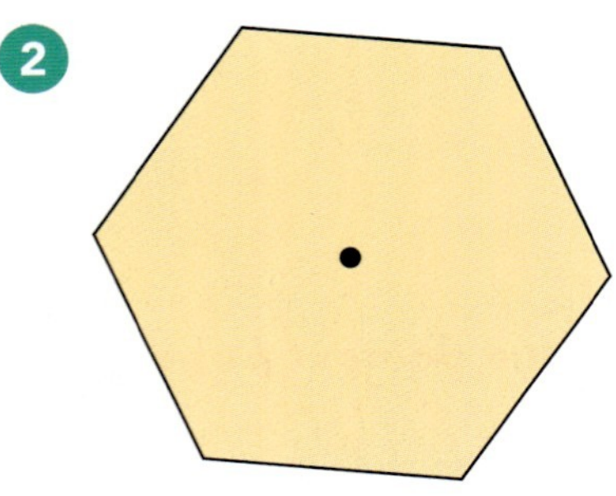

Complete.

3 Blake drew a regular pentagon with side lengths of 6 inches. He divided the pentagon into 5 identical triangles, and measured the height of one of the triangles to be 4.1 inches. Find the area of the pentagon.

Area of triangle $= \frac{1}{2}bh$

$= \underline{\ ?\ } \cdot \underline{\ ?\ } \cdot \underline{\ ?\ }$

$= \underline{\ ?\ }$ in.^{2}

Area of pentagon $= \underline{\ ?\ } \cdot$ area of triangle

$= \underline{\ ?\ } \cdot \underline{\ ?\ }$

$= \underline{\ ?\ }$ in.^{2}

The area of the pentagon is $\underline{\ ?\ }$ square inches.

4 Melanie drew a regular hexagon with side lengths of 28 centimeters. She divided the hexagon into 6 identical triangles, and measured the height of one of the triangles to be 24.2 centimeters. Find the area of the hexagon.

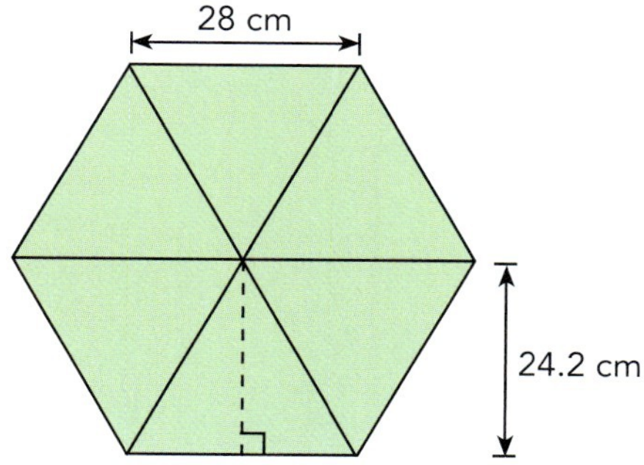

Area of triangle $= \frac{1}{2}bh$

$= \underline{\ ?\ } \cdot \underline{\ ?\ } \cdot \underline{\ ?\ }$

$= \underline{\ ?\ }$ cm^2

Area of hexagon $= \underline{\ ?\ } \cdot$ area of triangle

$= \underline{\ ?\ } \cdot \underline{\ ?\ }$

$= \underline{\ ?\ }$ cm^2

The area of the hexagon is $\underline{\ ?\ }$ square centimeters.

Practice 10.3

Give the minimum number of identical triangles you could divide each regular polygon into so that you could find the area of the polygon.

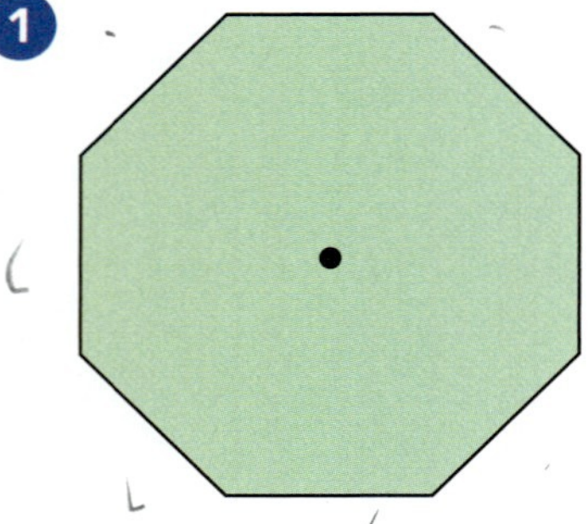

2

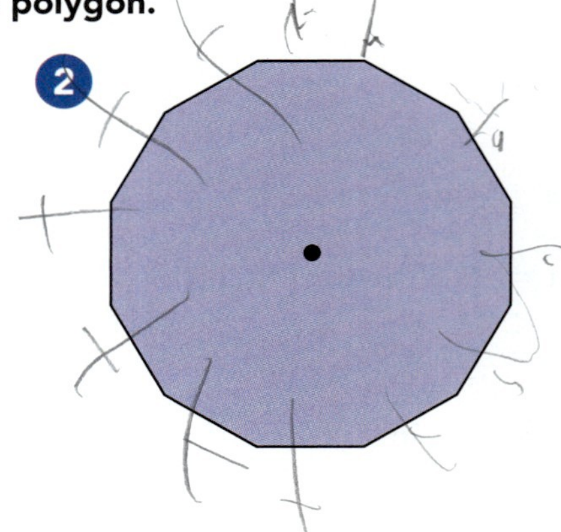

Solve.

3 Derrick drew a regular pentagon with side lengths of 8 centimeters. He divided the pentagon into 5 identical triangles, and measured the height of one of the triangles to be 5.5 centimeters. Find the area of the pentagon.

4 Lydia drew a regular hexagon. She divided it into 6 identical triangles, and measured the height of one of the triangles to be 4 inches. The area of the hexagon is 55.2 square inches. Find the length of each side of the hexagon.

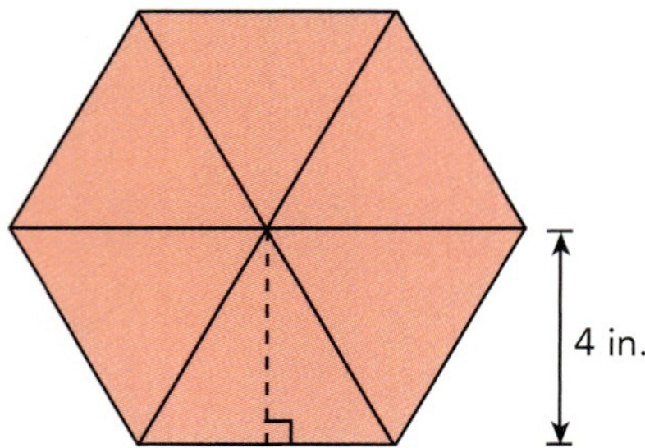

5 A floor tile is in the shape of a regular hexagon. Greg uses 187.5 floor tiles for a room. The area of the room is 450 square feet. Find the length of each side of the hexagon.

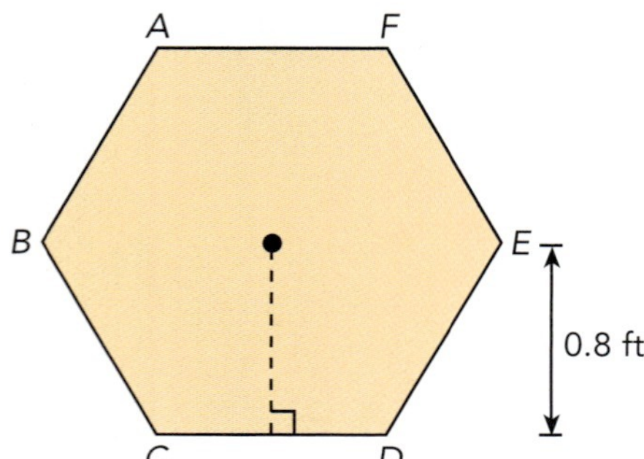

Use the given information to find the area of each regular polygon.

6 The shaded area is 9.7 square inches.

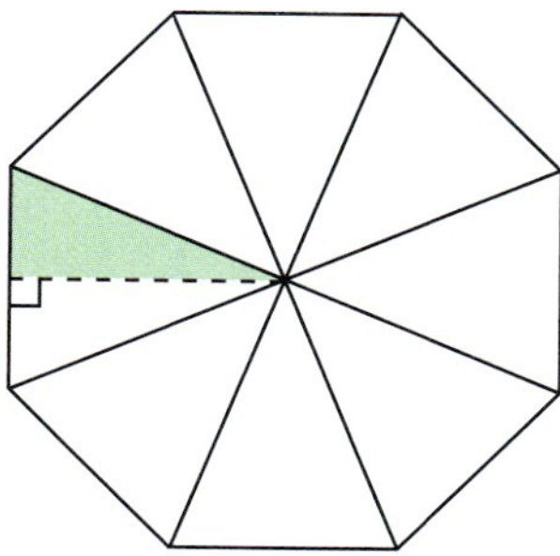

7 The shaded area is 12.8 square centimeters.

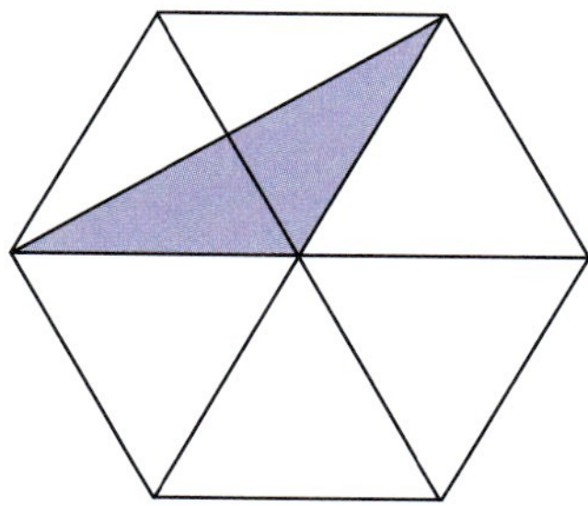

8 Suppose you have three identical equilateral triangles. Use a sketch to show how you can make each of the following from two or more of the triangles. Identify the quadrilateral.

a) a quadrilateral whose area is two times as great as an equilateral triangle.

b) a quadrilateral whose area is three times as great as an equilateral triangle.

Each figure is made from a regular polygon surrounded by identical triangles. Find the area of each figure.

9

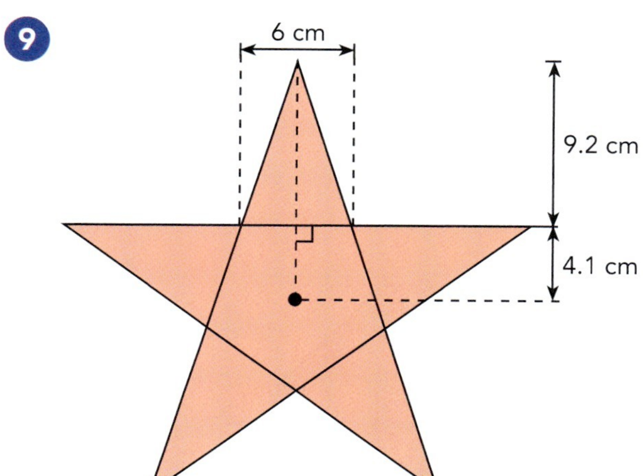

10

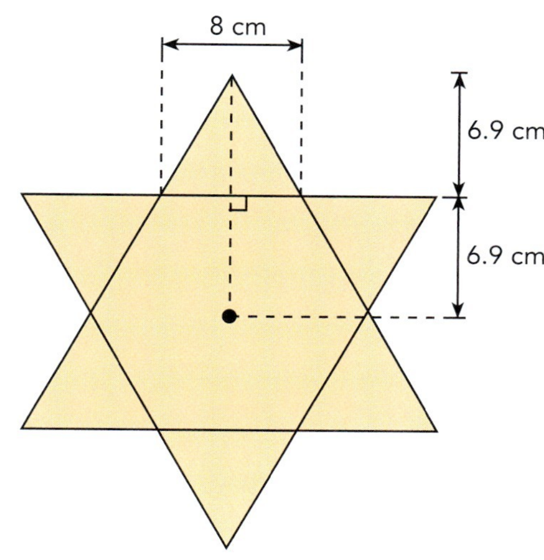

10.4 Area of Composite Figures

Lesson Objectives

- Recognize that a plane figure is made up of polygons.
- Solve problems involving areas of composite figures.

Learn **Recognize that a plane figure can be divided into other polygons.**

Trapezoid *PQRS* can be divided into many polygons.
It can be divided into a rectangle and a triangle.

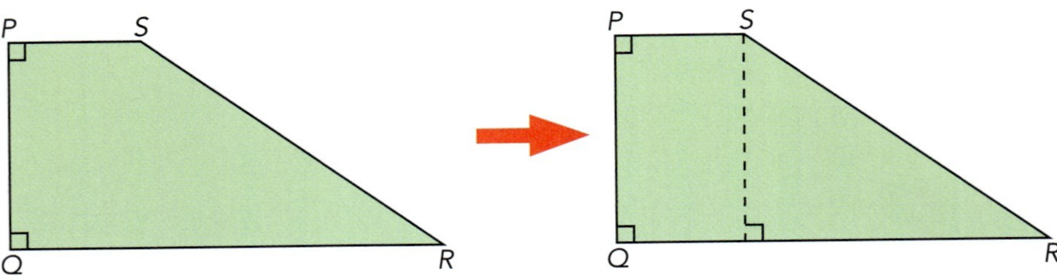

It can also be divided into three triangles.

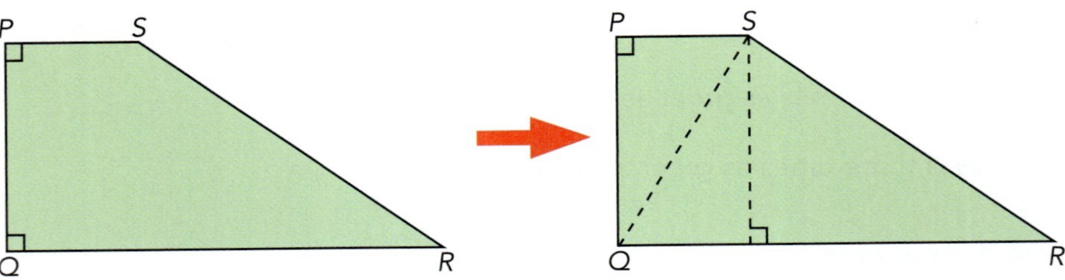

There are many other ways to divide trapezoid *PQRS*.

Guided Practice

Use graph paper. Copy the hexagon and solve.

1. Divide the hexagon into two identical triangles and a rectangle.

2. Divide the hexagon in another way. Name the polygons that make up the hexagon.

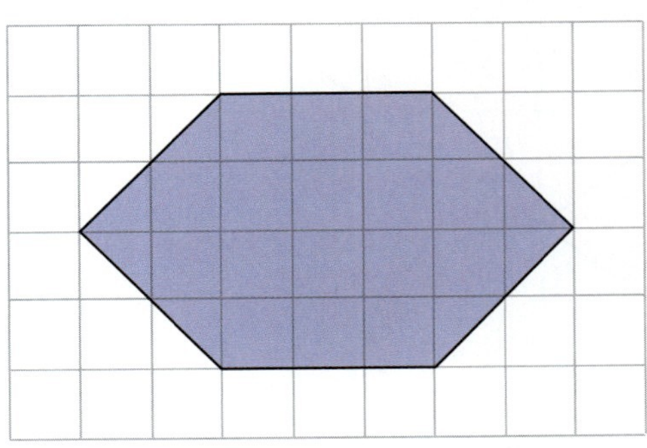

Learn Solve problems involving rectangles and triangles.

Trapezoid *ABDE* is made up of square *ABCE* and triangle *ECD*. The area of square *ABCE* is 64 square centimeters. The length of $\overline{CD}$ is 11 centimeters. Find the area of triangle *ECD*, and trapezoid *ABDE*.

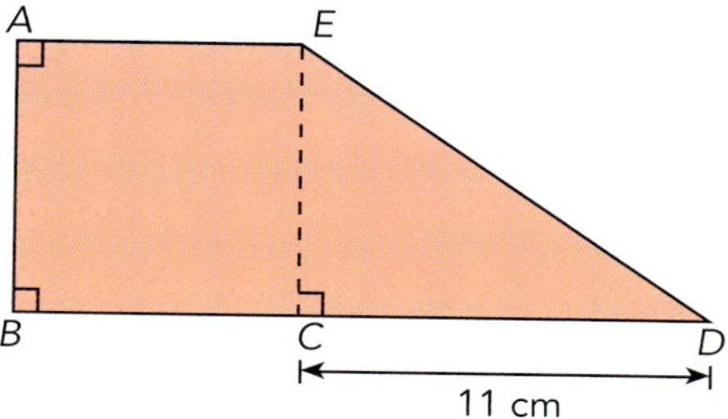

Area of square *ABCE* = 64 cm²

$\ell^2 = 64$, so
$\ell = \sqrt{64}$
$\ell = 8$

Use the fact that $EC = 8$ and is also the height of triangle *ECD*.

Area of triangle *ECD* $= \frac{1}{2}bh$ Write formula.

$= \frac{1}{2} \cdot CD \cdot EC$ Substitute.

$= \frac{1}{2} \cdot 11 \cdot 8$ Multiply.

$= 44 \text{ cm}^2$

The area of triangle *ECD* is 44 square centimeters.

Area of trapezoid *ABDE*
= area of square *ABCE* + area of triangle *ECD*
= 64 + 44
= 108 cm²

The area of trapezoid *ABDE* is 108 square centimeters.

Guided Practice

Complete.

3 Trapezoid *ABDE* is made up of square *ABCE* and triangle *ECD*. The area of triangle *ECD* is 60 square inches. The length of $\overline{CD}$ is 12 inches.

a) Find the height of triangle *ECD*.

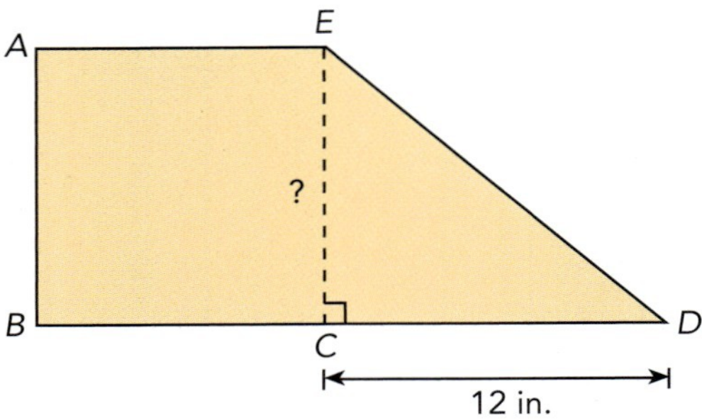

Area of triangle *ECD* = __?__ in.²

$$\text{Area of triangle } ECD = \frac{1}{2}bh$$

$$= \frac{1}{2} \cdot \underline{\ ?\ } \cdot EC$$

$$\underline{\ ?\ } = \underline{\ ?\ } \cdot EC$$

$$\underline{\ ?\ } \div \underline{\ ?\ } = \underline{\ ?\ } \cdot EC \div \underline{\ ?\ }$$

$$\underline{\ ?\ } = EC$$

The height of triangle *ECD* is __?__ inches.

b) Find the area of square *ABCE*.

$$\text{Area of square } ABCE = \ell^2$$

$$= \underline{\ ?\ }^2$$

$$= \underline{\ ?\ } \text{ in.}^2$$

The area of square ABCE is __?__ square inches.

c) Find the area of trapezoid *ABDE*.

Area of the trapezoid *ABDE*

= area of square *ABCE* + area of triangle *ECD*

$= \underline{\ ?\ } + \underline{\ ?\ }$

$= \underline{\ ?\ } \text{ in.}^2$

The area of trapezoid *ABDE* is __?__ square inches.

Learn Solve problems involving parallelograms, triangles, and rectangles.

Trapezoid $PQTU$ is made up of parallelogram $PQRV$, triangle VRS, and square $VSTU$. The area of trapezoid $PQSV$ is 99 square inches. Find the area of trapezoid $PQTU$.

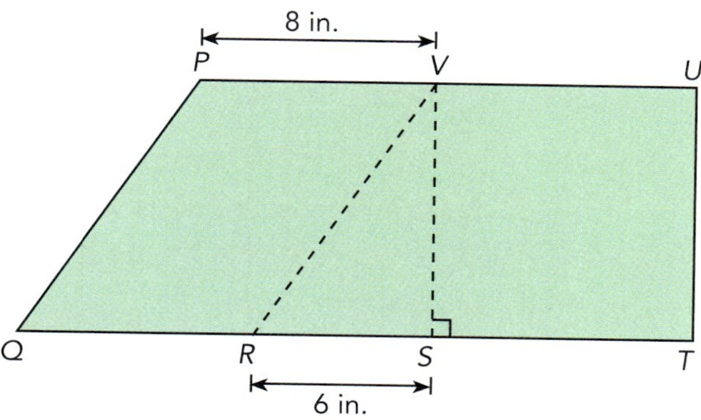

Apply the formula for the area of a trapezoid to find VS.

Area of trapezoid $PQSV$

$$= \frac{1}{2}h(b_1 + b_2)$$

$$= \frac{1}{2} \cdot VS \cdot (PV + QS)$$

$$= \frac{1}{2} \cdot VS \cdot (8 + 8 + 6)$$

$$= \frac{1}{2} \cdot VS \cdot 22$$

$$= 11 \cdot VS$$

Since area of trapezoid $PQSV = 99$ in.²,

Area of trapezoid $PQSV = 11 \cdot VS$	Write formula.
$99 = 11 \cdot VS$	Substitute.
$99 \div 11 = 11 \cdot VS \div 11$	Divide each side by 11.
$9 = VS$	Simplify.

Then find the area of square $VSTU$.

Area of square $VSTU = VS^2$

$$= 9^2$$

$$= 81 \text{ in.}^2$$

Then find the area of trapezoid $PQTU$.

Area of trapezoid $PQTU$ = area of trapezoid $PQSV$ + area of square $VSTU$

$$= 99 + 81$$

$$= 180 \text{ in.}^2$$

The area of trapezoid $PQTU$ is 180 square inches.

Guided Practice

Complete.

4 The area of parallelogram *ABEF* is 84 square meters.

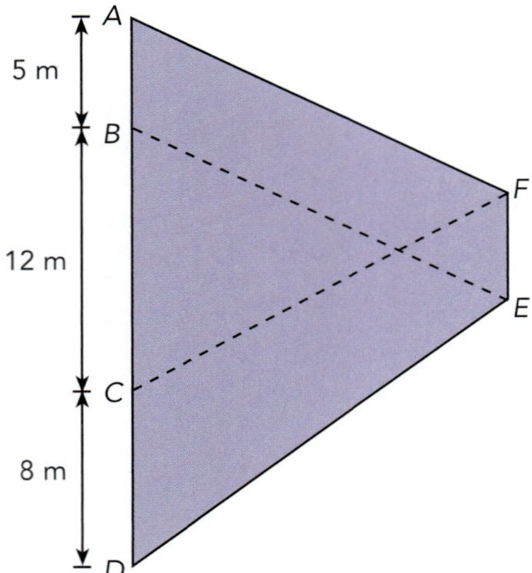

a) Find the area of triangle *BDE.*

Area of parallelogram *ABEF* $= bh$

$$\underline{\ ?\ } = \underline{\ ?\ } \cdot h$$

$$\underline{\ ?\ } \div \underline{\ ?\ } = \underline{\ ?\ }\ h \div \underline{\ ?\ }$$

$$\underline{\ ?\ } = h$$

The height of parallelogram *ABEF* is also the height of triangle *BDE.*

Area of triangle $BDE = \frac{1}{2}bh$

$$= \frac{1}{2} \cdot BD \cdot h$$

$$= \frac{1}{2} \cdot (\underline{\ ?\ } + \underline{\ ?\ }) \cdot \underline{\ ?\ }$$

$$= \underline{\ ?\ }\ \text{m}^2$$

The area of triangle *BDE* is $\underline{\ ?\ }$ square meters.

b) Find the area of trapezoid *CDEF.*

Parallelogram *ABEF* and trapezoid *CDEF* have the same height.

Area of trapezoid *CDEF* $= \frac{1}{2}h(b_1 + b_2)$

$$= \underline{\ ?\ } \cdot \underline{\ ?\ } \cdot (\underline{\ ?\ } + \underline{\ ?\ })$$

$$= \underline{\ ?\ }\ \text{m}^2$$

The area of trapezoid *CDEF* is $\underline{\ ?\ }$ square meters.

Practice 10.4

Copy each figure and draw straight lines to divide. Describe two ways to find the area of each figure.

1. Divide the figure into a rectangle and two right triangles.

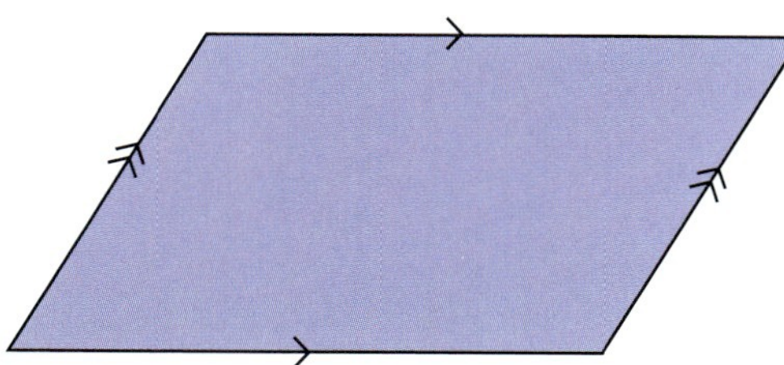

2. Divide the figure into a rectangle and two right triangles.

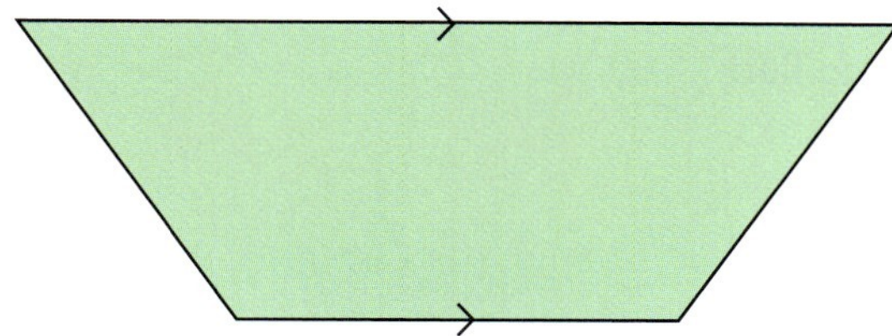

3. Divide the figure into a rectangle and a right triangle.

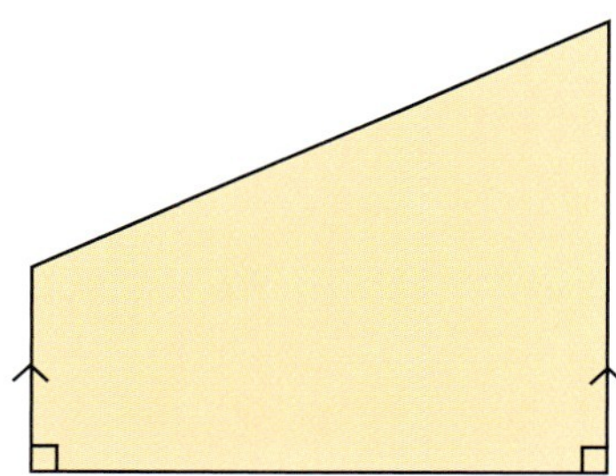

Copy each figure and draw straight lines to divide. Describe a way to find the area.

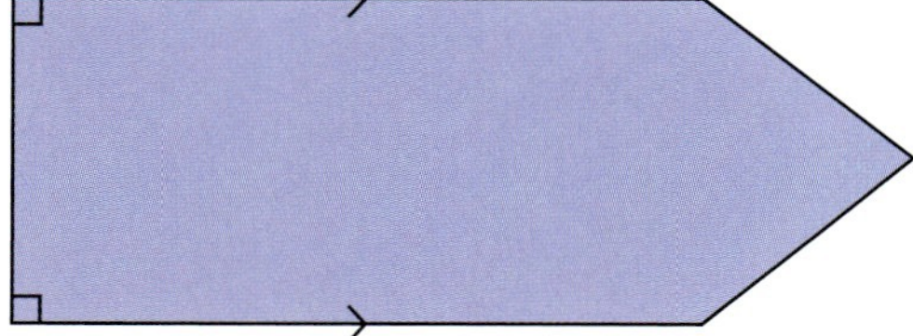

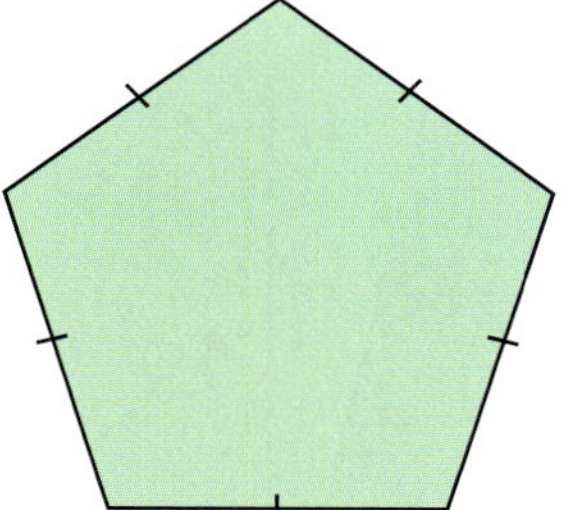

Find the area of each figure.

6. Parallelogram *ABDE* is made up of square *ACDF*, triangle *ABC*, and triangle *FDE*. Triangle *ABC* and triangle *FDE* are identical. The area of square *ACDF* is 36 square meters. Find the area of triangle *ABC*. Then find the area of parallelogram *ABDE*.

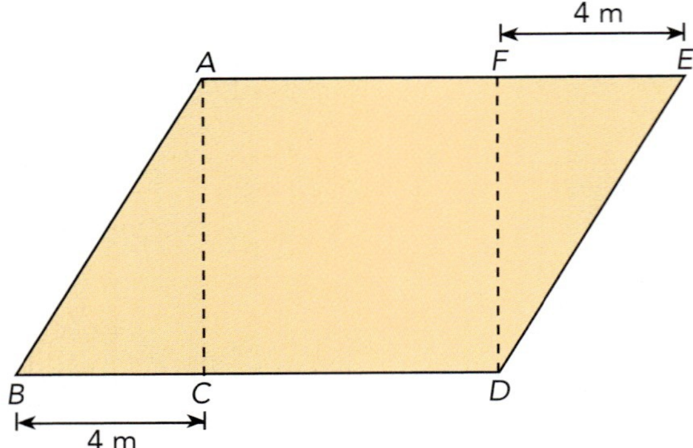

7. ***Math Journal*** Describe how you would divide the figure with straight lines. Which sides of the figure would you measure to find its area? Explain your answer.

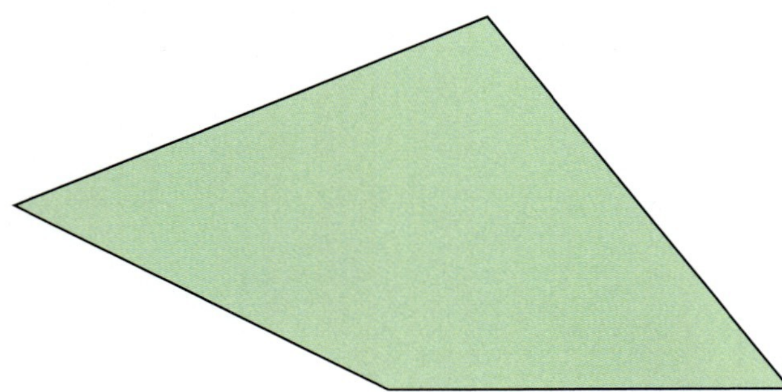

Find the area of triangle *EBC*.

8. In the figure below, trapezoid *ABDE* is made up of three triangles, and figure *ABCE* is a parallelogram. Find the area of triangle *EBC* if the area of trapezoid *ABDE* is 180 square centimeters.

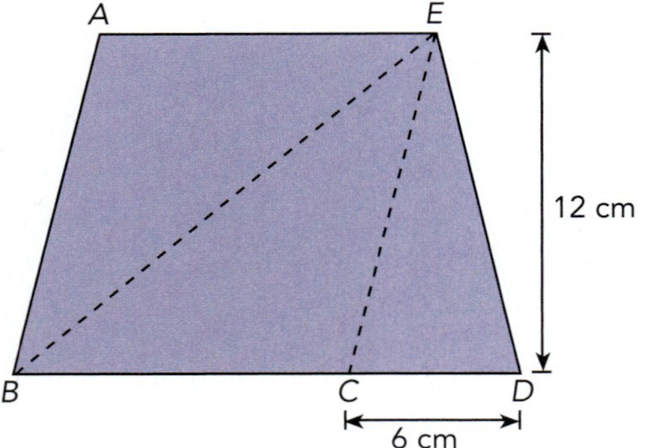

Solve. Use graph paper.

9 a) Plot the points $P(-2, 2)$, $Q(-2, -2)$, $R(-4, -5)$, $S(1, -5)$, and $T(3, -2)$ on a coordinate plane. Connect the points in order to form figure *PQRST*.

b) Find the area of figure *PQRST*.

c) Point *V* lies on along $\overline{QT}$. The area of triangle *PQV* is $\frac{2}{5}$ the area of triangle *PQT*. Give the coordinates of point *V*. Plot point *V* on the coordinate plane.

Find the area of trapezoid *MNRS*.

10 In the figure below, trapezoid *MNRS* is made up of trapezoid *MNPT*, triangle *TPQ*, and parallelogram *TQRS*. The area of triangle *TPQ* is 84 square feet. The lengths of $\overline{NP}$, $\overline{PQ}$, and $\overline{QR}$ are in the ratio 2 : 1.5 : 1. Find the area of trapezoid *MNRS*.

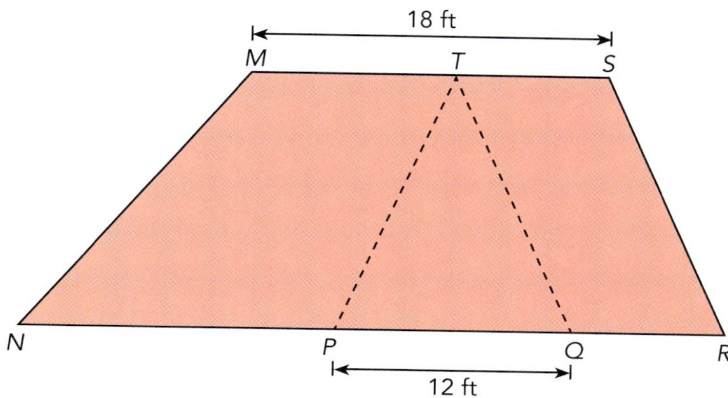

Find the area of triangle *BDE*.

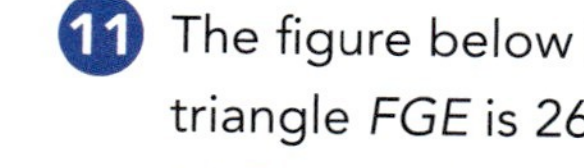

11 The figure below is made up of two trapezoids *ABEF* and *BCDE*. The area of triangle *FGE* is 26 square inches, and the area of trapezoid *BCDE* is 82.5 square inches. *BG* is equal to *GE*. Find the area of triangle *BDE*.

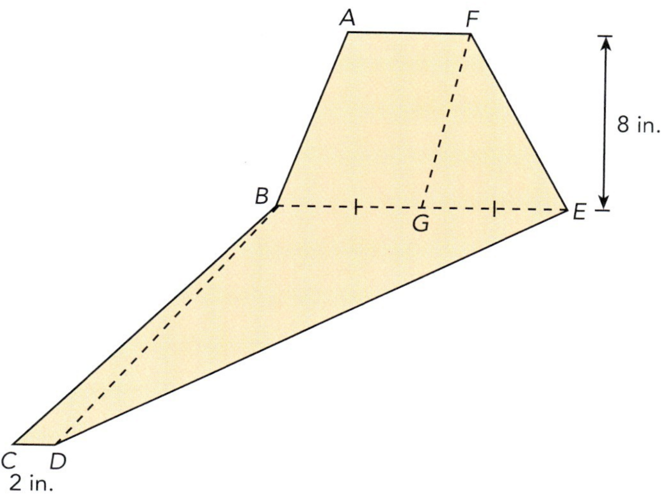

Find the area of the shaded region.

12 $\frac{3}{8}$ of the triangle is shaded.

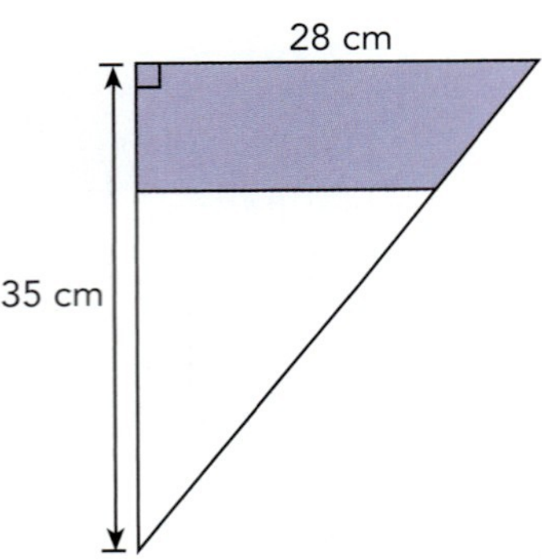

Find the height of trapezoid *PQRS*.

13 Trapezoid *PQRS* is made up of isosceles triangle *PQS* and triangle *SQR*. The area of triangle *PQS* is 16.5 square inches. The areas of triangle *PQS* and triangle *SQR* are in the ratio 2 : 3. Find the height of trapezoid *PQRS*.

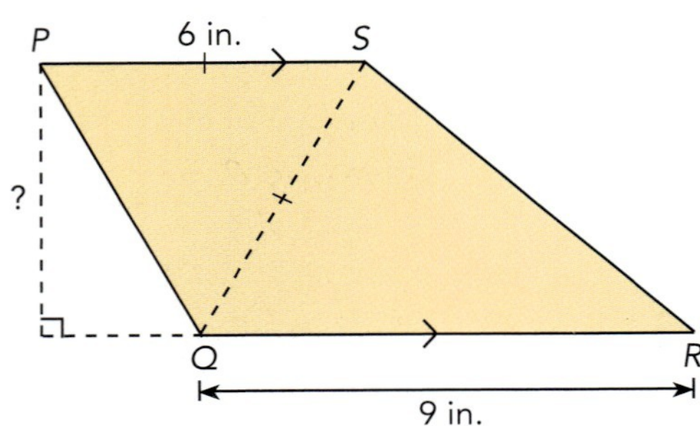

Find the area of each figure.

14 In the figure below, trapezoid *ABCD* is made up of square *BCDE* and triangles *ABF* and *AFE*. The area of square *BCDE* is 576 square feet. The ratio of *BF* to *FE* is 2 : 1. Find the area of triangle *ABF*.

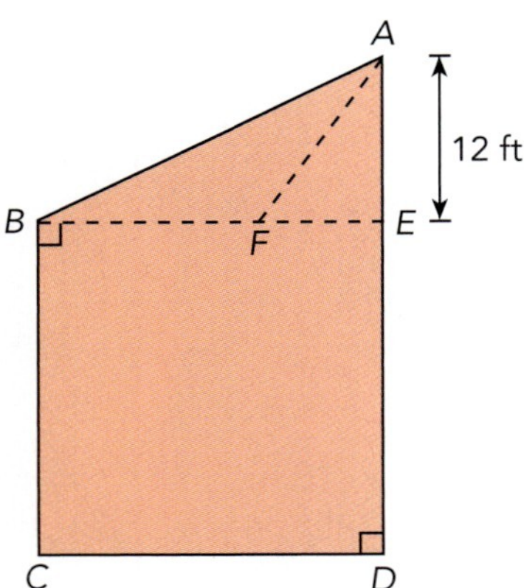

Brain @ Work

1 Figure *ABCD* is made up of square *PQRS* and four identical triangles. The area of triangle *APD* is 49 square feet. The lengths of $\overline{AP}$ and $\overline{PD}$ are in the ratio 1 : 2. Find the area of figure *ABCD*.

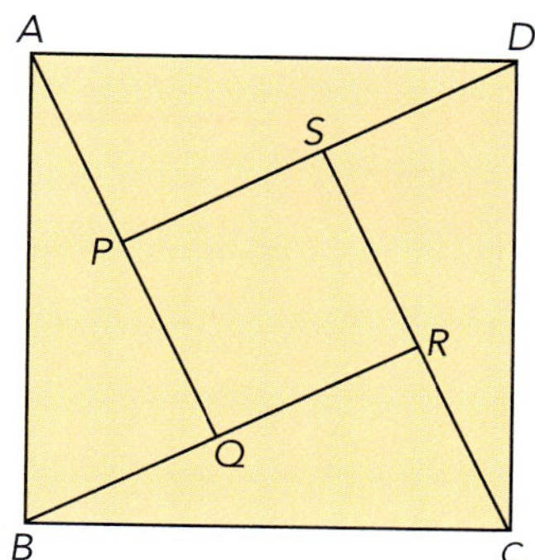

2 The figure is made up of squares *BCDE* and *AEFH*. The length of $\overline{DE}$ is 6 centimeters, and the length of $\overline{EF}$ is 12 centimeters.

a) Write the length of $\overline{FG}$ in terms of x.

b) Find the area of the shaded region in terms of x.

c) Give the value of x for which the shaded region has the greatest area. What is the shape of the shaded region for the value of x you have given?

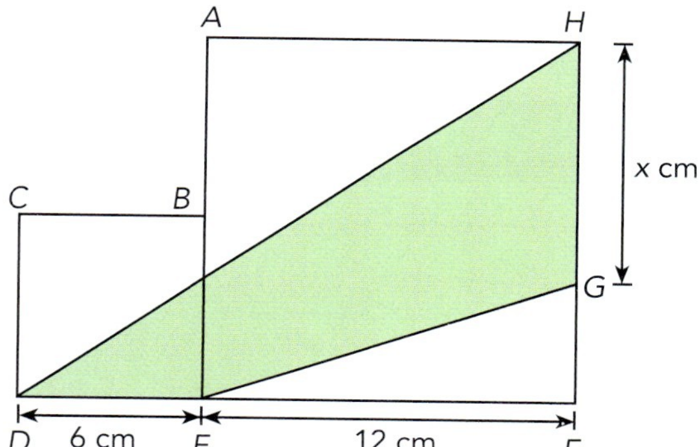

3 Figure *ABCD* is a square. Point *S* is in the middle of $\overline{AD}$, and point *T* is in the middle of and $\overline{CD}$. What fraction of the square is shaded?

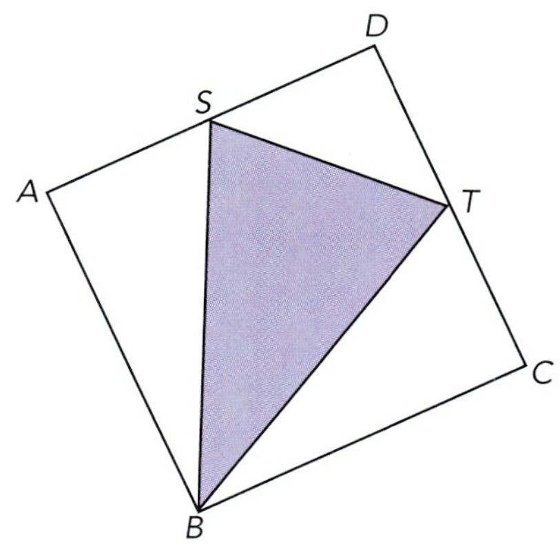

Chapter Wrap Up

Concept Map

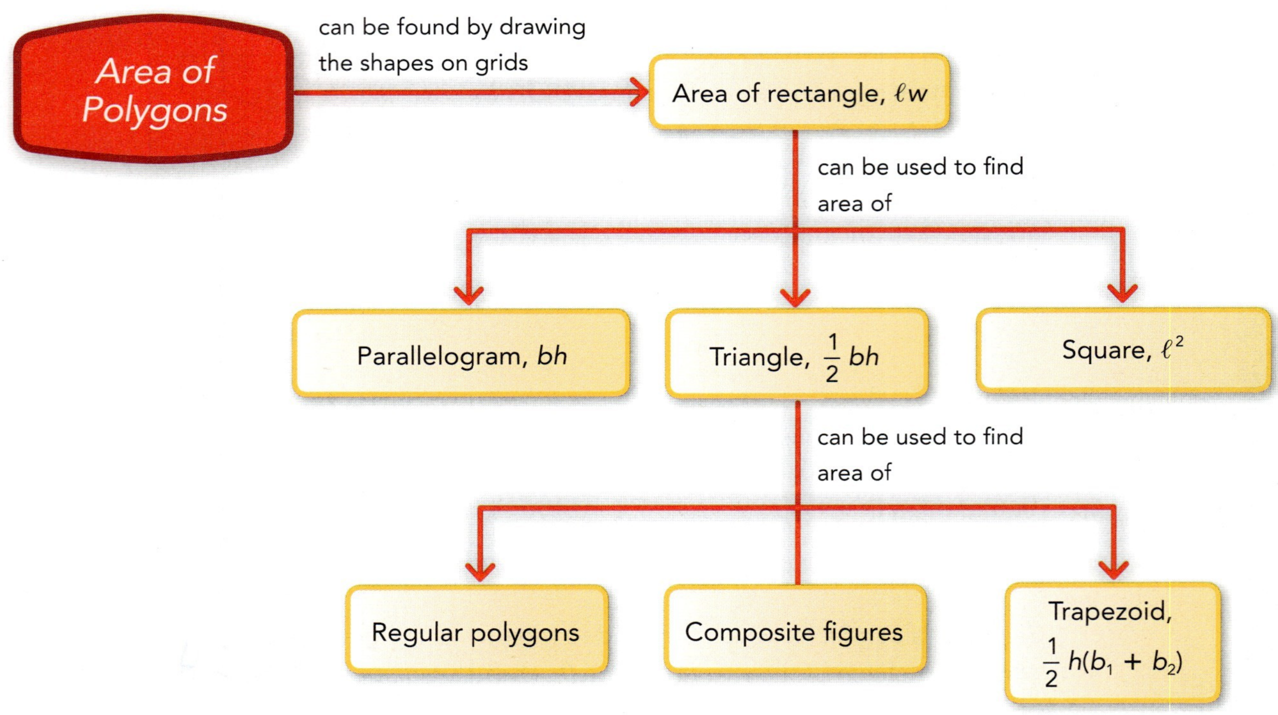

Key Concepts

- The area of a triangle is $\frac{1}{2}bh$.
- The area of a parallelogram is bh.
- The area of a trapezoid is $\frac{1}{2}h(b_1 + b_2)$.
- Any polygon can be divided into triangles. You can find the area of the polygon by calculating the sum of the areas of all the triangles that make up the figure.
- Composite figures can be divided into shapes such as triangles, parallelograms, and trapezoids.

Chapter Review/Test

Concepts and Skills

Identify a base and a height of each triangle.

1 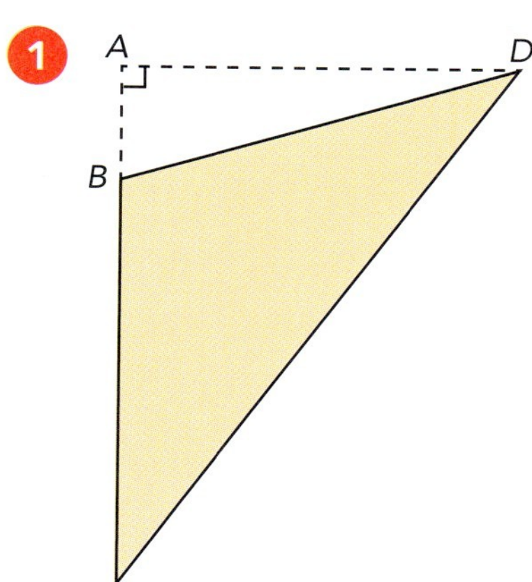

2 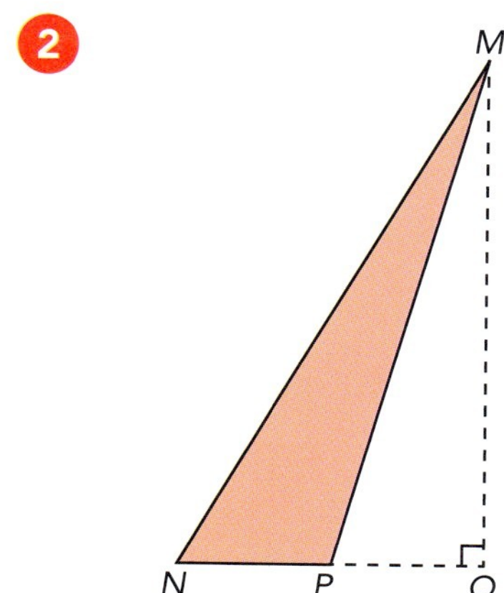

Find the area of each figure.

3 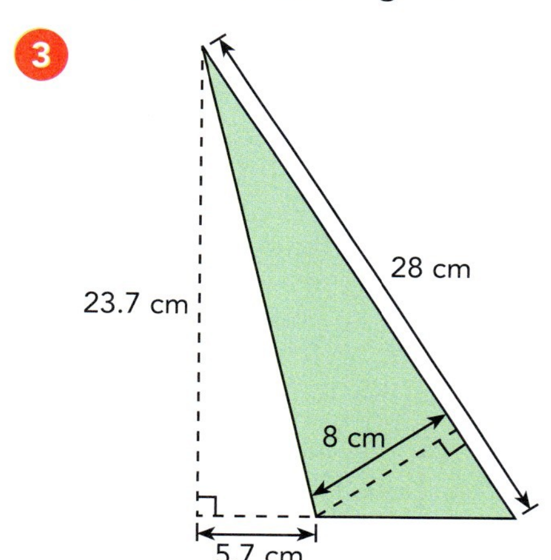

4 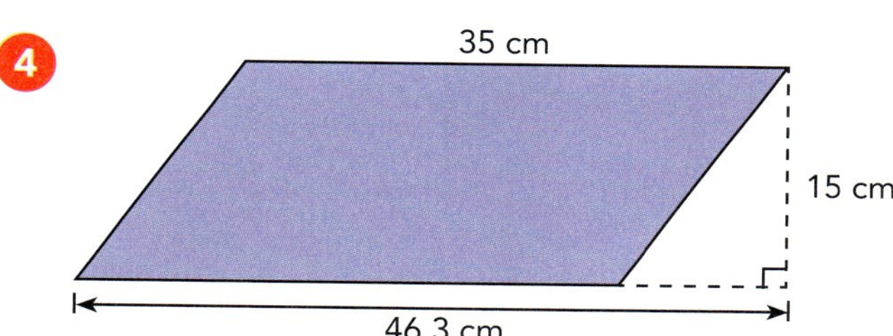

5 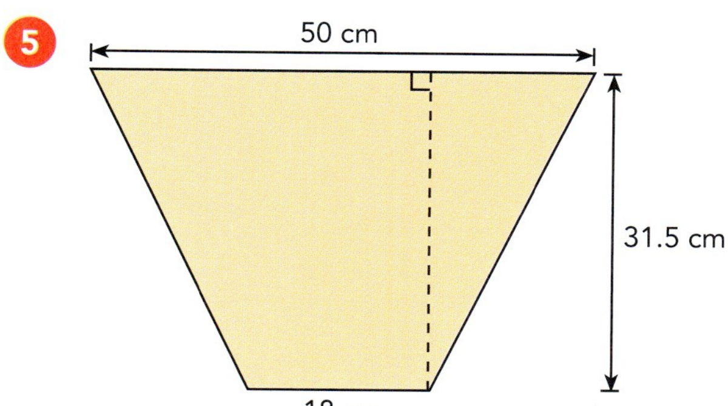

Find the area of the shaded region.

6 The area of the regular octagon below is 560 square inches.

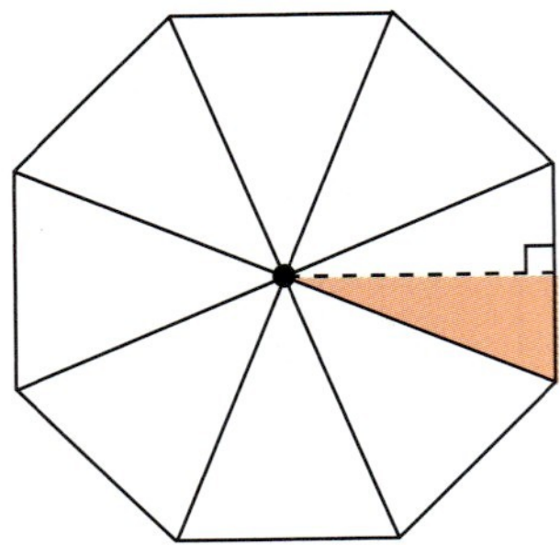

Problem Solving

Find the area of the shaded region.

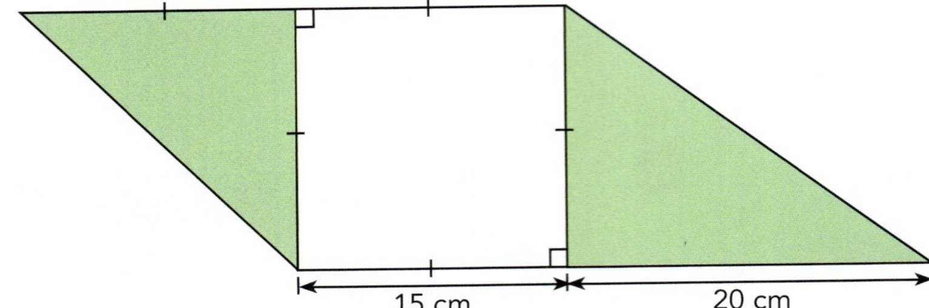

Solve.

8 Figure *ABCD* is a parallelogram. *BC* is 16 centimeters, *CD* is 12 centimeters, and *AH* is 10 centimeters.

a) Find the area of parallelogram *ABCD*.

b) Find the length of $\overline{AK}$. Round your answer to the nearest tenth of a centimeter.

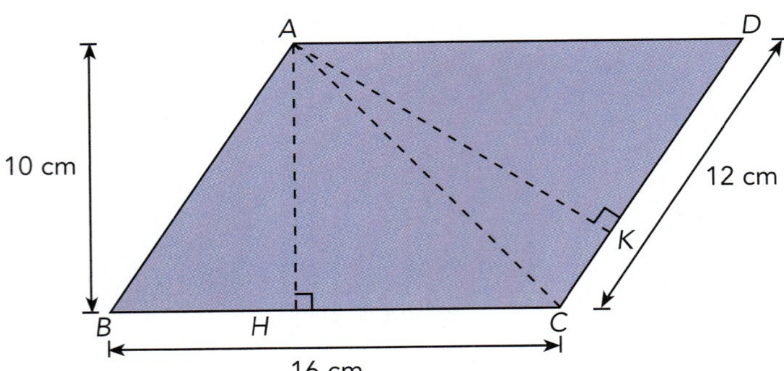

9 Figure *ABCD* is a trapezoid. The length of $\overline{BC}$ is 36 centimeters. The areas of triangles *ABC* and *ACD* are in the ratio 1.5 : 1. Find the length of $\overline{AD}$.

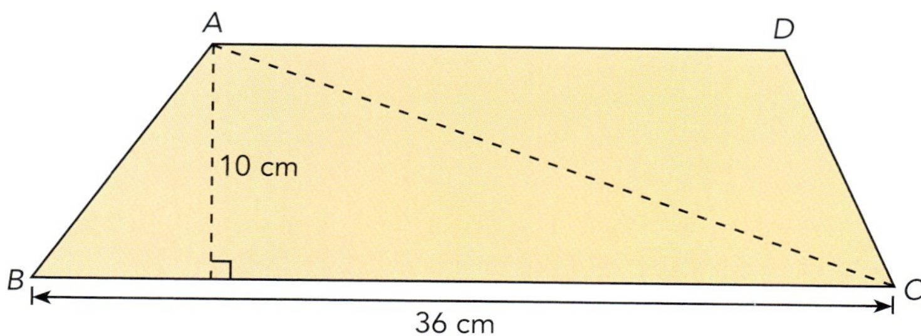

10 Parallelogram *PRTV* is made up of triangle *PQV*, triangle *QUV*, and trapezoid *QRTU*. The area of parallelogram *PRTV* is 96 square feet. The lengths of $\overline{TU}$ and $\overline{UV}$ are equal. Find the area of triangle *QUV*.

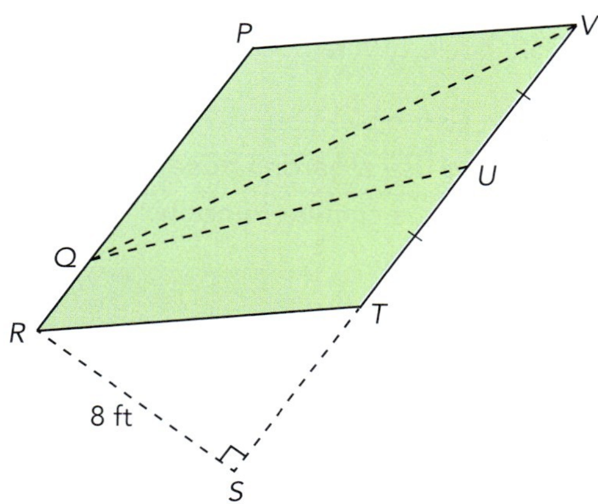

11 Charles drew a regular hexagon and divided it into two identical trapezoids. The side length of the hexagon is 16 centimeters, and the length of the diagonal shown is 32 centimeters. Charles measured the height of one of the trapezoids and found that the height was 13.9 centimeters. Find the area of the hexagon.

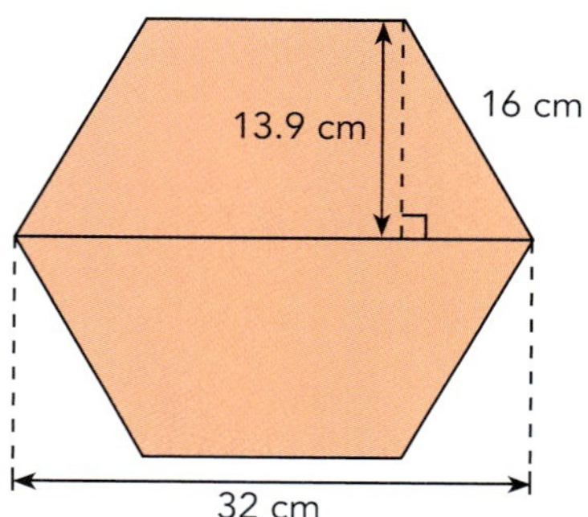

Circumference and Area of a Circle

▶ A circle is a geometric figure that has many useful applications in the real world.

Have you ever seen a rainbow?

A rainbow is an optical effect that occurs when light shines on water droplets suspended in the air. A good time to look for a rainbow is after a rain shower in the late afternoon or early evening. Stand with the sun behind you and look towards the horizon. If conditions are right, you might see a rainbow.

The shape of a rainbow is part of a circle. In fact, if you are flying in an airplane, you might see the whole circle of a rainbow out the window.

Under the right conditions, you can also make your own rainbow. Stand outdoors with the sun behind you and use a garden hose to spray water out in all directions. You might even see a circular rainbow.

Recall Prior Knowledge

Adding decimals

Find the value of 0.8 + 4.53.

STEP 1
Add the hundredths.

$$\begin{array}{r} 0.8 \\ +\ 4.53 \\ \hline 3 \end{array}$$

STEP 2
Add the tenths.

$$\begin{array}{r} \overset{1}{0}.8 \\ +\ 4.53 \\ \hline 33 \end{array}$$

STEP 3
Add the ones.

$$\begin{array}{r} \overset{1}{0}.8 \\ +\ 4.53 \\ \hline 5.33 \end{array}$$

The value of 0.8 + 4.53 is 5.33.

Quick Check

Add.

1. 0.451 + 3.12
2. 0.861 + 6.95
3. 13.74 + 3.791

Subtracting decimals

Find the value of 6.12 − 3.56.

STEP 1
Substract the hundredths.

$$\begin{array}{r} 6.\overset{0}{\cancel{1}}\,{}^{1}2 \\ -\ 3.5\,6 \\ \hline 6 \end{array}$$

STEP 2
Subtract the tenths.

$$\begin{array}{r} \overset{5}{\cancel{6}}.\,{}^{1}\overset{0}{\cancel{1}}\,{}^{1}2 \\ -\ 3.5\,6 \\ \hline 5\,6 \end{array}$$

STEP 3
Subtract the ones.

$$\begin{array}{r} \overset{5}{\cancel{6}}.\,{}^{1}\overset{0}{\cancel{1}}\,{}^{1}2 \\ -\ 3.5\,6 \\ \hline 2.5\,6 \end{array}$$

The value of 6.12 − 3.56 is 2.56.

Quick Check

Subtract.

4. 5.45 − 1.78
5. 12.795 − 0.816
6. 42.781 − 36.19

Multiplying decimals

Find the value of 2.45 × 6.

STEP 1
Multiply the hundredths.

```
      3
  2 . 4 5
×       6
---------
        0
```

STEP 2
Multiply the tenths.

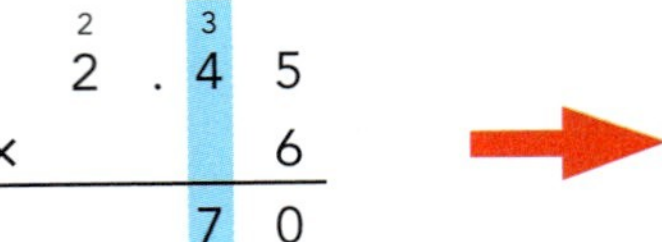

```
  2   3
  2 . 4 5
×       6
---------
      7 0
```

STEP 3
Multiply the ones.

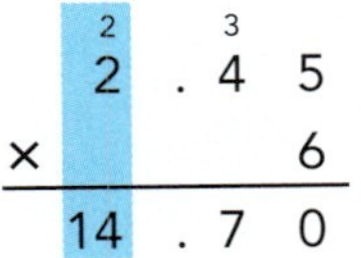

```
  2   3
  2 . 4 5
×       6
---------
 14 . 7 0
```

The value of 2.45 × 6 is 14.7.

Quick Check

Multiply.

 1.34 × 9

 4.246 × 2

 7.487 × 8

Dividing decimals

Find the value of 0.75 ÷ 6.

```
    0 . 1 2 5
6 ) 0 . 7 5
        6
      ---
        1 5
        1 2
        ---
          3 0
          3 0
          ---
            0
```

7 tenths ÷ 6 = 1 tenth R 1 tenth

Regroup the remainder 1 tenth.
1 tenth = 10 hundredths
10 hundredths + 5 hundredths = 15 hundredths
15 hundredths ÷ 6 = 2 hundreds R 3 hundredths

Regroup the remainder 3 hundredths.
3 hundredths = 30 thousandths
30 thousandths ÷ 6 = 5 thousandths

The value of 0.75 ÷ 6 is 0.125.

Quick Check

Divide.

10 2.56 ÷ 5

11 2.429 ÷ 7

12 1.143 ÷ 9

13 4.671 ÷ 9

14 0.656 ÷ 8

15 0.867 ÷ 3

Rounding numbers to the nearest whole number

Round 3.14 to the nearest whole number.

To round to the nearest whole number, look at the tenths digit.
Round up if the tenths digit is 5 or greater.
Round down if the tenths digit is less than 5.

In 3.14, the tenths digit is 1.
Because 1 is less than 5, 3.14 rounded to the nearest whole number is 3.

Quick Check

Round to the nearest whole number.

16. 4.56
17. 12.05
18. 26.48
19. 6.50
20. 14.15
21. 46.59

Rounding numbers to the nearest tenth

Round 10.58 to the nearest tenth.

To round to the nearest tenth, look at the hundredths digit.
Round up if the hundredths digit is 5 or greater.
Round down if the hundredths digit is less than 5.

In 10.58, the hundredths digit is 8.
Because 8 is greater than 5, 10.58 rounded to the nearest tenth is 10.6.

Quick Check

Round to the nearest tenth.

22. 7.68
23. 3.05
24. 19.92
25. 5.55
26. 8.17
27. 2.44
28. 43.65
29. 23.73
30. 17.51

11.1 Radius, Diameter, and Circumference of a Circle

Lesson Objectives

- Identify parts of a circle.
- Recognize that a circle's diameter is twice its radius.
- Use formulas to find the circumference of a circle.
- Identify semicircles and quarter circles, and find the distance around them.

Vocabulary

center	radius, radii
diameter	circumference
arc	semicircle
quadrant	

Learn **Identify the center and radius of a circle.**

These are circles.

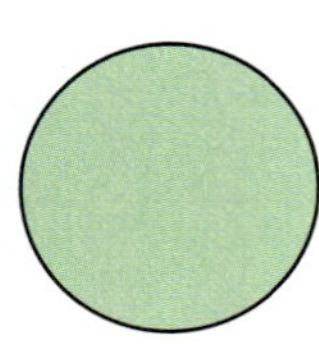

You can use a compass to draw a circle. Notice that all points on the circle are the same distance from the center.

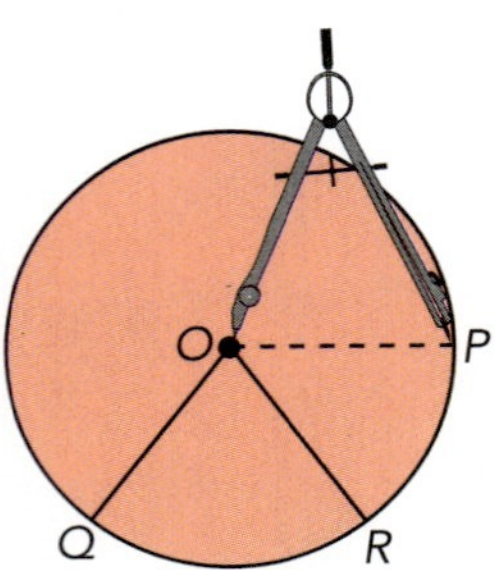

O is the center of the circle.

$\overline{OP}$ is a radius of the circle.

$\overline{OQ}$ and $\overline{OR}$ are also **radii** of the circle.

$OP = OQ = OR$

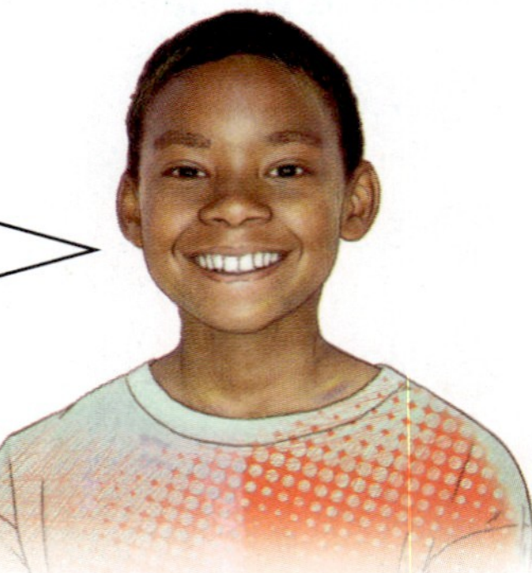

A radius is a line segment connecting the center and a point on the circle.

Learn Identify the diameter of a circle.

In the circle below, O is the center. The line segments $\overline{PQ}$ and $\overline{RS}$ pass through the center O. $\overline{PQ}$ is a diameter of the circle. $\overline{RS}$ is another diameter of the circle. $\overline{TU}$ is not a diameter.

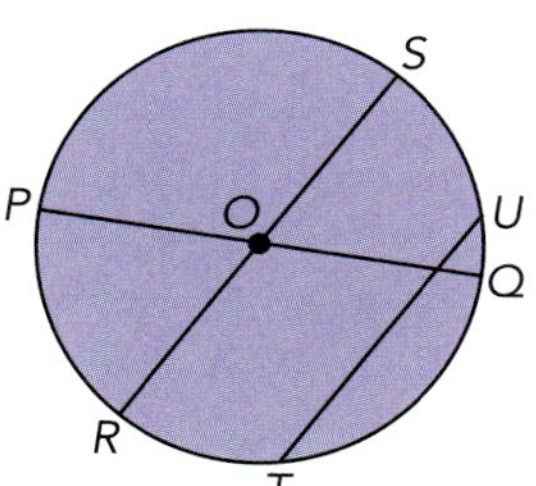

A diameter of a circle is a line segment that connects two points on the circle and passes through its center.

$\overline{OP}$, $\overline{OQ}$, $\overline{OR}$, and $\overline{OS}$ are radii of the circle.

$OP = OQ = OR = OS$

So $PQ = 2 \cdot OP$
$= 2 \cdot OQ$
$= 2 \cdot OR$
$= 2 \cdot OS$

Math Note

Diameter = 2 · radius
Radius = Diameter ÷ 2

Guided Practice

Complete.

1 In the figure, O is the center of the circle with $\overline{AB}$, $\overline{CD}$, and $\overline{ED}$ as shown.

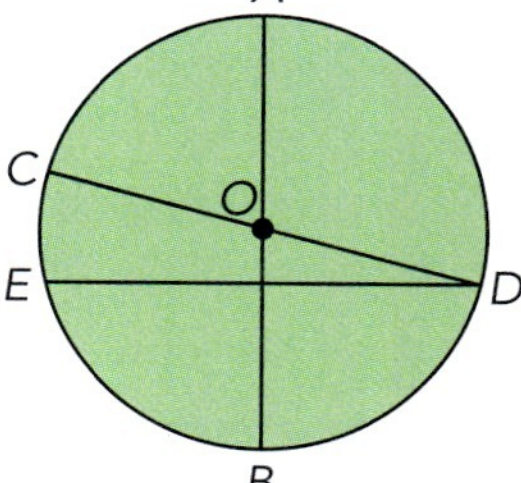

a) Name all the diameters that are drawn in the circle.

b) Which line segment that joins two points on the circle is not a diameter? Explain why it is not a diameter.

2 The radius of a circle is 6 centimeters. What is the length of its diameter?

Diameter = 2 · radius
= __?__ (?) __?__
= __?__ cm

The diameter of the circle is __?__ centimeters.

3 The diameter of a circle is 15 inches. What is the length of its radius?

Radius = diameter ÷ 2
= __?__ (?) __?__
= __?__ in.

The radius of the circle is __?__ inches.

Hands-On Activity

Material:
- compass

DRAWING CIRCLES USING A COMPASS

STEP 1 Measure 5 centimeters on a ruler with a compass.

Example

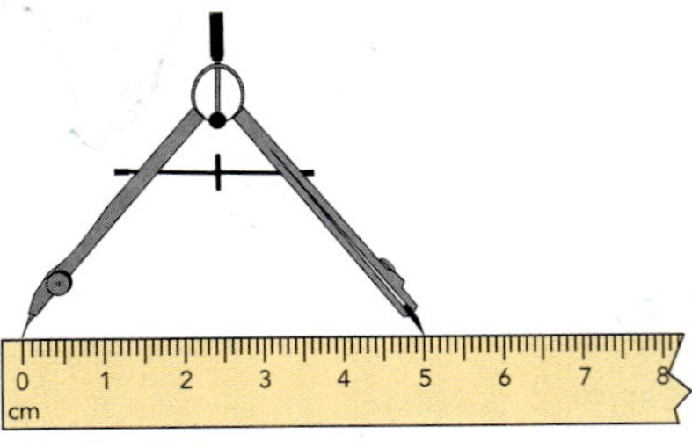

STEP 2 Then draw a circle. Draw and label the center O and four radii: $\overline{OP}$, $\overline{OQ}$, $\overline{OR}$, and $\overline{OS}$.

Example

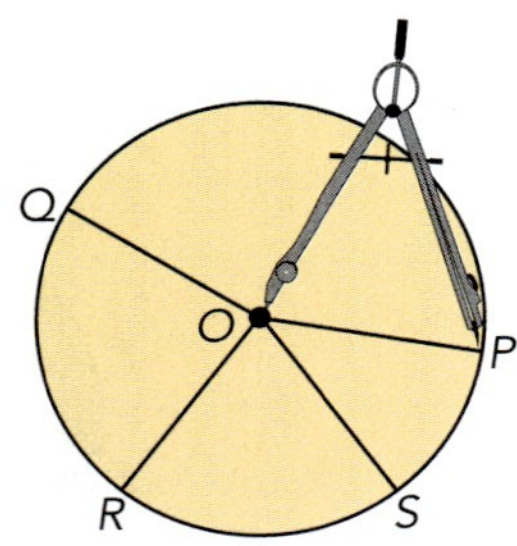

STEP 3 Measure the radii $\overline{OP}$, $\overline{OQ}$, $\overline{OR}$, and $\overline{OS}$. What can you say about the lengths of $\overline{OP}$, $\overline{OQ}$, $\overline{OR}$, and $\overline{OS}$?

Learn Identify the circumference of a circle.

The circumference of a circle is the distance around the circle.

The hoop in the photo has the shape of a circle.

The distance around the hoop is called its circumference.

Hands-On Activity

INVESTIGATING THE RELATIONSHIP BETWEEN THE CIRCUMFERENCE AND DIAMETER OF A CIRCLE

Lisa uses a string to measure the circumference of each circle to the nearest tenth of a centimeter and records it in a table.

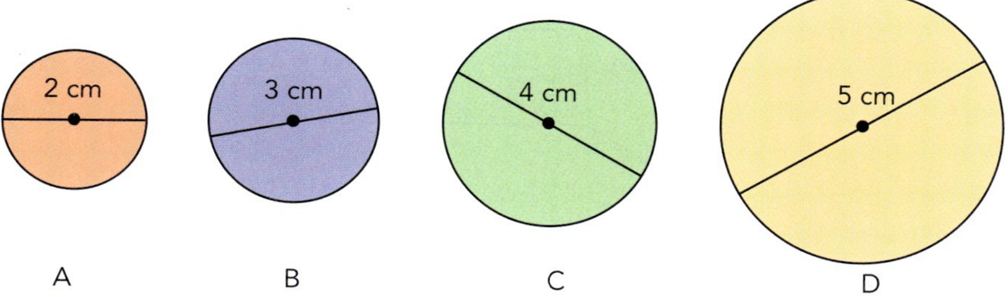

Copy the table. Divide the circumference of each circle by its diameter. Round your answers to the nearest tenth. Record your results.

Circle	Diameter (cm)	Circumference (cm)	Circumference ÷ diameter
A	2	6.2	?
B	3	9.4	?
C	4	12.5	?
D	5	15.6	?

What do you notice about the quotients in the last column?

The circumference of any circle divided by its diameter always gives the same value.

The Greek letter π is used to represent this value.

The letter π is pronounced "pie."

Continue on next page

STEP 2 To see the value of π up to 9 decimal places, press π ENTER on your calculator. Round the value of π to

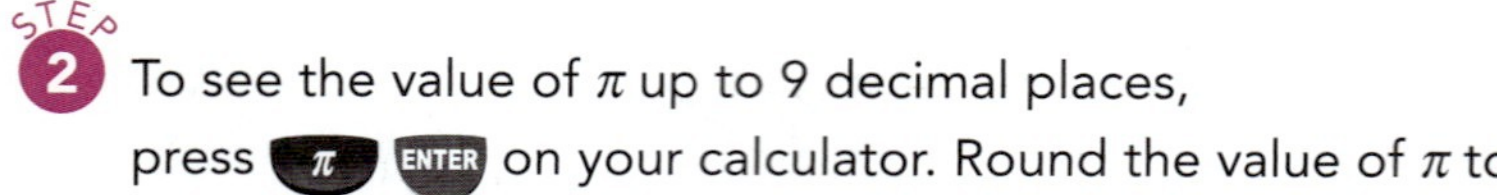

a) the nearest tenth.

b) the nearest hundredth.

c) the nearest thousandth.

STEP 3 In **STEP 1**, you learned that the circumference of any circle divided by its diameter is equal to π. You can use this fact to write a formula for the circumference of a circle. Complete the following statement.

Since circumference ÷ diameter = π,

Circumference = $\pi \cdot$ __?__

You also know that the diameter of a circle is 2 times its radius. You can use this fact to write a related formula for the circumference of a circle. Complete the following statement.

Circumference = $\pi \cdot$ diameter

= $\pi \cdot 2 \cdot$ __?__

= $2 \cdot \pi \cdot$ __?__

Using C for circumference, d for diameter, and r for radius, you can write these formulas as

$$C = \pi d$$
$$C = 2\pi r$$

Math Note

πd means $\pi \cdot d$ and $2\pi r$ means $2 \cdot \pi \cdot r$.

Learn Find the circumference of a circle.

a) Find the circumference of the plate shown. Use $\frac{22}{7}$ as an approximation for π.

Math Note

The symbol ≈ means "approximately equal to."

Circumference $= \pi d$	Write formula.
$\approx \frac{22}{7} \cdot 28$	Substitute.
$= \frac{22}{\cancel{7}_1} \cdot \frac{\cancel{28}^4}{1}$	Divide by the common factor, 7.
$= 22 \cdot 4$	Simplify.
$= 88$ cm	Multiply.

The circumference of the plate is approximately 88 centimeters.

b) The radius of a bicycle wheel is 10.5 inches. Find the circumference of the wheel. Use 3.14 as an approximation for π.

Circumference $= 2\pi r$	Write formula.
$\approx 2 \cdot 3.14 \cdot 10.5$	Substitute.
$= 65.94$ in.	Multiply.

The circumference of the bicycle wheel is approximately 65.94 inches.

Guided Practice

Copy and complete the table. Use $\frac{22}{7}$ as an approximation for π.

4

Circle	Radius (cm)	Diameter (cm)	Circumference (cm)
A	?	14	?
B	21	?	?
C	10.5	?	?

Copy and complete the table. Use 3.14 as an approximation for π.

Circle	Radius (cm)	Diameter (cm)	Circumference (cm)
D	?	25	?
E	16	?	?
F	8.25	?	?

Recognize that half of a circle is a semicircle and a quarter of a circle is a quadrant.

You can divide a circle into halves. Each half circle is called a semicircle.

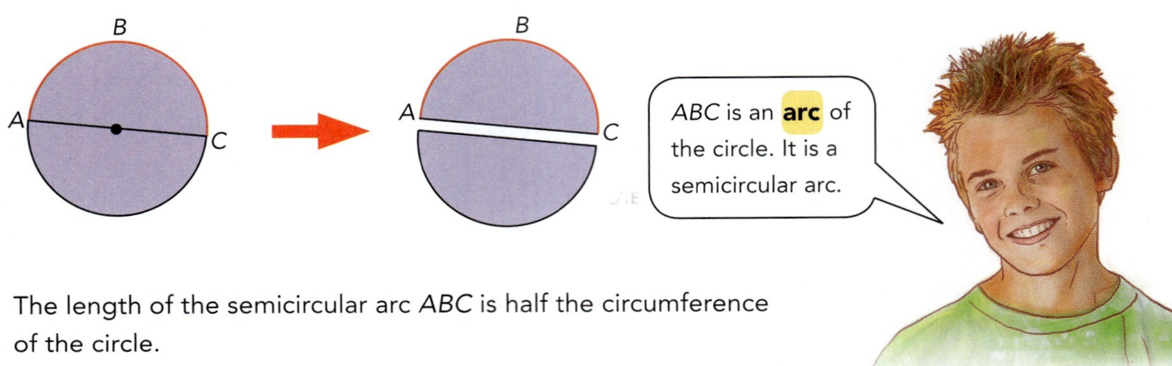

The length of the semicircular arc ABC is half the circumference of the circle.

You can divide a circle into quarters. Each quarter circle is called a quadrant.

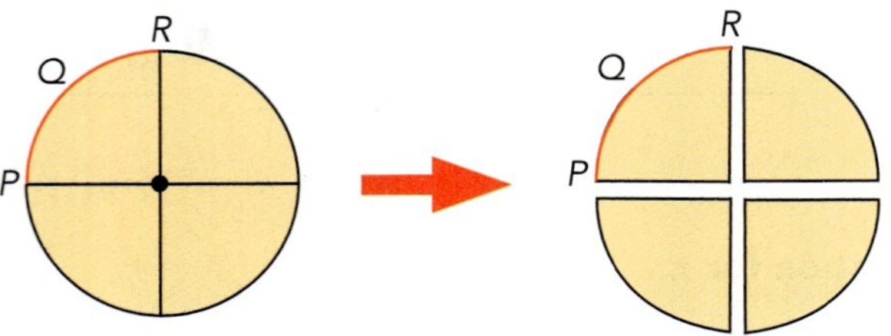

The length of arc PQR of the quadrant is one quarter the circumference of the circle.

Learn Find the lengths of a semicircular arc and the arc of a quadrant.

a) A length of wire is bent into a semicircular arc. The length of $\overline{EF}$ is 21 centimeters. Find the length of the wire. Use $\frac{22}{7}$ as an approximation for π.

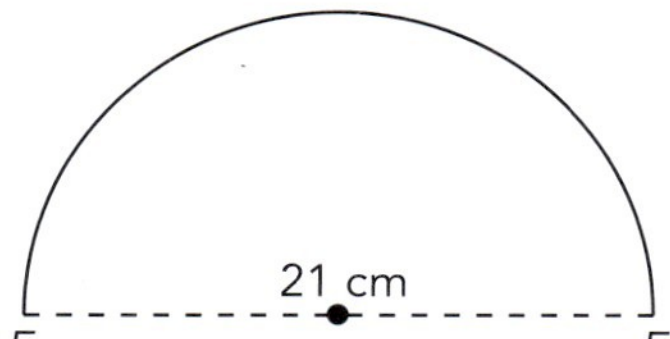

$$\begin{aligned} \text{Circumference} &= \pi d && \text{Write formula.} \\ &\approx \frac{22}{7} \cdot 21 && \text{Substitute.} \\ &= 66 \text{ cm} && \text{Multiply.} \end{aligned}$$

$$\begin{aligned} \text{Length of semicircular arc} &= \frac{1}{2} \times 66 \\ &= 33 \text{ cm} \end{aligned}$$

$$\begin{aligned} \text{Length of wire} &= \text{Length of semicircular arc} \\ &= 33 \text{ cm} \end{aligned}$$

The length of the wire is approximately 33 centimeters.

b) A circular ring of radius 5 inches is cut into four equal parts. Find the length of each arc of a quadrant. Use 3.14 as an approximation for π.

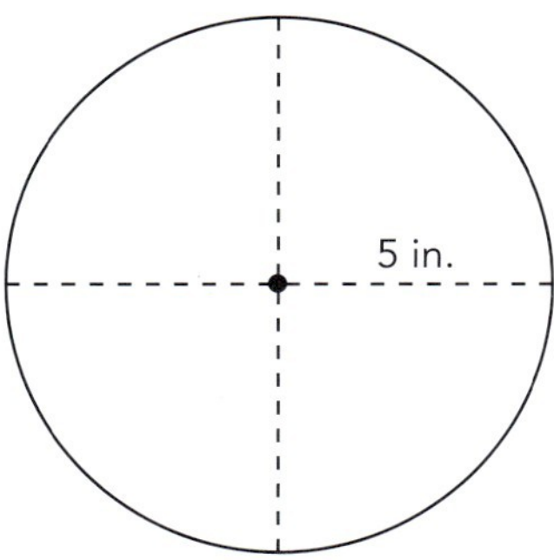

$$\begin{aligned} \text{Circumference} &= 2\pi r && \text{Write formula.} \\ &\approx 2 \cdot 3.14 \cdot 5 && \text{Substitute.} \\ &= 31.4 \text{ in.} && \text{Multiply.} \end{aligned}$$

$$\begin{aligned} \text{Length of each arc of the quadrant} &= \frac{1}{4} \times 31.4 \\ &= 7.85 \text{ in.} \end{aligned}$$

The length of each arc of a quadrant is approximately 7.85 inches.

Guided Practice

Complete.

6 A circular hoop is cut into two equal parts. Its diameter is 35 inches. Find the length of each semicircular arc. Use $\frac{22}{7}$ as an approximation for π.

Circumference of hoop $= \pi d$

$\approx \underline{\ ?\ }\ (?)\ \underline{\ ?\ }$

$= \underline{\ ?\ }$ in.

Length of each semicircular arc $= \frac{1}{2} \cdot$ circumference of hoop

$= \underline{\ ?\ }\ (?)\ \underline{\ ?\ }$

$= \underline{\ ?\ }$ in.

The length of each semicircular arc is approximately $\underline{\ ?\ }$ inches.

7 A quadrant is cut from a square. The side of the square is 10 centimeters. Find the length of the arc of the quadrant. Use 3.14 as an approximation for π.

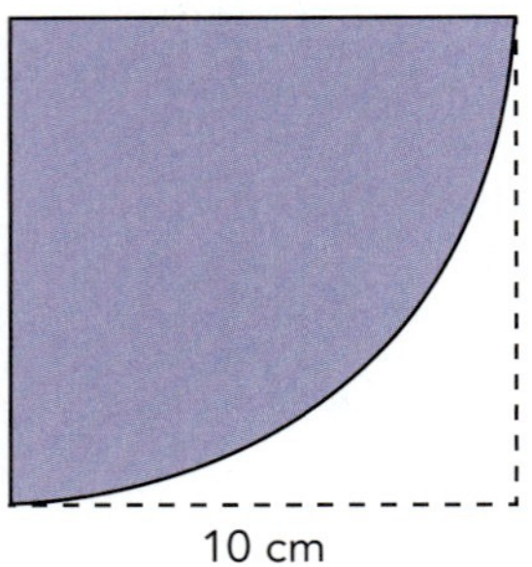

Circumference of circle $= 2\pi r$

$\approx 2 \cdot \underline{\ ?\ } \cdot \underline{\ ?\ }$

$= \underline{\ ?\ }$ cm

Length of the arc of the quadrant $=$ circumference $\div 4$

$= \underline{\ ?\ } \div \underline{\ ?\ }$

$= \underline{\ ?\ }$ cm

The length of the arc of the quadrant is approximately $\underline{\ ?\ }$ centimeters.

Hands-On Activity

Materials:

- compass
- drawing triangles
- ruler
- protractor

DRAWING SEMICIRCLES AND QUADRANTS

Use a compass to draw a circle of radius 2 inches. Label the center *O*.

Draw and label a diameter of the circle $\overline{PQ}$. What do you notice?

A diameter of a circle divides it into __?__ semicircles.

This figure is one of the semicircles.

Find the distance around the semicircle. Use 3.14 as an approximation for π.

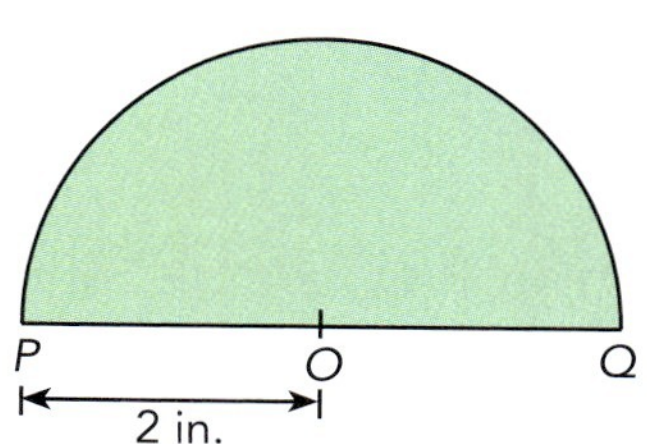

STEP 3

In your circle, draw a second diameter perpendicular to $\overline{PQ}$ using a ruler and protractor, or a drawing triangle. Label it $\overline{RS}$. What do you notice?

a) Two perpendicular diameters of a circle divide it into __?__ quadrants.

This figure is one of the quadrants.

Find the distance around the quadrant. Use 3.14 as an approximation for π.

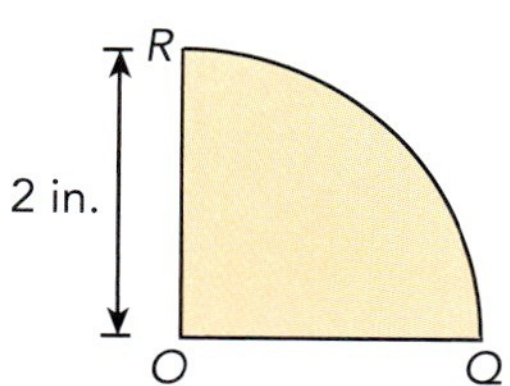

b) This figure is made up of the semicircular arc, the arc of a quadrant, and the radii $\overline{OR}$ and $\overline{OQ}$. Find the distance around the figure. Use 3.14 as an approximation for π.

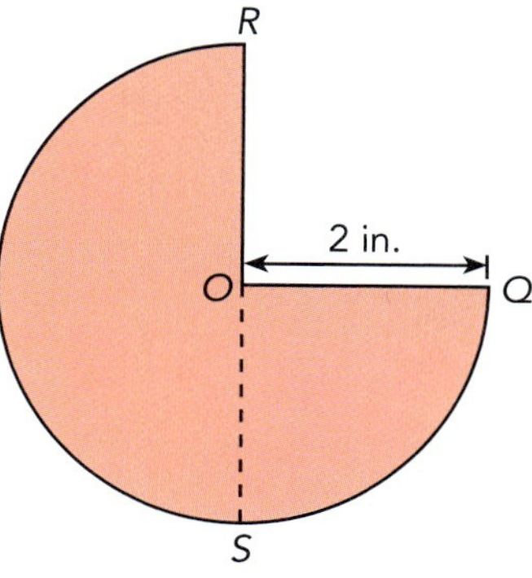

Practice 11.1

Use the figure to complete. In the figure, *O* is the center of the circle and $\overline{XY}$ is a straight line.

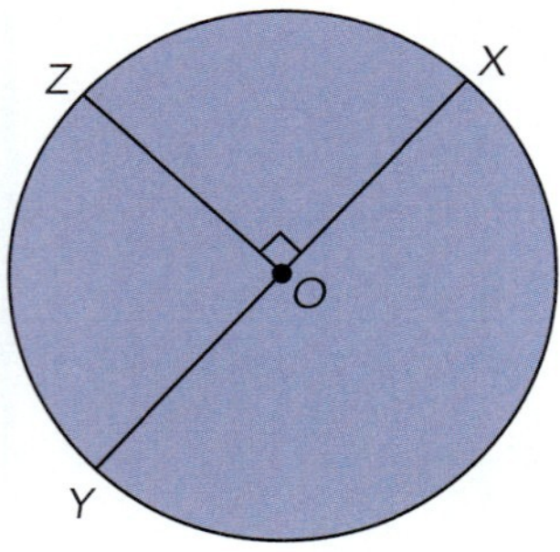

1. $\overline{OX}$, $\overline{OY}$, and $\overline{OZ}$ are __?__ of the circle.

2. $\overline{XY}$ is a __?__ of the circle.

3. $OX =$ __?__ $=$ __?__

4. $XY =$ __?__ $\cdot OZ$

5. Circumference of the circle $= \pi \cdot$ __?__

Find the circumference of each circle. Use $\frac{22}{7}$ as an approximation for π.

6.
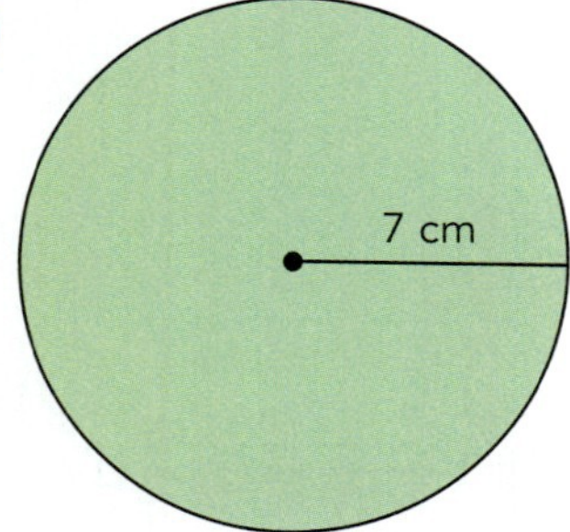

7.
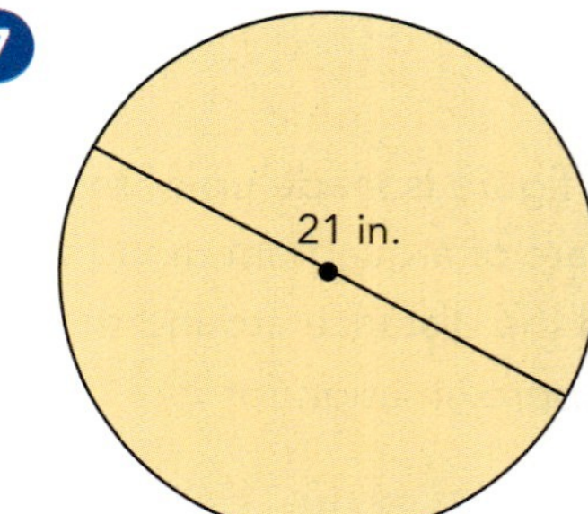

8.
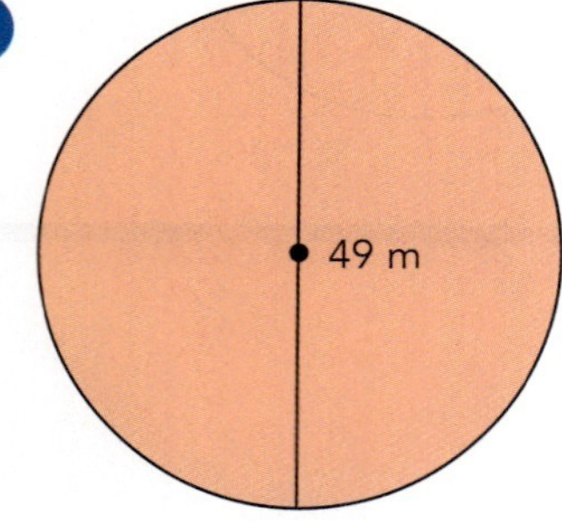

9.

Find the length of each arc. Use $\frac{22}{7}$ as an approximation for π.

10

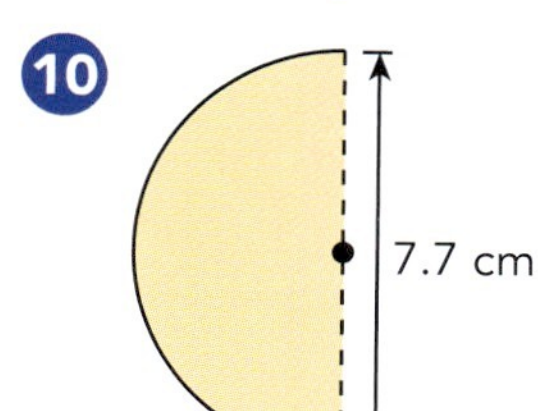

11

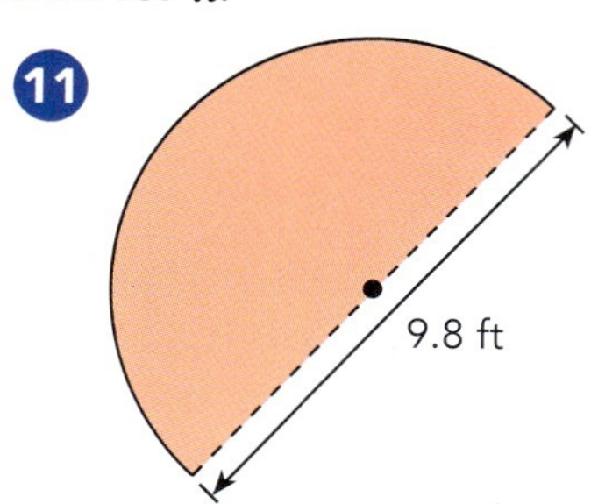

12

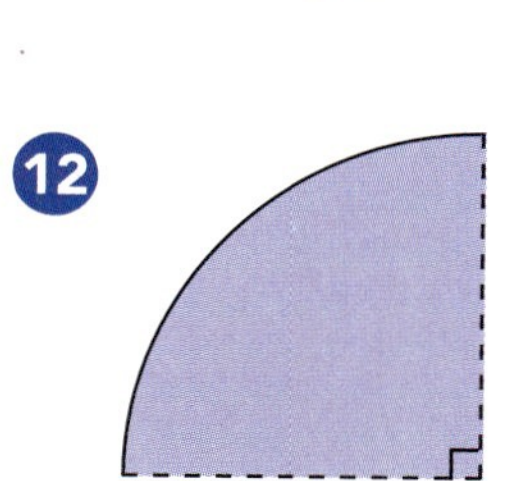

13

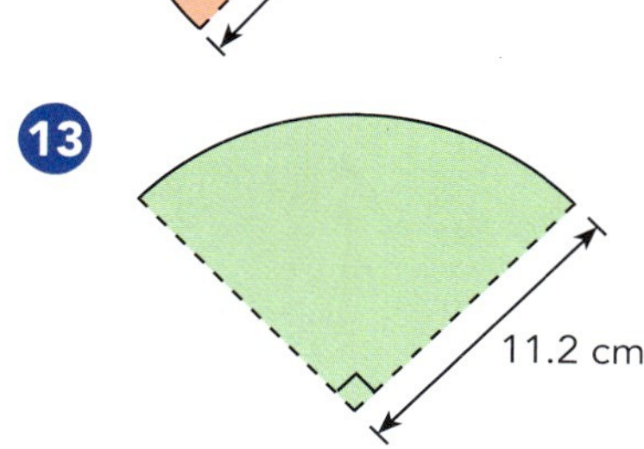

Find the distance around each semicircle. Use 3.14 as an approximation for π.

14

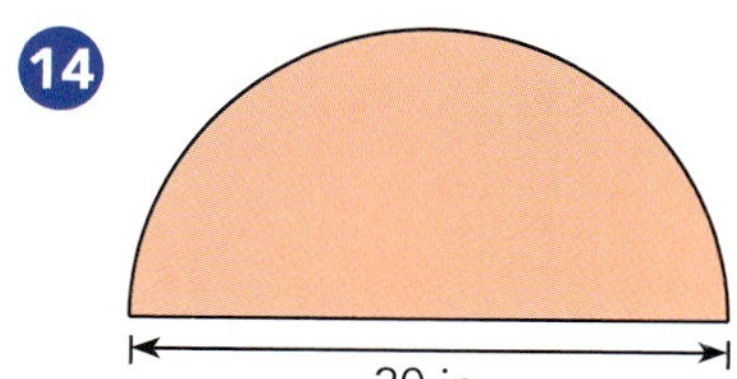

15

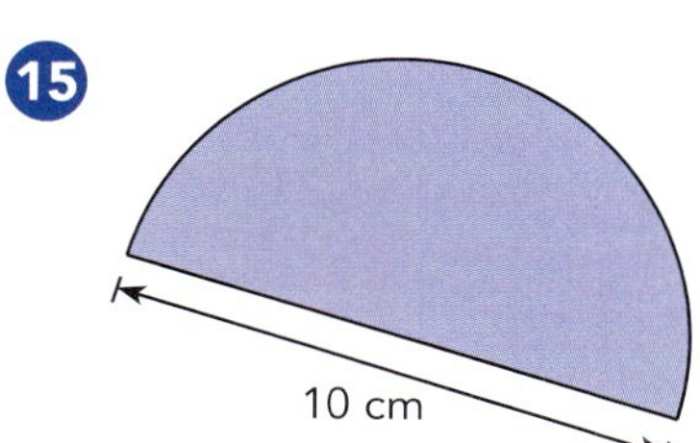

16

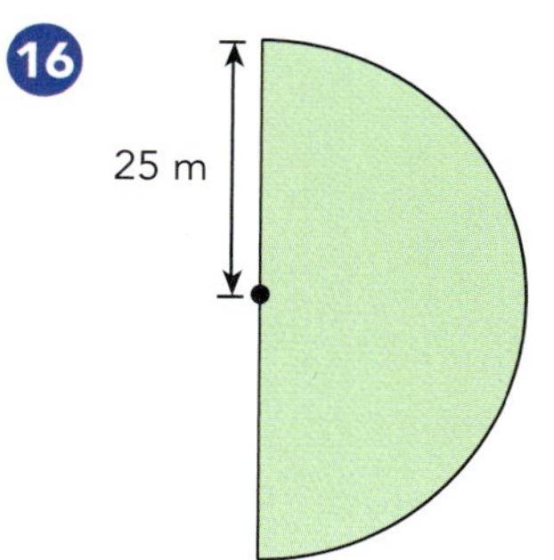

17

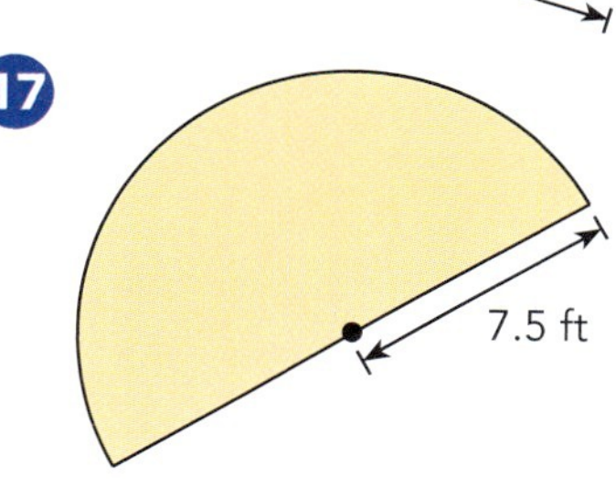

Find the distance around each quadrant. Use $\frac{22}{7}$ as an approximation for π.

18

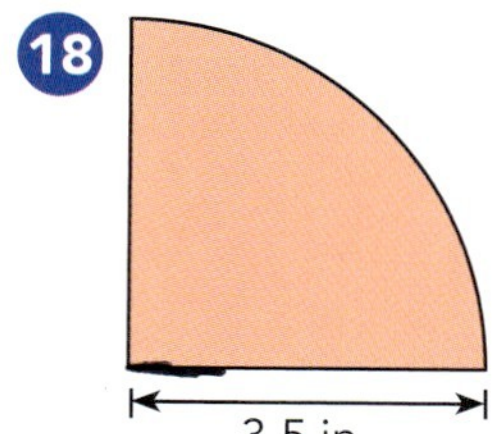

19

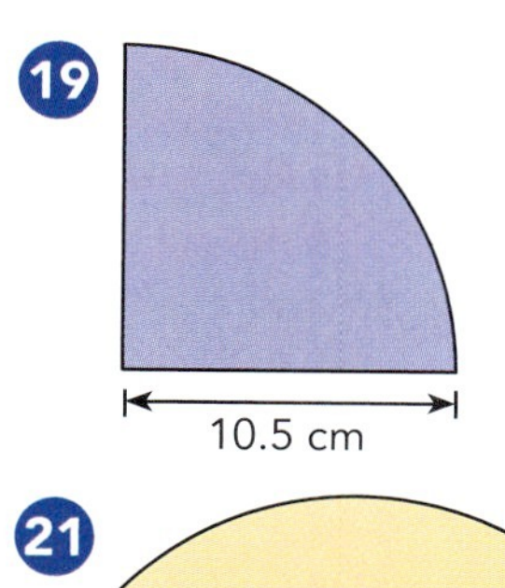

20

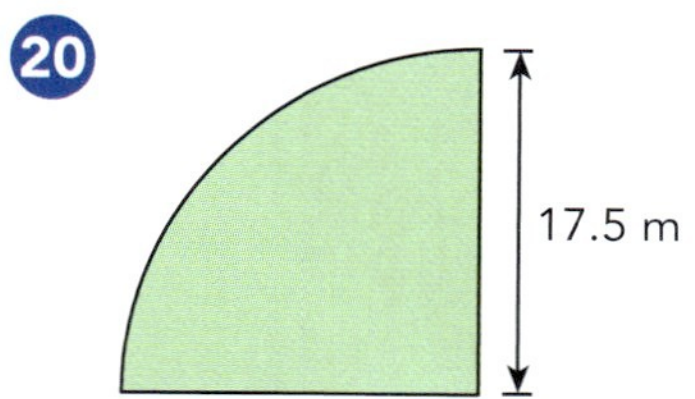

21

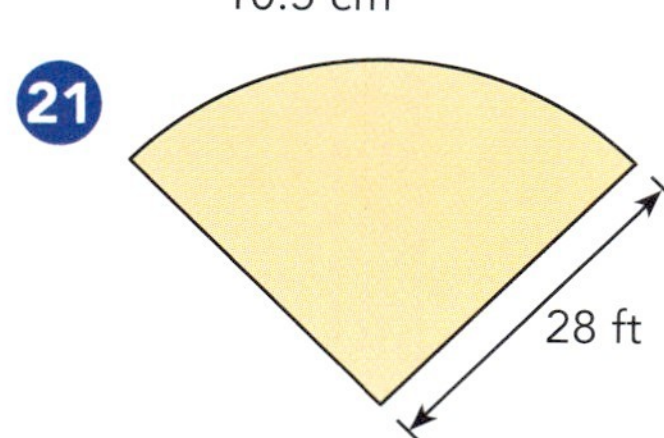

Solve. Show your work. Use 3.14 as an approximation for π.

22. A circular garden has a diameter of 120 feet. Find its circumference.

23. A circular coaster has a radius of 4 centimeters. Find its circumference.

24. The diameter of a roll of tape is $5\frac{1}{2}$ centimeters. Find its circumference.

25. The shape of a floor mat is a semicircle. Find the distance around the mat.

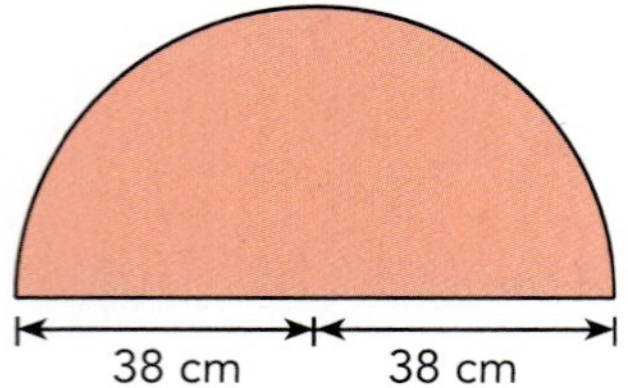

26. A small playground is shaped like a quadrant, as shown. Find the distance around the playground.

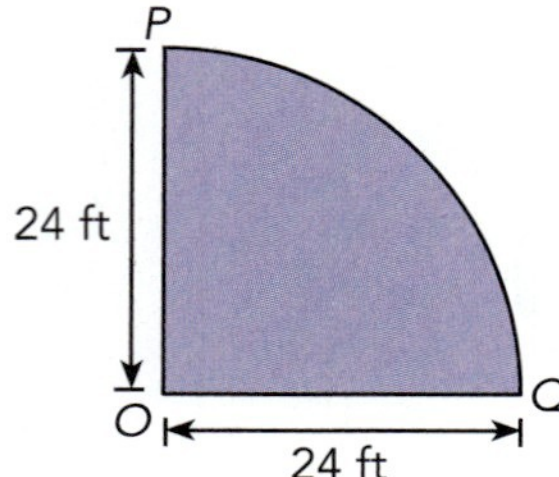

27. If the radius of a wheel is 14 inches, what is the distance traveled when the wheel turns around 100 times?

Find the distance around each figure. Use $\frac{22}{7}$ as an approximation for π.

28. The figure is made up of a rectangle and a semicircle.

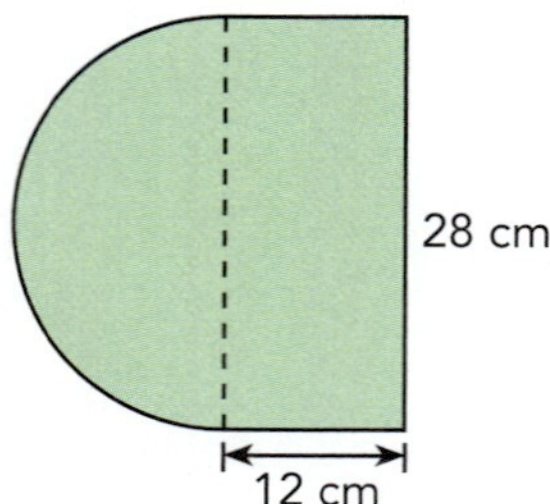

29 The figure is made up of an equilateral triangle and a semicircle.

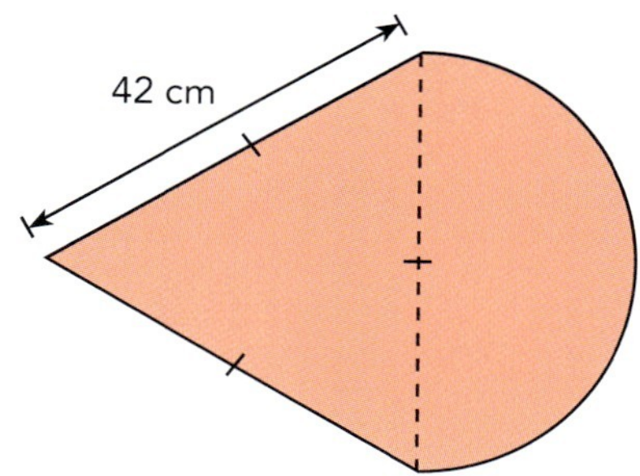

Find the distance around each figure. Use 3.14 as an approximation for π.

30 The figure is made up of a rectangle and two identical semicircles.

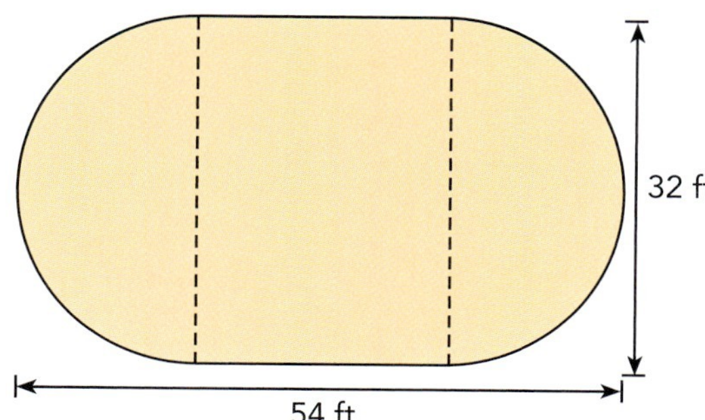

31 The figure is made up of two identical quadrants, a semicircle, and an equilateral triangle.

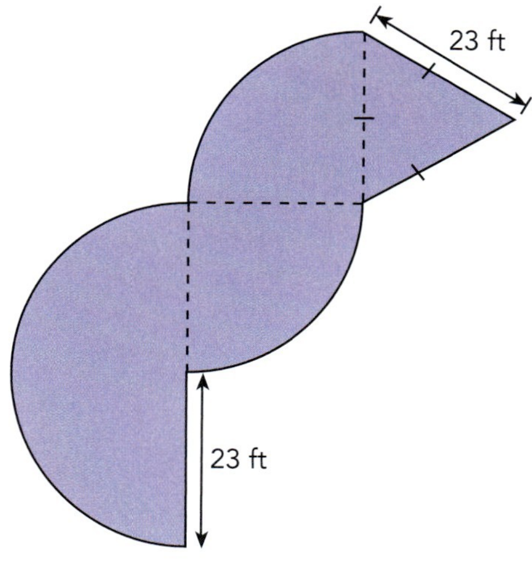

11.2 Area of a Circle

Lesson Objective

- Use formulas to calculate the areas of circles, semicircles, and quadrants.

Derive the formula for the area of a circle.

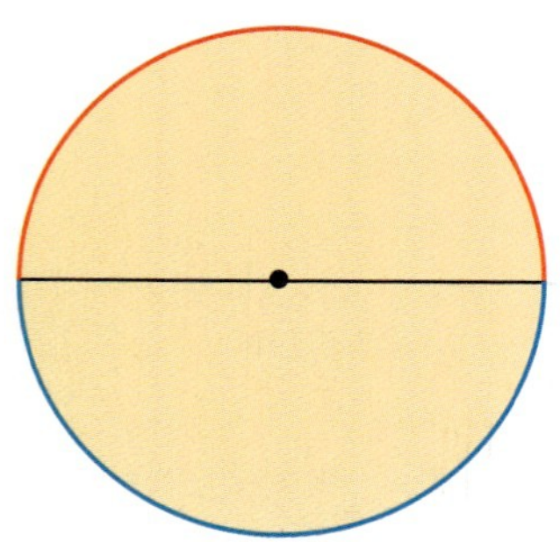

A diameter divides a circle of radius r into 2 semicircles.

$$\begin{aligned}\text{Length of semicircular arc} &= \frac{1}{2} \cdot \text{circumference of circle}\\ &= \frac{1}{2} \cdot 2\pi r\\ &= \pi r\end{aligned}$$

Suppose you cut a circle of radius r into 16 equal pieces.

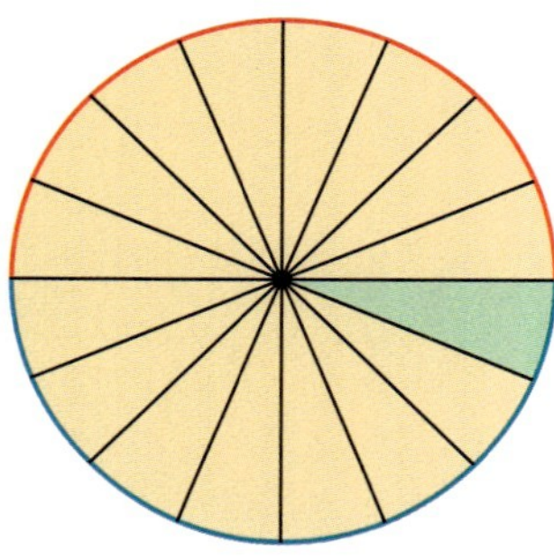

The cuts all go through the center of the circle.

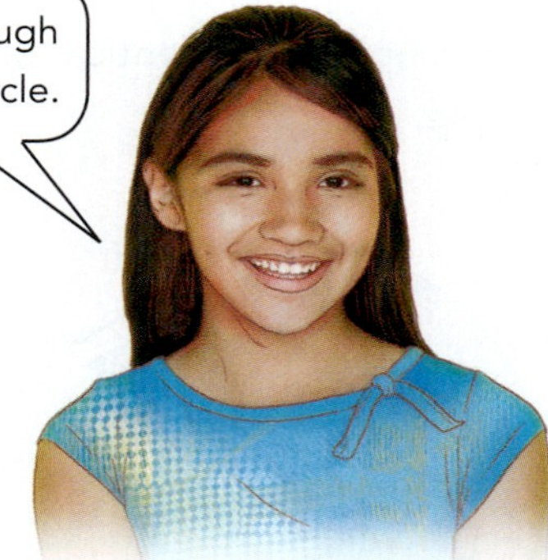

You can cut one of the pieces into 2 equal parts.

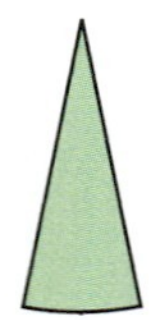

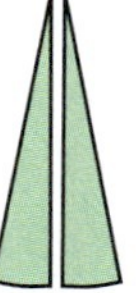

Arrange all the pieces to form the figure shown below. You can also label the dimensions of the figure.

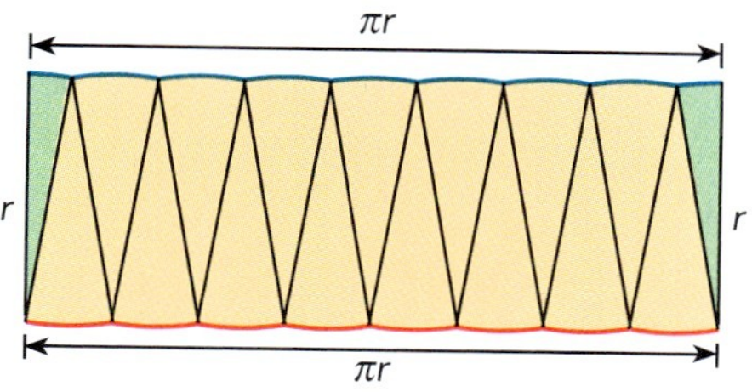

Area of circle = area of the figure

Now suppose you cut the circle into as many equal pieces as possible. You can form the figure shown at the right.

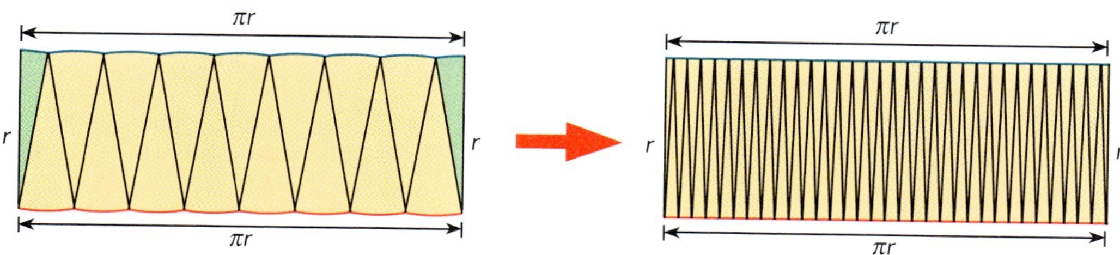

As the number of pieces keeps increasing, the top and bottom of the figure gradually become straight lines. Then the figure gradually becomes a rectangle of length πr and width r. You can write an expression for its area in terms of r. Because the rectangle is made up of the same pieces as the original circle, the area of the circle is equal to the area of the rectangle.

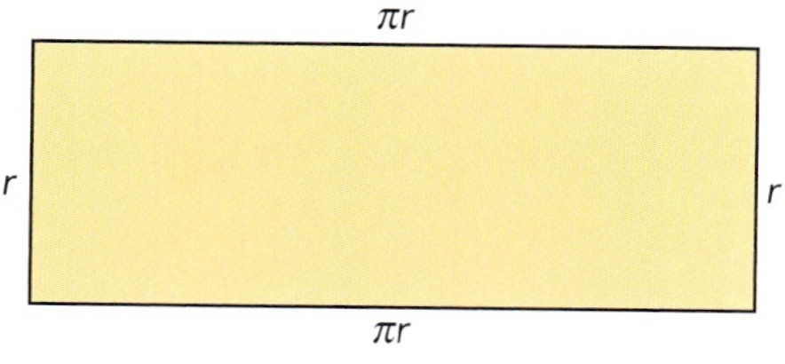

$$\begin{aligned}\text{Area of circle} &= \text{area of rectangle}\\ &= \pi r \cdot r\\ &= \pi \cdot r \cdot r\\ &= \pi r^2\end{aligned}$$

Your can write the formula as

Area of circle = πr^2

Learn Find the area of a circle.

a) The radius of a circular disc is 7 inches. Find its area. Use $\frac{22}{7}$ as an approximation for π.

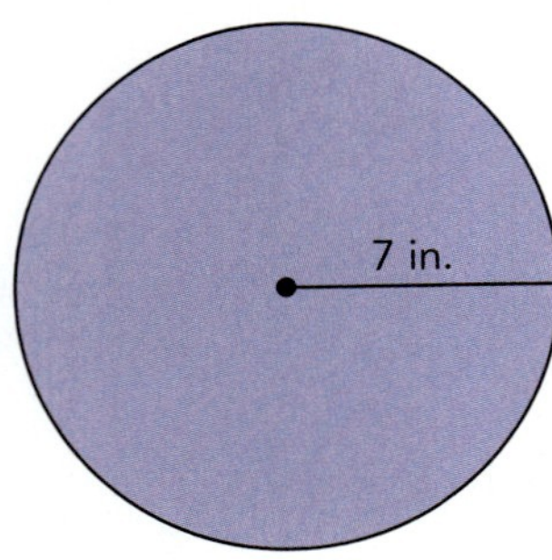

Area $= \pi r^2$	Write formula.
$\approx \frac{22}{7} \cdot 7^2$	Substitute.
$= \frac{22}{\cancel{7}_1} \cdot 7 \cdot \cancel{7}^1$	Divide by the common factor, 7.
$= 22 \cdot 7$	Simplify.
$= 154 \text{ in.}^2$	Multiply.

The area of the disc is approximately 154 square inches.

b) The diameter of a circle is 24 centimeters. Find its area. Use 3.14 as an approximation for π.

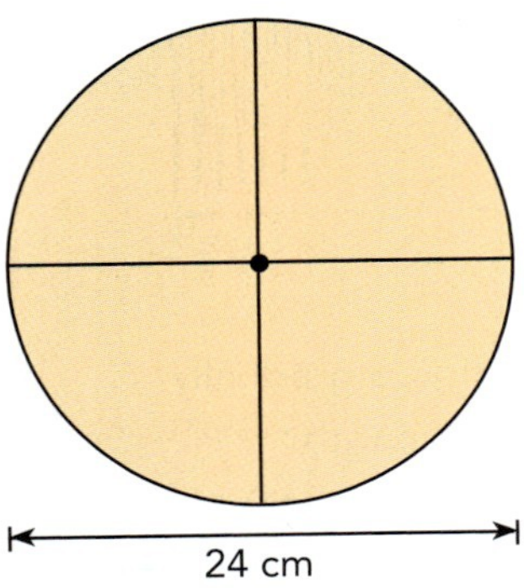

Radius of circle = diameter ÷ 2
= 24 ÷ 2
= 12 cm

Area $= \pi r^2$	Write formula.
$\approx 3.14 \cdot 12^2$	Substitute.
$= 3.14 \cdot 144$	Simplify.
$= 452.16 \text{ cm}^2$	Multiply.

The area of the circle is approximately 452.16 square centimeters.

Guided Practice

Complete. Use 3.14 as an approximation for π.

1 Find the area of a circle that has a radius of 18 centimeters.

Area $= \pi r^2$

$\approx$ __?__ $\cdot$ __?__^{2}

$=$ __?__ $\cdot$ __?__

$=$ __?__ cm^2

The area of the circle is approximately __?__ square centimeters.

2 Find the area of a circle that has a radius of 15 inches.

Area $= \pi r^2$

$\approx \underline{\ ?\ } \cdot \underline{\ ?\ }^2$

$= \underline{\ ?\ } \cdot \underline{\ ?\ }$

$= \underline{\ ?\ }$ in.^{2}

The area of the circle is approximately $\underline{\ ?\ }$ square inches.

3 Find the area of a circle that has a diameter of 26 centimeters.

Radius = diameter ÷ 2

$= \underline{\ ?\ } \div \underline{\ ?\ }$

$= \underline{\ ?\ }$ cm

Area $= \pi r^2$

$\approx \underline{\ ?\ } \cdot \underline{\ ?\ }^2$

$= \underline{\ ?\ } \cdot \underline{\ ?\ }$

$= \underline{\ ?\ }$ cm^2

The area of the circle is approximately $\underline{\ ?\ }$ square centimeters.

Learn

Find the area of a semicircle.

The diameter of a circle is 14 feet. Find the area of a semicircle. Use $\frac{22}{7}$ as an approximation for π.

Radius = diameter ÷ 2
= 14 ÷ 2
= 7 ft

14 ft

Area of semicircle $= \frac{1}{2} \cdot$ area of circle

$= \frac{1}{2} \cdot \pi r^2$ Write formula.

$\approx \frac{1}{2} \cdot \frac{22}{7} \cdot 7^2$ Substitute.

$= \frac{1}{\cancel{2}_1} \cdot \frac{\cancel{22}^{11}}{\cancel{7}_1} \cdot 7 \cdot \cancel{7}^1$ Divide by the common factors, 2 and 7.

$= 11 \cdot 7$ Simplify.

$= 77$ ft^2 Multiply.

The area of a semicircle is approximately 77 square feet.

Guided Practice

Complete. Use $\frac{22}{7}$ as an approximation for π.

4 Find the area of a quadrant.

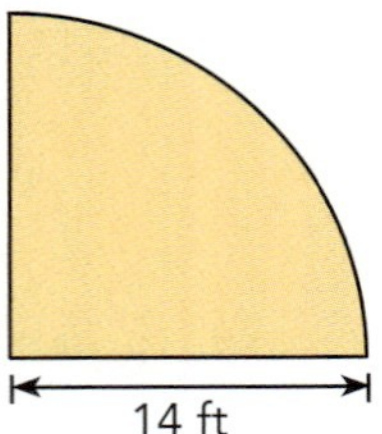

Area of quadrant $= \underline{?} \cdot$ area of circle

$= \underline{?} \cdot \pi r^2$

$\approx \underline{?} \cdot \underline{?} \cdot \underline{?}^2$

$= \underline{?} \cdot \underline{?} \cdot \underline{?} \cdot \underline{?}$

$= \underline{?}$ ft^2

The area of a quadrant is approximately $\underline{?}$ square feet.

5 The diameter of a circle is 42 inches. Find the area of a quadrant.

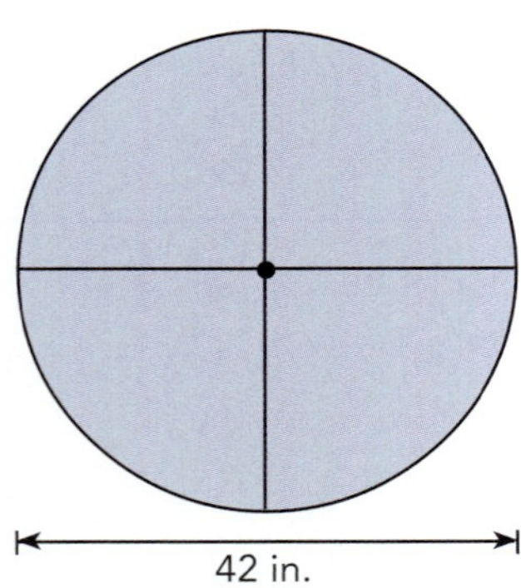

Radius = diameter ÷ 2

$= \underline{?} \div 2$

$= \underline{?}$ in.

Area of quadrant $= \underline{?} \cdot$ area of circle

$= \underline{?} \cdot \pi r^2$

$\approx \underline{?} \cdot \underline{?} \cdot \underline{?}^2$

$= \underline{?} \cdot \underline{?} \cdot \underline{?} \cdot \underline{?}$

$= \underline{?}$ in.^{2}

The area of a quadrant is approximately $\underline{?}$ square inches.

Practice 11.2

Find the area of each circle. Use 3.14 as an approximation for π.

1

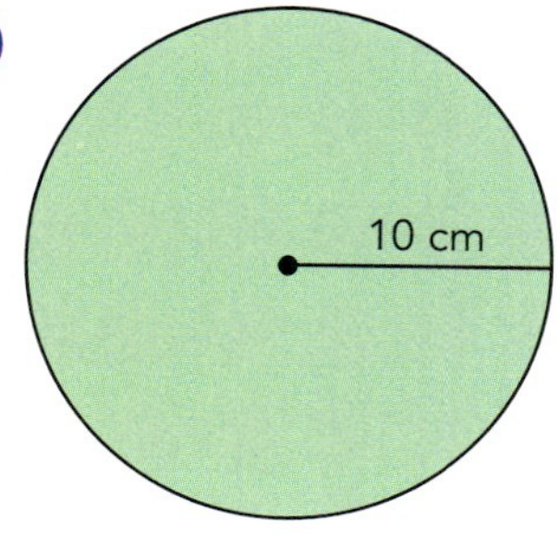

2

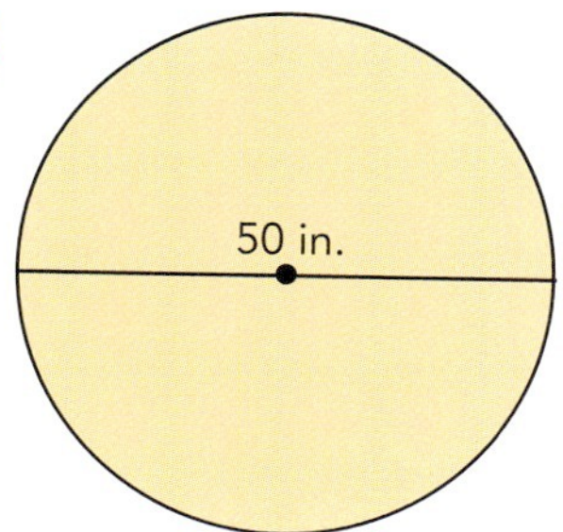

Find the area of each semicircle. Use $\frac{22}{7}$ as an approximation for π.

3

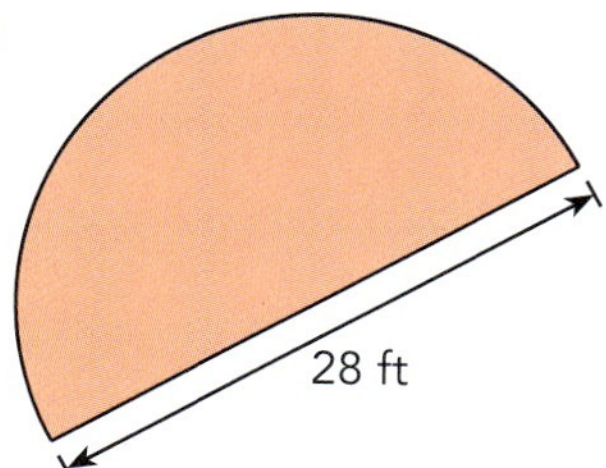

4

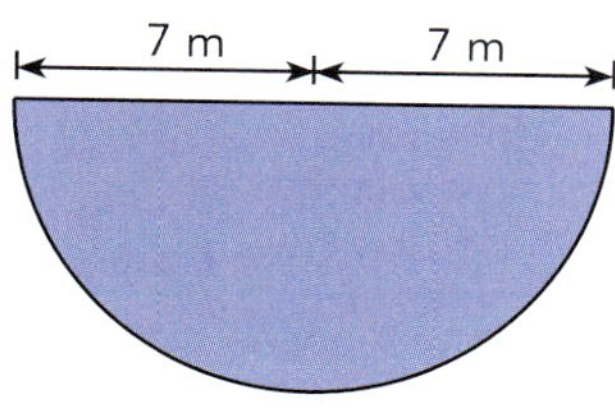

Find the area of each quadrant to the nearest tenth. Use 3.14 as an approximation for π.

5

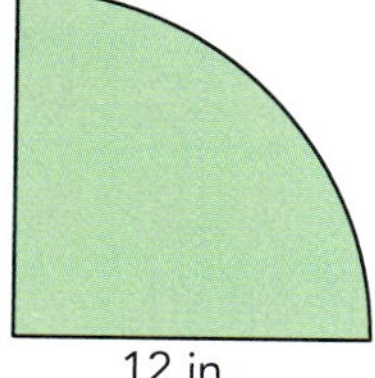

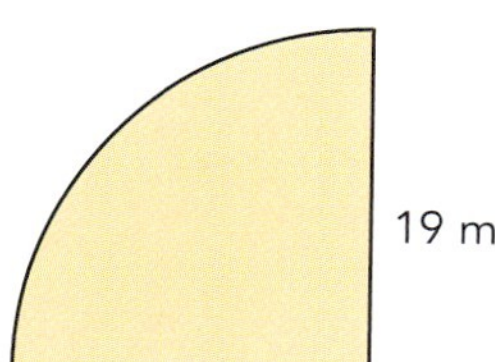

Solve. Show your work.

7 A circular pendant has a diameter of 7 centimeters. Find its area. Use $\frac{22}{7}$ as an approximation for π.

8 The shape of the stage of a lecture theater is a semicircle. Find the area of the stage. Use 3.14 as an approximation for π.

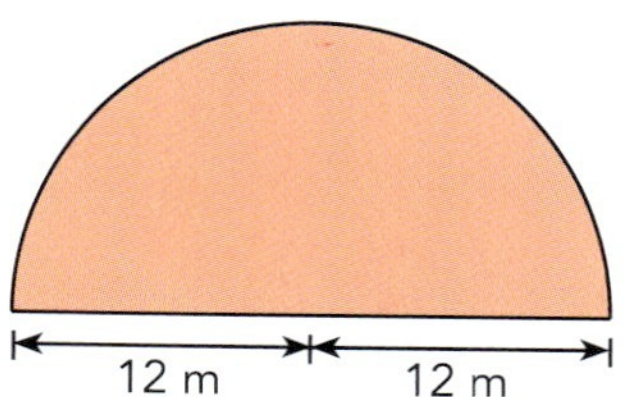

9 The shape of a balcony floor is a quadrant. Find the area of the balcony floor. Use 3.14 as an approximation for π.

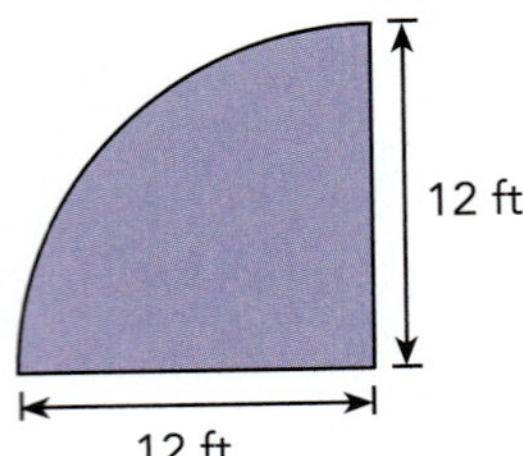

10 The cost of an 8-inch pizza is \$4. The cost of a 16-inch pizza is \$13. Use 3.14 as an approximation for π.

a) How much greater is the area of the 16-inch pizza than the area of the 8-inch pizza?

b) Which is a better deal? Explain your reasoning.

11 Four identical drinking glasses each have a radius of 5 centimeters. The glasses are arranged so that they touch each other as shown in the figure below. Find the area of the green portion. Use 3.14 as an approximation for π.

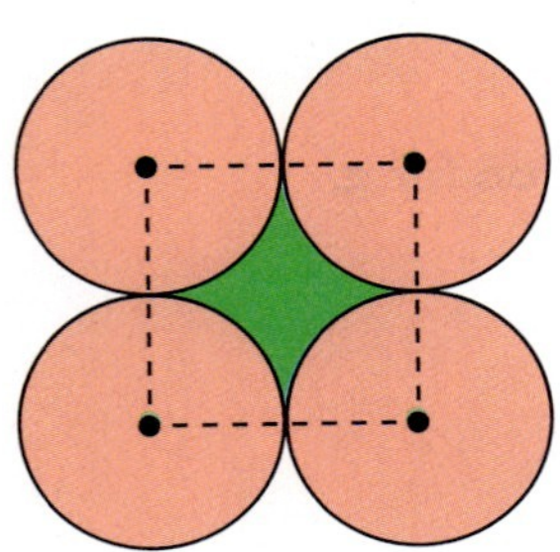

12 The figure is made up of trapezoid *ABCD* and a semicircle. The height of trapezoid *ABCD* is $\frac{5}{6}$ the length of $\overline{BC}$. Find the area of the figure. Use $\frac{22}{7}$ as an approximation for π.

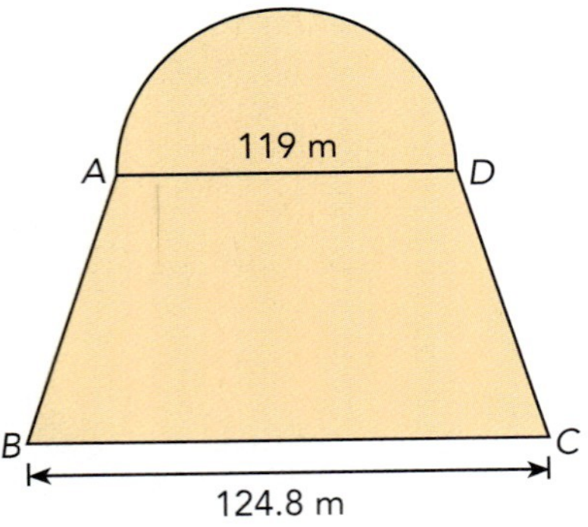

11.3 Real-World Problems: Circles

Lesson Objectives

- Solve real-world problems involving area and circumference of circles.
- Solve real-world problems involving semicircles, quadrants, and composite figures.

Learn Use the formula for circumference to solve real-world problems.

a) A circular mat has a diameter of 53 centimeters. Lily wants to sew a decorative braid around the mat. How many centimeters of braid does she need? Give your answer to the nearest tenth of a centimeter. Use 3.14 as an approximation of π.

Circumference of mat $= \pi d$	Write formula.
$\approx 3.14 \cdot 53$	Substitute.
$= 166.42$ cm	Multiply.
≈ 166.4 cm	Round to the nearest tenth of a centimeter.

Lily needs approximately 166.4 centimeters of decorative braid.

b) A metalworker cuts out a large semicircle with a diameter of 28 centimeters. Then the metalworker cuts a smaller semicircle out of the larger one and removes it. The diameter of the semicircular piece that is removed is 14 centimeters. Find the distance around the shape after the smaller semicircle is removed. Use $\frac{22}{7}$ as an approximation for π.

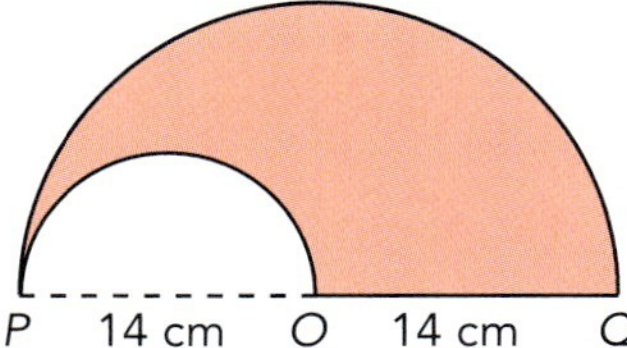

To find the distance around the shape, you need to add up the two arc lengths and OQ.

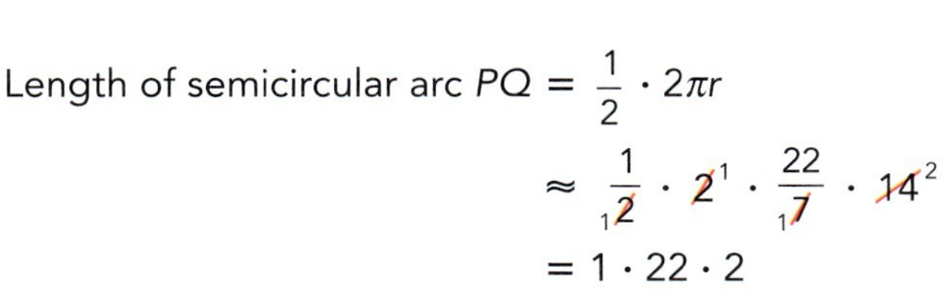

Length of semicircular arc $PQ = \frac{1}{2} \cdot 2\pi r$	Write formula.
$\approx \frac{1}{\cancel{2}_1} \cdot \cancel{2}^1 \cdot \frac{22}{\cancel{7}_1} \cdot \cancel{14}^2$	Substitute. Divide by the common factors, 2 and 7.
$= 1 \cdot 22 \cdot 2$	Simplify.
$= 44$ cm	Multiply.

Continue on next page

Length of semicircular arc $PO = \frac{1}{2} \cdot \pi d$ — Write formula.

$\approx \frac{1}{_1\not{2}} \cdot \frac{\not{22}^{11}}{_1\not{7}} \cdot \not{14}^{2}$ — Substitute. Divide by the common factors, 2 and 7.

$= 1 \cdot 11 \cdot 2$ — Simplify.

$= 22$ cm — Multiply.

Distance around the shape
= length of semicircular arc PQ + length of semicircular arc PO + OQ
$= 44 + 22 + 14$
$= 80$ cm

The distance around the shape is approximately 80 centimeters.

c) The shape of a table top is made up of a semicircle and a quadrant. Find the distance around the table top. Use 3.14 as an approximation for π.

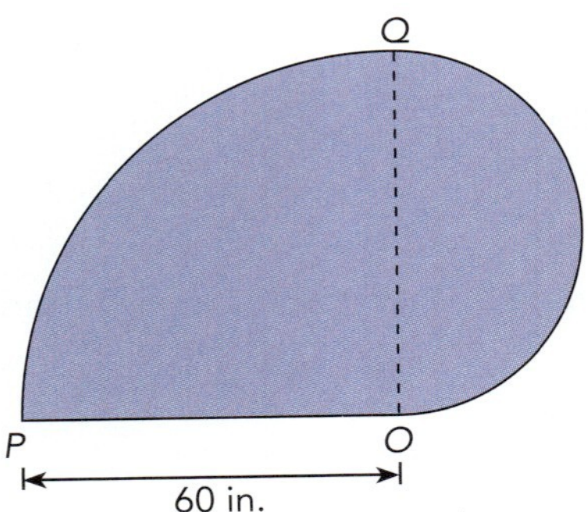

Length of semicircular arc $QO = \frac{1}{2} \cdot \pi d$ — Write formula.

$\approx \frac{1}{2} \cdot 3.14 \cdot 60$ — Substitute.

$= 94.2$ in. — Multiply.

Length of arc $PQ = \frac{1}{4} \cdot 2\pi r$ — Write formula.

$\approx \frac{1}{_1\not{4}} \cdot 2 \cdot 3.14 \cdot \not{60}^{15}$ — Substitute. Divide by the common factor, 4.

$= 1 \cdot 2 \cdot 3.14 \cdot 15$ — Simplify.

$= 94.2$ in. — Multiply.

Distance around the table top
= length of semicircular arc QO + length of arc PQ + PO
$= 94.2 + 94.2 + 60$
$= 248.4$ in.

The distance around the table top is approximately 248.4 inches.

Guided Practice

Complete. Use 3.14 as an approximation for π.

1 The circumference of the moon is the approximate distance around a circle with radius 1,736 kilometers. Find the circumference of the moon.

a) Round your answer to the nearest 10 kilometers.

Circumference of moon $= 2\pi r$

$\approx$? · ? · ?

= ? km

The circumference of the moon to the nearest 10 kilometers is ? kilometers.

b) Round your answer to the nearest 1,000 kilometers.

The circumference of the moon to the nearest 1,000 kilometers is ? kilometers.

2 A greeting card is made up of three semicircles. O is the center of the large semicircle. Sarah wants to decorate the distance around the card with a ribbon. How much ribbon does Sarah need? Round your answer to the nearest inch.

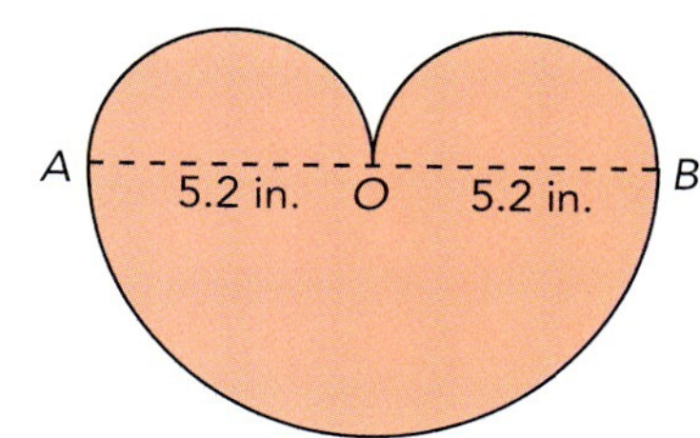

Length of semicircular arc $AB = \frac{1}{2} \cdot 2\pi r$

$\approx$? · ? · ? · ?

= 1 · ? · ?

= ? in.

Semicircular arcs AO and OB have the same length.

Total length of semicircular arcs AO and OB

$= 2 \cdot \frac{1}{2} \cdot \pi d$

$\approx$? · ? · ? · ?

= 1 · ? · ?

= ? in.

Distance around the card

= length of semicircular arc AB + total length of semicircular arcs AO and OB

= ? + ?

= ? in.

$\approx$? in.

Sarah needs approximately ? inches of ribbon.

3 As part of her artwork, Sally bends a length of wire into the shape shown. The shape is made up of a semicircle and a quadrant. Find the length of the wire.

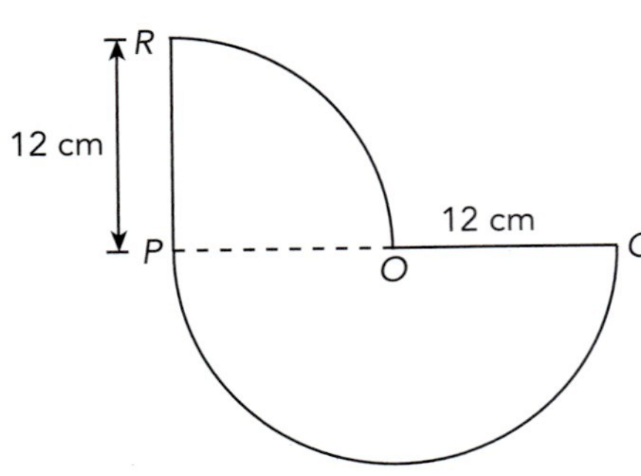

Length of semicircular arc PQ

$= \frac{1}{2} \cdot 2\pi r$

$\approx$ _?_ $\cdot$ 2 $\cdot$ _?_ $\cdot$ _?_

$= 1 \cdot$ _?_ $\cdot$ _?_

$=$ _?_ cm

Length of arc $RO = \frac{1}{4} \cdot 2\pi r$

$\approx \frac{1}{4} \cdot 2 \cdot$ _?_ $\cdot$ _?_

$=$ _?_ cm

Distance around the shape

= length of semicircular arc PQ + length of arc RO + RP + OQ

= _?_ + _?_ + _?_ + _?_

= _?_ cm

The length of the wire is approximately _?_ centimeters.

Learn Use the formula for area of a circle to solve real-world problems.

a) A jewelry designer is making a pendant. The pendant will be a circular disc (center O) with a circular hole cut out of it, as shown. The radius of the disc is 35 millimeters. Find the area of the pendant. Use $\frac{22}{7}$ as an approximation for π.

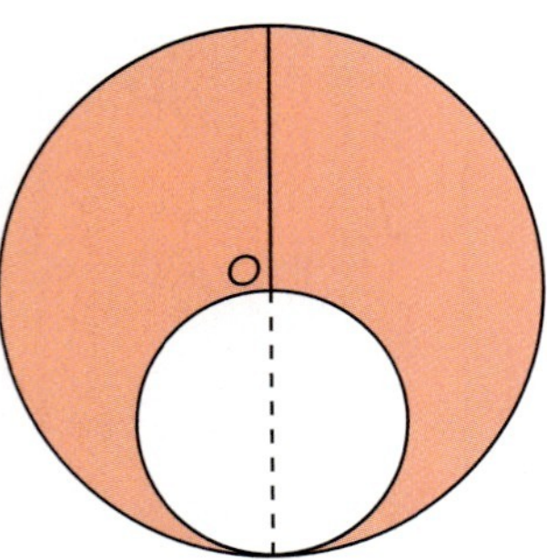

Area of disc $= \pi r^2$

$\approx \frac{22}{7} \cdot 35^2$

$= \frac{22}{\cancel{7}_1} \cdot 35 \cdot \cancel{35}^5$

$= 22 \cdot 35 \cdot 5$

$= 3{,}850 \text{ mm}^2$

Radius of hole = diameter ÷ 2

= 35 ÷ 2

= 17.5 mm

Area of hole $= \pi r^2$

$\approx \frac{22}{7} \cdot 17.5 \cdot 17.5$

$= 962.5 \text{ mm}^2$

Area of pendant = area of disc − area of hole

$= 3{,}850 - 962.5$

$= 2{,}887.5 \text{ mm}^2$

The area of the pendant is approximately 2,887.5 square millimeters.

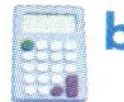

b) A graphic designer creates a design for a company logo. The design is a green semicircle with a white quadrant, as shown. Find the area of the green part of the design. Use 3.14 as an approximation for π.

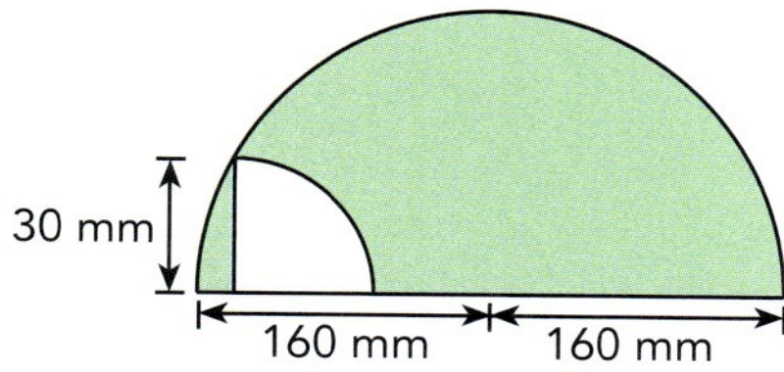

Area of semicircle $= \frac{1}{2} \cdot \pi r^2$

$\approx \frac{1}{2} \cdot 3.14 \cdot 160^2$

$= \frac{1}{\cancel{2}_1} \cdot 3.14 \cdot 160 \cdot \cancel{160}^{80}$

$= 1 \cdot 3.14 \cdot 160 \cdot 80$

$= 40{,}192 \text{ mm}^2$

Area of quadrant $= \frac{1}{4} \cdot \pi r^2$

$\approx \frac{1}{4} \cdot 3.14 \cdot 30^2$

$= \frac{1}{\cancel{4}_1} \cdot 3.14 \cdot \cancel{30}^{15} \cdot \cancel{30}^{15}$

$= 1 \cdot 3.14 \cdot 15 \cdot 15$

$= 706.5 \text{ mm}^2$

Area of green part

= area of semicircle − area of quadrant

$= 40{,}192 - 706.5$

$= 39{,}485.5 \text{ mm}^2$

The area of the green part of the design is approximately 39,485.5 square millimeters.

Guided Practice

Complete. Use $\frac{22}{7}$ as an approximation for π.

4 Judy baked a pizza and had part of it for lunch. After the meal, the shape of the remaining pizza is made up of a semicircle and a quadrant. Find the area of the remaining pizza.

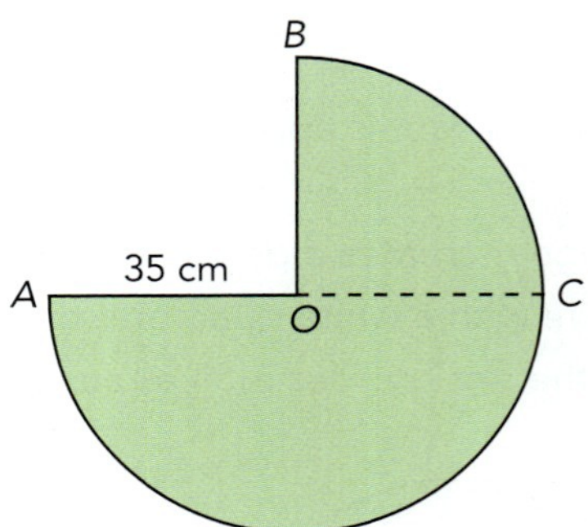

Area of quadrant $= \frac{1}{4} \cdot \pi r^2$

$\approx \frac{1}{4} \cdot \underline{\ ?\ } \cdot \underline{\ ?\ }^2$

$= \frac{1}{4} \cdot \underline{\ ?\ } \cdot \underline{\ ?\ } \cdot \underline{\ ?\ }$

$= \underline{\ ?\ }$ cm^2

Area of semicircle $= \frac{1}{2} \cdot \pi r^2$

$\approx \frac{1}{2} \cdot \underline{\ ?\ } \cdot \underline{\ ?\ }^2$

$= \frac{1}{2} \cdot \underline{\ ?\ } \cdot \underline{\ ?\ } \cdot \underline{\ ?\ }$

$= \underline{\ ?\ }$ cm^2

Area of remaining pizza = area of quadrant + area of semicircle

$= \underline{\ ?\ } + \underline{\ ?\ }$

$= \underline{\ ?\ }$ cm^2

The area of the remaining pizza is approximately $\underline{\ ?\ }$ square centimeters.

5 A rug is made up of a quadrant and two semicircles. Find the area of the rug.

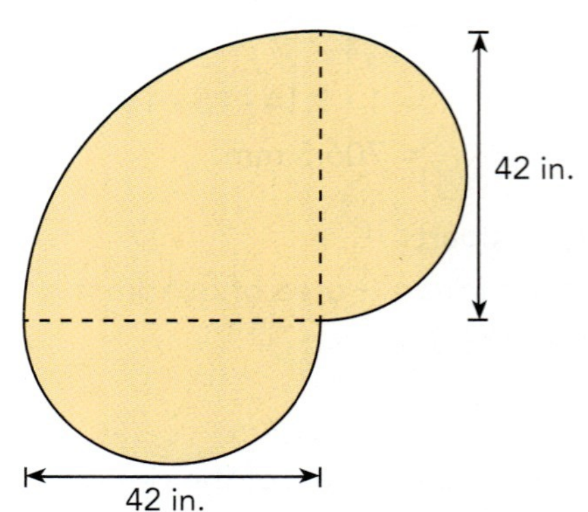

Area of quadrant $= \frac{1}{4} \cdot \pi r^2$

$\approx \frac{1}{4} \cdot \underline{\ ?\ } \cdot \underline{\ ?\ }^2$

$= \frac{1}{4} \cdot \underline{\ ?\ } \cdot \underline{\ ?\ } \cdot \underline{\ ?\ }$

$= \underline{\ ?\ }$ in.^{2}

Radius of semicircle = diameter ÷ 2

$= \underline{\ ?\ } \div \underline{\ ?\ }$

$= \underline{\ ?\ }$ in.

$$\text{Total area of two semicircles} = 2 \cdot \frac{1}{2} \cdot \pi r^2$$
$$\approx \underline{\ ?\ } \cdot \underline{\ ?\ } \cdot \underline{\ ?\ } \cdot \underline{\ ?\ }^2$$
$$= 1 \cdot \underline{\ ?\ } \cdot \underline{\ ?\ } \cdot \underline{\ ?\ }$$
$$= \underline{\ ?\ } \text{ in.}^2$$

Area of figure = area of quadrant + total area of two semicircles

$$= \underline{\ ?\ } + \underline{\ ?\ }$$
$$= \underline{\ ?\ } \text{ in.}^2$$

The area of the rug is approximately ___?___ square inches.

Learn Solve real-world problems involving rates and circles.

1 The tire of a car has a radius of 10.5 inches. How many revolutions does the tire need to make for the car to travel 13,200 inches? Use $\frac{22}{7}$ as an approximation for π.

$$\text{Circumference of tire} = 2\pi r$$
$$\approx 2 \cdot \frac{22}{7} \cdot 10.5$$
$$= \frac{22}{\cancel{7}_1} \cdot \cancel{21}^3$$
$$= 66 \text{ in.}$$

The car travels approximately 66 inches with one revolution of the tire.

$$\text{Number of revolutions} = \text{distance} \div \text{circumference of tire}$$
$$= 13{,}200 \div 66$$
$$= 200$$

The tire needs to make approximately 200 revolutions to travel 13,200 inches.

Continue on next page

2 A field is shaped like the diagram below. It is a rectangle with semicircles at the two ends. There is a running track around the field. Use 3.14 as an approximation for π.

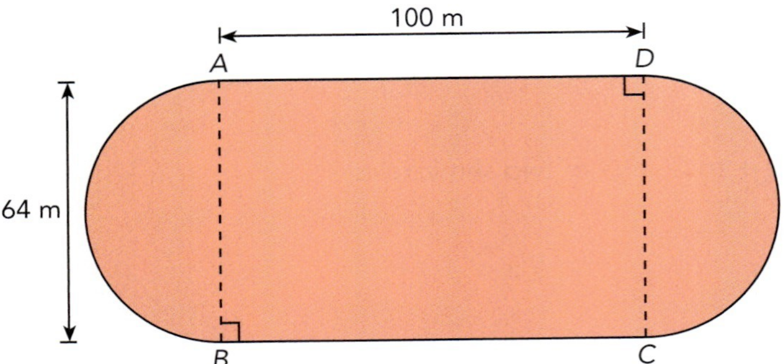

a) Find the length of the running track. Round your answer to the nearest ten meters.

Semicircular arcs AB and DC have the same length.

$$\begin{aligned}\text{Total length of semicircular arcs } AB \text{ and } DC &= 2 \cdot \frac{1}{2} \cdot \pi d \\ &= 1 \cdot \pi d \\ &\approx 1 \cdot 3.14 \cdot 64 \\ &= 200.96 \text{ m}\end{aligned}$$

$$\begin{aligned}\text{Length of running track } &= \text{total length of semicircular arcs } AB \text{ and } DC + AD + BC \\ &= 200.96 + 100 + 100 \\ &= 400.96 \text{ m} \\ &\approx 400 \text{ m} \qquad \text{Round to the nearest ten meters.}\end{aligned}$$

The length of the running track is approximately 400 meters.

b) An athlete ran around the track one time at an average speed of 8 meters per second. How many seconds did it take him to run around the track?

$$\begin{aligned}\text{Time taken } &= \text{distance} \div \text{speed} \\ &\approx 400 \div 8 \qquad \text{Substitute.} \\ &= 50 \text{ s} \qquad \text{Divide.}\end{aligned}$$

It took the athlete approximately 50 seconds to run one time around the track.

c) A gardener is hired to cut the grass in the field. She cuts the grass at an average rate of 40 square meters per minute. How many hours will she take to finish the entire field? Round your answer to the nearest hour.

The areas of the two semicircles are equal.

Radius of circle = diameter ÷ 2
= 64 ÷ 2
= 32 m

Total area of two semicircles $= 2 \cdot \frac{1}{2} \cdot \pi r^2$ Write formula.

$\approx {}^{1}\not{2} \cdot \frac{1}{{}_{1}\not{2}} \cdot 3.14 \cdot 32^2$ Substitute. Divide by the common factor, 2.

$= 1 \cdot 3.14 \cdot 32 \cdot 32$ Simplify.

$= 3{,}215.36 \text{ m}^2$ Multiply.

Area of rectangle $ABCD = \ell w$

$= 100 \cdot 64$ Substitute.

$= 6{,}400 \text{ m}^2$ Multiply.

Area of field = area of rectangle $ABCD$ + total area of two semicircles
= 6,400 + 3,215.36
= $9{,}615.36 \text{ m}^2$

Time taken by gardener = area of field ÷ rate of cutting grass

≈ 9,615.36 ÷ 40 Substitute.

= 240.384 min Divide by 60 to convert to hours.

= 4.0064 h

≈ 4 h Round to the nearest hour.

The gardener will take approximately 4 hours to finish the entire field.

Guided Practice

Complete. Use $\frac{22}{7}$ as an approximation for π.

6 The diameter of a bicycle wheel is 60 centimeters. How far does the wheel travel when it makes 35 revolutions? Give your answer in meters.

Circumference of wheel $= \pi d$

≈ __?__ · __?__

= __?__ cm

Distance traveled = circumference of wheel · number of revolutions

= __?__ · __?__

= __?__ cm

= __?__ m Divide by 100 to convert to meters.

The wheel travels approximately __?__ meters.

7 A park is shaped like the diagram below. It is a rectangle with semicircles at the two ends. There is a running track around the park.

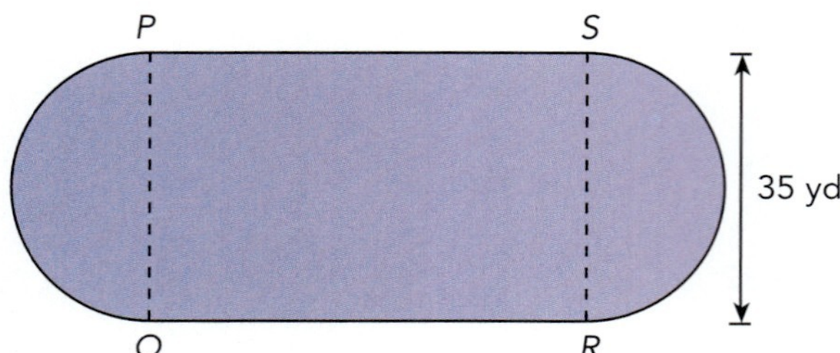

a) The total length of the track is 220 yards. Find the length of $\overline{PS}$.

The track is made up of semicircular arcs *PQ* and *SR*, and sides *PS* and *QR*. Semicircular arcs *PQ* and *SR* are equal.

Total length of semicircular arcs *PQ* and *SR*

$= 2 \cdot \frac{1}{2} \cdot \pi d$

$\approx 1 \cdot \underline{\ ?\ } \cdot \underline{\ ?\ }$

$= \underline{\ ?\ }$ yd

The length of $\overline{PS}$ and $\overline{QR}$ are equal.

Total length of track $= 220$

$PS + QR +$ total length of semicircular arcs PQ and $SR = 220$

$PS + QR + \underline{\ ?\ } = 220$ Substitute.

$PS + QR = 220$ (?) $\underline{\ ?\ }$ Solve equation.

$2 \cdot PS = \underline{\ ?\ }$

$PS = \underline{\ ?\ }$ (?) $\underline{\ ?\ }$

$= \underline{\ ?\ }$ yd

The length of $\overline{PS}$ is approximately $\underline{\ ?\ }$ yards.

b) A jogger runs once around the track in 125 seconds. What is his average speed in yards per second?

The jogger runs $\underline{\ ?\ }$ yards in 125 seconds.

125 seconds → $\underline{\ ?\ }$

1 second → $\underline{\ ?\ }$ (?) $\underline{\ ?\ }$

$= \underline{\ ?\ }$ yd

The average speed of the jogger is $\underline{\ ?\ }$ yards per second.

c) A gardener is hired to water the grass in the park. Using a machine, he waters 4 square yards per second. How many minutes will he take to water the entire park? Round your answer to the nearest minute.

Radius = diameter ÷ 2

= ___?___ ÷ 2

= ___?___ yd

The areas of the two semicircles are equal.

Total area of two semicircles $= 2 \cdot \frac{1}{2} \cdot \pi r^2$

$\approx 2 \cdot \frac{1}{2} \cdot$ ___?___ $\cdot$ ___?___^{2}

$= 1 \cdot$ ___?___ $\cdot$ ___?___ $\cdot$ ___?___

= ___?___ yd^2

Area of rectangle *PQRS* $= \ell w$

= ___?___ $\cdot$ ___?___

= ___?___ yd^2

Area of park = area of rectangle *PQRS* + total area of two semicircles

= ___?___ + ___?___

= ___?___ yd^2

Time taken = area of park ÷ rate of watering park

= ___?___ ÷ ___?___

= ___?___ s

= ___?___ min

≈ ___?___ min   Round to the nearest minute.

To find the time taken to water the park, think:
Rate of watering = area of park ÷ time taken
You can write this equation as:
Time taken = area of park ÷ rate of watering park
Remember to express the answer in minutes, not seconds.

The gardener will take approximately ___?___ minutes to water the entire park.

Practice 11.3

Solve. Show your work.

1. The radius of a circular pond is 8 meters. Find its area and circumference. Use 3.14 as an approximation for π.

2. The diameter of a metal disc is 26 centimeters. Find its area and circumference. Use 3.14 as an approximation for π.

3. The shape of a carpet is a semicircle. Use $\frac{22}{7}$ as an approximation for π.

   a) Find its area.

   b) Janice wants to put a fringed border on all sides of the carpet. How many feet of fringe are needed?

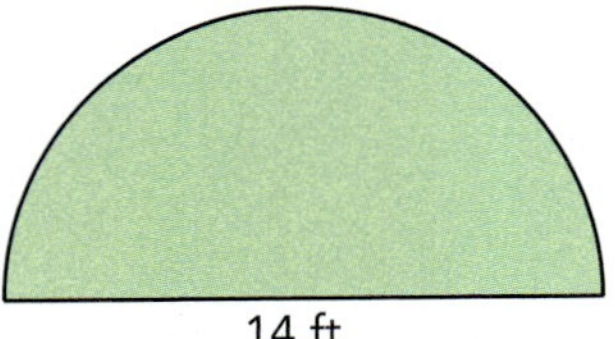

4. The circumference of the rim of a wheel is 301.44 centimeters. Find the diameter of the rim. Use 3.14 as an approximation for π.

5. A Japanese fan is made out of wood and cloth. The shape of the fan is made up of two overlapping quadrants. What is the area of the portion that is made of cloth? Use $\frac{22}{7}$ as an approximation for π.

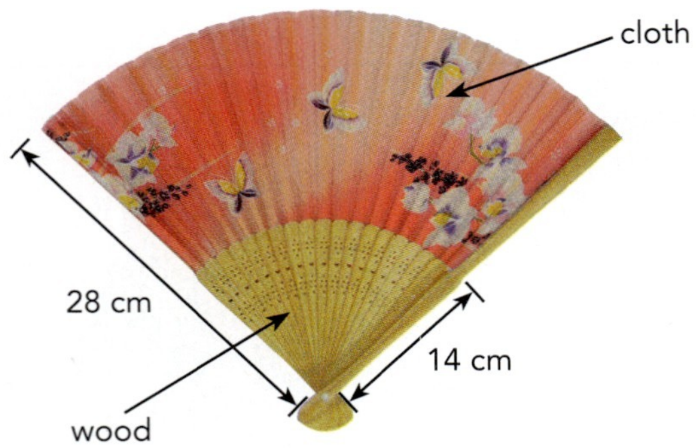

6 A pancake restaurant serves small silver-dollar pancakes and regular-size pancakes. Use 3.14 as an approximation for π.

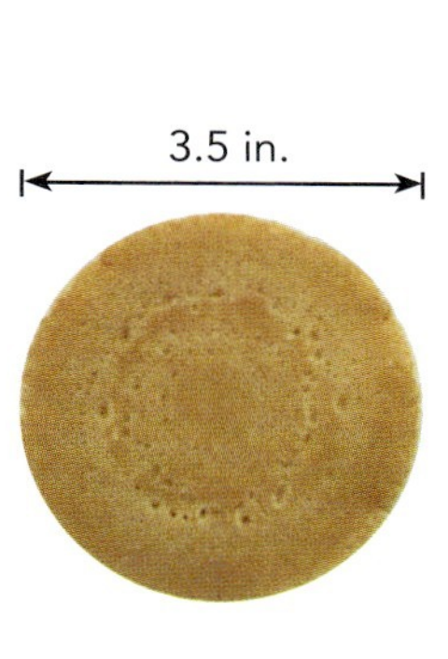

a) What is the area of a small silver dollar-pancake? Round your answer to the nearest tenth of an inch.

b) What is the area of a regular-size pancake? Round your answer to the nearest tenth of a square inch.

c) If the total price of 6 small silver-dollar pancakes is the same as the total price of 3 regular-size pancakes, which is a better deal?

7 A park is shaped like a rectangle with a semicircle on one end, and another semicircle cut out of one side.

a) Find the distance around the park.

b) Find the area of the park.

Use $\frac{22}{7}$ as an approximation for π.

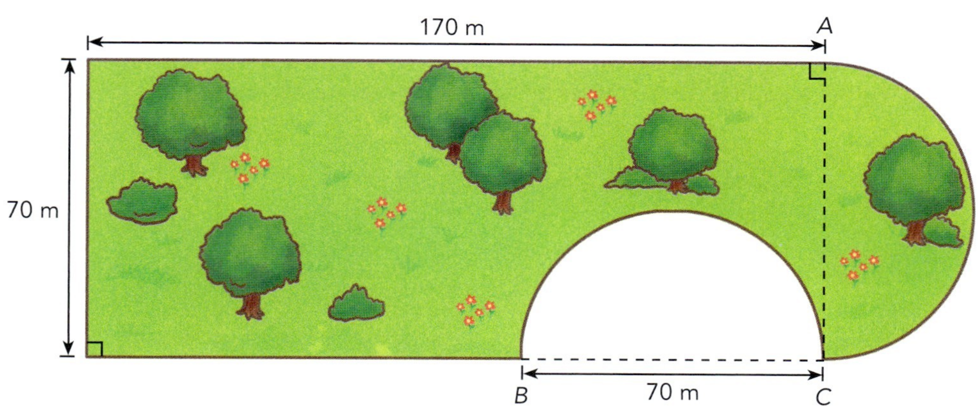

8 The diameter of a circular fountain in a city park is 28 feet. A sidewalk that is 3.5 feet will be built around the fountain. Use $\frac{22}{7}$ as an approximation for π.

a) Find the area of the sidewalk.

b) 0.8 bag of concrete will be needed for every square foot of the new sidewalk. What is the minimum number of bags needed?

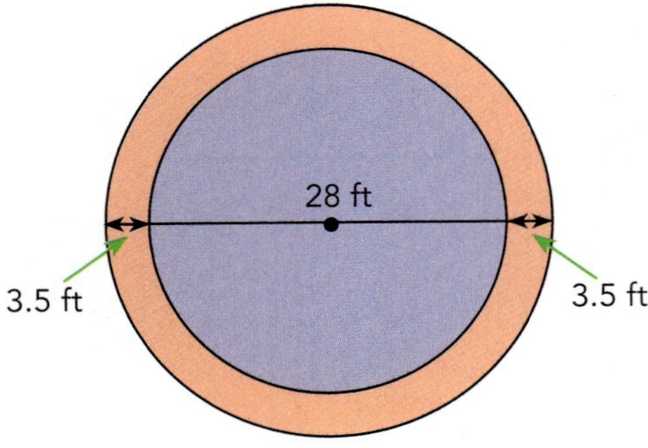

9 The diagram shows an athletic field with a track around it. The track is 4 feet wide. The field is a rectangle with semicircles at the two ends. Find the area of the track. Use 3.14 as an approximation for π.

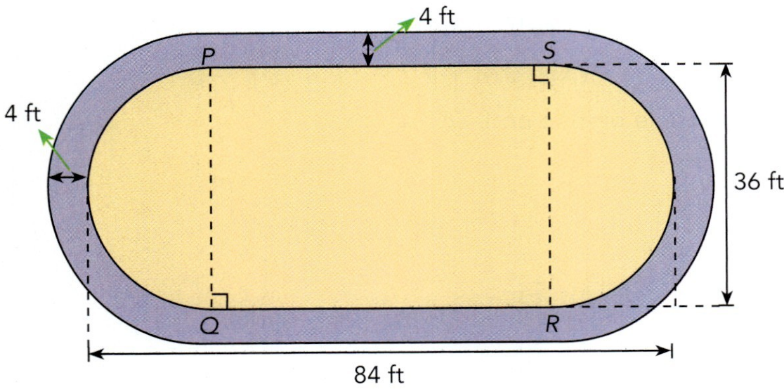

10 The petal of a paper flower is created by cutting along the outlines of two overlapping quadrants within a square. Use 3.14 as an approximation for π.

a) Find the distance around the shaded part.

b) Find the area of the shaded part.

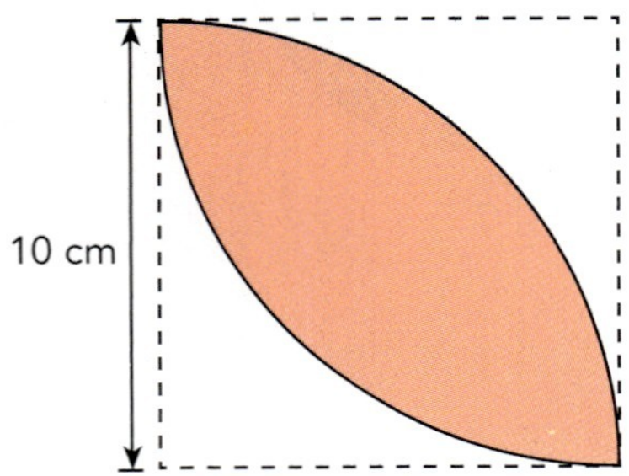

11 Wheels A and B are placed side by side on a straight road. The diameter of wheel A is 56 inches. The diameter of wheel *B* is 35 inches. Suppose each wheel makes 15 revolutions. Find the distance between the wheels after they have made these 15 revolutions.

Use $\frac{22}{7}$ as an approximation for π.

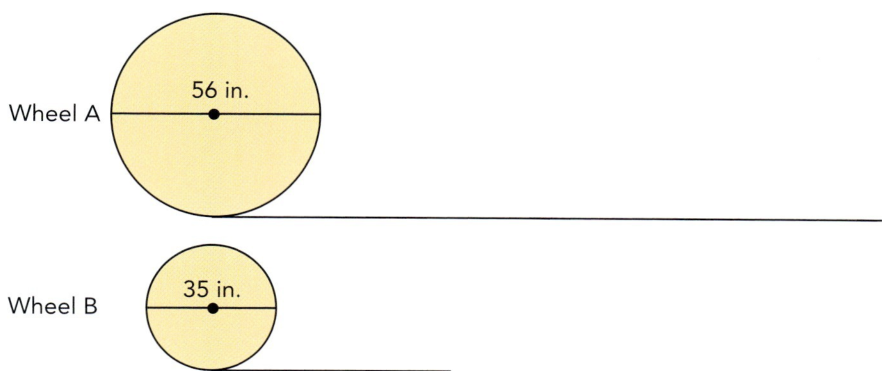

12 Nine identical circles are cut from a square sheet of paper whose sides are 36 centimeters long. If the circles are as large as possible, what is the area of the paper that is left after all the circles are cut out? Use 3.14 as an approximation for π.

13 A designer drew an icon as shown below. *O* is the center of the circle, and $\overline{AB}$ is a diameter. Two semicircles are drawn in the circle. If *AB* is 28 millimeters, find the area of the shaded part. Use $\frac{22}{7}$ as an approximation for π.

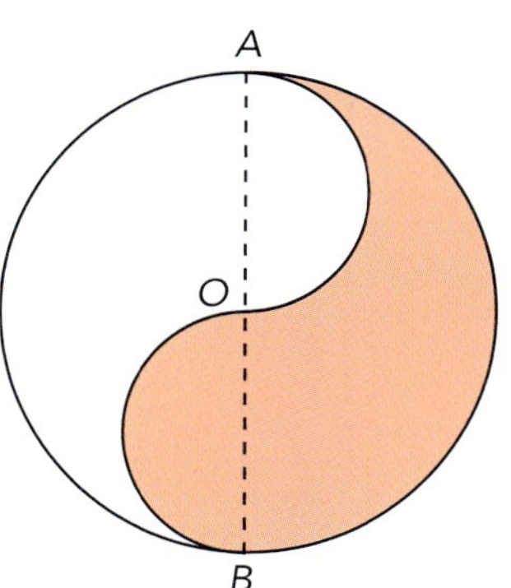

Use graph paper. Solve.

14 Mary wants to draw the plan of a circular park on graph paper. The coordinates of the center of the park are *A* (3, 4). The circle has a radius of 3 units.

a) Use a compass and draw the plan of the circular park on graph paper.

b) Assume that the *y*-axis points north and south. A barbecue pit is located at the northernmost part of the park. Plot and label the location of the barbecue pit as point *B*. Give the coordinates of point *B*.

c) Connect points *A*, *B*, and the origin to form a triangle. Find the area of the triangle.

15 A wire is bent to make the shape below. The shape is made up of four identical circles. Each circle intersects two other circles. The four circles meet at a common point T, which is the center of square $PQRS$. Use $\frac{22}{7}$ as an approximation for π.

a) Find the length of the wire.

b) Find the area of the whole shape.

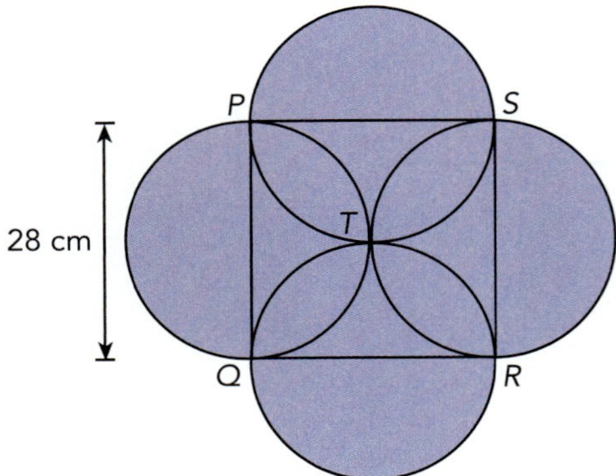

1 The figure shows two identical overlapping quadrants. Find the distance around the shaded part. Use 3.14 as an approximation for π. Round your answer to the nearest tenth of a centimeter.

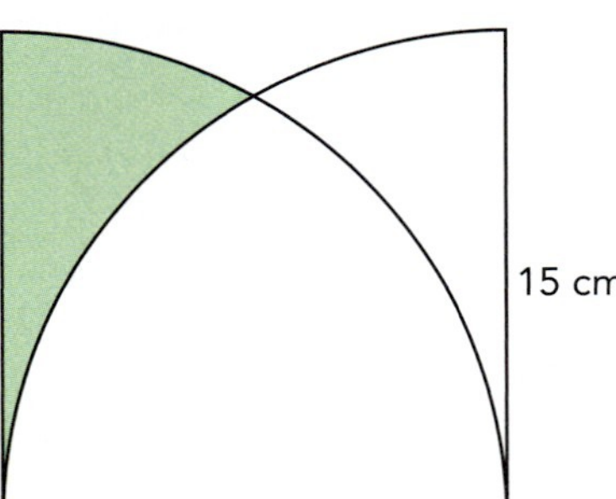

2. A cushion cover design is created from a circle of radius 7 inches, and 4 quadrants. Find the total area of the shaded parts of the design. Use $\frac{22}{7}$ as an approximation for π.

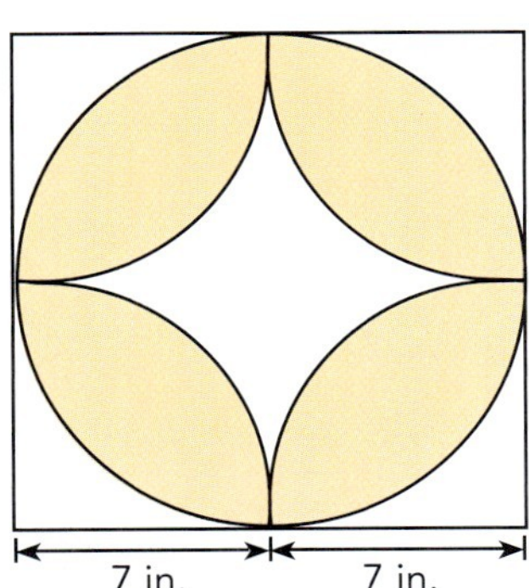

3. Two identical wheels are placed along a straight path so that their centers are 9.31 meters apart. The radius of each wheel is 3.5 centimeters. They are pushed towards each other at the same time, each making one revolution per second. How long does it take for them to knock into each other? Use $\frac{22}{7}$ as an approximation for π.

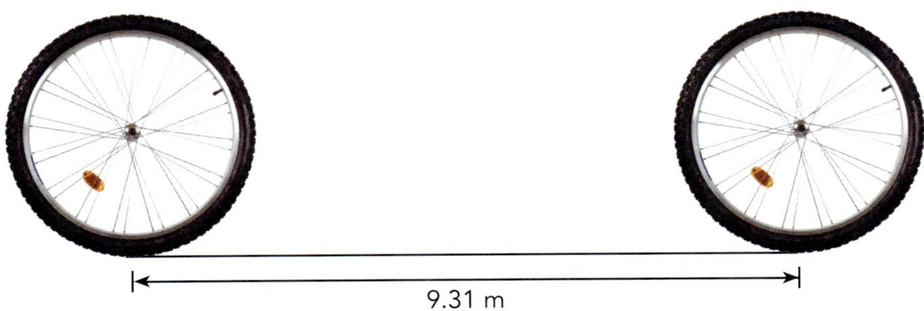

4. A stage prop is made up of a semicircle and a quadrant. Its area is 924 square inches. Find the value of x. Use $\frac{22}{7}$ as an approximation for π.

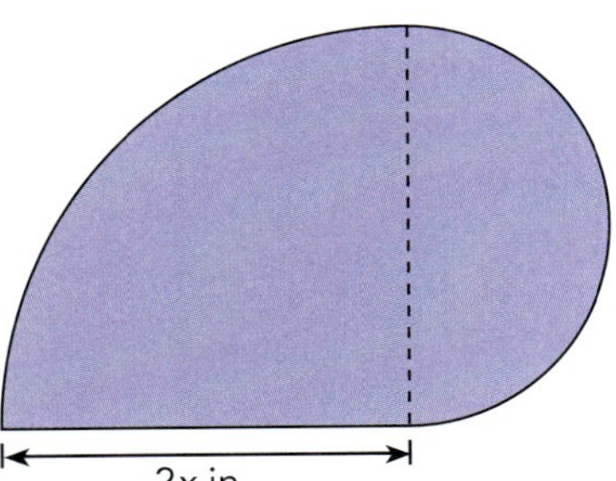

Chapter Wrap Up

Concept Map

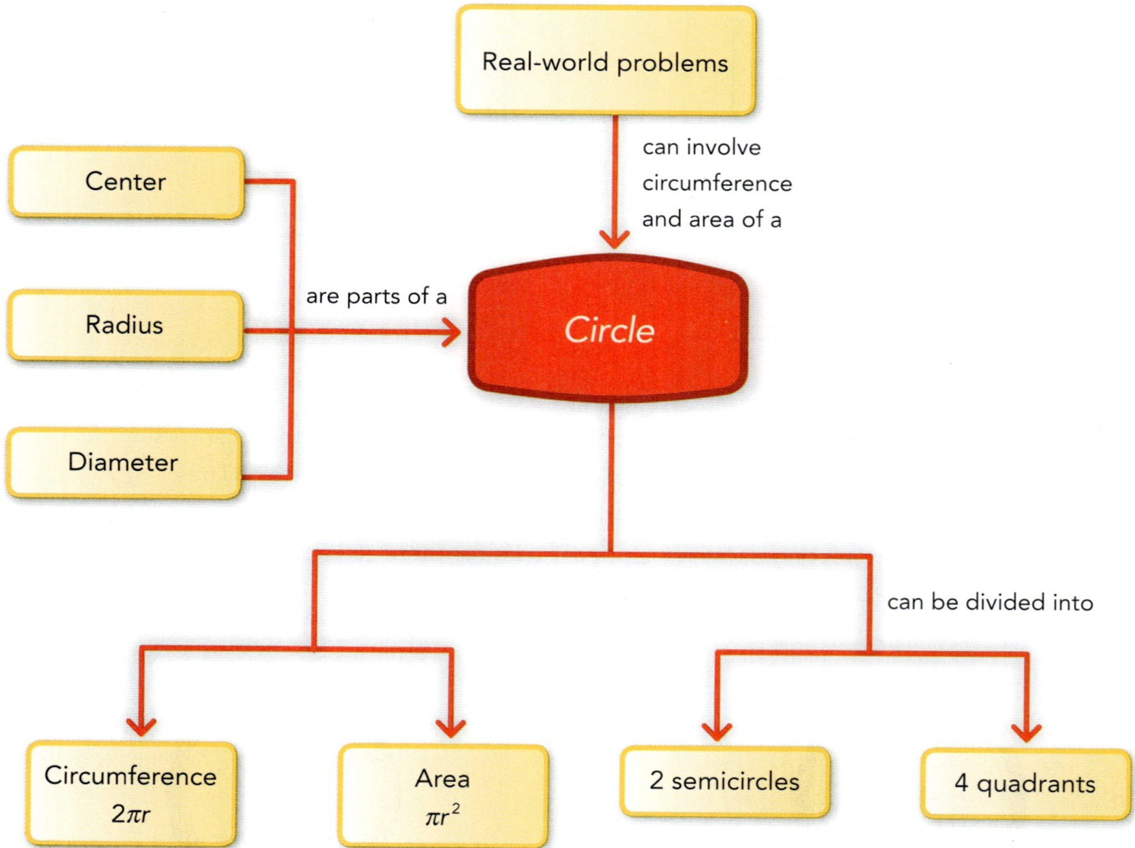

Key Concepts

- All radii of a circle are equal.
- A diameter of a circle is twice its radius.
- The number π is the ratio of the circumference to the diameter of a circle.

Chapter Review/Test

Concepts and Skills

Find the circumference and area of each circle. Use $\frac{22}{7}$ as an approximation for π.

1
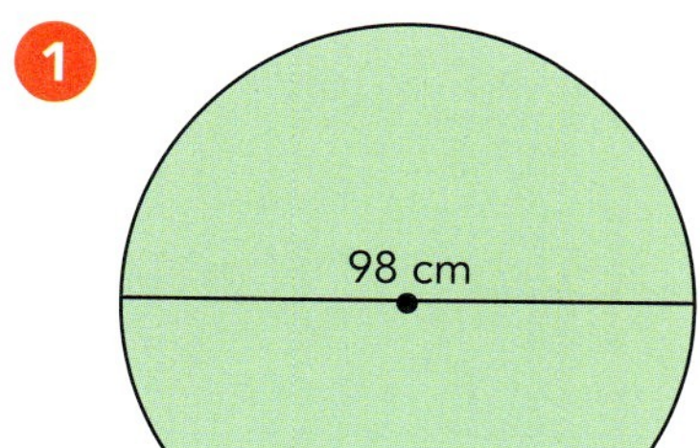

2
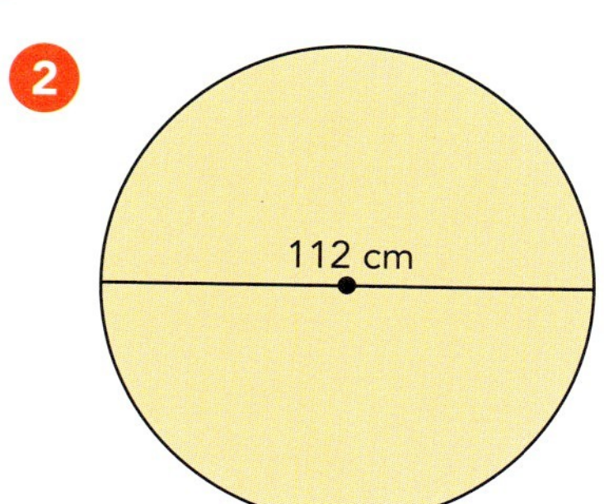

Find the distance around each semicircle. Use $\frac{22}{7}$ as an approximation for π.

3
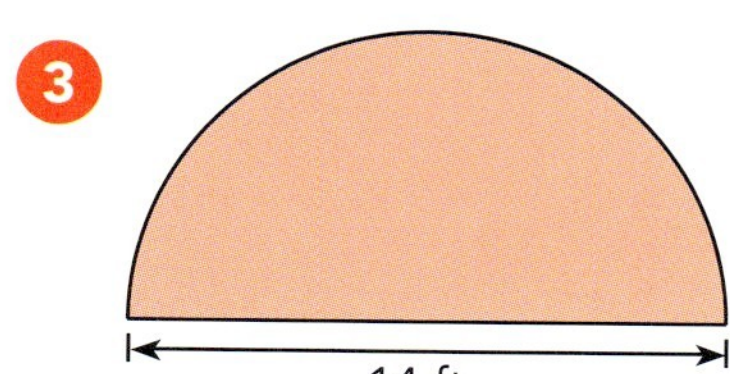

4
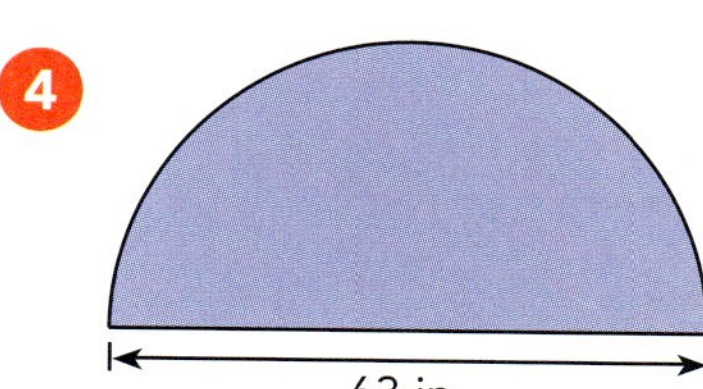

Find the distance around each quadrant. Round your answer to the nearest tenth. Use 3.14 as an approximation for π.

5
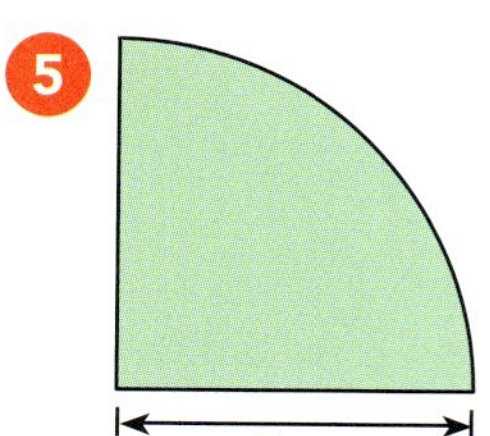

6
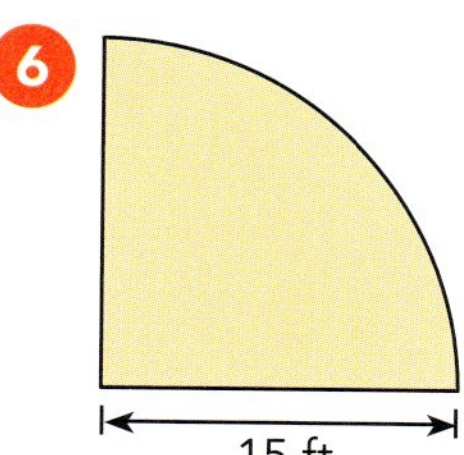

Solve. Show your work.

7. The diameter of a flying disc is 10 inches. Find the circumference and area of the disc. Use 3.14 as an approximation for π.

8. The area of a compact disc is $452\frac{4}{7}$ square centimeters. What is the diameter of the compact disc? Use $\frac{22}{7}$ as an approximation for π.

9. The circumference of a circular table is 816.4 centimeters. Find the radius of the table. Use 3.14 as an approximation for π.

Problem Solving

 **Solve. Show your work.**

10 A water fountain shoots up a jet of water. The water falls back down onto the ground in the shape of a circle. Michelle wants the circle of water on the ground to be 0.7 meter wider on each side. She gradually increases the strength of the water jet. The area of the circle of water increases at 0.2 square meter per second. Use $\frac{22}{7}$ as an approximation for π.

a) Find the area of the original circle of water.

b) Find the area of the larger circle of water.

c) How long does it take for the original circle of water to become the larger circle of water? Round your answer to the nearest second.

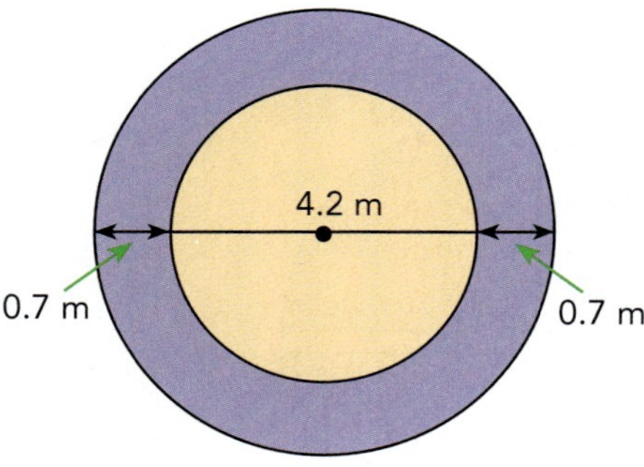

11 A machine in an assembly line stamps pieces of metal. The stamping plate on the machine travels in a path shaped like the arc of a quadrant as the stamping plate opens and closes. It takes the machine 5 seconds to open and close the stamping plate one time. Use $\frac{22}{7}$ as an approximation for π.

a) Find the total distance the outside edge of the stamping plate travels when the machine opens and closes one time.

b) Find the speed of the stamping plate's outside edge in centimeters per second.

c) Assume the machine starts and ends in an open position. How many seconds will it take the machine to stamp 500 pieces of metal?

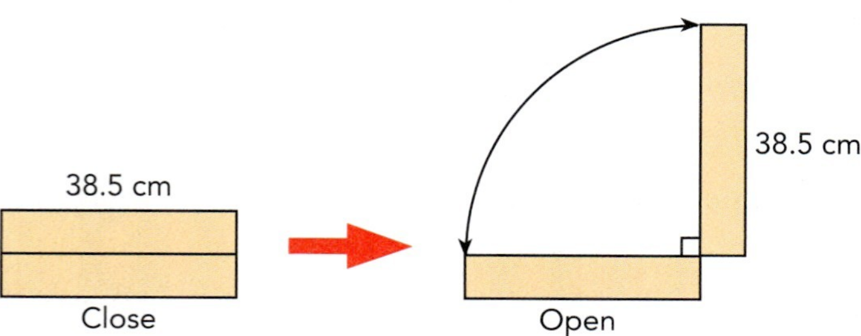

12 The figure shows four identical quadrants enclosed in a square. The side length of the square is 20 inches. Find the area of the blue part. Use 3.14 as an approximation for π.

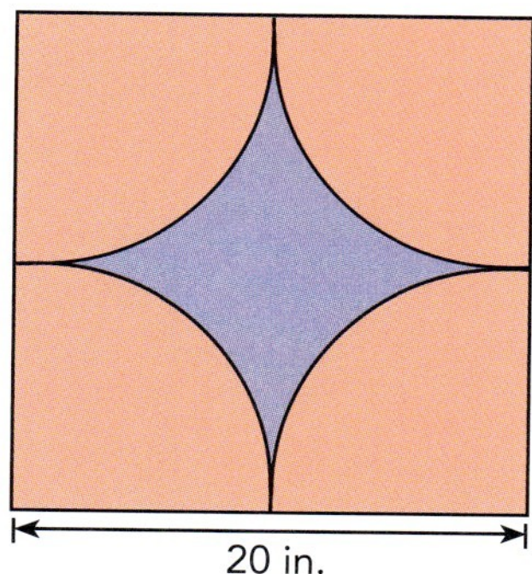

13 The figure shows 3 identical circles. X, Y, and Z are the centers of the circles, and the radius of each circle is 15 feet. $\frac{1}{6}$ of each circle is shaded. What is the total area of the shaded portion? Round your answer to the nearest tenth of a foot. Use 3.14 as an approximation for π.

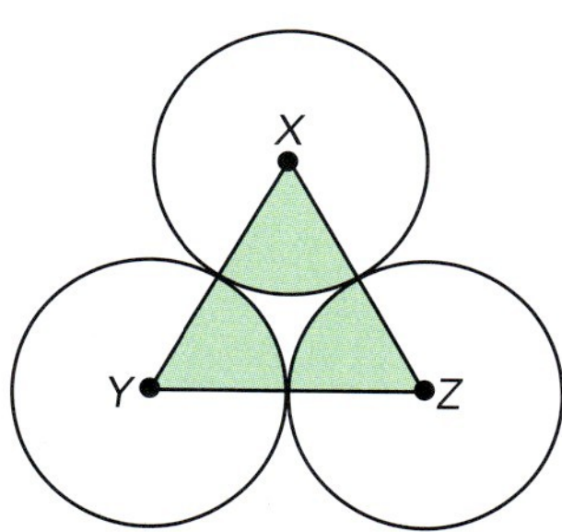

14 The figure is made up of one semicircle and two quadrants. The distance around the figure is 97.29 inches. Find the value of k. Use 3.14 as an approximation for π.

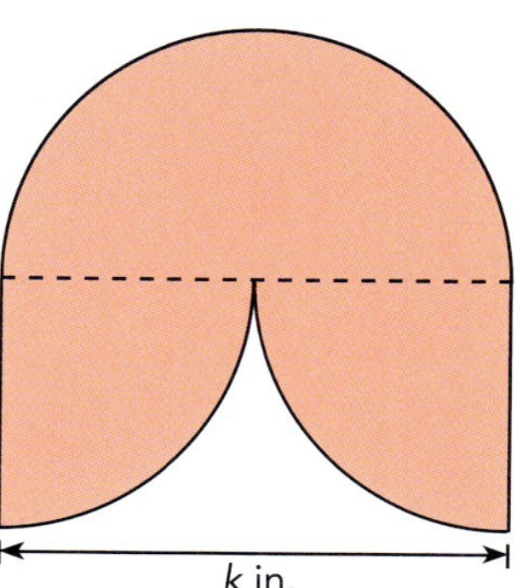

Cumulative Review Chapters 8–11

Concepts and Skills

Represent the solution set of each inequality on a number line. (Lesson 8.3)

1. $p \leq 35$
2. $q \geq 12.6$
3. $r < \frac{4}{5}$
4. $s > 13\frac{1}{2}$

Use graph paper. Plot the points on a coordinate plane and answer the question. (Lesson 9.1)

5. **a)** Plot points A (−2, −2) and B (−10, −2) on a coordinate plane. Connect the two points to form a line segment.

   b) Point C lies above $\overline{AB}$, and is 5 units away from the x-axis. If triangle ABC is an isosceles triangle with base $\overline{AB}$, find the coordinates of point C.

   c) Points D and E lie below $\overline{AB}$ such that $ABDE$ is a rectangle. If BD is 7 units, find the coordinates of points D and E.

Find the area of each figure. (Lesson 10.2)

6. 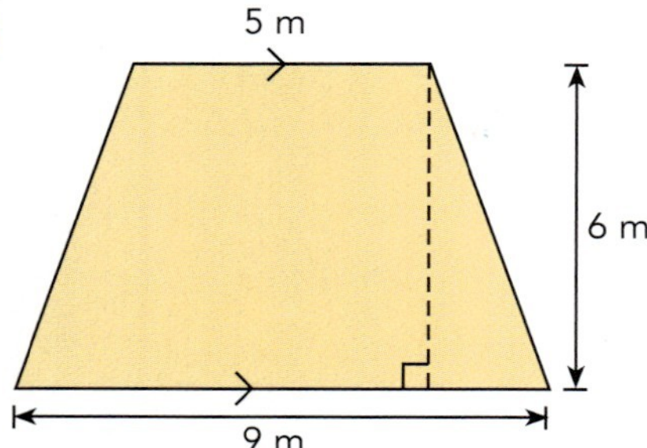

7. 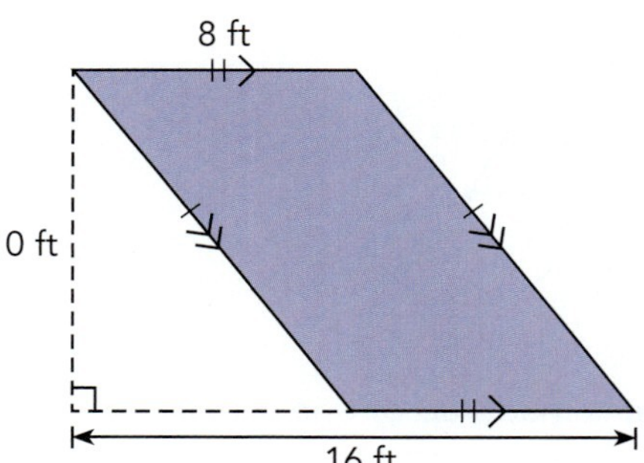

Solve. Show your work. (Lessons 8.2, 11.1, 11.2)

8. The cost of a shirt is p dollars. The cost of a pair of pants is twice the cost of the shirt. If the cost of the pair of pants is t dollars, express t in terms of p.

9. A can has a circular base of diameter 8 centimeters. Find the area of this base. Use 3.14 as an approximation for π.

10. The cross section of a bowl is in the shape of a semicircle. The area of the semicircle is 77 square centimeters. Find its radius. Use $\frac{22}{7}$ as an approximation for π.

11. The circumference of a platinum ring is 44 millimeters. Find its radius. Use $\frac{22}{7}$ as an approximation for π.

Problem Solving

Solve. Show your work.

12 Emily weighs x pounds. Jonathan weighs 3 times as much as Emily. If Jonathan weighs 81 pounds, write an equation in terms of x and solve it. (Chapter 8)

13 Kim has a bag of yo-yos. Some of the yo-yos are red. The rest are yellow. The ratio of the number of red yo-yos to the number of yellow yo-yos is 5 : 9. If Kim has a total of b yo-yos, how many more yellow yo-yos than red yo-yos are there? (Chapter 8)

14 The length of a rectangle is $4n$ centimeters, and it is twice as long as the width. The perimeter of the rectangle is twice as long as that of an equilateral triangle. Find the side length of the triangle in terms of n. (Chapter 10)

15 The length of the minute hand of a clock is 6.5 centimeters. How far does the tip of the minute hand travel in an hour? Use 3.14 as an approximation for π. (Chapter 11)

16 The area of trapezoid $ABCE$ is 36 square meters. Find the height of the trapezoid. (Chapter 10)

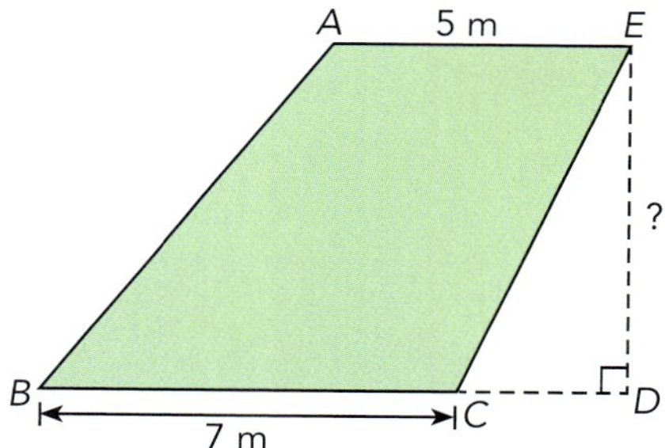

Find the area of the shaded region. (Chapter 10)

17

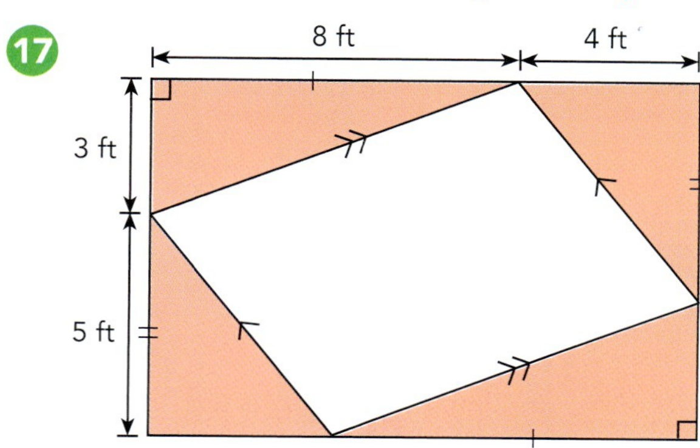

18

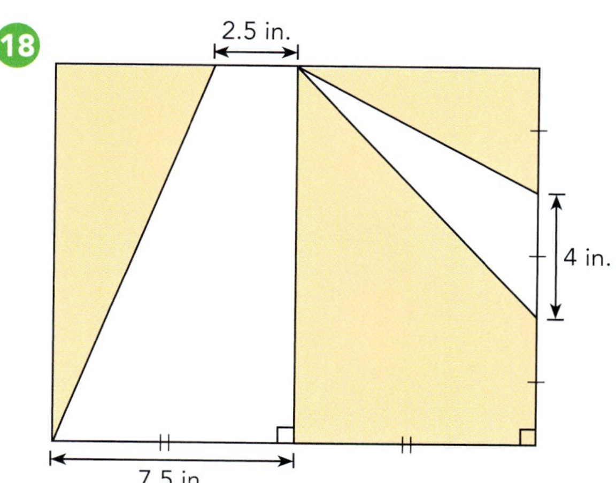

Find the area of the shaded region. Use 3.14 as an approximation for π. (Chapters 10, 11)

19 **20**

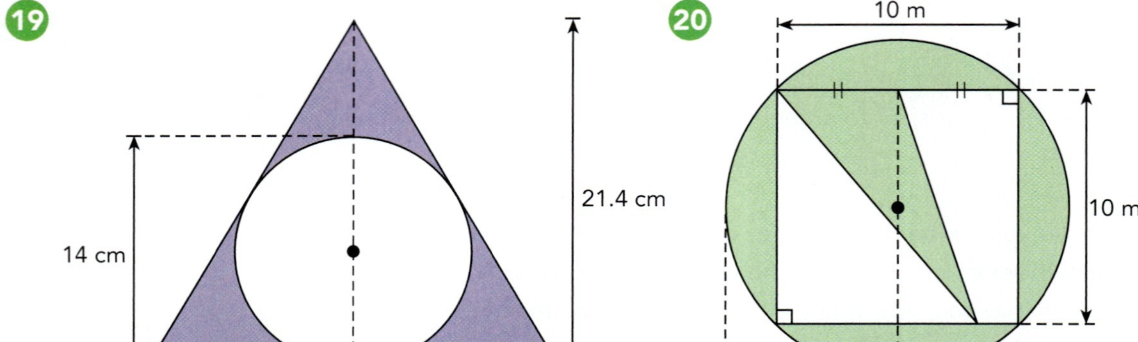

Solve.

21 The diagram shows the plan of a square garden. The side length of each grid square is 2 meters. (Chapters 9, 10)

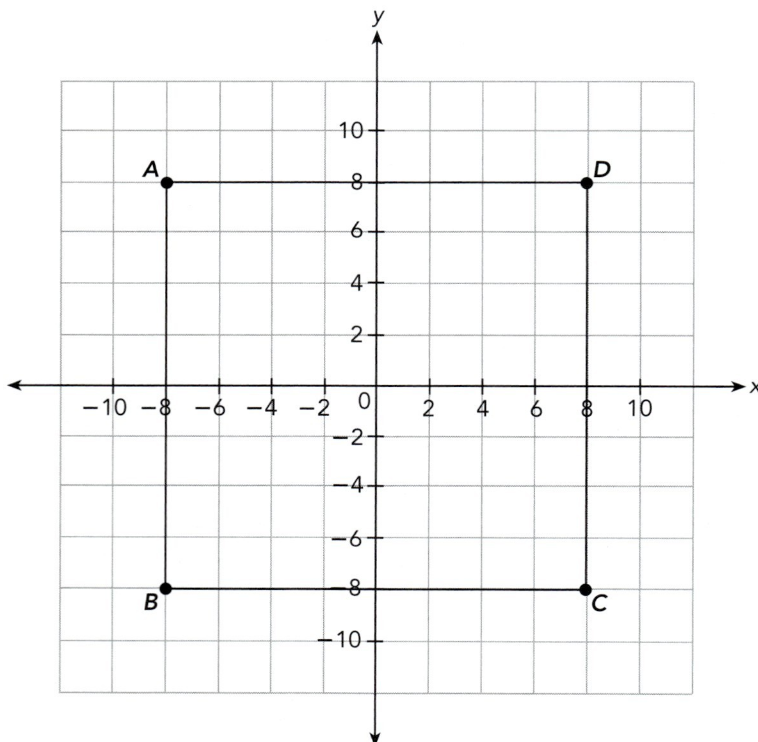

a) A triangular region ABP is surrounded with a wooden fence. The shortest possible distance from point P to $\overline{AB}$ is 8 meters, and triangle ABP is an isosceles triangle with base $\overline{AB}$. Find the coordinates of point P.

b) Find the area and perimeter of the garden.

c) Find the area of the garden that lies outside triangle ABP in square meters.

Solve. Use graph paper to answer the question.

22 An aspen tree is 300 centimeters tall. It grows 15 centimeters taller each month. The height of the tree, h centimeters, over t months is given by $h = 300 + 15t$. Copy and complete the table. Graph the relationship between t and h. Use 1 unit on the horizontal axis to represent 1 month and 1 unit on the vertical axis to represent 15 centimeters. Start your vertical axis at 300 centimeters. (Chapters 8, 9)

a)

Time *t* (months)	0	?	4	6	8
Height *h* (centimeters)	300	330	360	?	?

b) What is the height of the tree after 3 months?

c) Assuming the growth of the tree is constant for the next year, what is the height of the tree after 10 months?

d) If the tree is at least 360 centimeters tall, how many months have passed? Express your answer in the form of an inequality in terms of t, where t stands for the number of months that have passed.

e) Name the dependent and independent variables.

Solve. Show your work.

23 A circular garden is surrounded by a cement path that is 1.5 meters wide. Find the area of the path. Use 3.14 as an approximation for π. (Chapter 11)

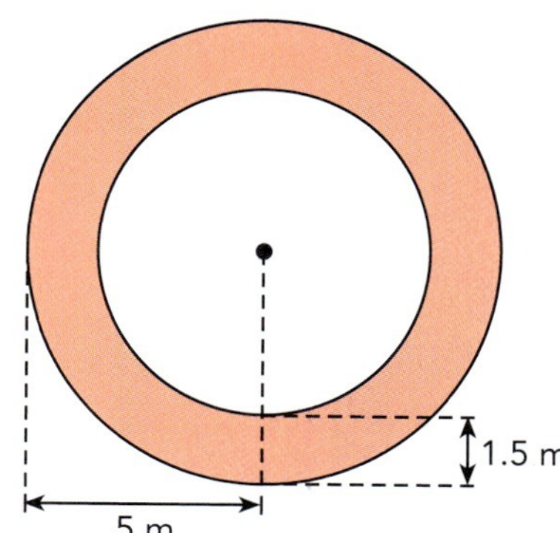

24 Figure $PRSV$ is a parallelogram. The length of $\overline{VU}$ and $\overline{UT}$ are equal. The area of parallelogram $QRSW$ is 30 square inches. The length of $\overline{RS}$ is 6 inches. (Chapter 10)

a) Find the height of parallelogram $QRSW$.

b) Find the area of triangle PRV.

c) If you did not know the length of $\overline{RS}$, explain how you could find the area of triangle PRV.

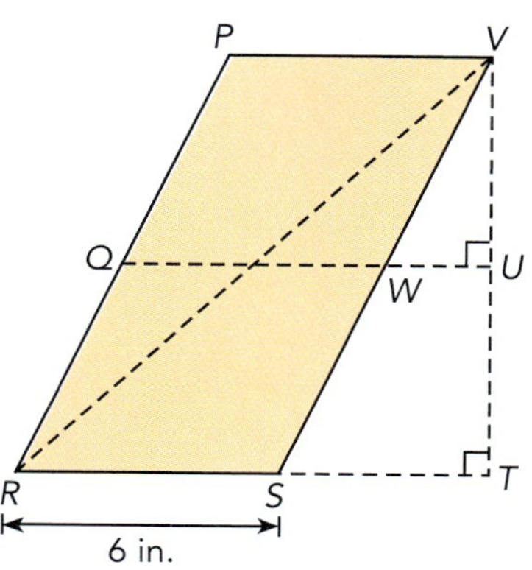

Surface Area and Volume of Solids

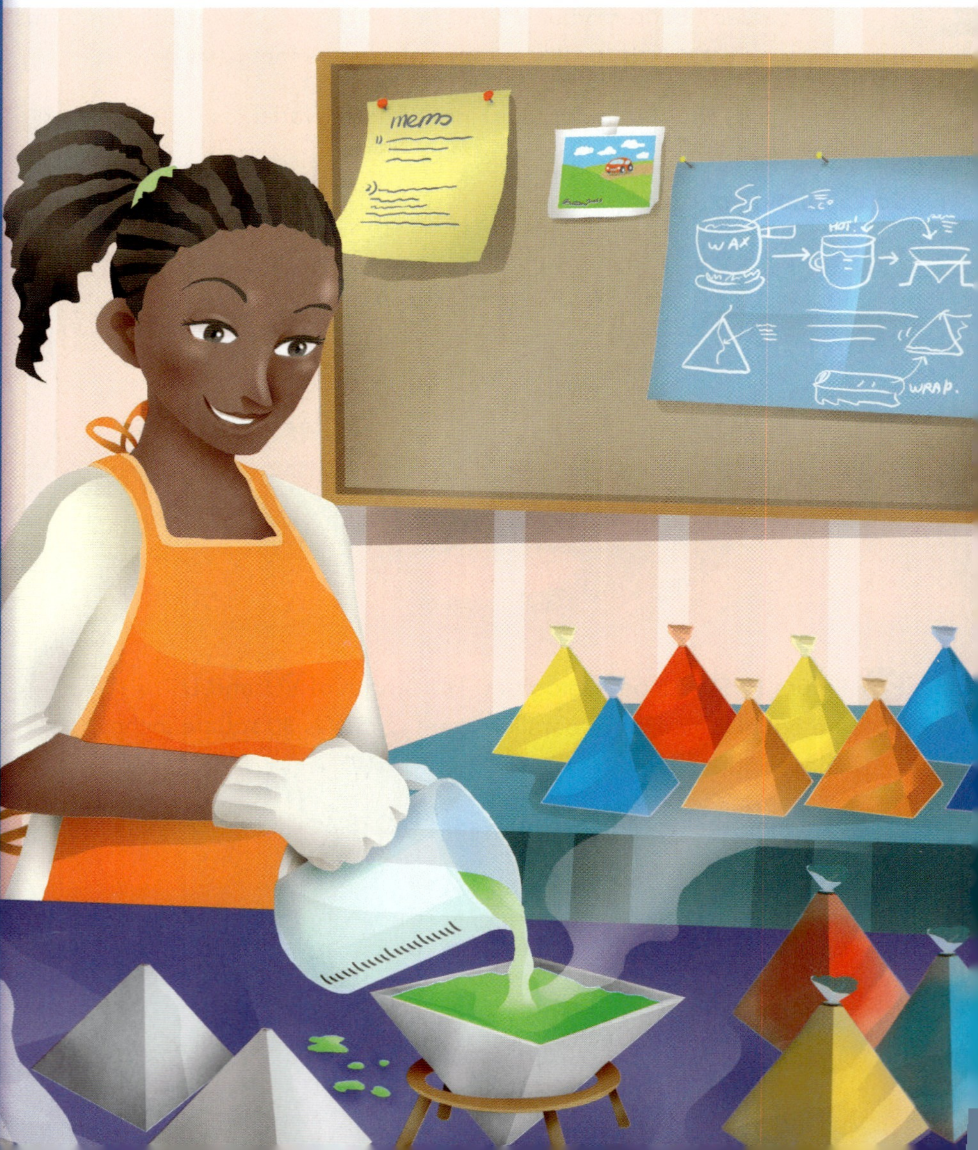

BIG IDEA

- Area is measured in square units, and the surface area of a prism or pyramid is the sum of the areas of its faces. Volume is measured in cubic units, and the volume of a prism is the area of its base times its height.

How can math help you make candles?

To make a candle, you need some wax, a mold, and a wick. Then you melt the wax, pour it into the mold, and insert the wick. When the wax has cooled and hardened, you can wrap the candle in plastic.

How much wax will you need? To find out, you can find the volume of the mold. How much plastic wrap will you need? To find out, you can find the surface area of the candle.

Recall Prior Knowledge

Identifying special prisms

A prism is a solid with two parallel congruent bases joined by faces that are parallelograms. A prism is named by the shape of its base.

Cube

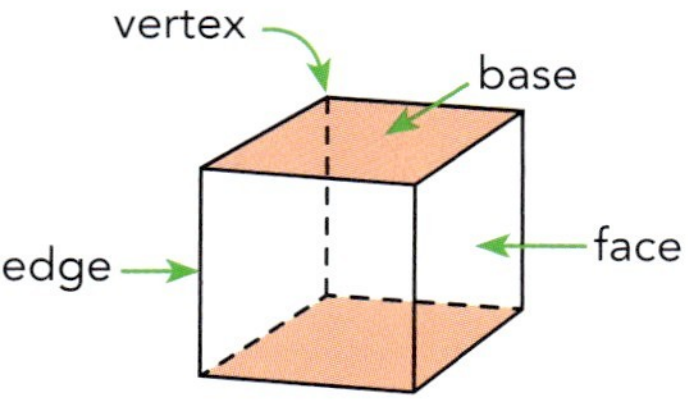

Each base of a cube is a square.

Rectangular prism

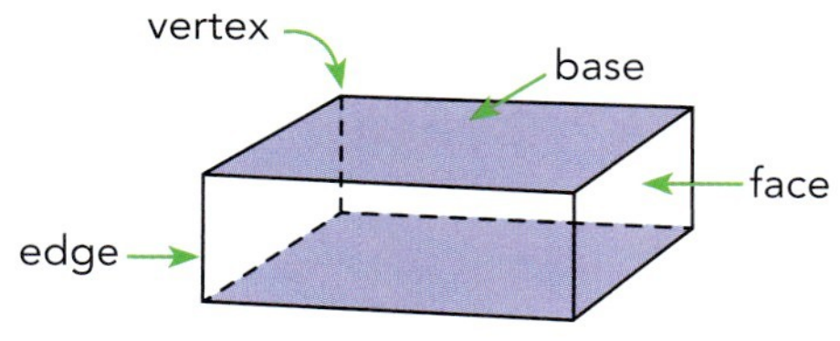

Each base of a rectangular prism is a rectangle.

Triangular prism

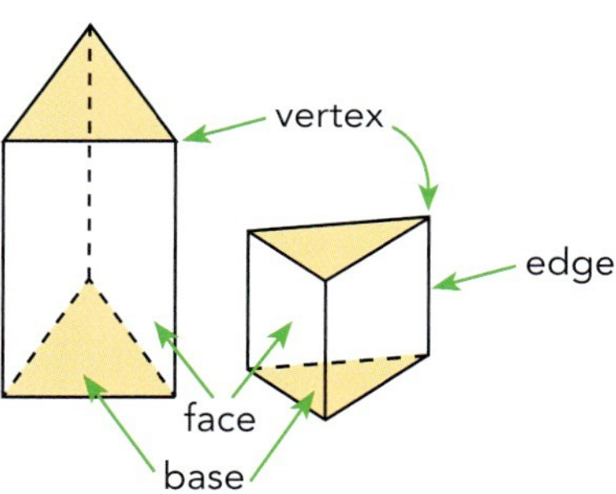

Each base of a triangular prism is a triangle.

Quick Check

Name each prism. In each prism, identify a base, a face, an edge, and a vertex.

1. 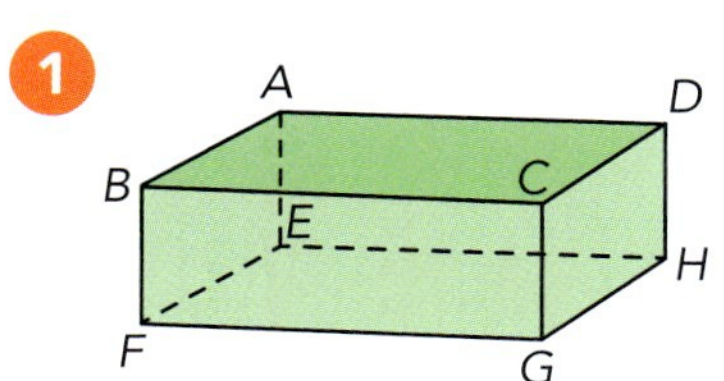

2. 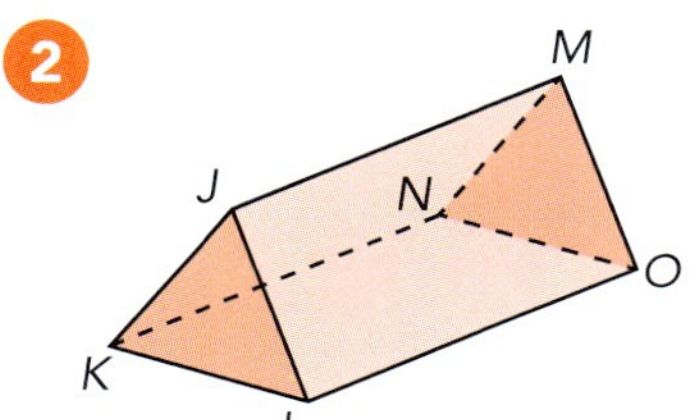

3. 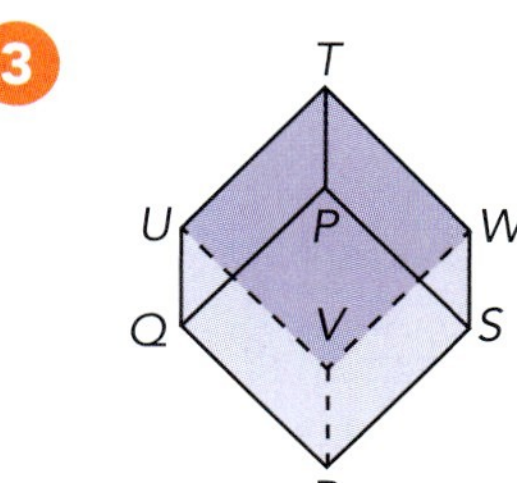

Finding the areas of rectangles, triangles, and trapezoids

Rectangle

width (w)

length (ℓ)

Area of rectangle

= length · width

$A = \ell \cdot w$ or ℓw

Triangle

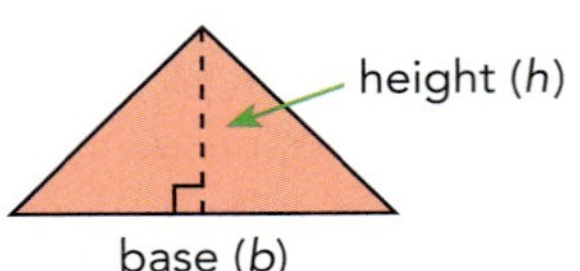

Area of triangle

$= \frac{1}{2} \cdot$ base · height

$A = \frac{1}{2} \cdot b \cdot h$ or $\frac{1}{2}bh$

Trapezoid

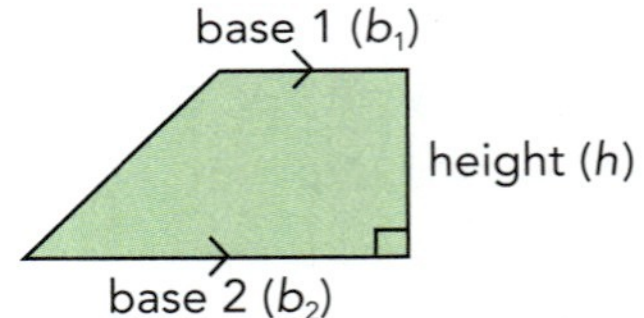

Area of trapezoid

$= \frac{1}{2} \cdot$ height · sum of parallel sides

$A = \frac{1}{2} \cdot h \cdot (b_1 + b_2)$ or $\frac{1}{2}h(b_1 + b_2)$

Quick Check

Find the area of each figure.

4

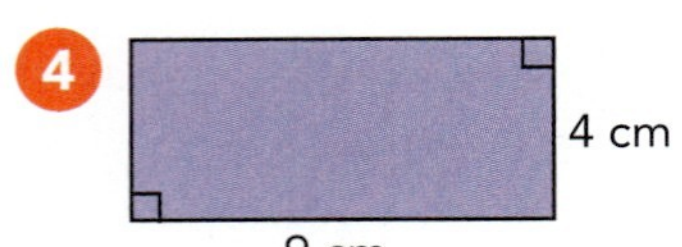

Area = ___?___ · ___?___

= ___?___ cm^2

5

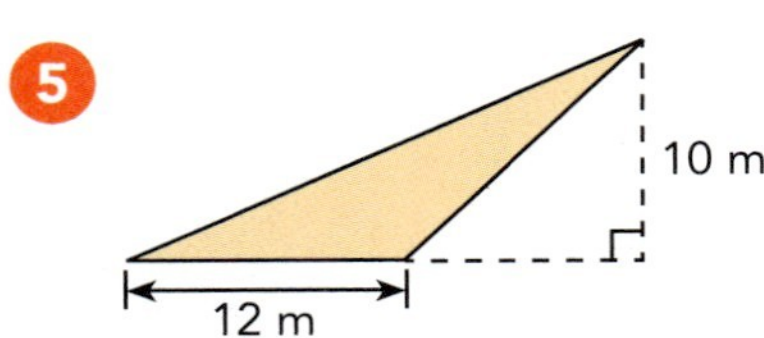

Area $= \frac{1}{2} \cdot$ ___?___ · ___?___

= ___?___ m^2

6

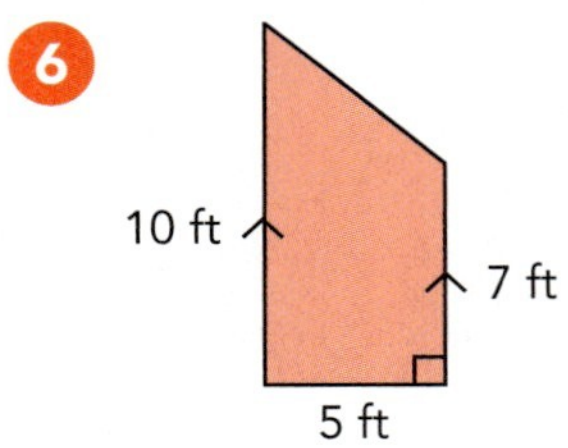

Area $= \frac{1}{2} \cdot$ ___?___ · (___?___ + ___?___)

$= \frac{1}{2} \cdot$ ___?___ · ___?___

= ___?___ ft^2

7

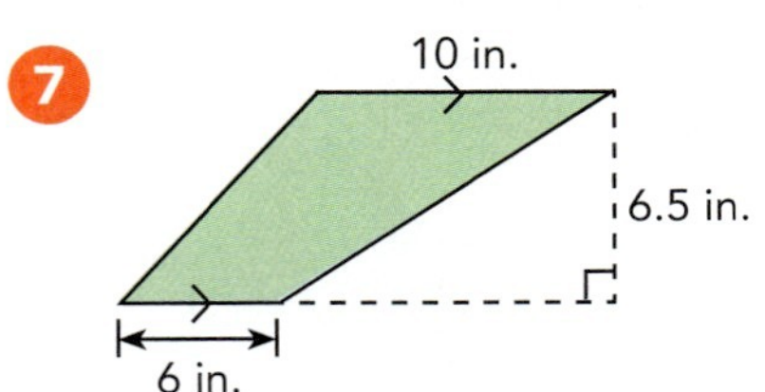

Area $= \frac{1}{2} \cdot$ ___?___ · (___?___ + ___?___)

$= \frac{1}{2} \cdot$ ___?___ · ___?___

= ___?___ in.^2

Finding the volumes of rectangular prisms

Cube

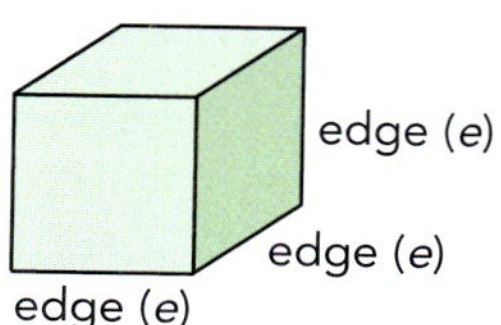

Volume of cube
= edge · edge · edge
$V = e \cdot e \cdot e$ or e^3

Rectangular prism

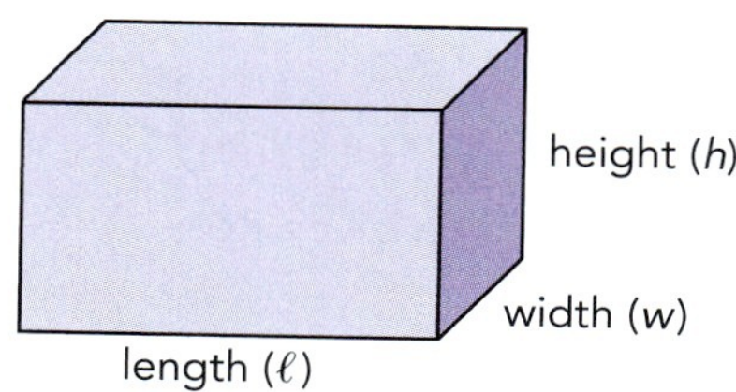

Volume of rectangular prism
= length · width · height
$V = \ell \cdot w \cdot h$ or ℓwh

Quick Check

Find the volume of each solid.

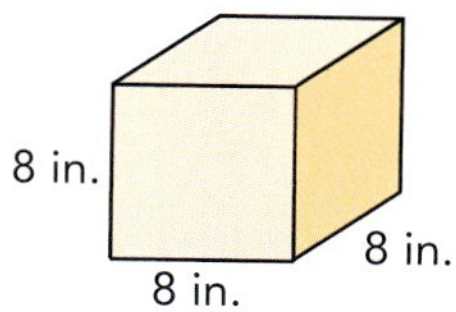

Volume = __?__ · __?__ · __?__

= __?__ in.^{3}

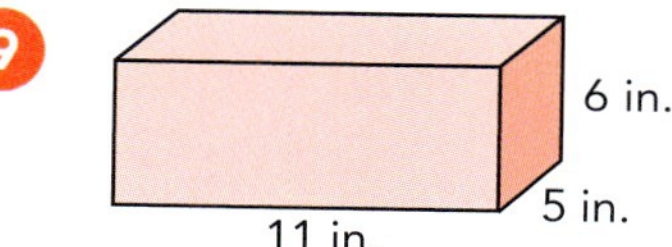

Volume = __?__ · __?__ · __?__

= __?__ in.^{3}

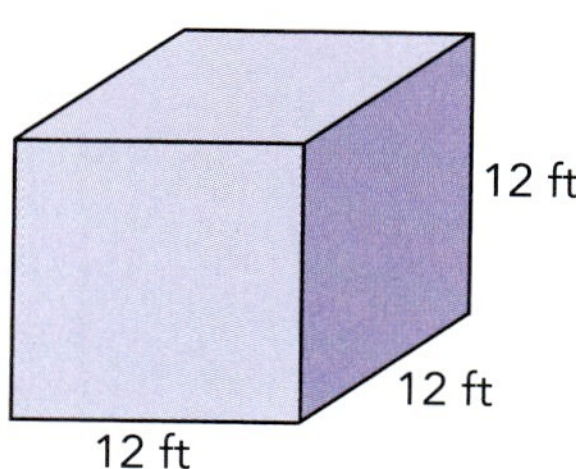

Volume = __?__ · __?__ · __?__

= __?__ ft^3

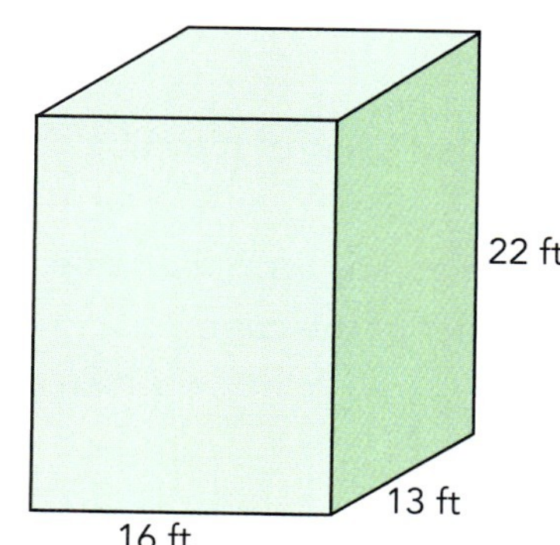

Volume = __?__ · __?__ · __?__

= __?__ ft^3

12.1 Nets of Solids

Lesson Objectives

- Identify the nets of a prism and a pyramid.
- Identify the solid formed by a given net.

Vocabulary

net pyramid

Learn Recognize the net of a cube.

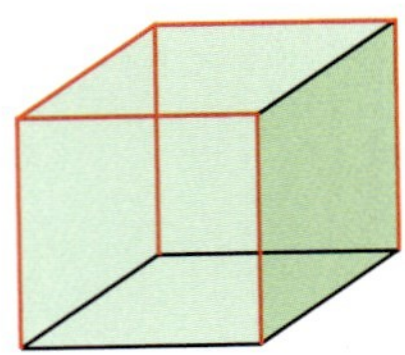

A cube is a type of prism. It can be cut along the red edges and flattened as shown.

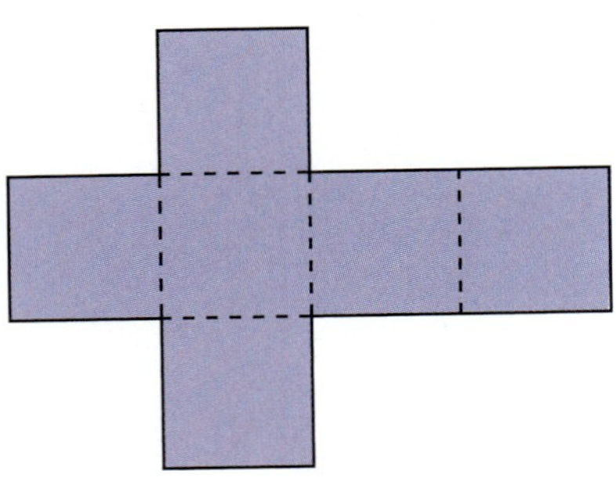

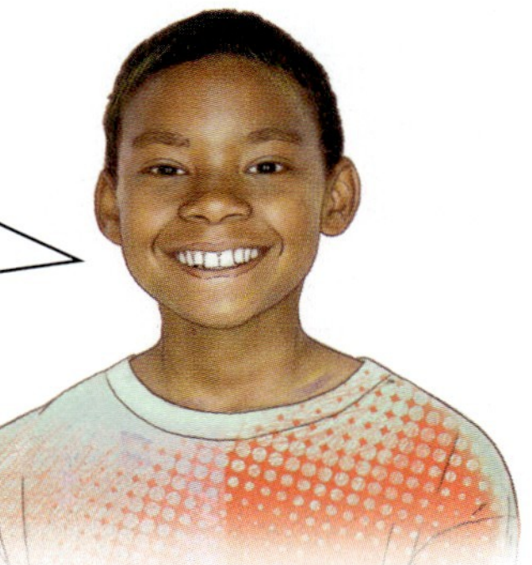

This figure is called a net of the cube.

More than one net may form the same solid figure. This is another net of the cube.

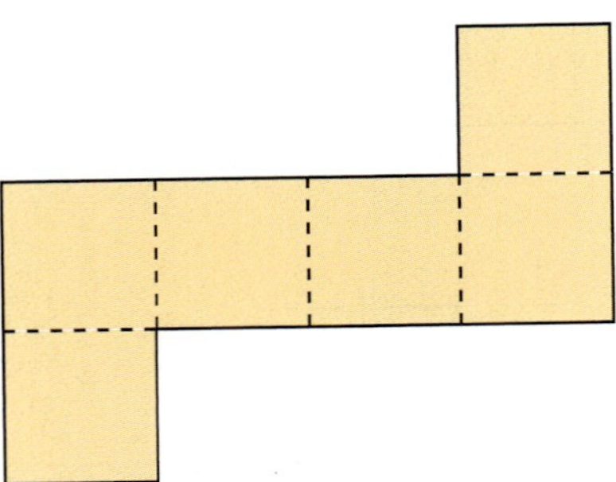

A net is a plane figure that can be folded to make a solid.

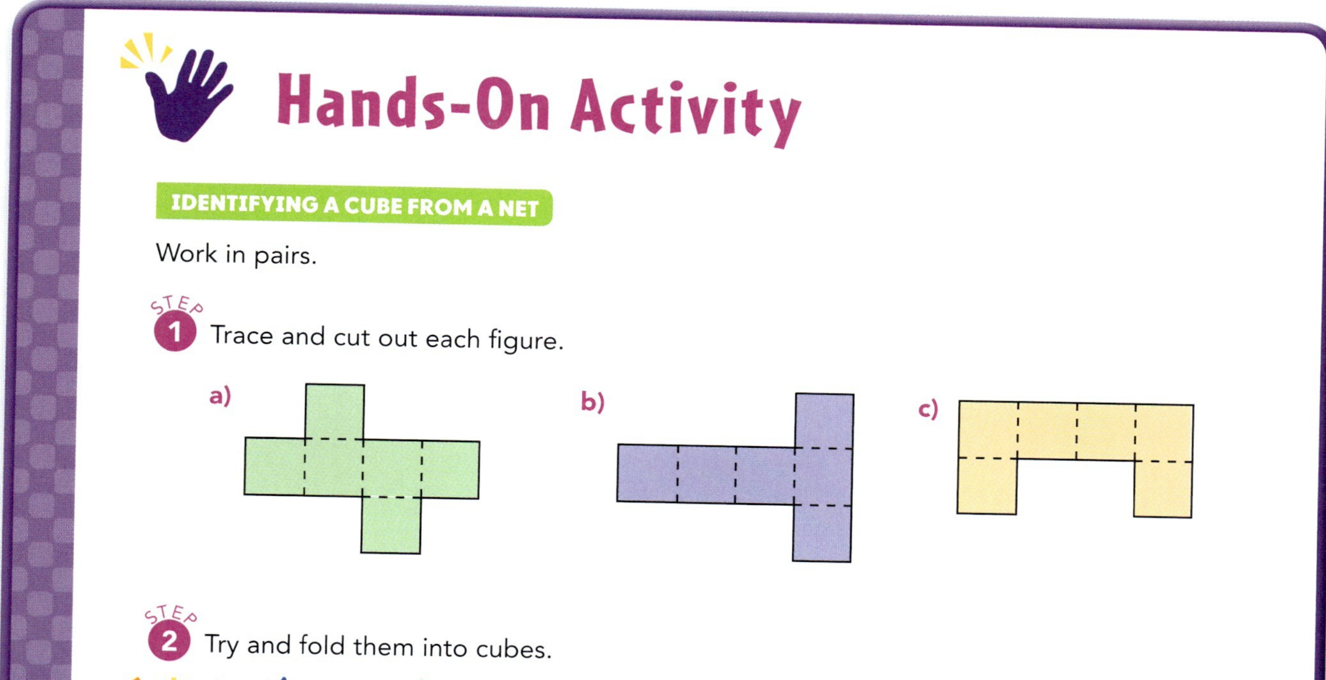

Hands-On Activity

IDENTIFYING A CUBE FROM A NET

Work in pairs.

STEP 1 Trace and cut out each figure.

a) b) c)

STEP 2 Try and fold them into cubes.

Math Journal Can you fold all the above figures into cubes? Discuss with your partner and explain your thinking.

Recognize the net of a rectangular prism.

This solid is a rectangular prism. It has six rectangular faces. Any two of the parallel faces can be its bases.

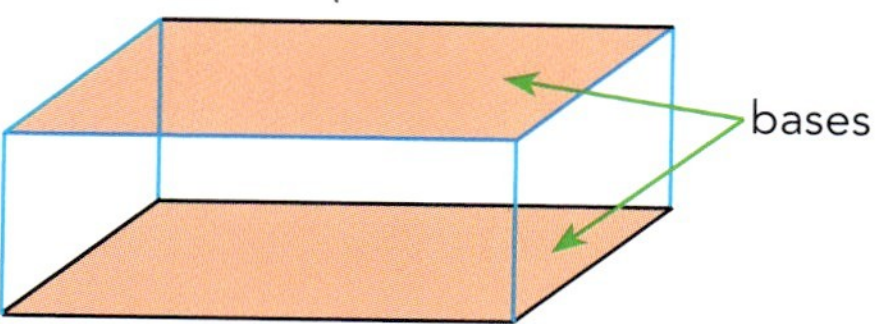

Math Note

In any prism, any pair of parallel faces can be considered bases.

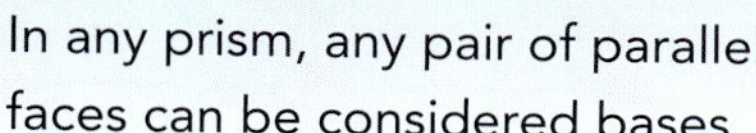

It can be cut along the blue edges and flattened as shown. This is a net of the rectangular prism.

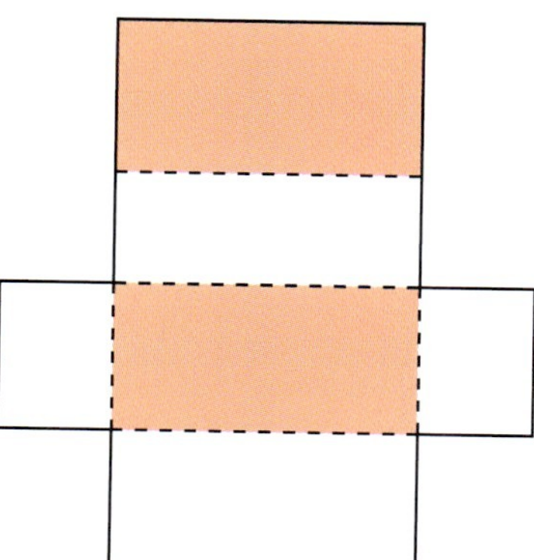

Learn Recognize the net of a triangular prism.

This solid is a triangular prism. It has three rectangular faces and two parallel triangular faces that are the same shape and size.

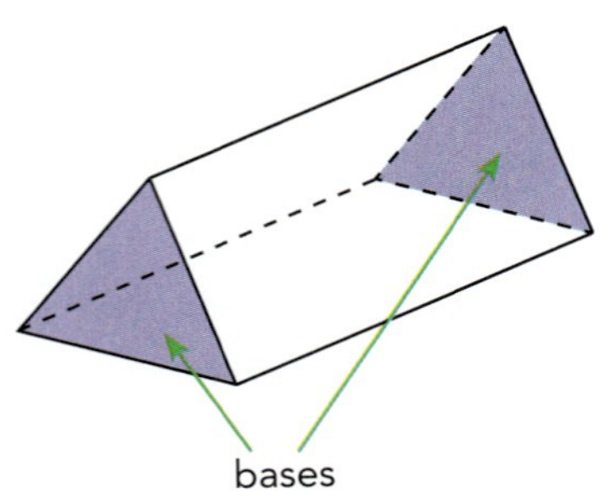

These are two nets of a triangular prism.

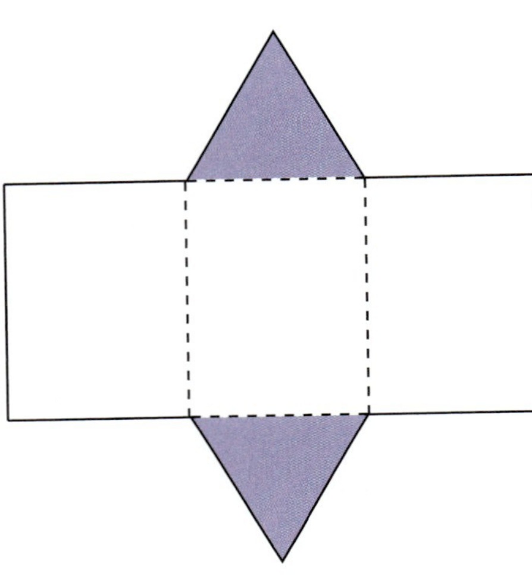

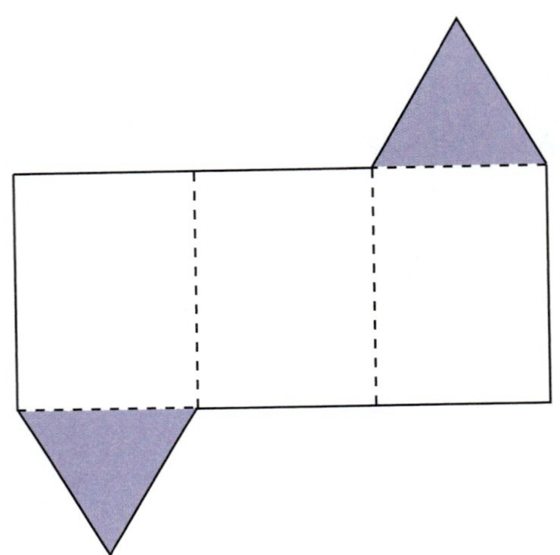

A triangular prism can also look like the one below.

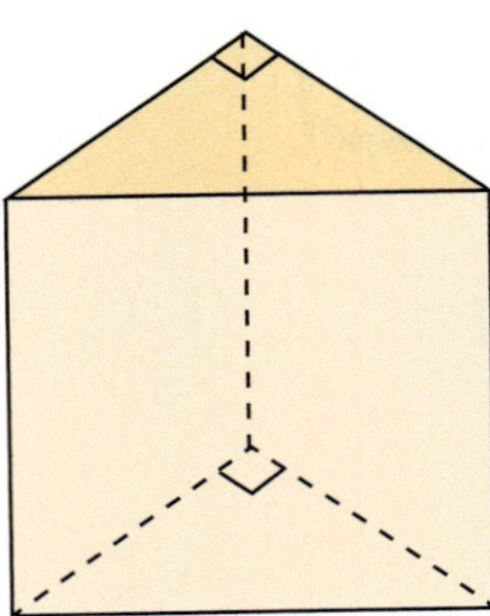

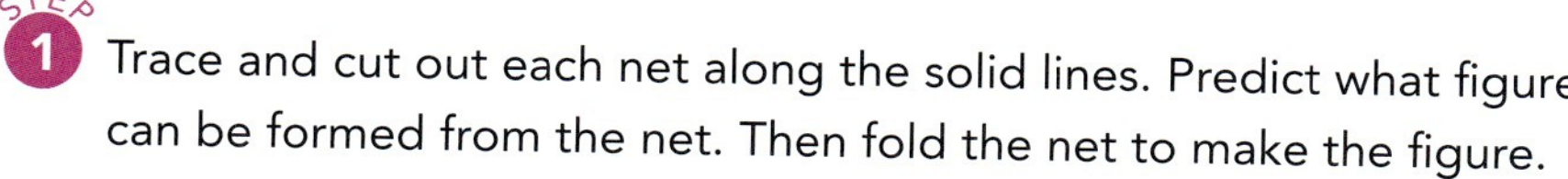

Work in pairs.

STEP 1 Trace and cut out each net along the solid lines. Predict what figure can be formed from the net. Then fold the net to make the figure.

a)

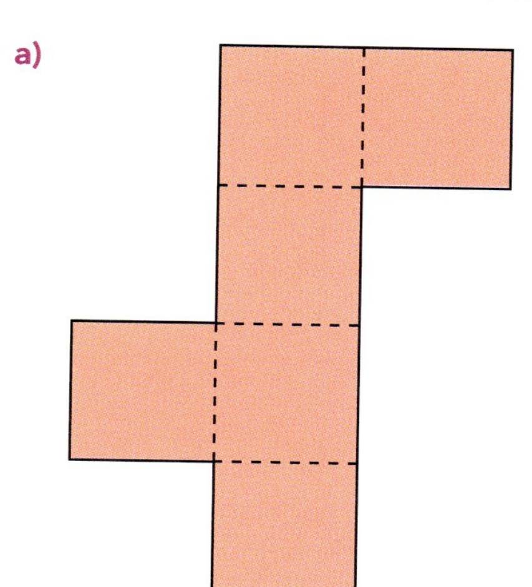

b)

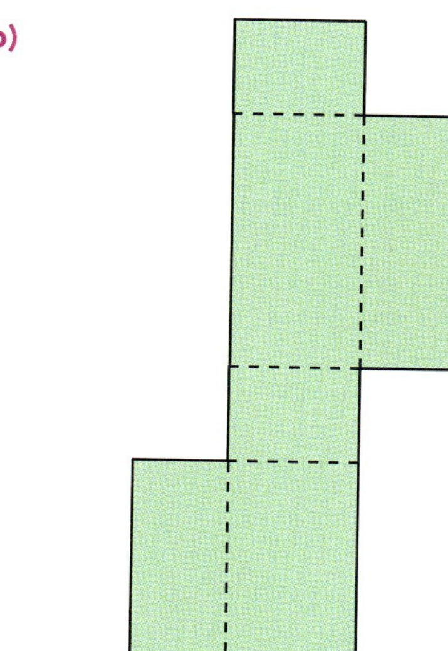

c)

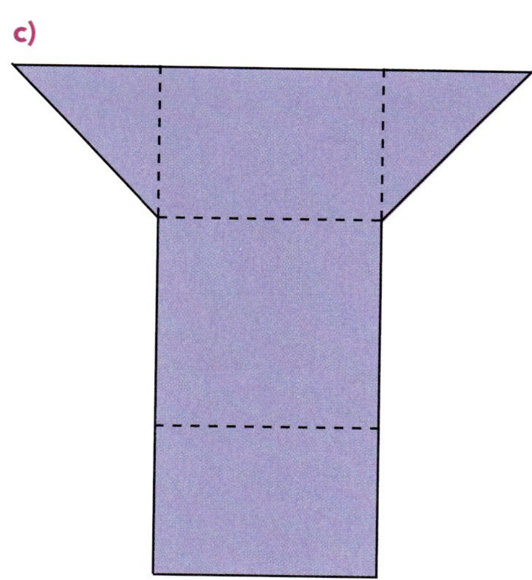

d)

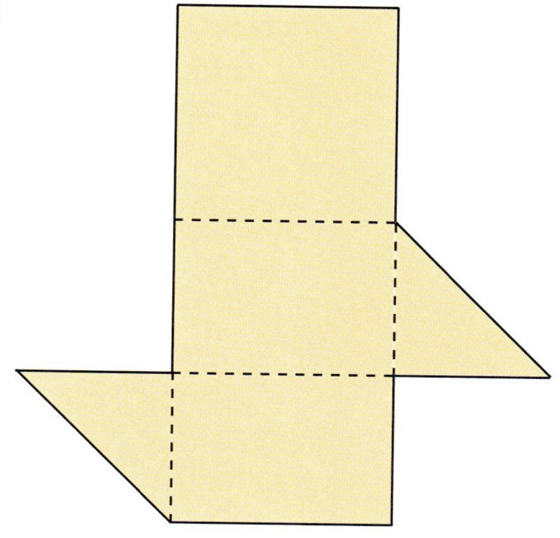

Name the solid that each net forms.

Guided Practice

Match each solid with its net(s). There may be more than one net of each solid.

1

Solid			
Net	*b*, ___?___	___?___	___?___

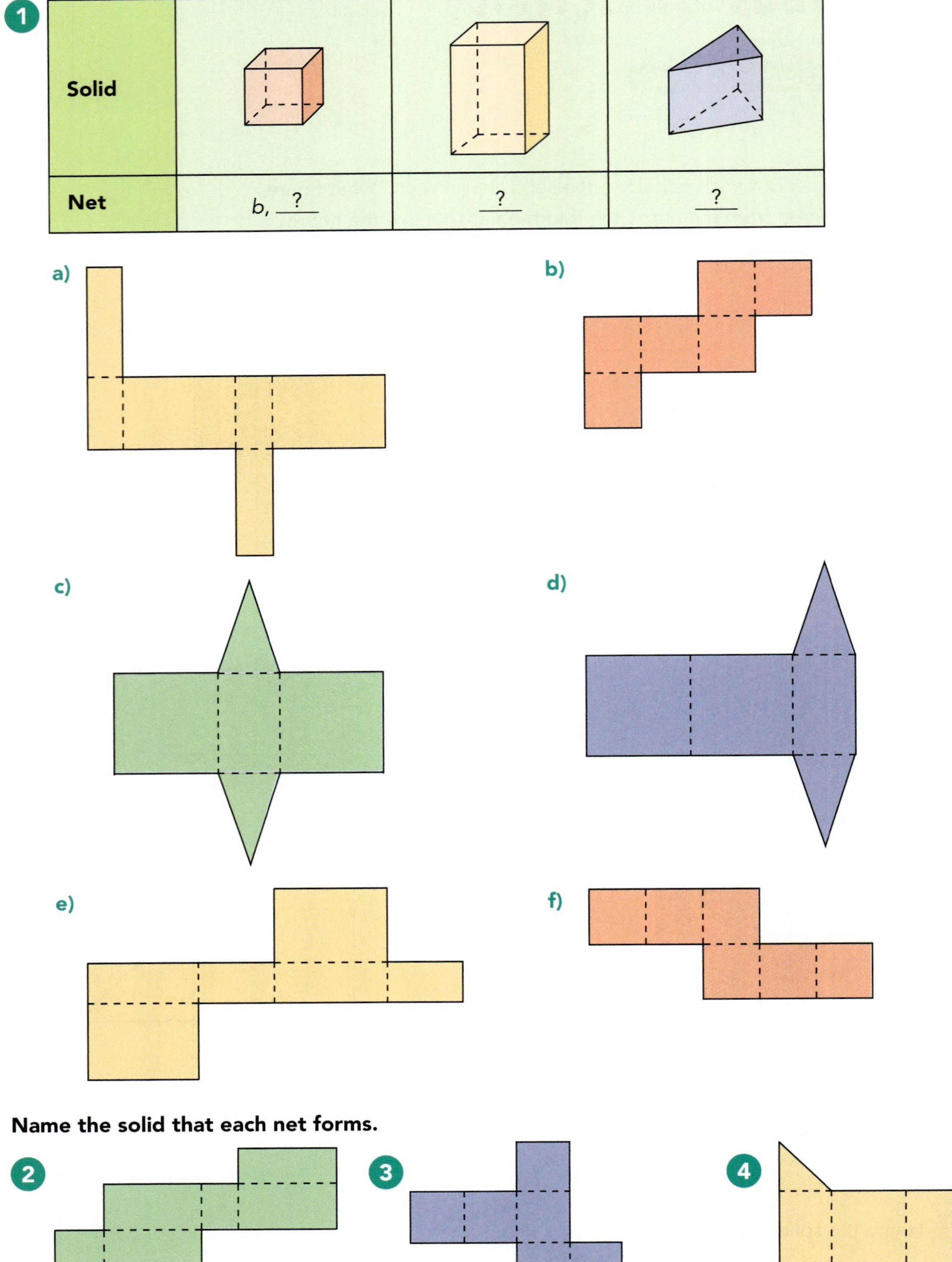

Name the solid that each net forms.

2

3

4

Learn

Recognize the net of a square pyramid.

A pyramid has one base that is a polygon. The other faces are triangles that meet at a common vertex.

The solid shown below is a square pyramid. It has a square face, called the base, and four faces that are congruent isosceles triangles.

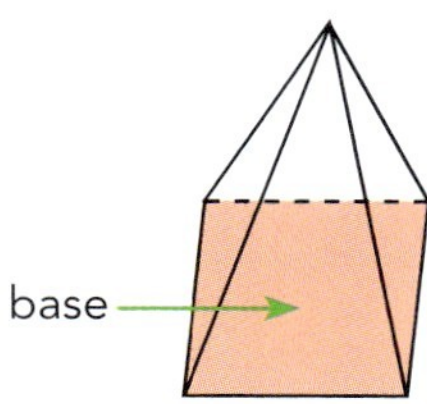

A pyramid is named by the shape of its base. So, this is a square pyramid.

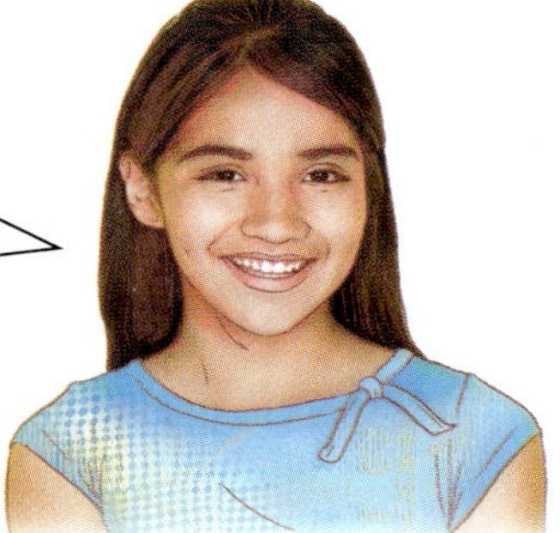

These are two nets of the square pyramid.

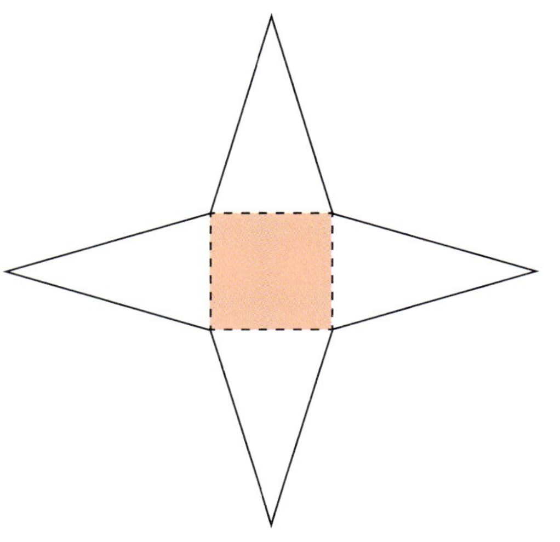

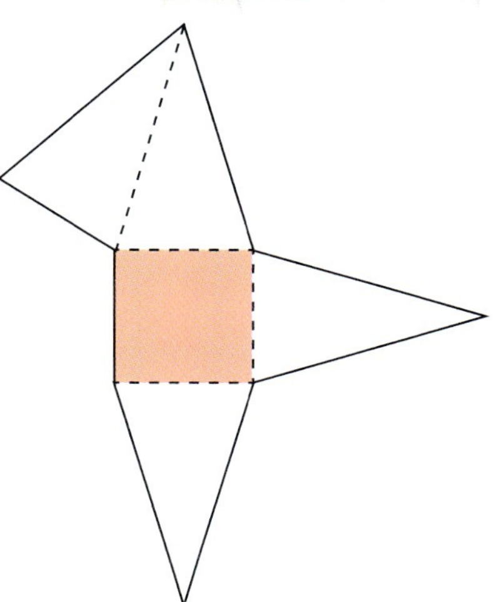

The solid shown below is a triangular pyramid.

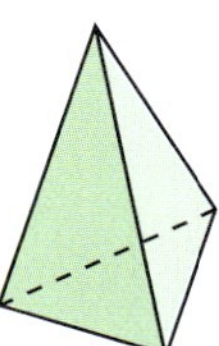

This triangular pyramid has an equilateral triangle for the base. The other three faces are congruent isosceles triangles.

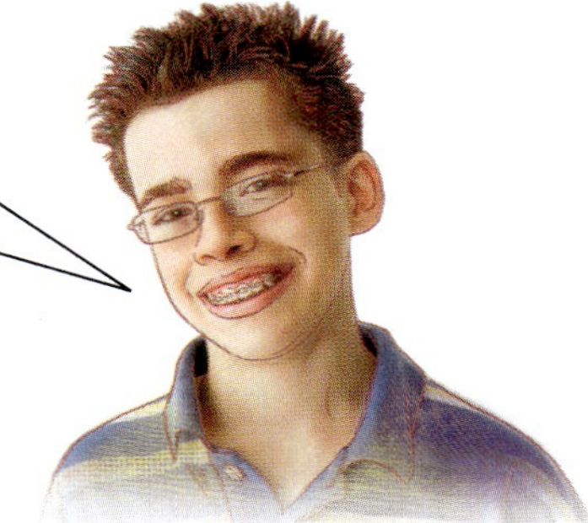

This is a net of the triangular pyramid.

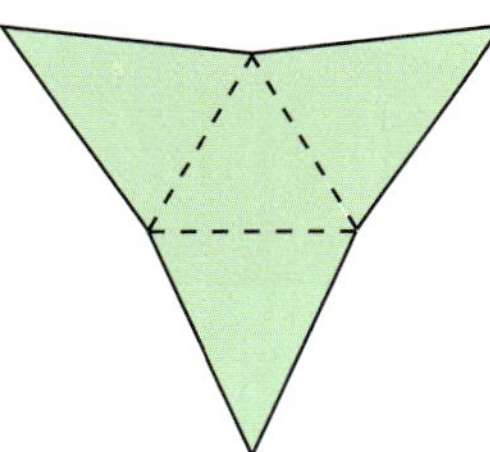

Hands-On Activity

CLASSIFYING PYRAMIDS

Work in pairs.

STEP 1 Trace, cut out, and fold the nets.

a)

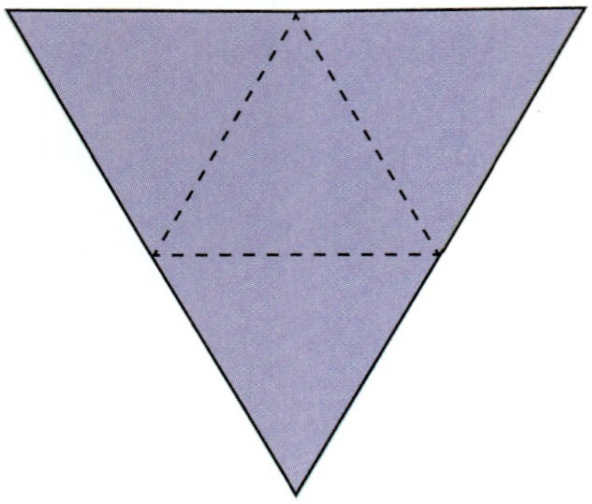

b)

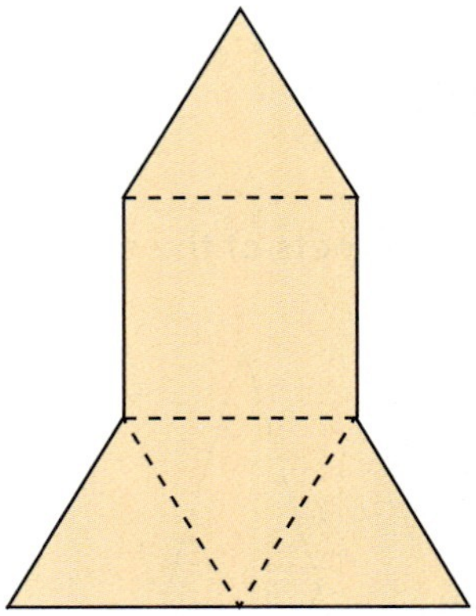

STEP 2 Name the solid that each net forms.

Guided Practice

Match each solid with its net(s). There may be more than one net of each solid.

5

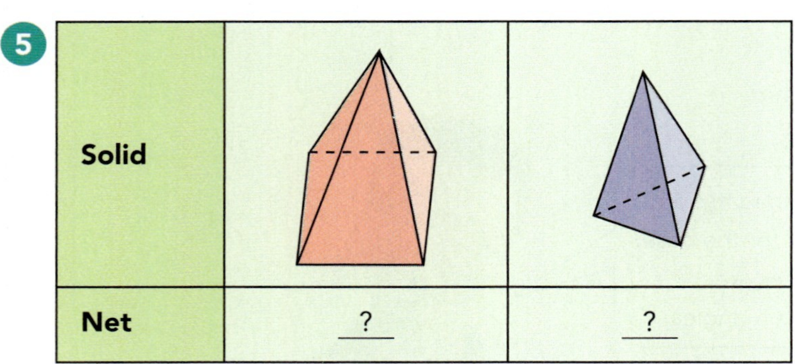

Solid		
Net	?	?

a) **b)**

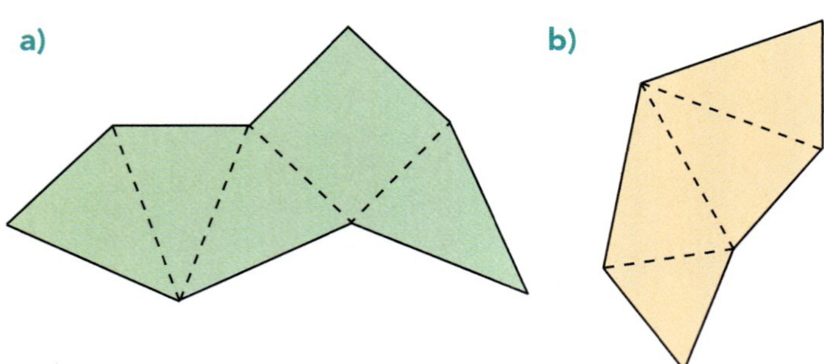

c)

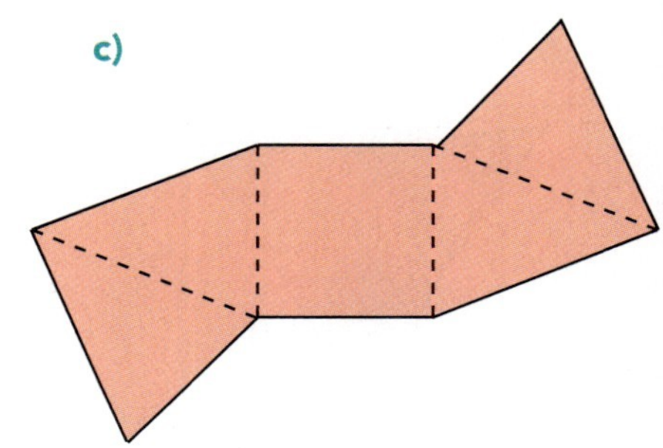

Practice 12.1

Name each solid. In each solid, identify a base and a face that is not a base.

1. 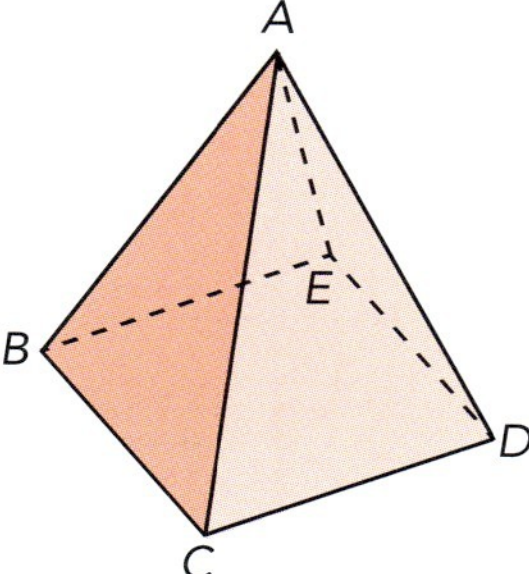

2. 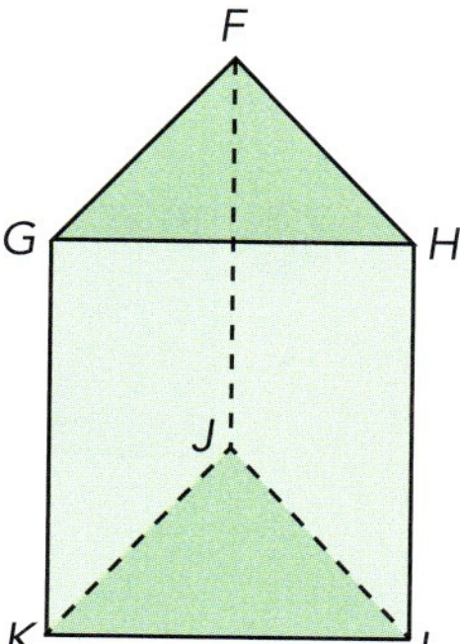

3. 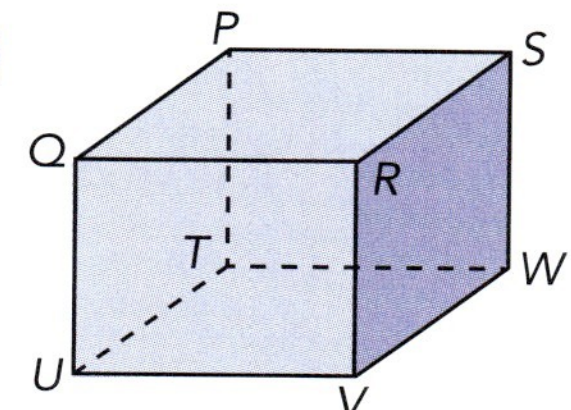

4. 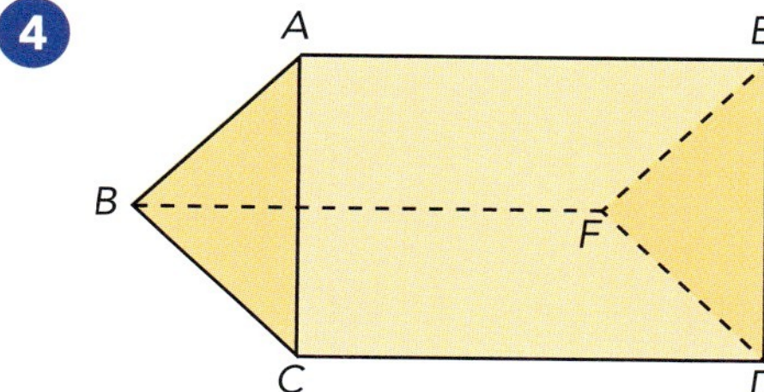

Name the solid that each net forms.

5. 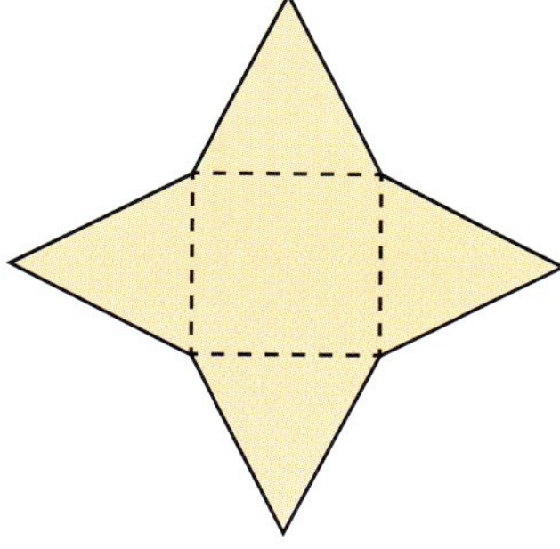

6. 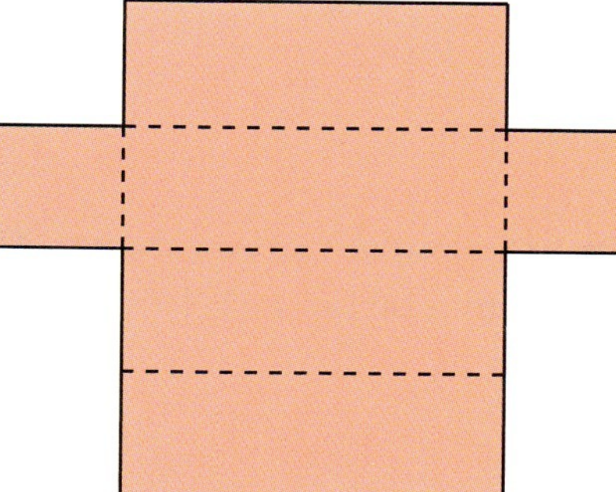

7. 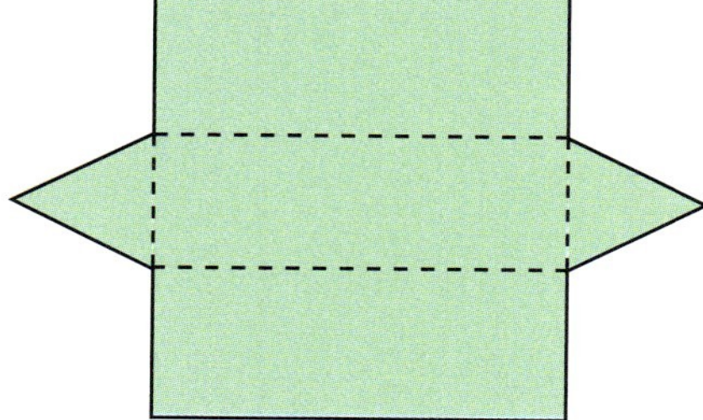

8. 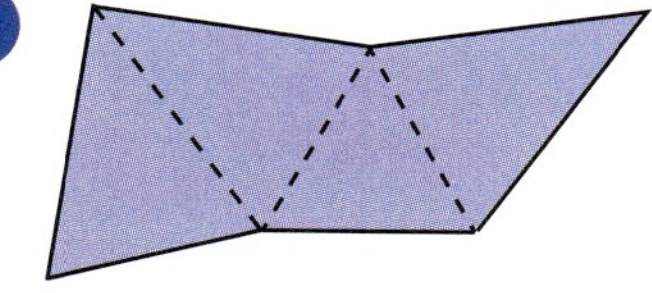

Decide if each net will form a cube. Answer Yes or No.

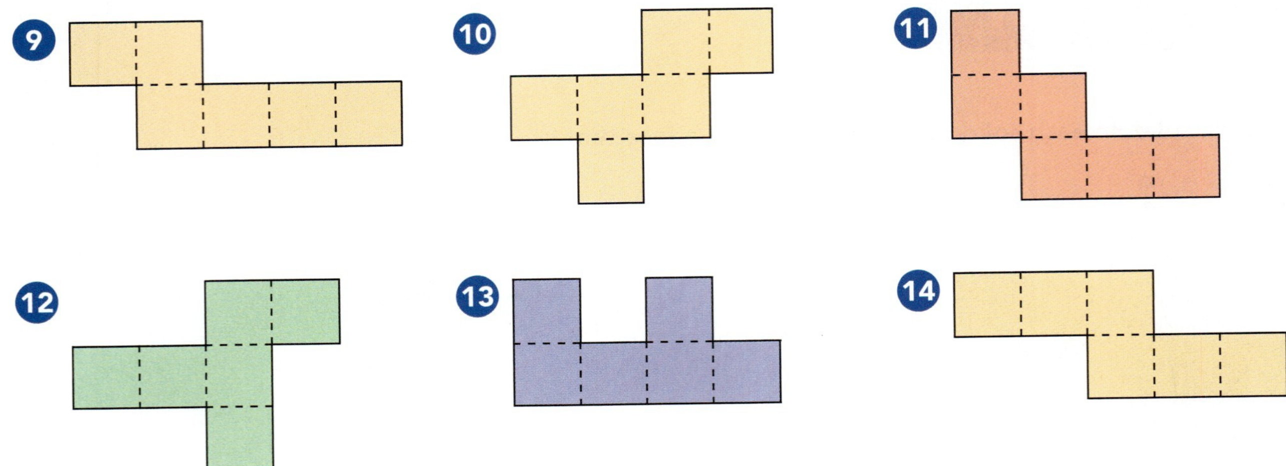

Solve. Use graph paper.

15 In Exercises **9** to **14**, you identified some possible nets for a cube. There are other possible nets. Find all of the other possible nets.

Decide if each net will form a prism. Answer Yes or No.

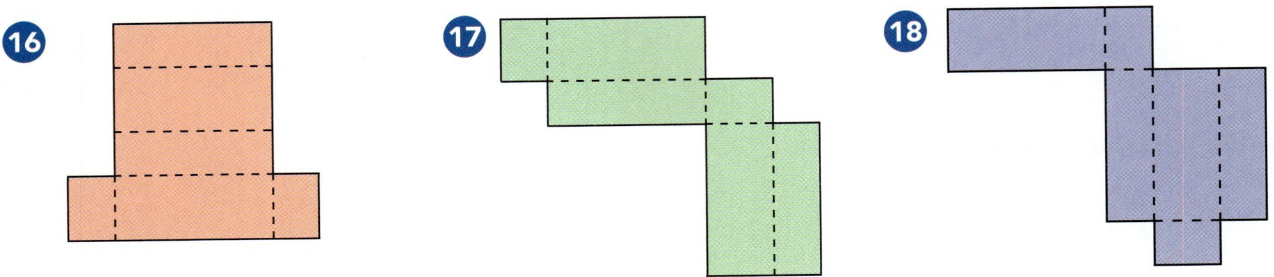

Copy the net of the rectangular prism shown. Then name the vertices that are not already labeled with a letter. Label the vertices.

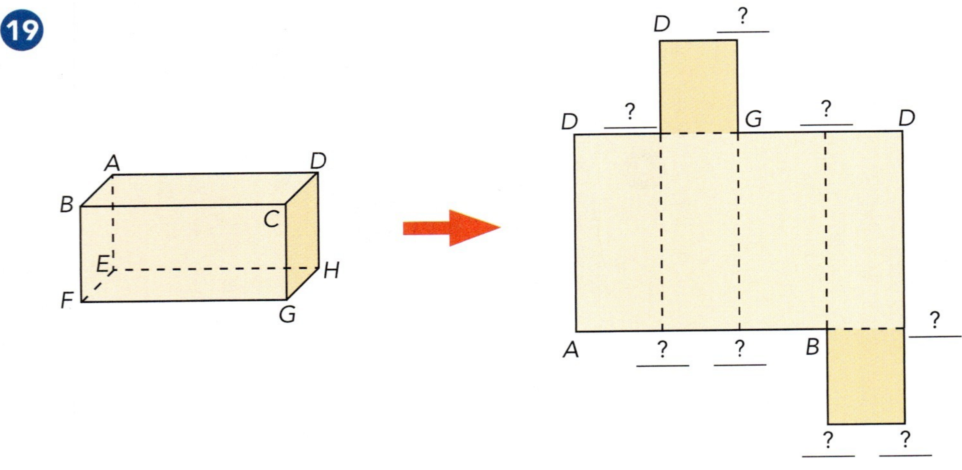

12.2 Surface Area of Solids

Lesson Objective

- Find the surface area of a prism and a pyramid.

Vocabulary

surface area

Learn Find the surface area of a cube.

A wooden box is painted green all over.

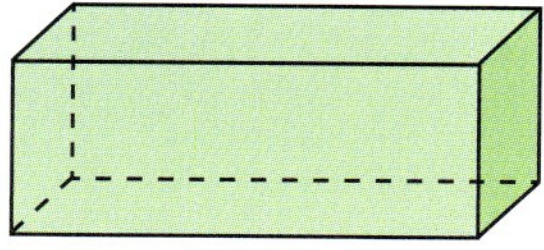

The total area painted green is the surface area of the box.

A wooden cube has edges measuring 5 centimeters each. Find the surface area of the cube.

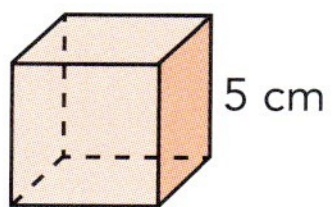

To find the surface area, you can draw a net of the cube.

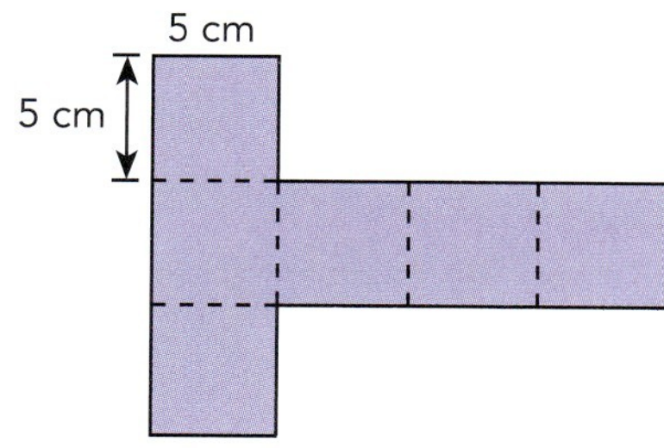

The surface area of a cube is the area of its net.

Area of one square face $= 5 \cdot 5$
$= 25 \text{ cm}^2$

Surface area of cube $= 6 \cdot 25$
$= 150 \text{ cm}^2$

Math Note

The surface area of a cube is equal to the sum of the areas of the six square faces.

If S is the surface area, and e is the length of an edge, then $S = 6e^2$.

Learn Find the surface area of a rectangular prism.

A rectangular prism is 12 inches long, 8 inches wide, and 4 inches high. Find the surface area of the rectangular prism.

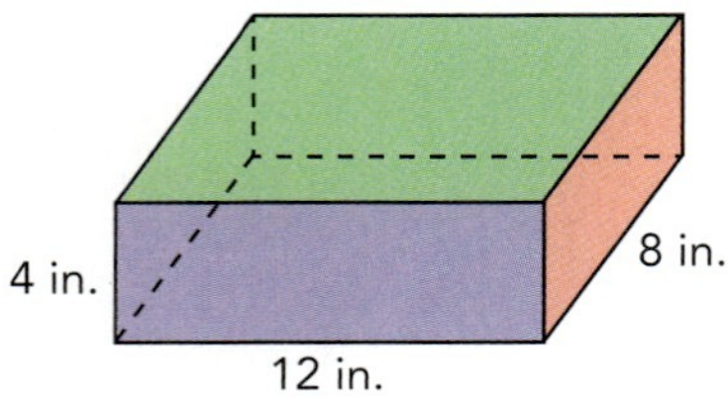

To find the surface area, draw a net of the rectangular prism.

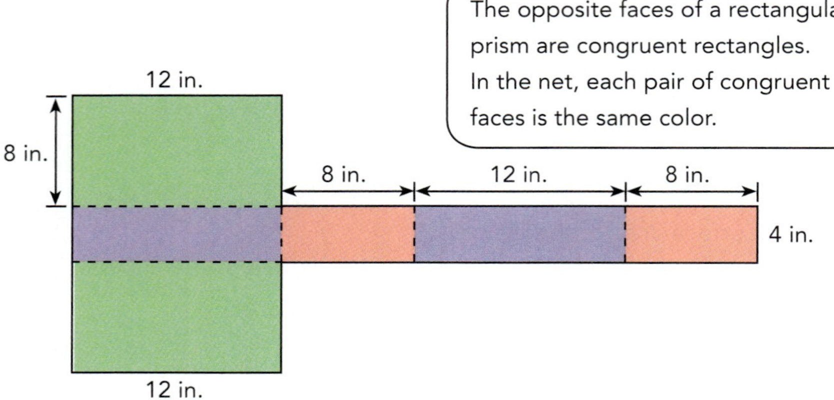

The opposite faces of a rectangular prism are congruent rectangles. In the net, each pair of congruent faces is the same color.

The surface area of a rectangular prism is the area of its net.

The total area of the two purple and two orange faces is equal to the area of the rectangle of length $12 + 8 + 12 + 8 = 40$ inches and width 4 inches.

Total area of these four faces
$= 40 \cdot 4$
$= 160$ in.^{2}

The length of the rectangle, $(12 + 8 + 12 + 8)$ inches, is the perimeter of the base of the prism. The width, 4 inches, is the height of the prism.

Area of two green rectangular bases
$= 2 \cdot (12 \cdot 8)$
$= 2 \cdot 96$
$= 192$ in.^{2}

Surface area of rectangular prism
$= 160 + 192$
$= 352$ in.^{2}

Math Note

The surface area of a prism is equal to the perimeter of the base multiplied by the height and then added to the sum of the areas of the two bases.

Guided Practice

Complete.

1 A cube has edges measuring 6 centimeters each. Find the surface area of the cube.

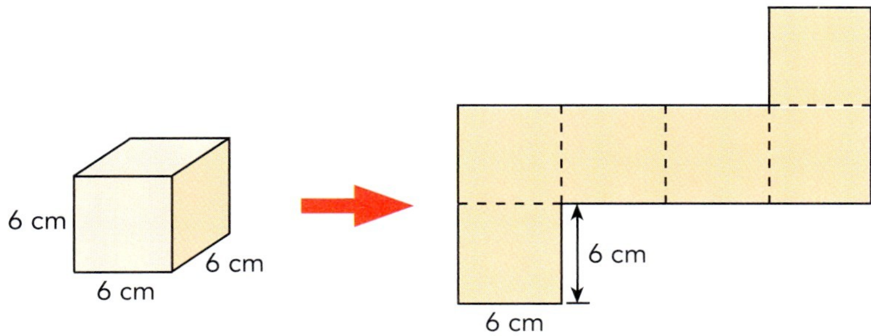

Area of one square face = $\underline{\ ?\ } \cdot \underline{\ ?\ }$

$= \underline{\ ?\ }$ cm^2

Surface area of cube = $\underline{\ ?\ } \cdot \underline{\ ?\ }$

$= \underline{\ ?\ }$ cm^2

2 A rectangular prism measures 7 inches by 5 inches by 10 inches. Find the surface area of the prism.

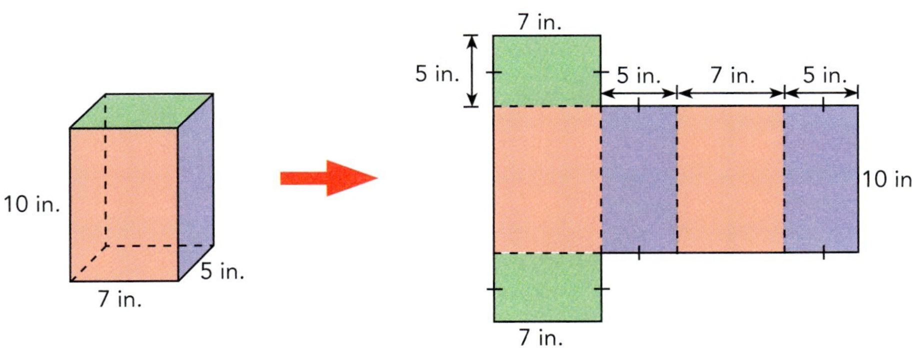

Total area of two orange and two purple faces = $(\underline{\ ?\ } + \underline{\ ?\ } + \underline{\ ?\ } + \underline{\ ?\ }) \cdot \underline{\ ?\ }$

$= \underline{\ ?\ } \cdot \underline{\ ?\ }$

$= \underline{\ ?\ }$ in.^{2}

Area of two green rectangular bases = $2 \cdot \underline{\ ?\ } \cdot \underline{\ ?\ }$

$= \underline{\ ?\ }$ in.^{2}

Surface area of rectangular prism = $\underline{\ ?\ } + \underline{\ ?\ }$

$= \underline{\ ?\ }$ in.^{2}

Learn

Find the surface area of a triangular prism.

The triangular prism shown has three rectangular faces. Its bases are congruent isosceles triangles. Find the surface area of the triangular prism.

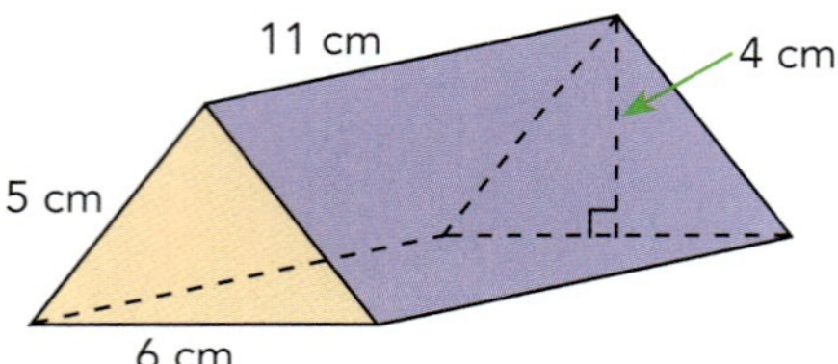

This is a net of the triangular prism.

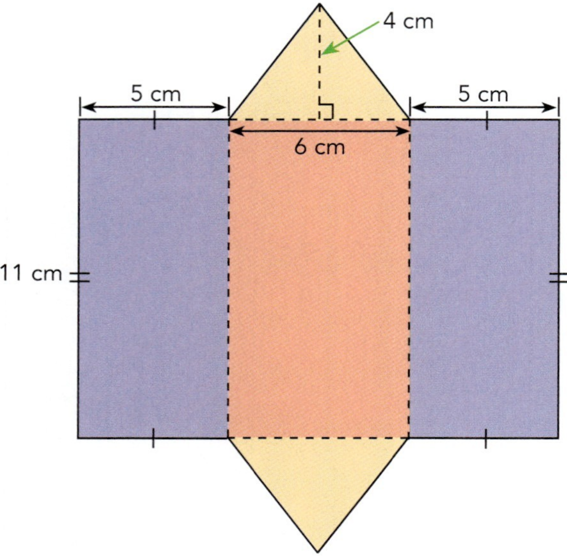

The surface area of a triangular prism is the area of its net.

$$
\begin{aligned}
\text{Total area of two purple rectangles and orange rectangle} &= (5 + 6 + 5) \cdot 11 \\
&= 16 \cdot 11 \\
&= 176 \text{ cm}^2
\end{aligned}
$$

$$
\begin{aligned}
\text{Area of two yellow triangular bases} &= 2 \cdot \left(\frac{1}{2} \cdot 6 \cdot 4\right) \\
&= 2 \cdot 12 \\
&= 24 \text{ cm}^2
\end{aligned}
$$

$$
\begin{aligned}
\text{Surface area of triangular prism} &= 176 + 24 \\
&= 200 \text{ cm}^2
\end{aligned}
$$

The surface area of the triangular prism is 200 square centimeters.

Learn Find the surface area of a pyramid.

This pyramid has a square base measuring 10 inches on each side. It has four faces that are congruent isosceles triangles. The height of each triangle is 12 inches. Find the surface area of the pyramid.

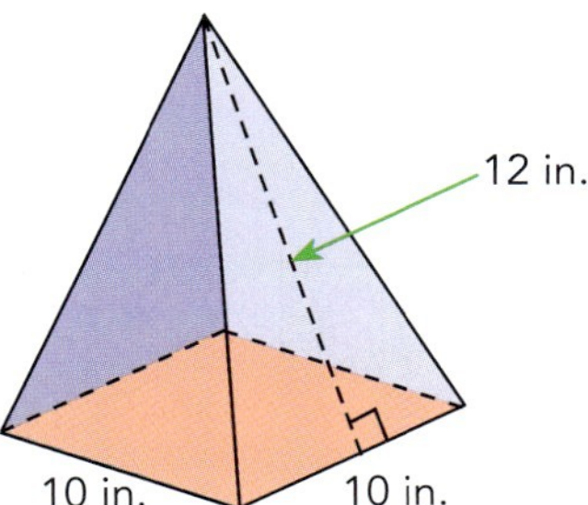

This is a net of the pyramid.

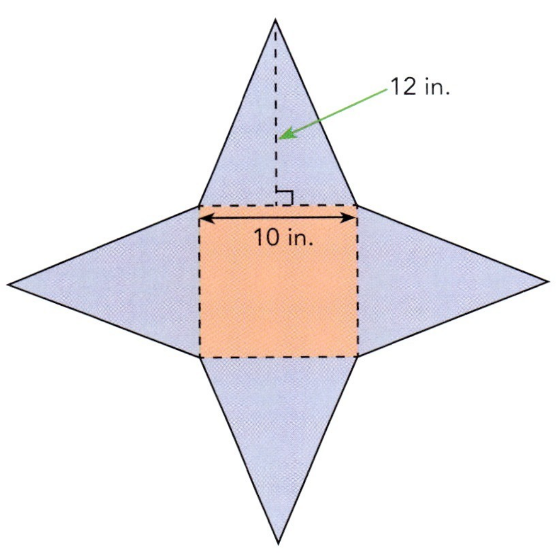

The surface area of a pyramid is the area of its net.

Area of square base

$= 10 \cdot 10$

$= 100 \text{ in.}^2$

Area of four triangles

$= 4 \cdot \left(\frac{1}{2} \cdot 10 \cdot 12\right)$

$= 4 \cdot 60$

$= 240 \text{ in.}^2$

Surface area of the pyramid

$= 100 + 240$

$= 340 \text{ in.}^2$

The surface area of the pyramid is 340 square inches.

Guided Practice

Complete.

3 The triangular prism shown has three rectangular faces. Its bases are congruent right triangles. Find the surface area of the triangular prism.

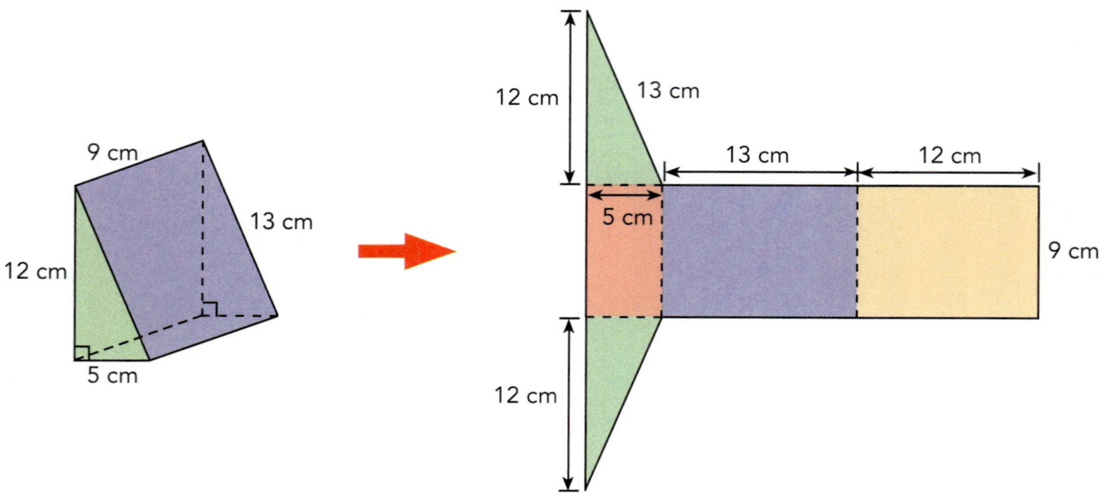

Total area of orange, purple, and yellow rectangles = (? + ? + ?) · ?

= ? · ?

= ? cm^2

Area of two green triangular bases = $2 \cdot \left(\frac{1}{2} \cdot \underline{?} \cdot \underline{?}\right)$ = ? cm^2

Surface area of triangular prism = ? + ? = ? cm^2

4 Alicia makes a pyramid that has an equilateral triangle as its base. The other three faces are congruent isosceles triangles. She measures the lengths shown on the net of her pyramid. Find the surface area of the pyramid.

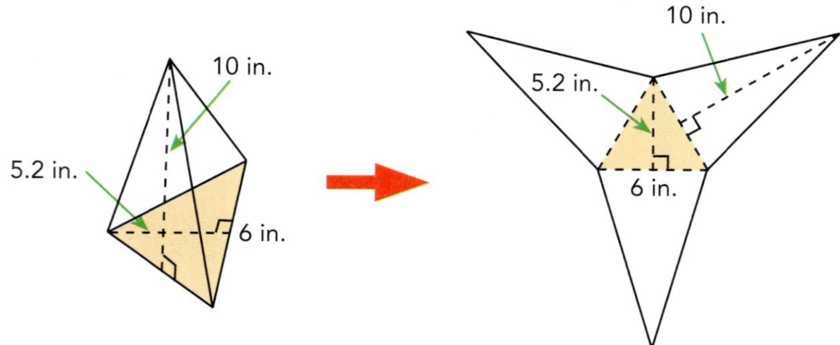

Area of yellow triangle = $\frac{1}{2} \cdot \underline{?} \cdot \underline{?}$ = ? in.^{2}

Area of three blue triangles = $3 \cdot \frac{1}{2} \cdot \underline{?} \cdot \underline{?}$ = ? in.^{2}

Surface area of triangular pyramid = ? + ? = ? in.^{2}

Practice 12.2

Solve.

1. A cube has edges measuring 6 centimeters each. Find the surface area of the cube.

2. The edge length of a cube is 3.5 inches. Find the surface area of the cube.

3. A closed rectangular tank measures 12 meters by 6 meters by 10 meters. Find the surface area of the tank.

4. A closed rectangular tank has a length of 8.5 feet, a width of 3.2 feet, and a height of 4.8 feet. Find the surface area of the tank.

5. A triangular prism with its measurements is shown. Find the surface area of the prism.

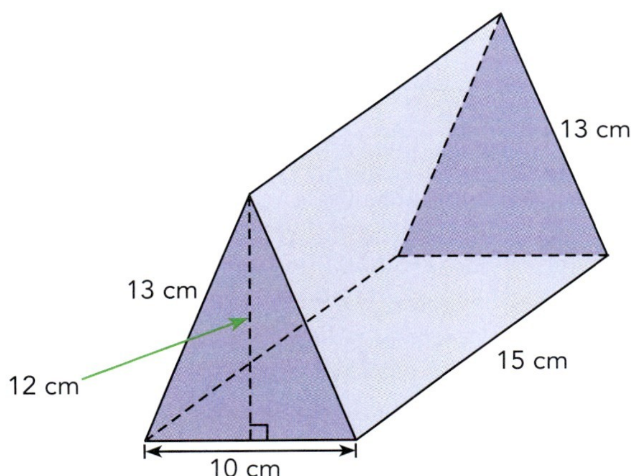

6. A triangular prism with its measurements is shown. Find the surface area of the prism.

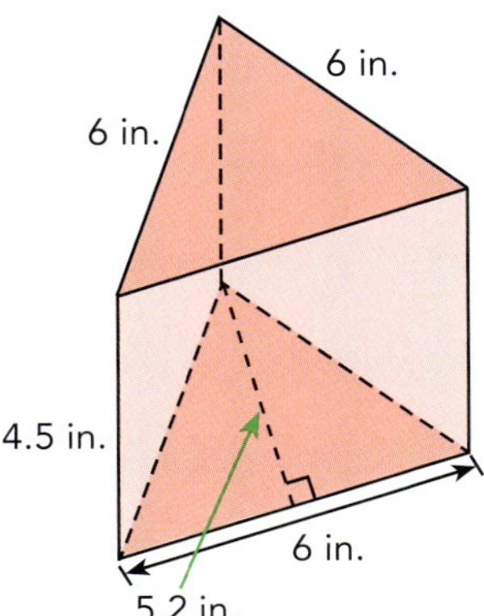

Solve.

7 A square pyramid has four faces that are congruent isosceles triangles. Find the surface area of the square pyramid if the base area is 169 square centimeters.

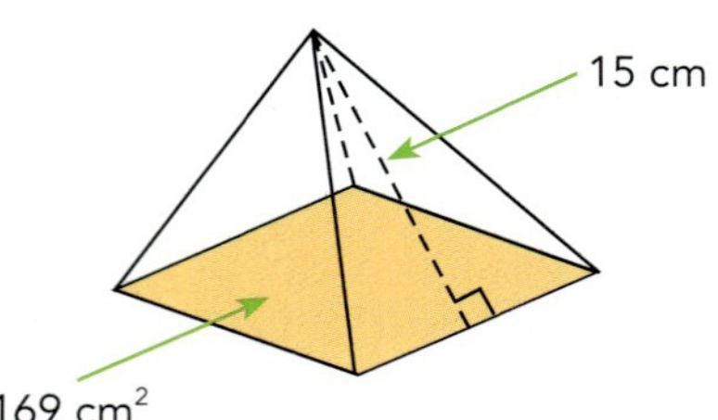

8 The faces of this solid consist of four identical trapezoids and two squares. The side lengths of the two squares are 4 centimeters and 8 centimeters. The height of each trapezoid is 12 centimeters. Find the surface area of the solid.

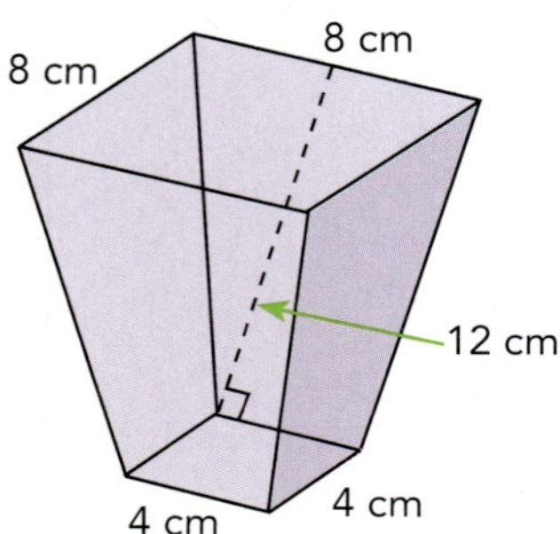

9 Ms. Jones wants to paint the walls of a rectangular room. The height of the room is 8 feet. The floor is 10.5 feet wide and 12 feet long. The doors and windows total 24 square feet and are not going to be painted. Find the total area of the walls that need to be painted.

10 The base of a prism has n sides. Write an expression for each of the following.

a) the number of vertices

b) the number of edges

c) the number of faces

11 The base of a pyramid has m sides. Write an expression for each of the following.

a) the number of vertices

b) the number of edges

c) the number of faces

12.3 Volume of Prisms

Lesson Objective

- Find the volume of a prism.

Vocabulary

cross section

Learn Derive the formula for the volume of a rectangular prism.

A rectangular prism is $4\frac{1}{2}$ inches long, 1 inch wide, and $1\frac{1}{2}$ inches high. Find its volume.

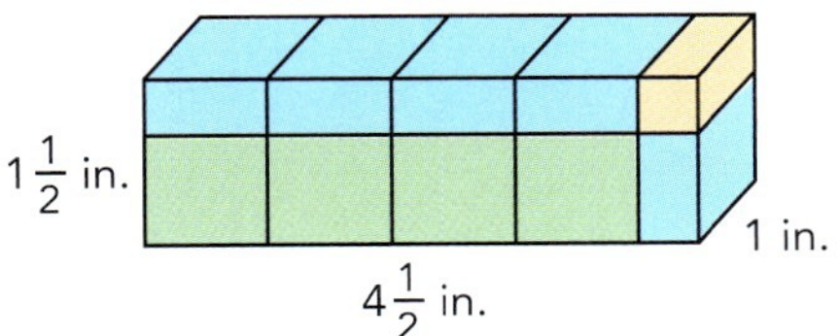

From the diagram, the prism is made up of four green cubes, five blue half cubes, and one yellow quarter cube.
To find the total volume of the different sized blocks:

Volume of one green cube = 1 in.^3

Volume of one blue half cube = $\frac{1}{2} \cdot 1 = \frac{1}{2} \text{ in.}^3$

Volume of one yellow quarter cube = $\frac{1}{4} \cdot 1 = \frac{1}{4} \text{ in.}^3$

$$\begin{aligned}\text{Volume of prism} &= (4 \cdot 1) + \left(5 \cdot \frac{1}{2}\right) + \left(1 \cdot \frac{1}{4}\right)\\ &= 4 + \frac{5}{2} + \frac{1}{4}\\ &= 6\frac{3}{4} \text{ in.}^3\end{aligned}$$

$$\begin{aligned}\text{Length} \times \text{width} \times \text{height} &= 4\frac{1}{2} \cdot 1 \cdot 1\frac{1}{2}\\ &= \frac{9}{2} \times 1 \times \frac{3}{2}\\ &= \frac{27}{4}\\ &= 6\frac{3}{4} \text{ in.}^3\end{aligned}$$

The volume of any rectangular prism of length ℓ, width w, and height h is given by

$$V = \ell wh$$

Learn Use a formula to find the volume of a rectangular prism.

A rectangular prism measures 8.4 centimeters by 5.5 centimeters by 9 centimeters. What is the volume of the rectangular prism?

$V = \ell wh$
$= 8.4 \cdot 5.5 \cdot 9$
$= 415.8 \text{ cm}^3$

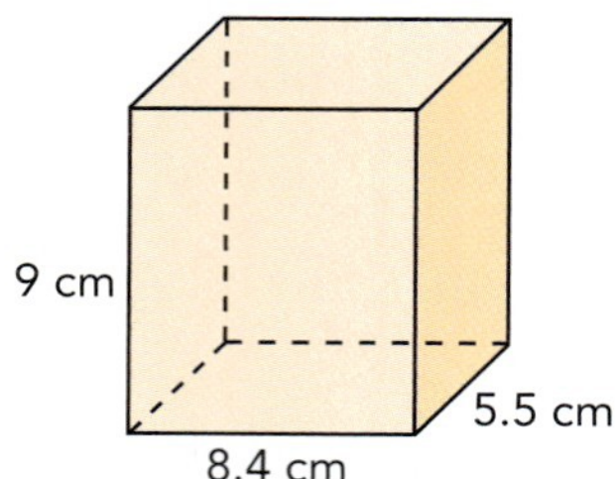

Guided Practice

Find the volume of each rectangular prism.

1 Length = $5\frac{1}{4}$ in.
Width = 6 in.
Height = 12 in.

$V = \ell wh$
$= \underline{?} \cdot \underline{?} \cdot \underline{?}$
$= \underline{?} \text{ in.}^3$

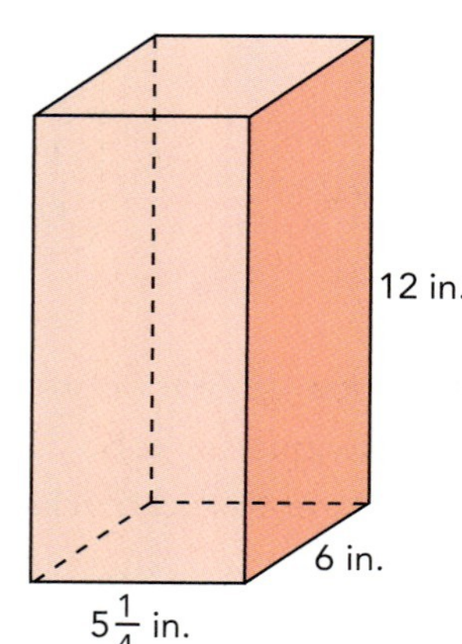

2 Length = 8 cm
Width = 7.2 cm
Height = 3 cm

$V = \ell wh$
$= \underline{?} \cdot \underline{?} \cdot \underline{?}$
$= \underline{?} \text{ cm}^3$

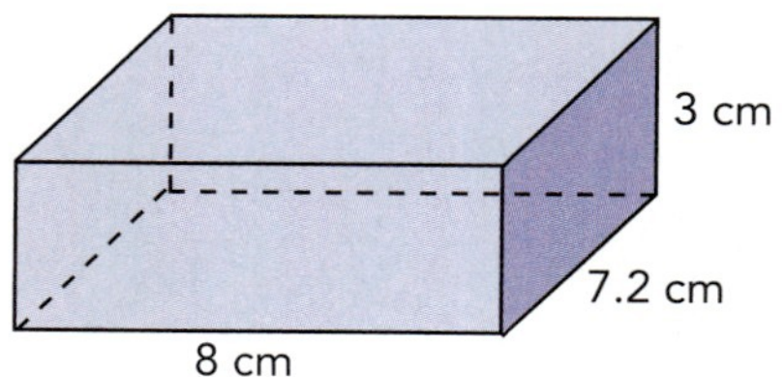

3 Length = 4 ft
Width = 3 ft
Height = $8\frac{1}{3}$ ft

Volume = $\underline{?}$
$= \underline{?} \cdot \underline{?} \cdot \underline{?}$
$= \underline{?} \text{ ft}^3$

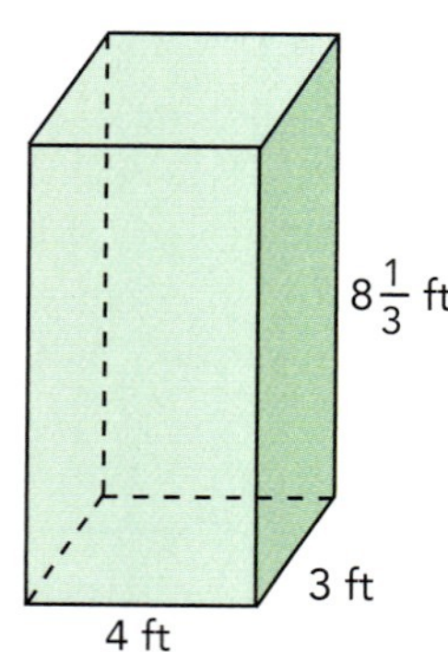

Learn Form cross sections of prisms.

The rectangular prism below is sliced in two places: along segment $\overline{AB}$ parallel to the bases and along segment $\overline{CD}$ parallel to the bases.

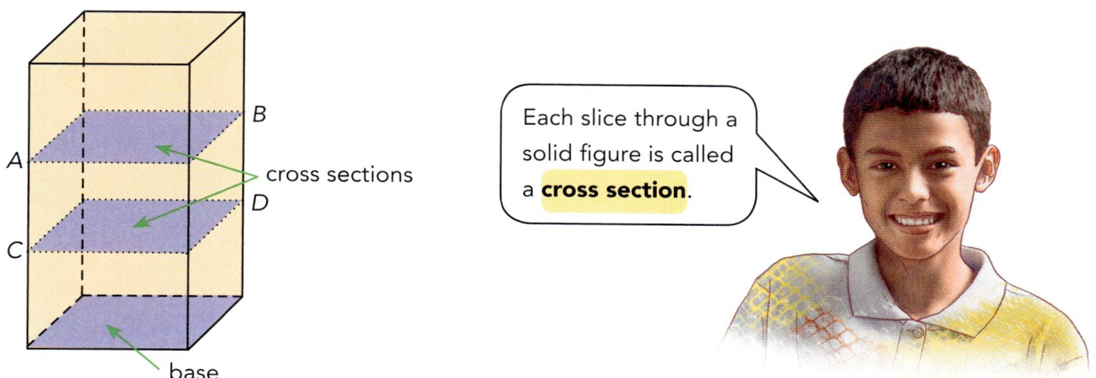

The cross section formed through $\overline{AB}$ is a rectangle that is congruent to each base.

The cross section through $\overline{CD}$ is also congruent to each base.

Any cross section of a rectangular prism that is parallel to the bases will be congruent to the bases. So, the prism has uniform cross sections.

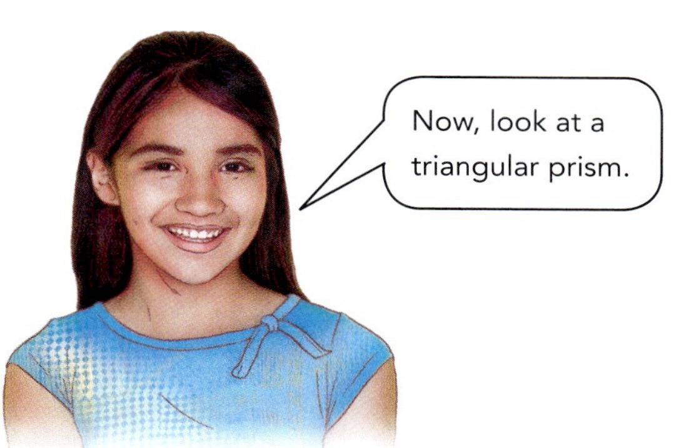

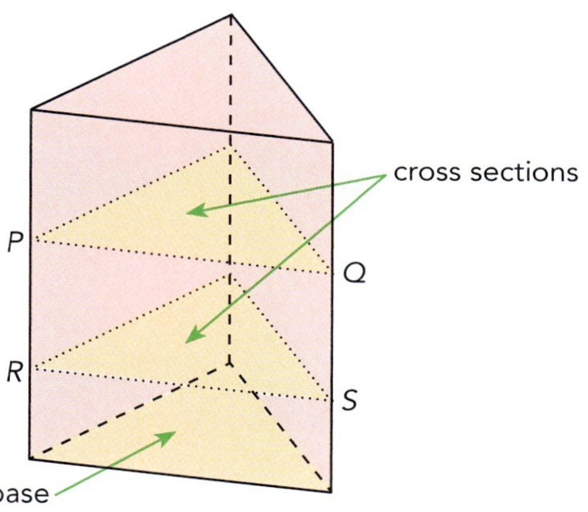

This triangular prism has right triangles for its bases. It is sliced through at both $\overline{PQ}$ and $\overline{RS}$ parallel to its bases. These cross sections are triangles that are congruent to the bases.

So, a triangular prism also has uniform cross sections when sliced parallel to the bases.

Math Note

In general, any prism has uniform cross sections when it is sliced parallel to the bases of the prism.

Guided Practice

Tell whether slices parallel to each given slice will form uniform cross sections. If not, explain why not.

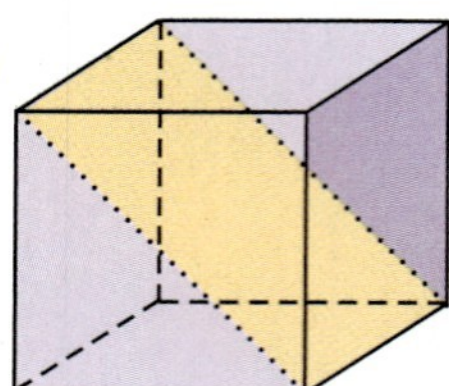

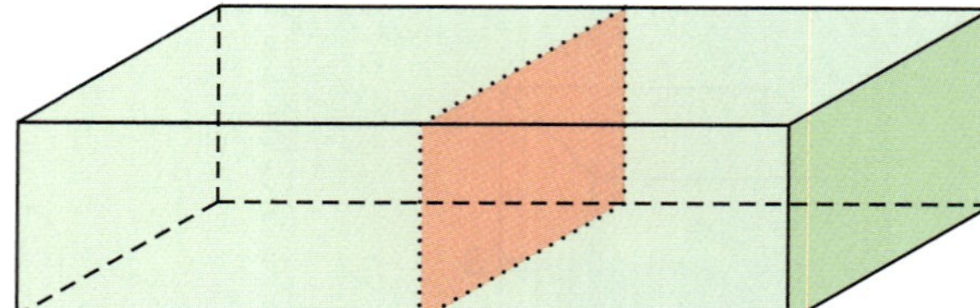

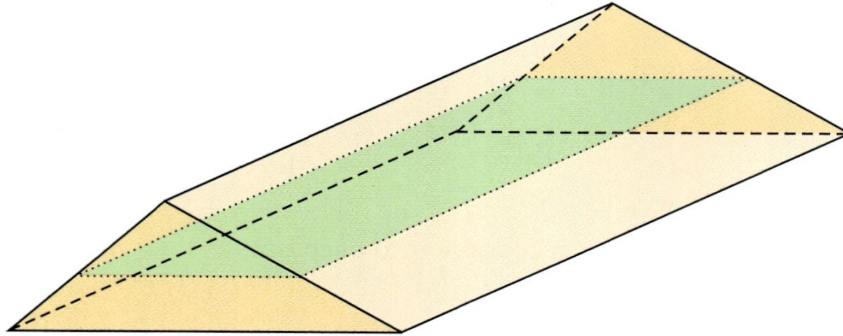

Learn

Use a formula to find the volume of any prism.

This is a rectangular prism.

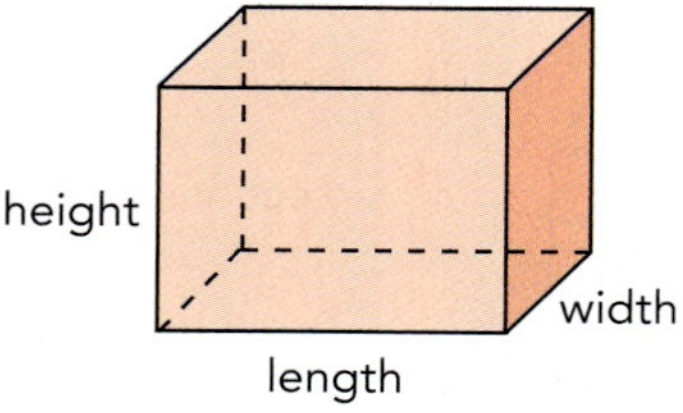

Volume of a rectangular prism = length · width · height
Since length · width = area of base,
volume of a prism = area of base · height.

Because all prisms have a uniform cross section when sliced parallel to the base, this formula applies to all prisms.

Volume of a prism with uniform cross sections
= area of base · height
or $V = Bh$

Caution

In the formula $V = Bh$, B represents the area of the base, not a length.

a) The prism shown has bases that are parallelograms. The area of a base is 20 square inches. The height of the prism is 4 inches. Find the volume of the prism.

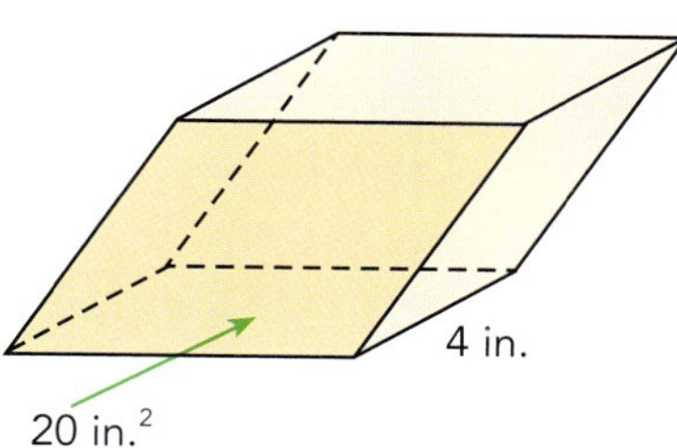

$$\begin{aligned} V &= Bh \\ &= 20 \cdot 4 \\ &= 80 \text{ in.}^3 \end{aligned}$$

The volume of the prism is 80 cubic inches.

b) A triangular prism with its measurements is shown. Find the volume of the prism.

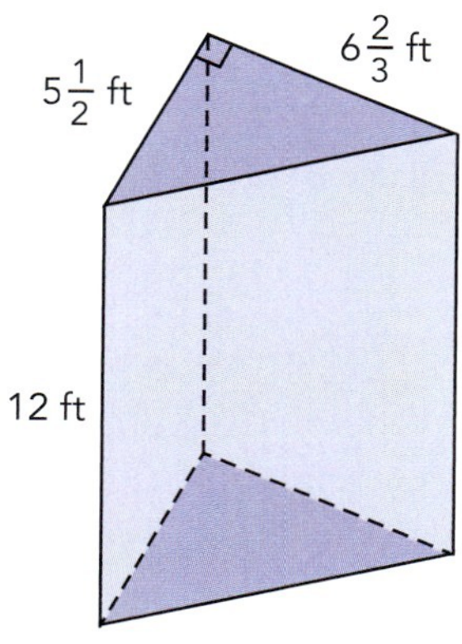

Area of right triangle base

$$\begin{aligned} &= \frac{1}{2} \cdot 5\frac{1}{2} \cdot 6\frac{2}{3} \\ &= \frac{1}{2} \cdot \frac{11}{2} \cdot \frac{20}{3} \\ &= \frac{55}{3} \text{ ft}^2 \end{aligned}$$

$$\begin{aligned} V &= Bh \\ &= \frac{55}{3} \cdot 12 \\ &= 220 \text{ ft}^3 \end{aligned}$$

The volume of the prism is 220 cubic feet.

Caution

The base b of the triangular base is not the same as the base B of the prism.

Guided Practice

Find the volume of each prism.

7 Length = 6 cm
Width = 5.5 cm
Height = 9 cm

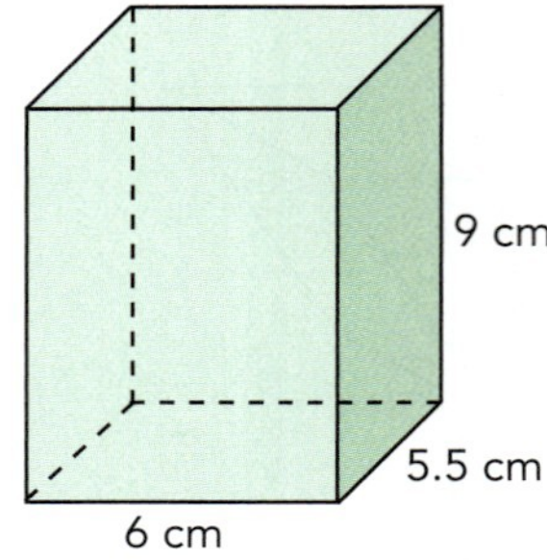

Area of base = $\underline{\ ?\ } \cdot \underline{\ ?\ }$

$= \underline{\ ?\ }$ cm^2

Volume of prism = $\underline{\ ?\ } \cdot \underline{\ ?\ }$

$= \underline{\ ?\ }$ cm^3

The volume of the prism is $\underline{\ ?\ }$ cubic centimeters.

8 Base of triangle = 10 in.
Height of triangle = $3\frac{1}{3}$ in.
Height of prism = 14 in.

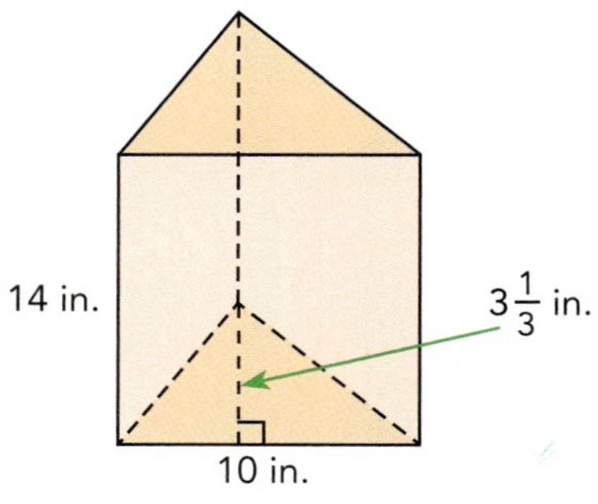

Area of base = $\frac{1}{2} \cdot \underline{\ ?\ } \cdot \underline{\ ?\ }$

$= \underline{\ ?\ }$ in.^{2}

Volume of prism = $\underline{\ ?\ } \cdot \underline{\ ?\ }$

$= \underline{\ ?\ }$ in.^{3}

The volume of the prism is $\underline{\ ?\ }$ cubic inches.

9 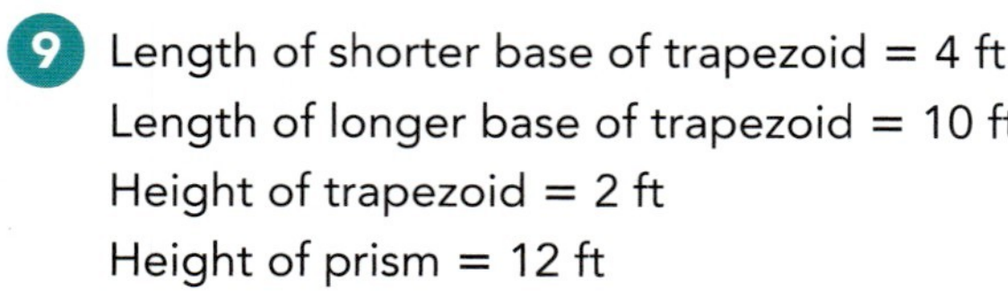
Length of shorter base of trapezoid = 4 ft
Length of longer base of trapezoid = 10 ft
Height of trapezoid = 2 ft
Height of prism = 12 ft

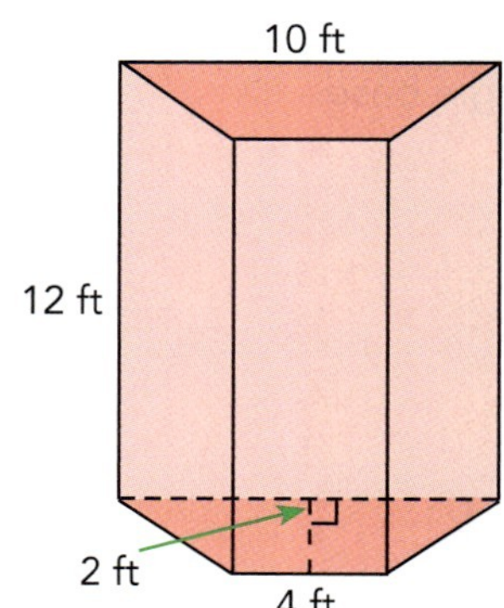

Area of base = $\frac{1}{2} \cdot \underline{\ ?\ } \cdot (\underline{\ ?\ } + \underline{\ ?\ })$

$= \frac{1}{2} \cdot \underline{\ ?\ } \cdot \underline{\ ?\ }$

$= \underline{\ ?\ }$ ft^2

Volume of prism = $\underline{\ ?\ } \cdot \underline{\ ?\ }$

$= \underline{\ ?\ }$ ft^3

The volume of the prism is $\underline{\ ?\ }$ cubic feet.

Hands-On Activity

Materials:

- 27 unit cubes

DETERMINING THE RELATIONSHIP BETWEEN VOLUME AND SURFACE AREA OF PRISMS

Work in pairs.

STEP 1 Build the cube and the rectangular prism using unit cubes.

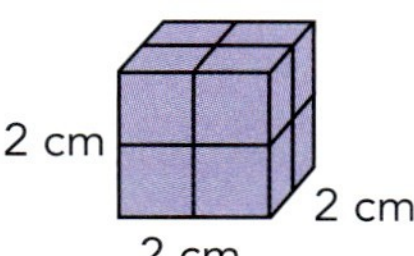

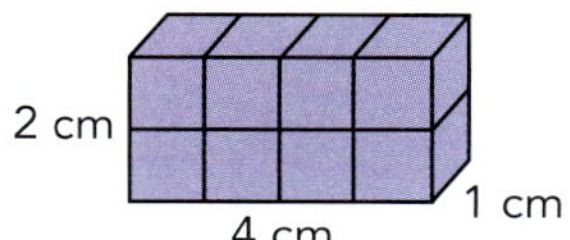

STEP 2 Find the volume of the cube.
Find the volume of the rectangular prism.
What can you say about the volumes of the cube and the rectangular prism?

STEP 3 Find the surface area of the cube. Draw its net if it helps you.
Find the surface area of the rectangular prism. Draw its net if it helps you.
What can you say about the surface areas of the cube and the rectangular prism?

STEP 4 Now, build these rectangular prisms using unit cubes.

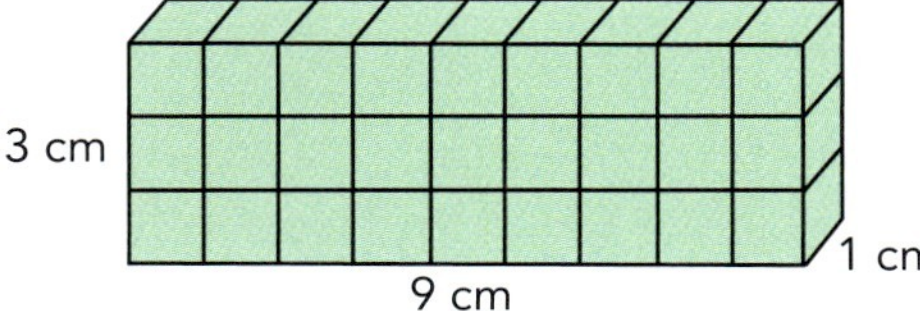

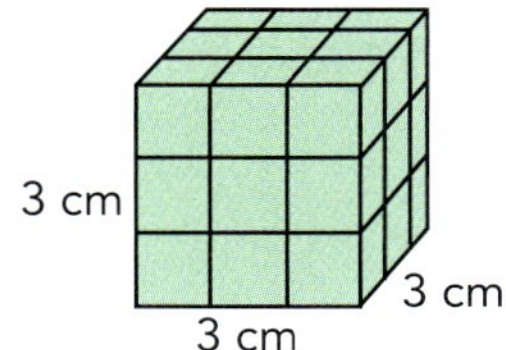

STEP 5 Find the volume of the cube. Find the volume of the rectangular prism.
What can you say about their volumes?

STEP 6 Find the surface area of the cube. Find the surface area of the rectangular prism. Draw their nets if it helps you. What can you say about their surface areas?

Math Journal Based on the activity, what can you conclude about prisms with the same volume? Discuss with your partner and explain your thinking.

Practice 12.3

Solve.

1. A cube has edges measuring 9 inches each. Find the volume of the cube.

2. A cube has edges measuring 6.5 centimeters each. Find the volume of the cube.

3. A storage container is shaped like a rectangular prism. The container is 20 feet long, 10 feet wide, and $5\frac{1}{2}$ feet high. Find the volume of the storage container.

4. Find the volume of the peppermint tea box on the right.

5. The solid below is made of idential cubes. Each cube has an edge length of 2 inches. Find the volume of the solid.

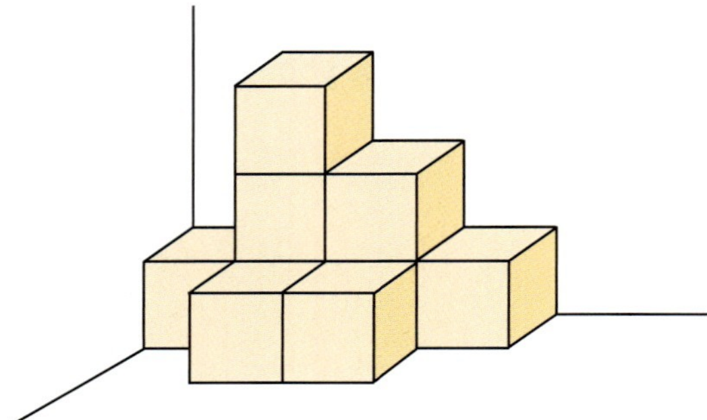

Find the volume of the triangular prism.

6.

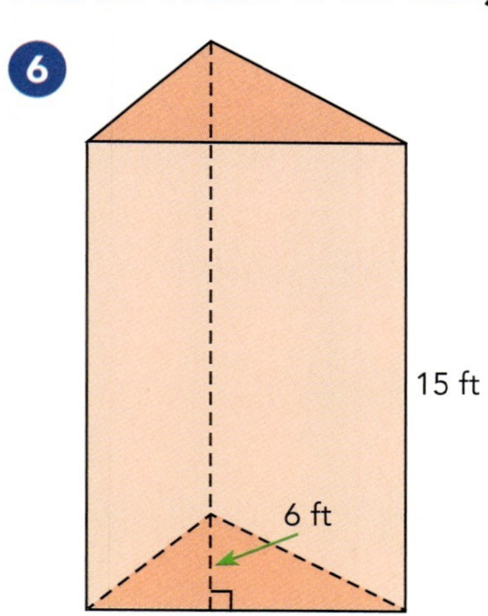

7.

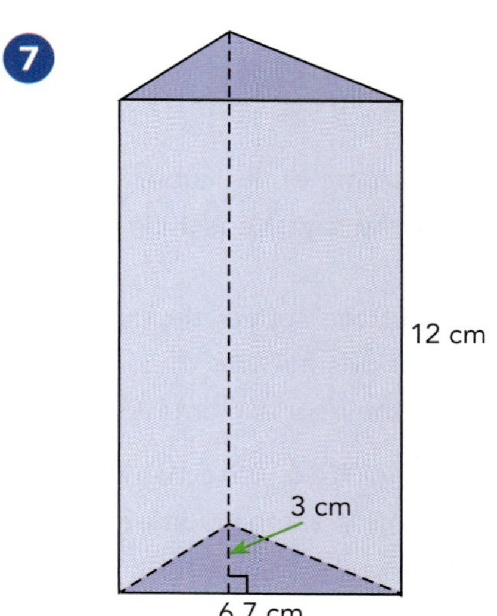

Tell whether slices parallel to each given slice will form uniform cross sections. If not, explain why not.

8 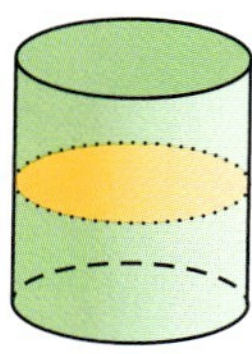

9 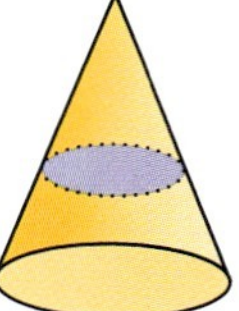

10 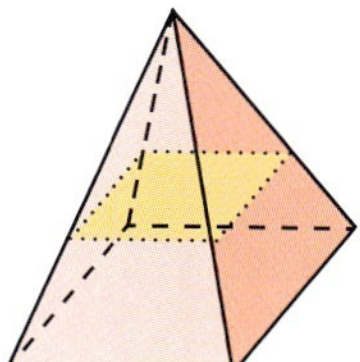

Copy the solid. Draw a slice that has the same cross section as the bases in each prism.

11 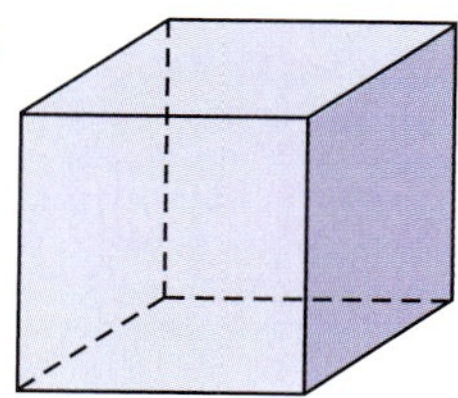

12 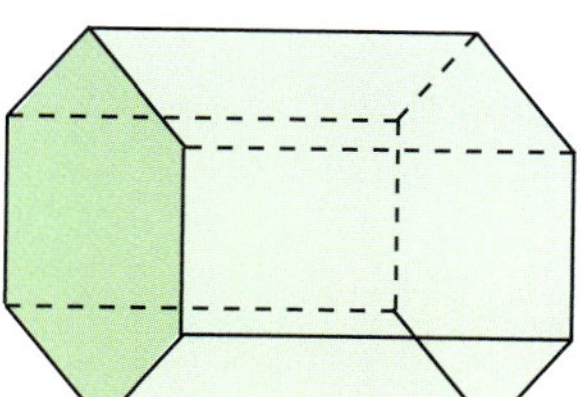

13 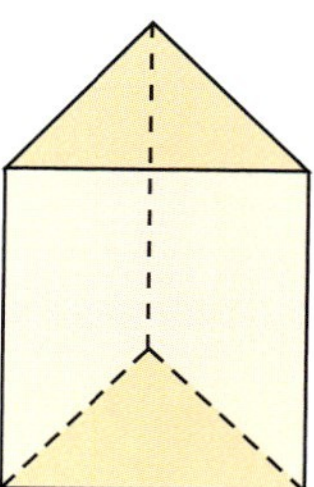

Solve.

14 The bases of the prism shown are trapezoids. Find the volume of the prism.

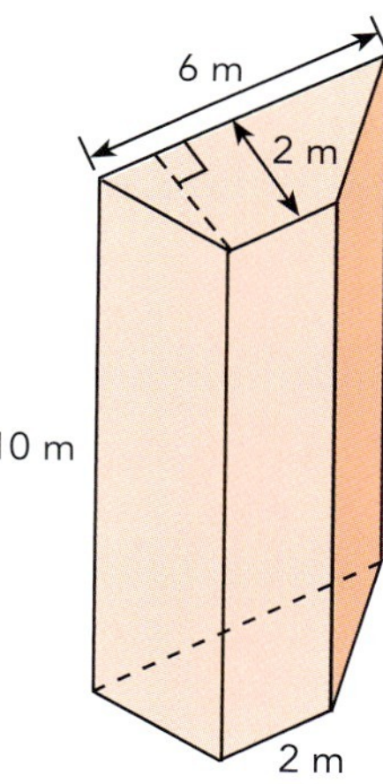

15 A cube has a volume of 125 cubic inches. Find the length of its edge.

16 The volume of a triangular prism is 400 cubic centimeters. Two of its dimensions are given in the diagram. Find the height of a triangular base.

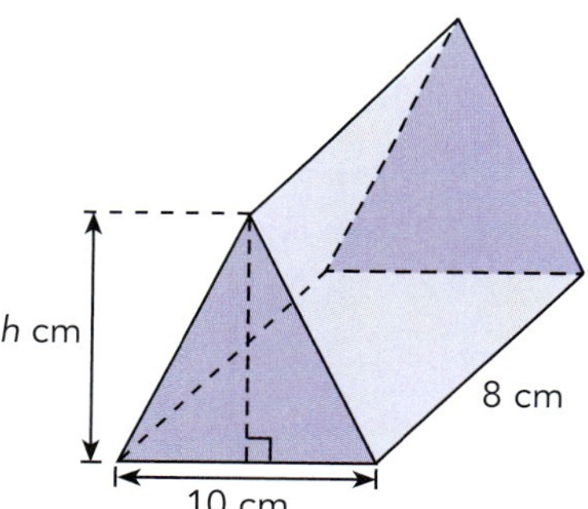

17 A cross section of the triangular prism shown below is parallel to a base. The area of the cross section is 24 square feet. The ratio of DM to MA is 3 : 5 and the length of $\overline{FO}$ is 6 feet. Find the volume of the triangular prism.

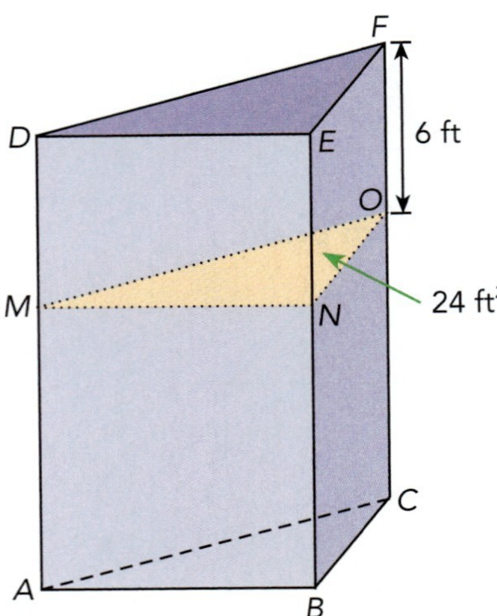

18 The volume of the rectangular prism shown below is 2,880 cubic inches. The cross section shown is parallel to a base. The area of the cross section is 180 square inches. The length of $\overline{AB}$ is x inches, and the length of $\overline{BC}$ is $4x$ inches.

a) Find the length of $\overline{AC}$.

b) Find the value of x.

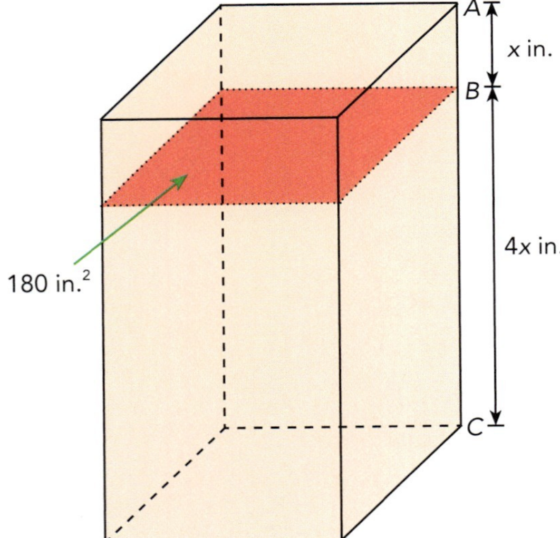

19 In the diagram of a cube shown below, points A, B, C, and D are vertices. Each of the other points on the cube is a midpoint of one of its sides. Describe a cross section of the cube that will form each of the following figures.

a) a rectangle

b) an isosceles triangle

c) an equilateral triangle

d) a parallelogram

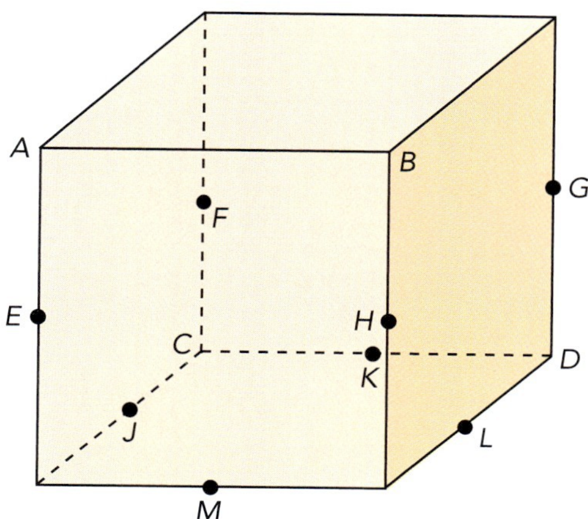

Solve. Use graph paper.

20 Points A, B, C, and D form a square. The area of the square is 9 square units.

a) Find the side length of square $ABCD$.

b) The coordinates of point A are (2, 6). Points B and C are below $\overline{AD}$. Point B is below point A, and point D is to the right of point A. Plot the points in a coordinate plane. Connect the points in order to draw square $ABCD$.

c) The points E, F, G, and H also form a square that is the same size as square $ABCD$. Point E is 4 units to the right of point A, and 3 units up. Points F and G are below $\overline{EH}$. Point F is below point E, and point H is to the right of point E. Plot the points in the coordinate plane. Draw $\overline{EH}$ and $\overline{GH}$ with solid lines, and $\overline{EF}$ and $\overline{FG}$ with dashed lines.

d) Draw $\overline{AE}$, $\overline{DH}$, and $\overline{CG}$ with solid lines, and $\overline{BF}$ with a dashed line. Use the solid and dashed lines to see the figure as a solid. Name the type of prism formed.

e) If the height of the prism is 7 units, find the volume of the prism.

12.4 Real-World Problems: Surface Area and Volume

Lesson Objective

- Solve problems involving surface area and volume of prisms.

Learn **Solve word problems about the volume of rectangular prisms.**

A rectangular fish tank 60 centimeters by 15 centimeters by 34 centimeters is $\frac{1}{3}$ full of water. Find the volume of water needed to fill the tank completely.

34 cm
15 cm
60 cm

Volume of water needed
= Volume of empty space in the tank

Height of empty space $= \frac{2}{3} \cdot 34$
$= \frac{68}{3}$ cm

Volume of water needed to fill the tank $= 60 \cdot 15 \cdot \frac{68}{3}$ Write equation.
$= 60 \cdot 5 \cdot 68$ Divide out common factor 3.
$= 20{,}400 \text{ cm}^3$ Multiply.

To fill the tank, 20,400 cubic centimeters more water are needed.

Guided Practice

Complete.

1 Find the volume of water needed to fill three fourths of the aquarium.

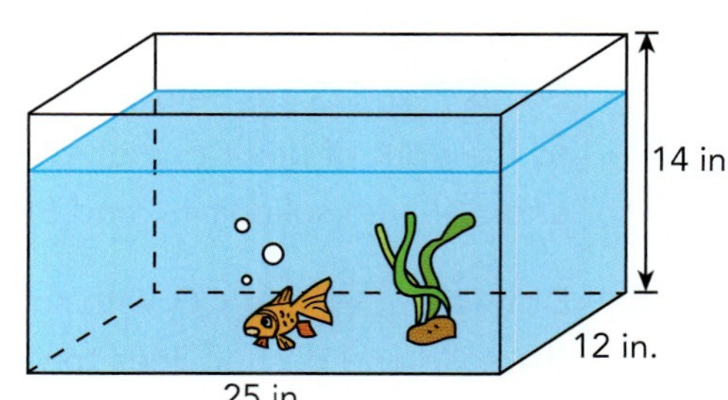

Height of water needed $= \frac{3}{4} \cdot$ ___?___
= ___?___ in.

Volume of water needed = ___?___ · ___?___ · ___?___
= ___?___ in.^{3}

The aquarium needs to have ___?___ cubic inches of water added to it to be $\frac{3}{4}$ full.

Learn Solve word problems about surface area and volume of non-rectangular prisms.

A block of wood is a prism and has the dimensions shown in the diagram below.

a) Find the volume of the block of wood.

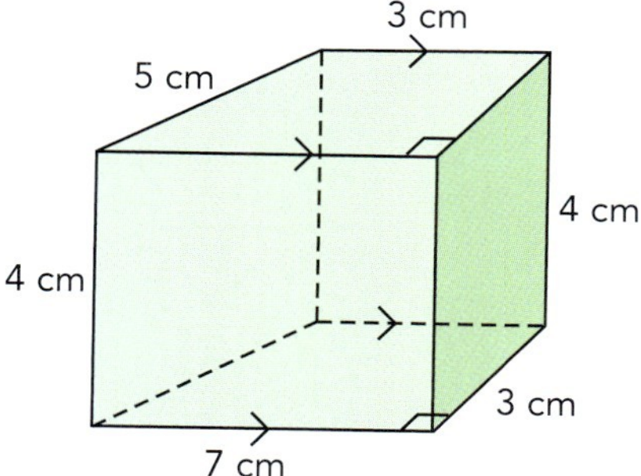

The base of the prism is a trapezoid.

Area of base

$= \frac{1}{2}h$(sum of lengths of parallel sides)

$= \frac{1}{2} \cdot 3 \cdot (3 + 7)$

$= \frac{1}{2} \cdot 3 \cdot 10$

$= 15 \text{ cm}^2$

Volume

$= Bh$

$= 15 \cdot 4$

$= 60 \text{ cm}^3$

Because all prisms have uniform cross sections when sliced parallel to the bases, you can use the formula $V = Bh$.

The volume of the block of wood is 60 cubic centimeters.

b) Find the surface area of the wooden block.

Surface area of wooden block

= perimeter of base · height + total area of two bases

$= (7 + 3 + 3 + 5) \cdot 4 + (2 \cdot 15)$

$= 18 \cdot 4 + 30$

$= 72 + 30$

$= 102 \text{ cm}^2$

The surface area of the wooden block is 102 square centimeters.

Guided Practice

Complete.

2 A metal bar has bases that are parallelograms.

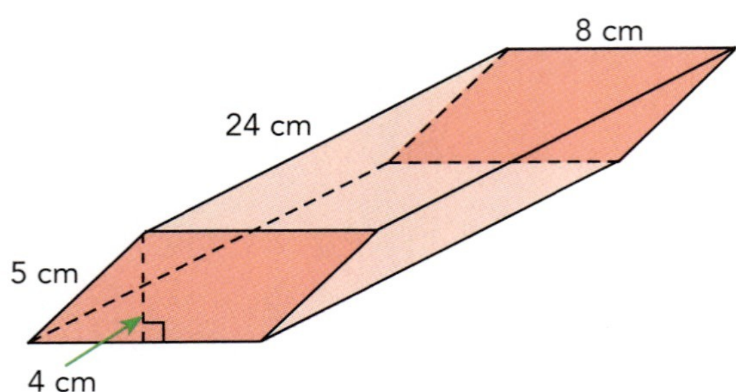

a) Find the volume of the metal bar.

Area of parallelogram
= base of parallelogram · height of parallelogram

= __?__ · __?__

= __?__ cm²

Volume of metal bar
= base of prism · height of prism

= __?__ · __?__

= __?__ cm³

The volume of the metal bar is __?__ cubic centimeters.

b) Find the surface area of the metal bar.

Surface area of metal bar
= perimeter of base · height + total area of 2 bases

= (__?__ + __?__ + __?__ + __?__) · __?__ + __?__ · __?__

= __?__ · __?__ + __?__

= __?__ + __?__

= __?__ cm²

The surface area of the metal bar is __?__ square centimeters.

Learn Solve word problems about prisms with missing dimensions.

A square prism of height 11 inches has a volume of 539 cubic inches.

a) Find the length of each side of the square base.

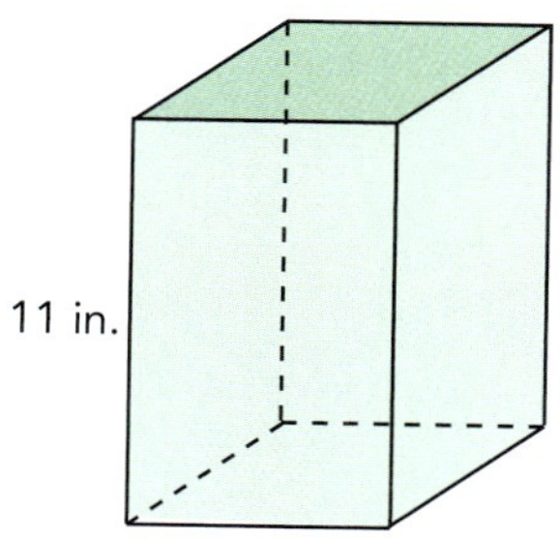

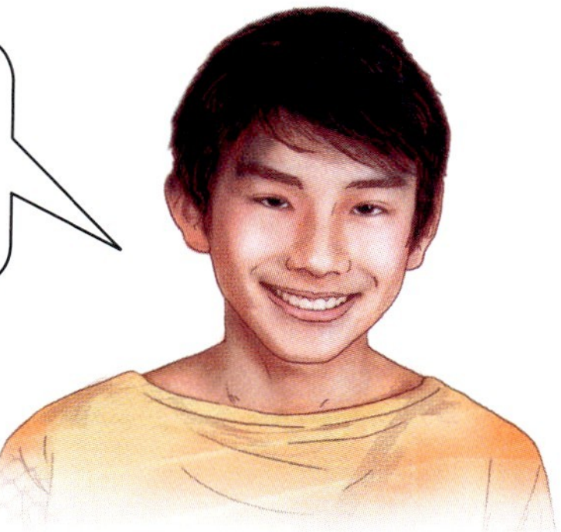

$V = Bh$ — Write formula.

$539 = B \cdot 11$ — Substitute.

$\frac{539}{11} = B \cdot \frac{11}{11}$ — Divide each side by 11.

$49 = B$ — Simplify.

The area of the square base is 49 square inches.

Length of each side of base $= \sqrt{49}$

$= 7$ in.

The length of each side of the square base is 7 inches.

b) Find the surface area of the prism.

Surface area of prism

= perimeter of base · height + area of two bases

$= (7 + 7 + 7 + 7) \cdot 11 + 2 \cdot 49$

$= 28 \cdot 11 + 98$

$= 308 + 98$

$= 406 \text{ in.}^2$

The surface area of the prism is 406 square inches.

Learn Solve word problems about non-rectangular prisms with missing dimensions.

Jacob is making a wooden birdhouse. The birdhouse is a prism with bases that are pentagons, and has the dimensions shown in the diagram. The volume of the prism is 720 cubic inches.

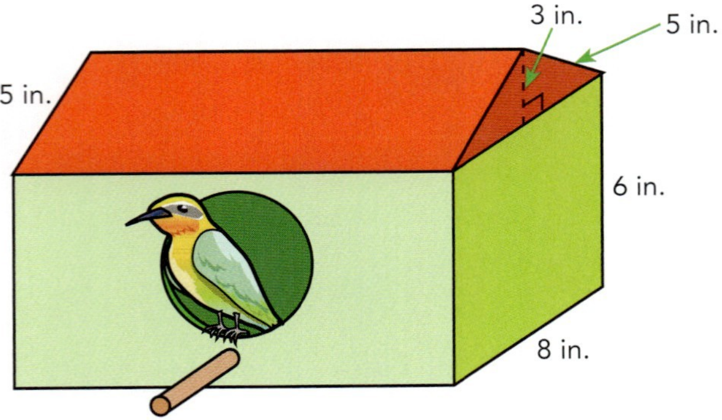

a) Find the height of the prism.

Area of pentagonal base

= area of triangle + area of rectangle

$= \left(\frac{1}{2} \cdot 8 \cdot 3\right) + 8 \cdot 6$

$= 12 + 48$

$= 60 \text{ in.}^2$

$V = Bh$	Write formula.
$720 = 60 \cdot h$	Substitute.
$\frac{720}{60} = h \cdot \frac{60}{60}$	Divide each side by 60.
$12 = h$	Simplify.

The height of the prism is 12 inches.

b) Find the surface area of the prism.

Surface area of the prism

= perimeter of base · height + area of two bases

$= (5 + 6 + 8 + 6 + 5) \cdot 12 + 2 \cdot 60$

$= 30 \cdot 12 + 120$

$= 360 + 120$

$= 480 \text{ in.}^2$

The surface area of the prism is 480 square inches.

Guided Practice

Complete.

3 A candle is a square prism. The candle is 15 centimeters high, and its volume is 960 cubic centimeters.

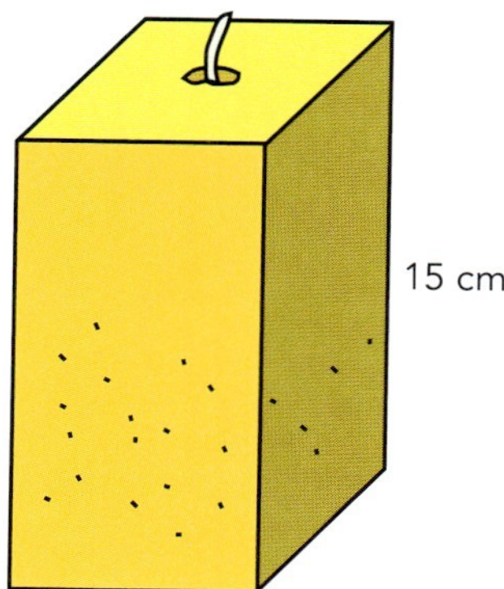

a) Find the length of each side of the square base.

$V = Bh$

$\underline{\ ?\ } = B \cdot \underline{\ ?\ }$

$\underline{\ ?\ } \div \underline{\ ?\ } = \underline{\ ?\ } \cdot B \div \underline{\ ?\ }$

$\underline{\ ?\ } = B$

Length of each side of base

$= \underline{\ ?\ }$

$= \underline{\ ?\ }$ cm

The length of each side of the square base is $\underline{\ ?\ }$ centimeters.

b) Find the surface area of the candle.

Surface area of candle
= perimeter of base · height + area of two bases

$= (\underline{\ ?\ } + \underline{\ ?\ } + \underline{\ ?\ } + \underline{\ ?\ }) \cdot \underline{\ ?\ } + \underline{\ ?\ } \cdot \underline{\ ?\ }$

$= \underline{\ ?\ } \cdot \underline{\ ?\ } + \underline{\ ?\ }$

$= \underline{\ ?\ } + \underline{\ ?\ }$

$= \underline{\ ?\ }$ cm^2

The surface area of the candle is $\underline{\ ?\ }$ square centimeters.

4 A storage chest is a prism with bases that are pentagons. The diagram shows some of the dimensions of the storage chest. The volume of the storage chest is 855 cubic inches.

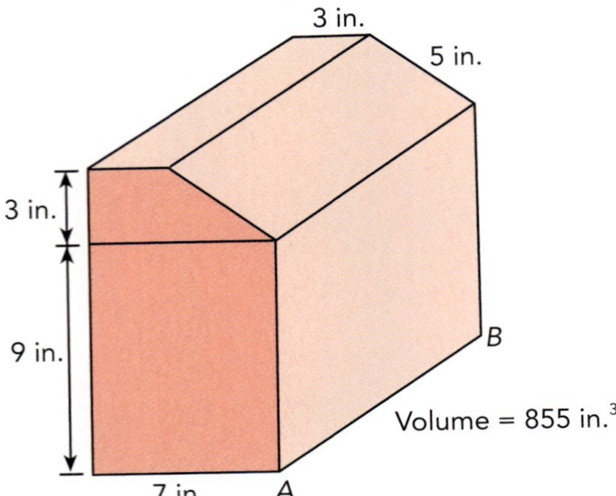

a) Find the height AB of the prism. Round your answer to the nearest hundredth.

Area of pentagonal base

= area of trapezoid + area of rectangle

$= \frac{1}{2} \cdot \underline{?} \cdot (\underline{?} + \underline{?}) + \underline{?} \cdot \underline{?}$

$= \underline{?} + \underline{?}$

$= \underline{?}$ in.²

$V = Bh$

$\underline{?} = \underline{?} \cdot h$

$\underline{?} \div \underline{?} = \underline{?} \cdot h \div \underline{?}$

$\underline{?} \approx h$

The height of the prism is approximately $\underline{?}$ inches.

b) Find the surface area of the prism. Round your answer to the nearest hundredth.

Surface area of prism

= perimeter of base · height + area of two bases

$\approx (\underline{?} + \underline{?} + \underline{?} + \underline{?} + \underline{?}) \cdot \underline{?} + \underline{?} \cdot \underline{?}$

$= \underline{?} \cdot \underline{?} + \underline{?}$

$= \underline{?} + \underline{?}$

$= \underline{?}$ in.²

The surface area of the prism is approximately $\underline{?}$ square inches.

Practice 12.4

Solve.

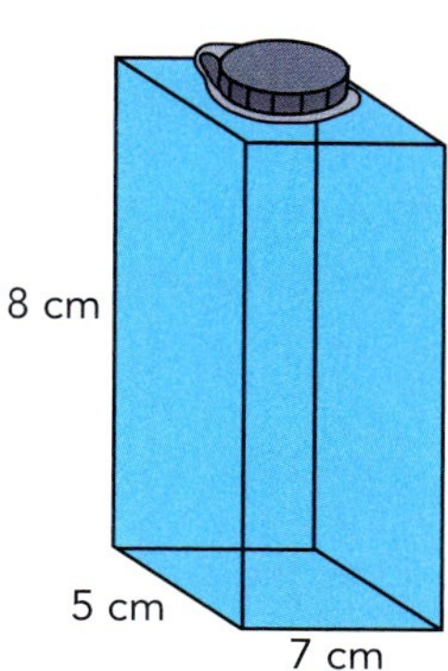

1. Savannah has a water bottle that is a rectangular prism. The bottle measures 7 centimeters by 5 centimeters by 18 centimeters and she filled it completely with water. Then, she drank $\frac{1}{4}$ of the volume of water in her water bottle. How many cubic centimeters of water were left in the water bottle?

2. A rectangular prism has a square base with edges measuring 8 inches each. Its volume is 768 cubic inches.

   a) Find the height of the prism.

   b) Find the surface area of the prism.

3. A triangular prism has the measurements shown.

   a) Find the volume of the prism.

   b) Find the surface area of the prism.

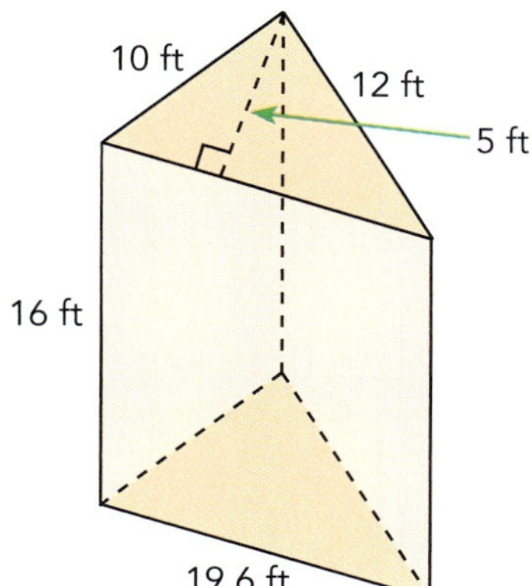

4. The volume of Box A is $\frac{2}{5}$ the volume of Box B. What is the height of Box A if it has a base area of 32 square centimeters?

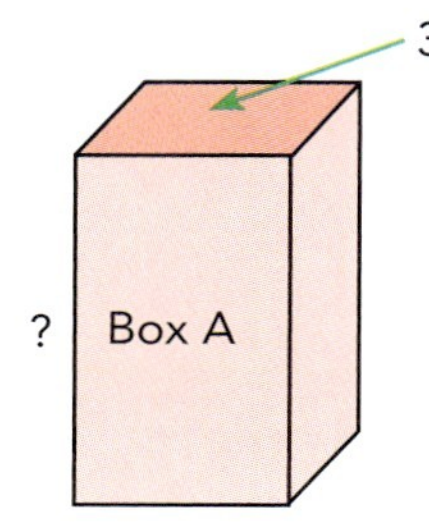

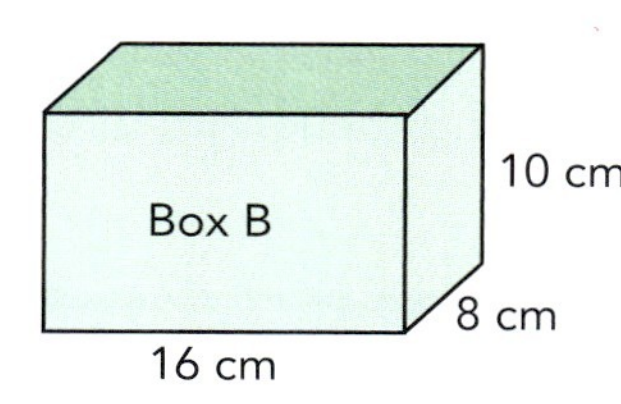

5 The ratio of the length to the width to the height of an open rectangular tank is 10 : 5 : 8. The height of the tank is 18 feet longer than the width.

a) Find the volume of the tank.

b) Find the surface area of the open tank.

6 Janice is making a gift box. The gift box is a prism with bases that are regular hexagons, and has the dimensions shown in the diagram.

a) Find the height *PQ* of the prism.

b) Find the surface area of the prism.

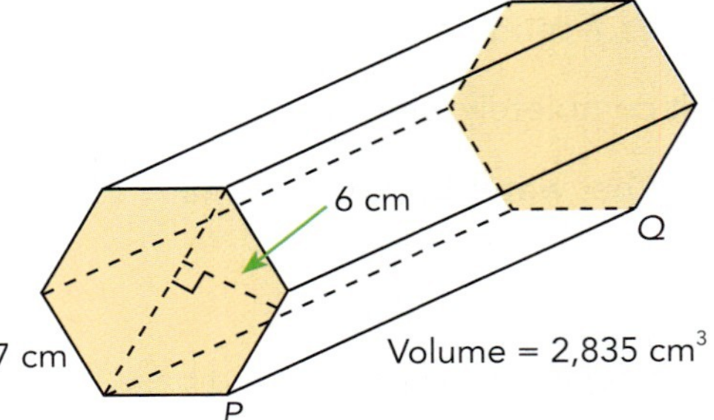

7 Container A was filled with water to the brim. Then, some of the water was poured into an empty Container B until the height of the water in both containers became the same. Find the new height of the water in both containers.

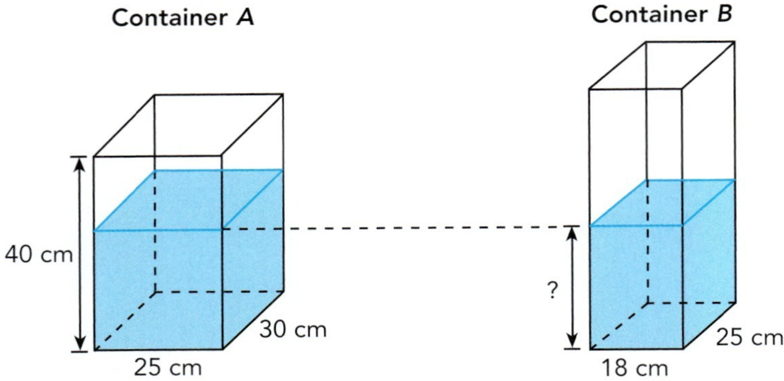

1 The volume of a cube is 100 cubic inches. If each of the edges is doubled in length, what will be the volume of the cube?

2 The volume of a cube is *x* cubic feet and its surface area is *x* square feet, where *x* represents the same number. Find the length of each edge of the cube.

Chapter Wrap Up

Concept Map

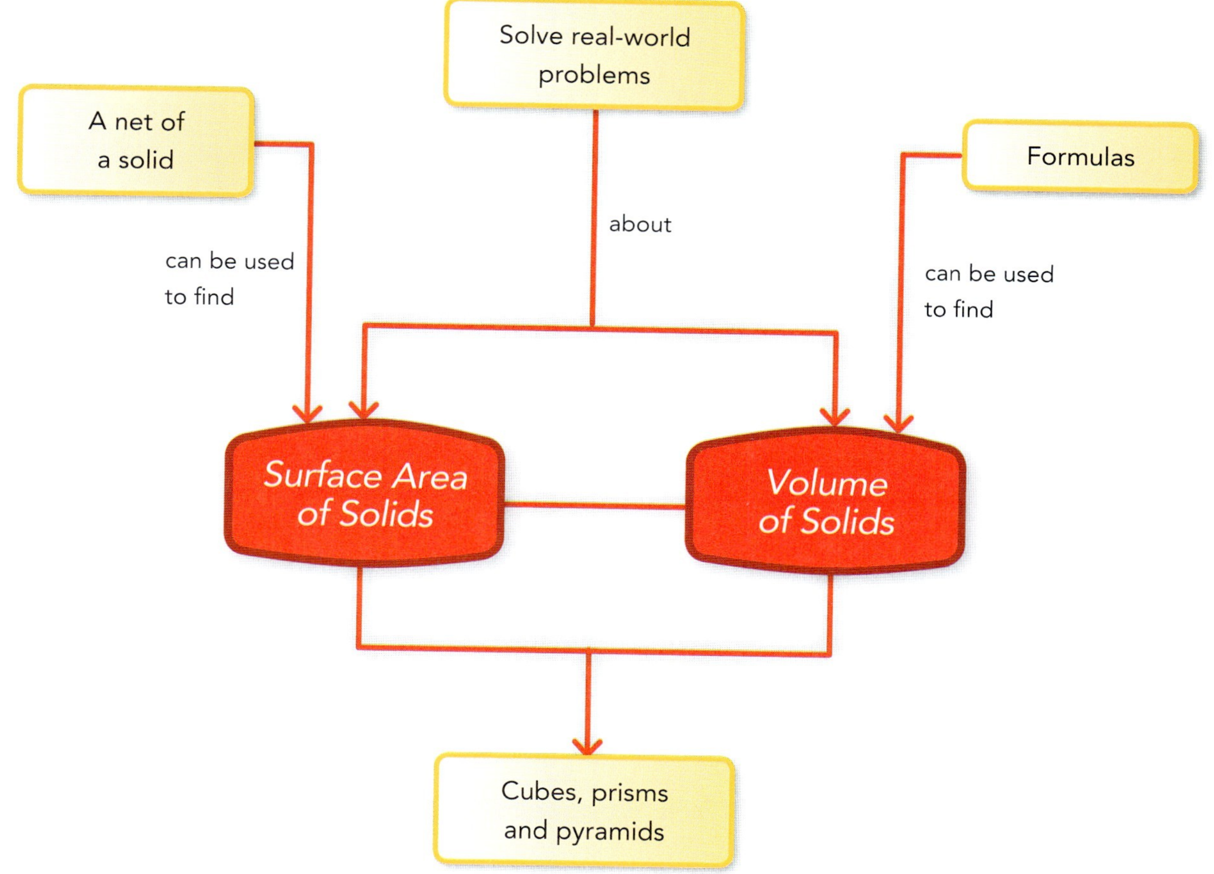

Key Concepts

- The volume of a rectangular prism is the product of its length, width, and height.
- The volume of any prism is the product of the area of its base and its height.
- The surface area of a prism or pyramid is the sum of the areas of its faces.

Chapter Review/Test

Concepts and Skills

Match each of the solid figures to its net.

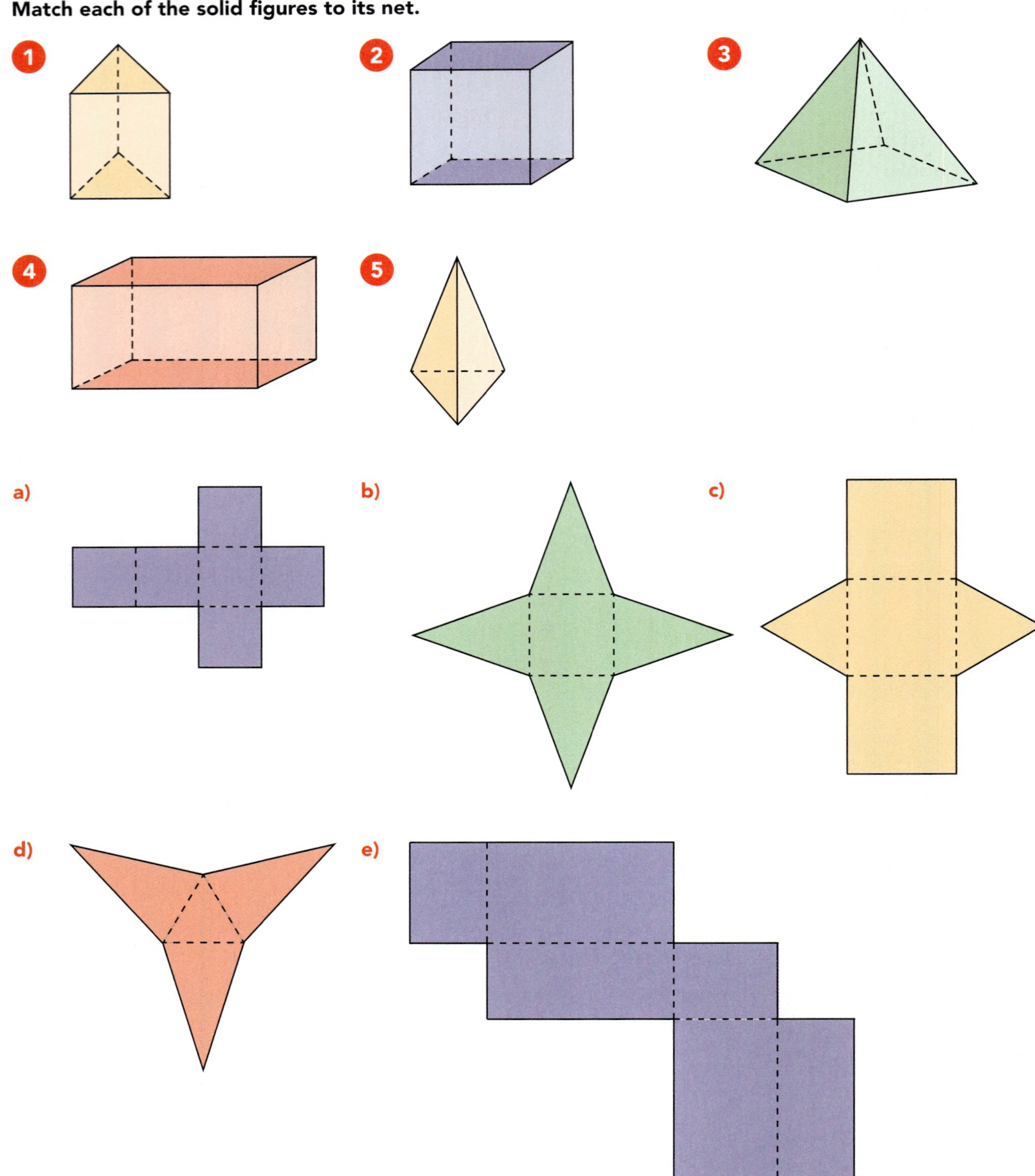

Find the surface area of each solid.

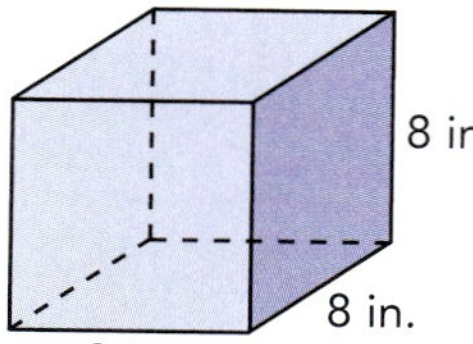

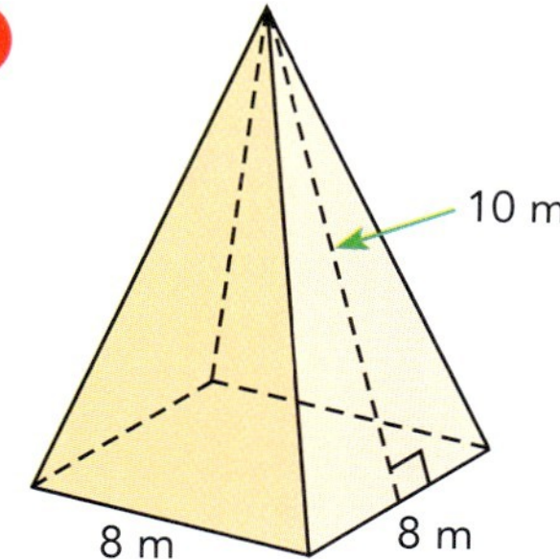

Find the volume of each prism.

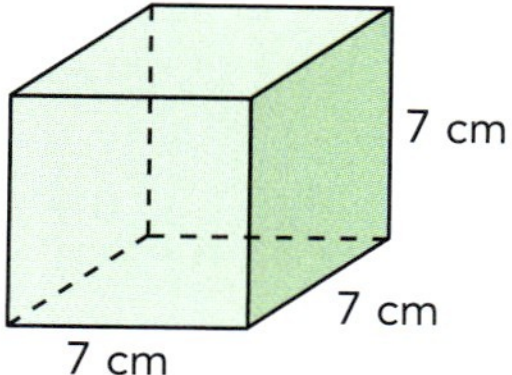

9

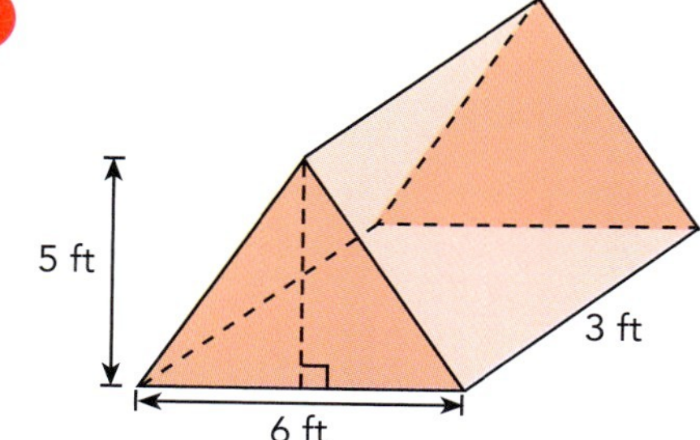

Solve.

10 The solid below is made up of cubes, each of which has an edge length of 3 inches.

a) What is the volume of one cube?

b) What is the volume of the solid figure?

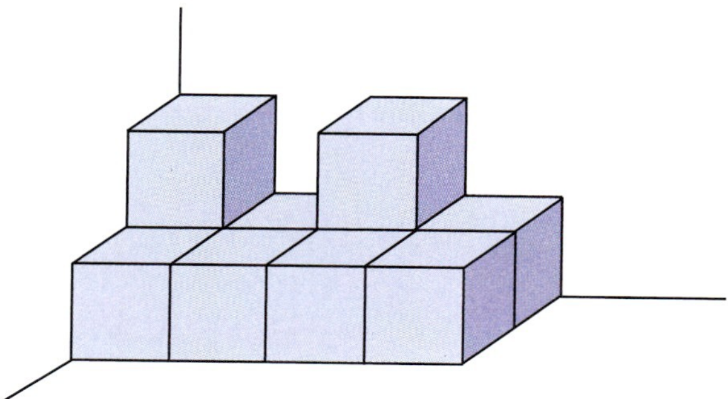

Problem Solving

Solve.

11 A fish tank is 50 centimeters long, 30 centimeters wide, and 40 centimeters high. It contains water up to a height of 28 centimeters. How many more cubic centimeters of water are needed to fill the tank to a height of 35 centimeters?

12 Find the surface area of a square pyramid given that its base area is 196 square inches and the height of each of its triangular faces is 16 inches.

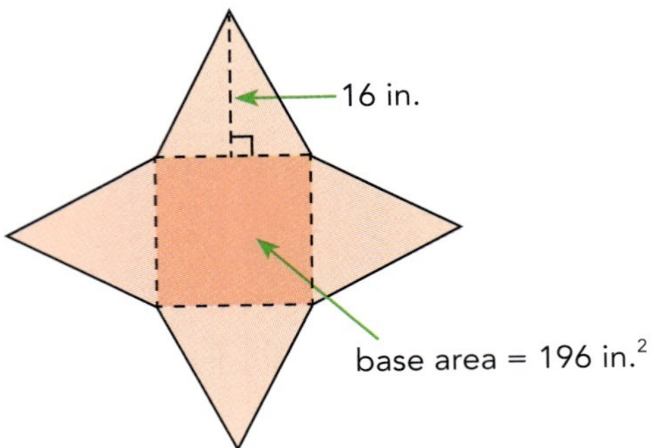

13 The volume of a rectangular prism is 441 cubic feet. It has a square base with edges that are 7 feet long.

a) Find the height of the prism.

b) Find the surface area of the prism.

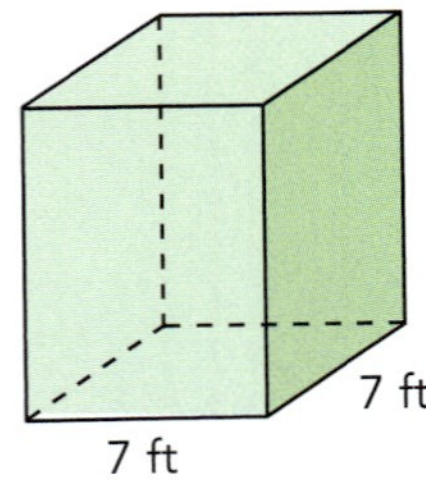

14 The volume of a rectangular tank with a square base is 63,908 cubic centimeters. Its height is 64 centimeters. Find the length of an edge of one of the square bases. Round your answer to the nearest tenth of a centimeter.

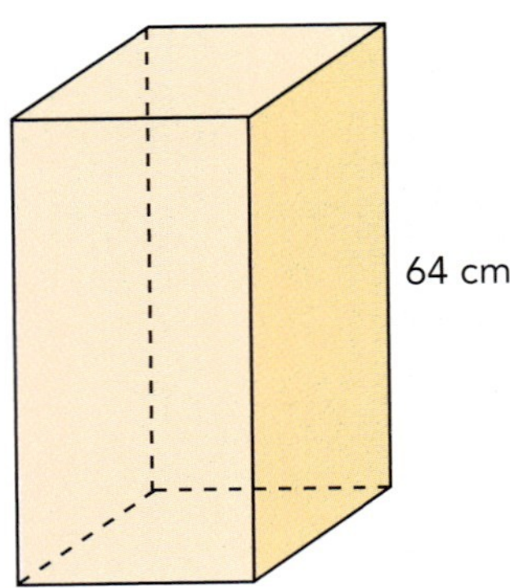

 **15** A rectangular container has a base that is 12 inches long and 8 inches wide. The container is filled with water to a height of 6 inches. If all the water is poured into a second container with a square base, it will rise to a height of 16 inches. What is the length of one edge of the square base of the second container?

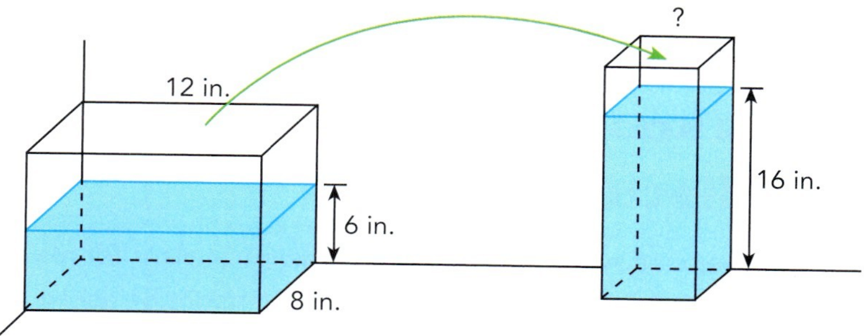

 **16** Find the surface area and the volume of the prism.

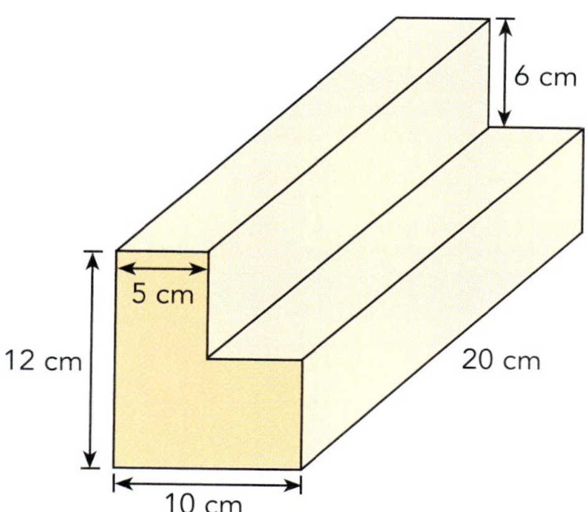

 **17** Find the surface area and the volume of the prism.

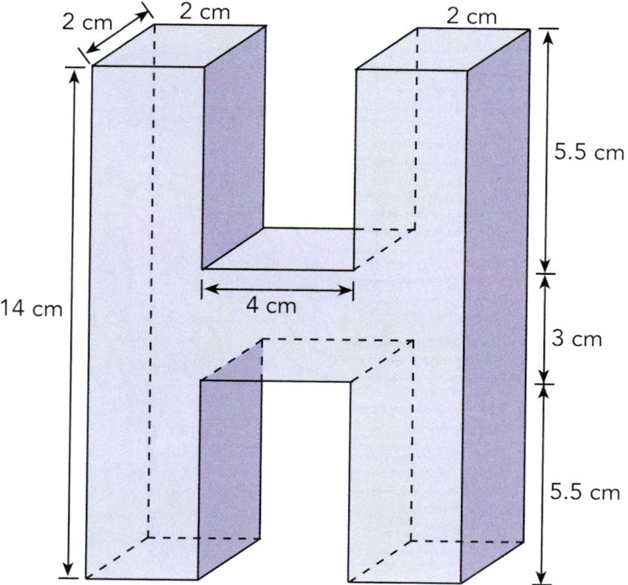

CHAPTER

13

Introduction to Statistics

BIG IDEA

▶ Statistics summarize data so that information or decisions can be gathered from the data.

Do you know why and how statistics are collected?

Have you ever wondered how a cafeteria manager plans for making food every day? Some statistical questions that might be asked about preparing food for the cafeteria are:

- How many students do we serve each day?
- How many students order pancakes for breakfast?

These are statistical questions because many pieces of data are needed to answer each question. Cafeteria managers need answers to questions such as these to find out how much food they will need to buy each week or how many cooks they will need to hire.

Once data have been collected, it needs to be organized so that patterns and trends can be seen. Data displays, such as graphs, can help summarize the data and make it easy to understand. Learning about statistics and data displays can help you understand and find solutions to real-world problems.

Recall Prior Knowledge

Interpreting data in a line plot

Michael surveyed a group of children in a music class to find out their ages. The table below shows the results of his survey.

Ages of Children

Name of Child	Age (yr)
Allen	12
Brooklyn	11
Eric	10
Gianna	12
Isabelle	12
Juan	12
Lauren	13
Miguel	12
Parker	11
Vanessa	11

Michael made a line plot to show the results of his survey.
Each × represents 1 student.

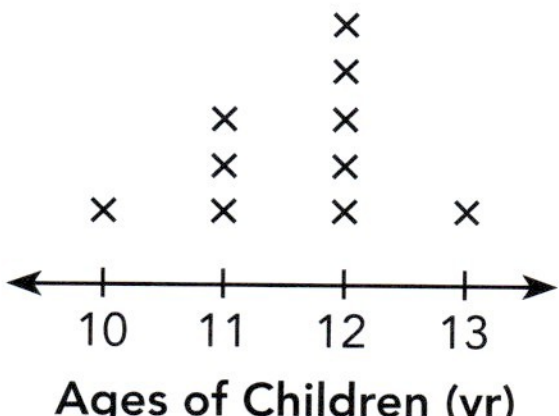

Three of the students are 11 years old.
The most common age is 12 years old.
The number of students who are 10 years old and 13 years old is the same.
The total number of students in the music class is 10.
Six of the students are older than 11 years.

Quick Check

Complete. Use the data in the line plot.

The line plot shows the weight, in pounds, of cartons of apples in a store. Each × represents 1 carton of apples.

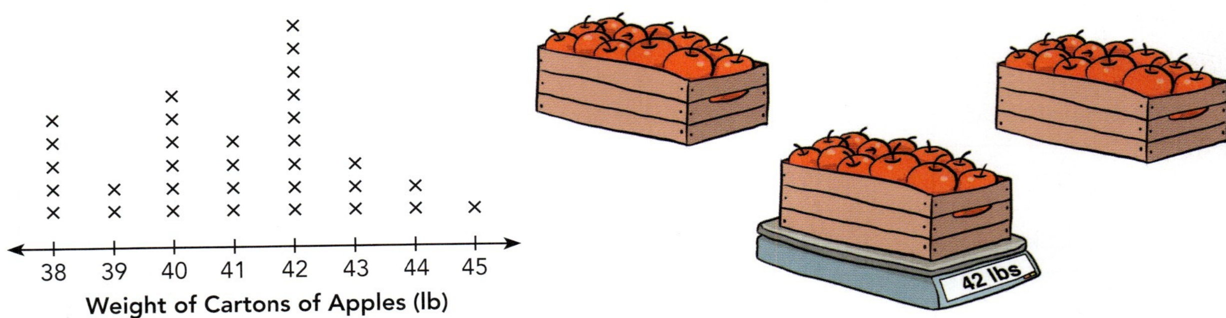

1. What is the weight of the lightest carton of apples?

2. What is the weight of the heaviest carton of apples?

3. What is the difference in weight between the heaviest carton of apples and the lightest carton of apples?

4. How many cartons weigh more than 41 pounds?

5. How many cartons weigh less than 40 pounds?

6. How many cartons weigh 44 pounds each?

7. How many cartons are there in all?

8. How many times as many cartons of apples weigh 40 pounds as the number of cartons of apples that weigh 43 pounds?

9. The ratio of the number of cartons of apples that weigh 42 pounds to the number of cartons of apples that weigh 40 pounds is __?__.

10. The number of cartons of apples that weigh 41 pounds is __?__ % of the total number of cartons of apples.

13.1 Collecting and Tabulating Data

Lesson Objective

- Collect, organize, and tabulate data.

Vocabulary
frequency

Collect and tabulate data.

Sean wants to find how students in his class get to school.

To do this, he can collect the data by using one of the three methods.

Method 1: Carrying out observations

Sean can stand at the school door in the morning to observe how his classmates arrive at school.

Which method is the most efficient?

Method 2: Conducting surveys through interviews

Sean can interview his classmates to find out how they get to school.

Method 3: Conducting surveys using a questionnaire

Sean can prepare a questionnaire for his classmates to complete, such as the one below.

How Do You Get to School?

Check (✓) the box next to how you usually come to school.
Choose only one option.

Walk ☐ Bus ☐

Bicycle ☐ Car ☐

Continue on next page

Sean uses a tally chart to record the results of his survey. Then he counts the tally marks to find how many students use each form of transportation.

How My Classmates Get to School

How Students Get to School	Tally	Frequency
Walk	~~////~~ ///	8
Bus	~~////~~ ~~////~~ ///	13
Bicycle	////	4
Car	~~////~~	5

Frequency refers to how often a piece of data, such as an item or a number, occurs.

Eight of Sean's classmates walk to school.
The most common form of transportation is by bus.
The least common form of transportation is by bicycle.
There is 1 more classmate who comes to school by car than by bicycle.
Sean collected data from 30 classmates altogether, excluding himself.

Guided Practice

Complete. Use the data in the table.

Emma used a questionnaire to find out the number of brothers or sisters her classmates have in their families.

Then she used a tally chart to record what she had found.

1. Copy and complete the table by counting the tally marks.

Number of Brothers or Sisters of Emma's Classmates

Number of Brothers or Sisters	Tally	Frequency
0	///	?
1	~~////~~ ////	?
2	~~////~~ //	?
3	~~////~~	?
4	//	?
5 or more	/	?

2. More of Emma's classmates have __?__ brother or sister than any other number.

3. __?__ of Emma's classmates have 3 brothers or sisters in their families.

4. __?__ of Emma's classmates have 4 brothers or sisters in their families.

5. How many more of Emma's classmates have 2 brothers or sisters than 5 or more brothers or sisters in their families?

6. Emma has __?__ classmates altogether.

Hands-On Activity

Materials:

- blank table
- ruler
- collection of pencils

COLLECT, TABULATE, AND INTERPRET DATA

Work in groups of three or four.

STEP 1 Collect a set of pencils of various lengths. Use a ruler to measure the length of each pencil to the nearest centimeter. Use tally marks to record the data.

STEP 2 Tally your results on a table like the one below. Then count the tally marks to complete the table.

Length of Pencil (cm)	Tally	Frequency
?	?	?
?	?	?
?	?	?
?	?	?
?	?	?

STEP 3 Write at least four questions about the data in the table using these phrases.

- how many pencils
- shortest
- longest
- fewer than
- more than
- altogether

Practice 13.1

Copy and complete the table. Solve.

1 A shampoo company wanted to find out more about its customers. So they asked 30 customers to indicate their income bracket:

Below $500 per week
$500–$1,000 per week
Over $1,000 per week

A tally chart was used to record the findings.

Weekly Income	Tally	Frequency
Below $500	~~////~~ //	?
$500–$1,000	~~////~~ ~~////~~ ~~////~~ ////	?
Over $1,000	////	?

How many customers have a weekly income of $1,000 or less?

2 Fifty students were asked their level of satisfaction with the school's music program. The following responses were the choices provided:

(a) very satisfied (b) satisfied (c) neutral (d) dissatisfied (e) very dissatisfied.

Level of Satisfaction	Tally	Frequency
Very satisfied	//	?
Satisfied	~~////~~ //	?
Neutral	~~////~~ ~~////~~ ~~////~~ ~~////~~ ////	?
Dissatisfied	~~////~~ ~~////~~ ////	?
Very dissatisfied	////	?

a) How many students are satisfied or very satisfied?

b) Based on the results of the survey, should the school think about changing the program? Explain your reasoning.

3 A mathematics teacher wanted to find out how many hours per week his students spent on math homework. The average number of hours reported by each student is shown.

5, 3, 6, 8, 2, 4, 2, 1, 9, 1, 9, 6, 4, 6, 5, 1, 10, 1, 5, 6, 7, 8, 6, 10, 7, 5, 2, 8

Arrange the numbers in ascending order.

Number of Hours	Tally	Frequency
0–3	?	?
4–7	?	?
8–10	?	?

How many students spent more than 3 hours per week on their math homework?

4 Shelly conducted a survey among her friends. She asked them to choose their favorite fruit from this list of fruits: apple, orange, strawberry, grapes, and peach. These are the data she collected:

Favorite Fruits

strawberry	peach	apple	apple
orange	strawberry	strawberry	grapes
strawberry	apple	strawberry	apple
peach	orange	grapes	orange
strawberry	apple	strawberry	grapes

Tabulate the data.

Fruit	Tally	Frequency
Apple	?	?
Orange	?	?
Strawberry	?	?
Grapes	?	?
Peach	?	?

What is the favorite fruit of Shelly's friends?

13.2 Dot Plots

Lesson Objective

- Display and analyze data using a dot plot.

Vocabulary

dot plot
symmetrical
skewed
range

Learn

Represent numerical data using a **dot plot**.

a) The number of text messages sent by some students one day is as follows. Represent the data on a dot plot.

12	11	10	15	13
15	12	11	12	11

The number of text messages spans from 10 to 15 messages.
To construct a dot plot of these numbers, draw a horizontal number line that extends from 10 to 15.

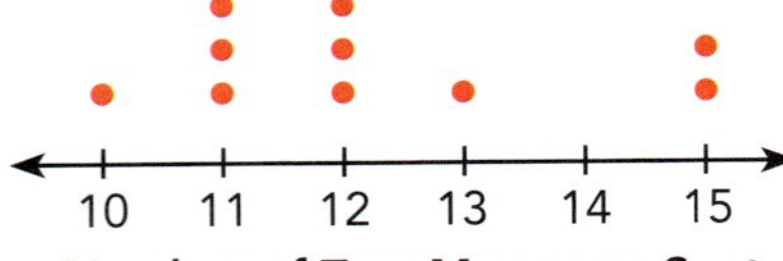

The data value 10 appears once, so place one dot above the number 10 on the number line. The data value 11 appears three times, so place three dots above the number 11.
The data value 14 is absent, so there is no dot above the number 14.

Dot plots are similar to line plots. Simply replace the ×s with dots.

b) Eugenia tossed a number cube, numbered 1 to 6, 20 times. She recorded the number in the table below. Represent the data on a dot plot.

Number	1	2	3	4	5	6
Frequency	2	3	6	1	5	3

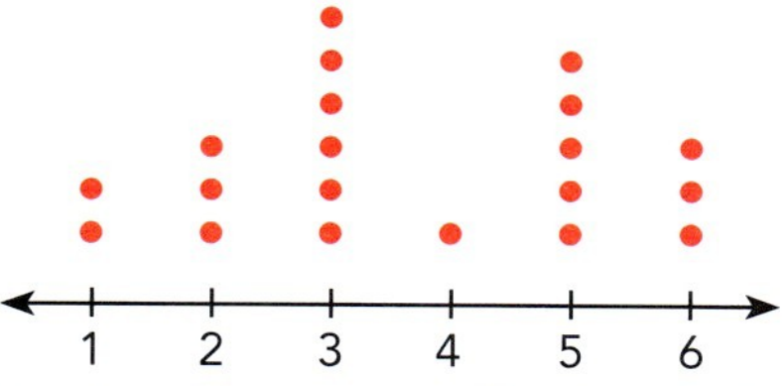

Numbers Tossed on a Number Cube

Guided Practice

Represent each set of data with a dot plot. Give each dot plot a title.

1. A group of 15 students was asked how many times they have traveled on a plane. The results are recorded in the table.

Number of Plane Trips	0	1	2	3	4	5	6
Number of Students	1	5	3	1	1	3	1

2. The results of the high jumps at a track meet are recorded in the table.

High Jump Results (cm)	150	151	152	153	154	155
Number of Students	1	4	3	1	0	2

Learn

Identifying the shape of a set of data.

The shape of a dot plot can be either **symmetrical** or **skewed**.

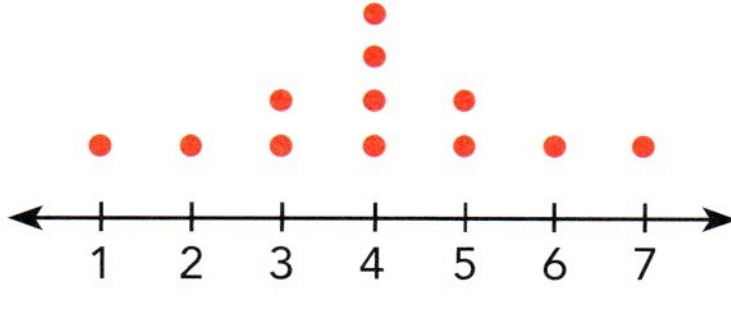

Most of the data is near the center of the range. The shape is symmetrical.

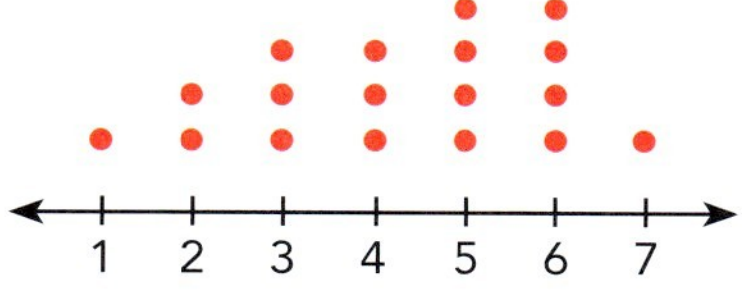

The dot plot has a "tail" on the left. The shape is left-skewed.

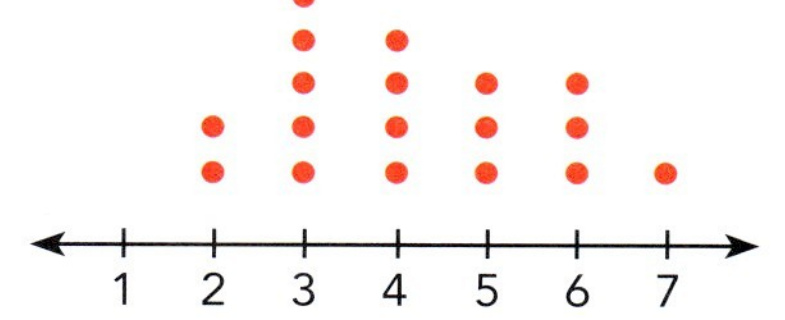

The dot plot has a "tail" on the right. The shape is right-skewed.

Learn Interpret data from a dot plot.

a) The money (in dollars) that 15 students earned by babysitting in one week is shown in the dot plot on the right. Briefly describe the distribution of the earnings of the students.

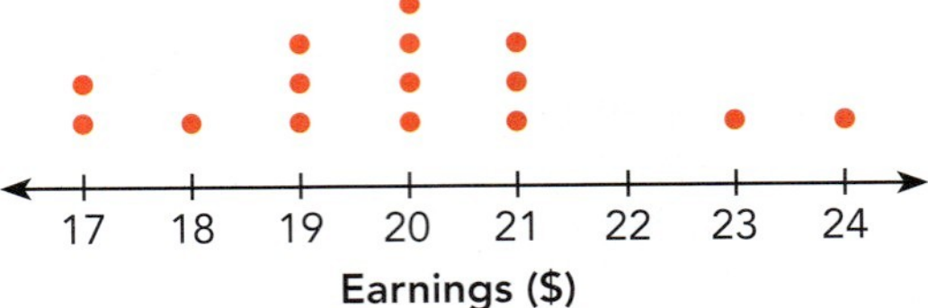

A dot plot can be described by its shape and its **range**.

This dot plot is nearly symmetrical.

These data show a nearly symmetrical dot plot centered around 20. Most of the data values are from 19 to 21.

The data values are from 17 to 24.

The range of the data is the difference of these numbers.

Range: $24 - 17 = 7$

From these characteristics, you can describe the weekly earnings of the babysitters. They typically earn from \$19 to \$21 each week, but their earnings range from \$17 to \$24.

b) The number of movies that 12 students saw last month is shown in the dot plot on the right. Briefly describe the number of movies seen by the students.

The 12 dots represent 12 students. The dot plot has a "tail" on the right. Most of the data value are from 4 to 6, and the distribution is skewed to the right. The data values are from 3 to 8.

Range: $8 - 3 = 5$

From the description of the dot plot, you know that the students saw about 4 or 5 movies last month, and all of them saw 3 to 8 movies.

Guided Practice

Describe the data.

3 The weekly savings (in dollars) of 10 students in a class are shown in the dot plot. Briefly describe the distribution of the weekly savings of the students.

4 The number of points scored by 12 members of a volleyball team in a game is shown in the dot plot. Briefly describe the number of points scored by the group of players.

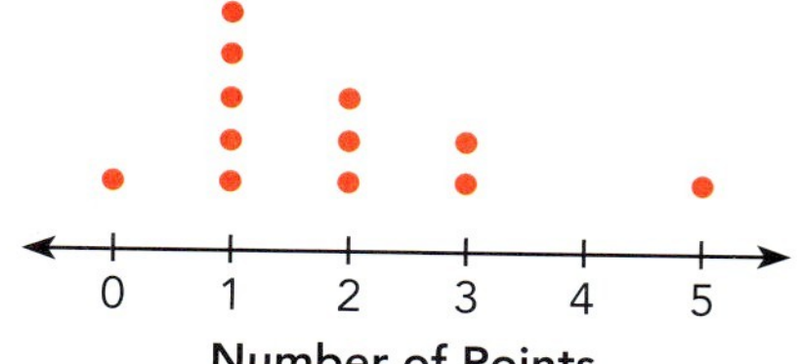

Hands-On Activity

Materials:

- 2 number cubes, numbered 1–6
- blank table

CONSTRUCTING A DISTRIBUTION

Work in pairs.

STEP 1 Toss two number cubes. Record the difference between the two numbers in a tally chart.

STEP 2 Repeat 20 times and add your results to another group's results. Record the results for 40 tosses in a copy of the table below.

Difference	0	1	2	3	4	5
Frequency	?	?	?	?	?	?

STEP 3 Represent the data with a dot plot.

STEP 4 Repeat **STEP 1** to **STEP 3**, but record the SUM of the two numbers each time.

a) What is the least sum you can get?

b) What is the greatest sum you can get?

Math Journal

a) Describe the distribution of the differences.

b) Describe the distribution of the sums.

c) Discuss with your partner why one distribution is skewed, and the other is symmetric (or nearly so). Why are the shapes of the two distributions different?

Practice 13.2

Represent each set of data with a dot plot.

1. The years of service for each of the 18 employees in a company are as follows:

7	8	4	3	10	3
2	10	7	6	8	2
1	4	11	12	6	9

2. A group of 24 students was asked how many states they have visited. The results are recorded in the table.

Number of States Visited	0	1	2	3	4	5	6	7
Number of Students	2	4	5	2	2	6	2	1

A group of teens was asked to indicate how many pairs of shoes they have in their closet. The results are shown in the dot plot. Use the dot plot to answer questions 3 to 5.

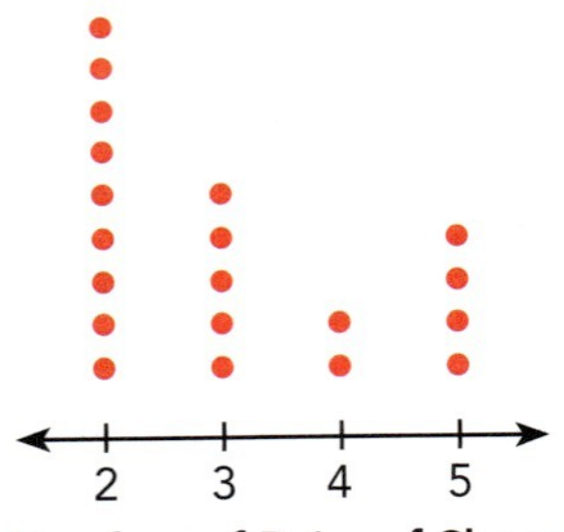

3. How many data values are there?

4. What conclusions can you draw with regard to the number of pairs of shoes the teens have?

5. What percent of the teens indicated 3 pairs of shoes in their closet?

The dot plot shows the number of weeks each movie that was number 1 at the box office during one year stayed in the number 1 position. Use the dot plot to answer questions 6 and 7.

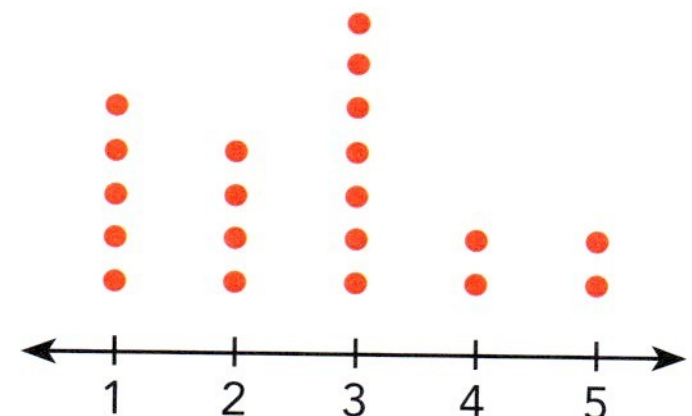

6 How many movies are represented by the dots altogether?

7 Give a reason why more dots are above the numbers 1 to 3 than above the numbers 4 and 5 on the horizontal axis.

Copy and complete the dot plot. Use the dot plot to answer each question.

8 The incomplete dot plot shows the result of a survey in which each student was asked how many dimes were in their pockets or wallets. The results for "4 dimes" are not shown. Each dot represents one student. It is known that 12.5% of the students had one dime.

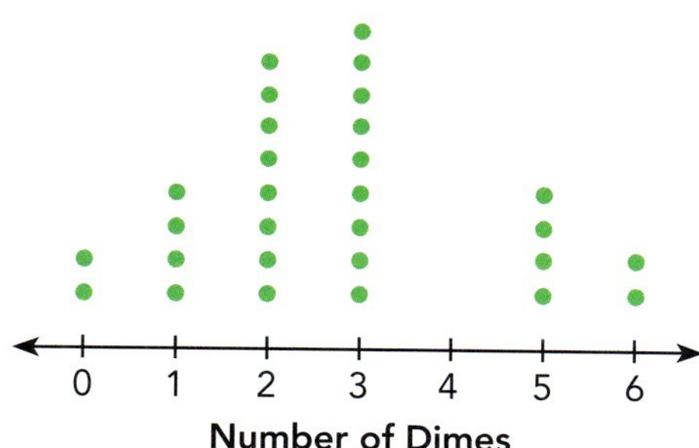

a) Find the number of students surveyed. Then complete the dot plot.

b) What percent of the students had either 0 or 6 dimes?

c) What percent of the students had either 1 or 5 dimes?

d) Briefly describe the distribution of the data.

13.3 Histograms

Lesson Objective

- Display and analyze data using a histogram.

Vocabulary

histogram outlier

Learn Represent numerical data using a histogram.

The table shows the number of minutes 25 students spent reading for pleasure one day.

Number of Minutes	0–29	30–59	60–89	90–119	120–149	150–179	180–209
Frequency	1	3	5	7	5	3	1

Draw a histogram to display this information.

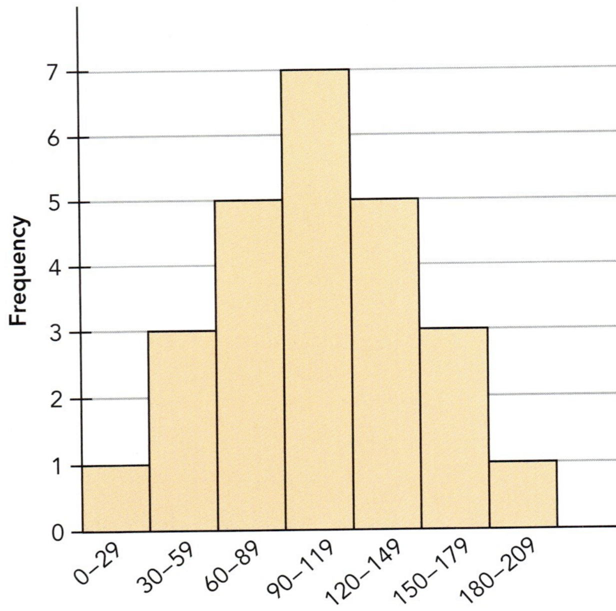

A histogram is a data display that divides the range of data into equal intervals and shows how often each interval occurs in the data set. It is usually used for large sets of data.

Math Note

Because the horizontal axis represents continuous intervals of time, there are no gaps between the bars.

Guided Practice

Draw a histogram for each set of data.

1. In a study of the length of several individuals of one species of fish caught, the following observations were recorded. The lengths were measured to the nearest centimeter.

Length of Fish (cm)	51–60	61–70	71–80	81–90	91–100	101–110
Number of Fish	4	5	7	4	2	4

2. The scores obtained by 40 students in a mathematics quiz are recorded in the table below.

Scores	1–2	3–4	5–6	7–8	9–10
Frequency	8	8	10	9	5

Learn

Choose an appropriate interval to organize data in a histogram.

The data show the heights (in inches) of students in a class.

50	66	67	61	68	59	63	69	64	73
56	68	56	65	67	66	66	59	68	70
62	64	57	67	60	65	60	67	59	66
60	65	61	66	58	63	64	68	61	68

a) Group the data into 4 intervals. Display the data in a histogram.

b) Group the data into 8 intervals. Display the data in a histogram.

c) Compare the two histograms.

The greatest value in the data is 73, and the least value in the data is 50.
Range: $73 - 50 = 23$.

To make 4 intervals, use $23 \div 4$, which you round up to 6 numbers in each interval. To make 8 intervals, use $23 \div 8$, or 3 numbers in each interval.

Continue on next page

a) 4 intervals

Height (in.)	50–55	56–61	62–67	68–73
Frequency	1	13	18	8

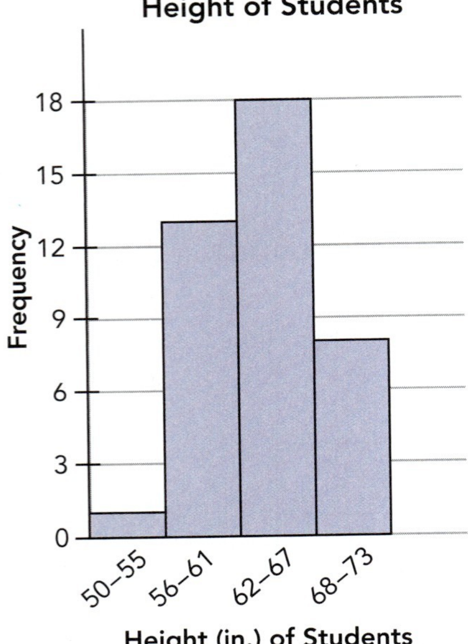

The first bar is $\frac{1}{3}$ the height between 0 and 3, so the frequency is 1.

b) 8 intervals

Height (in.)	50–52	53–55	56–58	59–61	62–64	65–67	68–70	71–73
Frequency	1	0	4	9	6	12	7	1

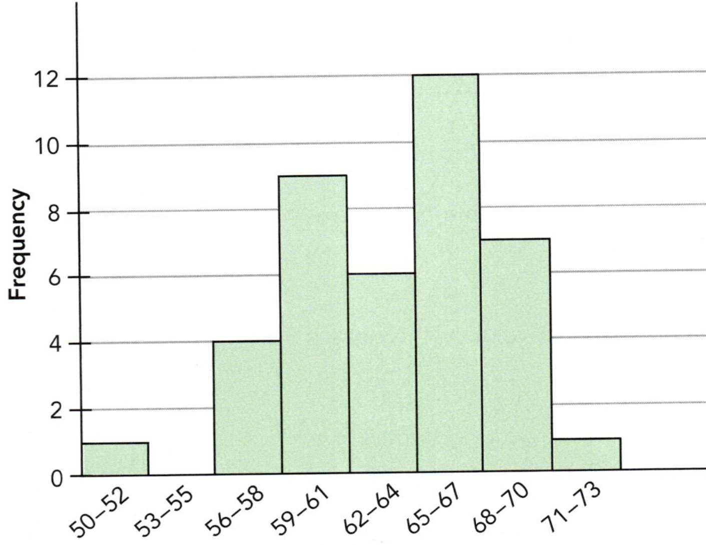

c) The 4-interval histogram is easier to group and draw than the 8-interval histogram. But the spread of the data is revealed better in the 8-interval histogram. The 8-interval histogram shows that the value 50 is an **outlier** from the data. It stands apart from all the other data.

From the two histograms, we see that using more intervals reveals more about the distribution of data.

An **outlier** is an extreme or rare occurrence of a value, which is usually excluded in data analysis.

Guided Practice

Draw a histogram for each set of data. Solve.

3. The cholesterol levels (in milligram per deciliter) of 40 men are listed below.

221	125	235	274	243	215	173	231	256	213
270	210	223	161	220	238	180	201	218	198
193	225	247	239	230	268	229	325	234	277
218	282	207	265	227	189	239	253	212	159

a) Group the data into suitable intervals and tabulate them. Explain your choice of intervals.

b) Draw a histogram using the interval.

4. The speeds in kilometers per hour of 40 cars on a highway were recorded as follows.

68	51	67	55	74	60	70	66	80	69
64	81	60	67	65	71	56	78	62	73
74	63	71	61	77	88	69	62	72	72
63	65	53	68	58	61	66	61	75	64

a) Group the data into suitable intervals and tabulate them. Explain your choice of intervals.

b) Draw a histogram using the interval.

Learn Interpret data from a histogram.

The histogram shows the number of digital music files each student in a class has on a computer or other electronic player. Briefly describe the data.

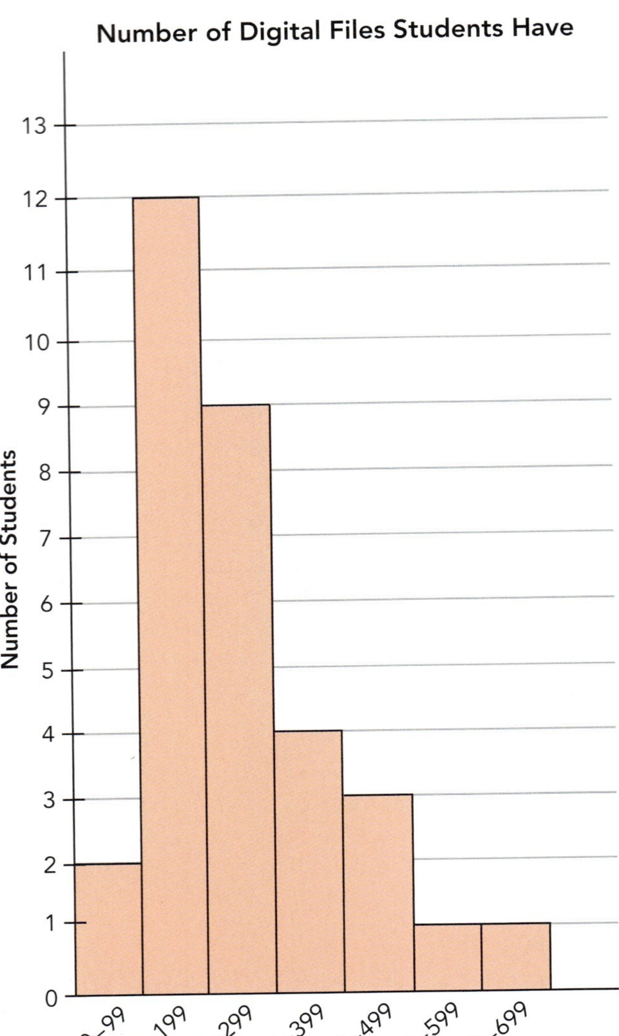

There are 32 students in the class.

Most students have 100 to 299 digital music files.

The range of the data is 699.

The histogram has a "tail" to the right.

Most of the data values are to the right of the most frequent value, so the shape of the histogram is right-skewed.

Guided Practice

Describe the data.

5 The histogram shows the number of representatives each state sent to the U.S. Congress in 2011. Briefly describe the data.

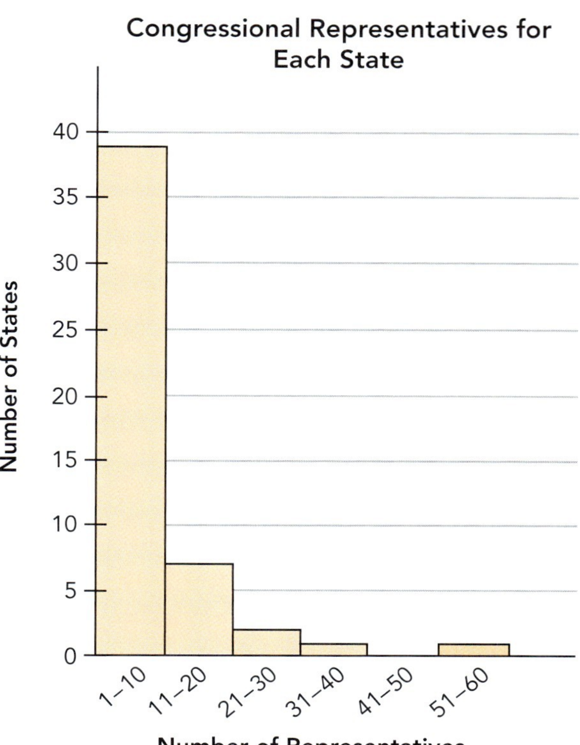

6 The histogram shows the highest temperature (in degrees Fahrenheit) recorded during December for one city. The temperature were recorded to the nearest degree. Briefly describe the data.

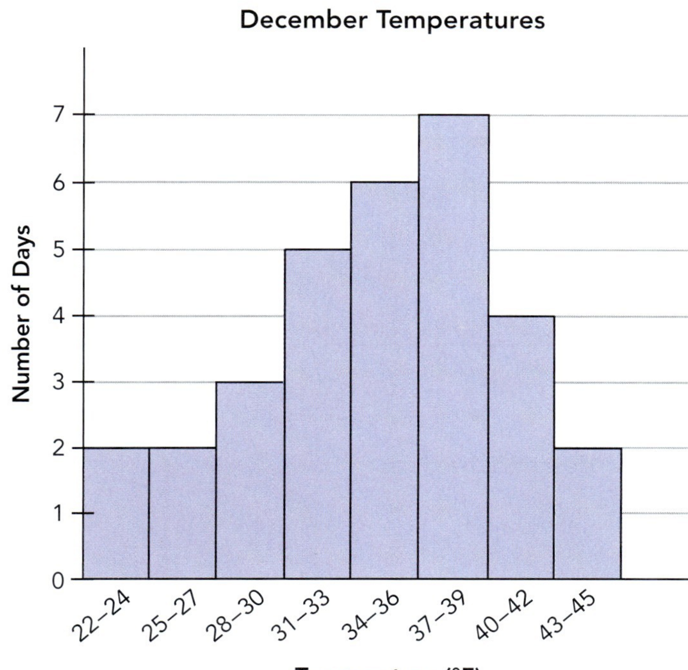

Practice 13.3

Draw a histogram for each set of data. Include a title.

1 The table shows the number of cans recycled by 25 households in a month.

Number of Cans	0–4	5–9	10–14	15–19	20–24	25–29	30–34
Frequency	1	1	3	6	8	4	2

2 The table shows the number of points scored by a football team in 20 games of one season.

Number of Points	0–5	6–11	12–17	18–23	24–29	30–35	36–41
Frequency	1	4	6	5	3	0	1

3 The table shows the keyboarding speed of 100 students in a beginning keyboarding class.

Words per Minute	20–29	30–39	40–49	50–59	60–69	70–79	80–89
Frequency	39	32	15	10	2	1	1

Draw a histogram for the set of data. Include a title. Solve.

4 The number of sunny days in a year for 200 cities are shown in the table.

Number of Sunny Days	140–148	149–157	158–166	167–175	176–184	185–193	194–202
Number of Cities	21	25	32	x	31	24	19

a) Find the value of x.

b) Draw a histogram to represent the data. Briefly describe the data.

c) What percent of the cities had fewer than 149 sunny days?

d) What percent of the cities had more than 184 sunny days?

The histogram shows the number of cars observed at one intersection at different times of the day. Use the histogram to answer questions 5 to 9.

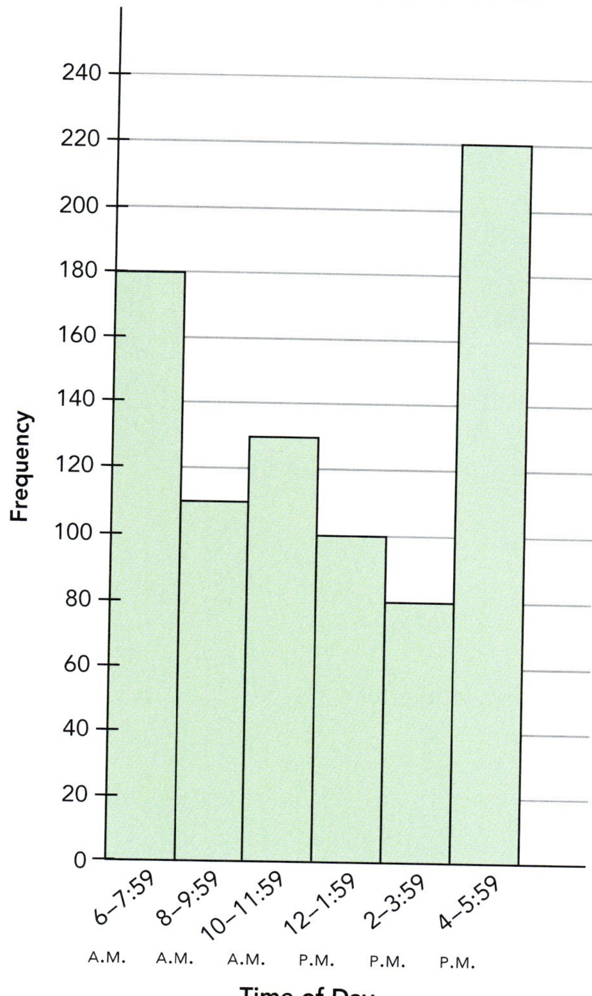

5 How many observations are there?

6 How many fewer cars passed the intersection from 6 A.M. to 7:59 A.M. than from 4 P.M. to 5:59 P.M.?

7 How many more cars passed the intersection from 10 A.M. to 11:59 A.M. than from 2 P.M. to 3:59 P.M.?

8 What percent of the number of cars that passed the intersection from 4 P.M. to 5:59 P.M. was observed from 8 A.M. to 9:59 A.M.?

9 What percent of the total number of cars that passed the intersection from 6 A.M. to 5:59 P.M. was observed from 4 P.M. to 5:59 P.M.? Round your answer to the nearest percent.

The histogram shows the number of books students in a class read last month. Use the histogram to answer the question.

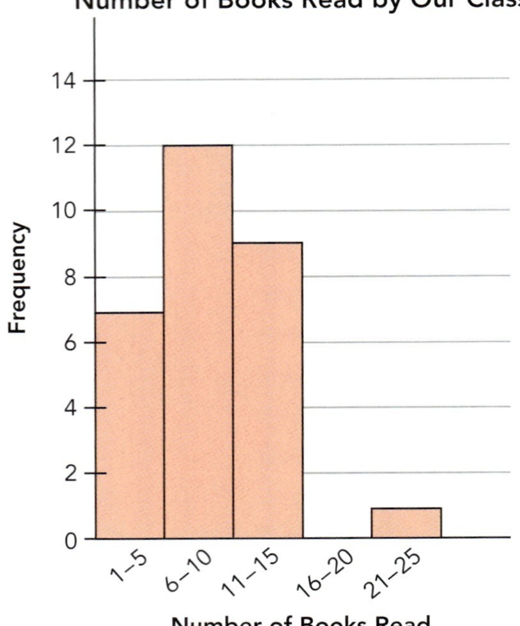

10 Briefly describe the data. Explain whether the histogram shows any outlier of the data set.

Draw a histogram for the set of data. Include a title. Solve.

11 The sales figures for 60 pairs of one style of shoe of various sizes at a department store are given in the table.

Size of Shoes	6	6.5	7	7.5	8	8.5	9	9.5	10
Number Sold	x	8	22	16	4	3	3	y	1

2 pairs of shoes of at least size 9.5 were sold.

a) Find the values of x and y.

b) What fraction of the shoes sold are smaller than size 8?

c) Draw a histogram using the intervals 6–6.5, 7–7.5, 8–8.5 and so on. Briefly describe the data.

d) If shoes were to be categorized as follows:
small – sizes 6 to 7; medium – sizes 7.5 to 8.5; large – sizes 9 to 10,
draw a histogram for the above data using the new categories.

e) Compare the two histograms. When would each one be more useful?

12 *Math Journal* A survey was carried out to find the number of players who scored a certain number of goals during soccer matches in a month. A histogram was drawn to display the results.

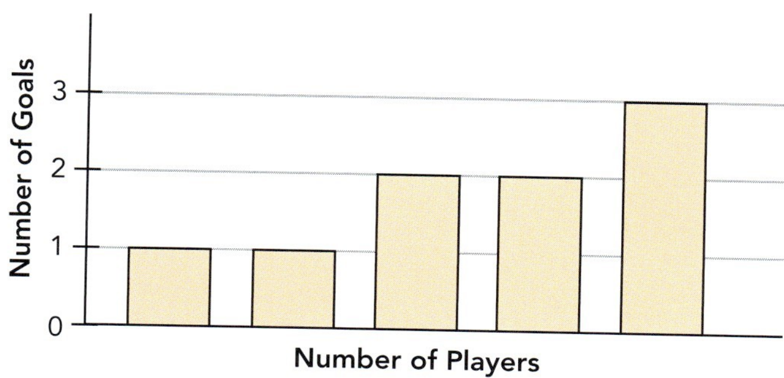

Is the histogram drawn correctly? Discuss with your partner and explain your thinking.

Brain @ Work

The table below shows the test scores for all the students in a Spanish I course.

Scores	94–100	87–93	80–86	73–79	66–72	59–65	52–58
Frequency	40	50	25	15	10	5	5

The following grades are used to represent the scores.

Scores	94–100	87–93	80–86	73–79	66–72	59–65	52–58
Grade	A	B	C	C	D	F	F

1. Draw a histogram to show the distribution of the scores.
2. Draw a bar graph to display the grades.
3. Five students increased their scores from 79 to 89.
   a) How would it change the histogram?
   b) How would it change the bar graph?

Chapter Wrap Up

Concept Map

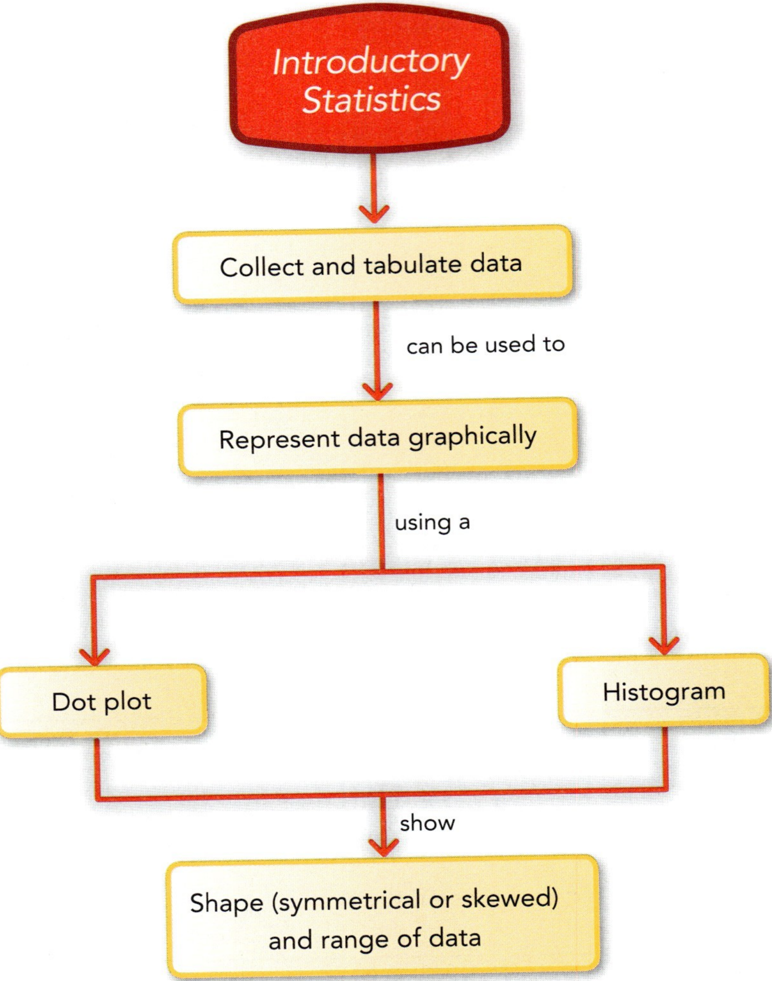

Key Concepts

- Statistical questions need many pieces of data to answer. The answers to these questions require collecting data and organizing it so that it can be easily interpreted.
- Data, when presented in a dot plot or histogram show patterns of shape, range, and outliers. The shape of the graph may be skewed to either end of the range, or it may be symmetrical about the middle of the range.
- The spread of data can be represented by the range shown on a number line that is part of a dot plot or a histogram.

Chapter Review/Test

Concepts and Skills

Copy and complete the table. Use the set of data.

1 The number of bedrooms in the units of a new apartment building ranged from 1 to 5. The number of bedrooms in each unit is as follows:

2	1	3	4	5
4	3	4	3	2
3	4	2	1	4
3	4	2	1	3
5	1	3	4	3
2	2	3	5	2

Tabulate the data.

Number of Bedrooms	Tally	Frequency
1	?	?
2	?	?
3	?	?
4	?	?
5	?	?

Draw a dot plot and a histogram for the set of data. Include a title.

2 The table below shows the number of hours 30 teachers in a school spent correcting students' assignments.

Number of Hours	1	2	3	4	5	6
Frequency	4	6	8	6	4	2

The histogram shows the ages of runners in a marathon. Use the histogram to answer questions 3 and 4.

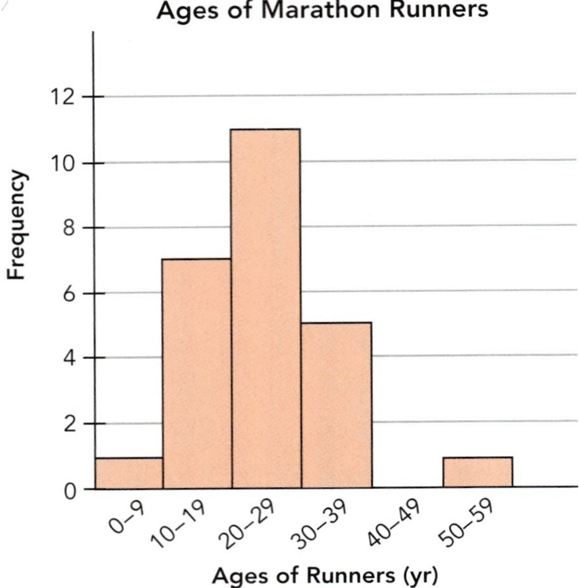

3 How many data values are there?

4 Briefly describe the distribution including any outliers in the data.

Problem Solving

The data show the lengths (in inches) of 50 trout caught in a lake during a fishing competition. Use the data to answer questions 5 and 6.

12	14	13	10	14	12	16	13	11	13
16	12	8	13	12	11	13	15	12	13
10	9	12	14	16	13	15	12	11	15
13	12	12	10	13	8	12	16	13	12
15	11	17	13	14	13	10	15	18	13

5 Group the data into suitable intervals and tabulate them.
Explain your choice of interval.

6 Draw a histogram using the interval. Briefly describe the data.

The data show the distances a golfer hits (in yards) in a long drive championship. Use the data to answer questions 7 and 8.

244	252	267	245	257	270	250	261	251	274
263	248	256	273	270	248	265	271	260	278
254	250	255	252	249	263	273	268	256	269

7. Group the data into suitable intervals and tabulate them. Explain your choice of interval.

8. Draw a histogram using the interval. Briefly describe the data.

The table shows the number of cars passing a traffic light during peak hours on a Friday morning. Use the data to answer questions 9 to 11.

Time	7:00–7:29	7:30–7:59	8:00–8:29	8:30–8:59	9:00–9:29	9:30–9:59
Number of Cars	22	45	64	57	27	25

9. How many cars were observed altogether?

10. Draw a histogram to display the data.

11. Describe the distribution of the data. Suggest why the histogram has the shape that it does.

The quiz scores of 94 students are shown in the table. Use the data to answer questions 12 to 14.

Score	14–16	17–19	20–22	23–25	26–28	29–31	32–34	35–37	38–40
Number of Students	17	x	3	5	12	15	17	10	8

12. Find the value of x.

13. Draw a histogram to represent the data. Describe the distribution of the data.

14. If the 5 students who scored 23–25 all scored 26 instead, would this change where most of the data occur? Justify your answer.

Measures of Central Tendency

How do blue jean companies know what customers will buy?

When blue jeans are manufactured, the quantity needed for each size depends on what retailers have ordered. It does not make economic sense to manufacture an equal number of jeans in all men's sizes from 24 inches to 44 inches. By finding a value around which most orders cluster, the production can be tailored to meet the demand. This helps to reduce waste in the manufacturing process.

In statistics, finding a value for a typical order is called finding a measure of central tendency. Learning how to find the various measures of central tendency is an important part of any production process from art prints to xylophones.

- Measures of central tendency can be used to summarize data distributions, and help you make decisions in real-world problems.

Recall Prior Knowledge

Dividing decimals by a whole number

Find the value of 29.1 ÷ 6.

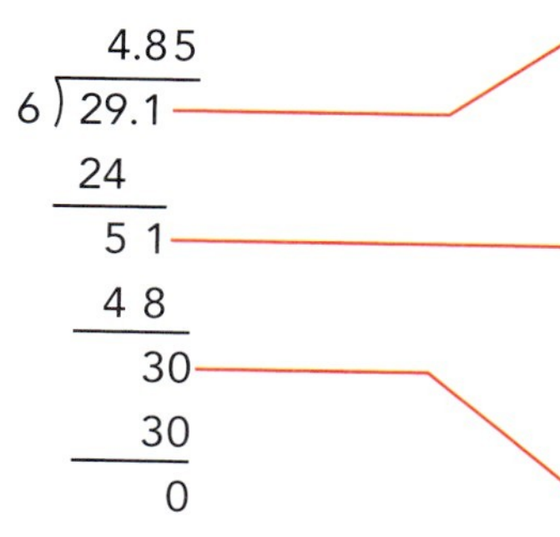

29 ones ÷ 6 = 4 ones R 5 ones

Regroup the remainder 5 ones.
5 ones = 50 tenths
Add the tenths.
50 tenths + 1 tenth = 51 tenths
51 tenths ÷ 6 = 8 tenths R 3 tenths

Regroup the remainder 3 tenths.
3 tenths = 30 hundredths
30 hundredths ÷ 6 = 5 hundredths

The value of 29.1 ÷ 6 is 4.85.

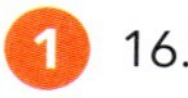

Quick Check

Divide.

1. 16.5 ÷ 2
2. 48.09 ÷ 7

Finding the average of each data set

Find the average of 12, 14, 18, 24, 36, and 40.

First, find the sum of the data values.

12 + 14 + 18 + 24 + 36 + 40 = 144

Then divide the sum by the number of data values.

The average is 144 ÷ 6 = 24.

Quick Check

Find the average of each data set.

3. 2, 4, 16, 18
4. 3, 5, 7, 8, 21, 31
5. \$14, \$30, \$32, \$50
6. 25 ft, 32 ft, 46 ft, 55 ft, 78 ft

14.1 Mean

Lesson Objectives
- Find the mean of a set of data.
- Use the mean of a set of data to solve problems.

Vocabulary
mean

Learn Understand the concept of mean.

Finding the mean of a set of data is one way to summarize all the values in a data set with a single number.

To find the mean of a set of items, find the sum of all the items and then divide the sum by the number of items.

$$\text{Mean} = \frac{\text{sum of a set of items}}{\text{number of items}}$$

For example, Aaron has the following three mathematics test scores.

Test	Score
1	65
2	74
3	80

One way to describe the set of test scores is to find the average or mean of the three test scores.

Math Note
Another word for average is mean.

Mean score for the three tests

$$= \frac{\text{total score for the three tests}}{\text{number of tests}}$$

$$= \frac{65 + 74 + 80}{3}$$

$$= \frac{219}{3}$$

$$= 73$$

So, Aaron's mean score for the three tests is 73.

Guided Practice

Complete.

Four boys have heights of 154 centimeters, 157 centimeters, 160 centimeters, and 165 centimeters.

1 What is the total height of the four boys?

Total height

= __?__ + __?__ + __?__ + __?__

= __?__ cm

The total height of the four boys is __?__ centimeters.

2 What is the mean height of the four boys?

Mean height

$= \frac{\text{total height}}{\text{number of boys}}$

= __?__ ÷ __?__

= __?__ cm

The mean height of the four boys is __?__ centimeters.

Complete. Use the data in the table.

The table shows the temperature at noon from Monday to Friday in one city.

Temperature in Degrees Fahrenheit (°F)

Monday	Tuesday	Wednesday	Thursday	Friday
52°F	51°F	49°F	48°F	54°F

3 What was the mean temperature at noon from Monday to Friday?

Mean temperature

$= \frac{\text{total temperature}}{\text{number of days}}$

$= \frac{\underline{?} + \underline{?} + \underline{?} + \underline{?} + \underline{?}}{\underline{?}}$

$= \frac{?}{?}$

= __?__ °F

The mean temperature at noon from Monday to Friday was __?__ °F.

Learn Find the mean of a data set using a dot plot.

There are six songs in an album. The dot plot shows the length of each song in minutes. Each dot represents 1 song.

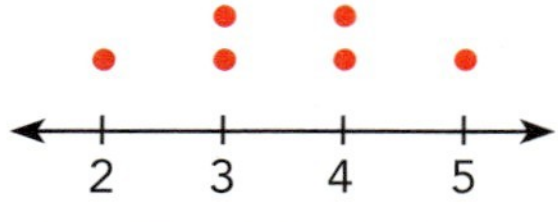

Length of Songs (min)

To find the mean, first calculate the total length of the six songs. Then divide the total length of the songs by the number of songs.

1 song of length 2 min ⟶ $1 \times 2 = 2$ min
2 songs of length 3 min ⟶ $2 \times 3 = 6$ min
2 songs of length 4 min ⟶ $2 \times 4 = 8$ min
1 song of length 5 min ⟶ $1 \times 5 = 5$ min

$$\begin{aligned} \text{Mean} &= \frac{\text{total length of songs}}{\text{number of songs}} \\ &= \frac{2 + 6 + 8 + 5}{6} \\ &= \frac{21}{6} \\ &= 3.5 \text{ min} \end{aligned}$$

The mean length of the six songs is 3.5 minutes.

Guided Practice

Complete. Use the data in the dot plot.

A group of volunteers was selling coupons to raise money for a food pantry. The dot plot on the right shows the number of coupons sold by each volunteer. Each dot represents 1 volunteer.

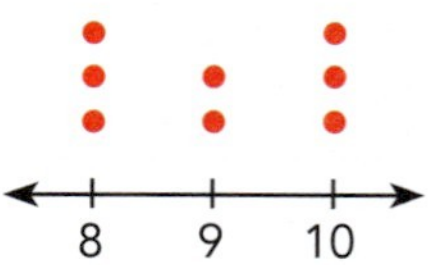

Number of Coupons

4 __?__ volunteers sold 8 coupons each. ⟶ __?__ × __?__ = __?__ coupons sold

5 __?__ volunteers sold 9 coupons each. ⟶ __?__ × __?__ = __?__ coupons sold

6 __?__ volunteers sold 10 coupons each. ⟶ __?__ × __?__ = __?__ coupons sold

7 __?__ coupons were sold altogether.

8 There were __?__ volunteers altogether.

9 The mean number of coupons sold by the group of volunteers was __?__.

Learn Find the total and a missing number from the mean.

Geraldine recorded a set of six numbers and found the mean to be 11.2. After she accidentally erased one of the numbers, she had only five numbers left: 2.3, 6.5, 8.8, 12.4, and 16.0. Find the missing number.

Total of the six numbers = mean × number of given numbers
= 11.2 × 6
= 67.2

Total of the five numbers left = 2.3 + 6.5 + 8.8 + 12.4 + 16.0
= 46

67.2 − 46 = 21.2

So, the missing number is 21.2.

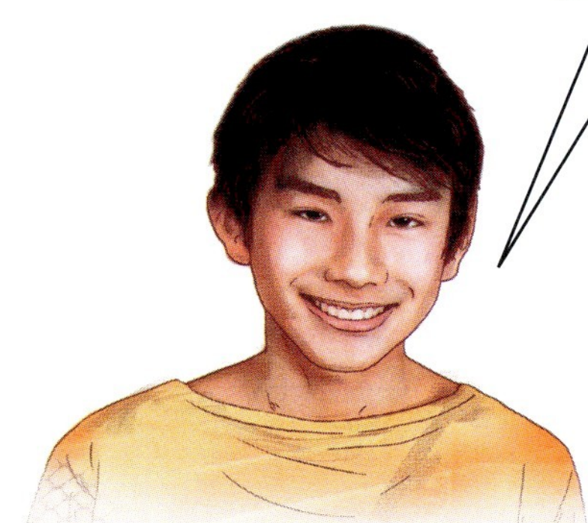

You can find the total of a set of items by multiplying the mean by the number of items.

Total of a set of items
= mean × number of items

Guided Practice

Solve.

10. Jay's mean score for four quizzes is 8. His scores for the first three quizzes are 7.5, 8, and 9. What is Jay's score for the last quiz?

Total score for the four quizzes = mean score × number of quizzes
= ? × ?
= ?

Total score for the first three quizzes = ? + ? + ?
= ?

? − ? = ?

Jay's score for the last quiz is ?.

11. Sarah's mean number of points scored for four video games is 7,500. How many points must she score in the fifth video game so that her mean score becomes 7,700?

Hands-On Activity

Materials:
- centimeter ruler
- blank table

FINDING MEAN AND USING MEAN TO SOLVE PROBLEMS

Work in groups of five.

STEP 1 Use a centimeter ruler to measure the length of each group member's hand to the nearest tenth of a centimeter. Record your answers in a copy of the table below.

Hand Size of Group Members

Name	Length of Hand (cm)
?	?
?	?
?	?
?	?
?	?

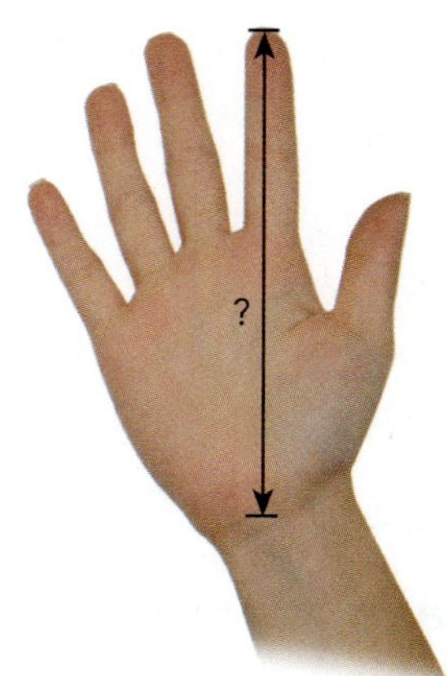

STEP 2 Use your data to answer the following questions.

What is the longest hand length? ?

What is the shortest hand length? ?

The mean hand length of the group is ? centimeters.

STEP 3 *Math Journal* Suppose a new student joins your group and the mean of the hand length of your group increases by 0.3 centimeter. Find the hand length of the new student to the nearest centimeter. Explain how you found your answer.

Practice 14.1

Find the mean of each data set.

1. 8, 7, 5, 9, 6, 13

2. 72 L, 91 L, 65 L, 81 L, 62 L, 83 L, 75 L, 88 L

3. 21.5 cm, 63.7 cm, 18.9 cm, 34.1 cm, 75.6 cm

Solve. Show your work.

4. The number of goals scored by seven forwards in one soccer season were 8, 6, 4, 8, 3, 1, and 5. Find the mean number of goals scored by the seven forwards.

5. The lengths of five ropes are 3.2 meters, 5.2 meters, 2.9 meters, 6.6 meters, and 4.5 meters. Find the mean length of these five ropes.

6. The masses of six chairs are 34.5 kilograms, 42.6 kilograms, 39.8 kilograms, 40.1 kilograms, 53.4 kilograms, and 33.8 kilograms. Find their mean mass.

Use the data in the table to answer the question.

The table shows a sprinter's times for the 100-meter dash at the first five meets of one season.

Time Clocked by the Sprinter

Meet Number	1	2	3	4	5
Time (s)	10.09	10.14	10.29	10.07	9.99

7. What was the sprinter's mean time for the 100-meter dash at these meets?

Use the data in the dot plot to answer questions 8 and 9.

Eight ice hockey teams competed in the quarter finals of a national championship. The dot plot on the right shows the number of goals scored by each team. Each dot represents 1 team.

8. What was the total number of goals scored by the eight teams?

9. What was the mean number of goals scored by each team?

Solve. Show your work.

10 The mean of five numbers 3, 7, 9, 12, and x is 8. Find the value of x.

11 The mean of a set of five numbers is 4.8. Given that the sixth number is x and the mean of these six numbers is 5.5, find the value of x.

12 In a race, the mean time for three runners was 12.4 seconds and the mean time for another six runners was 11.5 seconds. Calculate the mean time for all the nine runners.

13 The mean weight of nine apples is 7.5 ounces. Three of the apples have a mean weight of 8 ounces. Find the mean weight of the other six apples.

14 The mean of six numbers is 45. Four of the numbers are 40, 38, 46, and 51. If the remaining two numbers are in the ratio 2 : 3, find the two numbers.

15 A data set consists of three numbers, a, b, and c. Write an algebraic expression, in terms of a, b, and c, to represent the mean of the new set of numbers obtained by

a) adding 5 to every number in the set.

b) doubling every number in the set.

c) halving every number in the set.

16 The table shows the mean scores of three classes in a history test.

Mean Scores by Three Classes

Class	Mean Number of Points
A	8
B	6
C	9

The mean score of all the students in classes A and B combined is 6.8. The mean score of all the students in classes B and C combined is 7. If the number of students in classes A, B, and C are denoted by a, b, and c respectively, find the ratio $a : b : c$.

17 *Math Journal* Find five different numbers whose mean is 12. Explain your strategy.

14.2 Median

Lesson Objectives

- Find the median of a set of data.
- Use the median of a set of data to solve problems.

Vocabulary
median

Learn Understand the concept of median.

Barbara drew three number cards from a box and wanted to know the middle value, or median, of these values. The median is a second way to summarize the values in a data set with a single number.

First, she arranged the numbers from the least to the greatest.

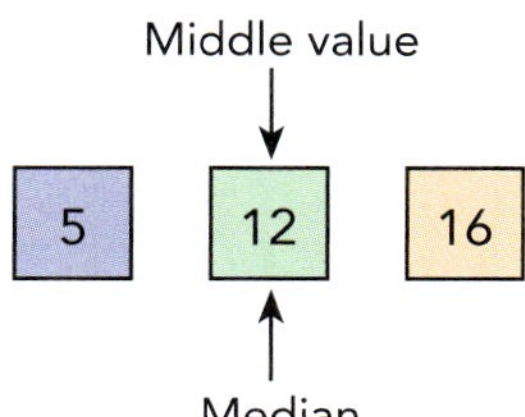

When a data set has an **odd** number of values, you can identify the middle value, or median, by inspection. The number of values less than the median equals the number of values greater than the median.

Then she identified the middle value, 12. So, the median of the three numbers is 12.

Barbara then picked another number, 19, from the box. She arranged these numbers in order again.

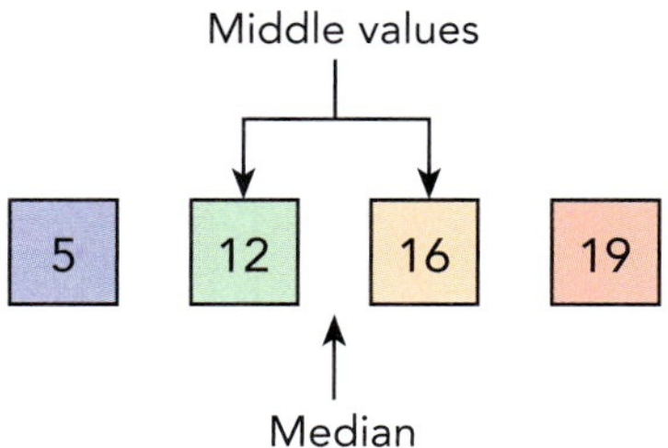

When a data set has an **even** number of values, identify the two middle values. The median is the mean of these two middle values.

$$\text{Mean of the two middle values} = \frac{12 + 16}{2} = \frac{28}{2} = 14$$

So, the median of the four numbers is 14.

Caution

Remember, the data must be in order before you look for the middle value or values. The data can be arranged from least to greatest, or greatest to least.

Guided Practice

Find the median of each data set.

1 The data set shows the weights of a group of students.

109 lb, 86 lb, 117 lb, 97 lb, 98 lb

Ordered from least to greatest:

__?__ lb, __?__ lb, __?__ lb, __?__ lb, __?__ lb

The median weight is __?__ pounds.

2 The data set shows the volumes of water (in fluid ounces) in some containers.

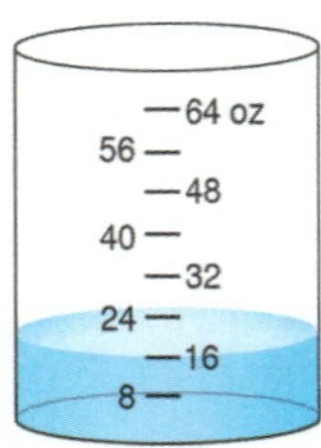

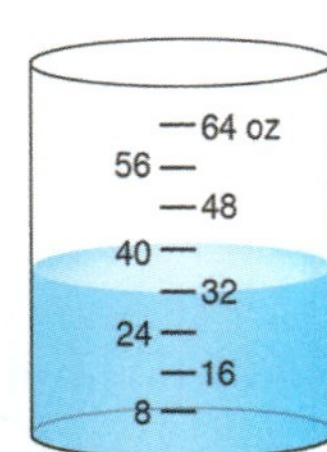

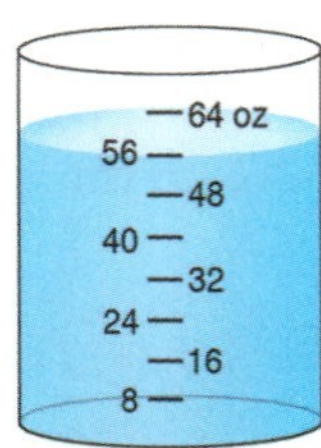

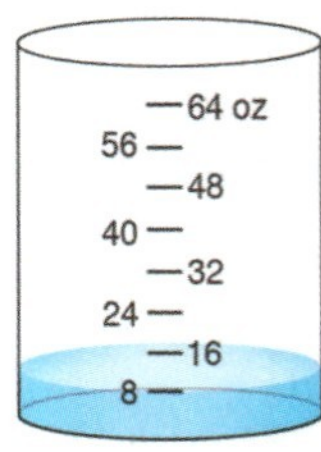

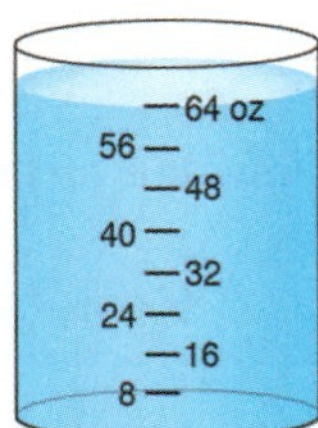

The median volume of water is __?__ fluid ounces.

3 The data set shows the ages of a group of people.

23 years, 36 years, 28 years, 43 years, 34 years, 29 years

The two middle values are __?__ years and __?__ years.

Mean of the two middle values $= \dfrac{\underline{\ ?\ } + \underline{\ ?\ }}{2} = \underline{\ ?\ }$ yr

The median age is __?__ years.

4 The data set shows the lengths of the tables that one company produces.

85 cm, 92 cm, 108 cm, 210 cm, 264 cm, 200 cm, 135 cm, 78 cm

The median length is __?__ centimeters.

5 The data set shows the distances that a group of students ran during an exercise.

$\frac{1}{2}$ mi, $\frac{7}{8}$ mi, $\frac{3}{4}$ mi, $\frac{5}{8}$ mi

The median distance was __?__ mile.

Learn Find the median of a data set using a dot plot.

a) The dot plot shows the number of children in seven families living in an apartment complex. Each dot represents 1 family.

To find the median, count the dots to find the middle values.

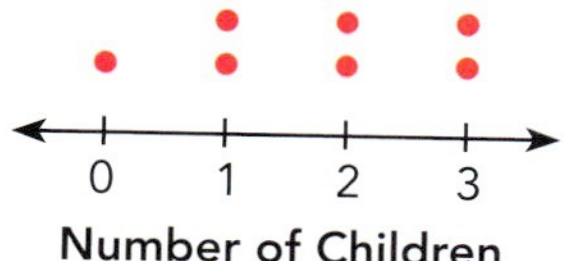

There are seven families altogether.
The fourth family is in the middle because there are three families to the left and to the right of this family.
So, the median number of children is 2.

b) The dot plot shows the number of hours eight children spend on exercise every week. Each dot represents 1 child.

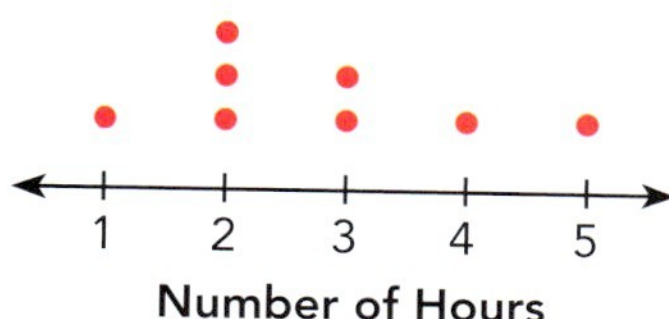

First, find the middle number of hours.

There are eight children altogether. Divide this into two equal groups.
There are four children in the upper half and four children in the lower half.
So, the fourth and fifth children are in the middle.
The fourth child spends 2 hours and the fifth child spends 3 hours on exercise every week.

Then find the median number of hours.

$$\text{Mean of the two values} = \frac{2 + 3}{2}$$
$$= 2.5 \text{ h}$$

So, the median is 2.5 hours.

Guided Practice

Complete. Use the data in the dot plot.

The dot plot shows the weights of a group of immature white-tailed deer fawn. Each dot represents 1 fawn.

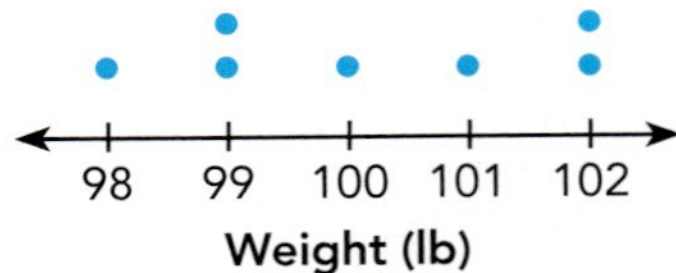

6 The median weight of the fawns is __?__ pounds.

7 A new fawn joins the group. It weighs 101 pounds.

a) Add a dot to a copy of the dot plot above to show this information.

b) Does this change the median of the data set?
What is the median of the data set now?

Learn Compare the mean and median of a data set.

Mrs. Brown took a survey to find out the number of hours the students in her class spent in the public library in two weeks. Each dot represents 1 student.

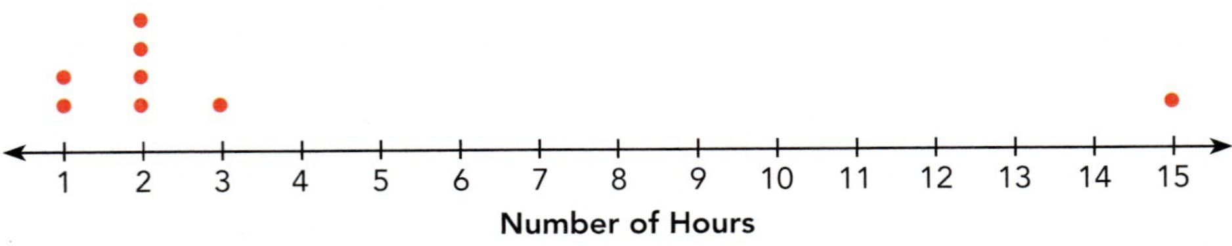

a) Find the mean and median.

$$\text{Mean} = \frac{\text{total number of hours}}{\text{total number of students}}$$

$$= \frac{2 \times 1 + 4 \times 2 + 1 \times 3 + 1 \times 15}{8}$$

$$= \frac{28}{8}$$

$$= 3.5 \text{ h}$$

The data set has an outlier, 15. This value makes the mean much greater than a typical value for these data.

The mean is 3.5 hours.

There are eight students altogether. The fourth and fifth students are in the middle. Each of those two students spent 2 hours at the library. So, the median is 2 hours.

b) Which one of the two measures of central tendency, the mean or the median, better describes the data set? Justify your answer.

The mean is 3.5 hours. However, all but one student visited the library for fewer than 3.5 hours during the two weeks. So, the mean does not describe the data set well.

The median is 2 hours. It describes the data set better because most of the data values cluster around 2 hours.

Guided Practice

Complete. Use the data in the dot plot.

The lowest temperatures in a town are recorded over a few days. The dot plot on the right shows these temperature readings. Each dot represents 1 temperature reading.

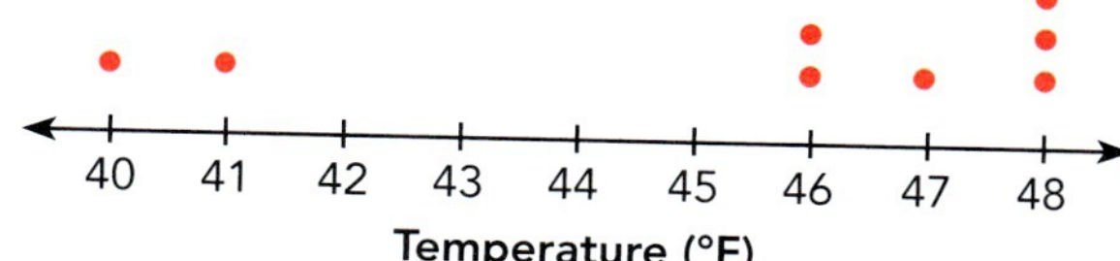

8 The mean temperature is ___?___ °F.

9 The median temperature is ___?___ °F.

10 ___?___ of the temperature readings recorded are higher than the mean temperature.

11 Which of the two measures of central tendency, the mean or the median, better describes the data set? Justify your answer.

Hands-On Activity

Materials:
- blank table

COLLECTING AND TABULATING DATA TO FIND MEDIAN

Work in pairs.

STEP 1 Refer to the first paragraph of the chapter opener. Count the number of times the letter 'e' appears in each line. Record your answers in a copy of the table below.

Number of Times the Letter 'e' Appears

Line	1	2	3	4	5	6
Number of Times	?	?	?	?	?	?

STEP 2 Find the mean and median number of times the letter 'e' appears in each line.

Practice 14.2

Find the median of each data set.

1. 9, 8, 7, 11, 7, 16, 3
2. 31, 43, 12, 25, 54, 18
3. 3.2, 1.5, 2.6, 3.5, 6.9, 5.8, 2.4
4. 32.6, 72.6, 28.7, 45.4, 83.6, 69.9

Solve. Show your work.

5. The number of points scored by seven students in a language test are 68, 46, 74, 58, 63, 91, and 85. Find the median score.

6. The data set shows the number of goals scored by a soccer team in eight matches.

   0, 2, 3, 1, 4, 2, 5, 2

   Find the median number of goals scored.

7. The costs of four cell phones are \$345, \$400, \$110, and \$640. Find the median cost.

8. The volumes of water, in liters, in eight containers are 3.1, 2.8, 3.2, 4.2, 3.9, 5.6, 3.7, and 4.5. Find the median volume.

Use the data in the dot plots to answer questions 9 and 10.

The dot plot shows the number of points scored by the members of a Quiz Bowl team in a competition between School A and School B. Each dot represents one student's points.

School A

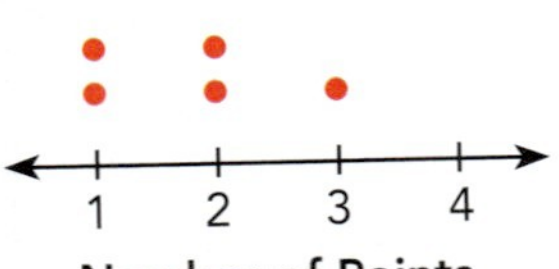

School B

1 2 3 4

Number of Points

9. How many team members did each school have?

10. What was the median number of points scored by the students from

    a) School A?

    b) School B?

Use the data in the dot plot to answer questions 11 to 13.

Janice bought some dinner rolls from a bakery. The dot plot shows the prices of the dinner rolls in cents. Each dot represents 1 dinner roll.

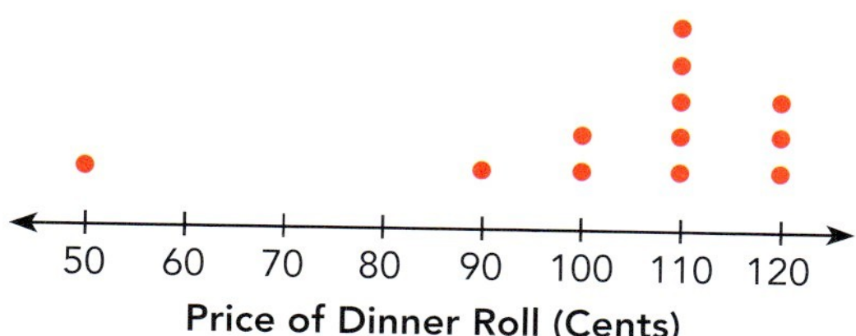

11 What is the mean price of the dinner rolls Janice bought? Round your answer to the nearest cent.

12 What is the median price of the dinner rolls she bought?

13 Which of the two measures of central tendency, the mean or the median, better describes the data set? Justify your answer.

Solve.

14 The median of a set of numbers is x. There are at least three numbers in the set. Write an algebraic expression, in terms of x, to represent the median of the new set of numbers obtained by

a) adding 3 to every number in the set.

b) doubling every number in the set.

c) dividing every number in the set by 5 and then subtracting 2 from the resulting numbers.

d) adding 2 to the greatest number in the set.

e) subtracting 3 from the least number in the set.

15 The median of a set of three unknown numbers is 5. If the number 3 is added to the least number in the set, give an example of the original set in which

a) the median of the new set of numbers will not be equal to 5.

b) the median of the new set of numbers will still be equal to 5.

16 The median of a set of three unknown numbers is 5. If the number 2 is subtracted from the greatest number in the set, give an example of the original set in which

a) the median of the new set of numbers will not be equal to 5.

b) the median of the new set of numbers will still be equal to 5.

14.3 Mode

Lesson Objectives

- Find the mode of a set of data.
- Use the mode of a set of data to solve problems.

Vocabulary
mode

Learn Understand the concept of mode.

Ryan tossed a number cube, numbered 1 to 6, and he recorded the data in the table.

Number Tossed on Number Cube

Number Tossed	Number of Times
1	1
2	2
3	2
4	1
5	3
6	2

The mode of a set of data is the value that appears most frequently. It is the third measure of central tendency.

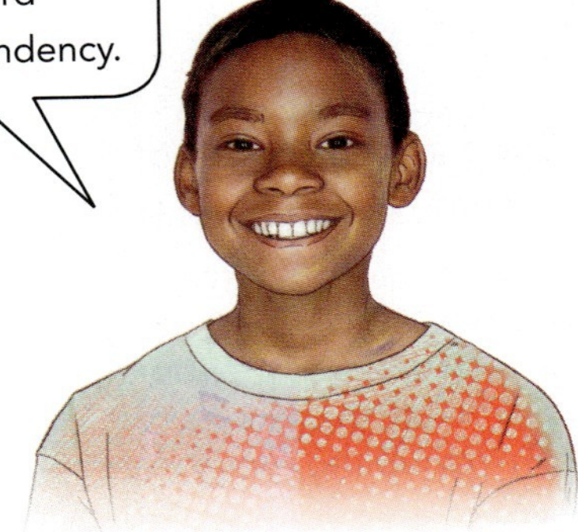

From the table, notice that the number 5 appears most frequently.
So, the number 5 is the mode of the set of data.

You can draw a dot plot to show that the number 5 is the mode of the set of data. Each dot represents 1 toss.

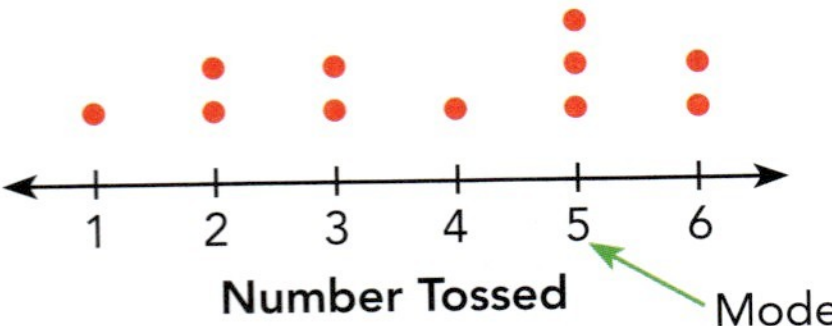

The dot plot shows clearly that the number 5 appears most frequently.
So, the number 5 is the mode of the set of data.

Math Note

A set of data can have more than one mode. If all the numbers in a set of data appear the same number of times, there is no mode.

Guided Practice

Use the data set to complete the table. Then complete the sentence.

Justin recorded the times for the ten runners on a track team when they ran the 100-meter dash. The data set shows the times that he recorded.

9.8 s, 9.9 s, 10.0 s, 9.9 s, 10.2 s, 10.1 s, 9.8 s, 10.3 s, 9.9 s, 10.1 s

Times of Ten Runners

Time (s)	Number of Times
9.8	2
?	?
10.0	?
?	?
?	?
?	?

1. The mode of this data set is ? seconds.

Complete. Use data in the dot plot.

Elsie likes to bowl. The dot plot shows her scores for each of the ten frames that she bowled in one game. Each dot represents her scores for one frame.

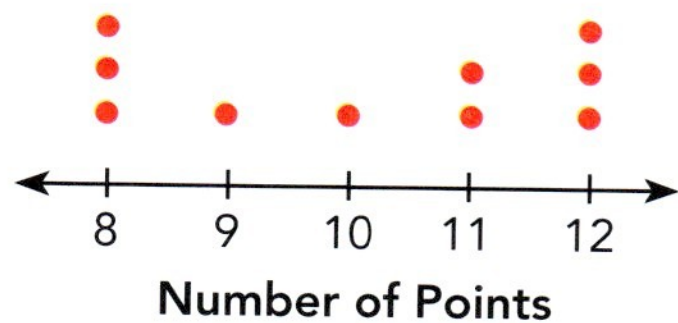

2. Elsie scored 11 points in each of ? frames.

3. The modes of this set of data are ? and ?.

When a data set has two modes, you can say that the data set is bimodal.

Learn Use mode to summarize a data set.

A farmer was placing chickens, ducks, and geese in a feeding pen. He recorded the type of birds as C, D, or G as they went into the pen. These are the data he recorded.

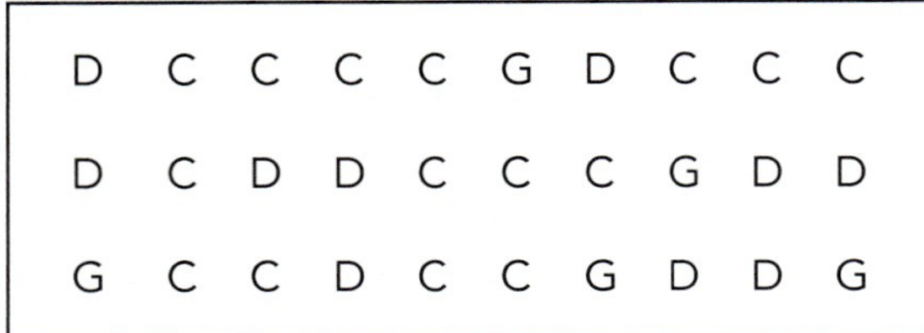

D	C	C	C	C	G	D	C	C	C
D	C	D	D	C	C	C	G	D	D
G	C	C	D	C	C	G	D	D	G

This data set is not numeric, so you cannot find the mean or median. However, you can find the mode of the data: chickens, because it is the data item that appears most often.

You can use a bar graph to show the mode.

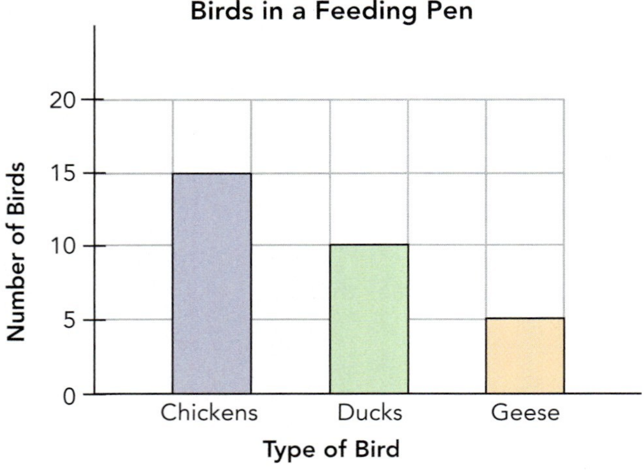

Notice that the bar representing the number of chickens has the greatest height. So, the number of chickens is the greatest and the mode is chickens.

Guided Practice

Find the mode of each set of data.

4. There are 9 teachers, 88 boys, and 79 girls at a school camp.

5. In a mall, there are 2 laundry shops, 14 garment shops, 3 photographic shops, 5 shoe shops, and 9 food stores.

6. The data set shows the masses of the school bags of some students.
5.5 kg, 6.6 kg, 4.8 kg, 4.3 kg, 5.5 kg, 4.3 kg, 5.5 kg, 6.6 kg, 4.5 kg, 5.5 kg

Hands-On Activity

Materials:

- net of a rectangular prism, with pairs of opposite faces numbered 10, 11, or 12
- blank table
- tape
- scissors
- centimeter ruler

FINDING MEAN, MEDIAN, AND MODE

Work in pairs.

STEP 1 Cut out, fold, and tape the net of the rectangular prism provided by your teacher.

STEP 2 Take turns to toss the rectangular prism 40 times and record the number tossed each time.

STEP 3 Copy and complete your results in a table like the one below.

Number Tossed	Tally	Frequency
10	?	?
11	?	?
12	?	?

STEP 4 From the set of data collected, find the

a) mean. **b)** median. **c)** mode.

STEP 5 **a)** Measure the area of each face to the nearest tenth of a square centimeter. Find the ratio of the total area of the faces numbered 10 to the total area of the faces numbered 11 to the total area of the faces numbered 12.

b) Find the ratio of the number of times the number 10 is tossed to the number of times the number 11 is tossed to the number of times the number 12 is tossed.

c) Compare the two ratios. Why do you think you get this result?

STEP 6 Compare your findings with the other pairs.

Practice 14.3

Find the mode or modes of each data set.

1. 5, 6, 4, 5, 8, 9, 9, 3, 4, 5

2. 13, 31, 12, 45, 6, 19, 21, 12, 31

3. 8.5, 6.5, 7.8, 6.5. 6.4, 2.3, 4.5, 5.4, 7.8, 5.5, 7.8

Find the mode.

4. The scores of a basketball team in a series of games are 76, 85, 65, 58, 68, 72, 91, and 68. Find the mode.

5. The table shows sizes of shoes and the number of pairs of shoes sold at a shop last month.

Number of Pairs of Shoes Sold

Size	6.5	7	7.5	8	8.5	9	9.5	10	10.5
Number of Pairs	5	15	21	30	30	31	13	8	3

Find the mode.

6. Tickets for a concert are priced at \$20, \$30, \$40, \$50, or \$100. The table shows the number of tickets sold at each price.

Number of Tickets Sold

Price (\$)	**Number of Tickets**
20	40
30	55
40	95
50	84
100	48

Find the mode.

Make a dot plot to show the data. Use your dot plot to answer each question.

The data set shows the number of goals scored by a soccer team in 17 matches.
3, 2, 1, 0, 2, 4, 1, 0, 2, 3, 4, 2, 3, 2, 1, 2, 5

7 What is the mean of the data set?
Round your answer to the nearest number of goals.

8 What is the median of the data set?

9 What is the mode of the data set?

Solve. Show your work.

10 A class of 15 students had a spelling test consisting of 10 words. The number of spelling mistakes made by each student in the class is listed in the data set.

1, 2, 1, 0, 3, 1, 2, 3, 1, 2, 0, 4, 2, 3, x

a) If there are two modes, what are the possible values for x?

b) If there is exactly one mode, write a possible value for x, and the mode.

11 The table shows the number of days of absences for 80 students in a school.

Number of Absent Days

Number of Days	Number of Students
0	x
1	25
2	17
3	y
4	8

a) Find the value of $x + y$.

b) If the mode for this set of data is 3, write the possible values for the pair of numbers (x, y).

c) If the mode is equal to the median, write two possible values of x.

14.4 Real-World Problems: Mean, Median, and Mode

Lesson Objective

- Solve problems that are related to the concepts of mean, median, and mode, including the selection of the measure of central tendency to be used for problems.

Learn Decide whether to use mean, median, or mode.

The table shows the sizes of in-line skates and the number of pairs of skates sold in a month.

Number of Pairs of In-Line Skates Sold

Size	Number of Pairs
6	12
7	15
8	18
9	9
10	6

a) How many pairs of in-line skates were sold?

$12 + 15 + 18 + 9 + 6 = 60$

60 pairs of in-line skates were sold.

b) What is the mean size of the in-line skates sold?

$$\begin{aligned}\text{Mean} &= \frac{\text{total of sizes of in-line skates sold}}{\text{total number of pairs sold}}\\ &= \frac{12 \times 6 + 15 \times 7 + 18 \times 8 + 9 \times 9 + 6 \times 10}{60}\\ &= \frac{462}{60}\\ &= 7.7\end{aligned}$$

The mean size of the shoes sold is 7.7.

c) What is the modal size of the in-line skates sold?

The size of in-line skates that was sold most frequently is 8.
So, the modal size of the in-line skates sold is 8.

d) What is the median size of the in-line skates sold?

First, you need to find the middle sizes.

60 pairs of in-line skates were sold. Divide the skates into two equal groups.
There are 30 pairs in the upper half and 30 pairs in the lower half.
So, the thirtieth and thirty-first pairs of skates are in the middle.
The sizes of the thirtieth and thirty-first pairs of skates are both 8.

So, the median size is the mean of the two middle sizes, which is 8.

e) Which measure of central tendency best describes the data set?
Justify your answer.

The mean size is 7.7. However, the usual sizes for in-line skates are either whole numbers or halves. So, the mean figure 7.7 may not be a realistic number for describing the data set.

The mode and median are both size 8, which is a realistic number for describing the data set. So, the mode and median may describe the data set best.

Guided Practice

Solve.

The table shows the sizes of T-shirts and the number of T-shirts displayed in a shop.

Number of T-Shirts Being Displayed

Size	8	10	12	14	16
Number of T-Shirts	7	14	22	15	2

1. How many T-shirts are displayed in the shop?

2. What is the mean size of the T-shirts being displayed?

3. What is the modal size of the T-shirts being displayed?

4. What is the median size of the T-shirts being displayed?

5. Which measure of central tendency best describes the data set?
Justify your answer.

Learn Relate the measure of center to a skewed distribution.

The dot plot shows the daily pocket money of a group of students. Each dot represents one student.

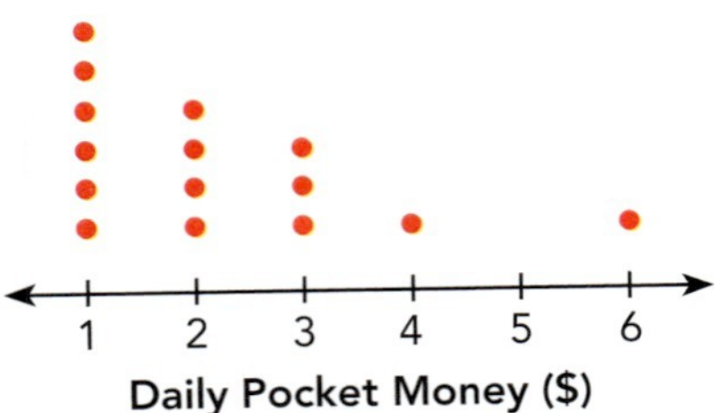

a) What is the mean daily pocket money?

$$\text{Mean} = \frac{\text{total amount of pocket money}}{\text{total number of students}}$$

$$= \frac{6 \times 1 + 4 \times 2 + 3 \times 3 + 1 \times 4 + 1 \times 6}{15}$$

$$= \frac{33}{15}$$

$$= \$2.20$$

b) What is the modal daily pocket money?

The greatest number of students has daily pocket money of $1.
So, the modal daily pocket money is $1.

c) What is the median daily pocket money?

There are 15 students altogether. The eighth student is in the middle, because there are 7 students to the left and 7 to the right of this student.
So, the median daily pocket money is $2.

d) Which measure of central tendency best describes the data set? Justify your answer.

The mode is $1, but it represents only 6 of the 15 students.
So, the mode does not describe these data well.
The mean is $2.20 and the median is $2.00. Both of these numbers might be used to describe this set of data. The mean takes into account the students who have more pocket money, but the median better describes what most students have in pocket money.

e) Relate the measures of center to the shape of the data distribution.

The shape of the data distribution is skewed to the right. The mean gives more weight to the values on the right than the median does. So, the mean is to the right of the median.

Guided Practice

Solve.

The dot plot shows the results of a survey on the number of children below 13 years old in each household. Each dot represents one household.

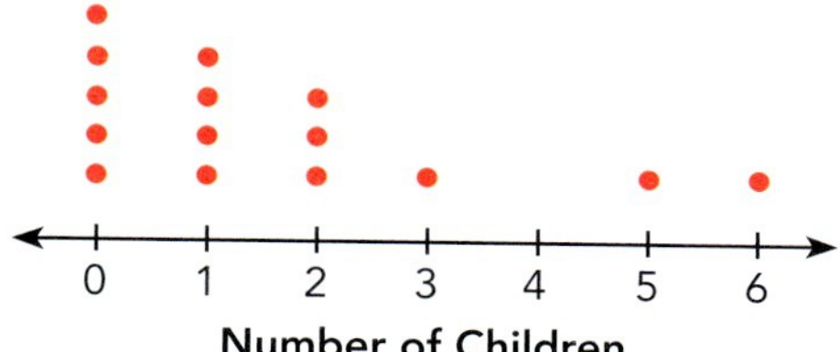

6. Find the mean, mode, and median of the data set.

7. Which measure of central tendency best describes the data set? Justify your answer.

8. Relate the measures of center to the shape of the data distribution.

Learn

Relate the measure of center to a symmetrical distribution.

The dot plot shows the ages of students, in years, on a basketball team. Each dot represents 1 student.

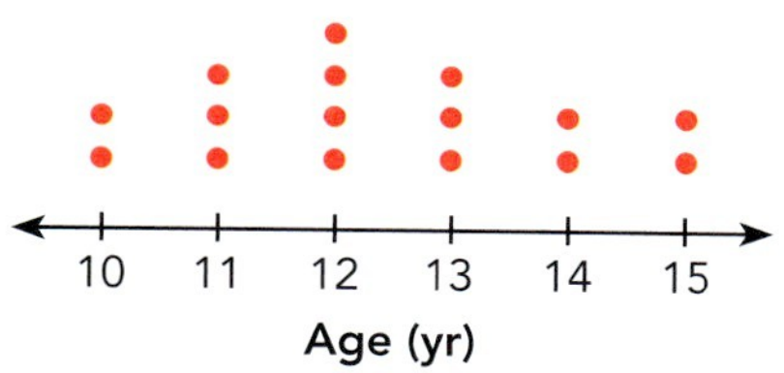

In a symmetric or nearly symmetric distribution, the mean, median, and mode are all equal, or nearly equal.

a) Find the mean.

$$\text{Mean age} = \frac{\text{total age of the students}}{\text{total number of students}}$$

$$= \frac{2 \times 10 + 3 \times 11 + 4 \times 12 + 3 \times 13 + 2 \times 14 + 2 \times 15}{16}$$

$$= \frac{198}{16}$$

$$= 12.375 \text{ yr}$$

The mean is 12.375 years.

b) Find the mode.

Most students are of age 12 years. So, the mode is 12 years.

Continue on next page

c) Find the median.

The two middles ages are both 12 years. So, the median is 12 years.

d) Relate the measures of center to the shape of the data distribution.

The data are well spread out and the shape of the data distribution is nearly symmetrical. Because the mode and median are the same, and the mean is slightly greater, the data set is likely to be more spread out for data greater than 12. The data set has a slight skew to the right.

Guided Practice

Solve.

The dot plot shows the number of feedback forms received by a mall over a ten-week period. Each dot represents one feedback form.

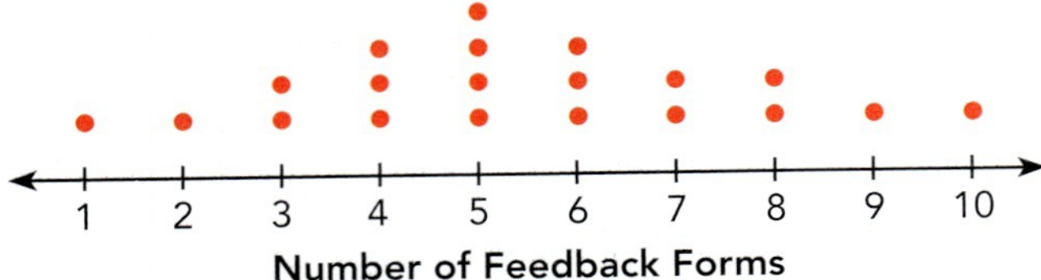

9 Find the mean, mode, and median of the data set.

10 Relate the measures of center to the shape of the data distribution.

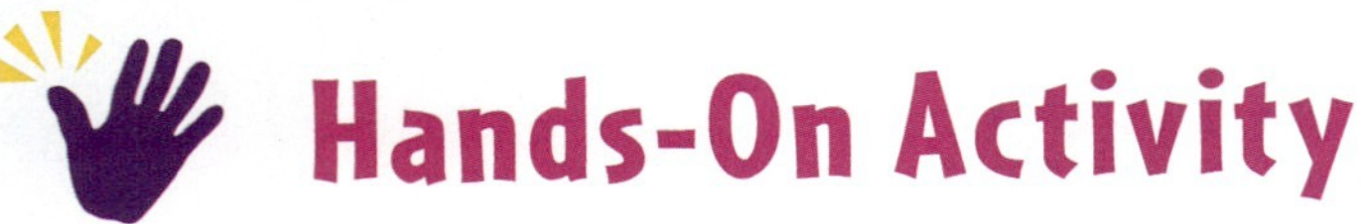

Hands-On Activity

FINDING POSSIBLE VALUES OF MEAN, MEDIAN, AND MODE

Work in pairs.

The lengths of 10 wallets have the same mean, median, and mode of 12 centimeters.

Explore and find a set of possible values for these lengths.

Show your work.
(Hint: You may use a dot plot to help you.)

Practice 14.4

Find the mean, median, and mode.

1 Eight students took a mathematics quiz. Their scores were 85, 92, 73, 85, 68, 82, 93, and 76. Find the mean, median, and mode.

Use the data in the table to answer questions 2 and 3.

The table shows the results of a survey carried out on 80 families.

Number of Children in 80 Families

Number of Children	0	1	2	3	4	5	6
Number of Families	8	17	21	13	13	6	2

2 Find the mean, median, and mode.

3 Which measure of central tendency best describes the data set? Justify your answer.

Solve. Show your work.

The data set shows the weights of ten gerbils in ounces.

5.49, 4.48, 4.57, 4.59, 4.61, 4.57, 4.98, 4.43, 4.45, 4.58

4 Find the mean, median, and mode.

5 Which one of the weights would you delete from the list if you want the mean to be closer to the median?

Use the data in the dot plot to answer questions 6 to 9.

The dot plot shows the number of hours nine students spent surfing the Internet one day. Each dot represents 1 student.

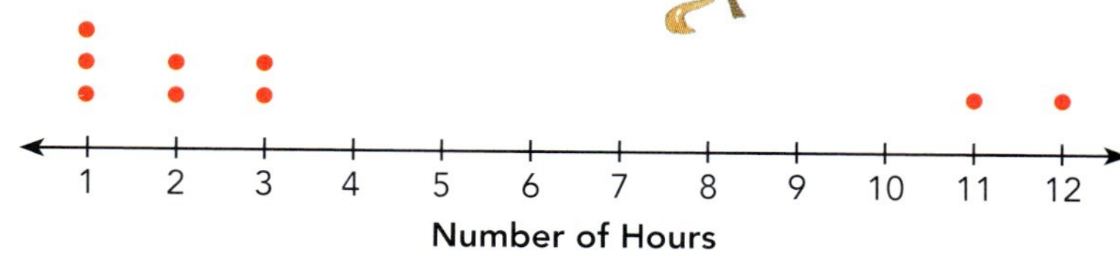

6 Find the mean, median, and mode.

7 Give a reason why the mean is much greater than the median.

8 Which measure of central tendency best describes the data set?

9 Relate the measures of center to the shape of the data distribution.

Use the data in the dot plot to answer the question.

The dot plot shows the results of a survey on the number of brothers or sisters each student in a class has. Each dot represents 1 student.

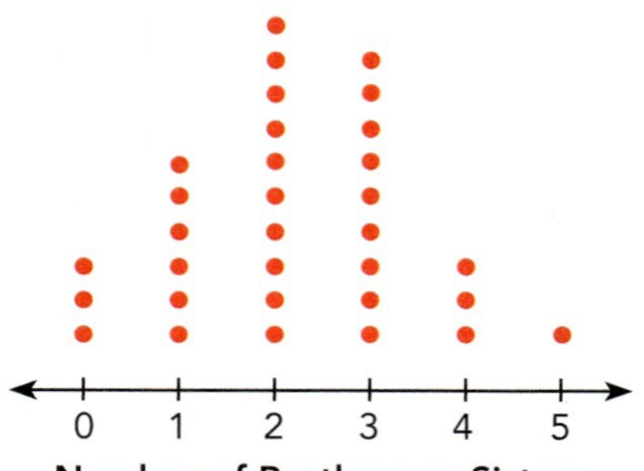

10 Briefly describe the data distribution and relate the measure of center to the shape of the dot plot shown.

Make a dot plot to show the data. Use your dot plot to answer questions 11 and 12.

A box contains cards each with a number 1, 2, 3, 4, or 5 on it. In an experiment, 20 students took turns drawing a card from the box. The number written on the card was recorded before it was put back into the box.

Alice, who was the last person to draw a card, was supposed to complete the dot plot below. However, she lost the record of the experiment's results. All she could recall was the following information.

(i) There were twice as many cards with the number '3' drawn as there were cards with the number '4' drawn.

(ii) There were an equal number of cards with the numbers '1' and '5' drawn.

(iii) 5 cards with the number '2' were drawn.

(iv) 8 students drew cards that show an even number.

11 Copy and complete the dot plot.

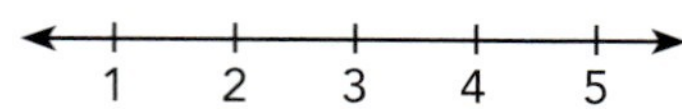

12 Briefly describe the data distribution and relate the measure of center to the shape of the dot plot shown.

Use the data in the table to answer questions 13 to 17.

The table shows the number of students absent from school over a 30-day period.

Number of Students Absent from School

Number of Students	0	1	2	3
Number of Days	8	7	10	5

13 What is the mode of this distribution?

14 Find the mean and median number of students absent from school over the 30 days.

15 It is found that the mean number of students absent from school over a subsequent 20-day period is 1. Find the mean number of students absent from school over the entire 50-day period.

16 If on one day of the 30-day period, 4 students were absent from school instead of 3, what should the mean of the distribution over the first 30-day period be? Round your answer to the nearest hundredth.

17 If on one day of the 30-day period, 2 students were absent from school instead of 1, would the median of the distribution over the 30-day period be affected? If so, what is the new median?

In a series of six class quizzes, Tim's first four quiz scores are 3, 5, 6, and 8. The mean score of the six quizzes is 6. If the greater of the missing quiz scores is doubled, the mean score becomes $7\frac{1}{3}$. What are the two missing quiz scores?

Tim's Test Scores

Test	First	Second	Third	Fourth	Fifth	Sixth
Score	3	5	6	8	?	?

Chapter Wrap Up

Concept Map

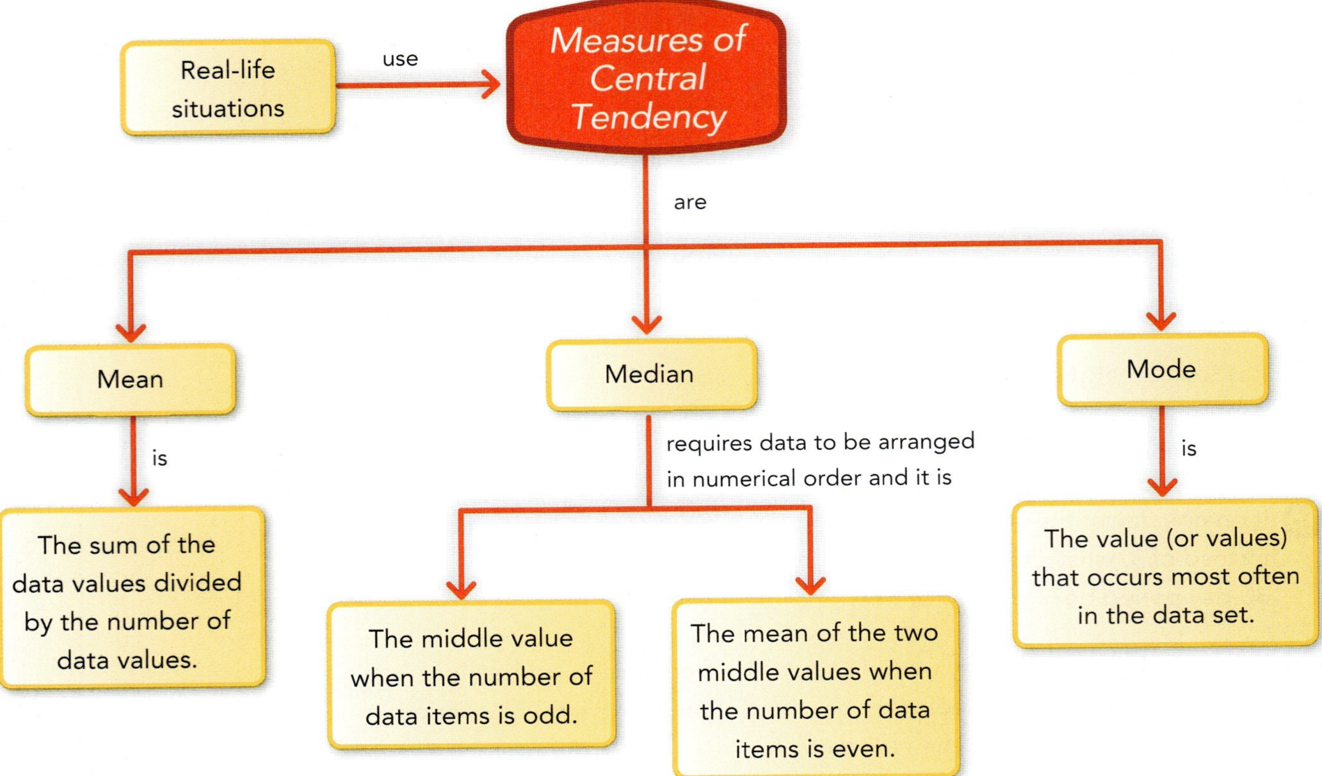

Key Concepts

- The three measures of central tendency are the mean, median, and mode. Each measure is a single number summarizing all the values in a data set.

- Mode is the only measure that can be used to describe non-numeric data.

- Mean and median are both used to describe the center of a set of numeric data. The mean gives more weight to outliers and extreme values than the median does.

- In a symmetric or nearly symmetric data set, the mean, median, and mode will be close together.

- In a skewed distribution, the median and mode will be close together, but the mean will move towards the outliers.

Chapter Review/Test

Concepts and Skills

Solve. Show your work.

1. The data set shows nine students' scores in a science quiz.

   9, 6, 6, 5, 9, 10, 1, 4, 10

   Find the mean and median score.

2. The mean of a set of four numbers is 3.5. If a fifth number, x, is added to the data set, the mean becomes 4. Find the value of x.

Make a dot plot to show the data. Use your dot plot to answer the question.

3. The data set shows the number of vehicles at a highway intersection during morning rush hour on 15 working days.

   12, 11, 4, 6, 9, 11, 4, 6, 12, 16, 11, 10, 8, 4, 5

   Find the mean, median, and mode of the data set.

Problem Solving

Solve. Show your work.

The data set shows the amount of money 10 children spent in a week.

\$16, \$13, \$11, \$19, \$17, \$28, \$15, \$11, \$13, \$11

4. Find the mean and median amount of money spent.

5. Which amount of money would you delete from the list if you want the mean to be closer to the median? Explain your answer.

Use the data in the table to answer the question.

6. Three classes in Grade 7 took a geography test last week. The table shows the mean score of the students in each class.

   The mean score of the students in classes A and B combined is 7.25. The mean score of all the students in the three classes is 6.5.

   Find the values of x and y.

Mean Score of Students in Three Classes

Class	A	B	C
Number of Students	x	25	20
Mean Score	6	8	y

Make a dot plot to show the data. Use your dot plot to answer questions 7 and 8.

The table shows the number of goals scored by a soccer team in 15 games.

Number of Goals Scored by a Soccer Team

Number of Goals	1	2	3	4	5	6	7
Number of Games	5	6	3	0	0	0	1

7 Find the mean, median, and mode of the data set.

8 Briefly describe the data distribution and relate the measure of center to the distribution.

Use the data in the dot plot to answer questions 9 to 13.

The dot plot shows the results of a survey to find the number of computers in 30 randomly chosen families. Each dot represents 1 family.

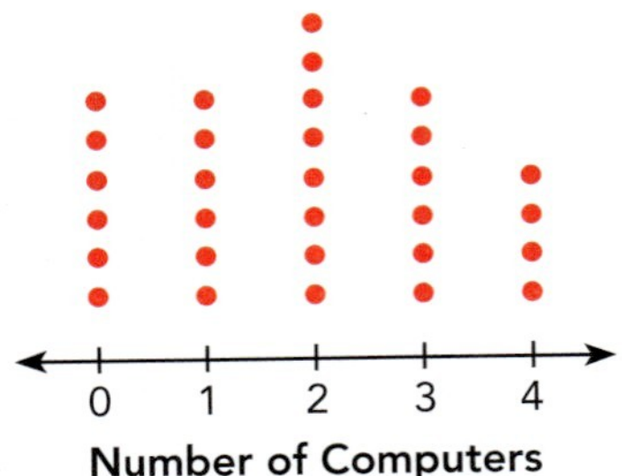

9 What is the modal number of computers?

10 What is the mean number of computers? Round your answer to the hundredths place.

11 What is the median number of computers?

12 Briefly describe the data distribution and relate the measure of center to the shape of the dot plot shown.

13 A similar survey is carried out on another 15 randomly chosen families and the mean number of computers is found to be 2. If the two data sets are combined, find the mean number of computers in the combined data set. Round your answer to the nearest hundredth.

Cumulative Review Chapters 12–14

Concepts and Skills

Match each of the solid figures to its net. (Lesson 12.1)

1 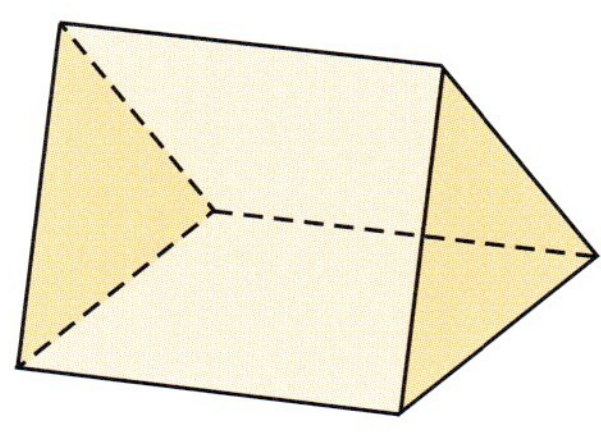

2 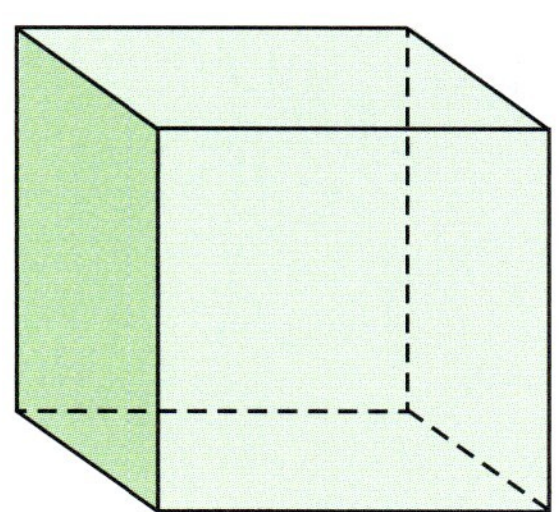

3 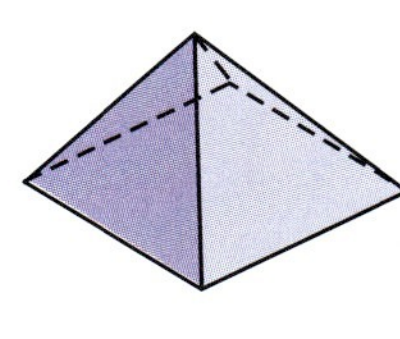

a) 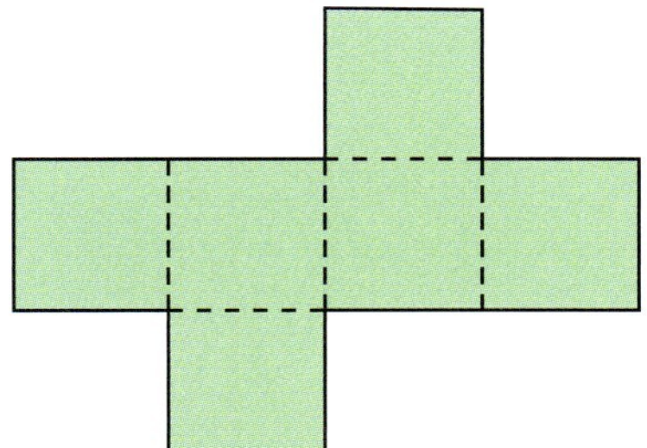

b) 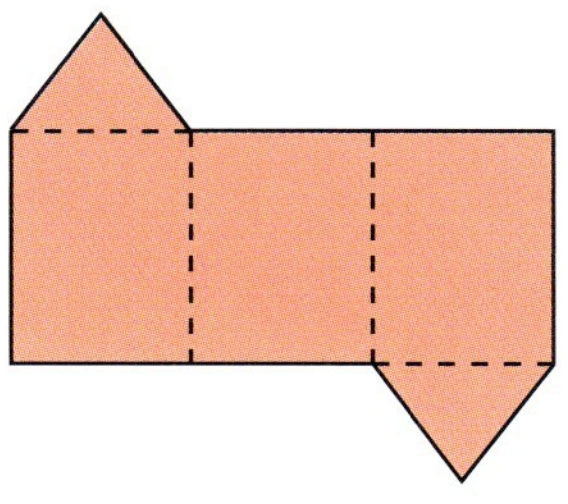

c) 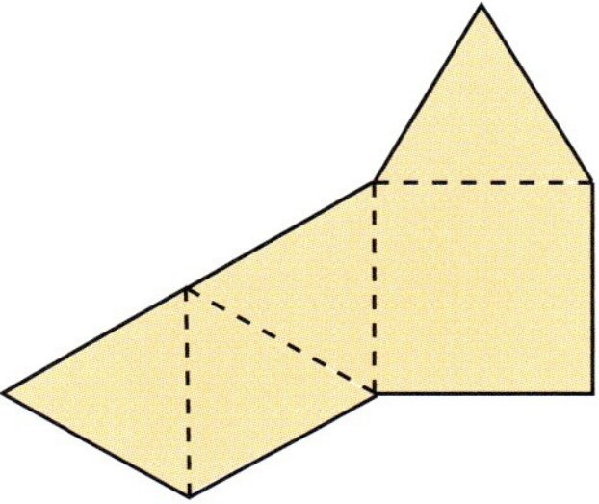

Find the surface area and volume of each prism. (Lessons 12.1, 12.2)

4 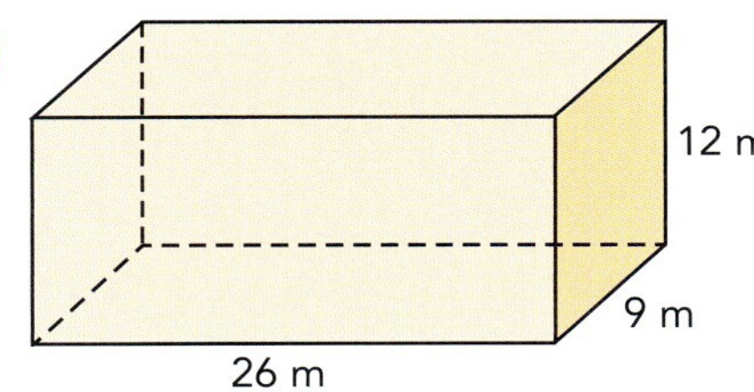

5 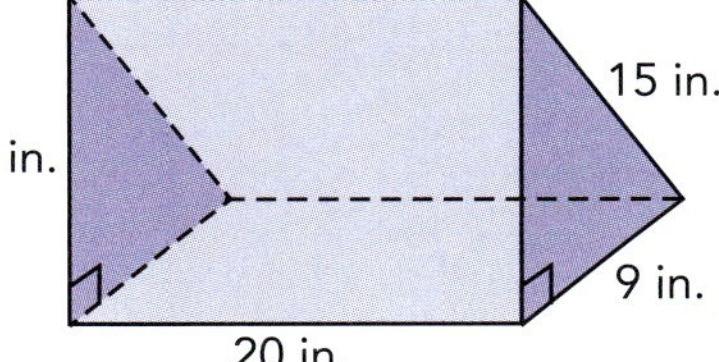

Solve. Show your work. (Lessons 14.1, 14.2)

6 The data set shows the lengths (in inches) of seven pieces of wire.
7.9, 6.8, 7.6, 9.9, 10.1, 9.1, 10.9
Find the mean and median lengths of these seven pieces of wire.

7 The data set shows the weights (in pounds) of 9 vases.
8.8, 8.3, 7.7, 11.6, 9.9, 8.9, 10.4, 9.6, 8.5
Find the mean and median weights of these 9 vases.

8 The data set shows the heights (in feet) of 8 trees.
53, 56, 65, 61, 67, 60, 52, 48
Find the mean and median heights of these 8 trees.

The volume of each triangular prism is 497 cubic feet. Find the height of the triangular base. Round your answers to the nearest tenth of a foot. (Lesson 12.3)

9 **10**

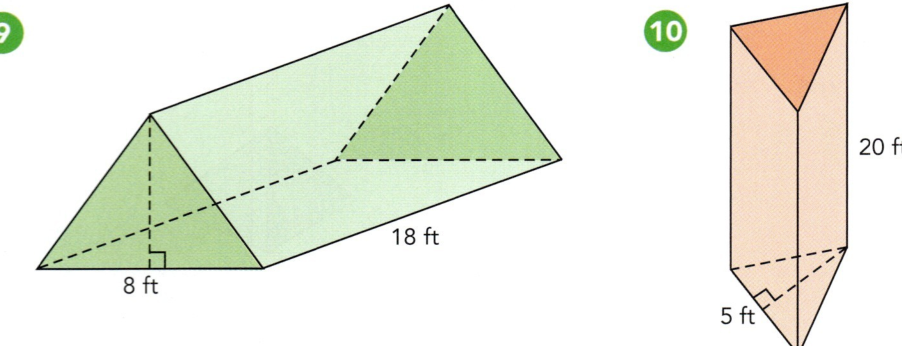

Solve. (Lesson 12.3)

11 The solid below is made of identical cubes. The volume of the solid is 405 cubic centimeters. Find the edge length of each cube.

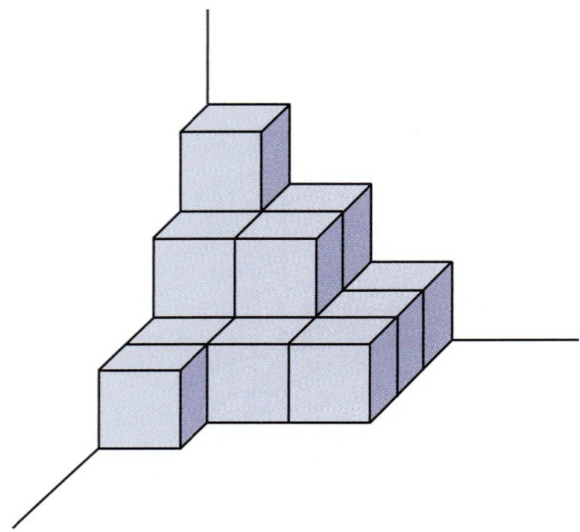

Draw a dot plot and a histogram for the set of data. Include a title. (Lessons 13.2, 13.3)

12 The number of pieces of fruits eaten in the past two days by each of 30 students was recorded below.

1	3	0	2	1	2	2	2	3	1
5	3	2	1	7	4	5	3	4	7
4	2	1	3	6	3	6	1	2	6

a) Represent the set of data with a dot plot.

b) Group the data into suitable intervals and tabulate them.

c) Draw a histogram using the intervals from part **b)**. Briefly describe the data.

Describe the data. (Lesson 13.3)

13. The histogram shows the number of floors each building has in a particular city. Briefly describe the data.

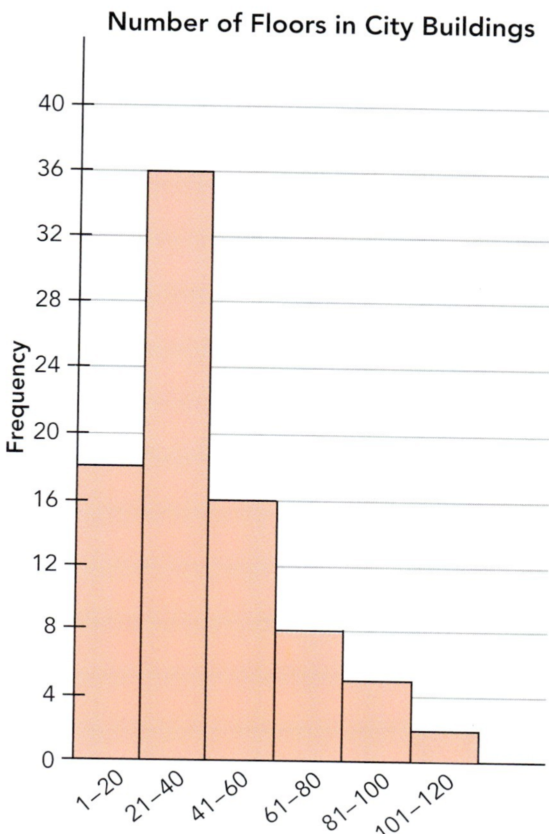

Problem Solving

Draw a dot plot for each set of data. Use your dot plot to answer each question. (Chapters 13, 14)

14. The data set shows the number of text messages sent by Emily in 14 days.

1	5	7	3	7	0	3
7	0	1	5	8	7	2

a) Represent the set of data with a dot plot.

b) Find the mean, median, and mode of the data set.

15 The data set shows the number of salads served in a cafe for each of 20 days.

23	22	24	26	19	21	24	26	21	16
22	20	18	24	25	17	22	23	19	24

a) Represent the set of data with a dot plot.

b) Find the mean, median, and mode of the data set.

Solve. Show your work. (Chapter 12)

16 The square pyramid shown has congruent triangular faces. The area of one triangular face is 48 square inches. Find the surface area of the pyramid.

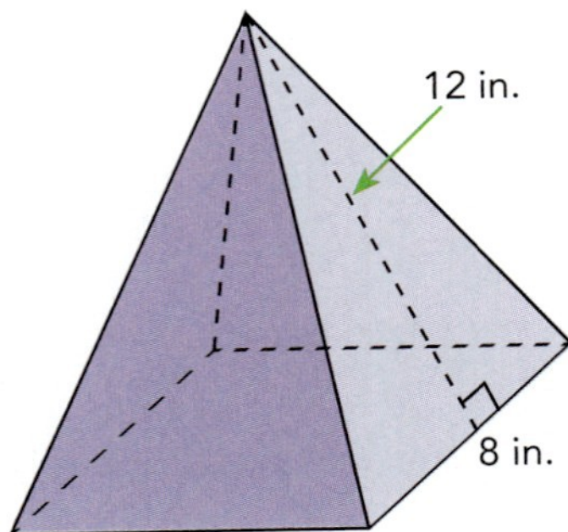

17 The length of the aquarium shown is two times its width. The height of the aquarium is 18 inches. The aquarium is filled with water to a height of 16 inches. The volume of the water is 7,200 cubic inches.

a) Find the length of the base of the aquarium.

b) Then find the amount of glass, in square inches, used to make the bottom and sides of the aquarium.

Solve. (Chapter 13)

18 The table shows the number of hours each of 120 students spent helping their community in two months.

Number of Hours	31 – 35	36 – 40	41 – 45	46 – 50	51 – 55	56 – 60	61 – 65	66 – 70	71 – 75
Number of Students	x	9	13	17	19	18	16	13	$2x$

a) Find the value of x.

b) Draw a histogram to represent the data.
Briefly describe the data.

c) What percent of the students spent more than 55 hours helping their community?

d) What percent of the students spent less than 46 hours helping their community?

Make a dot plot to show the data. Use your dot plot to answer each question. (Chapters 13, 14)

19 The table shows the results of a survey to find the number of television sets in 50 randomly chosen homes.

Number of Television Sets	0	1	2	3	4	5
Number of Homes	y	11	17	x	6	2

The total number of homes that have 0 or 1 television set is 15.

a) Find values of x and y. Then represent this set of data with a dot plot.

b) Find the mean, median, and mode of the data set.

c) Briefly describe the data distribution and relate the measure of center to the shape of the dot plot.

d) A similar survey is carried out on another 30 randomly chosen homes and the mean number of television sets is found to be 1.9. If the two data sets are combined, find the mean number of television sets in the combined data set.

Selected Answers

CHAPTER 8

Lesson 8.1, Guided Practice (pp. 6–11)

1. 1; 4; ≠; 2; 5; ≠; 4; 7; 4 **2.** $p = 7$ **3.** $r = 8$ **4.** $k = 17$ **5.** $m = 3$ **6.** $n = 5$ **7.** $z = 15$ **8.** –; 8; –; 8; 11 **9.** $f = 9$ **10.** $g = 15$ **11.** $w = 16$ **12.** $z = 30$ **13.** ÷; 3; ÷; 3; 9 **14.** $a = 7$ **15.** $b = 5$ **16.** $m = 72$ **17.** $n = 84$ **18.** –; $\frac{3}{7}$; –; $\frac{3}{7}$; $\frac{2}{7}$ **19.** Subtract $\frac{1}{8}$; $k = \frac{3}{4}$ **20.** Divide by 4; $p = \frac{3}{16}$

Lesson 8.1, Practice (p. 12)

1. $b = 3$ **3.** $k = 15$ **5.** $t = 7$ **7.** $k = 11$ **9.** $f = 40$ **11.** $m = 9$ **13.** $c = \frac{2}{3}$ **15.** $q = 1$ **17.** $d = \frac{1}{12}$ **19.** $f = 2\frac{2}{3}$ **21.** $x = 4.5$ **23.** $j = 24.1$ **25.** $z = 5.56$ **27.** $x = 1\frac{1}{4}$ **29.** $p = 3$ **31.** $y = 27$ **33.** $k = 18\frac{2}{3}$ **35.** Answers vary. Sample: 1, $\frac{2}{5}$; 2, $\frac{4}{5}$; 3, $1\frac{1}{5}$; 4, $1\frac{3}{5}$; 5, 2

Lesson 8.2, Guided Practice (pp. 14–19)

1a. $h + 7$ **1b.** h; 7 **1c.** h; k **2.** $t = p + 12$; Independent variable: p; Dependent variable: t **3.** $n = 30 - m$; Independent variable: m; Dependent variable: n **4.** $c = 7b$; Independent variable: b; Dependent variable: c **5.** $y = \frac{x}{12}$; Independent variable: x; Dependent variable: y

6a. $q = p - 2$; 2; 3; 5; 6

Length (p meters)	3	4	5	6	7	8
Width (q meters)	1	2	3	4	5	6

6b. Dimensions of a Rectangular Tank

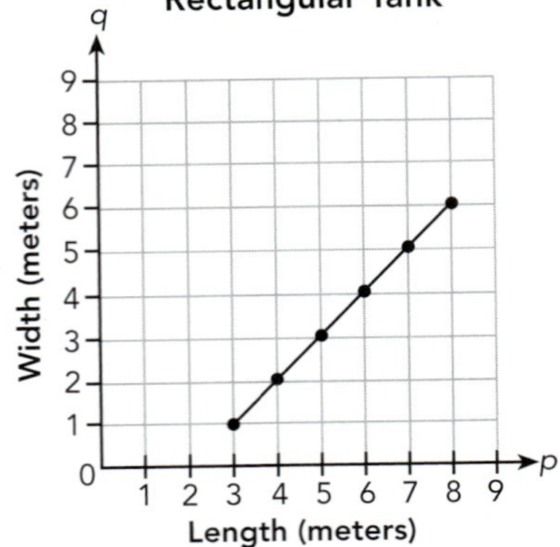

6c. Yes, the rectangular tank can have a length of 5.5 meters and a width of 3.5 meters.

7. 8; 10; 11; $y = x + 6$ **8.** 12; 16; 20; $r = 4b$

9. Journey

Distance Traveled (miles) / Time Taken (hours)

$d = 50t$

Lesson 8.2, Practice (pp. 20–21)

1a. $x = w + 3$ **1b.** Independent variable: w; Dependent variable: x **3a.** $m = 5k$ **3b.** Independent variable: k; Dependent variable: m **5a.** $y = x + 8$ **5b.** 18; 19; 20; 21; 22; 23 **7a.** $P = 6b$ **7b.** 6; 12; 18; 24; 30; 36

9a. $z = 4t$

9b.

Length of Square (t inches)	1	2	3	4	5	6	7	8	9	10
Perimeter of Square (z inches)	4	8	12	16	20	24	28	32	36	40

9c. Side Length and Perimeter of a Square

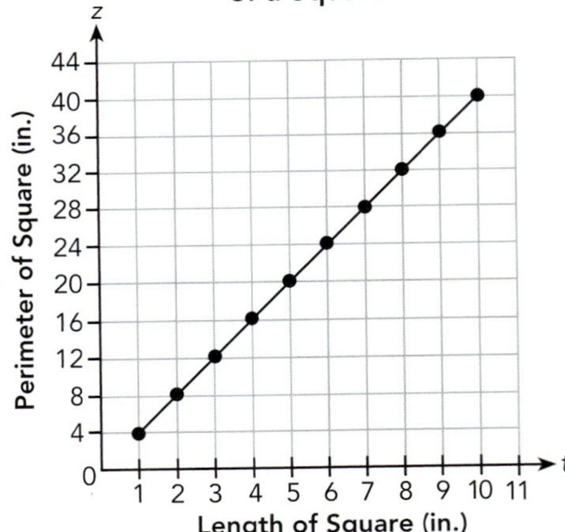

9d. Length: 3.5 inches, Perimeter:14 inches
Length: 7.5 inches, Perimeter: 30 inches

Lesson 8.3, Guided Practice (pp. 24–26)

1.

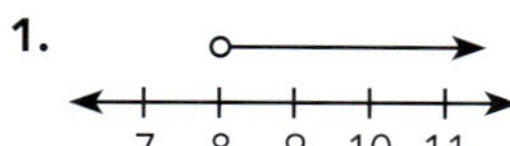

2.

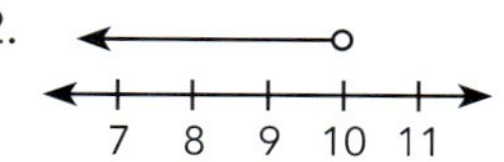

3.

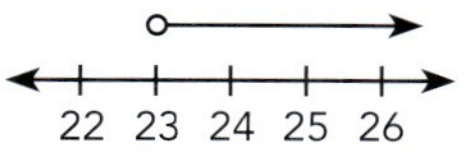

22 23 24 25 26

4.

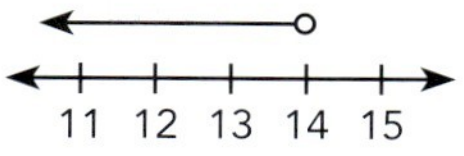

11 12 13 14 15

5.

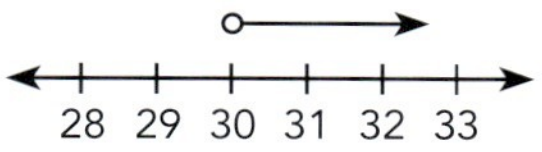

28 29 30 31 32 33

6.

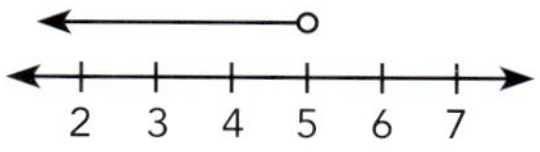

2 3 4 5 6 7

7.

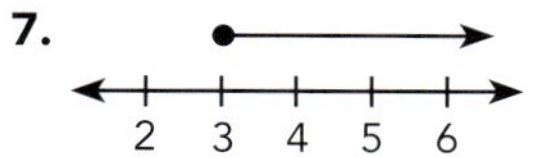

8.

9 10 11 12 13

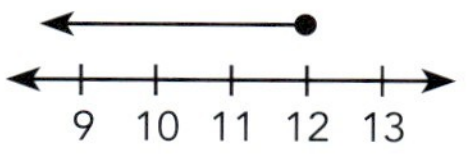

Answers vary. Sample: $q = 3, 4,$ or 5

9.

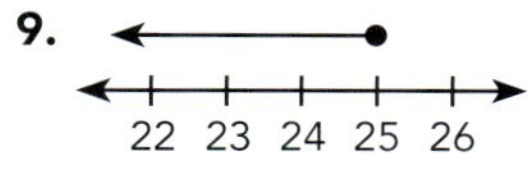

10.

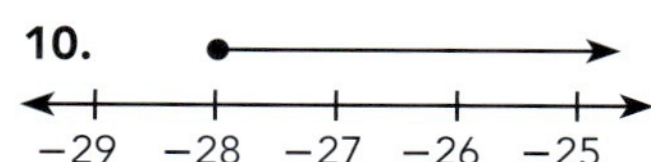

Answers vary. Sample: $k = 23, 24,$ or 25

11. b **12.** c **13.** d **14.** a

Lesson 8.3, Practice (pp. 27–28)

1. $k < 12$ **3.** $w \geq 17$ **5.** $x \geq 20$

7.

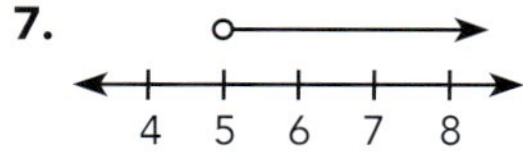

9.

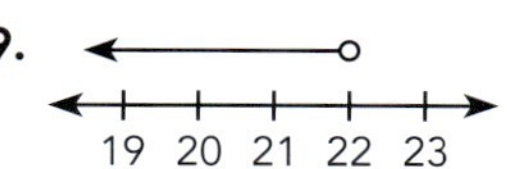

11. $x < 9$ **13.** $x \leq 11$

15.

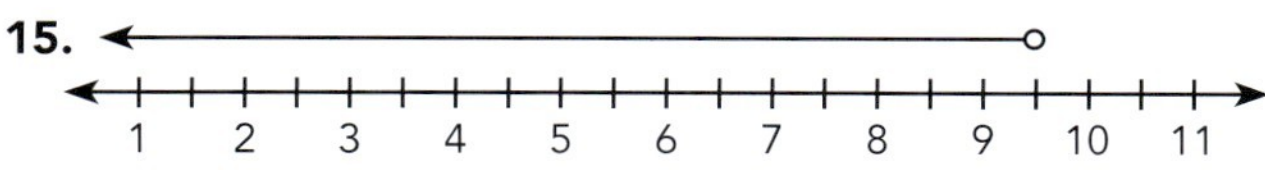

Answers vary. Sample: $p = 5, 6,$ or 7

17.

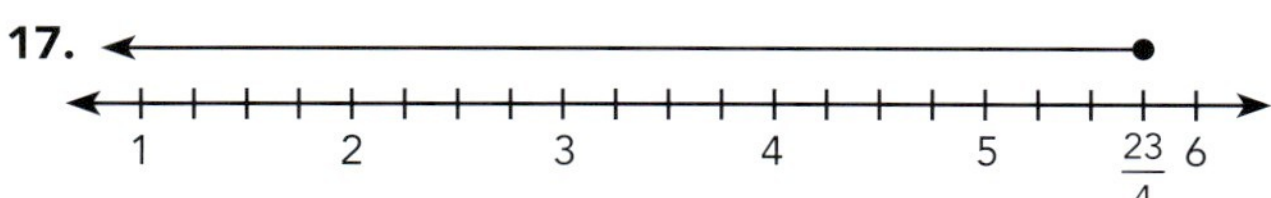

Answers vary. Sample: $b = 3, 4,$ or 5

19.

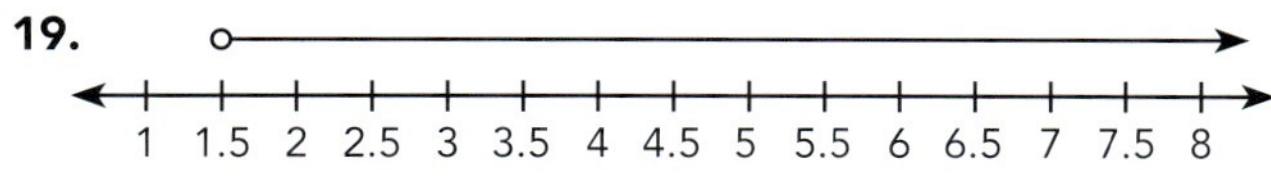

Answers vary. Sample: $g = 2, 3,$ or 4

21.

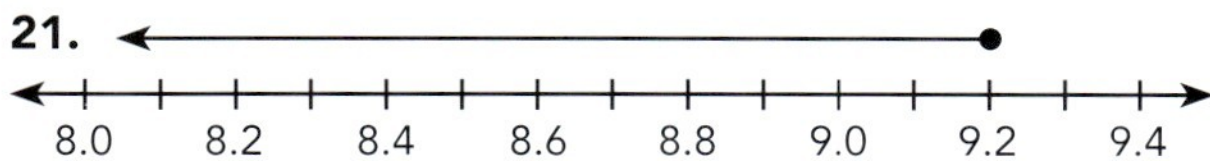

Answers vary. Sample: $z = 7, 8,$ or 9

23a. No. x is more than 9. **23b.** No. x is an integer.

25.

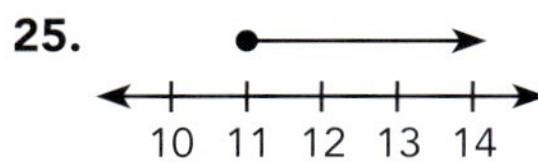

27.

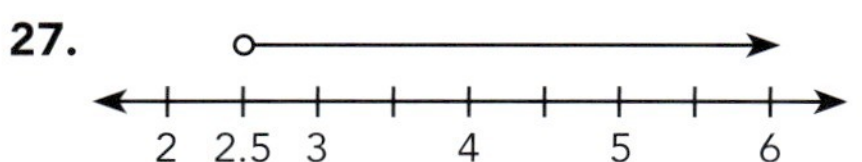

29.

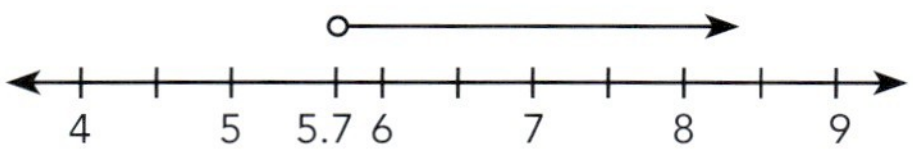

4 5 5.7 6 7 8 9

Lesson 8.4, Guided Practice (pp. 30–32)

1. 41; 23; 41; 23; 18; 18 **2.** 28 **3.** \$34 **4.** 17 green beads **5.** 125 quarters **6a.** $x \leq 55$ **6b.** 55 **7a.** $x > 35$ or $x \geq 36$ **7b.** 36 guests **8a.** $x < 50$ **8b.** 49 words **9a.** $x \leq 240$ **9b.** 240 tons **10a.** $x \geq 50$ **10b.** Alex

Lesson 8.4, Practice (pp. 33–34)

1. 65 **3.** 26 words per minute **5a.** $x > 40$;

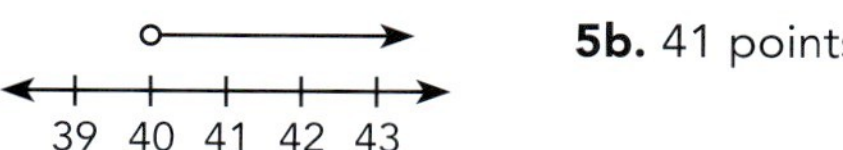

5b. 41 points

7. $\frac{3}{7}x = 24$; 56 mountain bikes

9. $0.3x = 42$; 140 comic books **11.** 54 marbles

13a. 60 participants **13b.** 96 participants

Lesson 8.4, Brain@Work (pp. 34)

5 cm

Chapter Review/Test (pp. 36–37)

1. $x = 19$ **3.** $f = 5.4$ **5.** $k = 3\frac{1}{3}$ **7.** $h = 14$

9. $P = 12\frac{1}{2}$

11.

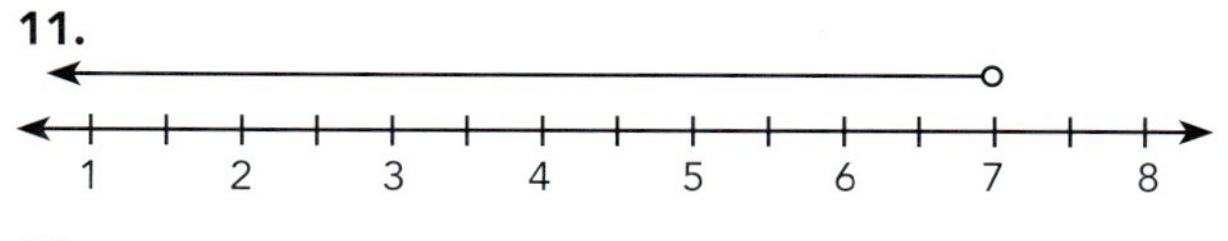

13.

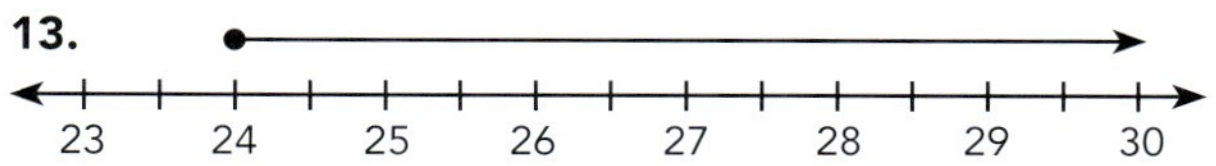

15.

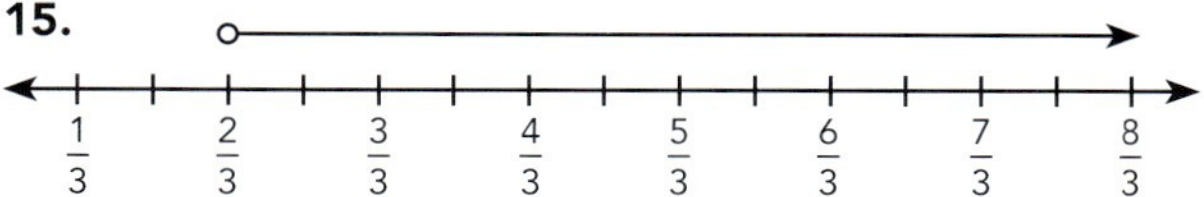

17.

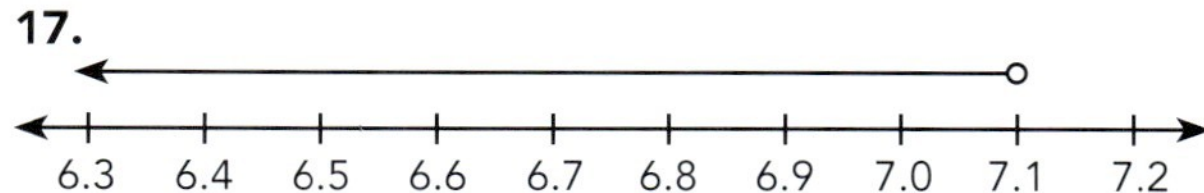

19. $x \geq 9$ **21.** $x < \frac{7}{10}$ **23.** $y = x + 9$ **25.** 4,030 mL

27. 119 pages **29.** 24 more green counters

31a. $x \geq 18$ **31b.** Perimeter: 66 cm; Area: 270 cm^2

CHAPTER 9

Lesson 9.1, Guided Practice (pp. 44–46)

1. $P(3, 0)$, $Q(-3, 3)$, $R(-5, 1)$, $S(-6, -4)$, $T(-4, -7)$, $U(4, -5)$, and $V(3, -2)$; Quadrant II: Points Q and R; Quadrant III: Points S and T; Quadrant IV: Points V and U; Point P lies on the x-axis. It is between Quadrant I and Quadrant IV.

2.

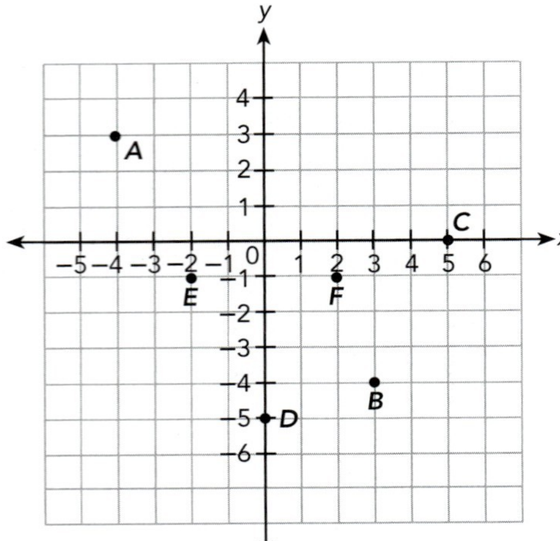

3a.

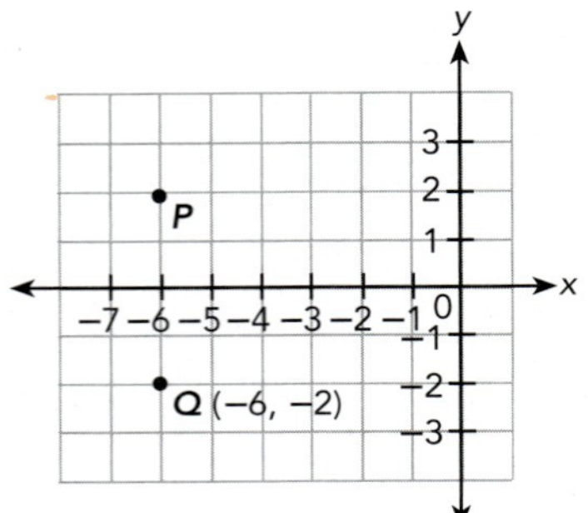

3b.

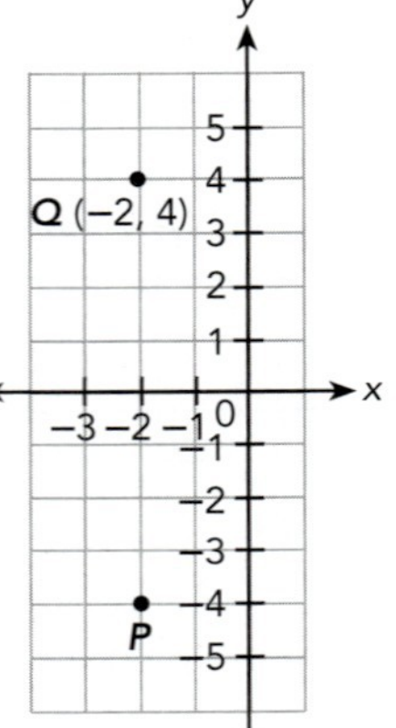

3c.

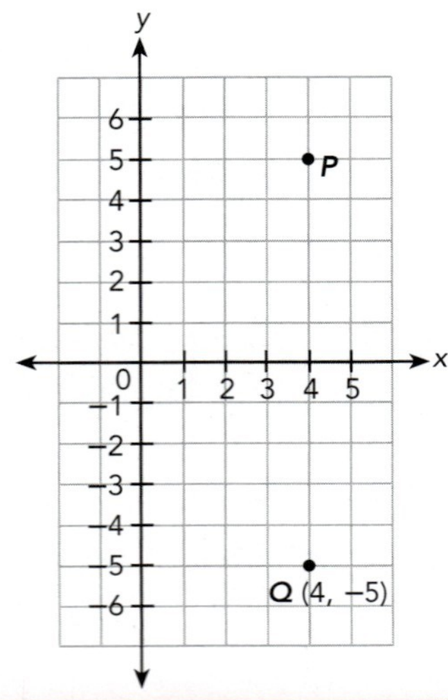

3d.

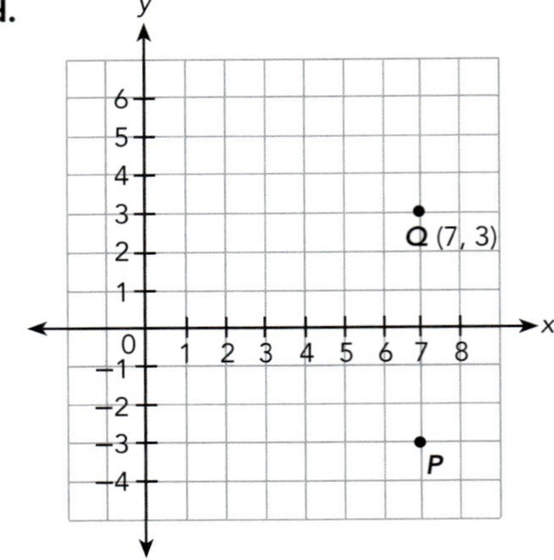

4a.

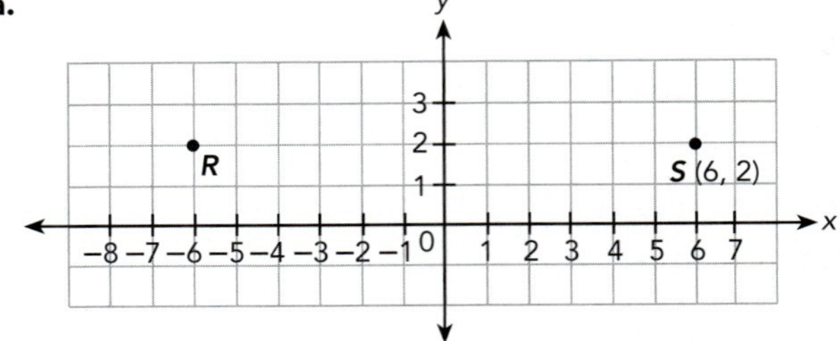

4b.

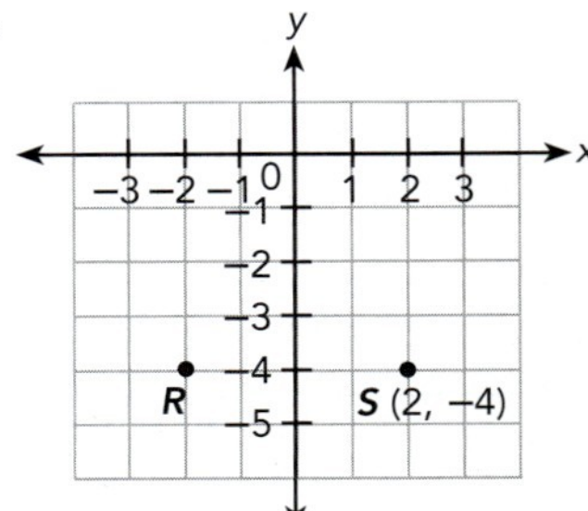

4c.

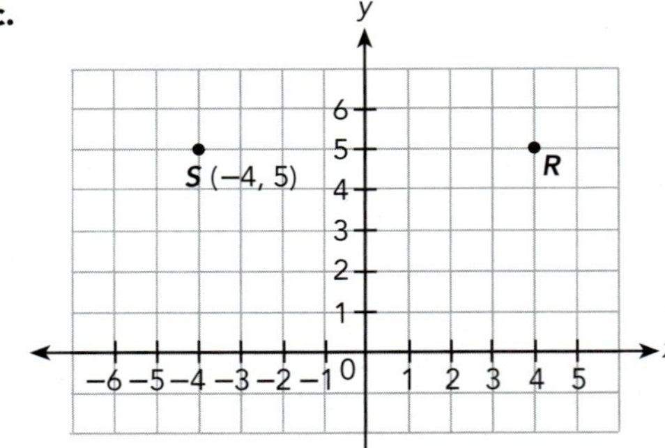

4d.

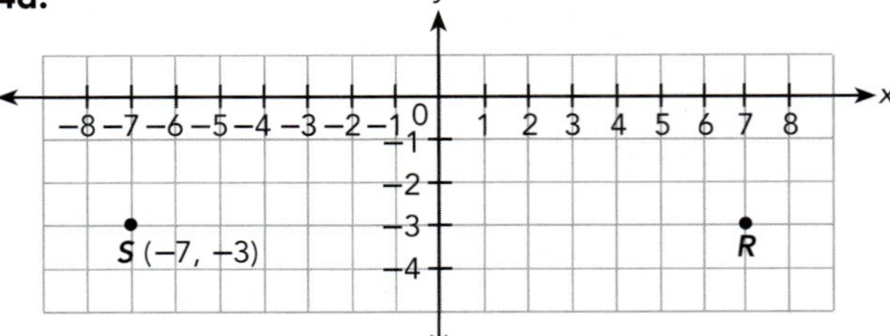

5.

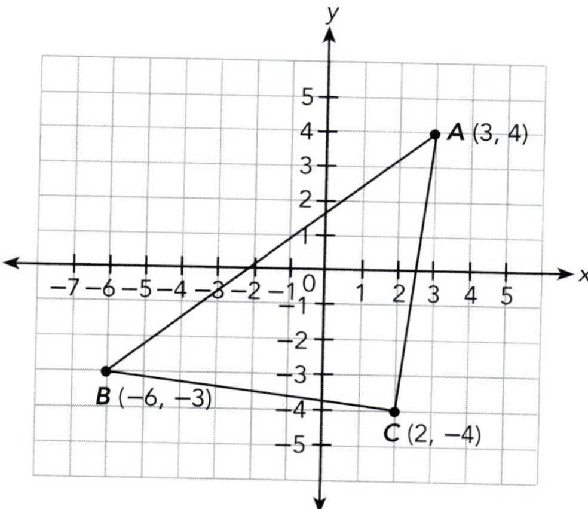

triangle

6.

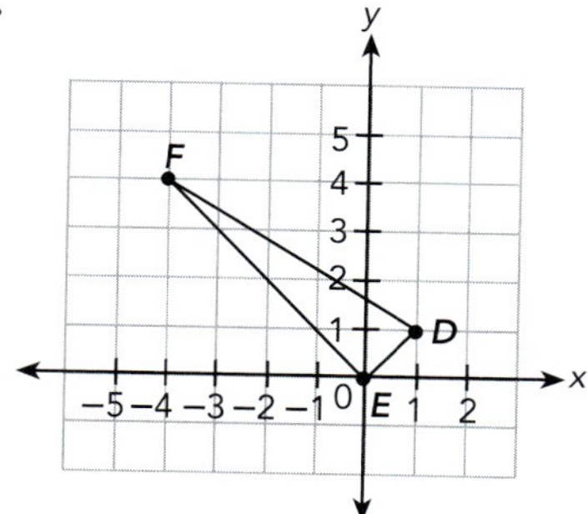

triangle

7.

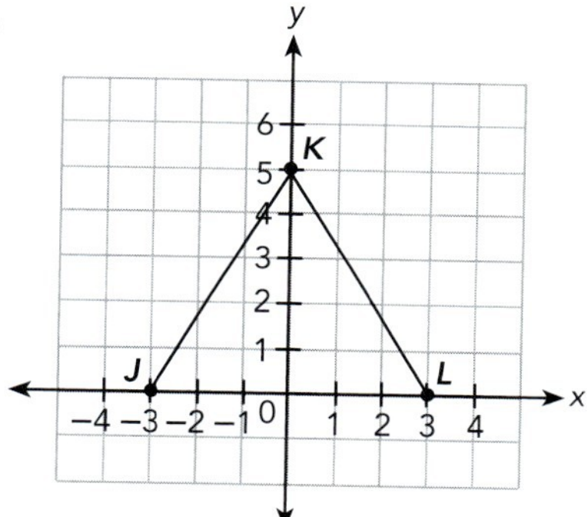

triangle

8.

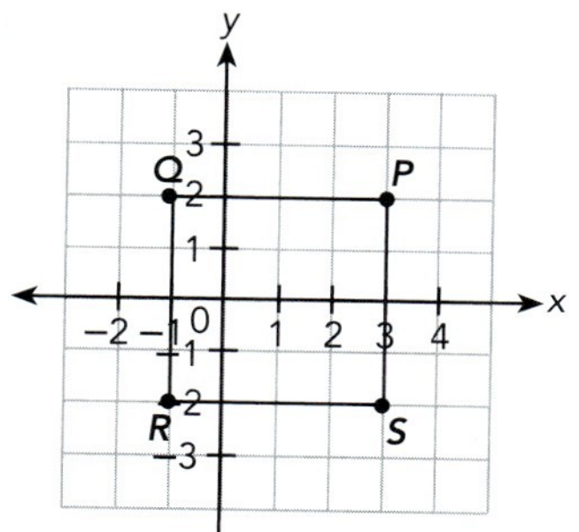

square

9.

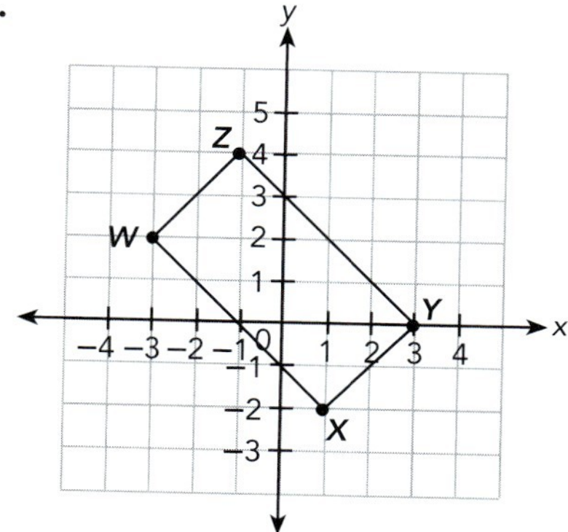

rectangle

10.

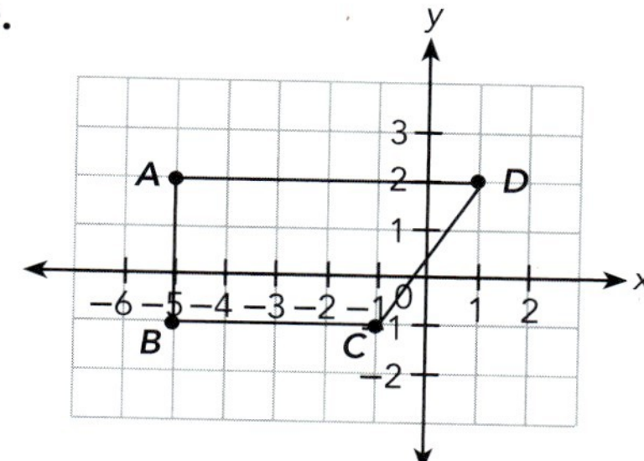

trapezoid

11.

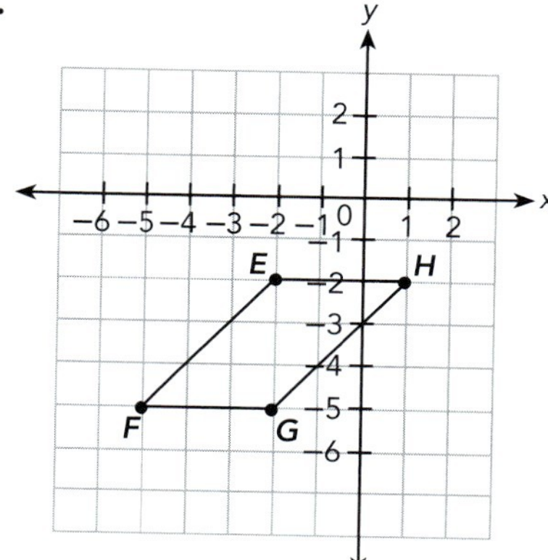

parallelogram

12.

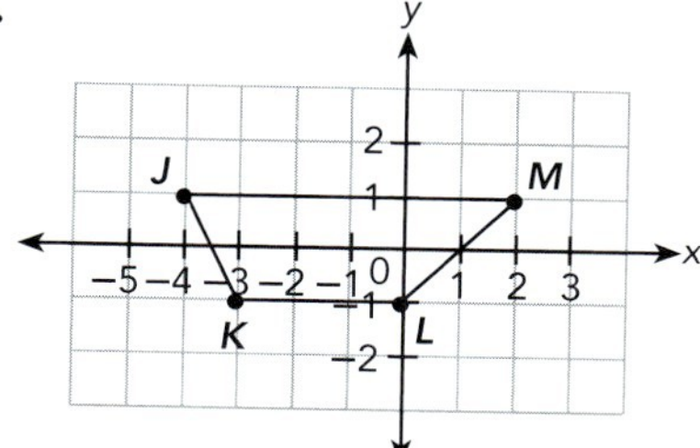

trapezoid

13.

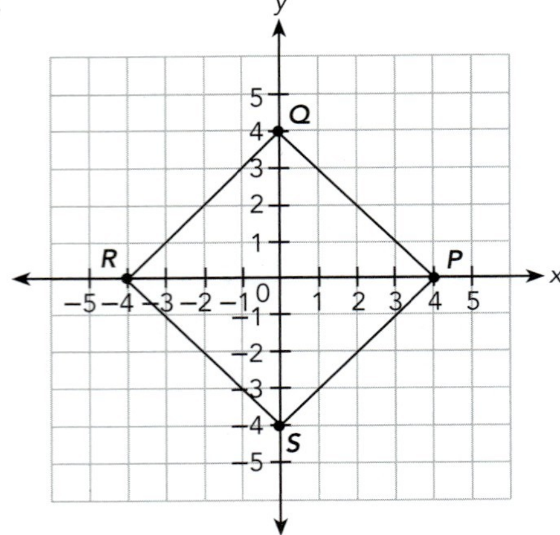

square

14.

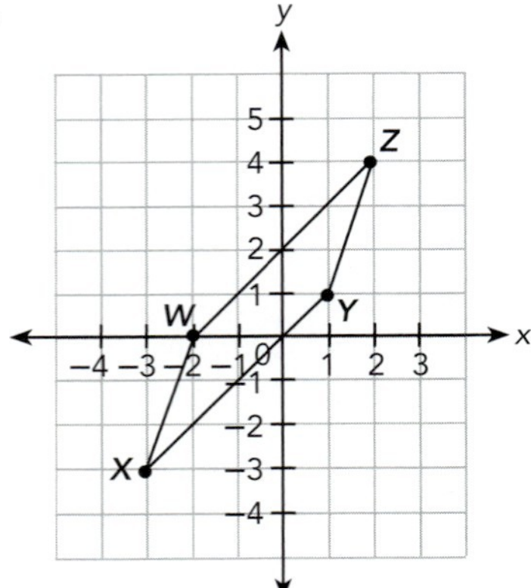

parallelogram

Lesson 9.1, Practice (pp. 48–49)

1. *A* (2, 6), *B* (6, 2), *C* (3, 0), *D* (4, −9), *E* (0, −2), *F* (−2, −4), *G* (−3, 0), and *H* (−1, 9); Quadrant I: Points *A* and *B*; Quadrant II: Point *H*; Quadrant III: Point *F*; Quadrant IV: Point *D*; Point *C* lies on the *x*-axis. It lies between Quadrant I and Quadrant IV. Point *G* lies on the *x*-axis. It lies between Quadrant II and Quadrant III. Point *E* lies on the *y*-axis. It lies between Quadrant III and Quadrant IV.

3.

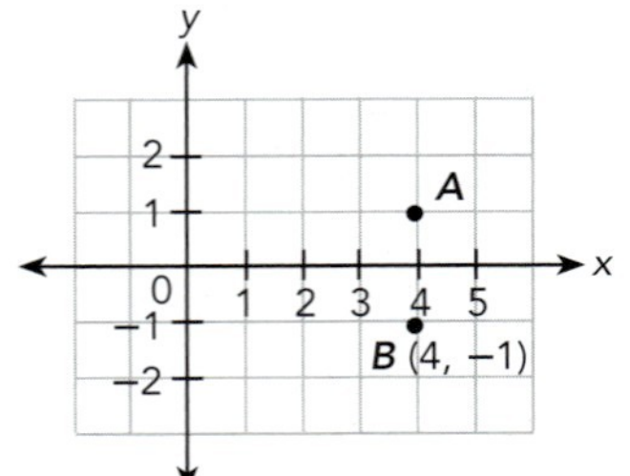

5.

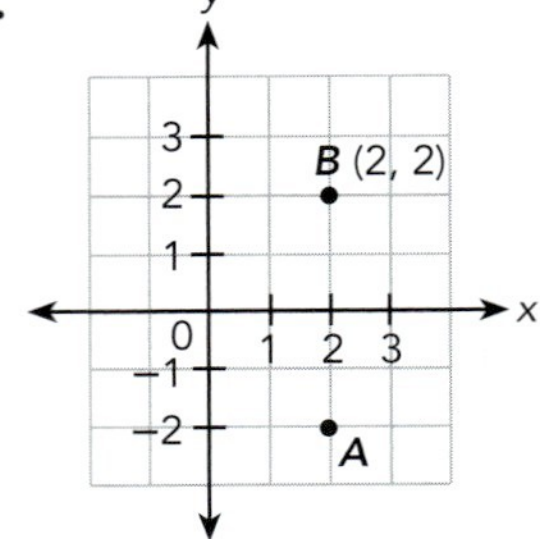

7.

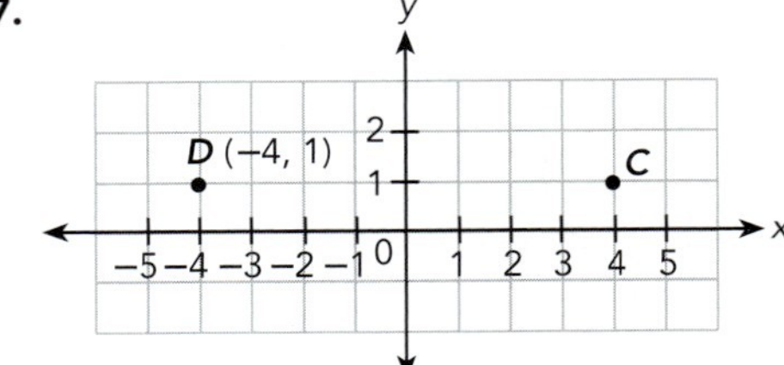

9.

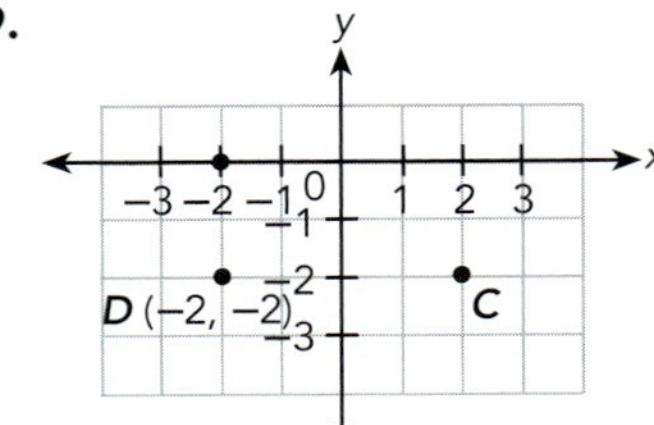

11.

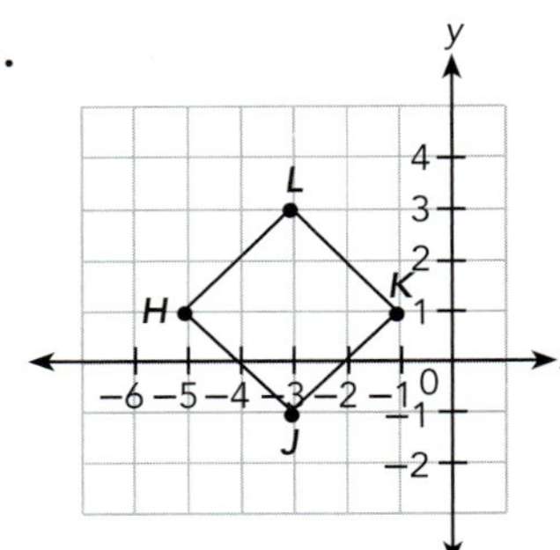

square

13.

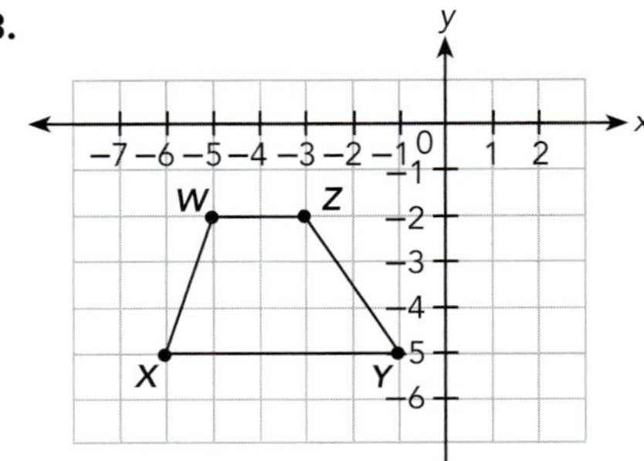

trapezoid

15a and **15b.**

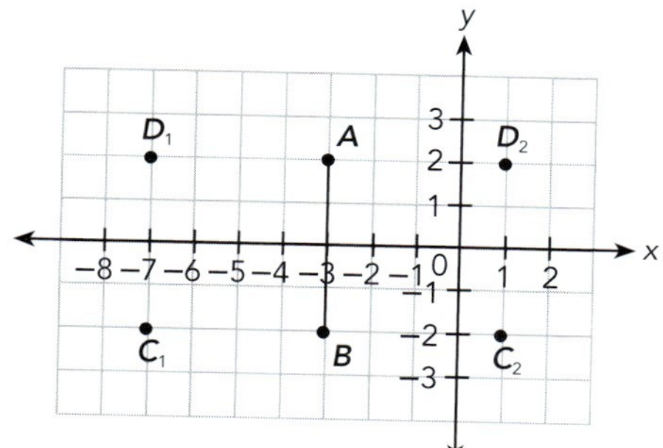

15c. C_1 (−7, −2), D_1 (−7, 2) and C_2 (1, −2), D_2 (1, 2)

17.

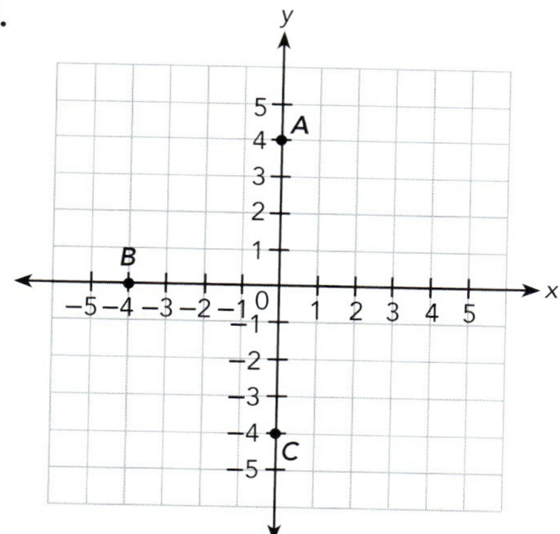

17a. right isosceles triangle

17b.

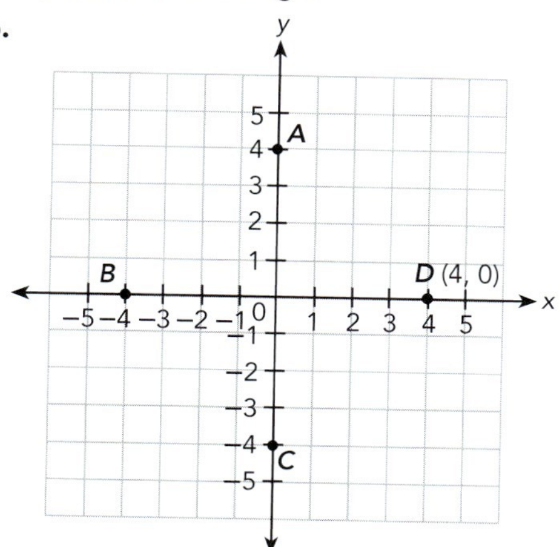

D (4, 0)

Lesson 9.2, Guided Practice (pp. 51–57)

1.

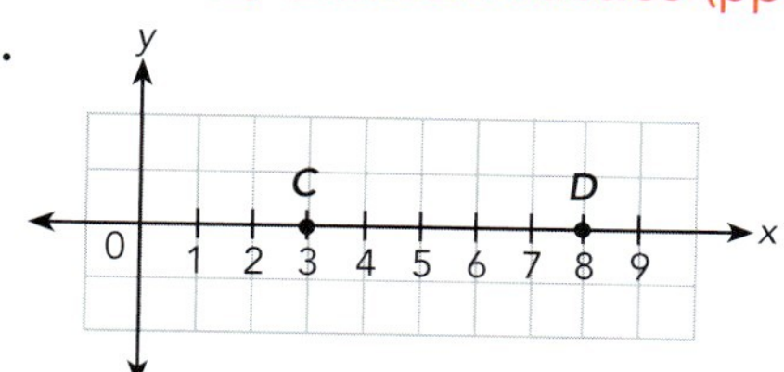

CD = 5 units

2.

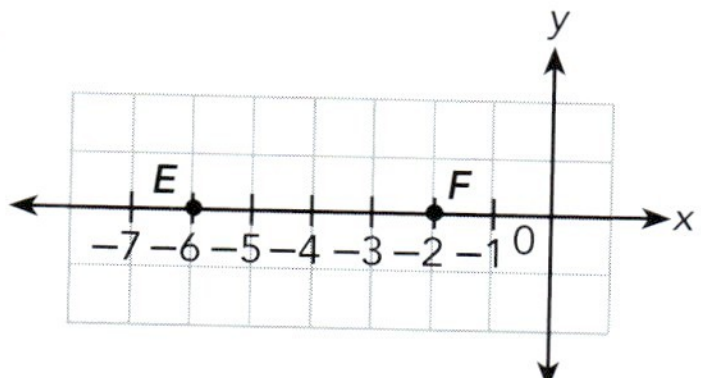

EF = 4 units

3.

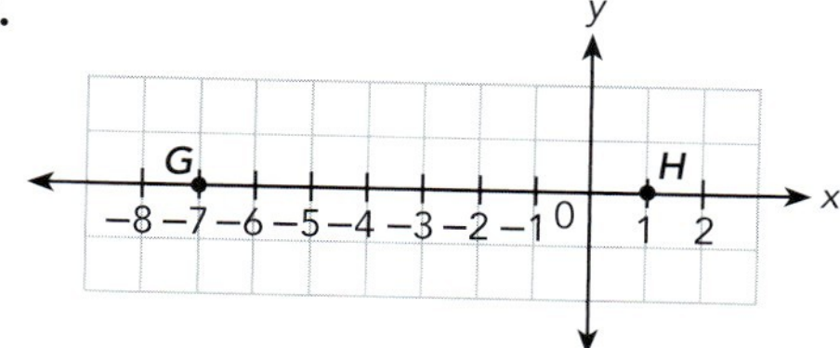

GH = 8 units

4.

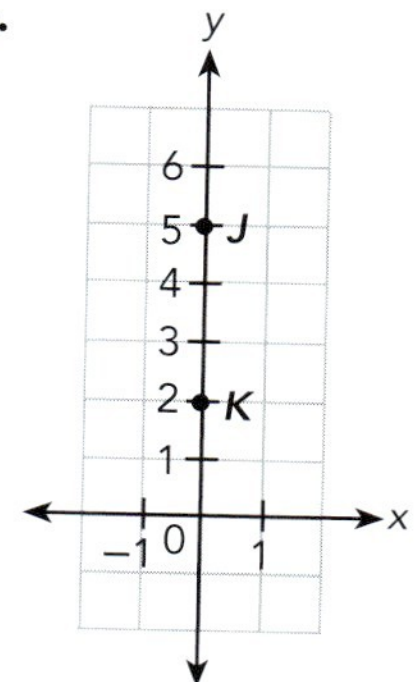

JK = 3 units

5.

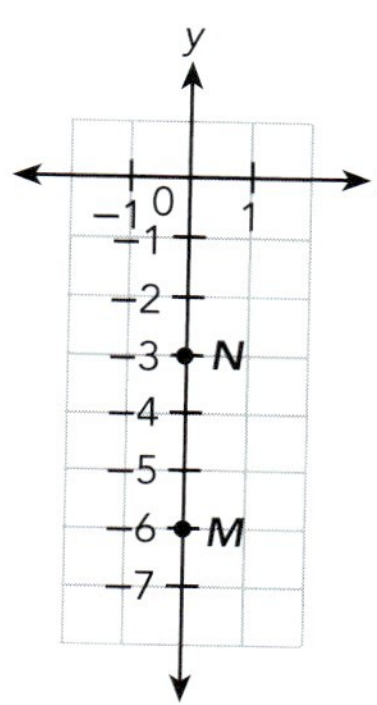

MN = 3 units

6.

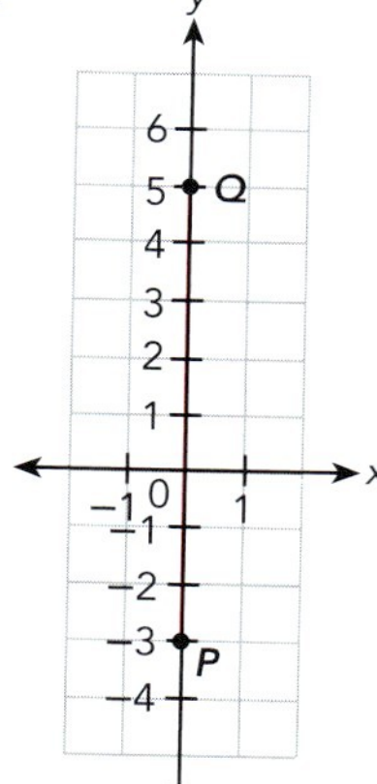

PQ = 8 units

7.

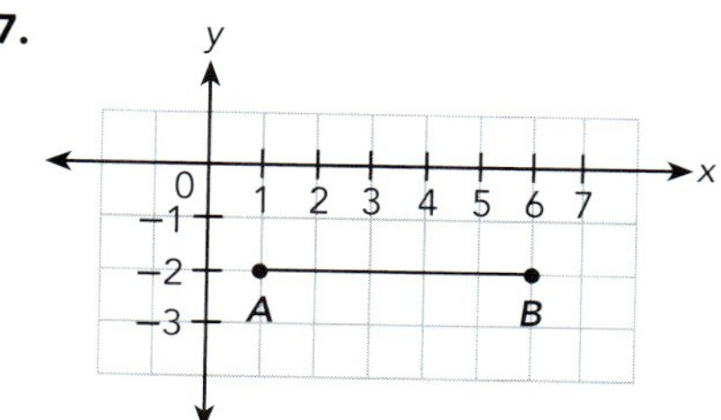

AB = 5 units

8.

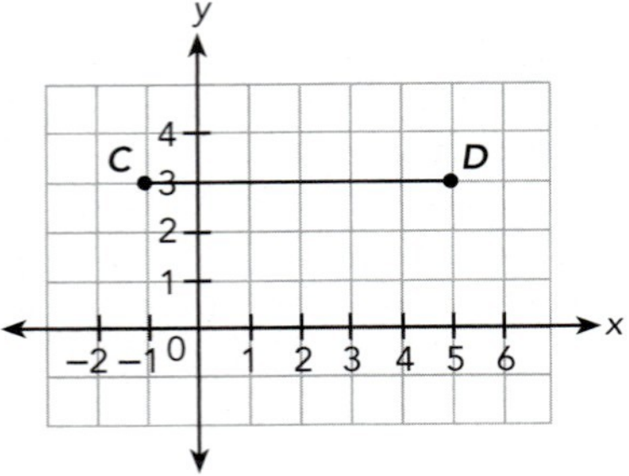

$CD = 6$ units

9.

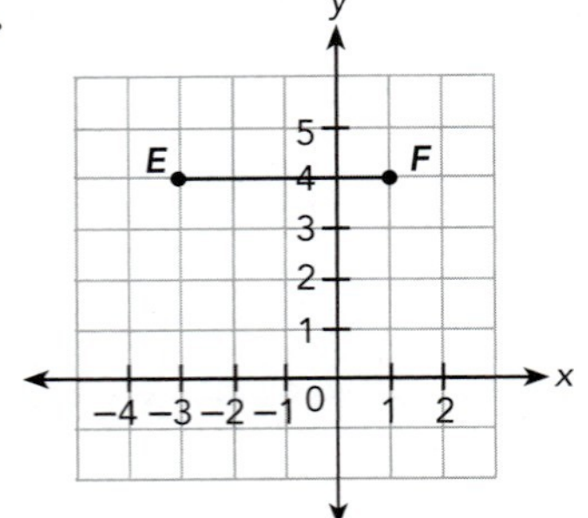

$EF = 4$ units

10.

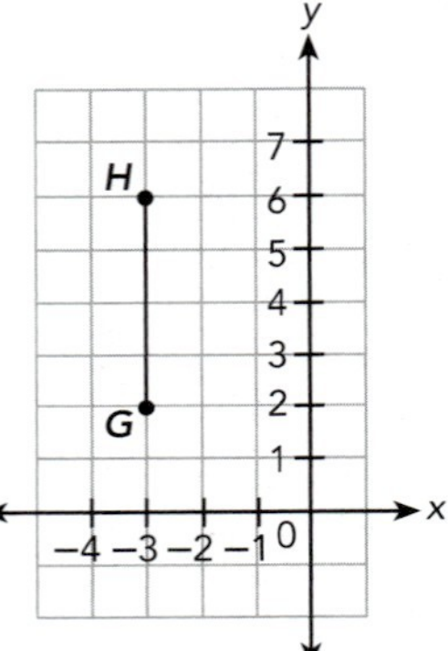

$GH = 4$ units

11.

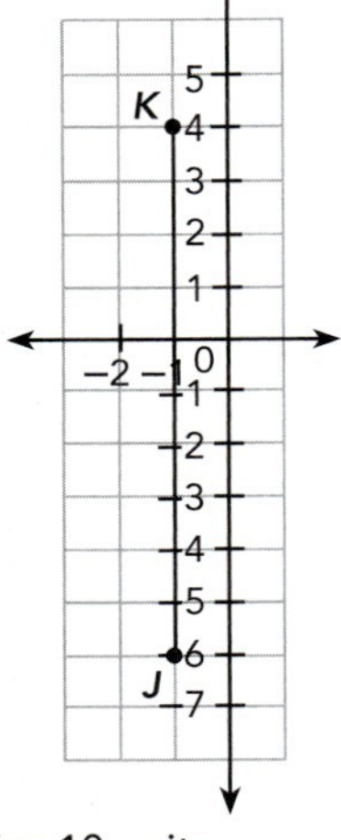

$JK = 10$ units

12.

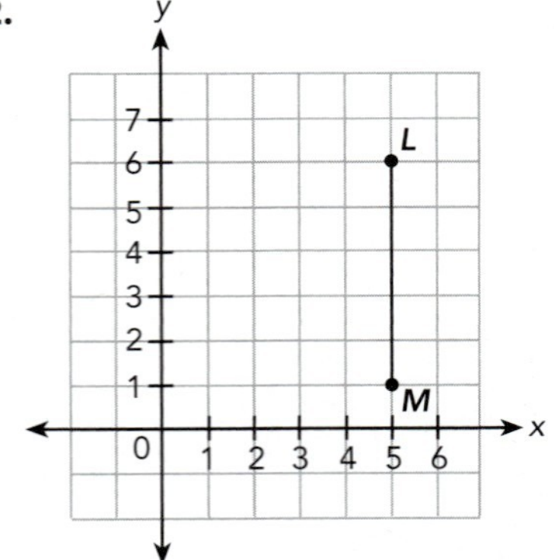

$LM = 5$ units

13. A (10, 20), B (10, 5), and C (30, 20) **14.** 20; 5; 15; 30; 10; 20; 15; 25; 20; 60; 60 **15.** 10; 2; 2; 2; 2; 4; 4; 5; 20; 1; 4; 1; 3; 3; 5; 15; 20; 15 **16.** P (16, 44), Q (16, 4), R (36, 4), and S (36, 44) **17.** 120 m **18.** T (16, 36)

Lesson 9.2, Practice (pp. 58–61)

1.

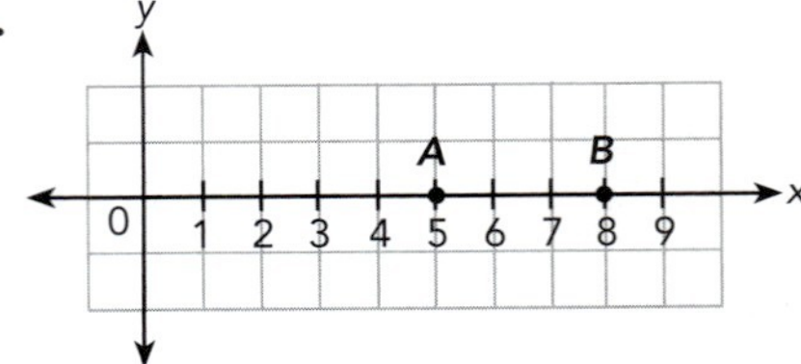

$AB = 3$ units

3.

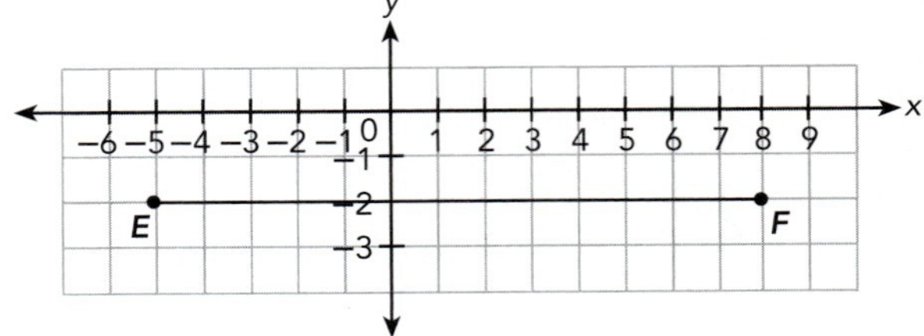

$EF = 13$ units

5.

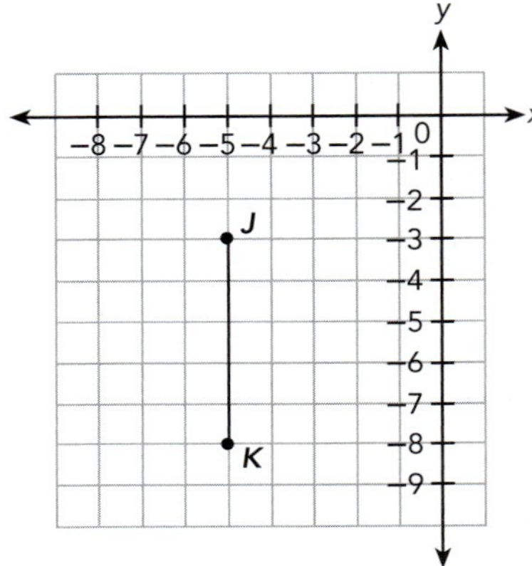

$JK = 5$ units

7a.

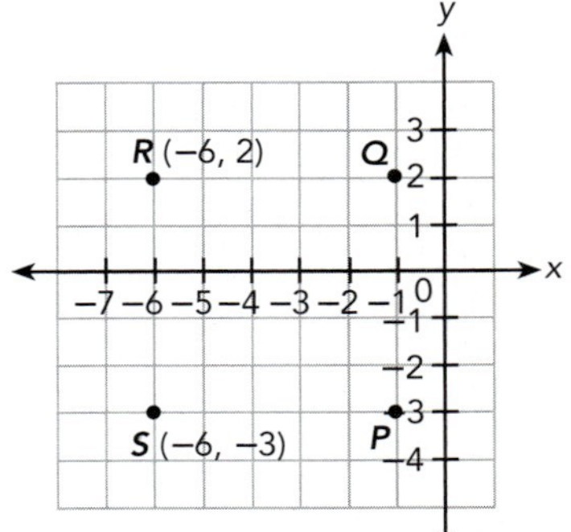

The coordinates of point R are (−6, 2). The coordinates of point S are (−6, −3).

7.b

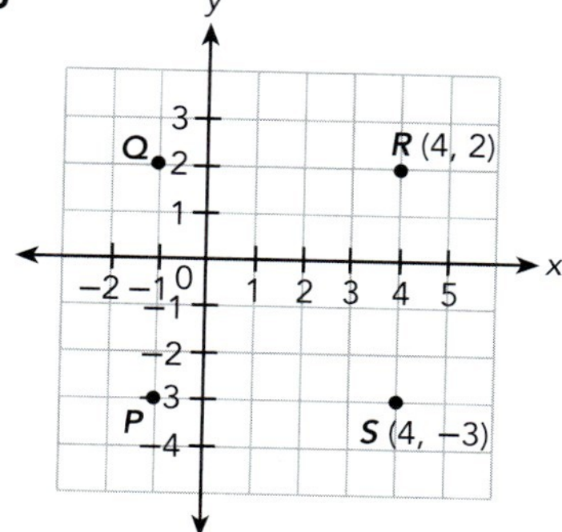

The coordinates of R are (4, 2). The coordinates of S are (4, −3).

9a.

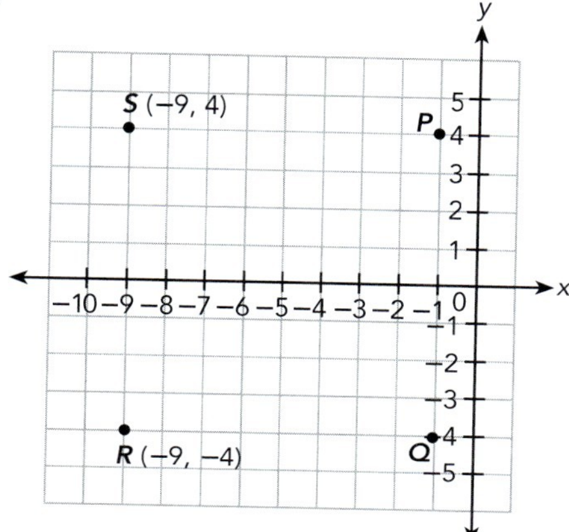

The coordinates of point R are (−9, −4). The coordinates of point S are (−9, 4).

9b.

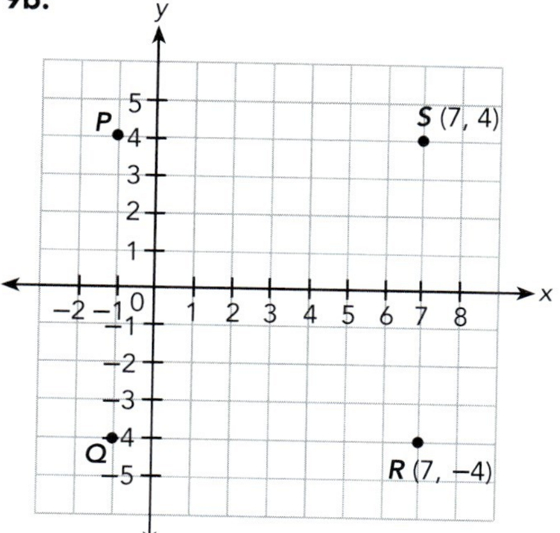

The coordinates of point R are (7, −4). The coordinates of point S are (7, 4).

11. A: 60 m; B: 60 m; C: 50 m; D: 50 m

13. Area: 15,400 m^2; Perimeter: 500 m

15.

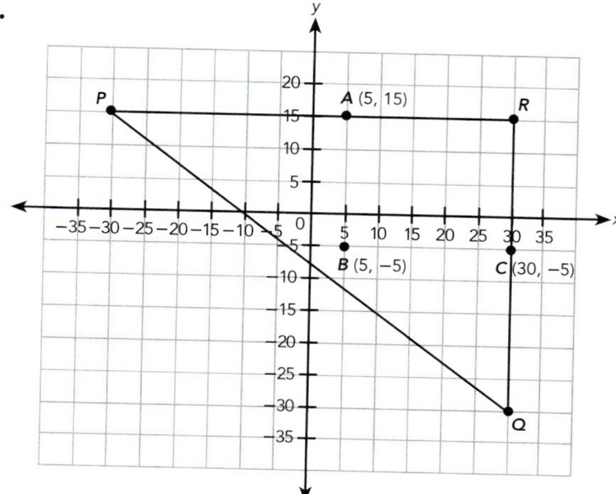

17. 500 m^2 **19.** 180 m **21.** 413

Lesson 9.3, Guided Practice (pp. 63–64)

1.

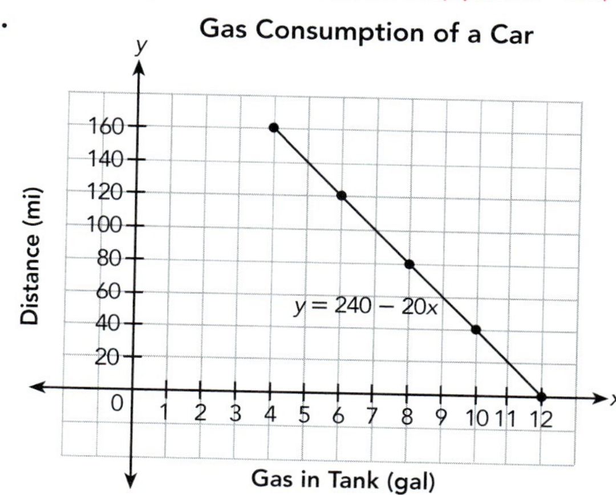

1a.

Amount of Gas (x gallons)	12	10	8	6	4
Distance Traveled (y miles)	0	40	80	120	160

1b. straight line or linear **1c.** 9 **1d.** 7 **1e.** 4; 20; 4; 20; 80; 80 **1f.** $x < 10$ **1g.** Dependent: y; Independent: x

2.

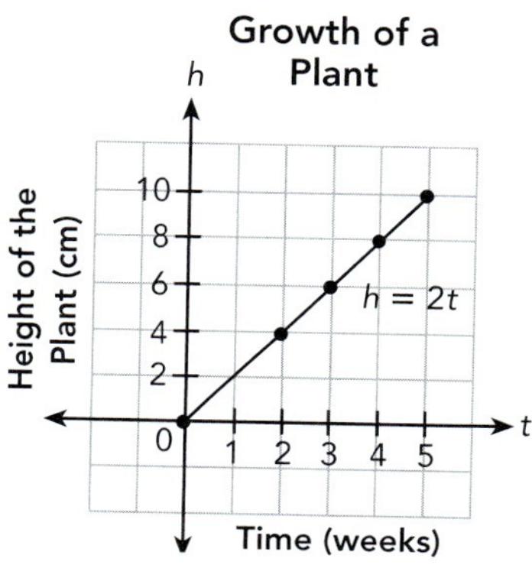

2a.

Time (*t* weeks)	0	1	2	3	4	5
Height (*h* centimeters)	0	2	4	6	8	10

2b. straight line graph or linear graph **2c.** 6 cm

2d. 10 cm **2e.** $h < 8$ **2f.** Dependent: *h*; Independent: *t*

Lesson 9.3, Practice (pp. 65–66)

1.

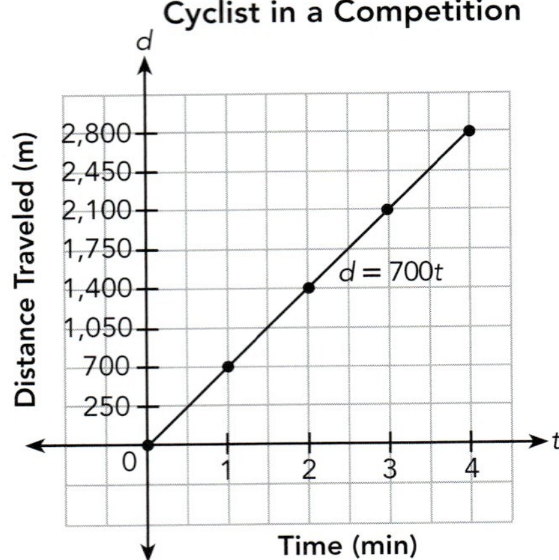

1a. straight line graph or linear graph **1b.** 1,750 m

1c. 2,450 m **1d.** 700 m/min **1e.** 4,900 m

1f. $t \geq 3$ **1g.** Dependent: *d*; independent: *t*

3.

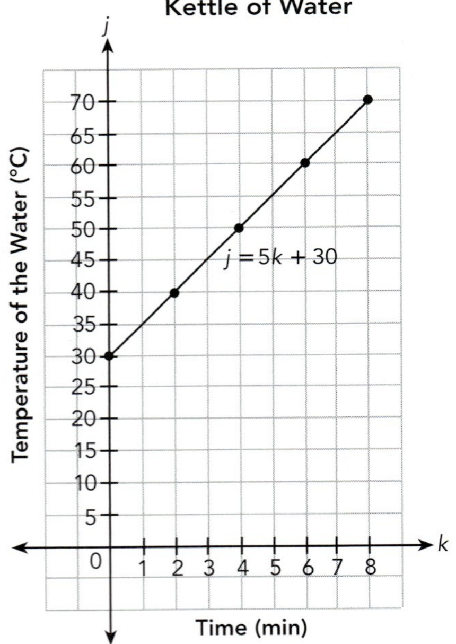

3a.

Time (*k* minutes)	0	2	4	6	8
Temperature (*j*°C)	30	40	50	60	70

3b. 55°C **3c.** 5°C/min **3d.** 80°C **3e.** $k \geq 14$

Lesson 9.3, Brain@Work (p. 66)

1.

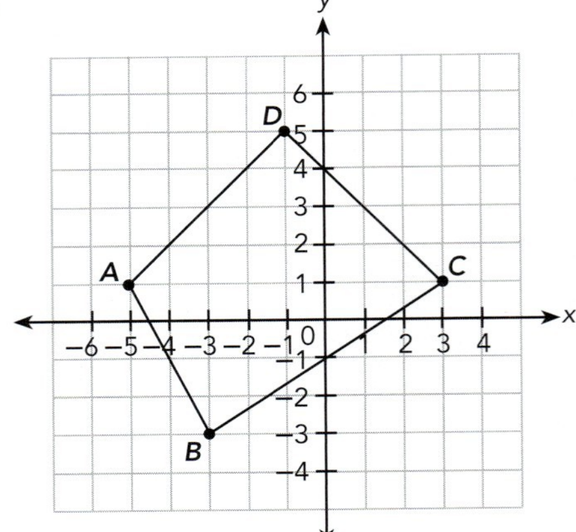

2.

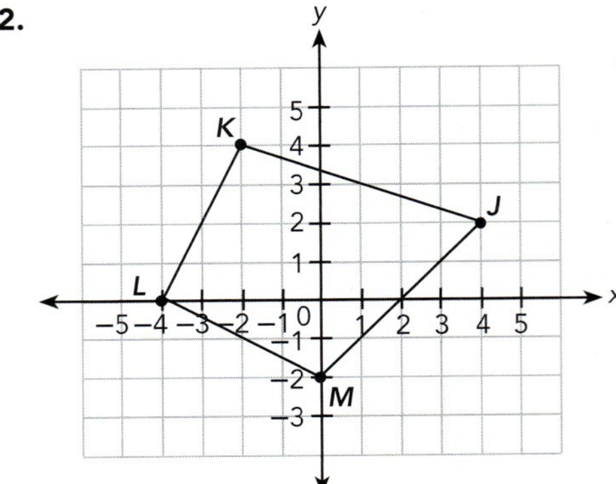

3.

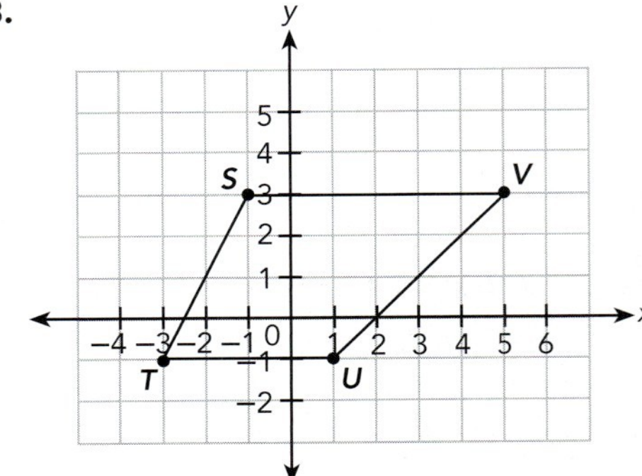

4. The figure formed is a quadrilateral.

5a.

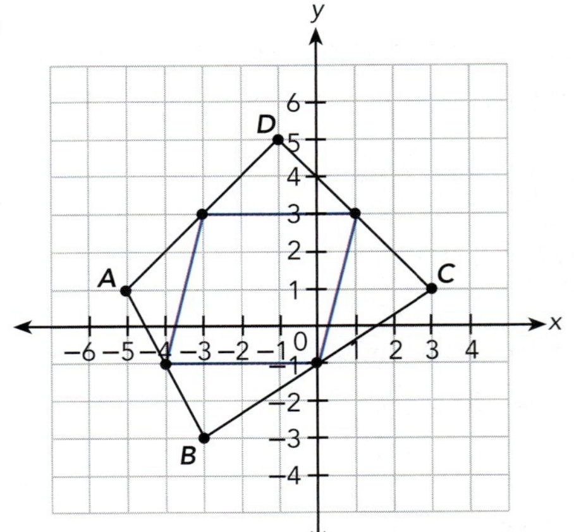

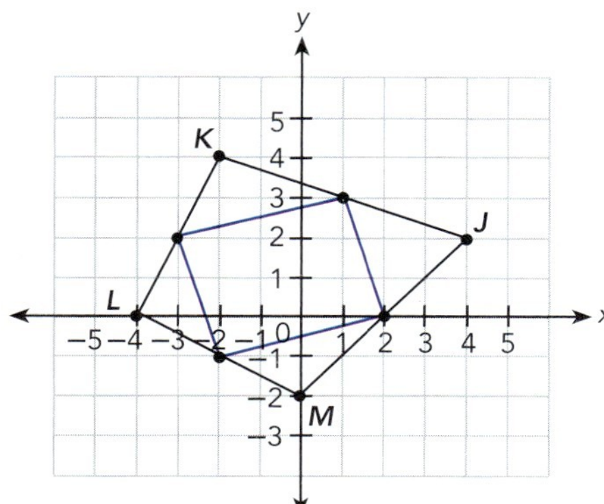

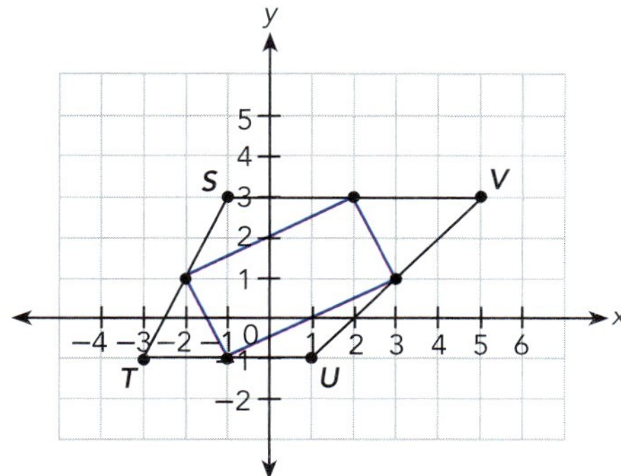

5b. Parallelograms. Both pairs of opposite sides are equal in length. Both pairs of opposite sides are parallel.

Chapter Review/Test (pp. 68–71)

1. *A* (−4, −3), *B* (0, −6), *C* (2, −4), *D* (6, 3), and *E* (−2, 3)

3.

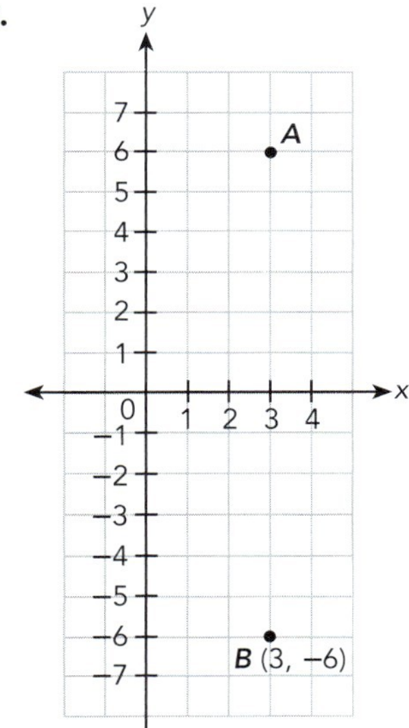

B (3, −6)

5.

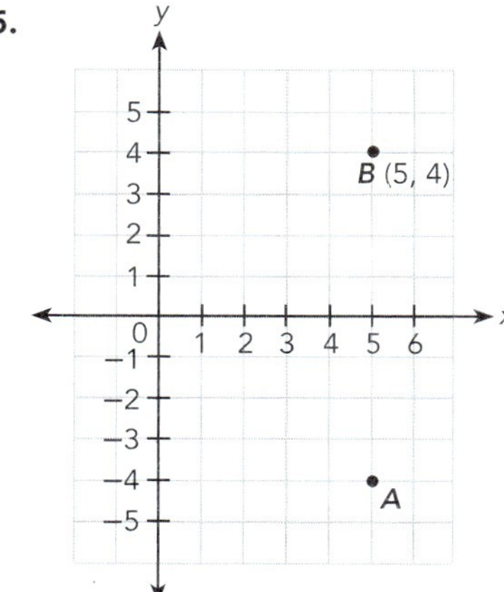

B (5, 4)

7.

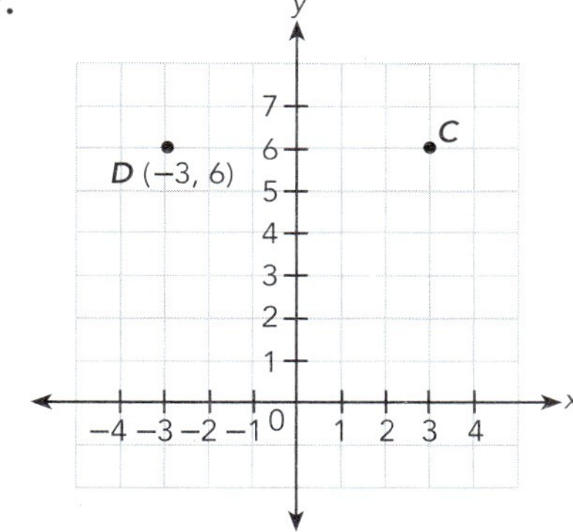

D (−3, 6)

9.

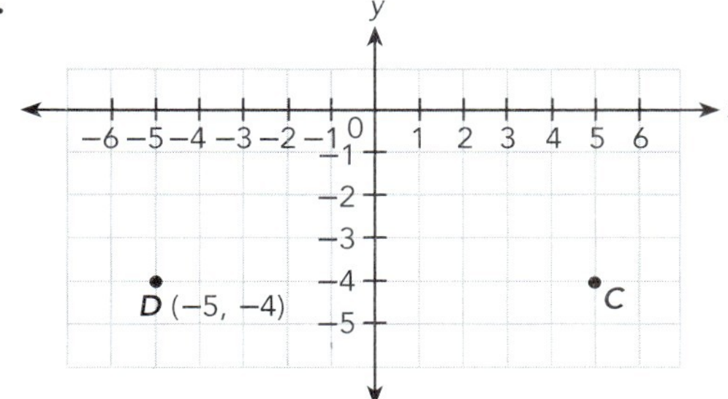

D (−5, −4)

11.

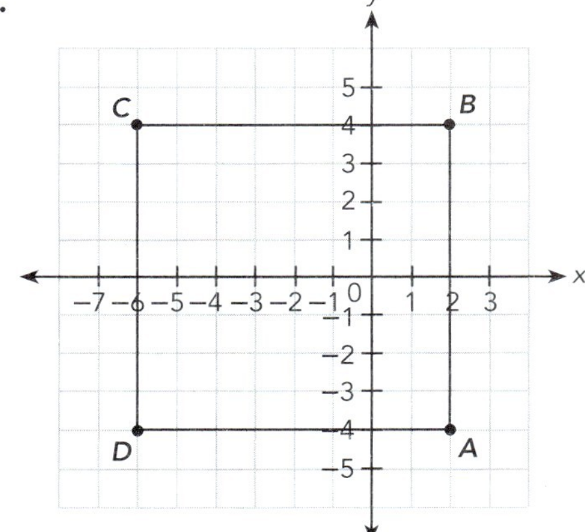

square

13.

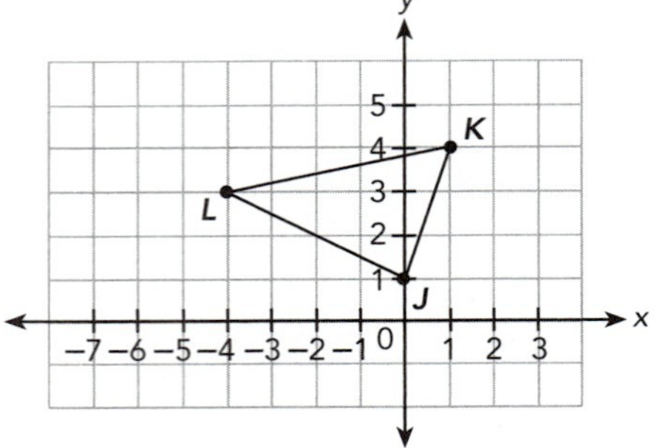

triangle

15.

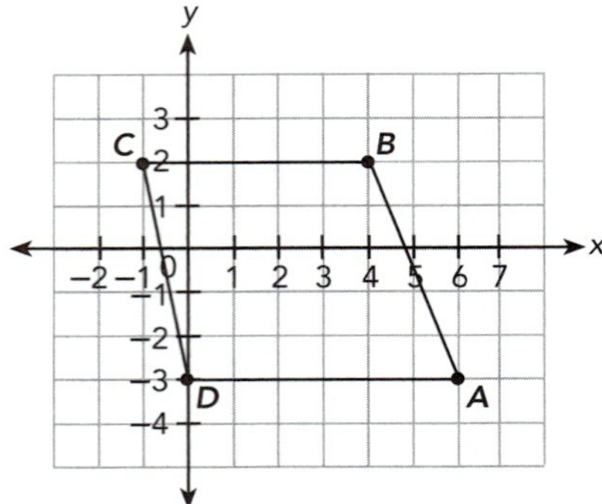

trapezoid

17.

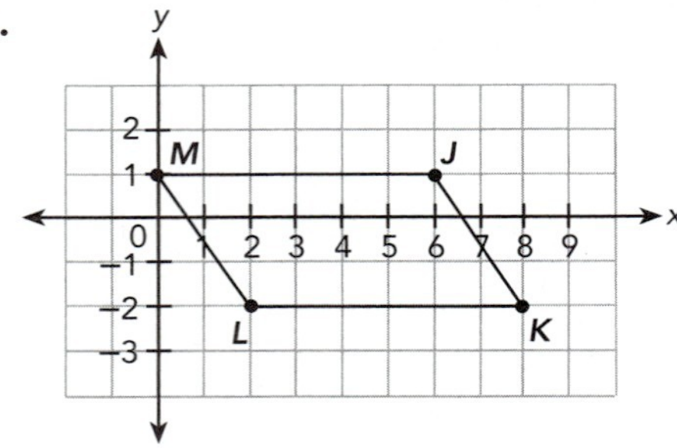

parallelogram

19.

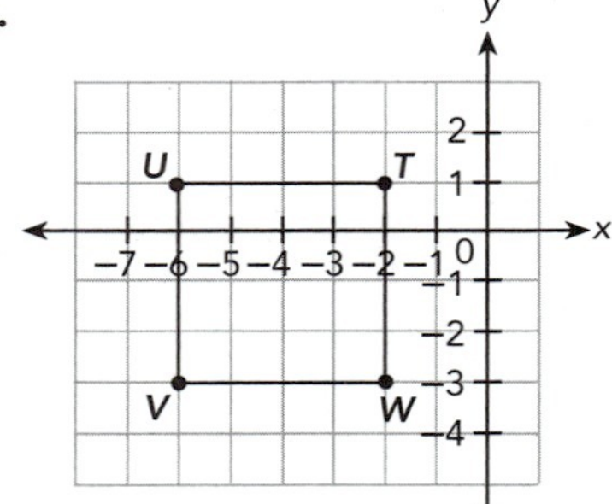

square

21.

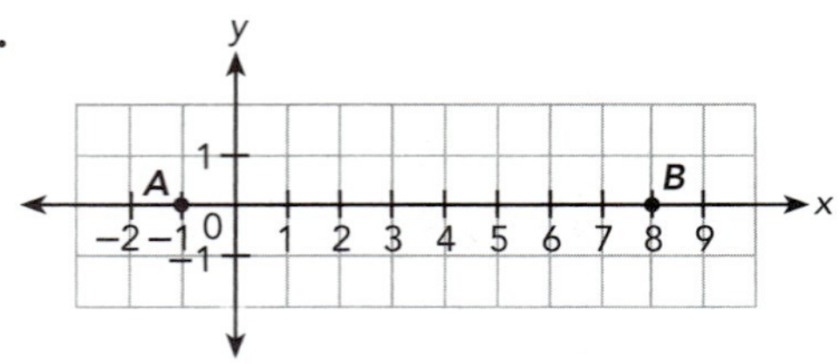

AB = 9 units

23.

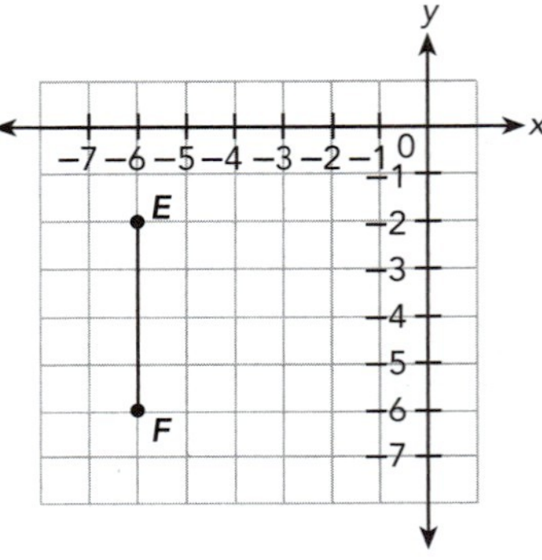

EF = 4 units

25.

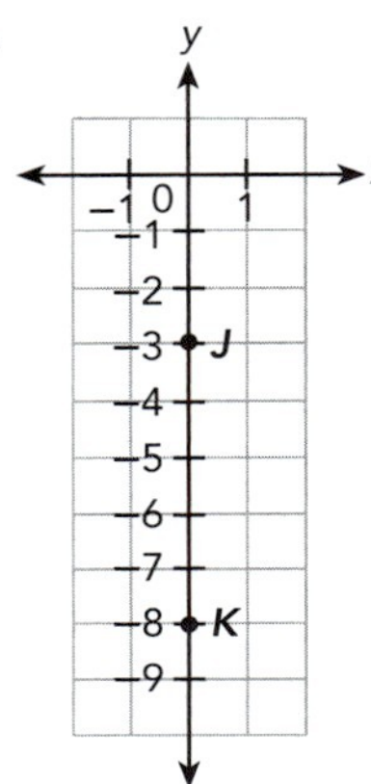

JK = 5 units

27. A (−40, 100), B (−40, 20), C (−60, 20), D (−60, −40), E (60, −40), F (60, 20), G (40, 20), and H (40, 100)

29. 160 ft

31.

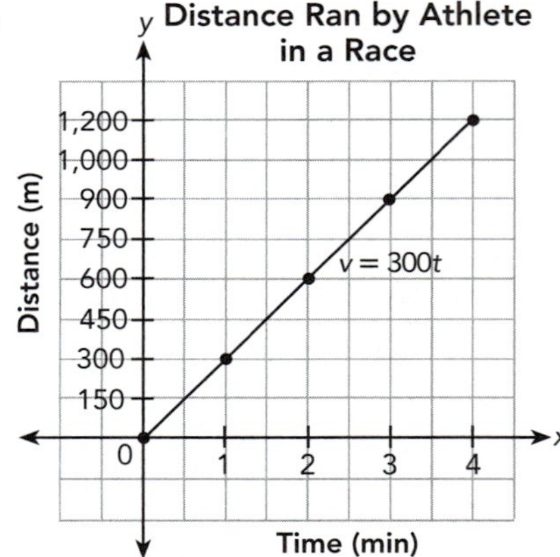

31a. straight line graph or linear graph **31b.** 1,050 m **31c.** 300 m/min **31d.** 2,400 m **31d.** Dependent: v; Independent: t

CHAPTER 10

Lesson 10.1, Guided Practice (pp. 79–82)

1. 5; 8; $\frac{1}{2}$; 5; 8; 20 **2.** 3; 4; $\frac{1}{2}$; 3; 4; 6 **3.** 2.1; 1.8; $\frac{1}{2}$; 2.1; 1.8; 1.89 **4.** 3.4; 2.7; $\frac{1}{2}$; 3.4; 2.7; 4.59 **5.** 35; $\frac{1}{2}$;

7; 35; 3.5; 35; 3.5; 3.5; 3.5; 10; 10 **6.** 36; $\frac{1}{2}$; 8; $\frac{1}{2}$; 8; 36; 4; 36; 4; 4; 4; 9; 9 **7.** 19.2; $\frac{1}{2}$; 9.6; $\frac{1}{2}$; 9.6; 19.2; 4.8; 19.2; 4.8; 4.8; 4.8; 4; 4

Lesson 10.1, Practice (pp. 83–87)

1. *b*: *BC*; *h*: *AB*

3.

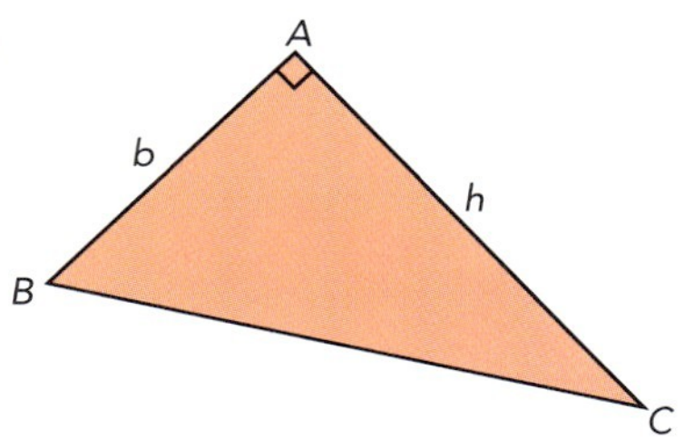

5.

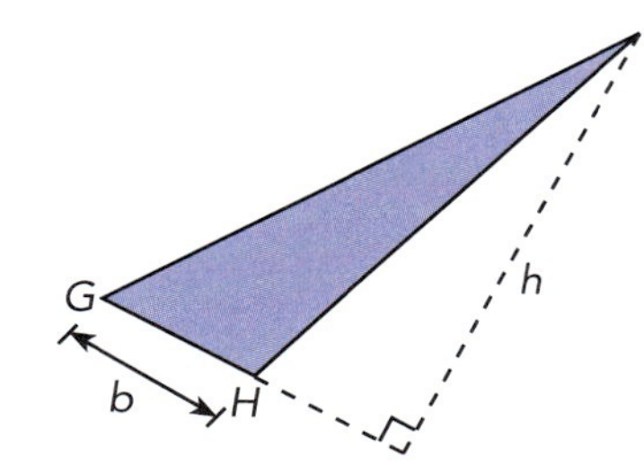

7. 50 cm^2 **9.** 9.7 in. **11.** 12.5 cm **13.** 12 cm **15.** 330 m^2 **17.** 264 cm^2 **19.** 54 cm^2

21.

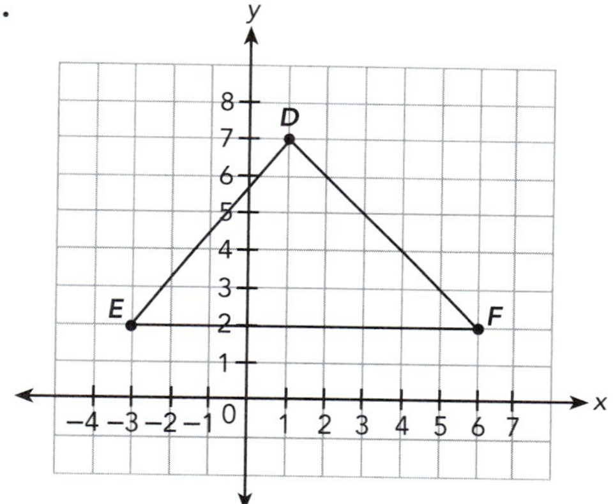

Area of triangle *DEF* = 22.5 units^2

23.

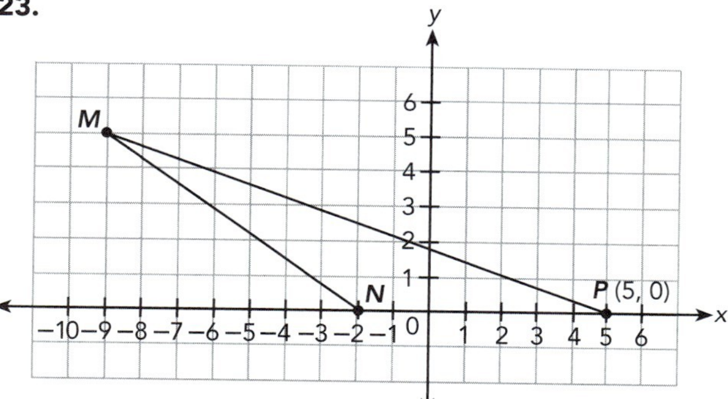

P (5, 0)

25.

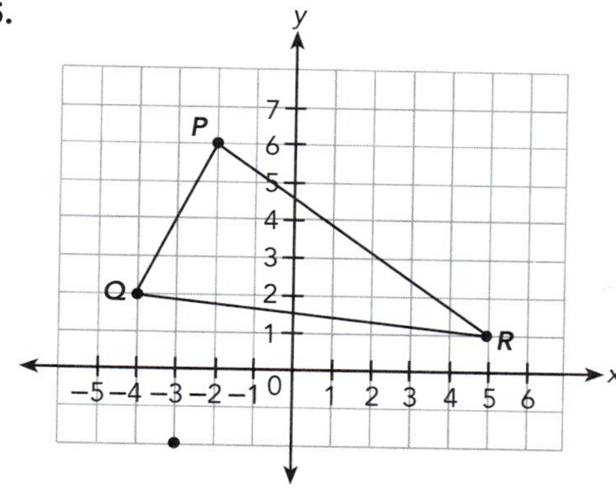

Area of triangle *PQR* = 19 units^2

27. 487.5 cm^2 **29.** 32 ft^2

Lesson 10.2, Guided Practice (pp. 89–95)

1. 4; 7; 4; 7; 28 **2.** 3; 7; 3; 7; 21 **3.** 4; 8; 4; 8; 32 **4.** 2; 8; 2; 8; 16 **5.** 21; 12; 21; 12; 252 **6.** 24; 14.5; 24, 14.5; 348 **7.** 3; 3; 7; 10; $\frac{1}{2}$; 3; 10; 15 **8.** 4; 1; 3; 4; $\frac{1}{2}$; 4; 4; 8 **9.** 7; 7; 4; 11; $\frac{1}{2}$; 7; 11; 38.5 **10.** 7; 3; 5; 8; $\frac{1}{2}$; 7; 8; 28 **11.** 39; 25; 13; 38; $\frac{1}{2}$; 39; 38; 741 **12.** 13; 10.6; 21; 31.6; $\frac{1}{2}$; 13; 31.6; 205.4 **13.** 22; 38; 60; 60; 30; 1,248; 30; 30; 1,248; 1,248; ÷; 30; 41.6; *DC*; 41.6; 22; 41.6; 457.6; 457.6

Lesson 10.2, Practice (pp. 96–98)

1.

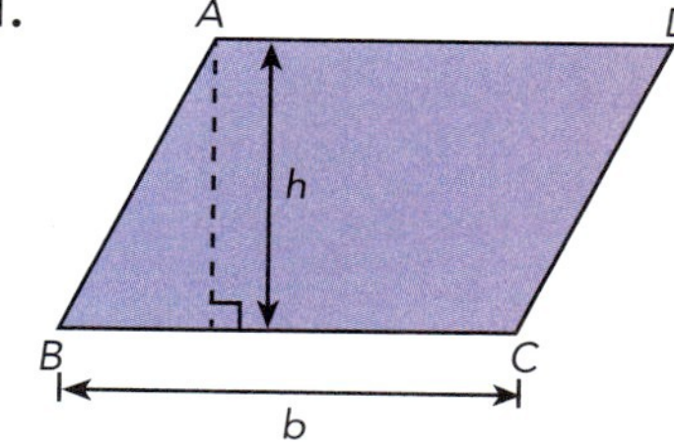

3.

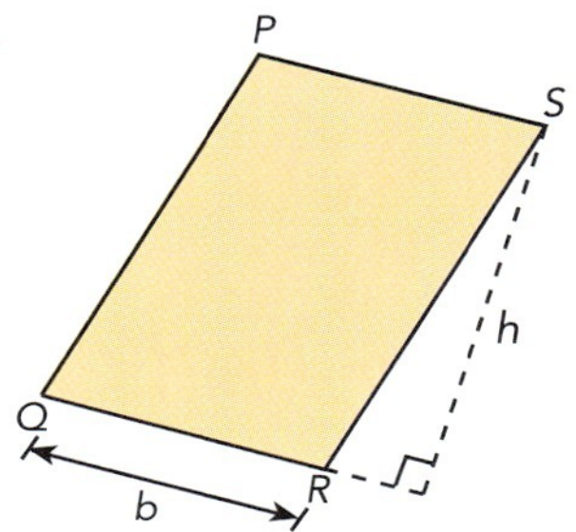

5. 420 in.^{2}

7.

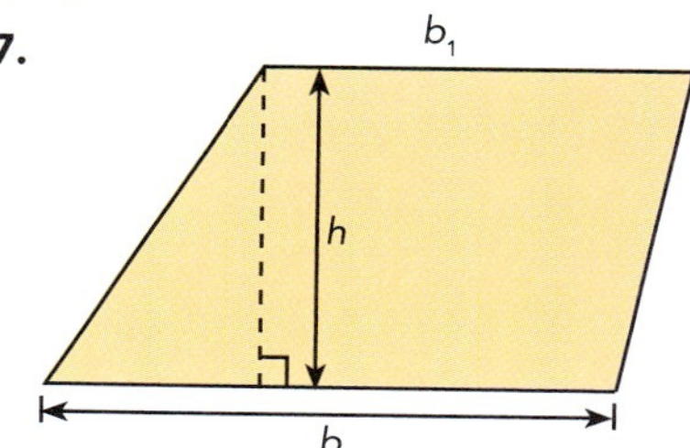

9.

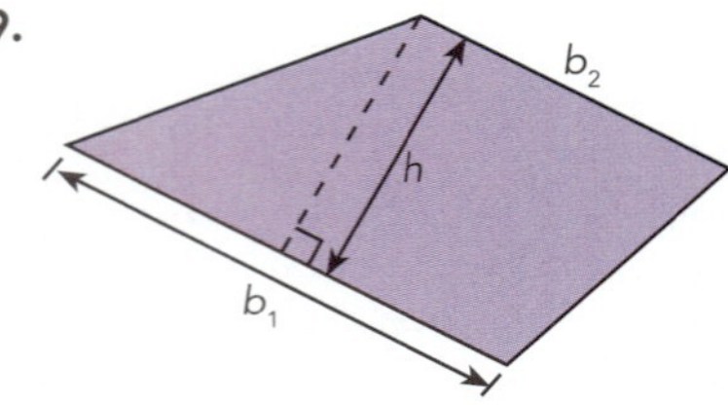

11. 110 cm^2 **13.** 9.1 in. **15.** 6.7 cm **17.** 21 cm

19.

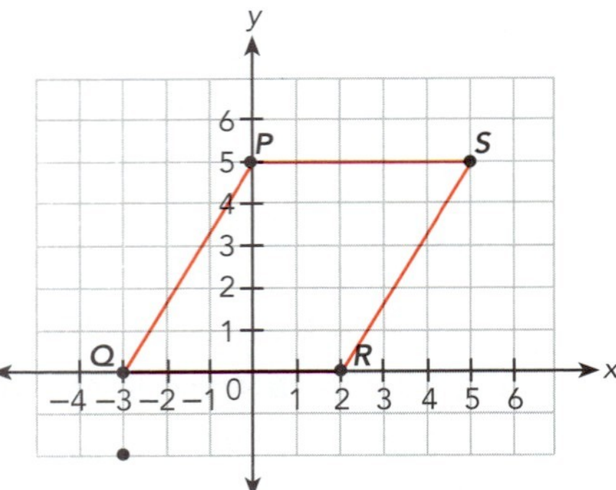

Area of parallelogram $PQRS$ = 25 units^2

21.

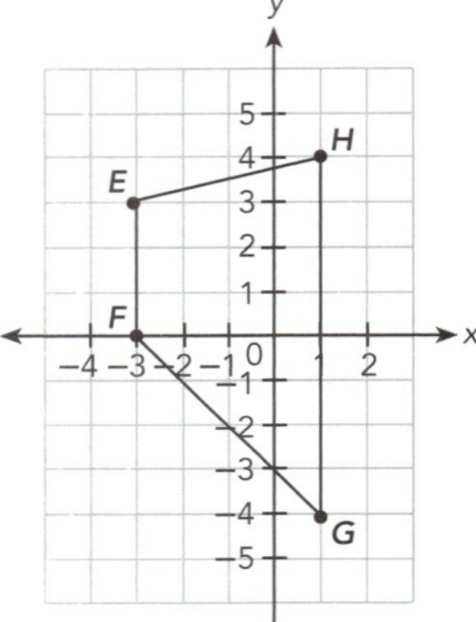

Area of trapezoid $EFGH$ = 22 units^2

23. 290 cm^2

Lesson 10.3, Guided Practice (pp. 100–101)

1. 5 **2.** 6 **3.** $\frac{1}{2}$; 6; 4.1; 12.3; 5; 5; 12.3; 61.5; 61.5

4. $\frac{1}{2}$; 28; 24.2; 338.8; 6; 6; 338.8; 2,032.8; 2,032.8

Lesson 10.3, Practice (pp. 102–103)

1. 8 **3.** 110 cm^2 **5.** 1 ft **7.** 76.8 cm^2 **9.** 199.5 cm^2

Lesson 10.4, Guided Practice (pp. 104–108)

1.

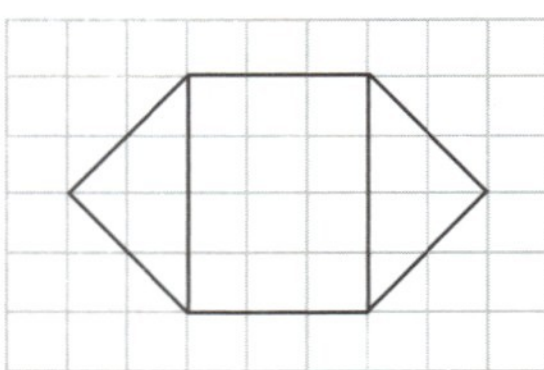

2. Answers vary. Sample: two trapezoids

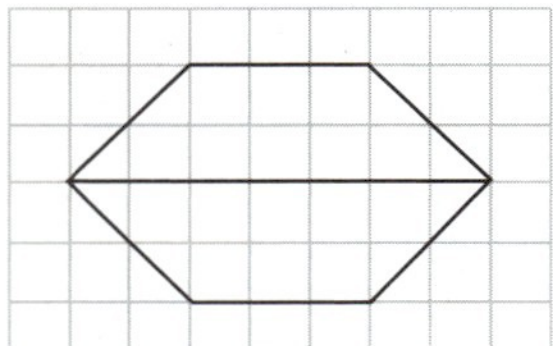

3a. 60; 12; 60; 6; 60; 6; 6; 6; 10; 10 **3b.** 10; 100; 100 **3c.** 100; 60; 160; 160 **4a.** 84; 5; 84; 5; 5; 5; 16.8; 12; 8; 16.8; 168; 168 **4b.** $\frac{1}{2}$; 16.8; 5; 8; 109.2; 109.2

Lesson 10.4, Practice (pp. 109–112)

1.

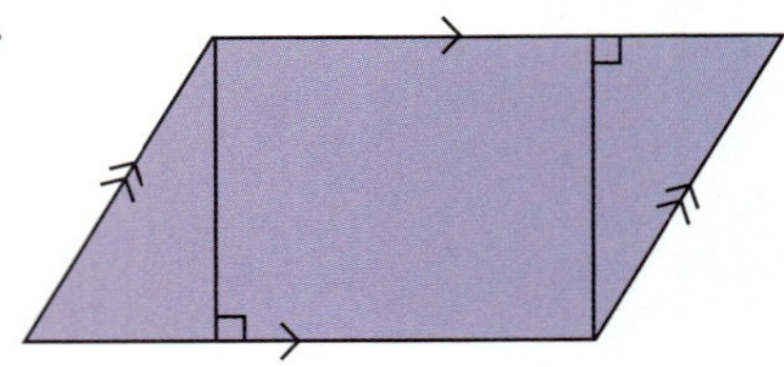

bh; sum of areas of the two right triangles and the rectangle

3.

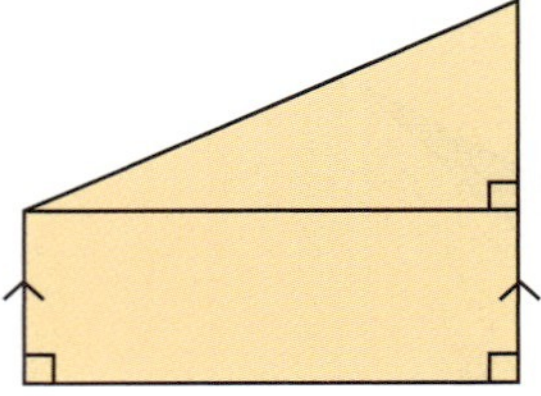

$\frac{1}{2}h(b_1 + b_2)$; sum of areas of the right triangle and the rectangle

5.

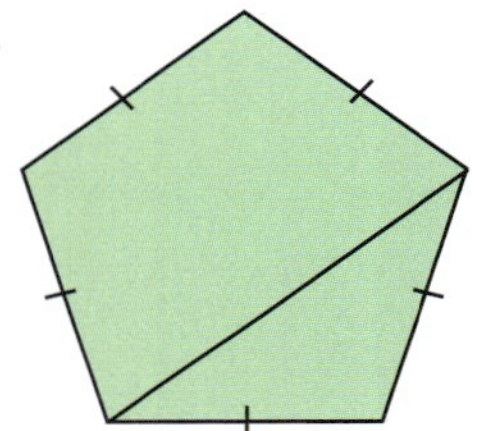

Answers vary. Sample: Sum of areas of the trapezoid and triangle

7. Answers vary. Sample: I would divide it into two triangles. I would measure the lengths of $\overline{BC}$, $\overline{AX}$, $\overline{AD}$, and $\overline{CY}$, so that I can find the areas of the two triangles.

9a.

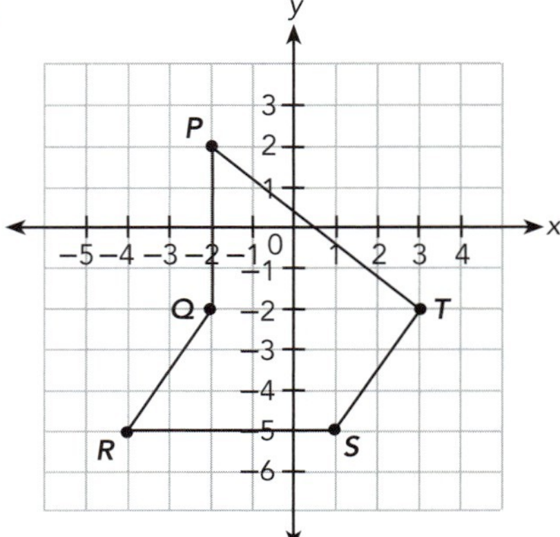

9b. Area of figure $PQRST$ = 25 units^2

9c.

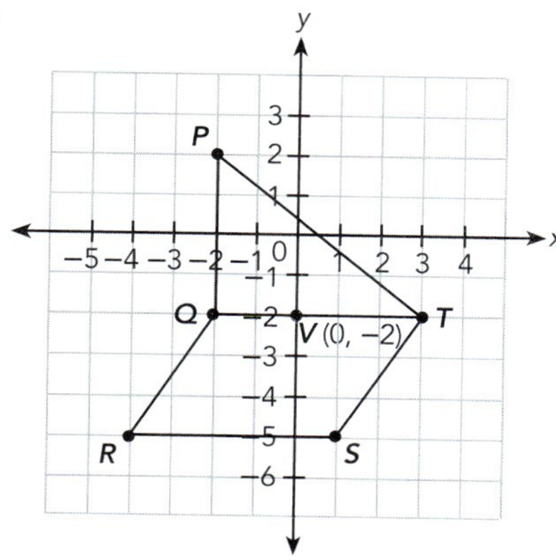

V (0, –2)

11. 71.5 in.^{2} **13.** 5.5 in.

Lesson 10.4, Brain@Work (p. 113)

1. 245 ft^2 **2a.** (12 − x) centimeters

2b. (36 + 6x) square centimeters **2c.** 12; triangle **3.** $\frac{3}{8}$

Chapter Review/Test (pp. 115–117)

1. b: BC; h: AD **3.** 112 cm^2 **5.** 1,071 cm^2

7. 262.5 cm^2 **9.** 24 cm **11.** 667.2 cm^2

CHAPTER 11

Lesson 11.1, Guided Practice (pp. 123–130)

1a. $\overline{AB}$ and $\overline{CD}$ **1b.** $\overline{ED}$. The line segment $\overline{ED}$ does not pass through the center, O. **2.** 2; ·; 6; 12; 12

3. 15; ÷; 2; 7

4.

Circle	Radius (cm)	Diameter (cm)	Circumference (cm)
A	7	14	44
B	21	42	132
C	10.5	21	66

5.

Circle	Radius (cm)	Diameter (cm)	Circumference (cm)
D	12.5	25	78.5
E	16	32	100.48
F	8.25	16.5	51.81

6. $\frac{22}{7}$; ·; 35; 110; $\frac{1}{2}$; ·; 110; 55; 55 **7.** 3.14; 10; 62.8; 62.8; 4; 15.7; 15.7

Lesson 11.1, Practice (pp. 132–135)

1. radii **3.** OZ; OY **5.** diameter or XY **7.** 66 in.

9. 17.6 ft **11.** $15\frac{2}{5}$ ft **13.** $17\frac{3}{5}$ cm **15.** 25.7 cm

17. 38.55 ft **19.** $37\frac{1}{2}$ cm **21.** 100 ft **23.** 25.12 cm

25. 195.32 cm **27.** 8,792 in. **29.** 150 cm **31.** 213.44 ft

Lesson 11.2, Guided Practice (pp. 138–140)

1. 3.14; 18; 3.14; 324; 1,017.36 **2.** 3.14; 15; 3.14; 225; 706.5; 706.5 **3.** 26; 2; 13; 3.14; 13; 3.14; 169; 530.66; 530.66 **4.** $\frac{1}{4}$; $\frac{1}{4}$; $\frac{1}{4}$; $\frac{22}{7}$; 14; $\frac{1}{4}$; $\frac{22}{7}$; 14; 14; 154; 154

5. 42; 21; $\frac{1}{4}$; $\frac{1}{4}$; $\frac{1}{4}$; $\frac{22}{7}$; 21; $\frac{1}{4}$; $\frac{22}{7}$; 21; 21; $346\frac{1}{2}$; $346\frac{1}{2}$

Lesson 11.2, Practice (pp. 141–142)

1. 314 cm^2 **3.** 308 ft^2 **5.** 113.0 in.^{2} **7.** $38\frac{1}{2}$ cm^2

9. 113.04 ft^2 **11.** 21.5 cm^2

Lesson 11.3, Guided Practice (pp. 145–153)

1a. 2; 3.14; 1,736; 10,902.08; 10,900 **1b.** 11,000

2. $\frac{1}{2}$; 2; 3.14; 5.2; 3.14; 5.2; 16.328; 2; $\frac{1}{2}$; 3.14; 5.2; 3.14; 5.2; 16.328; 16.328; 16.328; 32.656; 33; 33 **3.** $\frac{1}{2}$; 3.14; 12; 3.14; 12; 37.68; 3.14; 12; 18.84; 37.68; 18.84; 12; 12; 80.52; 80.52 **4.** $\frac{22}{7}$; 35; $\frac{22}{7}$; 35; 35; 962.5; $\frac{22}{7}$; 35; $\frac{22}{7}$; 35; 35; 1,925; 962.5; 1,925; 2,887.5; 2,887.5 **5.** $\frac{22}{7}$; 42; $\frac{22}{7}$; 42; 42; 1,386; 42; 2; 21; 2; $\frac{1}{2}$; $\frac{22}{7}$; 21; $\frac{22}{7}$; 21; 21; 1,386; 1,386; 1,386; 2,772; 2,772 **6.** $\frac{22}{7}$; 60; $188\frac{4}{7}$; $188\frac{4}{7}$; 35; 6,600; 66; 66 **7a.** $\frac{22}{7}$; 35; 110; 110; −; 110; 110; 110; ÷; 2; 55; 55 **7b.** 220; 220; 220; ÷; 125; 1.76 **7c.** 35; 17.5; $\frac{22}{7}$; 17.5; $\frac{22}{7}$; 17.5; 17.5; $962\frac{1}{2}$; 55; 35; 1,925; 1,925; $962\frac{1}{2}$; $2,887\frac{1}{2}$; $2,887\frac{1}{2}$; 4; 721.875; 12.03125; 12; 12

Lesson 11.3, Practice (pp. 154–158)

1. Area: 200.96 m^2; Circumference: 50.24 m **3a.** 77 ft^2

3b. 36 ft **5.** 462 cm^2 **7a.** 560 m **7b.** 11,900 m^2

9. 886.4 ft^2 **11.** 990 in. **13.** 308 mm^2 **15a.** 464 cm

15b. 2,016 cm^2

Lesson 11.3, Brain@Work (pp. 158–159)

1. 38.6 cm **2.** 112 in.^{2} **3.** 21 s **4.** 14

Chapter Review/Test (pp. 161–163)

1. Circumference: 308 cm; Area: 7,546 cm^2 **3.** 36 ft **5.** 17.85 m **7.** Circumference: 31.4 in.; Area: 78.5 $in.^2$ **9.** 130 cm **11a.** 121 cm **11b.** 24.2 cm/s **11c.** 2,500 s **13.** 353.3 ft^2

Cumulative Review Chapters 8–11 (pp. 164–167)

1.

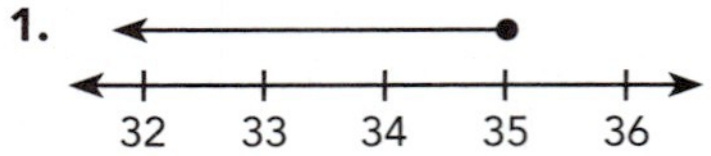

3.

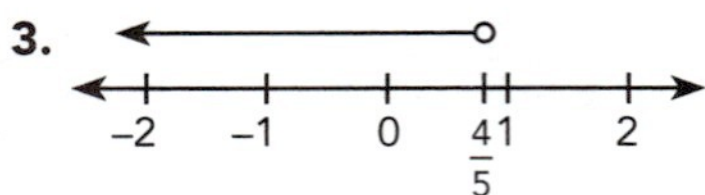

5a.

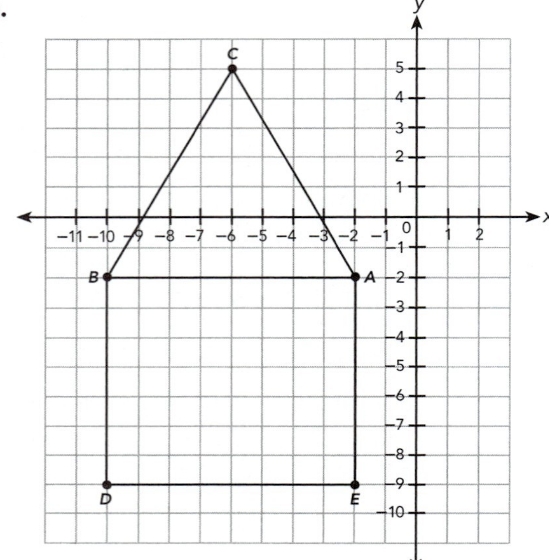

5b. (−6, 5) **5c.** *D* (−10, −9); *E* (−2, −9) **7.** 80 ft^2 **9.** 50.24 cm^2 **11.** 7 mm **13.** $\frac{2}{7}b$ **15.** 40.82 cm **17.** 44 ft^2 **19.** 113.64 cm^2 **21a.** *P* (0, 0) **21b.** Area: 256 m^2; Perimeter: 64 m **21c.** 192 m^2 **23.** 40.035 m^2

CHAPTER 12

Lesson 12.1, Guided Practice (pp. 176–178)

1. f; a and e; c and d **2.** rectangular prism **3.** cube **4.** triangular prism **5.** a and c; b

Lesson 12.1, Practice 12.1 (pp. 179–180)

1. pyramid; Base: *BCDE*; Lateral face: Answers vary. Sample: *ABC*; *ABE*; *ACD*; *AED* **3.** cube; Base: Answers vary. Sample: *PQRS*; *TUVW*; Lateral face: Answers vary. Sample: *PQUT*; *RSWV* **5.** square pyramid **7.** triangular prism **9.** No **11.** No **13.** No

15.

17. Yes

19.

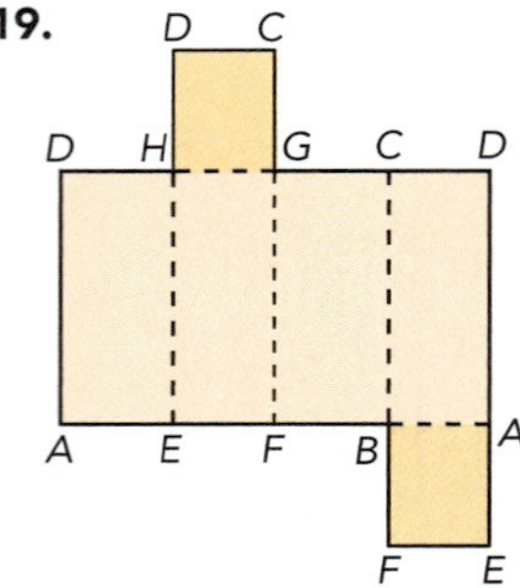

Lesson 12.2, Guided Practice (pp. 183–186)

1. 6; 6; 36; 36; 6; 216 **2.** 7; 5; 7; 5; 10; 24; 10; 240; 7; 5; 70; 240; 70; 310 **3.** 5; 13; 12; 9; 30; 9; 270; 12; 5; 60; 270; 60; 330 **4.** 6; 5.2; 15.6; 6; 10; 90; 15.6; 90; 105.6

Lesson 12.2, Practice 12.2 (pp. 187–188)

1. 216 cm^2 **3.** 504 m^2 **5.** 660 cm^2 **7.** 559 cm^2 **9.** 336 ft^2 **11a.** $m + 1$ **11b.** $2m$ **11c.** $m + 1$

Lesson 12.3, Guided Practice (pp. 190–194)

1. $5\frac{1}{4}$; 6; 12; 378 **2.** 8; 7.2; 3; 172.8 **3.** ℓwh; 4; 3; $8\frac{1}{3}$; 100 **4.** No. Rectangles will have different dimensions with other cuts. **5.** Yes. **6.** No. Rectangles will have different dimensions with other cuts. **7.** 6; 5.5; 33; 33; 9; 297; 297 **8.** $3\frac{1}{3}$; 10; $\frac{50}{3}$; $\frac{50}{3}$; 14; $233\frac{1}{3}$; $233\frac{1}{3}$ **9.** 2; 4; 10; 2; 14; 14; 12; 14; 168; 168

Lesson 12.3, Practice 12.3 (pp. 196–199)

1. 729 $in.^3$ **3.** 1,100 ft^3 **5.** 72 $in.^3$ **7.** 120.6 cm^3 **9.** No. Circles will have different diameters with other slices.

11.

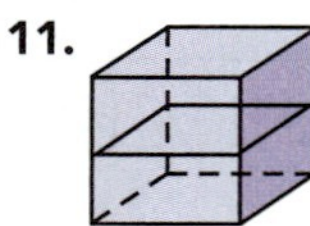

13.

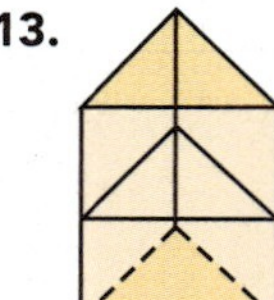

15. 5 in. **17.** 384 ft^3 **19a.** *ABDC* **19b.** *AJM* **19c.** *EJM* **19d.** *AHDF*

Lesson 12.4, Guided Practice (pp. 200–206)

1. 14; $\frac{42}{4}$; 25; 12; $\frac{42}{4}$; 3,150; 3,150 **2a.** 8; 4; 32; 32; 24; 768; 768 **2b.** 8; 5; 8; 5; 24; 2; 32; 26; 24; 64; 624; 64; 688; 688 **3a.** 960; 15; 960; 15; 15; 15; 64; $\sqrt{64}$; 8; 8 **3b.** 8; 8; 8; 8; 15; 2; 64; 32; 15; 128; 480; 128; 608; 608 **4a.** 3; 7; 3; 9; 7; 15; 63; 78; 855; 78; 855; 78; 78; 78; 10.96; 10.96 **4b.** 7; 9; 3; 3; 5; 9; 10.96; 2; 78; 36; 10.96; 156; 394.56; 156; 550.56; 550.56

Lesson 12.4, Practice (pp. 207–208)

1. 472.5 cm^3 **3a.** 784 ft^3 **3b.** 763.6 ft^2 **5a.** 86,400 ft^3 **5b.** 10,440 ft^2 **7.** 25 cm

Lesson 12.4, Brain@Work (p. 208)

1. 800 in.^{3}

2. Make a list and solve the problem using guess and check.

Length of edge of cube (ft)	Surface area (ft^2)	Volume (ft^3)
4	96	64
5	150	125
6	216	216

The length of each edge of the cube is 6 feet.

Chapter Review/Test (pp. 210–213)

1. c **3.** b **5.** d **7.** 224 m^2 **9.** 45 ft^3 **11.** 10,500 cm^3 **13a.** 9 ft **13b.** 350 ft^2 **15.** 6 in. **17.** Surface area: 268 cm^2; Volume: 136 cm^3

CHAPTER 13

Lesson 13.1, Guided Practice (pp. 218–219)

1. 3; 9; 7; 5; 2; 1 **2.** 1 **3.** 5 **4.** 2 **5.** 6 **6.** 27

Lesson 13.1, Practice (pp. 220–221)

1.

Weekly Income	Tally	Frequency
Below \$500	𝍸 //	7
\$500–\$1,000	𝍸 𝍸 𝍸 ////	19
Over \$1,000	////	4

3. 1, 1, 1, 1, 2, 2, 2, 3, 4, 4, 5, 5, 5, 5, 6, 6, 6, 6, 6, 7, 7, 8, 8, 8, 9, 9, 10, 10;

Number of Hours	Tally	Frequency
0–3	𝍸 ///	8
4–7	𝍸 𝍸 ///	13
8–10	𝍸 //	7

20

Lesson 13.2, Guided Practice (pp. 223–225)

1.

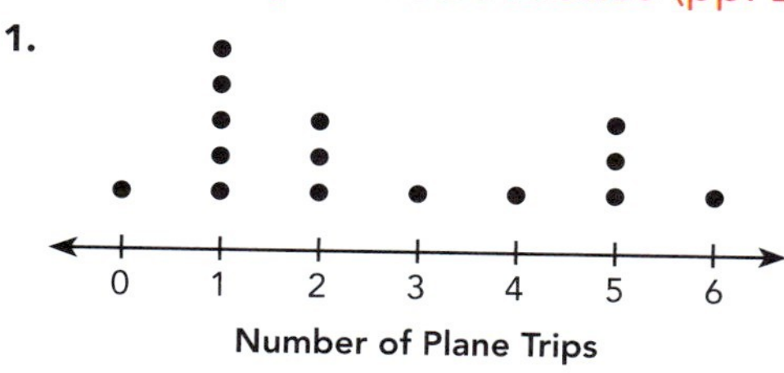

2.

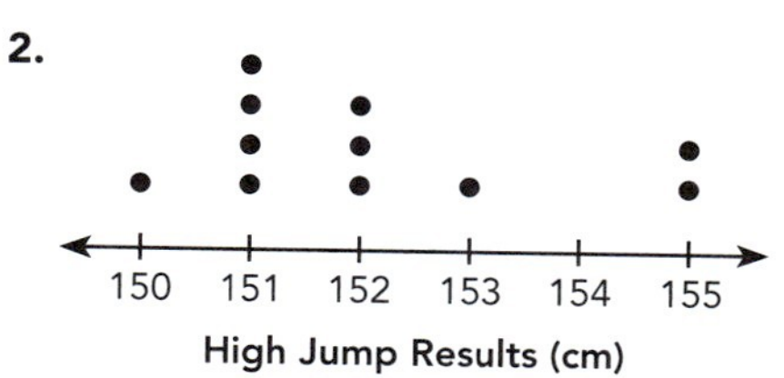

3. The dot plot has a "tail" on the left. The shape is left-skewed. The data values are from 1 to 5. Range: 5 − 1 = 4. The students saved about \$4 per week, and all of them saved \$1 to \$5 per week.

4. The dot plot has a "tail" on the right. The shape is right-skewed. The data values are from 0 to 5. Range: 5 − 0 = 5. Most of the players scored 1 point in the game, and all of them scored 0 to 5 points in the game.

Lesson 13.2, Practice (pp. 226–227)

1.

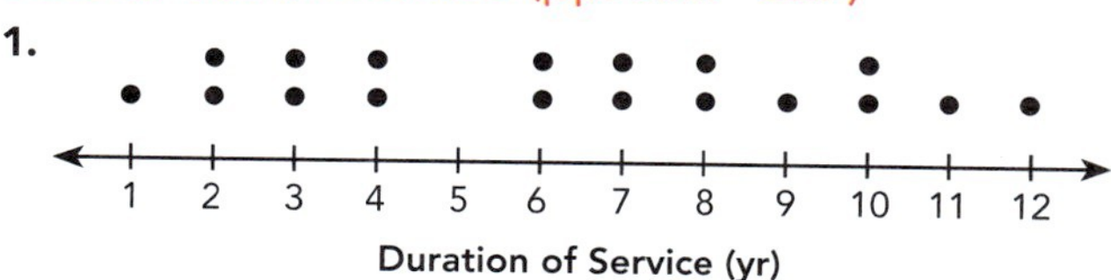

3. 20 **5.** 25% **7.** Answers vary. Sample: There are many good movies that come out regularly, so few movies stay at number 1 in the box office for a long time.

Lesson 13.3, Guided Practice (pp. 229–233)

1.

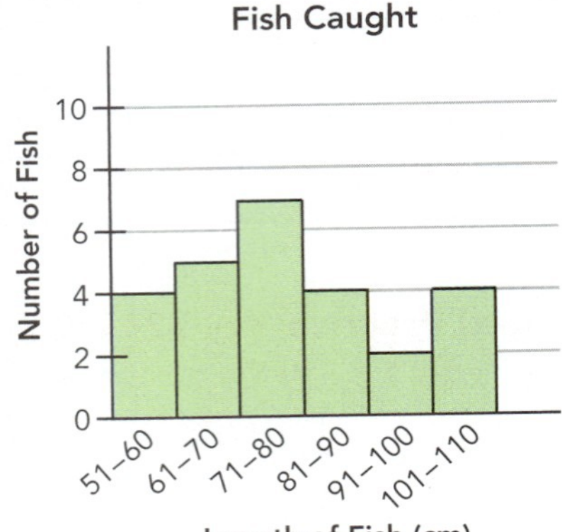

2.

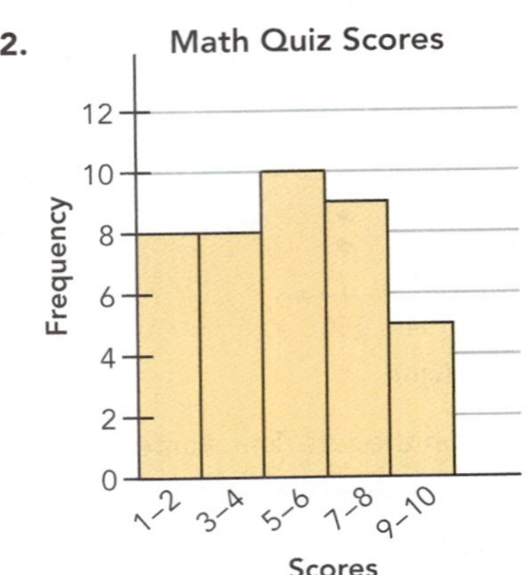

3a.

Cholesterol Level (mg/dL)	120–159	160–199	200–239	240–279	280–329
Frequency	2	6	21	9	2

For this set of data, it is suitable to use 5 intervals with a width of 40 since a cholesterol level less than 200 is desirable, a cholesterol level between 200 and 240 is borderline while a cholesterol level greater than 240 is considered high. The outlier is 125.

3b.

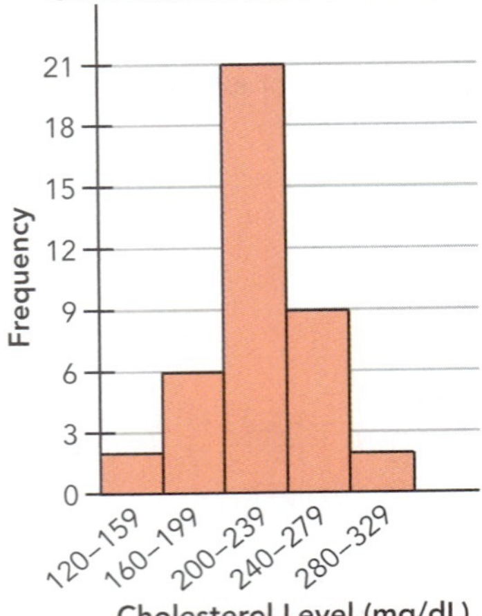

4a.

Speed (km/h)	50–54	55–59	60–64	65–69	70–74	75–79	80–84	85–89
Frequency	2	3	11	10	8	3	2	1

For this set of data, it is suitable to use 8 intervals with a width of 5 kilometers per hour since the tolerance for speeding is about 10% or 5 kilometers per hour above the speed limit. The outlier is 88.

4b.

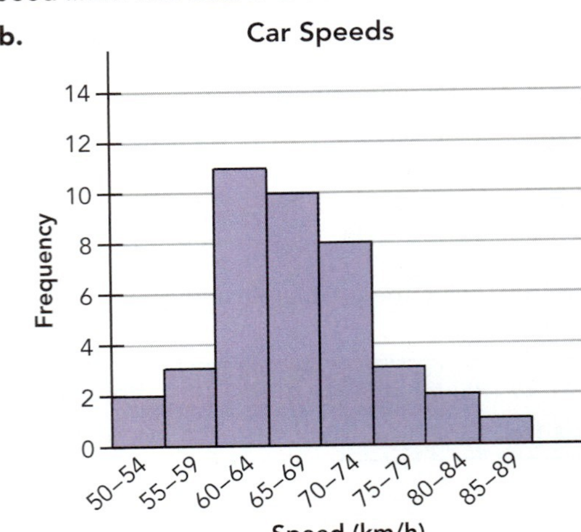

5. Most of the states sent 1 to 10 representatives to the U.S. Congress in 2011. The histogram is right-skewed. There is 1 state that sent 51 to 60 representatives, which is an outlier in the data. **6.** Most of the data values are from 31°F to 39°F. The data set has a "tail" to the left, and the distribution is left-skewed. The temperatures are from 22°F to 45°F, so the range is 23°F.

Lesson 13.3, Practice (pp. 234–237)

1.

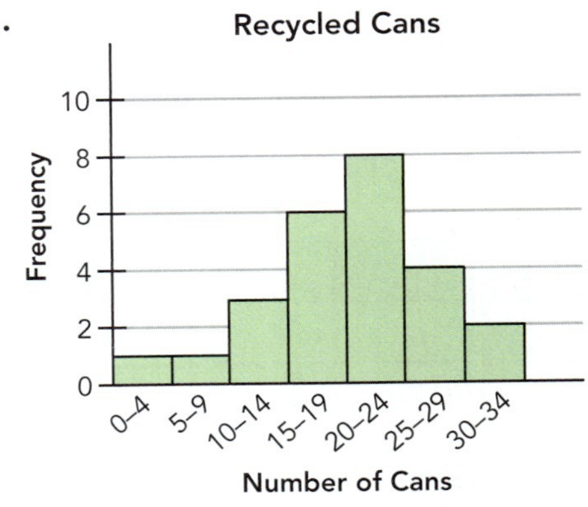

3.

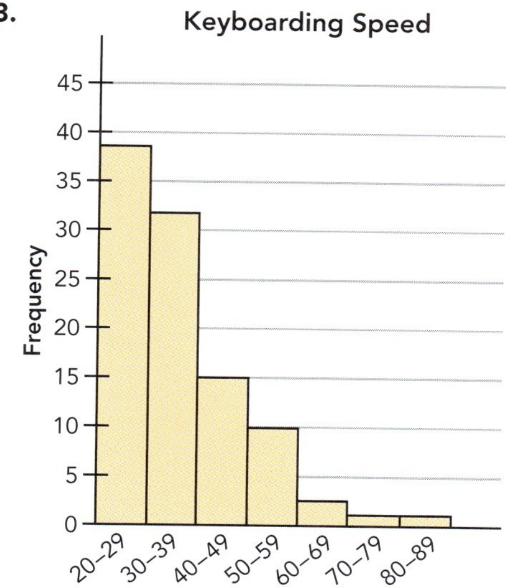

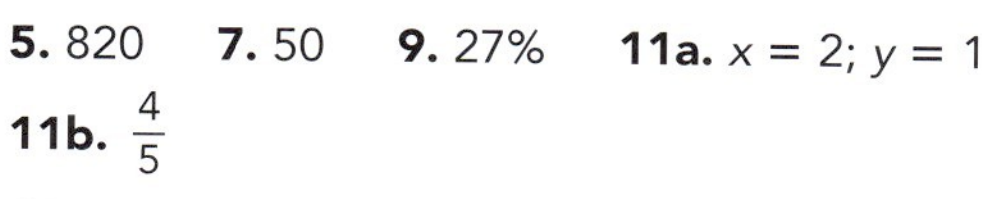

5. 820 **7.** 50 **9.** 27% **11a.** $x = 2$; $y = 1$

11b. $\frac{4}{5}$

11c.

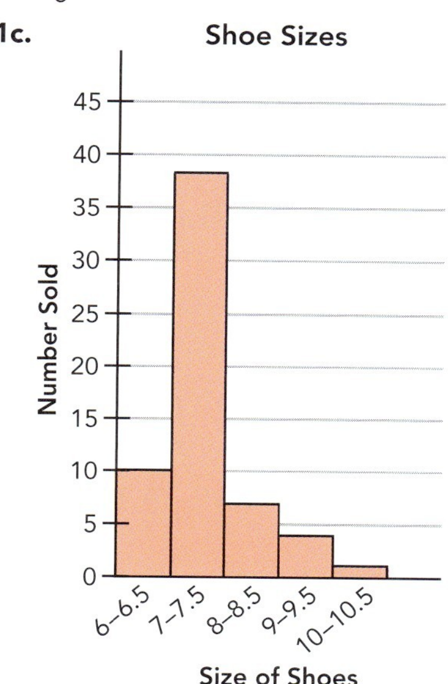

The department store sold the greatest number of shoes with sizes 7 or 7.5. The data set has a "tail" to the right, and so distribution is right-skewed.

11d.

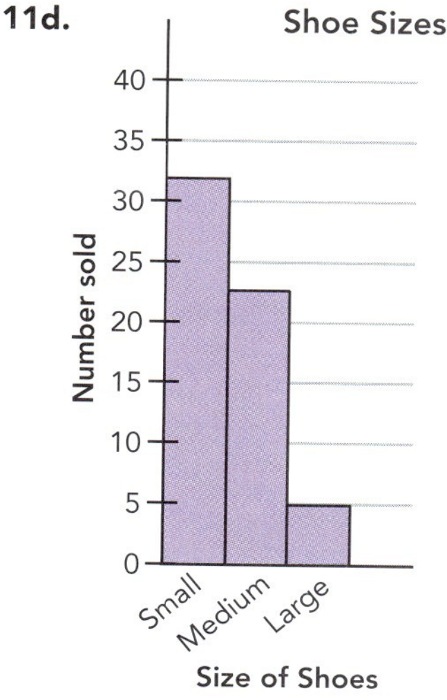

11e. The first histogram, which uses more intervals, reveals more about the distribution of data. It shows the two sizes of shoes that sold the most. This histogram will be more useful when you want to find out which two shoe sizes sold best.The second histogram, which uses fewer intervals with greater width, categorizes sizes into small, medium or large. This histogram will be more useful when you want general information on which shoe sizes to stock.

Lesson 13.3, Brain@Work (p. 237)

1.

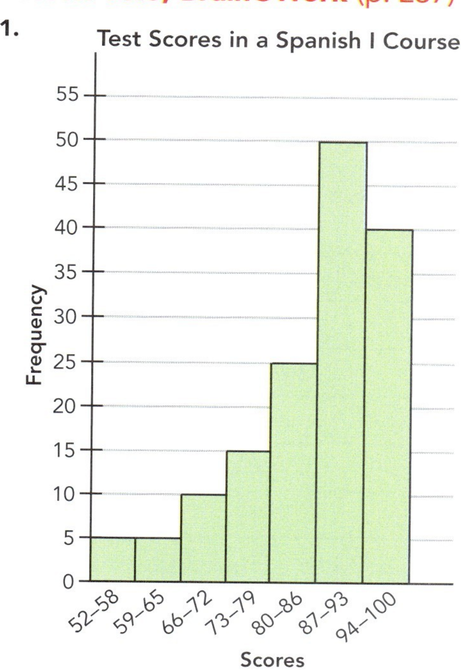

2.

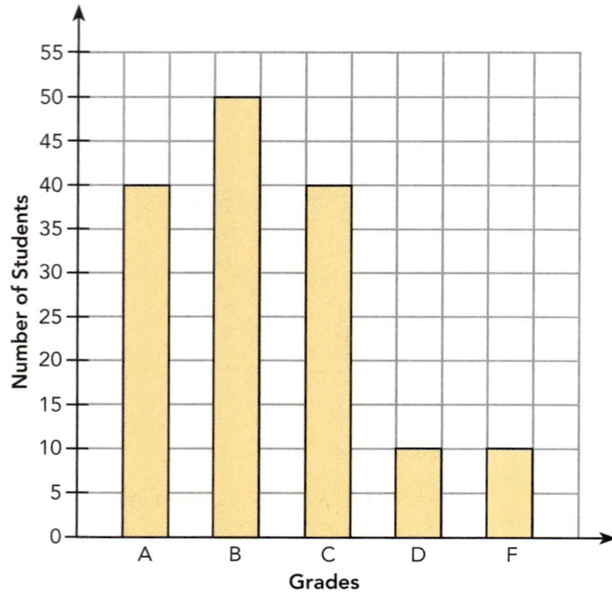

3a. If 5 students increased their scores from 79 to 89, then there would be 55 students with scores from 87 to 93, and 10 students with scores from 73 to 79. For the histogram, the height of the bar that represents the frequency for 87 − 93 will increase by 5, while the height of the bar that represents the frequency for 73 − 79 will decrease by 5. **3b.** For the bar graph, the height of the bar that represents the number of students who got a score of B will increase by 5, while the height of the bar that represents the number of students who got a score of C will decrease by 5.

Chapter Review/Test (pp. 239–241)

1.

Number of Bedrooms	Tally	Frequency
1	////	4
2	~~////~~ //	7
3	~~////~~ ////	9
4	~~////~~ //	7
5	///	3

3. 25

5.

Length of Trout (in.)	8–9	10–11	12–13	14–15	16–17	18–19
Number of Trout	3	8	24	9	5	1

The range is 18 − 8 = 10. Choosing an interval of 2 gives six intervals for the data set. A larger interval will give too few intervals, and you will not be able to see the distribution accurately.

7.

Distance of Long Drive (yd)	240–244	245–249	250–254	255–259	260–264	265–269	270–274	275–279
Frequency	1	4	6	4	4	4	6	1

The range is 278 − 244 = 34. Choosing an interval of 5 gives eight intervals for the data set. A larger interval will give too few intervals, and you will not be able to see the distribution accurately.

9. 240

11. The most frequent value is from 8:00 A.M. to 8:29 A.M. Most of the data values are to the right of 8:00 A.M. to 8:29 A.M., and the distribution is right-skewed. The second most frequent value is from 8:30 A.M. to 8:59 A.M. The third most frequent value is from 7:39 A.M. to 7:59 A.M. These three values are significantly higher than the rest of the time, because most companies start work from 8:00 A.M. to 9:00 A.M.

13.

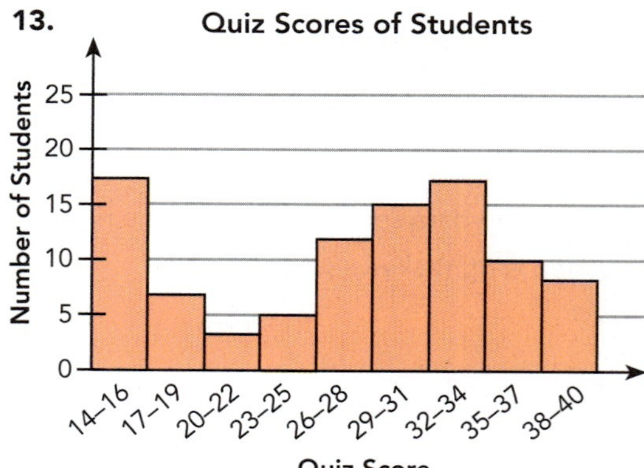

There are two peaks in the distribution of the data — one is for the interval 14–16, and the other is for the interval 32–34. Most of the data values are to the left of the interval 32–34, and the distribution is skewed to the left. The data values are from 14 to 40. Range: 40 − 14 = 26

CHAPTER 14

Lesson 14.1, Guided Practice (pp. 245–247)

1. 154; 157; 160; 165; 636; 636 **2.** 636; 4; 159; 159 **3.** 52; 51; 49; 48; 54; 5; $\frac{254}{5}$; 50.8; 50.8 **4.** 3; 3; 8; 24 **5.** 2; 2; 9; 18 **6.** 3; 3; 10; 30 **7.** 72 **8.** 8 **9.** 9 **10.** 8; 4; 32; 7.5; 8; 9; 24.5; 32; 24.5; 7.5; 7.5 **11.** 8,500 points

Lesson 14.1, Practice (pp. 249–250)

1. 8 **3.** 42.76 cm **5.** 4.48 m **7.** 10.116 s **9.** 3.25 **11.** 9 **13.** 7.25 oz **15a.** $\frac{a+b+c+15}{3}$ **15b.** $\frac{2a+2b+2c}{3}$ **15c.** $\frac{a+b+c}{6}$ **17.** Answers vary. Sample: 10, 11, 12, 13, and 14.

Lesson 14.2, Guided Practice (pp. 252–255)

1. 86; 97; 98; 109; 117; 98 **2.** 32 **3.** 29; 34; 29; 34; 31.5; 31.5 **4.** 121.5 **5.** $\frac{11}{16}$ **6.** 100

7a.

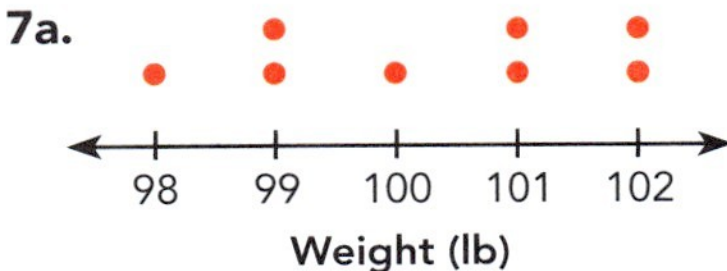

7b. Yes; 100.5 lb **8.** 45.5 **9.** 46.5 **10.** 6 **11.** Median, because most of the data values cluster around 46.5°F.

Lesson 14.2, Practice (pp. 256–257)

1. 8 **3.** 3.2 **5.** 68 **7.** $372.50 **9.** School A: 5; School B: 8 **11.** 104 cents **13.** Median, because most of the data values cluster around 110 cents.
15a. Answers vary. Sample: 4, 5, 8
15b. Answers vary. Sample: 1, 5, 8

Lesson 14.3, Guided Practice (pp. 259–260)

Times of Ten Runners

Time (s)	Number of Times
9.8	2
9.9	3
10.0	1
10.1	2
10.2	1
10.3	1

1. 9.9 **2.** 2 **3.** 8; 12 **4.** boys **5.** garment shops **6.** 5.5 kg

Lesson 14.3, Practice (pp. 262–263)

1. 5 **3.** 7.8 **5.** size 9 **7.** 2 **9.** 2 **11a.** 30
11b. (0, 30), (1, 29), (2, 28), (3, 27), (4, 26)
11c. Accept any number from 16 to 24.

Lesson 14.4, Guided Practice (pp. 265–268)

1. 60 T-shirts **2.** 11.7 **3.** 12 **4.** 12 **5.** Mode and median, because the T-shirt sizes are whole numbers and 12 is a realistic number for describing the data set.
6. Mean: 1.6; Mode: 0; Median: 1 **7.** The mode is 0, but it represents only 5 of the 15 households. So the mode does not describe the data well. The mean is 1.6 and the median is 1. Both of these numbers might be used to describe the set of data. The mean takes into account the households with 5 or 6 children, but the median better describes how many children most households have.
8. The shape of the data distribution is right skewed. The mean gives more weight to the values on the right than the median does. So, the mean is to the right of the median. **9.** Mean: 5.4; Mode: 5; Median: 5
10. The data are well spread out, and the shape of the data is symmetrical. Because the mode and median are the same, and the mean is slightly greater, the data set is likely to be more spread out for data greater than 5.

Lesson 14.4, Practice (pp. 269–271)

1. Mean: 81.75; Median: 83.5; Mode: 85 **3.** Median and mode. The mean number of children is 2.4. It is not a realistic number for describing the data set. The median and mode are both 2, which is a realistic number for describing the data set. So, the median and the mode best describe the data set. **5.** 5.49 oz **7.** Because there are two outliers, 11 and 12. **9.** The shape of the distribution is right-skewed. So, the measure of center is likely to be 2 hours, which is in the lower range.

11. 

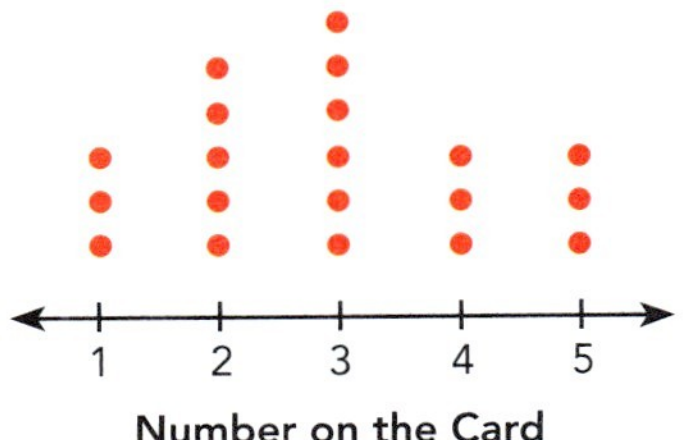

13. 2 **15.** 1.24 **17.** Yes; 2

Lesson 14.4, Brain@Work (p. 271)

Tim's Test Scores

Test	First	Second	Third	Fourth	Fifth	Sixth
Score	3	5	6	8	6	8

Chapter Review/Test (pp. 273–274)

1. Mean: $6\frac{2}{3}$; Median: 6

3.

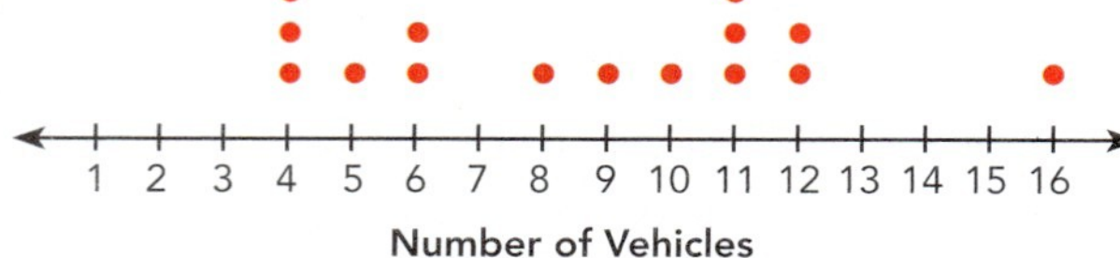

Mean: 8.6; Median: 9; Modes: 4 and 11

5. $28; Amounts at either extreme have more effect on the mean than the median.

7.

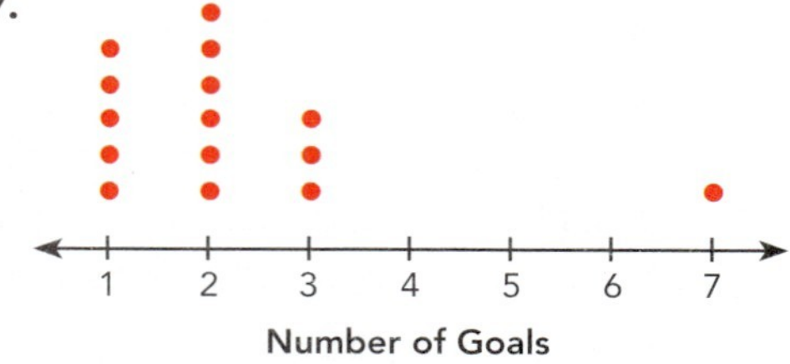

Mean: 2.2; Median: 2; Mode: 2

9. 2 **11.** 2 **13.** 1.91

Cumulative Review Chapters 12–14 (pp. 275–279)

1. b **3.** c **5.** Surface area: 828 in.^{2}; Volume: 1,080 in.^{3}

7. Mean: 9.3 lb; Median: 8.9 lb **9.** 6.9 ft **11.** 3 cm

13. There are 85 buildings in the city. Most buildings have 21 to 40 floors. The range of the data is 119. Most of the data values are to the right of the interval 21–40, and the shape of the histogram is right-skewed.

15a.

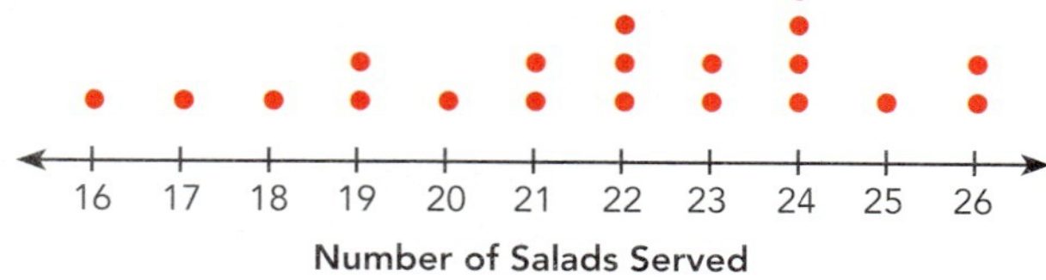

15b. Mean: 21.8; Median: 22; Mode: 24

17. Length: 30 in.; Surface area: 2,070 in.^{2}

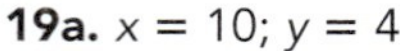
19a. $x = 10$; $y = 4$

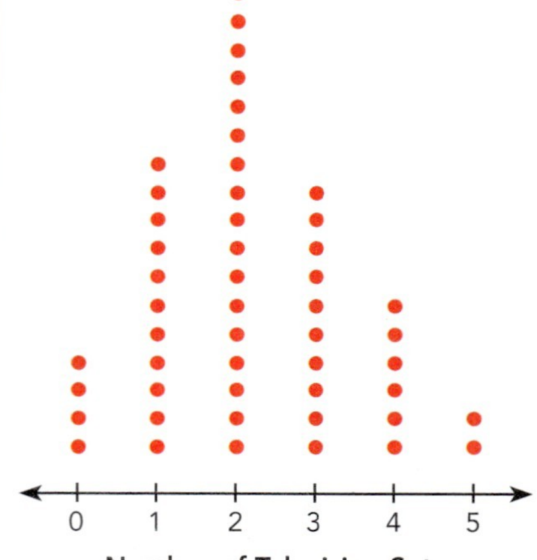

19b. Mean: 2.18; Median: 2; Mode: 2 **19c.** The data are well spread and the shape of the data distribution is nearly symmetrical. Because the mode and the median are the same, and the mean is slightly greater, the data set is likely to be more spread out for data greater than 12. The data set is slightly skewed to the right. **19d.** 2.075

Glossary

A

absolute value

The distance from a number to 0 on the number line. It is always positive or 0.

arc

A portion of a circle.

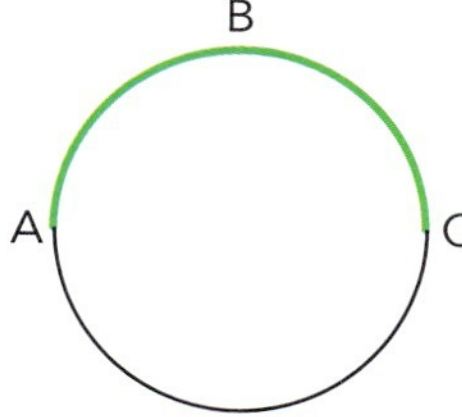

ABC is an arc.

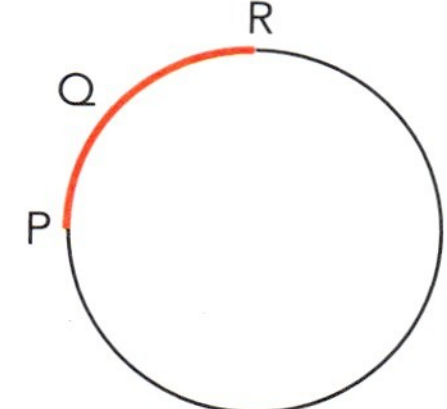

PQR is also an arc.

area

The number of square units covered by a figure. It is measured in units such as square centimeter (cm^2), square meter (m^2), square inch ($in.^2$), and square foot (ft^2).

B

base (of a triangle) (*b*)

Any side of a triangle from which the height of a triangle is measured.

C

center (of a circle)

A point within a circle that is the same distance from all points on the circle.

circumference

The distance around a circle.

congruent

Having the same size and shape.

coordinate plane

A grid formed by a horizontal number line, called the *x*-axis, and a vertical number line, called the *y*-axis, that intersect at right angles.

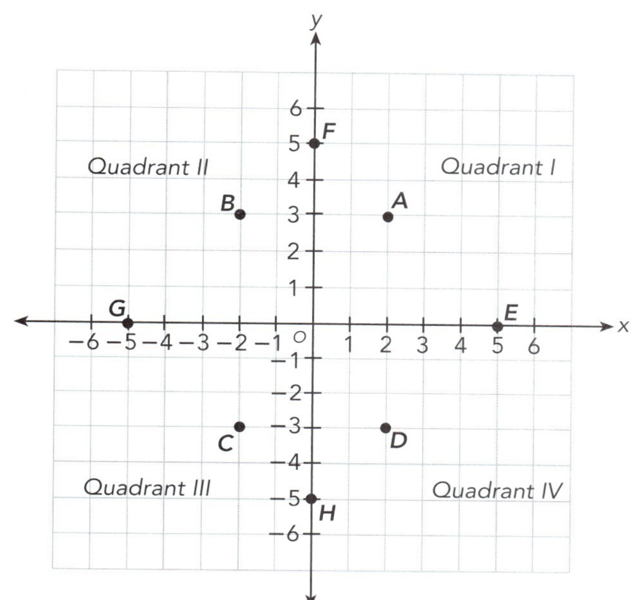

coordinates

An ordered pair of numbers that gives the location of a point on a coordinate plane.

cross section

The figure formed when a plane intersects a solid figure.

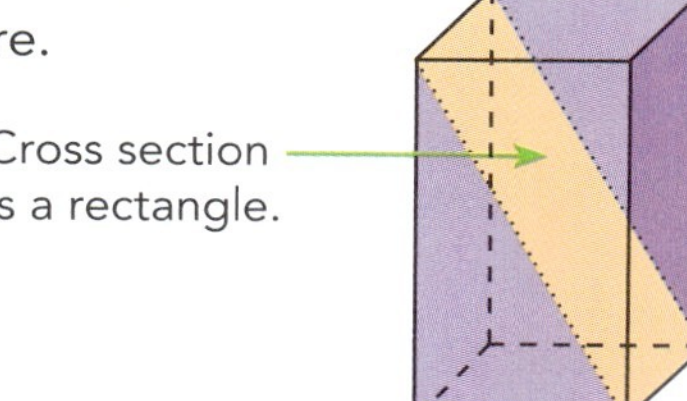

cube

A prism that has six congruent square faces.

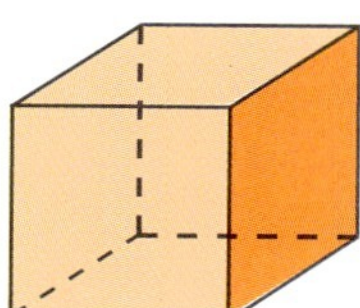

D

dependent variable

A variable whose value depends on the value of a related independent variable.

Example: In the equation $y = x + 10$, y is the dependent variable.

diameter of a circle

A line segment that connects two points on a circle and passes through its center; also the length of this segment.

dot plot

A data display similar to a line plot. It shows frequency of data on a number line using a ● to represent each occurrence.

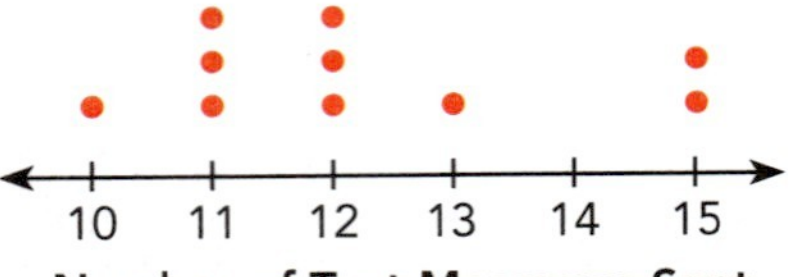

E

edge

The line segment formed where two faces of a solid figure meet.

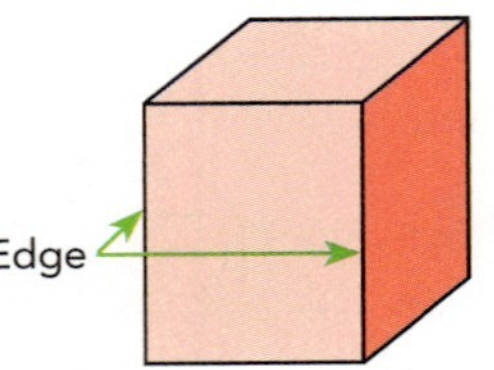

equation

A statement that two mathematical expressions are equal.

Example: $x + 5 = 8$, $4x = 12$ are equations.

F

face

A polygon that is a flat surface of a solid figure.

formula

A general mathematical equation or rule.

Example: Area of triangle $= \frac{1}{2}bh$

frequency

The number of times a piece of data, such as an item or a number, occurs.

H

height (of a triangle) (h)

The perpendicular distance from the base to the opposite vertex of a triangle.

histogram

A data display that divides the range of data into equal intervals and shows how often each interval occurs in the data set. It is usually used for large sets of data.

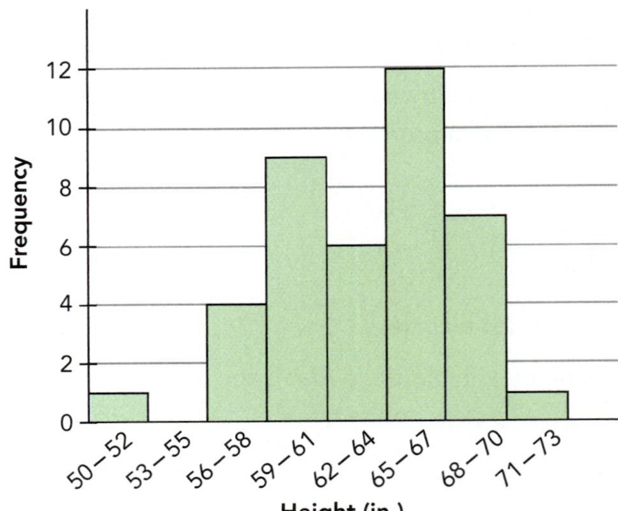

I

independent variable

A variable whose value determines the value of a related dependent variable.

Example: In the equation $y = x + 10$, x is the independent variable.

inequality

A mathematical sentence that compares two unequal expressions using one of the symbols $<$, $>$, $\leq$, $\geq$, or $\neq$.

L

linear equation

An algebraic equation that has a dependent and an independent variable. The variables have no exponents and are not multiplied together. The graph of a linear equation is a straight line.

Example: $y = x - 15$

linear graph

A straight line graph.

line plot

A diagram that shows frequency of data on a number line. Each × represents one occurrence.

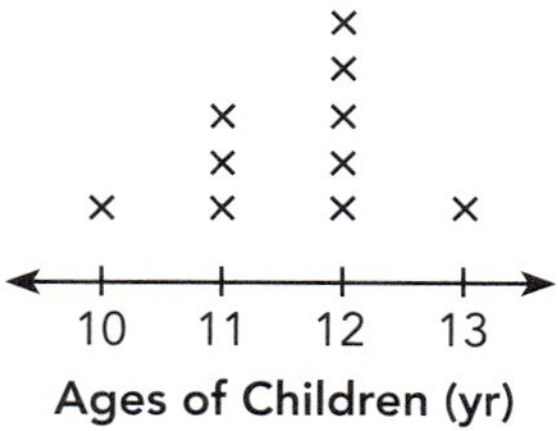

M

mean

One measure of the center of a set of data. It is found by dividing the sum of the data values by the number of data values.

$$\text{Mean} = \frac{\text{total of a set of items}}{\text{number of items}}$$

median

A measure of the center of a set of data. Once the data have been placed in numerical order, it is the middle value when the number of data items is odd, and the mean of the two middle values when the number of data items is even.

Examples:

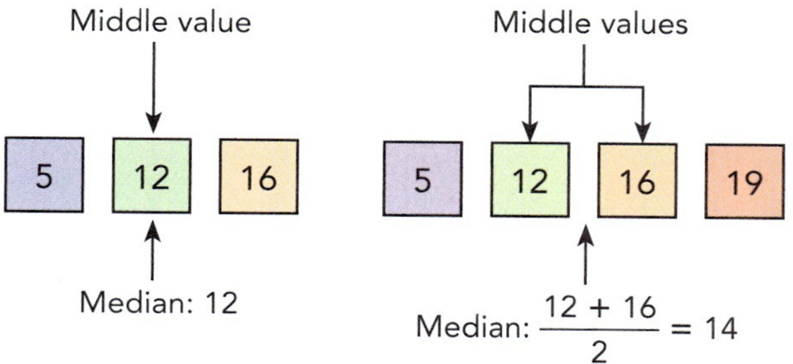

mode

A measure of the center of a set of data. It is the value (or values) that occurs most often in the data set.

Example:

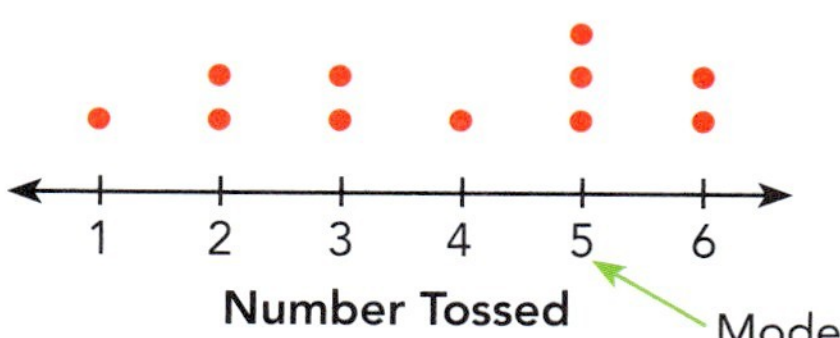

N

negative number

A number that is less than zero.

net

A plane figure that can be folded to make a solid.

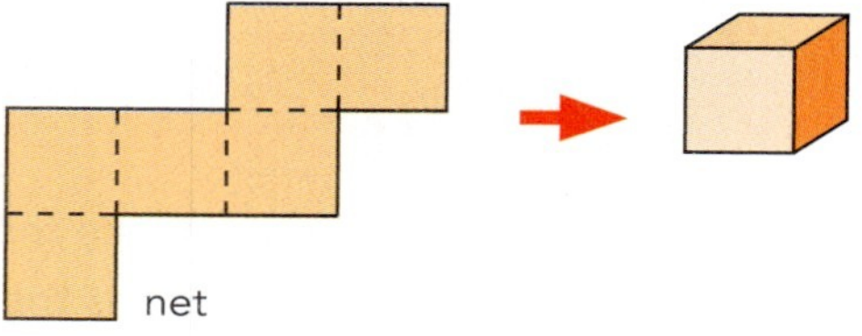

O

outlier

An extreme or rare occurrence of a value.

P

parallel

Always the same distance apart; planes or lines in the same plane that do not intersect.

parallelogram

A four-sided figure in which both pairs of opposite sides are parallel and congruent.

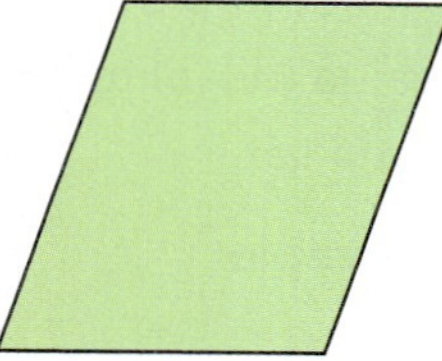

perimeter

The distance around a figure. It can be measured in units such as centimeter (cm), meter (m), inch (in.), or foot (ft).

prism

A solid with two parallel congruent polygons, called bases joined by faces that are parallelograms. A prism is named by the shape of its base.

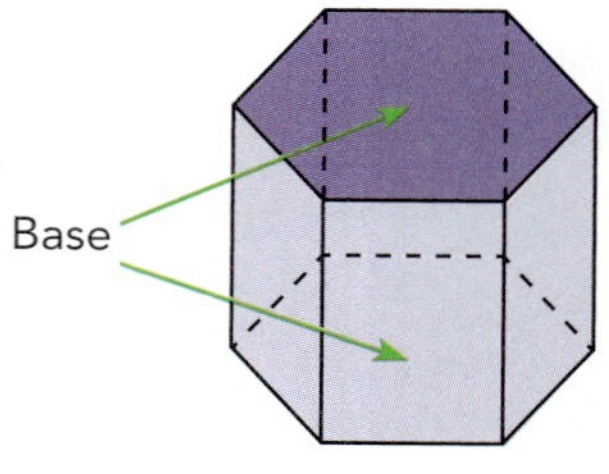

Hexagonal prism

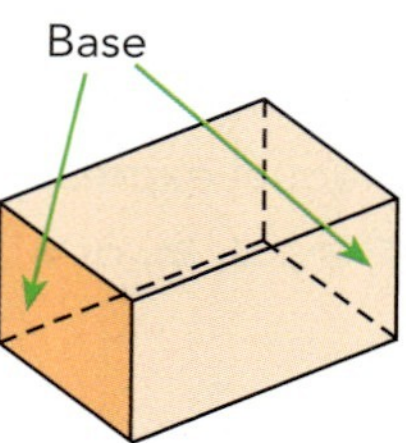

Rectangular prism

pyramid

A solid whose base is a polygon and whose other faces are triangles that share a common vertex.

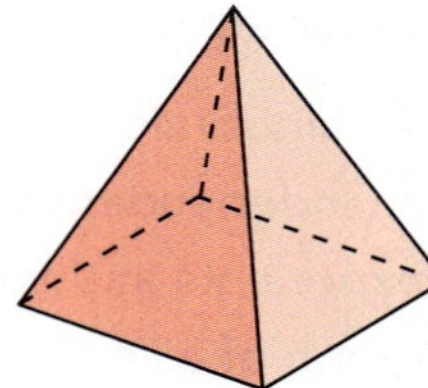

Q

quadrant of a circle

A quarter of a circle.

quadrants of a coordinate plane

The four sections of a coordinate plane formed by the axes. They are numbered Quadrant I, Quadrant II, Quadrant III, and Quadrant IV.

R

radius (r)

A line segment connecting the center and a point on the circle; also the length of this segment.

radii

Plural of *radius*.

range

The difference between the greatest and the least number in a set of data.

regular polygon

A polygon whose sides are all the same length, and whose angles are all the same measure.

Examples:

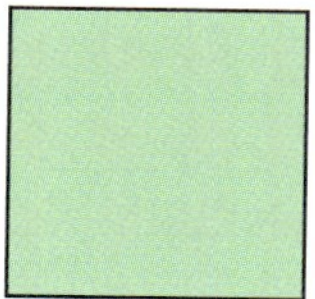

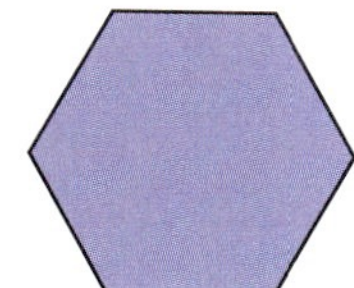

rhombus

A four-sided figure in which the opposite sides are parallel and the four sides are congruent.

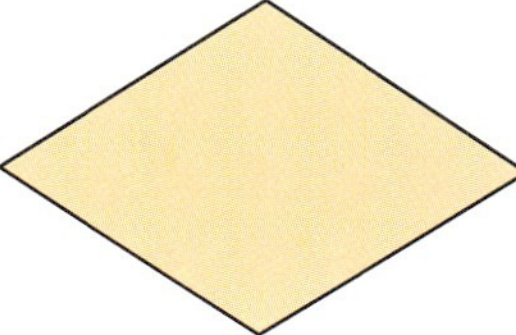

S

semicircle

A half of a circle.

skewed

A data set in which the mean, median, and mode are not all the same number.

Example:

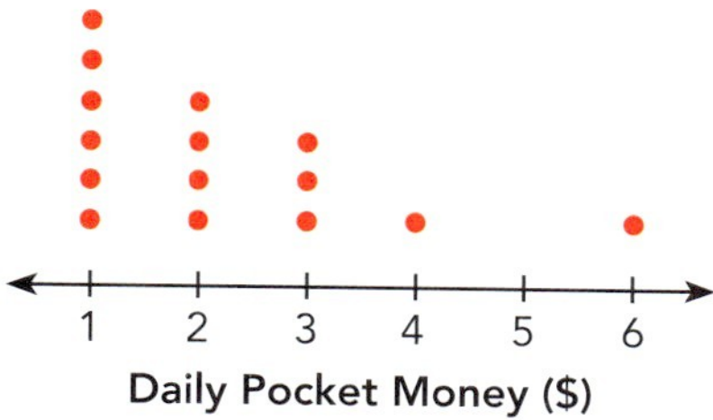

Mean	Median	Mode
2.2	2	1

So, the data set is skewed. The distribution has a "tail" on the right, so the data set is right-skewed.

solution

A value that makes an equation true when substituted for the variable.

Example: $4x = 12$

$x = 3$

The solution of the equation $4x = 12$ is 3.

surface area

The total area of the faces (including the bases) and curved surfaces of a solid figure.

symmetrical

A data set in which the mean, median, and mode are the same number.

Example:

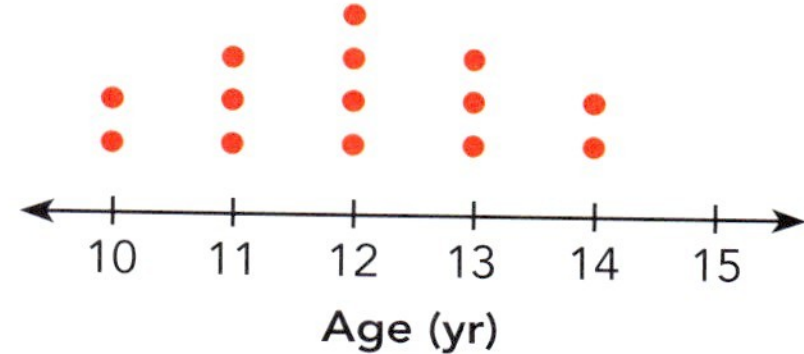

Mean	Median	Mode
12	12	12

So, the data set is symmetrical. The dot plot has most of the data near the center of the range.

T

trapezoid

A four-sided polygon with exactly one pair of parallel sides.

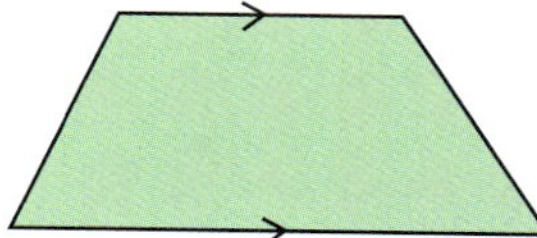

triangular prism

A prism composed of two triangular bases and three faces that are parallelograms or rectangles.

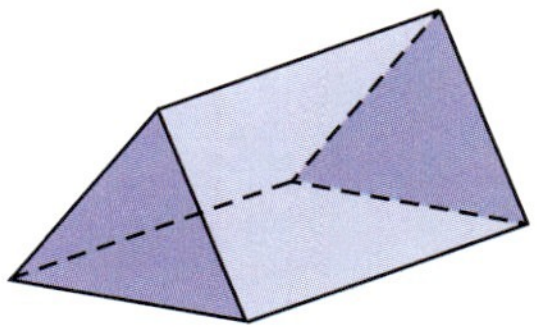

V

vertex

The point at which three edges of a prism meet.

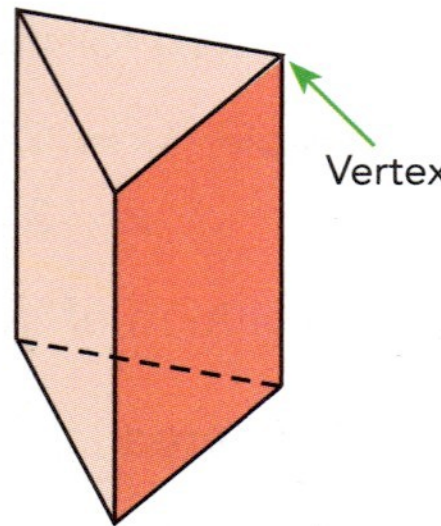

volume (*V*)

The number of cubic units it takes to fill a space. It is measured in units such as cubic centimeters (cm^3) or cubic inches ($in.^3$).

X

x-axis

The horizontal axis on a coordinate plane.

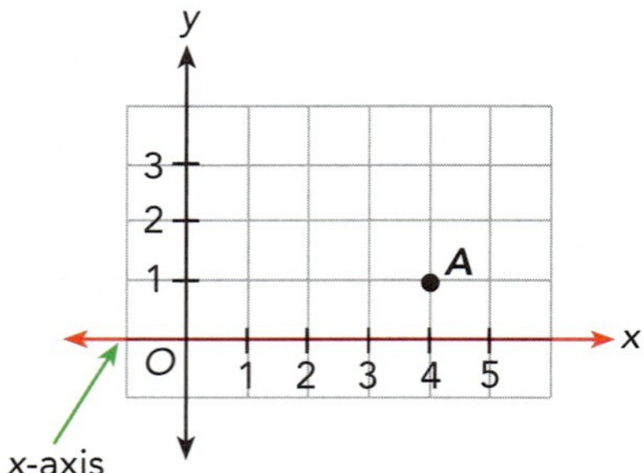

Y

y-axis

The vertical axis on a coordinate plane.

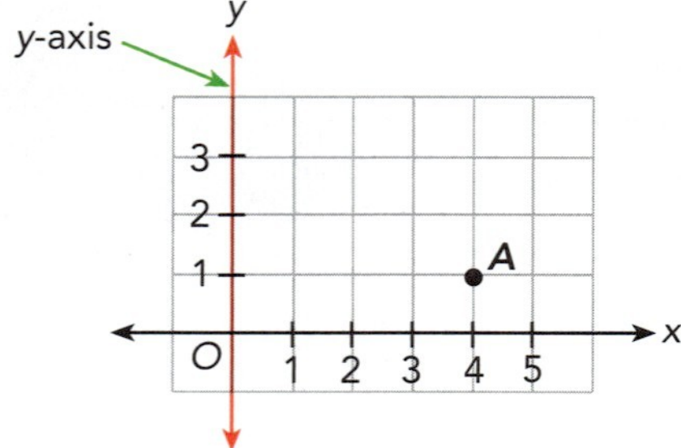

Table of Measures, Formulas, and Symbols

METRIC	CUSTOMARY
Length	
1 kilometer (km) = 1,000 meters (m)	1 mile (mi) = 1,760 yards (yd)
1 meter = 10 decimeters (dm)	1 mile = 5,280 feet (ft)
1 meter = 100 centimeters (cm)	1 yard = 3 feet
1 meter = 1,000 millimeters (mm)	1 yard = 36 inches (in.)
1 centimeter = 10 millimeters	1 foot = 12 inches
Capacity	
1 liter (L) = 1,000 milliliters (mL)	1 gallon (gal) = 4 quarts (qt)
	1 gallon = 16 cups (c)
	1 gallon = 128 fluid ounces (fl oz)
	1 quart = 2 pints (pt)
	1 quart = 4 cups
	1 pint = 2 cups
	1 cup = 8 fluid ounces
Mass and Weight	
1 kilogram (kg) = 1,000 grams (g)	1 ton (T) = 2,000 pounds (lb)
1 gram = 1,000 milligrams (mg)	1 pound = 16 ounces (oz)

TIME

1 year (yr) = 365 days	1 week = 7 days
1 year = 12 months (mo)	1 day = 24 hours (h)
1 year = 52 weeks (wk)	1 hour = 60 minutes (min)
leap year = 366 days	1 minute = 60 seconds (s)

Centimeters 0 1 2 3 4 5 6 7 8 9 10 11 12 13 14 15 16 17 18 19 20

CONVERTING MEASUREMENTS

You can use the information below to convert measurements from one unit to another.	
To convert from a smaller unit to a larger unit, divide.	To convert from a larger unit to a smaller unit, multiply.
Example: 48 in. = __?__ ft	Example: 0.3 m = __?__ cm

PERIMETER, CIRCUMFERENCE, AND AREA

Square

Perimeter $= 4\ell$

Area $= \ell^2$

Rectangle

Perimeter $= 2\ell + 2w$

$= 2(\ell + w)$

Area $= \ell w$

Circle

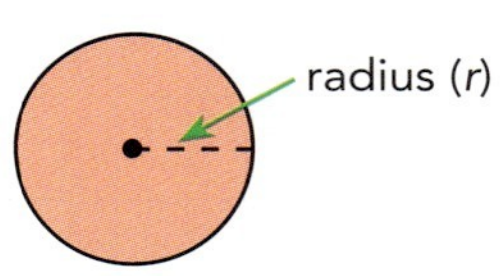

Circumference $= \pi d$

$= 2\pi r$

Area $= \pi r^2$

Triangle

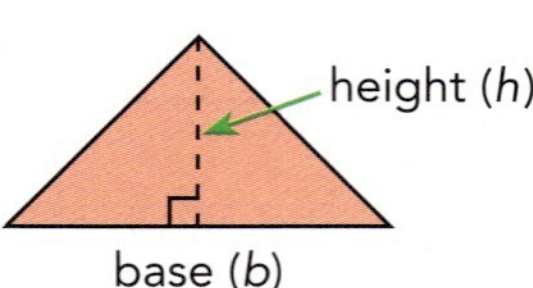

Area $= \frac{1}{2}bh$

Parallelogram

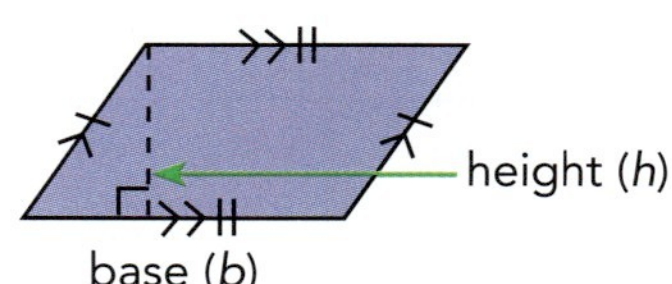

Area $= bh$

Trapezoid

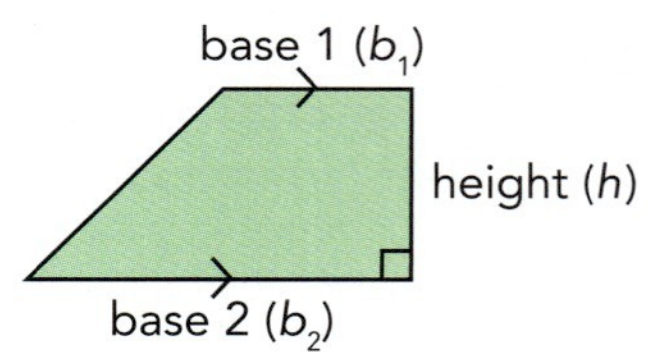

Area $= \frac{1}{2}h(b_1 + b_2)$

SURFACE AREA AND VOLUME

Cube

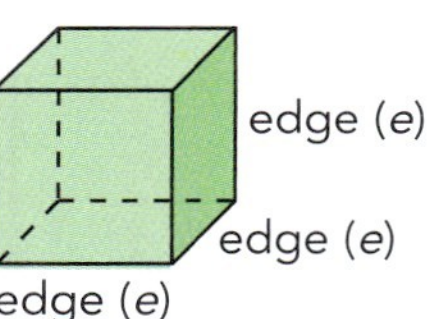

Surface Area $= 6e^2$
Volume $= e^3$

Rectangular Prism

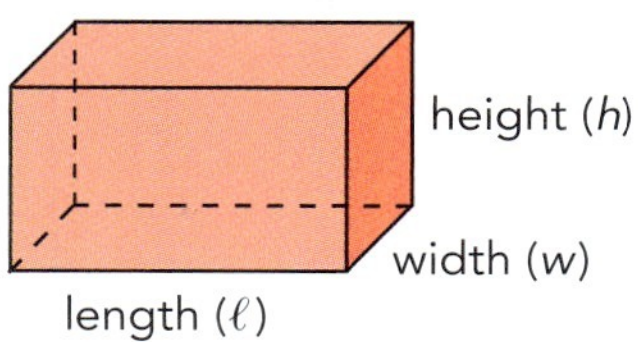

Surface Area $= 2(\ell w + wh + \ell h)$
Volume $= \ell wh = Bh$*

Prism

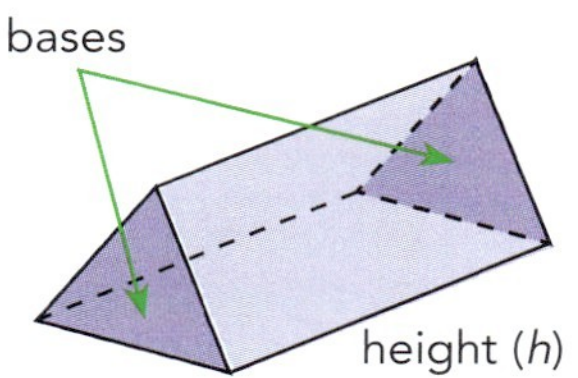

Surface Area
= Sum of the areas of the faces
= Perimeter of base × height + Area of two bases
Volume $= Bh$*

Pyramid

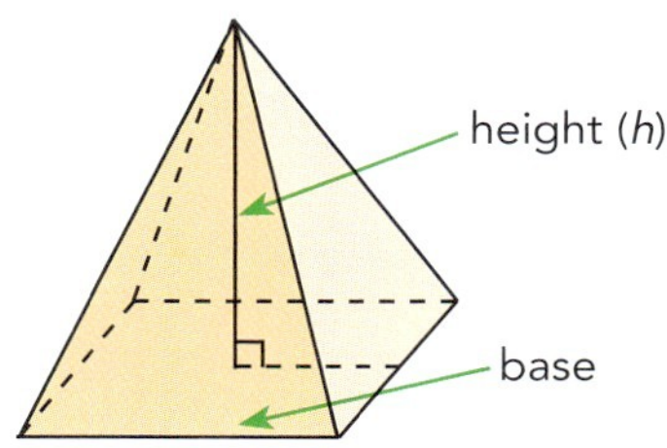

Surface Area = Sum of the areas of the faces
Volume $= \frac{1}{3}Bh$*

Cylinder

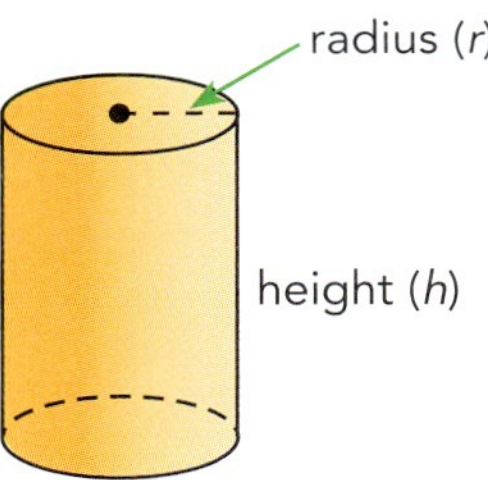

Surface Area $= 2\pi r^2 + 2\pi rh$
Volume $= \pi r^2 h$

Cone

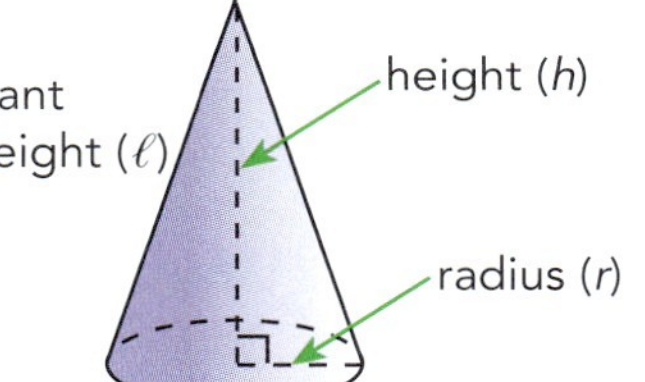

Surface Area $= \pi r(\ell + r)$,
where ℓ is the slant height
Volume $= \frac{1}{3}\pi r^2 h$

Sphere

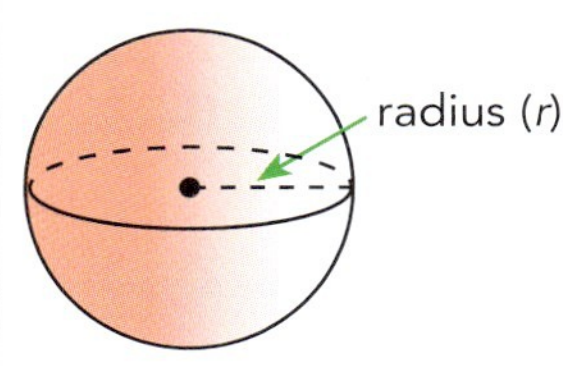

Surface Area $= 4\pi r^2$
Volume $= \frac{4}{3}\pi r^3$

*B represents the area of the base of a solid figure.

PYTHAGOREAN THEOREM

Right Triangle

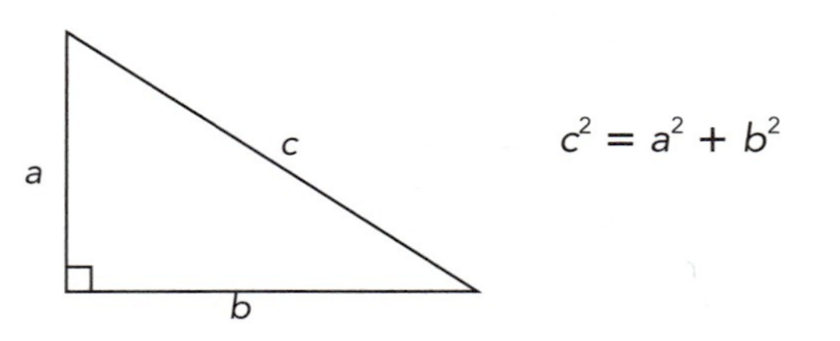

$$c^2 = a^2 + b^2$$

PROBABILITY

Probability of an event, A happening

$$P(A) = \frac{\text{Number of favorable outcomes}}{\text{Number of equally likely outcomes}}$$

Probability of an event not happening $= 1 - P(A)$

LINEAR GRAPHS

The slope, m, of a line segment joining points $P\ (x_1, y_1)$ and $Q\ (x_2, y_2)$ is given by

$m = \dfrac{y_2 - y_1}{x_2 - x_1}$ or $m = \dfrac{y_1 - y_2}{x_1 - x_2}$.

Given the slope, m, the equation of a line intercepting the y-axis at b is given by $y = mx + b$.

The distance, d, between two points $P\ (x_1, y_1)$ and $Q\ (x_2, y_2)$ is given by

$d = \sqrt{(x_2 - x_1)^2 + (y_2 - y_1)^2}$ or $d = \sqrt{(x_1 - x_2)^2 + (y_1 - y_2)^2}$.

RATE

Distance = Speed × Time

$$\text{Average speed} = \frac{\text{Total distance traveled}}{\text{Total time}}$$

Interest = Principal × Rate × Time

TEMPERATURE

Celsius (°C)	$C = \frac{5}{9} \times (F - 32)$
Fahrenheit (°F)	$F = \left(\frac{5}{9} \times C\right) + 32$

SYMBOLS

Symbol	Meaning	Symbol	Meaning
$<$	is less than	$\lvert a \rvert$	absolute value of the number *a*
$>$	is greater than	(x, y)	ordered pair
$\leq$	is less than or equal to	1 : 2	ratio of 1 to 2
$\geq$	is greater than or equal to	/	per
$\neq$	is not equal to	%	percent
$\approx$	is approximately equal to	$\perp$	is perpendicular to
$\cong$	is congruent to	$\parallel$	is parallel to
$\sim$	is similar to	$\overleftrightarrow{AB}$	line *AB*
10^2	ten squared	$\overrightarrow{AB}$	ray *AB*
10^3	ten cubed	$\overline{AB}$	line segment *AB*
2^6	two to the sixth power	$\angle ABC$	angle *ABC*
$2.\overline{6}$	repeating decimal 2.66666...	$m\angle A$	measure of angle *A*
7	positive 7	$\triangle ABC$	triangle *ABC*
-7	negative 7	$^\circ$	degree
$\sqrt{a}$	positive square root of the number *a*	π	pi; $\pi \approx 3.14$ or $\pi \approx \frac{22}{7}$
$\sqrt[3]{a}$	positive cube root of the number *a*	$P(A)$	the probability of the event *A* happening

Centimeters 0 1 2 3 4 5 6 7 8 9 10 11 12 13 14 15 16 17 18 19 20

Pages listed in black type refer to Book A.
Pages listed in blue type refer to Book B.
Pages in **boldface** type show where a term is introduced.

E

F

G

Pages listed in black type refer to Book A.
Pages listed in blue type refer to Book B.
Pages in **boldface** type show where a term is introduced.

Pages listed in black type refer to Book A.
Pages listed in blue type refer to Book B.
Pages in **boldface** type show where a term is introduced.